ADVANCED BIRD ID GUIDE

THE WESTERN PALEARCTIC

Every plumage of all 1,300 species and
subspecies recorded in Britain, Europe,
North Africa and the Middle East

NILS VAN DUIVENDIJK

In association with
BRITISH BIRDS

NEW
HOLLAND

Jimmy Carter
2012

First published in 2010 by New Holland Publishers
London • Cape Town • Sydney • Auckland
www.newhollandpublishers.com

Garfield House, 86-88 Edgware Road, London W2 2EA, United Kingdom
80 McKenzie Street, Cape Town 8001, South Africa
Unit 1, 66 Gibbes Street, Chatswood, NSW 2067, Australia
218 Lake Road, Northcote, Auckland, New Zealand

10 9 8 7 6 5 4 3

A CIP catalogue record for this book is available from the British Library.

ISBN 978 1 84773 607 9

Publisher: Simon Papps
Editor: Rob Fray
Artwork: Dirk Moerbeek
Cover photographs: Markus Varesvuo
Production: Melanie Dowland

Reproduction by Pica Digital (Pte) Ltd, Singapore
Printed and bound in India by Replika Press

Front cover: Montagu's Harrier
Spine: Common Redpoll
Back cover (left to right): Common Snipe, Shore Lark, Pied Flycatcher

Acknowledgements
I would like to thank Arend Wassink, Chris van Rijswijk, Dick Groenendijk, Diederik Kok, Edwin Winkel,
Henk van Rijswijk, Laurens Steijn, Martin Garner and Willem van Rijswijk for pointing me to certain ID
features, lending their photographs for study or the useful discussions we had about bird ID, Hein van
Grouw for letting me study the collection at the National Zoological Museum Leiden, Arnoud van den Berg
for answering all my questions regarding taxonomy and nomenclature, Simon Papps (Publisher, Natural
History, New Holland Publishers) for his help during the project, James Lidster for his support and help
looking for a British publisher, Roger Riddington for enabling the association with *British Birds* and for
checking pages, Norbert Bahr (co-editor of the Howard and Moore *Complete Checklist of the Birds of the
World*) for sharing his knowledgeable views with me about taxonomy, Dirk Moerbeek for permitting the
use his drawings of bird topography again, which he made for the Dutch edition of this book, and Diana
van Vliet for her support during the whole project.

Contents

Foreword	4
Introduction	5
Abbreviations and symbols	6
Bird topography	8
Species accounts	10
Non-passerines	
Swans, geese and ducks	10
Grouse, partridges, pheasants, quail and guineafowl	31
Divers	34
Albatrosses	36
Petrels	37
Shearwaters	40
Storm-petrels	43
Tropicbirds	45
Gannets	45
Cormorants and darters	46
Pelicans	48
Frigatebirds	49
Herons and egrets	49
Storks, ibises and flamingos	55
Grebes	57
Hawks, vultures, eagles and allies	58
Osprey	76
Falcons	76
Rails	83
Cranes	86
Bustards and buttonquails	87
Painted snipes, oystercatchers, stilts, crab-plover and thick-knees	88
Coursers and pratincoles	89
Plovers	90
Sandpipers and allies	98
Skuas	120
Gulls	123
Terns and skimmers	143
Auks	153
Sandgrouse	155
Pigeons	156
Mousebirds	158
Parakeets	158
Cuckoos	159
Barn owls	160
Owls	161
Nightjars	164
Swifts	166
Kingfishers	168
Bee-eaters, rollers and hoopoes	168
Woodpeckers	170

Passerines	
New World flycatchers	173
Vireos	173
Old World orioles	174
Shrikes	174
Crows	180
Kinglets	183
Penduline tits	184
Tits	184
Parrotbills	187
Larks	187
Swallows and martins	193
Bush warblers	196
Long-tailed tits	197
Babblers	197
Phylloscopus warblers	198
Sylvia warblers	204
Locustella warblers	212
Hippolais warblers and allies	214
Reed warblers	218
Cisticolas and allies	221
Waxwings	222
Wallcreeper, nuthatches and treeceepers	222
Wrens	225
Mockingbirds and allies	225
Starlings	225
Sunbirds	227
Dippers	227
Thrushes	227
'Brown' flycatchers	232
Scrub-robins and robins	233
Nightingales and Asian chats	234
Redstarts	236
Stonechats	238
Wheatears	240
Rock thrushes	246
Ficedula flycatchers	247
Accentors	249
Avadavats, silverbills and waxbills	250
Old World sparrows	250
Wagtails	253
Pipits	258
Finches	263
Buntings and New World sparrows	273
Icterids	285
New World warblers	286
Tanagers	291
Bibliography	292
Other Birding Books by New Holland	293
Index	294

Foreword

Looking at the enormous collection of bird identification features in this book, some people might be interested to know how this all started. Since I first met Nils, more than 15 years ago, he has not only been a fanatical birder but also an avid 'collector' of field characters. As a result of his constant striving to improve his identification knowledge, he was always on the look out for new features. This involved a countless number of evenings spent by Nils in his attic, swotting up on all available literature. In the field, when birding together with our regular group of friends, we not only noticed that his detailed knowledge was increasing, but also that his growing love for examining bird plumages in detail was becoming more obsessive, to such a (sometimes boring) extent that it earned the rather crude monicker of 'feather-f***ing'.

While assessing all the subtle features of a potential Pallid Swift is exciting, studying the variation in the tertial patterns of Mallards can be quite boring, at least for most of us … I think that none of us can even begin to imagine the number of hours that have been spent in researching and compiling the myriad of facts that have been included in this remarkable book – what a job! So many birds and bird photos were studied in extreme detail. Over the years, Nils became something of a walking encyclopedia of bird ID knowledge. Personally I made use of this encyclopedia on our many field trips together, in our identification discussions, and when we set up the mystery bird competition in the journal *Dutch Birding*. Quite frankly, it was both impressive and almost frightening to experience the amount of extremely detailed knowledge available in Nils's head. His expertise has led to the discovery of many rarities, and he has made important contributions to identification challenges in the Dutch birding scene and played a valuable role in the Dutch rarities committee.

Aiming to have an up-to-date overview of all the available sources combined, Nils started to order his collection of bird features systematically. To begin with this was just for his own use, but when he showed up with his set of pages when we were out birding, he obviously came under severe pressure to provide copies for his colleagues as well! After all, this was something completely new: a compact summary in 'bullet-point style' of all the relevant books, identification articles, his own experience and more. Urged by many birders, this led to several self-published titles in the late 1990s. This was followed, in 2002, by a complete guide to the birds of the Western Palearctic in Dutch: the *Dutch Birding Kenmerkengids*. Since its publication it has been an essential reference for anyone on the Dutch birding scene.

Combining all available literature from books and magazines, museum visits, internet sources and, last but not least, a lot of field experience, its comprehensiveness has built gradually over the years and through many different incarnations and editions. So much so that the English edition of the guide that you are now reading is again far more comprehensive than all the previous ones, and I am certain that it will become an essential reference for birders across Europe.

I am sure that with this book, Nils will succeed in his aim of assisting many birders in the field with the challenges of identifying, ageing and sexing the birds they find. I am also sure that Nils's passion for discovering more and new features will be never-ending. As I write I have no doubt that he is finding more features to add to future editions …

Good birding!

Diederik Kok, the Netherlands

British Birds

This book is proudly published in association with *British Birds*, a monthly magazine for everyone interested in the birds of the Western Palearctic. It publishes authoritative yet readable articles on a variety of topics, including identification, distribution, migration, conservation and taxonomy. The publication is widely regarded as *the* bird journal of record in Great Britain, and it has a continuous publication history stretching back more than 100 years. Visit the website www.britishbirds.co.uk to find out more and to download a free sample copy.

The British Birds Rarities Committee (BBRC)

The British Birds Rarities Committee (BBRC) was formed in 1959 under the aegis of the journal *British Birds*. Its main function is to apply uniform adjudication standards to claims of records of rare bird species in the United Kingdom. The Committee comprises 10 voting Members and a non-voting Chairman, Secretary, Archivist and Museum Consultant.

The BBRC aims to maintain an accurate database of records of the occurrence of rare bird taxa (species and sub-species) in Britain, providing an accurate and comprehensive annual report. It aims to assess all records of rare taxa in an independent, open, rigorous and consistent manner and to develop and publish criteria for the identification of rare taxa.

To help achieve these aims BBRC strives to work closely with county recorders, bird observatories, bird information services and observers. The work of the BBRC would not be possible without the efforts of all these groups and individuals, but in particular the observers who find and identify rare birds. James Lidster drew BBRC's attention to the Dutch version of this guide and it is satisfying to see this valuable resource becoming available in an English language edition. Whilst we endorse the author's view that bird identification knowledge is an evolving process and that therefore new features will be established or currently accepted criteria may be proved to be unreliable in due course, we are certain that this book will provide invaluable assistance to rarity hunting observers.

To find out more about the BBRC, visit our website www.bbrc.org.uk.

Adam Rowlands, BBRC Chairman

Introduction

This book presents the most important field marks of all bird species and distinguishable subspecies of the Western Palearctic. It is born from the idea that it would be handy to have a pocket-sized reference to check relevant features quickly and systematically when facing an ID problem in the field, when normally little or no information is available. In order to achieve this goal, the overall size of the book and the structure and format of the text have been designed so that it can be easily used in the field. In addition to its use as a field guide, it can also be consulted to make identifications from photographs or of birds in the hand.

The only illustrations are those which clarify the 'bird topography'. Therefore this guide is intended especially for birders who are already reasonably familiar with the main features of most species and forms likely to be encountered and it may be best used in addition to, or in combination with, a good illustrated field guide.

Features for each species are listed by plumage or subject. Note that in many species the features apply for the given plumage-type only. Since nowadays many birders carry a wide range of bird sounds with them on a small MP3-player, voices are given only when they are highly important for ID, so for species such as dowitchers and bonelli's warblers. Moreover, playable sounds are often much more useful than written descriptions of voices.

Our knowledge of bird ID is constantly evolving and developing. New features will be found and some known ones will be proven to be less reliable than they were initially considered to be. This book does not pretend to be fully complete or correct.

For this book we use the boundaries of the Western Palearctic as defined in *The Birds of the Western Palearctic* (Cramp *et al* 1977-1994). This area encloses the whole of Europe (including Spitsbergen, Franz Jozef Land and Novaya Zemlya, but excluding Greenland), the Middle East and North Africa. The eastern border is formed, from north to south, by the Ural mountain ridge, the western shore of the Caspian Sea via the west border of Iran up to Kuwait. The Middle East excludes Iran and the Arabian Peninsula. The southern border runs through North Africa, including all countries bordering the Mediterranean Sea but also the northern parts of Chad, Niger, Mali and Mauritania. In the west all Atlantic Island groups are included with the main boundary being the mid-Atlantic 40-degree-west line, but including also the most westerly of the Azores (which fall just outside this line).

Taxonomy and nomenclature

For this book we largely follow the rules set out by *Dutch Birding* and the Dutch committee for avian systematics (CSNA), which in turn are based on Howard & Moore (2003). Splits after this date have been adopted once they have been clarified and published in a scientific journal. Being primarily an ID guide, this approach has been chosen because it highlights certain distinct taxa which are sometimes not elevated to species level yet by other authorities, for example Scopoli's Shearwater, Hudsonian Whimbrel, Thayer's Gull, Siberian Stonechat, Moltoni's Warbler, Steppe Grey Shrike, Western and Eastern Black-eared Wheatears, orphean warblers and most taxa within the 'yellow wagtail' and 'white wagtail' complexes. Importantly, although no compromises are made for this reason in the book, full species status offers far greater protection in terms of international bird protection legislation for many of these birds. Other distinct taxa which are likely to deserve full species level too, like the chaffinch taxa of North Africa and the Atlantic Islands, are not split yet, mainly because there is no scientific evidence available to support this at present. The sequence of passerines follows Sangster *et al* in *Ibis* 152: 180-186, 2010.

Future editions

New Holland Publishers will endeavour to update future editions of the *Advanced Bird ID Guide* with the most up-to-date information available. Suggested amendments can be emailed to simon.papps@nhpub.co.uk.

Author Biography

Nils van Duivendijk lives in the Netherlands. He took his first steps into the world of birding at the age of 9 when on holiday on one of the Dutch Wadden Islands, and from this moment he developed a great interest in bird ID. Although birding has always been a very important part of his life, he has never had a professional job related to birds. From his mid-twenties he started to study bird ID in a more systematic way, became a member of, and then chairman of, the Dutch Rarities Committee and published the precursor to this book in Dutch in 2002. The Dutch Wadden Islands are still one of his favorite birding destinations.

Abbreviations and symbols

Abbreviations and symbols used in the margin

all plum	all plumages (from juvenile plumage onwards).
ad	adult
ad w	adult winter
ad s	adult summer
cy	calendar year
juv	juvenile
imm	immature (no specific age).
1w	first winter (2w = second winter, etc).
1s	first summer (2s = second summer, etc).
1w/2w	in both first summer and second winter (but not in first summer).
1s-2w	from first summer to second winter.
subad	subadult: near-adult still with some traces of immaturity.
⇒	important feature (key elements of the feature are sometimes highlighted in italics).
fl	flight: features mentioned are those which are either especially important or normally only visible in flight (leg-projection, secondary barring, etc).
behav	behaviour
geog var	geographical variation

Abbreviations and symbols used in the text

prim	primary/primaries, also in compound with other abbreviations or words, such as prim-cov, prim-projection, etc
sec	secondary/secondaries
scaps	scapulars
p1- p10	primaries 1 to 10: in non-passerines counted descendently, from the most innermost primary (next to the secondaries) outwards; in passerines counted ascendently, from the small outermost primary towards the secondaries
t1	tail-feather 1 (central tail-feather); tail-feathers always counted from the centre outwards

ind	individual
cov	covert/coverts, also in compound with other abbreviations or words, such as greater cov, undertail-cov, etc
incl	including
⇔	the feature described to the left of this symbol is a particularly reliable way of distinguishing the (sub)species in the account from the (sub)species mentioned to the right of the symbol
♂	male
♀	female
L	average length from tip of bill to tip of tail in centimetres (cm) and inches (")
WS	average wingspan in centimetres (cm) and inches (")

Glossary of other terms

distal	towards the end (away from the body)
eclipse	cryptic/camouflage plumage during flight-feather moult in ducks (during summer)
'grinning patch'	gap between cutting edges of upper and lower mandible in the closed bill of some geese
gular patch	area of bare skin below lower mandible, the shape of which is useful for identifying certain (sub)species, e.g. cormorants
intergrade	population or individual which shows mixed characters of different subspecies
jizz	general impression of size and posture
Kodak greyscale	grey hues ranging from white (0) to black (20), used in the ID of (sub)adult large gulls
morph	distinct plumage type of a species which is unrelated to age, sex or geographical variation, e.g. Snow Goose
moult-limit	visible contrast between old and new feathers in the same feather tract by different colour, length and/or wear (e.g. new inner, old outer greater coverts) or between feather tract (e.g. old greater coverts, new median coverts)
nominate	first named subspecies (in a polytypical species)
orbital-ring	narrow line of skin directly around eye, often prominent in *Sylvia* warblers and large gulls
prim-flash	primary-flash: pale area on upperside of hand mainly caused by pale inner webs of primaries, visible when the wing is spread
prim-projection	primary-projection: distance between the tip of the longest tertial and the tip of the longest primary, expressed as a % of the length of the visible part of the tertials
speculum	characteristic pattern of sec and greater cov in dabbling ducks; 'upper border' of speculum refers to the stripe formed by the pale tips of the greater cov; 'lower border' refers to the trailing edge of the arm, formed by pale tips of the sec
subspecies	geographic population which is separable by plumage, voice and/or measurements from other populations within the same species
subterminal	close to the end (e.g. subterminal tail-band)
tail projection	part of tail that reaches beyond wing-tip
'vulture stripe'	pale line along the underwing-coverts of certain vulture species
wing-projection	part of wing that reaches beyond tail-tip
WP	Western Palearctic (as defined by Cramp)

Other notes

a) The subjects in the margin follow a consistent order; all plum is followed by all adult plumages, beginning with the 'most advanced' male plumage and finishing with the 'least advanced' female plumage. Following this is the youngest plumage (juv) progressing through to subadult, e.g. all plum, ad ♂, ad ♀, ad s, ad w, juv, imm, 1w, 1s, 2w, etc, fl all plum, fl ad, fl ad ♂, etc, ending with moult, behaviour, voice, notes (not all the subjects listed here are given for every species).

b) Features per plumage/subject are listed from the most important to the least important.

c) When another species is mentioned with the same family name in a species account, this name is given in full only in the first instance, e.g. in the species account for Lesser Spotted Eagle, Greater Spotted Eagle and Steppe Eagle will be mentioned as Greater Spotted and Steppe respectively after the first time. However, other birds, e.g. Common Buzzard in a species account of an eagle, will have their species names written in full every time.

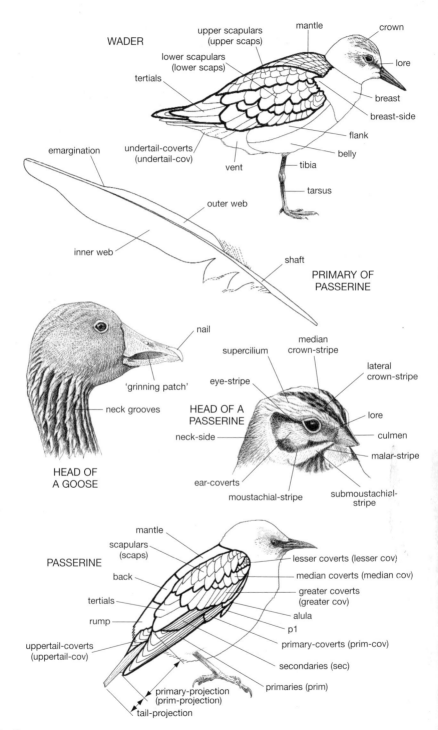

WADER

upper scapulars (upper scaps)

lower scapulars (lower scaps)

tertials

mantle

crown

lore

breast

breast-side

flank

belly

tibia

tarsus

undertail-coverts (undertail-cov)

vent

emargination

outer web

inner web

shaft

PRIMARY OF PASSERINE

nail

'grinning patch'

neck grooves

HEAD OF A GOOSE

supercilium

eye-stripe

median crown-stripe

lateral crown-stripe

lore

culmen

malar-stripe

HEAD OF A PASSERINE

neck-side

ear-coverts

moustachial-stripe

submoustachial-stripe

PASSERINE

mantle

scapulars (scaps)

back

tertials

rump

uppertail-coverts (uppertail-cov)

lesser coverts (lesser cov)

median coverts (median cov)

greater coverts (greater cov)

alula

p1

primary-coverts (prim-cov)

secondaries (sec)

primaries (prim)

primary-projection (prim-projection)

tail-projection

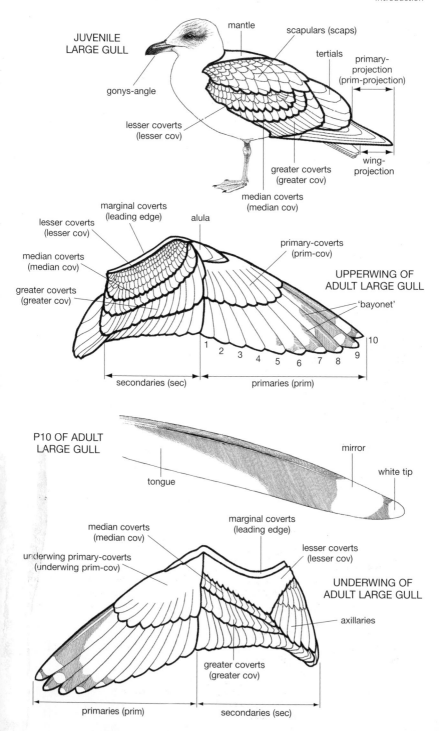

JUVENILE
LARGE GULL

mantle

scapulars (scaps)

tertials

primary-projection
(prim-projection)

gonys-angle

lesser coverts
(lesser cov)

greater coverts
(greater cov)

median coverts
(median cov)

wing-
projection

marginal coverts
(leading edge)

alula

lesser coverts
(lesser cov)

median coverts
(median cov)

greater coverts
(greater cov)

primary-coverts
(prim-cov)

UPPERWING OF
ADULT LARGE GULL

'bayonet'

10

1 2 3 4 5 6 7 8 9

secondaries (sec)

primaries (prim)

P10 OF ADULT
LARGE GULL

mirror

white tip

tongue

median coverts
(median cov)

marginal coverts
(leading edge)

lesser coverts
(lesser cov)

underwing primary-coverts
(underwing prim-cov)

UNDERWING OF
ADULT LARGE GULL

axillaries

greater coverts
(greater cov)

primaries (prim)

secondaries (sec)

NON-PASSERINES

Swans, geese and ducks

Fulvous Whistling Duck *Dendrocygna bicolor*   L 51cm 20"

all plum	• Striking structure with long legs and neck. Erect posture.
	• Legs and bill dark grey.
ad	• Orange-brown head and underparts.
	• Neck paler than head and breast, often with greyish wash.
	• Upperparts blackish with broad rufous tips to scaps.
	• Obvious pale striping along flanks and whitish undertail-cov.
fl all plum	• Very dark underwing.

Lesser Whistling Duck *Dendrocygna javanica*   L 42cm 16.5"

all plum	• Smaller size than Fulvous Whistling Duck but structure and posture similar.
ad	• Narrow dark line over crown through hind-neck, rather sharply defined.
	• Deep rufous uppertail-cov; central part of underparts deeper rufous than rest of underparts.
	• Unstreaked or indistinctly pale streaked flank ⇔ Fulvous.
	• Deep rufous lesser cov.

White-faced Whistling Duck *Dendrocygna viduata*   L 48cm 19"

all plum		• Structure similar to Fulvous Whistling Duck.
		• Legs dark grey.
ad	⇒	• Finely *barred flanks*.
		• *White face* and crown sharply demarcated from black rear-head and hind-neck.
		• Dark chestnut breast.
		• Black bill with blue-grey subterminal mark.
note		• Records in WP probably not of wild origin.

Mute Swan *Cygnus olor*   L 153cm 60"

all plum	• Curved neck ⇔ straighter in Bewick's Swan and Whooper Swan.
	• *Long pointed* tail ⇔ in Bewick's and Whooper shorter and more straight cut.
	• Back normally more bulky than in Bewick's and Whooper.
ad	• Orange-red bill with black base and knob on forehead (ad ♂ with larger knob than ad ♀).
juv	• Variable amount of grey-brown on whole plumage; normally warmer and less diffusely patterned than in other juv swans. Pure 'Polish-type' juv completely white, in other ind white plumage from mid 2cy.
	• Dark brown-grey bill, gradually turning to orange in course of 2cy.
fl all plum	• Long *pointed* tail reaching behind legs ⇔ in other swans legs reach to or slightly beyond tail-tip.

Whistling Swan *Cygnus columbianus*   L 130cm 51"

ad	⇒	• At most 1/8 of bill yellow (see note). In large majority yellow on bill like 'teardrop' on or just below lore and hardly larger than eye. Yellow on bill often almost absent.
		• Yellow on bill often paler than in Bewick's Swan.
		• Bill often a little longer than in Bewick's with flatter culmen (more Whooper Swan-like).
		• Generally a little larger than Bewick's with slightly longer neck.
note		• Assumed diagnostic amount of yellow on bill based on only one study.

Bewick's Swan *Cygnus bewickii*   L 122cm 48"

all plum		• Smaller than Whooper Swan with slightly shorter neck, slightly shorter bill and rounder head.
ad	⇒	• Yellow on bill highly variable but rounded and bordered by black part of bill (basal part of culmen normally black) ⇔ Whooper. At least 1/4 of bill yellow (see note)
		• Variable amount of orange-red on basal part of cutting-edge (possibly caused by sexual dimorphism) ⇔ in Whooper none.
juv-1w		• Bill-pattern much like Whooper (see below) but often more black on base of gape.
		• Rather uniform grey-brown like Whooper.

Whooper Swan *Cygnus cygnus*   L 153cm 60"

all plum	⇒	• Very long, nearly straight neck.
		• Triangular head-profile ('Common Eider-like'), caused by long bill ⇔ Bewick's Swan.
		• Bill longer and slightly flatter on lower side than in Bewick's with straighter culmen.
		• Breast often bulging (especially when swimming) ⇔ Bewick's.
ad	⇒	• More yellow on bill than Bewick's; *yellow angular, bordered* with black and extends below nostril ⇔ Bewick's.
		• Basal part of culmen always yellow ⇔ most Bewick's.
juv-1w		• Pale dull yellow basal part of bill becoming pinkish on distal part; cutting-edge and bill-tip black.
		• Evenly grey-brown ⇔ Mute Swan juv.
fl all plum		• Short tail; legs project beyond tail ⇔ Mute.
		• Very long and slender neck.

Snow Goose *Anser caerulescens*   L 73cm 29"

ad	• White morph entirely white except black prim and grey prim-cov (like Ross's Goose ad).
	• Blue morph with dark grey to brown-grey upperparts and underparts (except vent and undertail cov);

	head and upperside of neck white, dark hind-neck and underside of neck. Flight-feathers dark; tertials and rear greater cov *black-centred with well-defined pale fringes*. Tail white to very pale grey, cov pale grey ⇔ most hybrids.
	• Legs and bill orange-pink in both morphs.
juv	• White morph largely pale grey-brown, cov and tertials with narrow dark centres. Dark eye-stripe.
	• Blue morph largely dark grey to dark brown-grey with pale grey cov.
	• Bill and legs dark in both morphs.
1w	• Like ad but in white morph dark centres of sec and variable amount of dark patterning elsewhere.
fl juv	• White morph with dark grey prim and paler grey sec.
fl all plum	• Underwing-cov always white, sharply contrasting in blue morph all plum.
note	• See also Ross's Goose.

geog var	**Lesser Snow Goose** *A.c. caerulescens*
all plum	• Rather small bill with distinct 'grinning patch'.
	• Intermediates between blue and white morph occur (tertial pattern normally exclude hybrids).

geog var	**Greater Snow Goose** *A.c. atlanticus*
all plum	• Large bill with distinct 'grinning patch'; head-shape more triangular than in Lesser.
	• Generally larger than Lesser but very variable; Lesser ♂ nearly as big as Greater ♀; Lesser ♀ much smaller than Greater ♂ which approaches Greylag Goose in size.
note	• Blue morph very rare (or possibly only as intergrade with Lesser).

Ross's Goose *Anser rossii*   L 59cm 23"

all plum ⇒	• Small bill with *grey base*.
	• No 'grinning patch' ⇔ Snow Goose.
	• Border between bill and head-feathering (nearly) straight ⇔ in Snow curved, pointed on forehead.
	• Relatively short neck, slightly broadening from head to breast.
	• Head pure white (as Snow often with yellowish wash).
	• Somewhat rounder crown than Snow.
ad	• In blue morph (rare) strong contrast between almost black mantle and back and *almost white cov* (creating white line) ⇔ in Snow ad blue morph cov indistinctly grey.
	• In blue morph entirely dark hind-neck and crown and distinct white face ⇔ Snow ad blue morph.
juv	• White morph paler than Snow juv white morph with only pale grey upperparts and indistinct darker markings on tertials and greater cov. Blue morph as Snow juv but *cov white*. Central part of belly, vent and undertail-cov white.
	• White morph with weak dark eye-stripe.
	• Dark nail, paler later in winter.
fl all plum	• As Snow but neck shorter and thicker.

Juvenile 'grey geese'

	• Feathers of upperparts and underparts with slightly rounded tips and in most species rather indistinct yellow-brown fringes ⇔ in ad straight cut off tips and sharp white fringes along tips.
	• Bill-pattern normally duller than in ad with more dark patterning, especially on nail (paler later in winter).
	• Underparts less obviously barred than in ad (absence of barring especially obvious on rear flanks).
	• Indistinct neck grooves.

Taiga Bean Goose and Tundra Bean Goose

all plum	• Dark head and neck gradually merge into paler breast ⇔ in Pink-footed Goose more sharply defined dark head.
	• Dark tail with narrow white frame ⇔ Pink-footed.
	• Broad white fringes on scaps, cov and tertials ⇔ in other 'grey geese' less obvious.
	• Outer greater cov often slightly paler than rest of cov (but no strong contrast as in Pink-footed).
	• Legs deep orange.
juv	• See introduction to Juvenile 'grey geese'.
fl all plum	• Dark, uniform under- and upperwing ⇔ Pink-footed has pale upperwing-cov.
note	• On current knowledge, both Taiga Bean Goose and Tundra Bean Goose are rather variable in bill-structure and -pattern. Only ind showing full suite of specific characters are identifiable with certainty.

Taiga Bean Goose *Anser fabalis*   L 83cm 32.5"

all plum	• See introduction to Taiga Bean Goose and Tundra Bean Goose.
	• Long, triangular bill, seemingly more pointed than Tundra Bean Goose. Lower mandible narrow, often 'disappearing' below upper mandible towards bill-tip. Virtually no 'grinning patch'.
	• Larger than Tundra with longer neck and rear-end. Can be almost size of small Greylag Goose.
	• Variable amount of orange on bill, on average distinctly more orange than in Tundra. Sometimes nearly all orange bill with only dark basal part of culmen.
	• Often narrow white rim or pale band at bill-base ⇔ Tundra.
	• Head normally somewhat paler than in Tundra, contrasting less with neck.
juv	• See introduction to Juvenile 'grey geese'.

geog var	*A.f. johanseni* (western Siberia)
	• As *fabalis*, but bill generally larger with relatively little orange; often only orange band like in Tundra but wide overlap with *fabalis*.

Swans, geese and ducks

note geog var	• Overall size, bill-size and amount of dark on bill increases from *fabalis* in west, via *johanseni* to *middendorffii* in East Asia. As yet no other differences known, so field identification of *johanseni* in WP probably not possible with certainty.

Tundra Bean Goose *Anser serrirostris*   L 75cm 29.5"

all plum	• See introduction to Taiga Bean Goose and Tundra Bean Goose. • Fairly short, often rather stumpy bill, lower mandible visible up to bill-tip ⇔ Taiga Bean Goose. • Dark bill with subterminal band ('cigar-band'). Some ind with more orange on bill. • Bill with obvious 'grinning patch' ⇔ in Taiga and Pink-footed Goose less obvious. • Rather deep bill-base; somewhat concave culmen. • Short, thick neck.
juv	• See introduction to Juvenile 'grey geese'.

Pink-footed Goose *Anser brachyrhynchus*   L 71cm 28"

all plum ⇒	• (Very) broad white-framed tail (similar to Greylag Goose) ⇔ Tundra Bean Goose, Taiga Bean Goose and White-fronted Goose. • Narrow, dark bill with pinkish subterminal band; bill-band normally extending into *narrow line along cutting-edge of upper mandible* towards bill-base ⇔ Tundra. • *Pale buff breast* contrasting strongly with dark head, especially striking at distance. • Greater cov grey, obviously paler than dark rear flanks (greater cov sometimes not visible in non-flying bird) ⇔ in Tundra and Taiga less or no contrast. • Legs dark pinkish. • Upperparts greyish with whitish fringe on cov and tertials creating conspicuous pale wash on upperside. • Very dark head; often very little contrast with dark parts of bill ⇔ in Tundra and Taiga normally more contrast between less dark head and dark parts of bill. • Short neck.
juv	• See introduction to Juvenile 'grey geese'.
fl all plum	• Pale, grey-blue cov creating large pale patch on upperwing.

White-fronted Goose *Anser albifrons*   L 71cm 28"

all plum ad	• Legs bright orange. • White forehead blaze. • Very variable amount of black belly markings.

geog var	**Eurasian White-fronted** Goose *A.a. albifrons*
ad juv	• Bill pink. • See introduction to Juvenile 'grey geese'. • Little or no dark belly markings; little or no white forehead blaze (like Lesser White-fronted Goose juv).
fl all plum	• Tail with less white on tip than in ad. • Dull grey upperside of hand and cov slightly paler than sec. • Relatively long, narrow wings.

geog var	**Greenland White-fronted** Goose *A.a. flavirostris* L 74cm 29"
all plum ⇒ ⇒	• Yellow-orange bill, bulky and long. • Tail normally very narrowly white-framed (narrower than in *albifrons*). • Upperparts darker than in *albifrons* with narrower, indistinct buff fringes to cov and tertials (sometimes lacking on tertials) ⇔ *albifrons*. • Dark head, neck and breast ⇔ *albifrons*. • Narrower and shorter white flank stripe than *albifrons*. • Generally larger than *albifrons* with slightly longer neck. • Back and rump very dark brown-grey.
ad	• Some ind with bold black patterned underparts but in most not different from *albifrons* in this respect. • White forehead blaze often extends to underside of bill.
juv	• See *albifrons* juv. • Little or no dark belly markings; little or no white forehead blaze (like *albifrons* juv).

geog var	*A.a. frontalis* (Alaska, northern Canada and eastern Siberia)
all plum	• Larger than *albifrons*, especially ind from population of northern Canada which approach Greylag Goosein size (see note). • Long bill, often tending towards orange. • Head and upperside darker brown than in *albifrons*, underparts with brown background ⇔ in *albifrons* whiter background. • Tail with little white (almost as in Greenland White-fronted Goose).
notes	• Possible vagrant in WP. • Population of Alaska and northern Canada sometimes considered as separate taxon *albicans*.

geog var	*A.a. gambeli* (northern Canada)
all plum	• Very large size with long neck and tarsus (larger than *frontalis*). • Dark plumage with brown background (darker than *frontalis*). • Bill long, tapering to narrow tip and sometimes tending towards orange.
ad	• Obvious yellow or orange orbital ring. • Tail with little white (similar to *frontalis* and almost as in Greenland White-fronted Goose).

| notes | • White forehead blaze often larger than in other taxa.
• Often relatively little black belly-markings (but highly variable in all taxa).
• Breeds in taiga and winters mainly in aquatic habitats.
• Probably vagrant in WP. |

Lesser White-fronted Goose *Anser erythropus* L 62cm 24.5"

all plum ⇒ ⇒	• Dark pink bill, narrow and short. • Distinct yellow eye-ring. • White forehead blaze reaching higher up (onto crown) and more pointed than in White-fronted Goose (not present in most 1w). • Wing-tips reach obviously beyond tail (wing-projection) ⇔ e.g. White-fronted. • Rather small dark head and short dark neck (dark neck sometimes recalls Pink-footed Goose); often less obvious black vertical border between dark head and white forehead blaze White-fronted. • White flank-line often narrower but more well-defined than in White-fronted.
juv	• Tail fairly narrowly white-framed (slightly broader than in White-fronted). • See Juvenile 'grey geese'. • Little or no dark belly markings; little or no white forehead blaze (like White-fronted juv).
fl all plum	• Pale upperside of fore-wing more contrasting than in White-fronted due to darker rest of wing.

Greylag Goose *Anser anser* L 79cm 31"

all plum	• Legs orange-pink. • Orange orbital ring. • Tail broadly white-framed.
juv	• See introduction to Juvenile 'grey geese'.
fl all plum ⇒ ⇒	• Underwing contrastingly two-toned (whitish underwing-cov). • Contrast between pale grey uppertail-cov/rump and dark back/mantle. • Upperside of fore-wing pale blue-grey contrasting strongly with brown upperparts and brown patch on cov.
geog var	*A.a. anser* (western and northern Europe)
all plum	• Large bill, entirely yellow-orange to orange-pink.
geog var	*A.a. rubrirostris* (eastern Europe to central Asia)
ad	• Bill pinker and bulkier than anser; greyer plumage with more obvious whiter fringes to upperside feathers and stronger barred rear-flanks.
note geog var	• Status and identification in western Europe muddied by introductions and occurrence of intermediate types due to interbreeding with native population.

Canada Goose and Cackling Goose

Identification of these geese in Europe is often very difficult, especially as suspected vagrants are often lone individuals, and birds not showing all features consistent with a certain taxon are probably best left unidentified. Moreover, identification to (sub)species level is further muddied by frequently occurring intermediates due to suspected integration zones at the edges of the breeding range of some taxa in North America. In Europe intermediates may arise due to hybridisation with introduced or escaped ind. Many forms are not generally accepted as having occurred in a wild state in the WP.

In general, forms darken in North America from east to west and become bigger from north to south. Identification of all forms should be based on the following combination of field marks:

• size and general structure;
• bill structure;
• colour and dark/pale intensity of upperparts and underparts;
• presence or absence of dark line across white throat.

Canada Goose *Branta canadensis*

all plum	• See introduction to Canada Goose and Cackling Goose.
geog var	**Atlantic Canada Goose** *B.c. canadensis* L 105cm 41"
all plum	• Pale breast contrasting with dark flanks. • Often complete pale collar, sharply defined against black neck. • Slightly darker than palest forms, e.g. pale *parvipes* and Cackling Goose. • Broad pale fringes to feathers of upperparts and flanks (strongest pale barred form).
geog var	**Todd's Canada Goose** *B.c. interior* L 100cm 39"
all plum	• Fairly dark upperparts, without paler rear-side to collar (dark mantle continuing uninterrupted to black neck). • Often conspicuously pale breast. • Indistinct pale fringes to feathers of upperparts. • Large long bill. • Long, almost swan-like neck. • Most similar to *taverneri* but upperparts browner and only very lightly barred pale. • In western populations often dark line down centre of white throat.

Swans, geese and ducks

geog var	*B.c. maxima*	L 112cm 44"
all plum	• Very pale, especially on underparts. Plumage nearly as canadensis but very large broad white cheek-patch reaching higher up. • Somewhat narrower pale fringes to feathers of upperparts and flanks than in *canadensis*. • Often some white on forehead. • Long neck. • Large bill.	
note	• Not recorded as wild in the WP.	
geog var	*B.c. moffitti*	L 112cm 44"
all plum	• Plumage very like *maxima* but sometimes even paler. Underparts very pale, breast sometimes nearly white. • Sometimes with broad but incomplete collar. • Some white on forehead (more often in *maxima*). • Often dark line across throat.	
note	• Not recorded as wild in the WP.	
geog var	Intermediate Canada Goose *B.c. parvipes*	L 91cm 36"
all plum	• Larger than Cackling Goose with long body; size similar to or slightly larger than White-fronted Goose. • Plumage similar to pale Cackling (darker and smaller in extreme north-west). • Longer, more pointed bill than in Cackling with deep base. • Relatively short neck but longer than in Cackling. • Regularly with pale collar as in Cackling. • No dark gular line down throat dividing white cheek-patches.	
geog var	*B.c. occidentalis*	L 90cm 35.5"
all plum	• Fairly narrow bill in relation to size. • Plumage similar to *fulva* but in general slightly paler and more often with pale collar. • Only very narrow pale fringes to feathers of upperparts and underparts, looks uniformly dark from a distance. • Upperside of breast dark, fading into black neck (as often in hybrids with Barnacle Goose).	
note	• Not recorded as wild in the WP.	
geog var	Dusky Canada Goose *B.c. fulva*	L 95cm 37.5"
all plum	• Rather evenly coloured dark rufous-brown, little contrast between underparts and upperparts. • Underparts (especially flanks) deeper coloured, as in minima. • Rather narrow white cheek-patch (sometimes dark line across throat). • Normally no pale collar.	
note	• Not recorded as wild in the WP.	

Cackling Goose *Branta hutchinsii*

all plum	• See introduction to Canada Goose and Cackling Goose.	
geog var	Hutchins's Cackling Goose *B.h. hutchinsii*	L 69cm 27"
all plum ⇒	• Smallest of pale forms; size and structure (short neck and compact body) as Barnacle Goose, sometimes slightly smaller. • Typically angular head-shape with steep forehead and flattened crown. • Small, Barnacle Goose-like bill; slightly longer and more slender than in *minima*. • Pale breast conspicuous (sometimes with brownish wash), often almost white, creating normally palest part of underparts. • White cheek-patch often indented at eye level (sometimes in other Cackling and Canada Goose taxa too, especially *parvipes*). • Sometimes weak pale collar, not bordered by black on lower edge. • Cov rather plain, without obvious black subterminal band. • Often appears short-legged.	
geog var	Taverner's Cackling Goose *B.h. taverneri*	L 89cm 35"
all plum	• Bill somewhat smaller (shorter and thicker) than in Canada Goose *parvipes* and bill-line normally runs more or less evenly into sloping forehead; rounded crown. • Broad white cheek-patch; dark line across throat often present (as e.g. in *minima*). • Fairly long slender neck. • Rather dark brown upperparts. • Rather pale grey underparts, breast only a little paler. • Almost never shows pale collar.	
geog var	Dark Cackling Goose *B.h. minima*	L 63cm 25"
all plum	• Underparts dark, nearly as dark as upperparts. Lower breast and upper belly typically warm purple brown in adult. • Very small, triangular bill. • Small, rather rounded head, but when alert more square. • Very short neck. • Legs relatively long. • Sometimes broad pale collar, bordered by black on lower edge. • Rather narrow white cheek-patch; dark line across throat often present ⇔ e.g. hutchinsii.	

| ad ⇒ | • Feathers on upperparts have pale grey bases with black subterminal bands and white tips creating rather bold pattern slightly similar to Barnacle Goose (and hybrids!) ⇔ in juv and all plum of most other taxa less contrasting due to no or hardly any black subterminal bands and less white on tips. |
| note | • Not recorded as wild in the WP. |

Aleutian Cackling Goose *B.h. leucopareia*   L 67cm 26"

geog var

all plum	• Broad pale collar often very conspicuous; broad in front, often strongly narrowing backwards, normally lacking on rear side of neck.
	• Dark, sometimes rufous-brown underparts, only slightly paler than upperparts.
	• Angular head with steep forehead ⇔ *minima*.
	• Small thick bill, but not as small as in *minima*.
	• Short neck, but often longer than in *minima*.
	• Dark line across throat often present, as e.g. in *minima* ⇔ e.g. *hutchinsii*.
note	• Not recorded as wild in the WP.

Barnacle Goose *Branta leucopsis*   L 65cm 25.5"

all plum	• Black neck and breast contrast strongly with nearly white underparts (in Canada and Cackling Geese breast pale and only neck black).
juv	• Diffusely spotted rear-flank ⇔ in ad faintly barred.
	• Rather diffuse loral-stripe ⇔ in ad well-defined.
fl all plum	• Pale grey upperside to wings; pale underwing-cov.

Red-breasted Goose *Branta ruficollis*   L 57cm 22.5"

all plum	• Chestnut-red breast and fore-side of neck. White-outlined chestnut-red patch on side of head.
	• Upperparts black, conspicuous broad white flank-line, belly black.
juv-1w	• 3-5 narrow pale lines along cov ⇔ in ad often 3, of which 1-2 conspicuous broad white lines.
	• Belly and upperparts dark grey ⇔ in ad deep black.
	• Belly often with pale scales.
	• Chestnut-red patch on head-side sometimes still rather restricted (especially in 1cy), outlined by much white ⇔ ad.
fl all plum ⇒	• White flank-stripe conspicuous.
	• Short thick neck.
	• Very dark underwing.

Dark-bellied Brent Goose *Branta bernicla*   L 59cm 22"

all plum	• Dark grey underparts and black head and neck (the latter a feature of all brent geese).
	• Flanks variably barred whitish (belly always darker ⇔ Pale-bellied Brent Goose).
	• Upperparts uniform dark lead-grey.
ad	• White patch on neck-side ⇔ in juv absent.
juv	• Pale tips to cov create multiple white wing-bars.
	• No neck-side patch.
	• Upperparts paler than in ad.
1w	• Like juv but developing variable ad characters.

Pale-bellied Brent Goose *Branta hrota*   L 59cm 22"

all plum ⇒	• Like Dark-bellied Brent Goose but underparts rather evenly pale, strongly contrasting with black breast and neck.
	• *No dark area between legs* ⇔ paler ind of Dark-bellied.
	• Somewhat bulkier and more compact than Dark-bellied, and with shorter neck.
	• Upperparts slightly paler and browner than Dark-bellied, with slightly darker feather centres and vague paler fringe. Often also rather messy mix of paler and darker feathers ⇔ in Dark-bellied more uniform.
juv	• See Dark-bellied.
	• Flanks and belly uniform mid (brown-)grey.
1w	• Juv scaps and cov with pale fringes retained into late winter ⇔ Dark-bellied and Black Brant.

Black Brant *Branta nigricans*   L 59cm 22"

all plum	• Like Dark-bellied Brent Goose with white rear-flank (white often crossed by dark lines), strongly contrasting with very dark upperparts and belly ⇔ in Dark-bellied pale flank-patterning less white.
	• (Nearly) no contrast between black breast/neck and very dark central part of belly.
	• Very dark upperparts, in winter normally distinctly darker than in Dark-bellied (in summer often bleached). (In winter) nearly no contrast between upperside and visible black prim ⇔ Dark-bellied.
	• Large white patch on neck-side often connecting in front (in early winter sometimes smaller) ⇔ Dark-bellied.
juv	• Slightly less contrasting than ad (belly less dark) but often already clearly different from Dark-bellied. See Dark-bellied for other juv characters.
1w	• Neck-side patch sometimes already large (juv cov retained until spring).

'Grey-bellied Brent Goose' *[still without scientific name]* (western arctic Canada)

geog var

all plum	• Mostly resembles Pale-bellied but with solid *grey-brown* central part of underparts, extending to between/behind legs.
	• Flank conspicuously densely whitish streaked (as in Black Brant) but less contrasting due to less dark belly and upperparts (like 'washed-out' Black Brant).
	• Upperparts sometimes pale as in Pale-bellied but normally darker, like Dark-bellied but typically more brown.

1w notes	• White neck-side patch relatively large, often approaching size of patch of Black Brant. • See Pale-bellied. • Plumage-wise intermediate between Black Brant and Pale-bellied (and possibly stable hybrid population between latter but ongoing DNA investigations suggest valid (sub)species). • Probably very difficult or even impossible to distinguish from hybrid Pale-bellied x Dark-bellied, but known hybrids have grey instead of brown upperparts and less solid and greyer central part of underparts.

Egyptian Goose *Alopochen aegyptiaca* L 68cm 27"

all plum ad	• Pale iris. • Grey head and neck; dark patch through eye (creating mask). • Cream-coloured breast with dark spot in centre. • White cov creating white wing-panel (sometimes concealed by dark scaps). • Legs red-orange.
juv	• Head, neck and breast uniformly pale with no dark markings.
fl all plum ⟹	• White cov creating large white wing-panel on both upper- and underwing as in Ruddy Shelduck, but dark tips to median cov creating dark stripe on white panel of upperwing ⇔ Ruddy Shelduck. • Rounded wings.
note	• In grey form weak dark mask and paler upperparts and underparts.

Ruddy Shelduck *Tadorna ferruginea* L 64cm 25.5"

ad ad ♂	• Deep cinnamon-rufous upperparts and underparts (♂ darker and deeper coloured than ♀). • Black collar (in eclipse collar absent). • Cov sometimes with pale rufous wash ⇔ ad ♀.
ad ♀/juv juv	• White face (in ♂ head more uniform cream-coloured). • As ad ♀ but body more grey-brown; cov with pale greyish wash.
fl all plum	• Completely white cov (but see ad ♂ and juv) creating large white panel on both upper- and underwing, strongly contrasting with black flight-feathers (sec with green gloss).
note	• Cape Shelduck *T. cana* (South Africa) and Paradise Shelduck *T. variegata* (New Zealand) superficially similar to Ruddy and have occurred as escapes in WP. Both species have wing-pattern as Ruddy but Cape ad ♂ has uniform grey head, ad ♀ has head-pattern recalling Long-tailed Duck ♀ w. Paradise ad ♀ has sharply demarcated entirely white head (ad ♂ completely sooty-brown and not like Ruddy at all).

Common Shelduck *Tadorna tadorna* L 60cm 23.5"

ad ♂ ad ♀/1w ♂	• Large red knob at bill-base. • Less advanced knob than ad ♂. • Sometimes pale forehead and eye-ring (especially in 1s ♀).
juv-1w	• White forehead, lores and throat. • Whitish eye-ring. • Greater cov with grey tips ⇔ in ad wholly white. • Upperparts scalloped pale grey-brown. • Breast-band broken in centre (in juv completely absent); rest of underparts white (lacking adult's dark central band along underparts).
fl ad fl juv-1s	• Dark flight-feathers contrast with white cov. • Pale trailing edge along sec and inner prim ⇔ ad.

Spur-winged Goose *Plectropterus gambensis* L ♂100 cm 39"

all plum ad	• Large size (♂ larger than ♀). • Upperparts blackish with crow-like green-blue gloss. • Central part of underparts patchily white, contrasting with dark brown flanks and breast-sides. • White head-side. • Large red bill and bare red face.
ad ♂ fl all plum	• Reddish heightened shield on forehead ⇔ ad ♀. • Broad, strongly rounded wings. • Pale underwing-cov.

Cotton Pygmy-goose *Nettapus coromandelianus* L 33cm 13"

all plum	• Very small size (as Common Teal) but totally different structure with short thick neck and triangular goose-like bill.
ad ♂	• White head, neck and breast. Black bill, median crown-stripe, upperparts and stripe on breast-side. Grey flanks.
ad ♀	• Finely greyish patterned head, neck and breast. Black median crown-stripe and eye-stripe. Dark brown upperparts, pale brown flanks. • Dark bill with yellow cutting edge.

Eclipse plumage

Most species of duck develop an eclipse plumage from midsummer until (in some species) winter. Besides different feather-patterns (camouflage-patterns caused by complete moult of flight-feathers), the bill-pattern usually becomes less conspicuous (often completely dark). In most species the ad ♂ changes markedly in appearance, often resembling the ad ♀. In this book, ad ♂ s refers to breeding-plumage which is evident from autumn/winter until the next eclipse period. The upperwing-pattern of ad ♂ eclipse remains unchanged and is a good difference with 1w ♂ and ♀.

Red-crested Pochard *Netta rufina*

ad ♂ s	• Pale flanks contrast with dark upperparts and black vent and breast.
	• White wedge at front of mantle.
ad ♂ eclipse	• Resembles ad ♀ but iris red and bill remains wholly red ⇔ in ♀ dark iris and only red bill tip.
ad ♀	• Dark crown and blackish mask contrasts with pale head-side.
	• Pale subterminal spot on upper mandible.
	• Pale flanks contrast with darker mantle and scaps.
juv	• Complete dark bill ⇔ ad ♀.
	• No obvious dark mask ⇔ ad ♀.
fl all plum	• Broad, conspicuous pale bar over entire wing-length (resembles Ferruginous Duck).
	• Largely white underwing with narrow dark trailing edge.
fl ad ♂	• White leading edge.

Southern Pochard *Netta erythrophthalma*   L 51cm 20"

all plum	• Large, dark, *Aythya*-like duck with grey bill and dark nail.
ad ♂	• Sooty-black head and breast. Upperparts dark brown; flanks warm-brown, slightly paler than upperparts.
	• Eye red.
ad ♀	• Characteristic patterned head with large whitish patch in front of bill-base and whitish C-shaped patch on read side of head.
	• Undertail-cov white.
fl all plum	• Pale wing-bar along whole wing length, especially on underwing *strongly contrasting with very dark underwing-cov*

Common Pochard *Aythya ferina*   L 46 cm 18"

all plum ⇒	• Characteristic head-profile: concave culmen runs in even line from bill to forehead. Highest point of crown above eye.
ad	• Pale bill-mark more or less diagonal (in eclipse bill totally dark).
ad ♂	• Uniform pale grey upperside and flanks.
	• Black vent and breast.
	• Chestnut head.
ad ♀	• Brown-grey, diffusely spotted upperparts and flanks contrasting with dark brown breast and rear-end (uppertail-cov and undertail-cov). Becomes more brown during spring and early summer.
	• Warm brownish head with pale eye-stripe, dark line running from gape to cheek, pale eye-ring and pale area at bill-base.
juv	• More uniform and browner than ad ♀ in winter; head lacks dark markings.
juv-1w	• Underparts patchy ⇔ ad.
1w ♂	• Largely as ad ♂ but wings still juv with dark tertials.
fl all plum	• Completely greyish upperwing; black rear-side of hand.
note	• For further field marks, see Canvasback and Redhead.

Canvasback *Aythya valisineria*   L 54 cm 21"

all plum ⇒	• *Wholly black*, long bill (in Common Pochard imm and eclipse have dark bill as well).
	• *Deep bill-base* tapering to relatively fine bill-tip.
	• Forehead runs in straight or even slightly bulging line down to culmen.
	• Highest point of crown often behind eye.
	• Long neck.
ad ♂	• Flanks and upperparts (incl tertials) paler than in Common Pochard (sometimes nearly whitish).
	• Forehead and crown darker (blackish) than rest of head ⇔ in Common Pochard ♂ head more uniform.
	• Pale flanks usually reach further into black breast than in Common Pochard, creating sloping border ⇔ in Common Pochard vertical.
♀/imm	• Resembles Common Pochard ♀ but slightly paler on upperparts and flanks contrast stronger with dark breast.
	• Normally lacks Common Pochard's dark line running from gape to cheek; head, incl lores, more uniform than Common Pochard.
	• Pale flanks usually reach further into dark breast than in Common Pochard.
	• In 1w ♂ dark tertials.
fl all plum	• Long neck conspicuous.

Redhead *Aythya americana*   L 48 cm 19"

all plum ⇒	• Grey bill (in ad ♂ pale grey, in other plumages dark grey, but paler than in Common Pochard) with diffuse whitish subterminal band and *large straight-cut black tip*. Pale bill-band *nearly vertical* ⇔ in Common Pochard and some look-alike hybrids pale bill-band more diagonal and black tip extends along edge of upper mandible.
	• Characteristic head-shape with steep forehead and bulbous peak just above or before eye. Head-shape sometimes resembles Eurasian Wigeon.
	• Long nail sometimes conspicuous.
	• Often sits relatively high on water.
	• Border between bill feathering and side of upper mandible almost straight or only slightly convex (bulging) ⇔ in Common Pochard strongly convex.
ad ♂	• Orange-yellow iris ⇔ in Common Pochard ♂ darker orange-red.
	• Bright chestnut-red head.
	• Black breast extends well into grey flanks.
	• Upperparts rather dark grey.

ad ♀/1w ♀	• More like Ring-necked Duck ♀ than Common Pochard ♀ due to pale eye-ring, pale eye-stripe (but more faint) and bill-pattern but head rufous-brown instead of greyish. • Often very little or no contrast between flanks and breast (sometimes breast slightly darker) ⇔ in Common Pochard obvious contrast between dark brown breast and greyish flanks. • At distance rather uniform warm brown appearance, at closer range sometimes numerous pale feather-tips visible, giving strongly variegated impression. Other ind much more plain. • Dark, sometimes chestnut crown contrasts with rather pale head-side (sometimes even resembling Common Scoter ♀). • Area around bill-base pale, lacking dark line extending from gape to cheek normally present in Common Pochard. • Whitish undertail-cov often conspicuous due to tail usually being raised ⇔ in Common Pochard tail normally depressed and held at water-level meaning undertail-cov not visible.
1w	• Dark tertials. • Uniform dark bill.
fl all plum	• Rather pale grey wing-bar contrasts fairly strongly with dark front side of wing (cov), similar to Common Pochard.

Ring-necked Duck *Aythya collaris*   L 42cm 16.5"

all plum		• Egg-shaped head caused by high and rounded crown. • Relatively long tail often reaches above surface. • Rather pointed bill.
ad	⇒	• Grey bill with pale subterminal band and large black tip (in ♀ bill normally darker than in ♂).
ad ♂	⇒	• White line around bill-base.
♀	⇒	• Grey flanks with *conspicuous white 'tooth'* on front-side. • Brown collar (characteristic feature but difficult to see). • Bright yellow iris.
ad ♂ eclipse		• Black parts of ad ♂ s browner, flanks rufous-brown. • Pale iris retained ⇔ in 1w dark iris.
imm/ad ♀ ⇒		• Conspicuous pale 'spectacles' (pale eye-ring connected with pale eye-stripe). • (Rufous-)brown flanks contrasting with dark upperparts. • Lacks Common Pochard's dark line extending from gape to head-side. • Dark crown contrasts with greyish head-side. • Dark yellow-brown to red-brown iris ⇔ ♂. • Often diffuse pale vertical stripe on border of breast and flank (ghosting 'tooth' of ad ♂ s). • Diffuse pale area surrounding bill (in imm often conspicuous).
juv-1w		• Dark, normally somewhat red-brown iris. • Almost completely dark bill with diffuse paler subterminal band ⇔ in ad conspicuous pale subterminal band.
1w		• Underparts patchy ⇔ ad. Later in winter mainly as ad.
fl all plum ⇒		• Wing-bar grey on entire upperwing. • Underwing darker than congeners with more teal-like pattern; grey with white axillary and central-band (white medium cov and lesser cov, grey greater cov).
note		• Hybrids often identified by pattern of bill and in the case of Ring-necked x Tufted Duck by presence of some sort of crest.

Ferruginous Duck *Aythya nyroca*   L 41cm 16"

all plum	⇒	• Sharply defined, *black outlined*, totally white undertail-cov. • Strongly rounded head with highest peak in middle of crown. • Dark grey bill with variable amount of black on and directly around nail. Often diffuse pale, nearly vertical, subterminal bill-band (see ad ♀/imm) but very variable. In summer uniform dark bill. • Culmen curves high up near base in smooth line to forehead. • Breast and flanks uniform (in 1w ♂ sometimes slight colour difference) ⇔ in nearly all hybrids x Ferruginous clear contrast between breast and flanks. • No white before bill-base (lores often slightly paler brown in summer) ⇔ most Tufted ♀. • Under-edge of bill from base to tip nearly straight, only faintly extending up near tip (as in Common Pochard) ⇔ e.g. in Tufted Duck obvious upward bend near bill-tip.
ad		• Sharply demarcated white belly-patch (flight) ⇔ imm.
ad ♂		• White iris. • Dark brown-red head and flanks. • Black on bill-tip often restricted to nail. • In summer ill-defined pale spot on lores.
ad ♀/imm		• Dark iris ⇔ ad ♂. • Dark rufous-brown head and underparts; lores and ear-coverts paler (especially in summer). • Black on bill-tip more extensive than in ad ♂. Pale subterminal bill-mark often more diffuse and less vertical than in most ad ♂.
juv-1w	⇒	• Belly much darker than in ad, slightly paler belly ill-defined and contrasting little (especially in juv ♀) ⇔ ad. Dark belly retained well into 2cy. • 1w ♂ with pale iris from end of summer. • Bill dark grey; 1w ♂ with large dark bill-tip ⇔ ad ♂. • In juv dark patterning on undertail-cov.
fl all plum ⇒		• *Broad white wing-bar* along entire wing-length (in ♀ white wing-bar slightly narrower than in ♂ caused by larger dark tips to prim). • Very pale underside of wing, narrow dark framed.
fl ad ♂		• White leading edge.
note		• Some hybrids, especially Common Pochard x Ferruginous Duck ♀, can strongly resemble pure Ferruginous but in this hybrid-type pale subterminal bill-band more obvious and more diagonal, and there is more dark on bill-tip.

Tufted Duck *Aythya fuligula*

all plum ⇒	• Crest (or part of it) nearly always present ⇔ all other *Aythya*.
	• Relatively large amount of black on bill-tip; black often stretches along edge of bill-tip.
ad ♂	• Plumage black with sharply demarcated white flanks and belly. Long crest to hind-neck.
	• Purple gloss on head (gloss can vary under different circumstances).
ad ♂ eclipse	• Black parts of ad s ♂ browner; flanks spotted grey-brown.
ad ♀	• Amount of white at bill-base very variable, from absent to nearly as much as in typical Lesser/Greater Scaup but often less sharply defined.
	• Very variable amount of white on undertail-cov, from absent to nearly as in typical Ferruginous Duck, but white not surrounded by black as in Ferruginous.
1w	• By early winter already nearly as ad (e.g. iris-colour); in 1w ♂ flanks not entirely white. Wing still juv (as in all ducks 1w) with dark tertials.
note	• For further field marks, see Lesser Scaup and Greater Scaup.

Greater Scaup *Aythya marila*

all plum	• Black on bill-tip restricted to nail (ad ♂) or nail and its direct surrounding (imm and ♀); less black on bill-tip than in Tufted Duck.
	• Very rounded head-shape with highest point on front of crown.
	• Broad, blue-grey bill with deep base (broader than in Tufted Duck and Lesser Scaup).
	• Breast often more protruding than in Tufted Duck.
ad ♂ ⇒	• Entirely pale grey upperparts.
	• Green gloss on head ⇔ Tufted Duck (gloss can vary under different circumstances).
ad ♂ eclipse	• Black parts of ad s ♂ browner; upperparts darker brown-grey.
	• Flanks spotted brown-grey.
	• Pale iris retained ⇔ young 1w.
ad ♀/juv	• Pale spot on ear-coverts (appearing from late winter; in autumn normally absent).
	• Sharply demarcated, broad white patch surrounding bill (in juv-1w ♀ *browner* and often bordered more faintly).
	• Only little contrast between somewhat paler flanks and darker upperparts (as in Lesser) ⇔ Tufted Duck ♀-type.
ad ♀	• Slightly paler with grey wash on upperside and flanks. Breast and front of flanks warmer brown than in Tufted Duck ♀-type.
1w ♂	• Dark scaps and upperparts with variable amount of ad ♂-type grey feathers.
	• Brown and grey patterning on pale flanks (later in winter like ad).
	• Belly and breast brown (black later in winter).
	• Head wholly dark and lacks greenish gloss ⇔ in ad ♀ at least weak pale patch on side of head.
	• Tertials wholly dark ⇔ in ad fine pale patterning on some tertials.
1w	• Yellow-brown iris becoming yellow later in winter (ad-type iris-colour in ♀ develops much later than in ♂).
fl all plum	• Upperwing: broad white wing-bar on sec (slightly broader than in Tufted Duck) gradually becoming grey on prim (as in Tufted Duck).
fl ad ♂	• Grey cov ⇔ in Tufted Duck ♂ black.

Lesser Scaup *Aythya affinis*

all plum ⇒	• Bump on rear-crown; *angled or peaked rear-head* ⇔ Greater Scaup.
	• Sharply demarcated, very small rectangular black spot on nail. Black does not 'leak' to side of nail; in rear-view no black on bill-tip visible. In most Greater ad ♂ also very little black on nail.
	• Slightly smaller bill (slightly narrower and shorter) than Greater but slightly broader and deeper than Tufted Duck.
	• Slightly longer tail than Tufted Duck and Greater but rarely useful.
ad ♂	• Pale upperside with *quite obvious dark lines*, often somewhat coarser towards rear ⇔ in Greater ad ♂ finer and more evenly patterned.
	• Normally purple head-gloss (gloss can vary under different circumstances, sometimes seems to show green gloss).
	• Pale grey-blue bill.
	• Often very weak grey vermiculations on white flanks (only visible from close range).
	• Bright yellow eye (in 1w ♂ somewhat duller) ⇔ some hybrids.
ad ♂ eclipse	• As Greater ad ♂ eclipse but often slightly darker with coarser markings on upperside.
♀ s	• Diffuse pale spot on head-side, usually less distinct than in Greater ♀.
♀	• Sharply demarcated white spot surrounding bill-base (as in Greater ♀) but white narrows at gape, hardly extending down below bill.
	• Little contrast between slightly paler flanks and darker upperparts (as in Greater) ⇔ Tufted Duck ♀-type.
	• Head often distinctly darker than body ⇔ Tufted Duck ♀.
	• Bill darker grey than in ad ♂ (but normally paler than in Tufted Duck ♀).
	• Slightly paler than Tufted Duck ♀ with grey wash on upperside and flanks (grey wash not in juv). Breast and front of flanks warmer brown than in Tufted Duck ♀-type.
1w	• Dark, normally somewhat red-brown of brown-yellow iris, becoming gradually paler later in winter.
1w ♂	• See Greater 1w ♂.
fl all plum ⇒	• White wing-bar on sec *turns sharply into grey or pale brown on prim* (sometimes however very little difference in shade between sec and inner prim).
	• Underwing slightly darker than in Tufted Duck and Greater; grey base of greater cov contrast somewhat with white median cov and darker lesser cov and flight-feathers (two white bars on grey underwing). In Ring-necked Duck stronger contrast between darker grey base of greater cov and white median cov and lesser cov.

Mandarin Duck *Aix galericulata*
L 45cm 17.5"

ad ♂	• Unmistakable multi-coloured duck with bold white mask, strongly elongated orange feathers on sides of head (creating long 'whiskers') and central tertials developed to form large orange 'sails'.
ad ♀	• Large, rounded pale spots on flanks ⇔ in Wood Duck small spots.
	• Fine pale streaking on cheeks ⇔ in Wood Duck none.
	• Pale nail ⇔ in Wood Duck dark.
	• Pale inner-edge of tertials ⇔ in Wood Duck none.
	• Narrow white eye-stripe (creating narrow line) ⇔ in Wood Duck creating rather broad mask.
fl all plum	• Underwing-cov uniform dark ⇔ Wood Duck.
note	• Introduced in Britain, Germany, the Netherlands and other countries.

Wood Duck *Aix sponsa*
L 46cm 18"

all plum	• Long tail.
	• White outer-edge of prim (as in Mandarin Duck).
ad ♂	• White stripe on breast-sides, neck-side and ear-coverts; white throat.
	• Dark neck and head with long crest (with green gloss) to hind-neck.
	• Brown-yellow flanks.
	• Red bill, iris and eye-ring.
ad ♀	• Dark with pale mask and throat.
	• Dark brown flanks with fine pale speckles.
fl all plum	• Dark underwing; underwing-cov with fine grey spots creating slight contrast against dark flight-feathers.
	• White trailing edge along arm.
notes	• Frequently kept in captivity and regularly seen as a proven escape.
	• Introduced Mandarin ♀ rather similar to Wood ♀, for further differences see Mandarin Duck account.

Ruddy Duck *Oxyura jamaicensis*
L 39cm 15.5" incl tail

all plum	• Structure similar to White-headed Duck but smaller size and with concave culmen lacking 'swollen' base.
	• Undertail-cov white ⇔ in White-headed brown (concolorous with flank).
ad ♂	• White ear-coverts and throat with black crown and hind-neck. Black crown extending below eye ⇔ White-headed ad ♂.
1w/ad ♀	• Flank diffusely barred ⇔ in White-headed uniform.
note	• Not accepted as wild in WP; introduced in Britain and has spread to other countries.
	• See White-headed Duck account for further differences.

White-headed Duck *Oxyura leucocephala*
L 45cm 17.5" incl tail

all plum ⇒	• Strongly swollen basal part of culmen (in ♂ slightly more so than in ♀).
	• Little or no contrast between red-brown flanks and upperparts.
	• Long tail like Ruddy.
ad ♂	• White head with narrow black crown; dark eye surrounded by white.
ad ♂ eclipse	• Black crown sometimes adjoins top of eye (but does not extend below eye as in Ruddy).
ad ♀/1w ⇒	• Narrow, well-defined pale stripe on head-side ⇔ in Ruddy diffuse.
	• Sharp border between white throat and dark breast ⇔ Ruddy.
1w ♂	• White more extensive on head-side than in ♀.
imm	• Pale tips to tail-feathers.
note	• Hybridises quite commonly with Ruddy; hybrids always show less or even no swollen bill-base, and intermediate head-pattern.

Common Eider *Somateria mollissima*
L 64cm 25"

all plum	• *Drawn out and triangular head-profile* caused by long triangular bill.
ad ♂ s ⇒	• Black underparts; white upperparts and breast (breast often with pink wash) ⇔ in King Eider ad ♂ s mainly black upperparts.
ad ♂ eclipse	• Mainly black with white cov (cov creating long white vertical bar).
ad ♀	• Strongly barred flanks ⇔ dabbling ducks.
	• (Rather) obvious pale wing-bar on greater cov (like most King).
juv	• More uniform and colder grey-brown plumage than ad ♀.
	• Faint and finely barred flanks.
	• Broad diffuse supercilium ⇔ in ad ♀ often narrow but more sharply defined.
1w	• Flanks and scaps fresh, contrasting with juv belly and wings.
1w-1s ♂	• Black-brown with white breast and some white patterning on mantle and back. Cov wholly dark ⇔ ad ♂ eclipse.
2w-2s	• Similar to ad ♂ but cov, mantle and neck with variable amount of dark spots.
fl all plum	• Relatively slow wing-beats (compared with scoters).
fl ♀	• Almost uniform dark upperwing with pale lines along tips of greater cov and sec. Breadth of pale lines rather variable.
	• Pale axillaries and fairly pale bar over underwing-cov; underwing generally darker than in King.

geog var	**Northern Eider** *S.m. borealis* (Arctic waters from Spitsbergen to north-east Canada)
ad ♂ ⇒	• Rear scaps normally somewhat curled up, creating 'sails' on upperside, comparable with King ad ♂ but smaller and often less pointed. Visibility of 'sails' depends on behaviour.
	• Bill and shield mainly orange-yellow (see note), shield often rather broad ⇔ in *mollissima* shield narrow, grey to green-greyish or sometimes brown-yellow.
	• Tertials longer and more curled than in *mollissima*.
	• Black cap often more straight bordered with white side of head than in *mollissima*.
ad ♀	• When small 'sails' present then indicative of north-western origin.

ad ♂ eclipse note	• Often retained longer than in *mollissima*; may still be in full eclipse late into October.
	• Variable in colour and shape of shield with gradually more typical ind towards north-west of range. Ind from north-western Europe probably intermediate.

geog var   **Dresser's Eider** *S.m. dresseri* (North America)

ad ♂ ⟹	• Shield grey-greenish to orange (depending on season; orange in winter/spring) and *very broad, ending much more strongly rounded* on forehead than in *mollissima* and *borealis*. Shield reaches close to eye.
	• Green edge below black cap.
	• Black on lores narrow and parallel along lower edge of shield ⇔ in *mollissima* and *borealis* extending in a point.
	• White 'sails' often present.
	• Culmen often with concave kink.
	• Tertials long and curled down.
ad ♀	• Patch on rear-head greyish to yellow-green and ill-defined.
note	• When small 'sails' present then indicative of north-western origin.
	• Occurrence in WP recently confirmed.

geog var   **Pacific Eider** *S.m. v-nigra* (arctic Canada)

all plum	• Large size.
ad ♂ ⟹	• Bill wholly bright yellow-orange.
	• Shield narrow and short.
	• Green edge below black cap (as in *dresseri*).
	• White 'sails' often distinctly present (but sometimes absent).
	• Bill pointed and tip slightly downcurved.
	• Underside of black cap strongly curved.
	• Often dark V-shaped mark on throat, sometimes difficult to see.
note	• Not recorded in WP, but possible vagrant.

geog var   *S.m. faeroeensis* (Shetland and Faroe Islands)

ad ♂	• Relatively small, dark green-grey bill.
	• Shield relatively short, ending pointed (as in *mollissima*).

King Eider *Somateria spectabilis*   L 57cm 22.5"

all plum	• Smaller, shorter bill than Common Eider.
ad ♂	• Large yellow-orange bill-shield; front nearly vertical (in 2w-2s ♂ shield smaller, front not vertical).
ad ♂ s ⟹	• Mainly black upperside (black scaps but mantle white) and underparts; white thigh-patch conspicuous.
	• Pale blue crown and hind-neck.
	• Breast deep salmon-coloured (sometimes most eye-catching feature in group of eiders, but some Common with pink breast).
	• Rear scaps turned upwards, often pointed.
♂ eclipse	• Plumage nearly completely dark with white cov when ad (when wings closed creating narrow white vertical bar); in 1s-(some)2s ♂ still has entirely dark cov.
	• Shield slightly smaller than in ♂ s.
ad ♀ ⟹	• Dark bill, darker than head ⇔ in Common ♀ bill normally paler than head.
	• Broad, diffuse pale eye-ring and surround to gape (the latter creating 'smile' effect).
	• V-shaped flank-markings ⇔ in Common ♀ more straight.
	• Often small 'sails' present (upturned rear scaps). Also preent in some Common ♀ of north-western origin.
	• Main colour generally warmer orange-brown than in Common ♀ -type (but some Common ad ♀ occasionally conspicuously rufous-brown).
juv	• Juv-type flank-feathers with large dark centres and pale edges; juv ♂ with pale centres to breast-feathers.
	• Plumage more greyish than ad ♀.
1w	• Flanks and scaps fresh, contrasting with juv belly and wings.
1w-1s ♂ ⟹	• *Orange* sides of shield, bill yellowish to pinkish.
	• Upperparts wholly dark; whitish breast and, when present, thigh-patches only pale parts ⇔ in Common 1s ♂ besides whitish breast also variable whitish patterning on upperparts.
2w-2s ♂	• Shield less high than in ad.
fl all plum	• Shorter, thicker neck than Common.
	• Pale axillaries and pale underwing-cov often more obvious than in Common.
fl ad ♂	• White area on cov relatively small and separated by black scaps and leading edge of wing ⇔ in other eiders ad ♂ wholly white cov and scaps.
fl 2w-2s ♂	• Often less white on cov than ad, rarely still completely dark cov.
fl ♀	• Almost uniform dark upperwing with narrow pale lines along tips of greater cov and sec (generally narrower than in Common ♀).

Spectacled Eider *Somateria fischeri*   L 55cm 21.5"

all plum	• Bill-feathering reaches to upper mandible; no shield.
	• Structure more like Common Eider, less compact than King Eider.
ad ♂ s	• Black underparts incl breast; white upperparts. White patch on rear-flank small ⇔ Common and King ad ♂ s.
ad ♀/imm ♀	• Large pale area around eye and large dark area on lores.
	• No or very narrow pale wing-bar ⇔ Common and King ♀.
	• Shape of flank markings more like Common (nearly straight) ⇔ King.
fl ♀/imm	• Axillaries and underwing-cov grey ⇔ white in Common and King.

Steller's Eider *Polysticta stelleri*

L 46cm 18"

all plum ⇒	• *Plump, swollen bill with blunt tip*; no bill-feathering ⇔ other eiders.	
	• Often angular head with steep forehead and strongly flattened crown. Ad with bump on rear-head.	
ad ♂ s	• Brown-orange underparts with small dark spot on breast-sides.	
	• White head (green patch on rear-head and lores) with black neck-band and throat.	
ad ♂ eclipse	• Similar to ad ♀ but with large white area on cov and larger pale tips to tertials.	
ad ♀	• Dark, slightly drooping tertials with pale tips or streaks (in imm ♀ shorter, straighter tertials without white patterning). Colour and gloss like speculum.	
	• Pale head-side and diffuse broad pale eye-ring.	
♀ ⇒	• Dark brown plumage with (when visible) only *white borders of blue speculum* obvious (white wing-bar along greater cov and sec).	
	• Variable white, triangular marking on tertial-tips ⇔ juv-1w	
juv-1w	• As ad ♀ but speculum less or not at all blue and narrowly but evenly bordered white (in Common Eider narrowing towards outer side of arm).	
	• Tertials short without gloss. No or hardly any white on tertial-tips.	
2w ♂	• Similar to ad ♂ but variable amount of dark patterning on white cov.	
fl all plum ⇒	• Contrasting *white underwing-cov*.	
	• Blue speculum bordered white on both sides.	
	• Rear-end looks conspicuously full, especially rump. Neck short and thick.	

Harlequin Duck *Histrionicus histrionicus*

L 41cm 16"

all plum	• Small greyish bill, often becoming paler towards tip.	
	• Fairly long pointed tail.	
	• Steep forehead.	
ad ♂	• Mainly blue-grey, variably patterned with white stripes on neck, breast and scaps; large white patch on front of head and rufous flank.	
juv/♂ ⇒	• Clear white spot on rear-side of ear-coverts.	
	• Large pale patch on front of head (normally dark lores).	
	• Except head-pattern, wholly uniform black-brown (reminiscent of small Velvet Scoter ♀).	
fl all plum	• Dark wings; very dark underwing-cov contrast slightly with paler underside of flight-feathers.	
	• Rear-body long and tapering to point.	

Common Scoter *Melanitta nigra*

L 49cm 19"

ad ♂	• Entirely black plumage.	
	• Bill-knob rather small and steep.	
	• Variable amount of yellow on culmen; in ind with extensive yellow, yellow reaches over bill-knob as broad stripe to forehead. In rare cases 1w ♂ with much yellow, superficially similar to Black Scoter but *yellow at base more restricted to culmen, not broadly connected to bill-base; sides of knob black*.	
	• Long tail ⇔ Velvet Scoter and Surf Scoter.	
ad ♀	• Dark brown plumage; pale head-side contrasts with dark crown.	
imm	• Pale belly. 1w ♀ with brown wings.	
fl all plum ⇒	• Prim paler than rest of wing ⇔ Surf.	
	• Thin neck appears pinched behind head ⇔ Velvet and Surf.	
behav	• During wing-flapping holds head down ⇔ Velvet and Surf.	
	• Normally dives with leap and closed wing ⇔ Velvet and Surf.	
note	• See Black for more features.	

Black Scoter *Melanitta americana*

L 49cm 19"

all plum	• Neck thicker and tail shorter than in Common Scoter.	
	• Nail rather strongly hooked and often reaching below lower mandible ⇔ Common.	
	• Often sits higher in water than Common.	
ad ♂ ⇒	• Bill-knob much larger and less steep than in Common (at least reaching over half of upper mandible.	
⇒	• Knob completely yellow with only *narrow black line below yellow knob*; yellow stretches *along complete base of upper mandible* ⇔ in Common ♂ (incl 1w ♂) at most broad yellow stripe over knob reaching base of upper mandible (broad black area below yellow knob).	
	• Culmen more strongly concave than in Common; upper mandible slightly raised at nail.	
	• Nostril nearer bill-tip than in Common, behind basal part of upper mandible.	
	• Eye-ring inconspicuous greyish ⇔ in Common yellow.	
1w ♂	• Bill-structure and colour not yet as ad ♂ but from Nov/Dec onwards already much yellow-green around bill-base; from 2cy bill gradually like ad ♂, with colour developing more quickly than structure.	
	• Plumage like ad ♀ in autumn but during winter gradually like ad ♂; wings remain brown. Moult timing and extent variable, some ind very ♀-like until spring.	
ad ♀/1w	• Bill often slightly shorter than in Common with more swollen base and upper mandible raises more off nail.	
	• Head shape slightly less rounded than in Common with steeper forehead and flatter crown (more square head shape).	
	• Dark crown extending more obviously and broader through nape than in Common, often ending more or less angular ⇔ in Common ends more pointed.	
	• Bill feathering above gape sharply angled (right-angled or sharper) and feathering adjoining upper mandible concave ending on side of upper mandible (latter variable and only useful in obvious cases) ⇔ in Common angle of bill feathering above gape more rounded and feathering adjoining bill normally convex along side of upper mandible.	
	• Cheeks often cleaner than in Common with at most very weak vertical dark smudge.	
imm	• See Common.	
note	• See Common for main features.	

Surf Scoter *Melanitta perspicillata*   L 51cm 20"

all plum	⇒	• Angular head-profile with flat crown.
		• Bill-base reaching high up; no bill-feathering ⇔ Velvet Scoter.
		• Size like Common Scoter but head looks much larger due to large bill.
		• Legs orange-red (also useful in flight in group of Commons).
ad ♂	⇒	• Multi-coloured bill.
	⇒	• White patches on rear-head/hind-neck and on forehead.
1s-2w ♂		• Lacks ad's white patch on forehead and bill less vividly coloured.
ad ♀		• Faintly bordered, white patch on rear-head/hind-neck (clearer in older ind).
		• Often rather pale iris ⇔ juv-1w ♀.
ad ♀/1w		• Dark crown contrasts with pale rest of head (in ad ♀ often less strong contrast than in imm).
		• Diffuse pale spot before bill-base and on ear-coverts. Spot before bill-base forms narrow vertical ellipse ⇔ in Velvet ad ♀ broader and more horizontal ellipse.
juv-1w ♀		• Large pale area before bill-base and on ear-coverts (larger and whiter area than in ad ♀, sometimes creating completely pale head-side, rather similar to Common ♀).
imm		• Pale belly to 2nd part of 2cy. 1w ♂ with brown wings.
fl all plum		• Completely dark wings ⇔ Common.
		• Large head and thick hind-neck creating rather different silhouette compared to Common.
		• Often flies very low over surface, largely following waves.
behav		• Tail often raised when swimming.
		• Often dives with open wings ⇔ Common.

Velvet Scoter *Melanitta fusca*   L 54cm 21"

all plum		• Sec completely white (often visible when swimming).
		• Legs red.
ad ♂		• Black plumage with white sec and white crescent below eye.
		• Yellow on upper mandible mainly concentrated above cutting-edge and on nail; basal part of culmen dark ⇔ in Common Scoter ad ♂ yellow concentrated on culmen.
ad ♀		• Completely sooty-black with white sec and diffuse pale spot on lores and ear-coverts. Pale spots on head-side sometimes nearly absent ⇔ juv-1w ♀.
juv-1w ♀		• Pale spots on head-side often slightly larger and whiter than in ad ♀.
imm		• Pale belly up to 2nd part of 2cy. 1w ♂ with brown wings.
fl all plum	⇒	• Very conspicuous white speculum formed by white sec.
		• Thick neck ⇔ Common.
behav		• Dives with open wings without any form of leap.

White-winged Scoter *Melanitta deglandi*   L 53cm 21"

all plum		• Bill feathering sags deeply over basal part of bill and ends rectangular on upper mandible ⇔ in Velvet Scoter ends higher (sags less deeply) and runs more diagonal.
		• Bill feathering prolonged over base of culmen, often ending pointed ⇔ Velvet and Stejneger's.
		• White sec and red legs as in Velvet.
ad ♂	⇒	• Coloured part of bill red-orange and *concentrated on distal part, not reaching bill-base* (more black on bill-base than in Velvet, as in Stejneger's).
	⇒	• White crescent below eye also extending high above eye to rear (as in Stejneger's) ⇔ Velvet.
		• Flanks dark grey-brown spotted, in spring and summer sometimes becoming very pale by bleaching (see geog var) ⇔ Stejneger's. Breast and undertail-cov black.
		• Nostril very large (as in Stejneger's).
ad ♀/imm		• Bill-knob larger than in Velvet (in ad ♂ much larger) with obvious angle between bill and forehead ⇔ in Stejneger's culmen runs in more or less straight line over forehead, in Velvet in smooth concave line.
		• Tip of bill feathering reaches level of nostril (like Stejneger's) ⇔ in Velvet much shorter.
juv-1w ♀		• Large white spot on ear-coverts, larger than in most Velvet juv and some Velvet ad ♀.
imm		• Sharply demarcated white belly (as in Velvet and Stejneger's imm).

geog var		**Stejneger's Scoter** *M.d. stejnegeri* (north-east Asia)
all plum		• Bill-feathering mainly as in *deglandi*.
		• White sec and red legs as in Velvet Scoter.
ad ♂	⇒	• Yellow stripe along rim below red central part of upper mandible (yellow below red) ♀ in *deglandi* *yellow above red* on upper mandible.
		• Bill-knob often tall and well defined (sometimes creating prominent 'chimney') ⇔ in *deglandi* knob angular. In younger ad ♂ knob-shape often similar to that of *deglandi*.
♂		• Flatter but 'fuller' forehead than *deglandi* extends in an almost straight line to the bill-knob ('*swollen forehead*') ⇔ in *deglandi* forehead descends steeply to bill and appears 'pinched in'.
		• Wholly black flank as in Velvet ad ♂ ⇔ *deglandi*.
♀		• Angle between culmen and forehead less sharp than in *deglandi*, often nearly straight line from forehead to culmen, as in Surf Scoter ♀.
note		• See *deglandi* for other differences with Velvet.

Long-tailed Duck *Clangula hyemalis*   L 44cm 17.5" excl central tail-feathers of ad ♂

all plum		• Short bill with deep base.
ad ♂		• Pink spot on central part of bill (by late summer completely black).
		• Strongly elongated central tail-feathers.
ad ♂ w		• White crown and neck; grey face.
ad ♂ s		• Black breast, neck and head; white mask.
ad ♀ s		• Dark head with grey-brown face ⇔ in ad w face white.

juv	• Like ad ♀ w but often greyer on upperparts. Ageing often surprisingly difficult; some ind retain juv plumage up to spring of 2cy, others moult in winter towards ad w plumage type.
1w ♂	• Often pink wash over bill or indistinct subterminal pink bill-band ⇔ ♀ w.
	• Very variable, sometimes head-pattern like ad ♀ w but with more white on sides (e.g. smaller dark spot on sides).
	• From 2cy onwards develops long whitish scaps ⇔ ♀ w.
1s ♂	• Often already strongly resembles ad s ♂, but black on breast extends less towards belly and wings still juv (more worn and with shorter cov than in ad).
ad ♀ w/1w ♀	• Brown-grey breast.
	• Dark crown.
	• Grey bill with dark nail.
fl all plum ⇒	• Entirely dark under- and upperwing.
	• White rump- and tail-sides contrast with black band along middle of back and through rump and tail.
	• Fast flight with vigorous shallow wing beats, often switching from side to side (similar to auks); head often held up ⇔ other ducks.
moult	• Complex and variable; in ad some feather-groups such as scaps and body-feathers of head and neck moulted three times per year, other body-feathers one or two times per year resulting in very variable plumages year round.

Bufflehead *Bucephala albeola*   L 36cm 14"

all plum	• Very rounded head-shape with high crown.
	• Small pale grey bill.
ad ♂ s ⇒	• Large white area on rear head-side.
	• Completely white underparts; upperparts dark.
ad ♂ eclipse	• Similar to ad ♀ except wings (see flight ad ♂).
1w ♂	• Like ♀ but *uppertail-cov paler grey*, contrasting obviously with upperside.
	• White patch on ear-coverts as in (1w) ♀.
1s ♂	• White underparts like ad s ♂ but head still mainly as in 1w.
ad ♀/1w ♀ ⇒	• Entirely dark brown head with oval white spot on rear head-side (smaller in juv-1w).
	• Grey flanks contrasting rather weakly against dark grey-brown scaps and upperparts.
fl all plum	• Fairly dark grey-brown underwing with paler underwing-cov ⇔ in Barrow's and Common Goldeneye underwing-cov darker.
fl ad ♂	• Broad white band extending over complete arm.
fl ad ♀	• Dark wing with white inner sec.

Barrow's Goldeneye *Bucephala islandica*   L 47cm 18.5"

all plum	• Slightly larger with relatively bulkier head than Common Goldeneye.
	• Slightly shorter bill with higher base than Common; nail can appear somewhat raised (bill overall looks heavier).
	• Crown less pointed than in Common, in direct comparison fairy obvious (highest point of head about above eye ⇔ in Common behind eye). Forehead nearly vertical, rather flat crown.
	• Fuller rear-head than Common.
ad ♂ ⇒	• Large white loral-patch reaches above level of bill and eye and ends in point ⇔ Common.
⇒	• Dark vertical stripe on breast-sides.
⇒	• White scaps creating row of white spots.
	• Purple gloss on head ⇔ Common.
ad ♀	• Often much orange-yellow on bill, normally extending above whole cutting-edge (*orange-yellow below nostril*) ⇔ in Common ♀ yellow normally not below nostril. In North American population bill often entirely orange-yellow.
	• Head very dark brown, often darker than in Common ♀.
	• Breast and flanks sometimes slightly darker grey than in Common ♀.
	• Whitish to dull yellow iris ⇔ in Common ad ♀ more variable and often brighter yellow.
ad ♀/imm⇒	• Dark of head extends to upper part of neck like balaclava below helmet ⇔ in Common neck completely white and head seems glued on top of neck.
imm	• No yellow on bill.
fl all plum	• White speculum smaller than in Common all plum, 3-6 white sec ⇔ in Common 7-8.
fl ad ♂	• White patch on median cov rather small ⇔ in Common nearly complete white median cov (greater cov in both species mainly white). Wing-pattern resembles Common 1w ♂.
fl ad ♀	• Pale patch on lesser cov small and indistinct. White inner sec and greater cov separated by dark line. Wing-pattern resembles Common 1w ♀.

Common Goldeneye *Bucephala clangula*   L 44cm 17.5"

sec	• Somewhat pointed crown with highest point slightly behind eye.
ad ♂	• White flanks and neck.
	• Dark head with green gloss.
	• Round white loral-spot.
	• Scaps white with narrow black stripes.
juv	• Like ad ♀ but pale neck-band less distinct or absent.
ad ♀/juv	• Brown head.
	• Wholly greyish upperparts, neck and breast.
fl all plum	• Large thick head and small bill conspicuous.
fl ad ♂	• White inner sec, greater cov and central part lesser cov creating large solid white area.
fl ad ♀	• Inner 6-7 sec white, creating large white speculum; inner greater cov white with distinct dark tips (in 1w ♀ and 1w ♂ absent or at most indistinct); central median cov white, thus upperwing has three white areas, separated by two dark lines (dark lines often also visible when not flying).

fl 1w ♂	• White inner sec and greater cov; often very little dark on tips of greater cov; central lesser cov grey. Overall large white area with somewhat broken dark mid-line; grey central lesser cov isolated from white wing-patches ⇔ ad ♂.
fl 1w ♀	• Like ad ♀ but no dark tips to greater cov and central median cov indistinct grey-brown. Overall one pale area (sec and greater cov).
note	• See Barrow's Goldeneye for other field marks.

Smew *Mergellus albellus*   L 41cm 16"

all plum ⇒	• Short bill with rather deep base.
ad ♂ s	• Mainly white with fine black lines on rear-head and breast-sides; flank pale grey, mantle black.
ad ♂ eclipse	• Like ad ♀ but crown white and mantle, leading edge of wing and prim blacker (wing as ad s).
♀/1w	• Lores blackish in ad ♀, brown in 1w.
	• Rufous-brown crown sharply bordered by white head-side.
	• Brown-grey upperparts and flanks.
1w ♂	• From late winter crown and flanks become whiter with dark lines on fore-flanks breaking through.
fl all plum	• Dark sec with white trailing edge, white line along greater cov and white patch on cov. Pale patterning on underwing-cov.

Hooded Merganser *Lophodytes cucullatus*   L 46cm 18"

ad ⇒	• Large 'square' head caused by broad full crest at rear of head.
	• Blackish upperparts.
	• Tertials with broad white longitudinal stripes.
ad ♂	• Black head with large white area on ear-coverts extending to rear-head.
	• White breast and vertical black-white-black band on breast-sides.
	• Rufous flanks.
	• Yellowish eye.
ad ♀	• Pale lower mandible and cutting-edge.
	• Grey head with diffuse rufous ear-coverts and rear-head.
	• Dark grey flanks, becoming slightly darker at rear.
ad ♀/juv	• Red-brown eye, sometimes paler in ad ♀.
juv-1w	• Pale line on tertials vague dirty-white to grey-brown ⇔ in ad bright white.
fl all plum	• Relatively dark underwing ⇔ Red-breasted and Goosander.
	• Narrow wing 'positioned' more in middle of body ⇔ Red-breasted Merganser and Goosander.
fl juv-1w	• Greater cov with small pale centre, creating incomplete and patchy stripe ⇔ in ad complete white stripe, in ♂ broader than in ♀.

Red-breasted Merganser *Mergus serrator*   L 55cm 21.5"

all plum	• Bill more slender and largely parallel-shaped (only bill-base heightened) ⇔ Goosander.
	• Tip of hook of upper mandible does not reach below lower mandible ⇔ Goosander.
ad	• Iris rather pale red ⇔ in Goosander ad dark.
ad ♂ s	• Dark brown-spotted breast, white collar and grey flank ⇔ in Goosander ad ♂ underparts uniform pale.
ad ♂ eclipse	• Like ad ♀ but wing as ad ♂ (white cov creating large white wing-panel); mantle and scaps darker.
ad ♀ ⇒	• Diffuse border between brown head and grey neck ⇔ Goosander ♀.
	• Loose, spiky crest ⇔ Goosander ♀.
1w	• 1w ♀ nearly as ad ♀; 1w ♂ gradually has more ad ♂ s features coming through on head, neck and flanks (juv wing with dark cov retained to 1s).
fl all plum	• Elongated and slim silhouette with thin neck ⇔ in Goosander heavier body with thicker hind-neck; resembling silhouette of a small diver.
fl ad ♂	• Three separated white areas on upperwing: lesser and median cov, greater cov and sec ⇔ in ♀ and imm ♂ no white area on lesser cov and median cov.
fl ♀/imm ♂	• Dark tips of greater cov creating dark stripe on white wing-panel ⇔ in Goosander ♀ none (ad ♀) or very small (imm ♀).

Goosander *Mergus merganser*   L 63cm 25"

all plum	• Bill-tip slightly hooked (with tip of upper mandible extending below lower mandible) ⇔ Red-breasted Merganser.
ad	• Relatively deep bill-base ⇔ Red-breasted Merganser.
	• Eye dark ⇔ Red-breasted Merganser.
ad ♂ s	• Whitish underparts, often with variable yellowish or pinkish wash.
ad ♂ eclipse	• Like ad ♀ but wing as ad ♂ (white cov creating large white wing-panel).
ad ♀	• Red-brown head sharply demarcated from grey to white neck-side and breast ⇔ Red-breasted Merganser ad ♀.
	• Sharply demarcated pale throat-patch ⇔ Red-breasted Merganser ad ♀.
	• In eclipse variable pale loral line (resembling juv) and shorter crest.
juv	• Almost as ad ♀ eclipse but loral line normally longer and more sharply demarcated.
	• Pale iris ⇔ ad.
1w	• Nearly as ad ♀ but duller and with pale line over lores up to below eye.
	• 1w ♀ almost as ad ♀; in 1w ♂, ad ♂ s features start to appear but normally less advanced than in Red-breasted Merganser (juv wing, with grey cov, retained to 1s).
fl all plum	• See Red-breasted Merganser flight all plum.
fl ad ♀	• Grey cov contrast with black prim ⇔ in Red-breasted Merganser ad ♀ cov darker, barely any contrast.
note	• See Red-breasted Merganser for other field marks.

geog var	**Common Merganser** *M.m. americanus* (North America)

all plum
- Bill-feathering extends in nearly straight vertical line from culmen to lower mandible ⇔ in Goosander pointed ending at base of lower mandible. In ♀ and 1w less obvious than in ad ♂.
- Higher base of upper mandible reaches further along bill than in Goosander.
- Forehead profile often slightly less steep than in Goosander.

ad ♂
- Dark band on base of greater cov (also sometimes in Goosander 2w).
- Underparts normally pure white to 2nd half of winter, from then on more pinkish or yellowish wash ⇔ in Goosander pinkish or yellowish present from beginning of winter.
- Bill somewhat pinkish-red ⇔ in Goosander more pure red.

note
- Not recorded in WP, but possible vagrant.

Eurasian Wigeon *Anas penelope* — L 48cm 19"

ad ♂ s
- Red-brown head and yellow forehead/crown-stripe (often variable greenish mask).
- Grey flanks and upperparts.
- Brown-pinkish breast.

ad ♂ eclipse
- Variable, often with rufous-orange flanks, orange-brown head without pale forehead/crown-stripe. Wing as ad ♂ s.

ad ♀
- Nearly entirely grey-brown, sometimes more rufous-brown on flanks. Ad ♀ s occurs in rufous and grey forms.
- Belly pure white.

1w ♂
- Like ad ♂ s but normally brown juv feathers on upperparts and dark patterning on breast. Juv wings with mainly brown-grey cov to 1s (but often some white ad-type cov).

fl all plum ⇒
- Poorly contrasting grey underwing ⇔ and Northern Pintail.
- Speculum: in ♂ wholly blackish with green gloss without pale borders. In ♀ blackish but with rather narrow pale grey upper and lower borders.
- Well-defined white belly.
- Pointed tail.
- Hand rather strongly hooked backwards (more so than other ducks except American).

note
- See American for other field marks.

American Wigeon *Anas americana* — L 50cm 19.5"

all plum
- Often fairly obvious vertical black line at base of upper mandible (in ♂ often more so than in ♀).
- Tail slightly longer than in Eurasian Wigeon, reaching beyond wing-tip (in Eurasian tail-tip and wing-tip falling roughly level.
- Head-profile often slightly different than in Eurasian caused by steeper forehead and rounder crown.

ad ♂
- Greyish, finely spotted head, variable dark mask with green gloss and white to pale cream-coloured forehead and crown extending up to hind-neck (absent in eclipse). Pale crown often ill-defined at sides.
- Pinkish-brown breast, flanks and scaps.
- White rear-flanks more obvious than in Eurasian caused by stronger contrast with darker flank.
- For other field marks see hybrid American/Eurasian x Chiloe Wigeon *A. sibilatrix* and hybrid Eurasian x American.

eclipse ♂
- Flanks warmer, more orange-coloured than in ad s (see hybrids).
- Green glossy mask absent, from autumn onwards mask develops beginning from eye to rear-head. From December mask often complete but much variation.
- Crown-stripe (nearly) absent.

ad ♀ ⇒
- Grey head with fine dark spots (Eurasian ♀ only shows obvious dark spots in midsummer, at other times pattern is, at most, diffuse).
- Rather sharp division between greyish head and rufous flanks (flank-colour resembles ad ♂ ⇔ Eurasian ♀). Some Eurasian ♀ grey form also have grey head but against that also greyer flanks.
- White base and dark tip to greater cov; other cov with broad pale fringes, often visible when not flying (in flight stands out as white band over cov). Cov sometimes mainly white ⇔ Eurasian ♀.
- Dark mask rather conspicuous (resembling ad ♂) against fairly pale (grey) forehead.
- Outer web of tertials often blacker and outer fringes whiter than in Eurasian ad ♀.
- Breast often with bold dark spots.
- Outer web of inner sec grey ⇔ in Eurasian more white.

1w
- Basal part of greater cov pale grey ⇔ in Eurasian 1w darker.
- Inner and outer web of tertials black (with white fringes) ⇔ in ad inner web wholly grey (in ♀ less clear).

1w ♂
- Like ad ♂ s but wings as juv with mainly pale brown-grey cov with paler base until 1s (often multiple pure white ad-type cov) ⇔ in Eurasian 1w ♂ darker cov.

fl all plum
- Speculum: like Eurasian but in ad ♀ more diffuse and broader upper border caused by pale bases to greater cov.
- Pure white axillaries (in Eurasian axillaries have variable grey patterning but under field conditions can sometimes appear white).
- Whitish median cov forms distinct white stripe on underwing which contrasts more strongly than in Eurasian (more teal-like).

note
- Chiloe Wigeon *A. sibilatrix* (southern South America, escape in WP) is commonly kept in captivity. Both sexes have white foreheads, green heads, orange flanks and scaled black-and-white breasts and upperparts.

Hybrid ♂ wigeon: American Wigeon/Eurasian Wigeon x Chiloe Wigeon and Eurasian Wigeon x American Wigeon

Each of the features below point to hybrid origin. Some ind show lots of hybrid features, others (possibly multiple generation hybrids) strongly resemble pure American.

ad ♂
- Flanks warm-rufous and fade towards breast ⇔ in pure American colder pinkish-brown and uniformly coloured (except in eclipse, then warmer).

- In Chiloe-type hybrid undertail-cov not vertical and not straight cut with white vent.
- Pale around bill-base.
- Cream-coloured crown-stripe not extending to rear-head (also in pure American eclipse).
- Absence of vertical black line at base of upper mandible.
- Red-brown merged in dark mask or red-brown wash on cheeks and neck-side.
- Obvious yellow wash on pale forehead and crown.
- Mainly grey mantle and scaps without obvious brown wash.
- Green on mask very strong and glossy, connected on rear head-side.

Cape Teal *Anas capensis*
L 48cm 19"

ad	• Underparts completely and very strongly scaled (dark base to feathers with very broad whitish edges). From a distance very pale with dark spotted underparts.
	• Red bill with dark base and diffuse grey tip.
	• Eye red.
	• Head pale greyish with fine dark speckles.
	• Upperside dark with pale (somewhat rufous) fringes to scaps and tertials.
	• Sexes similar.
fl all plum ⇒	• Speculum: green with broad white upper and lower border (outer sec nearly white).

Falcated Duck *Anas falcata*
L 51cm 20"

all plum	• Entirely dark bill.
ad ♂	• Green head-side faintly bordered by dark brown crown and lores. Throat and upper part of breast white with black horizontal stripe.
	• Very long tertials hanging down behind tail (not in eclipse).
	• Grey upperparts and underparts.
	• Vent yellow, encircled black (similar to Common Teal ♂).
ad ♀	• Grey, rather uniform head with fine stripes, often slightly paler around bill-base.
	• Greater cov pale grey with white tips (often creating conspicuous pale wing-panel)
	• Tertials with pale grey outer web, broadening towards base.
	• Paler side of undertail-cov forms stripe on base of tail as in Common Teal ♀-type but often less distinct.
	• Full neck.
1w	• See Common Teal 1w ♂
	• Crest shorter than in ad ♂.
	• During body moult from juv to 1w head of ♂ with variable yellow-brown parts.
fl all plum	• Speculum: in ad ♂ blackish, strongly contrasting with paler (grey) rest of upperwing. In ♀ blackish with green gloss; upper border broad, lower border narrow white.
	• Poorly contrasting grey underwing ⇔ other teals.

Gadwall *Anas strepera*
L 51cm 20"

all plum	• Legs yellow to pale orange.
	• No clear white in tail (outer tail-feathers in juv/ad ♀ brown-yellow) ⇔ Northern Shoveler and Mallard.
	• Fairly steep forehead reminiscent of teals or wigeons.
ad	• White, unmarked belly.
ad ♂ s	• Mainly grey (tertials palest part of upperside) with black uppertail-cov and undertail-cov.
ad ♂ eclipse	• Like ad ♀ but tertials uniform pale grey (as in ad ♂ s).
ad ♀ ⇒	• *Blackish greater cov* (on swimming in often visible between scaps and tertials).
⇒	• Pale, orange bill with *wholly dark culmen* ⇔ Mallard ad ♀.
	• Rather uniform grey head with fairly distinct eye-stripe and dark crown.
	• Uniform grey tertials (in breeding season browner and somewhat patterned).
	• Pale stripe along tail-base like Common Teal ♀-type but less obvious.
juv	• White belly with fine markings.
	• Relatively rufous-brown body contrasting with uniform, greyish head.
	• Distinctly striped breast.
1w ♂	• Mainly like ad ♂ moulting into breeding plumage, but juv flank feathers long, pointed and creating regular band ⇔ in ad moulting into breeding plumage flank feathers rounder, shorter and creating more messy band. Shape of flank feathers also useful in ♀.
fl all plum ⇒	• Speculum: in both ♂ and ♀ white (in ♀ and imm narrower, only few white inner sec).
	• White underwing-cov as in Mallard.
behav	• Tail vertical during dabbling.

Baikal Teal *Anas formosa*
L 41cm 16"

all plum	• Relatively long, pointed tail compared to Common Teal.
	• Legs dull yellow-brown.
	• Long wings resulting in long prim-projection.
	• Small dark bill.
ad ♂ s	• Characteristic pied head-pattern with yellow forehead-side and vertical dark line below eye; green rear head-side; dark crown and throat.
	• Grey flanks with white vertical stripe on fore-flanks (as in Green-winged Teal ♂).
	• Long scaps hang down along flanks (not in eclipse).
	• Black undertail-cov.
	• Moults from eclipse to breeding plumage later than in most other *Anas* species. Full breeding plumage from Dec.
ad ♀/1w ⇒	• Pale loral-spot completely encircled by dark.
⇒	• Pale throat and pale vertical wedge on rear head-side.
	• Dark eye-stripe, especially distinct behind eye.

	• Pale, broken eye-ring. • uppertail-cov dark, forming dark line between tail and rump ⇔ in Common uppertail-cov, rump and back rather uniform dark with obvious pale feather-fringes. • Weak pale stripe along tail-base. • Scaps elongated often with uniform dark centre. In some ad ♀ very long overhanging scaps with deep red-brown fringes like ad ♂.
juv	• Like ad ♀ but breast with red-brown ground-colour and head-pattern less marked (can recall miniature Northern Pintail ♀).
1w	• See Common 1w ♂. • Newly moulted scaps elongated with uniform dark centres ⇔ Common (juv-type scaps short and with rounded tips as in Common).
fl all plum ⇒	• Speculum: in both ♂ and ♀ green at inner side of arm, rest black; *upper border narrow buff*, lower border conspicuous broad white, much broader than upper border. • Very dark leading edge to underwing (lesser cov and marginal cov) often darker than in Common.

Common Teal *Anas crecca*　　　　　　　　　　　　　　　　　　L 35cm 14"

all plum	• Small bill. • Legs dark grey-brown.
ad ♂ s ⇒	• White horizontal stripe along scaps. • Red-brown head with large green mask. • Undertail-cov yellow, encircled black.
ad ♂ eclipse	• Nearly as ad ♀ but bill wholly dark.
ad ♀/juv ⇒	• White outer-edge of undertail-cov forms *pale stripe along tail-base* ⇔ other teals (in Falcated Duck ♀ and Baikal Teal juv/♀ often occurring faintly). • Tertials with blackish outer webs (fringes) and paler greyish inner webs (and white fringes). • Almost uniform head with narrow dark eye-stripe.
juv	• Upperparts darker than in ad ♀. • Larger amount of orange-yellow on and above cutting-edge than in ad ♀ (in ad ♀ often restricted to cutting-edge alone and duller orange-yellow).
1w ♂	• Mainly like ad ♂ moulting into breeding plumage, but juv flank feathers long, pointed and creating regular band ⇔ in ad moulting into breeding plumage flank feathers rounder, shorter and creating more messy band. Shape of flank feathers also useful in ♀. • Tertials shorter and narrower than in ad ♂. • Retained juv scaps with complete dark centres and narrow rufous fringes ⇔ in ad pale, often V-shaped patterning in centre and broad pale fringes.
fl all plum	• Speculum: green; upper border broad (broadening towards hand) white to buff (see Garganey), lower border slightly narrower white. In juv-1w upper and lower border narrower than in ad. • Underwing: see Garganey flight all plum.

Green-winged Teal *Anas carolinensis*　　　　　　　　　　　　　L 34cm 14"

all plum ad ♂ s ⇒	• Tips of greater cov deeper buff than in Common Teal (forms deeper buff wing-bar). • White vertical stripe at border of breast and flank. • No white horizontal stripe along scaps ⇔ Common. • Grey flanks nearly uniform (minutely barred) ⇔ in Common finely grey patterned, often paler towards rear flanks. • Tertials more uniform than in Common with only narrow dark shaft-streak ⇔ in Common diffuse dark centres. • Front-side of breast deeper cream-coloured than in Common. • Hardly any pale surround to green mask. • Forehead sometimes slightly darker than in Common.
ad ♂ eclipse ad ♀	• See Common. • Breast and fore-flanks densely dark spotted; darker and browner general appearance than Common. • Often rather well-defined head-pattern with obvious eye-stripe and pale spot on lores (sometimes resembling Garganey or Blue-winged Teal) ⇔ Common. • Very little or no orange-yellow at bill-base.
1w	• See Common 1w ♂
fl all plum note ad ♀	• Speculum: like Common but upper border (tips to greater cov) often deeper buff. • Above-mentioned features are only indicative. Definite identification in WP as yet not possible.

Mallard *Anas platyrhynchos*　　　　　　　　　　　　　　　　　L 56cm 22"

ad ♂ s ad ♂ eclipse	• Dark head (with green gloss), white collar, dark brown breast and pale grey underparts and flanks. • Greyish head; feathers of upperparts and underparts dark with narrow pale fringes. Yellow bill throughout year. • Wing as in ad s with grey cov ⇔ ad ♀.
ad ♀ ad ♀/juv	• Orange bill with mainly dark culmen and dark pattern along cutting-edge. • Patterned belly ⇔ Gadwall (flight). • Relatively pale tertials.
1w	• Greater cov have half-rounded black tips, not forming uniform black line above speculum ⇔ in ad more diamond-shaped tips, forming uniform black line above speculum. • See Common Teal 1w ♂.
fl all plum ⇒	• Speculum: in both sexes deep blue; both sides bordered *broadly* white. • White underwing-cov, as in Northern Shoveler and Gadwall.
behav	• Tail horizontal during dabbling.

American Black Duck *Anas rubripes* L 48cm 19"

all plum ⇒	• No white in tail.
	• Rather pale, brown-greyish head-side sharply bordered by dark breast; dark crown and eye-stripe.
	• Underparts wholly dark ⇔ dark Mallard.
	• Legs orange-red (in Mallard orange).
ad ♂	• Scaps and flank-feathers with uniform dark centres and narrow pale fringes (no pale patterning in centre).
	• Greenish-yellow bill from winter onwards (darker in eclipse).
	• Uppertail-cov, rump and back almost uniform black.
	• Tertials with large amount of pale grey around shaft ⇔ in ♀ normally only some grey directly along shaft.
ad ♀ /juv	• Often very similar to ♂ but rather dark, dull green-grey bill, often with yellow wash. Culmen often with dark patterning ⇔ ♂.
	• Whole plumage browner than ad ♂.
	• Uppertail-cov, rump and back dark brown with weak patterning.
fl all plum ⇒	• Speculum: *purple-blue*; normally *no pale borders at all* (variable narrow pale lower border can exist).
⇒	• Dark patterning at base of prim-cov on underwing, creating dark crescent ⇔ in Mallard ♂ absent, in Mallard ♀ some dark feathers sometimes present but not creating obvious dark line.
	• Dark body strongly contrasting with pale underwing-cov and axillaries.
note	• Hybrid American Black Duck x Mallard frequently occurrs and variable. One or more of following features at least conspicuous in hybrids: some pale patterning in dark feather-centres (e.g. flanks and scaps), in ♂ some green on head and/or uppertail-cov, pale patterning on outer tail-feathers, largely grey tertials, white tipped greater cov and warm-brown fringe on breast-feathers.

Northern Pintail *Anas acuta* L 56cm 22" excl central tail-feathers of ♂

all plum ⇒	• Long, grey-blue bill with black culmen.
	• Long pointed tail.
	• Legs dark grey.
	• Long neck.
ad ♂	• Dark brown head; white front-side of neck and breast.
	• Grey flanks (rear flanks yellowish).
♂ eclipse	• Rear flanks heavily barred, contrasting with paler and more uniform remainder of flanks/belly. Grey-blue upper mandible except culmen throughout year.
♀	• Uniform dull cinnamon head.
	• Fairly dark tail with pale barring.
1w	• See Common Teal 1w ♂
fl all plum	• Speculum: in ad ♂ blackish; upper border yellow-brown, lower border broadly white. In ad ♀ brown, upper border narrowly bordered whitish, lower border conspicuously broad white (in juv this is notably narrower).
	• Dark underwing with white central band (especially very dark leading edge). In imm underwing much more uniform and lacks white central band (middle of underwing only slightly paler).
	• Slim and elongated silhouette with long neck, tail and wing.

Red-billed Duck *Anas erythrorhyncha* L 48cm 18.5"

ad	• Strongly scalloped underparts.
	• Pinkish-red bill with dark culmen (in ad ♀ duller).
	• Very dark crown and hind neck contrasting strongly with pale head-side.
	• Legs dark.
fl all plum	• Speculum: wholly pale brown-yellow (nearly gold-coloured).
	• Yellow-brown sec contrasting strongly with dark rest of upperwing.

Garganey *Anas querquedula* L 38cm 15"

all plum	• Uniform dark grey bill.
	• Legs dark grey.
	• Relatively long tail compared to Common Teal.
ad ♂ s ⇒	• Brown head and breast with very long and broad white supercilium, grey flanks.
ad ♂ eclipse	• Like ad ♀ but head markings stronger and pale iris.
ad ♀ ⇒	• Dark eye-stripe and *stripe over ear-coverts*.
	• Obvious supercilium.
	• Pale spot on lores and pale unpatterned throat.
	• Dark tertials with sharp white fringes ⇔ Common Teal.
	• Pale background to entire plumage.
juv	• Ground-colour of plumage more brown-yellow than in ad and narrow pale fringes to scaps.
1w	• See Common Teal 1w ♂
fl all plum ⇒	• Pale grey inner web of sec, prim and prim-cov; upperwing conspicuously grey overall, especially head.
	• Speculum ad: in ♂ dull dark green, both sides broadly bordered white. In ♀ dark grey, both sides bordered white (narrower than in ad ♂), lower border often broader ⇔ Common Teal.
	• Speculum juv: in ♀ rather narrow pale front and rear border, in ♂ broader but especially rear side not as broad as in ad ♂.
	• Solid, well-defined, very dark leading edge of underwing (lesser cov and marginal cov) contrasts strongly with pale median cov and greater cov, like other teal species, especially Blue-winged Teal and Baikal Teal; in Common Teal contrast slightly less strong.
fl ad ♀	• Cov paler than mantle ⇔ Common Teal.

Blue-winged Teal *Anas discors*
L 40cm 15.5"

all plum ⇒	• Legs yellow (orange-yellow in ♂, dull yellow in ♀). • Long, uniform dark bill.
ad ♂	• Dark head with large white vertical spot in front of bill-base (see note). • Rounded white patch on rear flanks.
ad ♂ eclipse	• Like ad ♀ but black bill (in ad ♀ s paler); sometimes weak pale crescent-shaped spot in front of bill. • Throat wholly patterned ⇔ in ad ♀ pale uniform throat.
1w ♂	• Mainly like ad ♂ moulting into breeding plumage, but juv flank feathers long, pointed and creating regular band ⇔ in ad moulting into breeding plumage flank feathers rounder, shorter and creating more messy band. Shape of flank feathers also useful in ♀. • Tertials shorter and more narrow than in ad ♂.
1s ♂	• Like ad ♂ but with subterminal dark spot on (white, inner) greater cov.
ad ♀/juv ⇒	• Obvious, pale *broken eye-ring*. • Pale loral-spot (not completely framed by dark ⇔ Baikal Teal). • Dark tertials with pale shaft and sharp white fringe (Northern Shoveler ♀ -type like pattern). • Conspicuous dark eye-stripe.
fl all plum	• Speculum: dark green, in ♂ upper border broadly white. In ad ♀/imm upper border ill-defined grey; in both sexes very little or no or pale lower border. • Conspicuous pale grey-blue cov. • Underwing: see Garganey flight all plum.
note ad ♂	• Australian Shoveler *A. rhynchotis* (escape in WP) ad ♂ also has large white vertical crescent in front of bill-base but size and structure like Northern Shoveler, pale iris, deeper rufous flanks and more green-blue head.
note ♀	• Green-winged Teal ♀ can approach head-pattern of Blue-winged ♀.

Cinnamon Teal *Anas cyanoptera*
L 41cm 16"

all plum ⇒	• Long, dark *spatula-shaped* bill sometimes with pink-orange cutting edge ⇔ Blue-winged Teal.
ad ♂ ⇒	• Uniform bright dark red-brown head and underparts; undertail-cov black.
ad ♀/juv	• Mostly resembles Blue-winged Teal ♀ but underparts rufous-brown and rufous head-side, head-pattern less distinct, only faint dark eye-stripe, indistinct eye-ring and often weaker pale spot in front of bill-base.
1w ♂	• Mainly like ad ♂ moulting into breeding plumage, but juv flank feathers long, pointed and creating regular band ⇔ in ad flank feathers rounder, shorter and creating more messy band. Shape of flank feathers also useful in ♀. • Tertials shorter and more narrow than in ad ♂.
fl all plum	• Speculum: as in Blue-winged.
note	• Western American species which occurs relatively frequently in captivity; in WP not yet accepted as occurring in wild, but a potential vagrant.

Northern Shoveler *Anas clypeata*
L 49cm 19.5"

all plum	• Large spatula-shaped bill. • Legs orange. • Much white in outer-tail.
ad ♂ s ⇒	• Dark head (with green gloss), white breast and red-brown flanks.
ad ♂ eclipse	• Diffuse orange flanks, grey head. Pale yellowish iris throughout year ⇔ ad ♀.
1s ♂	• Like ad but with subterminal dark spot on (white, inner) greater cov.
♀/imm ⇒	• Tertials with well-defined, narrow white fringes (not in ad ♂ s) and *pale shafts*. • In juv ♂ uniform blue-grey front side of arm (as in ad ♂) ⇔ in juv ♀ uniform greyish with pale fringes to cov. • Imm has dark scaps with narrow pale fringes.
1w ♂	• Like ad ♂ s but variable amount of dark patterning on head, breast, flanks and scaps. Strongly resembles ad ♂ in 'post-eclipse' (see note moult) but wings as juv with dull blue-green speculum ⇔ in ad ♂ 'post-eclipse' speculum glossy blue-green.
fl all plum ⇒	• Speculum: in ad ♂ blue-green, in ad ♀ less bright green than in ad ♂, in imm dull green to black; upper border broad white, *narrowing to inner-side*. Very faint or no lower border. • Blue (♂) or blue-grey (♀) front-side of arm. • White underwing-cov contrast with dark, patterned belly.
fl ♀/imm	• Dark belly, no contrast between belly and rest of underparts ⇔ most Mallards.
note moult	• In ad complicated moult from eclipse to ad s. Moults after eclipse into variable 'post-eclipse' (either only recognisable in ♂ or only occurring in ♂), in some ind 'post-eclipse' retained to winter, others moult directly to ad s. Ad ♂ 'post-eclipse' resembles incomplete ad ♂ s (or 1w ♂) with variable amount of dark patterning on head and underparts and often pale vertical band between bill and eye.

Marbled Duck *Marmaronetta angustirostris*
L 41cm 16"

all plum	• Broad dark stripe through eye forms conspicuous mask.
ad	• Flanks, cov and scaps with large white, rounded spots. • Short cross-striped crest on rear-crown (in ♀ shorter than in ♂).
juv	• Pale spots on upperparts smaller, more buff and scale-shaped. On flanks much more diffuse and buff (less contrasting) than in ad. • Mask less dark than in ad. Crest lacking (and no dark cross-bars on rear-crown).
fl all plum	• Pale sec contrast with dark tips to prim. • Pale underwing with narrow dark leading edge and trailing edge of hand.
note	• No eclipse.

Grouse, partridges, pheasants, quail and guineafowl

Hazel Grouse *Tetrastes bonasia*   L 36cm 14"

all plum	• Pale underparts completely peppered with dark spots; rufous fore flanks.
ad ⇒	• Grey rump and tail; tail with *black terminal band (fringed white)*.
ad ♂	• Black throat-patch.
	• Back and rump almost uniform grey.
ad ♀	• Spotted throat.
	• Back and rump grey with dark patterning.
juv	• Mainly as ad ♀ but lacks black tail-band.
behav	• When disturbed, often does not fly far and normally perches in a tree.

Willow Grouse *Lagopus lagopus*   L 39cm 15.5"

all plum	• Relatively strong bill in which length-depth ratio ± one ⇔ in Ptarmigan length-depth ratio ± 1.5.
ad ♂ ⇒	• Breast and neck in summer *uniform chestnut-brown, sharply bordered* by white belly.
	• In all patterned plumages more red-brown than Ptarmigan.
	• In s broad red comb above eye ⇔ ♀
ad ♀	• In all patterned plumages more evenly patterned with sharper border to white belly than Ptarmigan.
juv	• Mainly like ad ♀ but prim brown except white p9 and p10.
1w	• Complete moult to winter plumage completed in Nov but juv p9 and p10 retained, being more narrow and more pointed than p9 and p10 in ad.
w	• Completely white except outer tail-feathers.

Red Grouse *Lagopus scoticus*   L 35cm 14"

all plum	• Entirely red-brown plumage throughout year, no major plumage-changes as in Ptarmigan and Willow Grouse.
	• Bill structure as in Willow.
ad ♂	• Deep dark chestnut.
	• In s broad red comb above eye ⇔ ♀.
ad ♀	• Paler, more grey-brown than ad ♂.
fl all plum ⇒	• Brown wings ⇔ Ptarmigan and Willow.

Ptarmigan *Lagopus muta*   L 33cm 13"

all plum ⇒	• Relatively slender bill (see Willow Grouse).
ad ♂ ⇒	• Black lores, especially visible in winter plumage.
	• Plumage in spring, summer and autumn cold grey-yellow-brown with white and black patterning.
	• In spring and summer broad red comb above eye ⇔ in ♀ very narrow at most.
ad ♀	• Underparts and upperparts unevenly spotted and colder, *more greyish-coloured* than in Willow Grouse ad ♀.
ad w	• Wholly white plumage (except black tail).
juv	• Mainly like ad ♀ but prim brown except white p9 and p10.
1w	• In autumn, like autumn-plumage of ad ♀ but part of prim still brown. In winter like ad w but retained p9 and p10 with dark tip.

geog var	*L.m. millaisi* (Scotland)
ad s	• Upperparts more uniform and greyer than in *muta*.
ad w	• Often retains some dark feathers ⇔ *muta*.

Black Grouse *Tetrao tetrix*   L ♂ 55cm 21.5", ♀ 43cm 17"

ad ♂	• Almost completely blackish plumage with blue gloss; vent and undertail-cov white; outer tail-feathers curved outwards.
	• Brief eclipse plumage attained in midsummer: similar to ♀ plumage but more uniform brown, black back and weakly outcurved outer tail-feathers.
ad ♀	• Underparts and upperparts very densely and evenly barred.
	• Small red comb above eye.
	• Tail slightly forked.
1w	• Resembles ad of equivalent sex but ♂ with variable brown patterning on wing, head and body. 1w ♀ often more grey-brown than ad. Both sexes with p9 and p10 narrower, more pointed and with brown patterning on tips ⇔ ad.
fl all plum	• White underwing-cov ⇔ Capercaillie ♀.
	• White wing-bar (broad in ♂, narrow in ♀).

Caucasian Black Grouse *Tetrao mlokosiewiczi*   L ♂ 53cm 21", ♀ 40cm 15.5"

ad ♂	• Entirely black plumage, also undertail-cov (only tiny white spot on shoulder as in Black Grouse) ⇔ in Black white undertail-cov.
	• Longer tail than Black; outer tail-feathers less curved.
	• Brief eclipse plumage attained in midsummer like Black Grouse.
ad ♀	• Much more uniform and slightly greyer than Black ♀.
	• Long tail.
1w	• See Black.
fl all plum ⇒	• Upperwing uniform ⇔ in Black white wing-bar.

Grouse, partridges, pheasants, quail and guineafowl

Capercaillie *Tetrao urogallus*   L ♂ 81cm 32", ♀ 58cm 23"

all plum	• Very large. • Heavy bill with sharp hook.
ad ♂	• Upperparts, underparts and head blackish with blue-purple gloss; cov and scaps brown. • Long tail.
ad ♀ ⇒ ⇒	• Uniform brown-orange breast ⇔ Black. • Pale tips to scaps form conspicuous pale stripe. • Obvious red comb above eye ⇔ in Black ♀ small or absent. • More contrastingly patterned than Black ♀. • Rufous upperside of tail with broad dark bars ⇔ in Black ♀ tail more finely barred on less warm ground-colour. • Rump with grey ground-colour ⇔ in Black ♀ brown.
1w	• p9 and p10 narrower, more pointed and with brown patterning on tips ⇔ ad.

Caucasian Snowcock *Tetraogallus caucasicus*   L 55cm 21.5"

all plum	• Large and bulky grouse (like Capercaillie ♀).
ad	• Whole plumage (except head and white undertail-cov) finely barred (but if viewed from some distance plumage appears uniform). • Rufous and white head markings; *rufous hind-neck*, especially in ♂.
	• Flanks with black patterning ⇔ Caspian Snowcock.
♀	• Slightly less distinctly patterned than ♂ with hardly any rufous on hind-neck.
1w	• Mainly as ad but p8-10 retained; shorter, narrower and more pointed than in ad.
fl all plum	• Prim white with black tip (as in Caspian Snowcock). • Tail-feathers with orange tips (as in Caspian).
voice	• Very clear and far-carrying series of whistles as in all snowcocks, but last note lower in pitch ⇔ Caspian.

Caspian Snowcock *Tetraogallus caspius*   L 59cm 23"

ad ⇒	• *Broad, pale grey collar*, extending towards breast(side), contrasting with dark upperparts ⇔ Caucasian. • Overall paler, greyer and less finely patterned than Caucasian.
♀	• Slightly less distinctly patterned than ♂.
1w	• See Caucasian.
fl all plum	• See Caucasian.
voice	• See Caucasian.

Chukar Partridge *Alectoris chukar*   L 33cm 13"

ad ⇒	• Throat and upper-side of breast pale buff ⇔ Rock Partridge. • Supercilium widens behind eye. • Pale lores. • Dark band extends out to become V-shaped over breast. • Brown-grey upperparts.
1w	• Post-juv moult almost complete, only p9 and p10 retained; shorter, narrower, more pointed and more worn than in ad.

Rock Partridge *Alectoris graeca*   L 34cm 13.5"

ad ⇒	• White throat and upper-side of breast. • Very narrow supercilium. • Dark lores. • Dark band extends out to become rounded over breast. • Greyish upperparts.
1w	• See Chukar Partridge.
geog var	*A.g. whitakeri* (Sicily)
all plum	• Upperparts duller and darker grey-brown than in *graeca* and *saxatilis* (Alps). • Uppertail-cov and central tail-feathers finely patterned dark. • Black band over breast narrower and less round than in other subspecies.

Red-legged Partridge *Alectoris rufa*   L 33cm 13"

ad ⇒	• Black *striped and spotted* breast and neck. • Supercilium broad and conspicuous ⇔ in Chukar Partridge and Rock Partridge narrower and more diffuse. • Brown back, mantle, hind neck and crown ⇔ Chukar and Rock.
1w	• See Chukar Partridge.

Barbary Partridge *Alectoris barbara*   L 33cm 13"

ad ⇒	• Contrasting, *dark brown* crown-stripe. • White-spotted dark brown breast-band. • Mainly brown flank-barring.
fl all plum	• Wings slightly raised.
1w	• See Chukar Partridge.

See-see Partridge *Ammoperdix griseogularis*   L 23cm 9"

all plum ad ♂	• Strongly barred flanks (diffuse in ad ♀) as in Sand Partridge. • Black forehead and supercilium. • Very finely white spotted head- and neck-side.

ad ♀	• Like faintly patterned ad ♂; head uniform brown-grey. • Difficult to distinguish from Sand ad ♀ but at close range pale spots sometimes visible on head-side and neck-side (see also note under Sand).
1w	• See Chukar Partridge.
voice	• Song surprisingly similar to Spotted Crake, but calls very rhythmic in rather fast succession (about 1 per sec), slightly lower pitched and more drawn out.

Sand Partridge *Ammoperdix heyi*   L 23cm 9"

all plum	• Strongly barred flanks (diffuse in ad ♀) as in See-see Partridge.
ad ♂	• Uniform grey-blue head with white spot on lores and rear-side of ear-coverts.
ad ♀	• Like faintly patterned ad ♂ without white spots on head.
1w	• See Chukar Partridge.
note	• Distribution of both Sand and See-see Partridge are not well known. Definite identification of ♀-types in area between northern Israel and southern Turkey should be carried out with great caution.
voice	• Song very rhythmic like See-see, but single notes more monotone, rather similar to single note at beginning of song of Little Crake.

Black Francolin *Francolinus francolinus*   L 34cm 13.5"

all plum	• Orange legs.
ad ♂	• Black head with large white spot on ear-coverts. • *Broad rufous collar.* • Black underparts with many white speckles along entire flanks and breast-sides.
ad ♀	• Red-brown patch on neck-side. • Underparts and upperparts heavily spotted. • Yellow-brown undertail-cov and vent. • Yellow-brown head-side and supercilium.

Double-spurred Francolin *Pternistis bicalcaratus*   L 31cm 12"

ad	⇒	• Bold blackish striped underparts. • Long, whitish supercilium. • Ill-defined orange-brown crown and hind neck; paler throat.
1w		• See Chukar Partridge.
note		• In WP only represented by endemic subspecies *ayesha* in Morocco.

Grey Partridge *Perdix perdix*   L 30cm 12"

ad		• Grey-blue neck, crown and underparts. • Orange face, throat and supercilium. • Brown barred flanks. • Pale grey bill.
ad ♂	⇒	• Large black-brown, often horseshoe-shaped patch on belly. • Head-pattern more obvious and better defined than in ad ♀; orange and grey-blue both deeper.
ad ♀		• Dark belly-patch more narrow than in ♂, sometimes completely absent. • Head-pattern weaker than in ad ♂, supercilium often shorter and more obviously fading away behind eye. • Upperside with less chestnut than in ad ♂.
juv		• Longitudinal stripes on flanks (like Common Quail but no dark head-stripes) ⇔ in ad flanks barred. • Underparts buff-brown with paler belly.
1w		• See Chukar Partridge.

Common Quail *Coturnix coturnix*   L 17cm 6.5"

all plum	• Broad, dark longitudinal stripes on flanks.
ad ♂	• Long supercilium, eye-stripe and moustachial-stripe. • Dark stripe(s) over throat (see note). • Brown streaking on flanks.
ad ♀	• Unmarked pale throat. • Black spotting or short barring on flanks.
1w	• Early partial moult of inner prim (before outer ones fully grown) in breeding range and suspended. Body-moult complete. Central prim moulted in winter range.
1s	• Outer 3 (2-4) prim retained juv feathers and strongly worn.
fl all plum	• Size, relatively heavy body and long wings sometimes recalls large lark.
notes	• Japanese Quail *C. japonica* (escape and introduced in WP) similar to Common but slightly larger and no prim-projection; in ad ♂ uniform rufous-brown throat, ear-coverts and lores (no moustachial- and submoustachial-stripe). Breast warm buff ⇔ in Common yellow-brown. Common ad ♂ of so-called brown morph extremely similar to Japanese due to overall warmer brown plumage and mainly chestnut-brown head with less obvious chestnut-brown neck-side and throat-stripes. Only difference with Common ad ♂ brown morph: throat uniform chestnut-brown, lacks black throat-stripes and breast is more solidly warm buff. • In southern Europe at least, hybridisation occurs between Japanese and Common; these hybrids are sometimes very difficult or impossible to separate from Common.

Common Pheasant *Phasianus colchinus*   L incl tail ♂ 81cm 32", ♀ 62cm 24.5"

ad ♂	• Very variable due to 3 main factors; 1) many subspecies, 2) mixing of native population with different introduced Asian subspecies and 3) mixing of different introduced Asian populations among themselves. Native *'colchicus'*-group without white collar and with chestnut rump. Ind from introduced Asian *'torquatus'*-group with white collar and grey rump.

- Part of the *'colchicus'*-group, septentrionalis (north Caucasus) paler and more yellow-brown overall than more purple-orange nominate.

ad ♀
- Mainly brown with fine and complex patterning on cov and feathers of upperparts (see other pheasants ad ♀).

note
- It is possible that populations east of Black Sea and in north Caucasus (septentrionalis) are still original and not affected by introductions.

Golden Pheasant *Chrysolophus pictus*
L incl tail ♂ 97cm 38", ♀ 70cm 27.5"

all plum
- Legs yellow.

ad ♂
- Unmistakable with golden-yellow crown and rump, wholly red underparts and uppertail-cov and grey-blue wings.

ad ♀
- Darker and more uniform than Common Pheasant ♀. Belly hardly any paler than rest of underparts ⇔ Common ♀.
- Body and wing wholly finely barred. Barring extending onto belly ⇔ in Lady Amherst's Pheasant belly unmarked.
- Long, full tail with heavily barred central tail-feathers, rest of tail-feathers with variable fine barring.
- Rump plain brown ⇔ in Lady Amherst's spotted dark.

note
- Introduced in Britain, although population may not be self sustaining.

Lady Amherst's Pheasant *Chrysolophus amherstiae*
L incl tail ♂ 113cm 52", ♀ 70cm 27.5"

all plum
- Blue-grey bare skin around eye; in ♀ only as eye-ring.
- Legs grey.

ad ♂
- Unmistakable with dark fore-side of head and upper-breast and grey-white, dark scaled full hind-neck, white belly and lower-breast, blue back and wings, yellow rump and red uppertail-cov and patch on rear-crown.
- Extremely long grey tail, barred black.

ad ♀
- Mainly dark, barred rufous-brown.
- Pale eye-ring.
- Tail-feathers broad and rounded with pale and dark barring ⇔ in Golden more pointed and only with dark barring.
- Pale belly unmarked ⇔ Golden.

note
- Introduced in Britain, although population may not be self sustaining.

Reeves's Pheasant *Syrmaticus reevesii*
L incl tail ♂ 150cm 59", ♀ 75cm 28.5"

ad ♂
- Unmistakable. Background cinnamon-brown with black fringes to almost all body-feathers, creating strongly scaled appearance.
- Scaps greyish with broad black fringes.
- Head pale grey with broad black mask and broad pale 'half moon' below eye.
- Black collar ⇔ in ad ♀ none.
- Long tail mainly grey and broadly barred.

ad ♀
- In contrast to ♀ of many other pheasant species, resembles ad ♂, of which it is duller version with whitish background colour to underparts.
- White unmarked belly and neck.
- Flanks cinnamon-brown, spotted and without dark feather fringes.
- Grey tail with at most weak patterning.

note
- Introduced in several European countries but probably nowhere well established.

Helmeted Guineafowl *Numida meleagris*
L 63cm 25"

all plum
- Large thickset game bird with very narrow neck and small head.
- Whole plumage dark with purple wash and numerous small rounded pale spots.
- Bare head with brown crown and blue rear-side of head.

ad
- Upright bony point on crown.

Divers

Red-throated Diver *Gavia stellata*
L 62cm 24.5"

all plum
- Slender bill with straight culmen; lower mandible upturned towards tip of upper mandible.
- Breast stands in nearly vertical line on water surface, no strongly protruding breast as in other divers.
- Flat or somewhat rounded crown, no steep forehead as often in other divers.

ad s
- Blue-grey head- and neck-side; red throat.
- Upperparts uniform brown ⇔ other divers ad s.

w ⇒
- White of head-side and neck extends far back; *narrow* dark line through rear-neck.
⇒
- Well-defined pale spots on feathers of upperparts, *no scaled appearance* ⇔ other divers w.
- Eye situated below or level with dark crown and *large white spot in front of eye* (except juv) ⇔ in Black-throated Diver more dark on crown, eye situated in dark of crown (eye hardly visible).
- Upperparts greyish ⇔ in Black-throated blackish.
- Dark parts of head often paler than in Black-throated ad w/imm.
- Dark hind-neck often finely striped (especially in ad) ⇔ other divers ad w/imm.

juv
- Darker on ear-coverts and neck than ad w; often diffuse white spot on ear-coverts.
- Dark parts of (rear)neck ill-defined with pale fore-neck ⇔ in ad w and Black-throated ad w/imm well-defined border between dark and pale parts of neck.

juv-1w
- Pale markings on upperside less well-defined and less contrasting than in ad w but differences are slight.
- Pale bill ⇔ in ad w darker, at beginning of winter sometimes still black.

1s	• Nearly as ad s but variable amount of white around eye and lores ⇔ in other divers distinctly more immature-looking 1s plumage.
fl all plum	• Moves head regularly in vertical direction ⇔ Black-throated moves head much less. • Legs less conspicuous than in Black-throated.

Black-throated Diver *Gavia arctica*　　　　　　　　　　　　　　　　L 69cm 27"

all plum	• Culmen bent towards bill-tip ⇔ in most Great Northern Diver and nearly all Red-throated Diver culmen straighter. • Often steep forehead and sharp angle between forehead and crown (sometimes obvious knob on forehead as in White-billed Diver and Great Northern).
ad s ad w/imm ⇒	• White blocks on upperparts; grey head and rear-neck. • *White rear-flank* often visible when swimming. • Dark parts of head paler than upperparts ⇔ Great Northern. • Normally narrow, diffuse pale eye-ring ⇔ in Great Northern ad w/juv more obvious and better defined. • Grey head often with dark lores ⇔ in Great Northern head is darker overall and lores are not conspicuously darker. • In ad w grey bill-base and dark culmen and tip ⇔ in 1w more uniform grey.
juv-1w	• Scaled upperparts (but often less strongly patterned than in Great Northern and White-billed) ⇔ Red-throated ad w/imm. • Feathers of upperparts have rounded tips ⇔ in ad more straight cut. • Juv end summer has pale cheeks surrounded by darker ear-coverts and throat, like Red-throated juv (dark smudge on ear-coverts and throat in autumn disappear more rapidly than in Red-throated juv). • Pale grey bill ⇔ in ad w darker, especially culmen and distal part; at start of winter sometimes still black.
1s fl all plum	• No summer plumage but as bleached 1w ⇔ Red-throated. • Legs conspicuous (like Great Northern) ⇔ Red-throated. • Wings more centrally placed than in Red-throated. • Pale uniform axillaries, sharply bordered by dark flank-line (differences with other divers often hard to see but in Red-throated axillary darker and less contrasting with dark flank-line). • Shallow wing-beats ⇔ in Red-throated deeper.
fl ad w/1w	• Contrast between dark upperparts and pale underparts stronger than in Red-throated (similar to Great Northern).

Pacific Diver *Gavia pacifica*　　　　　　　　　　　　　　　　　　　L 63cm 25.5"

all plum ⇒	• When swimming, dark flank side runs *uninterrupted and evenly broad* along side of vent up to dark undertail-cov (no bulging white patch on rear flank) ⇔ in Black-throated Diver dark flank line strongly narrows at side of vent creating white patch on rear flank. • Bill shorter and more slender than in Black-throated. • Smaller size than Black-throated with shorter body (obvious when compared with Black-throated). • Head rounder than in Black-throated, without obvious knob on forehead. • Thicker and shorter neck than in Black-throated with especially 'fuller' hind-neck. • Rear head and hind-neck pale grey, paler than in Black-throated.
ad s	• White vertical stripes on neck-side much thinner than black stripes ⇔ in Black-throated about of same breadth. Variable in both species, only useful in extremes.
imm/ad w	• Well-defined dark throat-line connected with neck-side, but lacking in about half of 1w (when present in Black-throated often broader but very diffuse). • In imm often almost mono-coloured grey bill ⇔ in ad and Black-throated all plum often dark tip. • In 1w pale tips to scaps often more prominent than in Black-throated 1w. • In imm ear-coverts dirty grey ⇔ in Black-throated imm normally paler.

Great Northern Diver *Gavia immer*　　　　　　　　　　　　　　　　　L 80cm 31.5"

all plum	• Large size (like Cormorant); smallest ind overlap in size with largest Black-throated Diver. • Heavy bill with dark culmen and bill-tip (culmen rarely partially pale). In ad s completely black. • Often nearly straight culmen, at tip only slightly decurved. Bill-structure often only slightly different from White-billed Diver (but angled under-ridge of lower mandible extending up to bill-tip, see White-billed). • Steep forehead with angular bump (like White-billed and sometimes Black-throated). • 20 tail-feathers. • Highest part of back often close behind head ⇔ White-billed. • Bill-feathering reaches at most to middle of nostril ⇔ White-billed.
ad ad s	• Cov with white speckles ⇔ juv-1w and 2w. • Approximately 13 stripes on neck-side, towards hind neck stripes longer ⇔ White-billed. • European population retains summer plumage until well into autumn. North American population moults at breeding site and develops winter plumage sooner.
ad w	• Sometimes retains summer feathers, normally scaps up to mid-winter. • Bill often still partially black, often around tip and cutting-edges. Black parts well-defined against pale parts ⇔ in juv-1w mainly pale grey with dark culmen.
ad w/imm ⇒ ⇒	• Crown and hind-neck as dark or darker than upperparts ⇔ Black-throated. • Pale indentation above broad dark half-collar (like White-billed). • Pale, broken eye-ring (like White-billed). • Fairly dark, often diffusely mottled ear-coverts ⇔ in Black-throated ad w/imm often uniformly pale ear-coverts, roundly bordered by dark crown.
juv-1w 1s 2w fl all plum	• Scaled upperparts with rounded tips to feathers (like White-billed juv-1w) ⇔ ad. • See White-billed but normally not a very dark half-collar. • See White-billed. • Holds head (and bill) slightly downwards ⇔ all other divers. • Silhouette: see White-billed.

White-billed Diver *Gavia adamsii* L 90cm 35.5"

all plum ⇒	• Completely yellow-white bill (also with pale culmen and cutting-edge but sometimes basal half of culmen darker, especially in ad w) ⇔ Great Northern Diver.
	• Nearly straight culmen (slightly downturned near tip in most ind). Distal part of underside of lower mandible flattened ⇔ in Great Northern angled (normally only visible in the hand).
	• Generally larger than Great Northern.
	• Lower mandible with obvious gonys-angle.
	• Holds bill tilted slightly upwards most of the time ⇔ Great Northern.
	• 18 tail-feathers ⇔ Great Northern.
	• Highest part of back often in middle ⇔ Great Northern.
	• Eye slightly smaller than in Great Northern.
	• Bill-feathering reaches at least to middle of nostril ⇔ Great Northern.
ad	• Cov with white speckles ⇔ juv-1w and 2w.
ad s	• Approximately 10 stripes on neck-side, stripes on neck-side broader than in Great Northern.
	• White blocks on upperparts larger than in Great Northern.
ad w	• Often retains some summer-feathers, normally scaps.
ad w/imm	• Neck-side and side of head *pale brown* (in ad darker), contrasting with darker crown and hind-neck. *In imm only narrow dark line on rear head and neck* ⇔ Great Northern. Dark eye clearly visible against pale head-side ⇔ Great Northern.
⇒	• Dark spot on rear of head-side.
juv-1w	• Upperparts relatively pale ⇔ in Great Northern dark to blackish.
	• Upperparts strongly and evenly scaled, feathers on upperparts have rounded tips (like Great Northern juv-1w) ⇔ ad.
1s	• Like bleached 1w, often with conspicuous dark half-collar. Continuing moult from 1w to 2w very variable with pattern of new feathers in between ad w and juv.
2w	• Like ad w but no small white spots on cov.
fl all plum	• Pale shafts of flight-feathers ⇔ in Great Northern dark.
	• Elongated silhouette with 'beer-belly' and often prominent legs.
	• Regular head movements like Red-throated Diver but less flexible.

Albatrosses

Black-browed Albatross *Thalassarche melanophris* L 88cm 34.5", WS 225cm 89"

all plum	• Upperwing blackish; mantle, back and tail normally paler (dark grey); rump/uppertail-cov white.
	• Narrow black eye-stripe (in imm normally shorter or even absent).
ad ⇒	• Uniform, pale orange bill.
juv	• Dark bill with (often difficult to see) black tip.
	• Grey neck (sometimes still distinct up to 5cy).
2w	• Mainly grey-brown bill with dark tip.
3w	• Bill-pattern very variable, normally orange-yellow with dark tip (sometimes nearly entirely dark).
fl (sub)ad ⇒	• White mid-panel on underwing and dark leading and trailing edge, *leading edge broader than trailing edge.*
fl juv-1s	• All prim 1st generation.
	• Pale mid-panel on underwing indistinct or almost absent (sometimes also less distinct in older ind up to ad).
fl 2w	• p8-p10 (normally also p1) fresh, remainder old.
	• Pale mid-panel on underwing often narrow.
fl 3w	• p8-p10 old and worn, remainder fresh.
	• Pale mid-panel on underwing variable but often distinct.
fl 4w	• p8-p10, normally also p1-p2 (p4) fresh, p5-p7 old.
	• Pale mid-panel on underwing variable but often difficult to tell apart from ad.
notes	• Campbell Islands Albatross *T. impavida* (until recently regarded as subspecies of Black-browed, not recorded in WP) differs from Black-browed by pale brown iris, broader and longer dark eye-stripe (extending to lores) and less white on underwing.
	• Grey-headed Albatross *T. chrysostoma*, not recorded in WP, has underwing pattern similar to Black-browed (sub)ad but dark bill with yellow culmen (like Atlantic Yellow-nosed Albatross) and yellow under-ridge of bill; ad has grey head and paler upperwing and mantle than Black-browed.

Atlantic Yellow-nosed Albatross *Thalassarche chlororhynchos* L 76cm 30", WS 225cm 89"

all plum	• Upperside blackish, tail grey, rump and uppertail-cov white (scaps not or only slightly paler than upperwing ⇔ Black-browed Albatross and Shy Albatross).
	• Dark around eye, creating small triangular mask, but in most imm hardly present.
ad ⇒	• *Dark bill* with yellow culmen.
	• Pale grey head and hind-neck, crown whitish (in imm still white). Some worn ad with almost white head and hind-neck.
imm	• Plumage like ad but entirely white head and hind-neck and dark bill with only indistinct brown-grey culmen-ridge. With increasing age culmen-ridge becomes yellow (about about 6-7 years); sometimes yellow culmen-ridge develops earlier (see note).
fl all plum ⇒	• White underwing with *narrow* dark leading and trailing edge (leading edge distinctly broader than trailing edge) ⇔ in Black-browed very broad dark leading edge; in Shy evenly narrow leading and trailing edge.
	• More slender than Black-browed with longer neck and tail and narrower wings.
note	• Indian Yellow-nosed Albatross *T. carteri*, not recorded in WP, resembles Atlantic but in all plumages shows white head and hind-neck and narrower pale culmen-ridge, narrowing to a fine point towards base. Hardly any dark around eye. Some Atlantic imm have yellow culmen-ridge but still white head

and hind-neck. Structure of base of culmen diagnostic: in Atlantic border between culmen and forehead round, in Indian angular with feathering of forehead ending in weak tip onto base of culmen.

Shy Albatross *Thalassarche cauta*   L 94cm 37", WS 245cm 97"

all plum	• Upperwing, mantle, back and tail dark grey; uppertail-cov white.
ad ⇒	• Pale grey wash over head-side; crown white.
	• Yellow-grey bill.
imm	• Grey bill with black tip.
	• Diffuse pale grey collar contrasting with darker upperparts.
fl all plum ⇒	• Characteristic *elongated black mark* at corner of body and leading edge of underwing.
	• Paler grey mantle contrasting with dark upperwing.
	• White underwing with narrow dark leading and trailing edge, *evenly broad*.
	• Relatively broad wings.

Wandering Albatross *Diomedea exulans*   L 115cm 45", WS 300cm 118" (max 350cm 138")

all plum	• Large, wholly pale pinkish bill.
ad ⇒	• Pale upperparts.
⇒	• Legs greyish.
ad ♂	• White plumage incl large part of cov, except black flight-feathers.
ad ♀ /	• More numerous dark cov than ad ♂; some dark tail-feathers, fine grey-brown patterning on
subad ♂	feathers of upperparts, neck and sometimes crown.
juv/imm	• Juv wholly chocolate-brown with white face. With increasing age brown gradually replaced by white.
	• Dark tail.
fl all plum	• White underwing with very narrow black trailing edge and large black wing-tip (flight-feathers black, (long) underwing-cov white).
	• Legs project beyond tail (legs sometimes retract, then no leg-projection).

Petrels

Southern Giant Petrel *Macronectes giganteus*   L 87cm 34", WS 195cm 77"

all plum ⇒	• Large, orange-yellow bill with diffuse greenish tips to both upper and lower mandibles (see Northern Giant Petrel). From some distance bill looks *uniform* yellowish.
ad	• Two colour-morphs: on dark morph pale head and breast (without darker crown and hind neck; see Northern); underparts as dark or slightly paler than dark grey-brown upperparts. On very old ind sometimes white head and breast, pale grey underparts and mid-grey upperparts.
	• White morph white with some uneven scattered dark spots. Rarely completely white.
	• Definite ad plumage obtained only after about 10 years.
imm	• Juv completely black-brown (like Northern); imm grey-brown, head gradually becomes paler with age.
	• White morph as ad, no confusion with Northern possible.
fl ad ⇒	• On dark morph pale leading-edge of underwing ⇔ dark Northern ad.
	• Pale underwing.
note	• There have been some sightings of giant petrels in WP but it is uncertain to which species these ind belonged.

Northern Giant Petrel *Macronectes halli*   L 87cm 34", WS 190cm 75"

all plum ⇒	• Large, yellow-orange bill with dark (reddish) tip to upper mandible and dark tip to lower mandible. From some distance bill looks orange with *darker tip*.
ad ⇒	• Pale face with *dark crown and hind neck*.
	• Pale iris, in imm iris generally paler than in Southern Giant Petrel; in both species iris-colour becomes paler with age.
	• Underparts very variable from wholly grey to wholly dark; most with pale spotted underparts.
	• Often distinct contrast between pale underparts and dark upperparts ⇔ Southern.
	• Definite ad plumage obtained only after about 10 years.
imm	• Juv completely black-brown (like Southern); older ind grey-brown, head and underparts become gradually paler with age, starting with head.
fl ad	• Rather dark underwing but in very pale ind pale underwing like Southern ad.
note	• No white morph ⇔ Southern.
	• There have been some sightings of giant petrels in WP but it is uncertain to which species these ind belonged.

Fulmar *Fulmarus glacialis*   L 46cm 18", WS 110cm 43.5"

all plum	• Thick grey-yellowish bill (all morphs).
fl all plum ⇒	• Conspicuous pale base of inner prim (but see note).
	• Grey upperparts and upperwing contrast with white, thick neck and head and short, pale grey tail (see note).
	• Pale underwing with broad diffuse dark surrounding of hand (see note).
	• Short glides interspersed with series of fast, stiff and relatively shallow wing-beats. In strong winds changes into 'shearwater-flight' with regular series of wing-beats (⇔ most other seabirds). 'Shearwater-flight' with higher arcs and often 'more relaxed' than other seabirds.
	• Holds wings relatively straight, often with obvious forward-pushed carpal-corner.
note	• Occurs in variable dark morph (mainly in Arctic) with darker underwing, darker tail and (brown-)grey body and head. Bill often with broader subterminal dark band (very narrow or absent in pale morph). So-called 'double-dark morph' has deep (brown-)grey plumage with only slightly paler base of inner prim and dark lores. Neck, head and tail nearly concolorous with upperparts (creating no contrast).

Cape Petrel *Daption capense* L 39cm 15.5", WS 34cm 13.5"

all plum	• Pied black and white with dark head and terminal tail-band. Upperparts are finely dark spotted. Underparts white.
	• Structure and flight action like Northern Fulmar but smaller size.
fl all plum	• Upperwing black and white with large white area at base of hand and patchy white area at base of arm.
	• Underwing white with patchy dark leading edge and dark trailing edge.

Atlantic Petrel *Pterodroma incerta* L 43cm 17", WS 104cm 41"

all plum	• Heavy bill.
fl all plum ⇒	• Pale belly, sharply bordered by uniformly dark breast and head; belly more diffusely bordered with dark undertail-cov.
	• Upperparts, head and upperwing dark (brown-black), forehead, throat and hind-neck sometimes paler.
	• Underwing completely dark.

Soft-plumaged Petrel *Pterodroma mollis* L 34cm 13.5", WS 89cm 35"

all plum	• Very like Zino's Petrel, Desertas Petrel and Fea's Petrel but with *complete broad breast-band*. When breast-band not complete (rare) then broad dark breast-side patches larger and darker than in Zino's, Desertas and Fea's.
	• Bill often slightly less heavy than in Desertas/Fea's (about between Desertas/Fea's and Zino's).
	• Crown usually obviously paler than mask and concolorous with upperparts ⇔ Zino's, Desertas and Fea's.
	• Slightly bulkier, less slender build than Zino's, Desertas and Fea's.
fl all plum ⇒	• Uppertail-cov concolorous with rest of upperparts and tail ⇔ in Zino's, Desertas and Fea's rump, uppertail-cov and tail paler.
	• Underwing dark but paler than in Desertas, Fea's and some Zino's.
	• Paler and more pure grey upperparts than Zino's, Desertas and Fea's (Zino's, Desertas and Fea's often with brown wash).

Zino's Petrel, Desertas Petrel and Fea's Petrel

These species share the following features:

fl all plum	• Long, narrow wings (with pointed hand ⇔ in Zino's often slightly more stumpy; p10 slightly or not at all longer than p9).
	• Dark diagonal band over upperwing and dark hand creating dark 'M' over complete width of flying bird (often difficult to see due to very dark upperwing).
	• Dark breast-sides but no complete breast-band ⇔ Soft-plumaged Petrel.
	• Dark grey underwing with black diagonal band on underwing-cov (very difficult to see due to overall dark underwing except in some Zino's).
	• Mantle and back sometimes brownish (probably only in worn ind) ⇔ in Soft-plumaged cold-grey.
	• Pale tail and uppertail-cov contrast with dark upperparts ⇔ Soft-plumaged.
	• Flight-action sometimes resembles pratincole; fast, flexible, powerful wing-beats interspersed with often high arcs.
	• Hand often swept backwards with obvious carpal-corner.

Zino's Petrel *Pterodroma madeira* L 32cm 12.5", WS 82cm 32.5"

all plum ⇒	• Short, stumpy, relatively slender bill, especially less heavy than in Desertas/Fea's Petrel with slightly flatter, shorter nose-tube; distance between end of nose-tube and beginning of hook on culmen longer and flatter than in Desertas/Fea's, as long or longer than nose-tube.
	• See introduction to Zino's Petrel, Desertas Petrel and Fea's Petrel.
	• Smaller and more slender than Desertas/Fea's .
	• Crown often slightly paler than mask making mask slightly more conspicuous ⇔ Desertas/Fea's .
fl all plum	• Upperwing without distinct dark arm-diagonal ⇔ in Desertas/Fea's often rather marked.
	• Underwing sometimes with stronger contrast than in Desertas/Fea's ('*Pterodroma*-pattern' weakly shining through) to more conspicuous pale central band and pale 'triangle' at base of forewing.
moult	• Moults prim in September-February, imm earlier than ad. See Desertas and Fea's.
note	• Differences with Desertas/Fea's in plumage very slight and overlapping, very difficult to judge at sea.

Desertas Petrel *Pterodroma deserta* L 36cm 14", WS 100cm 39.5"

all plum ⇒	• Thick stumpy bill with prominent nose-tube (distance between end of nose-tube and beginning of hook on culmen short, shorter than nose-tube) ⇔ Zino's Petrel.
	• See introduction to Zino's Petrel, Desertas Petrel and Fea's Petrel.
	• Size about as Sooty Shearwater but heavier impression.
	• Dark mask connected with dark crown (mask hardly darker than crown, like most Zino's).
	• Crown darker than hind-neck and mantle; crown normally as dark as mask.
moult	• Moults prim in December-May, imm earlier than ad. See Zino's and Fea's Petrel
note	• See note under Zino's.
	• Breeds on Bugio Island (Madeira) in July/August; young leave nest-hole in December.

Fea's Petrel *Pterodroma feae* L 35cm 14", WS 95cm 37.5"

all plum	• See introduction to Zino's Petrel, Desertas Petrel and Fea's Petrel.
	• At present hardly any morphological differences with Desertas Petrel known, but generally slightly smaller size with slightly smaller bill (in between Desertas and Zino's Petrel) but of no use in the field, further see note.

moult	• For differences with Zino's Petrel, see account of that species.
note	• Moults prim in April-September, imm earlier than ad.
	• Breeding season (and hence moult strategy, see above) and voice markedly different from Desertas.
	• Breeds on Cape Verde Islands in December/January.

Bermuda Petrel *Pterodroma cahow* L 38cm 15", WS 92cm 36"

all plum	• Somewhat intermediate between 'soft-plumaged petrels' (ie Fea's, Zino's, Desertas and Soft-plumaged Petrels) and Black-capped Petrel. Upperparts more uniform and darker grey (tail very dark ⇔ 'soft-plumaged petrels') but underwing-pattern almost as in Black-capped.
	• Black mask and crown creating large dark cap; lores and forehead white, patchily bordered with dark crown.
	• Breast-band variable but normally broad; often hint of pale collar but rarely complete, when complete then narrow. Palest ind resemble darkest Black-capped.
	• Bill less heavy than in Black-capped and 'soft-plumaged petrels'.
fl all plum	• Underwing like Black-capped (see account for that species) but trailing and leading edge broader ⇔ 'soft-plumaged petrels'.
	• Relatively slender body with long pointed tail.
	• Rump and tail blackish with normally paler but not completely white uppertail-cov ⇔ in Black-capped uppertail-cov always completely white.
	• Upperwing nearly uniform, only somewhat darker leading edge of arm.

Black-capped Petrel *Pterodroma hasitata* L 40cm 15.5", WS 95cm 37.5"

all plum ⇒	• Dark crown bordered by broad white collar and white forehead (sometimes collar very narrow and grey, see note).
	• Underparts white with variable dark patch on breast-side (see note).
	• Upperparts dark grey.
	• Heavy bill.
fl all plum ⇒	• Typical *Pterodroma* underwing-pattern: short black diagonal band on white underside of arm, not reaching axillaries (see also Bermuda Petrel).
⇒	• White uppertail-cov and large part of rump creating *large white 'U'-shaped* area on uppertail.
	• White underwing with black trailing edge and black underside of hand, connected with diagonal band on white underside of arm.
	• White underparts with variable dark stripe on breast-side.
	• Dark grey to blackish upperwing and upperparts; mantle paler grey.
fl juv	• Like ad but pale tips to coverts creating narrow pale wing-bar(s).
moult	• Ind of all ages moult prim in April-August, imm earlier than ad. Pale type generally moults 1-2 months earlier than dark type, see note.
note	• At least two types distinguishable: pale and dark type (and possibly an intermediate type) which probably represent different populations.
	• Pale type generally larger with more white in face: white forehead extends to above eye (creating supercilium) and white ear-coverts. Narrow or no dark patch on breast-side, narrower black diagonal band on underside of arm, broad white collar (in dark type narrower and often grey) and broader white area on uppertail.

Herald Petrel *Pterodroma arminjoniana* L 37cm 14.5", WS 95cm 37.5"

all plum	• Wholly dark plumage of dark morph with pale band on underwing also reminiscent of Sooty Shearwater but pale band on prim instead of cov, flight-style and structure very different.
	• Rather long tail.
	• Short bill with prominent nose-tube.
	• Upperparts and upperwing uniform dark brown (sometimes faint dark band over upperwing).
fl all plum ⇒	• Pale base of both prim-cov and (outer) prim on underwing, often creating broad and long band on underwing.
	• Dark morph entirely dark brown to dark grey-brown (but belly and throat often mottled pale).
	• Pale morph with pale underparts; dark breast(side) and pale throat. Underwing with broad pale band on basal part of sec, prim, greater cov and prim-cov and isolated pale stripe over lesser cov.

Bulwer's Petrel *Bulweria bulwerii* L 26cm 10", WS 67cm 26.5"

all plum	• Heavy bill.
	• Entirely dark, at close range looks very dark brown.
	• Head evenly rounded, without peaked forehead as in storm-petrels.
fl all plum	• Long narrow tail and wings; tail longer than wing-width and even when held closed relatively full due to broad tail-feathers.
	• Relatively long neck conspicuous.
	• Faint (sometimes stronger) pale band over cov (mainly over greater cov); pale band curved.
	• Glides with carpal pushed forward and arched wing.
	• Head often held slightly upwards.
	• Often relatively pale upperside of hand ⇔ small storm-petrels.

Jouanin's Petrel *Bulweria fallax* L 31cm 12", WS 79cm 31"

all plum	• Completely dark brown-black (at short distance sometimes diffuse pale band on cov visible).
	• Very long wings and long pointed tail resembles Bulwer's Petrel but larger size (as Manx Shearwater).
	• Can resemble Wedge-tailed Shearwater dark morph but bill short and entirely dark (in Wedge-tailed Shearwater long with pale base).
behav	• Bill often held downwards.

Shearwaters

Scopoli's Shearwater and Cory's Shearwater

These species share the following features:

all plum ⇒	• Pale, yellowish bill.
	• Dark head (especially Cory's) *ill-defined* by white throat and breast-sides.
	• Upperside rather pale brown; scaled effect created by dark feather centres and paler fringes.
fl all plum	• Usually pale uppertail-cov, creating pale 'U' above tail, but variable.
	• When not banking, flexible wing-beats; almost 'lazy flight' with pushed forward carpal-corner and swept back hand (normal flight-style for all *Calonectris* ⇔ *Puffinus*).
	• Bulging trailing edge of arm.

Scopoli's Shearwater *Calonectris diomedea*　　　　L 44cm 17.5", WS 108cm 42.5"

all plum	• See introduction to Scopoli's Shearwater and Cory's Shearwater.
	• Smaller size and lighter build than Cory's Shearwater.
	• Pale neck; head very ill-defined with dark upperparts ⇔ Cory's.
	• Face normally not obviously darker than rest of head.
	• Bill somewhat shorter and especially more slender than in Cory's.
fl all plum	• Partially whitish inner web of outer prim (tongue), normally at least on p6-p10, therefore pale part of underwing (underwing-cov) ill-defined and *extending up to bases of prim* ⇔ most Cory's (see that account). Long white tongues on p6-p10 characteristic.
	• Normally lacks dark spot on 2nd outermost prim-cov on underwing ⇔ Cory's (see that account).
note	• Features mentioned in all plum only apparent in favourable conditions and in direct comparison with Cory's.

Cory's Shearwater *Calonectris borealis*　　　　L 48cm 19", WS 120cm 47"

all plum	• See introduction to Scopoli's Shearwater and Cory's Shearwater
	• Slightly darker face than Scopoli's Shearwater.
	• For structural differences see Scopoli's.
fl all plum	• Pale part of underwing (formed by underwing-cov) sharply demarcated by dark underside of hand ⇔ Scopoli's. *However, some ind have more than one (often) short white tongue on outer prim.*
	• Slightly stronger contrast between upperparts and underparts than in Scopoli's.
	• Dark spot on outer 2 prim-cov on underwing (2nd spot falling outside dark leading edge of underwing and therefore conspicuous) and dark leading edge of underside of hand slightly broader and more messy ⇔ in Scopoli's normally only dark spot on most outer prim-cov (spot falling within dark leading edge and therefore not conspicuous) and dark leading edge of underside of hand narrow and smooth.

Cape Verde Shearwater *Calonectris edwardsii*　　　　L 42cm 16.5", WS 106cm 42"

all plum ⇒	• Slender, *grey to yellow-greyish* and relatively long bill with dark tip.
	• Diffuse dark crown, darker than in Cory's Shearwater and Scopoli's Shearwater (somewhat capped-appearance), contrasting with pale mantle and darker rear-scaps and back.
	• Smaller size than Cory's and Scopoli's with relatively smaller head.
	• Pale eye-ring more distinct than in Cory's and Scopoli's.
fl all plum	• Narrower, more pointed wings and longer tail than Cory's and Scopoli's.
	• Upperwing darker grey-brown than Cory's and Scopoli's with dark, diffuse diagonal band over arm.
	• Underwing as in Cory's.
	• White uppertail-cov normally creating obvious pale 'U', usually more distinct than in most Cory's and Scopoli's.

Streaked Shearwater *Calonectris leucomelas*　　　　L 48cm 19", WS 112cm 44"

all plum ⇒	• Pale *patchy* face; broad white eye-ring.
	• Like Cory's and Scopoli's Shearwaters but slightly darker and more uniform on upperparts and hind-neck.
	• Dark neck-side more sharply bordered and contrasts more strongly with white underparts than in Cory's and Scopoli's.
fl all plum ⇒	• Mainly pale underwing-cov but *outer prim-cov dark* (creating dark spot on underside of base of hand) ⇔ all other large shearwaters with pale underwing-cov.
	• Broad dark trailing edge of arm.
	• Wings narrower than in Cory's and Scopoli's.

Wedge-tailed Shearwater *Puffinus pacificus*　　　　L 43cm 17", WS 101cm 40"

all plum	• Relatively long yellowish bill with dark tip (in dark morph usually only pale base).
fl all plum	• Long, strongly wedge-shaped tail ⇔ all shearwaters in WP.
	• Hand distinctly swept backwards (dark morph ⇔ Flesh-footed Shearwater).
fl all plum	• Pale tips to all cov creating 3-4 narrow but distinct pale bars on upperwing.
pale morph	• Head like Cory's Shearwater and Scopoli's Shearwater (dark cap diffusely merges into pale throat).
	• Pattern of underwing as in Cory's but hand blacker and contrasts more strongly with pale parts of underwing.
	• No pale spot on uppertail-cov as e.g. in Cory's and Scopoli's.
fl all plum	• Entirely sooty black-brown, underparts sometimes with grey wash.
dark morph	• Pale legs and bill but not as conspicuous as in Flesh-footed.

Flesh-footed Shearwater *Puffinus carneipes*   L 43cm 17", WS 103cm 40.5"

all plum	• Entirely sooty black-brown plumage.
	• Pale flesh-coloured bill and legs conspicuous, bill with dark tip.
	• Size like Sooty Shearwater (but heavier body and broader wings), slightly smaller than Great Shearwater, Cory's Shearwater and Scopoli's Shearwater.
fl all plum	• Under certain lighting conditions, underside of flight-feathers paler than underwing-cov.
	• Underwing-cov completely dark ⇔ Sooty.
	• Straight wings (as Great) ⇔ Sooty.

Great Shearwater *Puffinus gravis*   L 46cm 18", WS 112cm 44"

all plum ⇒	• Sharply demarcated dark cap separated from dark breast-sides by *broad white wedge*.
	• Upperside in autumn rather strongly scaled by dark feather centres and pale fringes (in Cory's Shearwater and Scopoli's Shearwater less marked due to relatively paler feather centres).
fl all plum	• Stiffer wing-beats than in Cory's and Scopoli's.
	• Dark diagonal band over axillaries and some well-defined dark markings on lesser cov contrast with pale underwing.
	• Pale, often 'U'-shaped patch on uppertail-cov (more conspicuous than in most Cory's and Scopoli's).
	• Black-framed pale underwing.
	• Nearly straight rear-side of arm ⇔ Cory's and Scopoli's.
	• Wings usually held nearly straight and project straight out of body ⇔ Cory's and Scopoli's.
	• Pale tips to cov and paler, often greyish greater cov creating relatively pale arm contrasting with black hand (only visible under good viewing conditions).
	• Diffuse, dark belly-patch; undertail-cov dark.

Sooty Shearwater *Puffinus griseus*   L 44cm 17.5", WS 102cm 40"

all plum	• Brown-black (underparts uniform dark ⇔ dark Balearic Shearwater).
fl all plum	• Relatively large size, only slightly smaller than 'large shearwaters' with relatively heavy body compared to narrow wings.
	• Pale silvery underwing-cov visible under good viewing conditions.
	• Long pointed wings in strong winds slightly swept back (sometimes resembling a large swift) ⇔ Manx Shearwater.
	• 'Shearwater-flight' usually with higher and faster arcs than in Manx.
	• In spring normally pale sec and/or cov by bleaching. In fresh plumage also paler outer sec and outer greater cov.
note	• See also Balearic.

Manx Shearwater *Puffinus puffinus*   L 32cm 12.5", WS 78cm 30.5"

all plum	• Pale crescent behind ear-coverts.
	• Uniform (brown-)black upperside; underparts white.
	• Front-side of legs pink, rest dark.
ad	• From end of summer more brownish upperparts and upperwing (moults in wintering area).
fl all plum	• Underwing white, usually without obvious dark axillary-patch (but present in some ind; see Yelkouan Shearwater).
	• Completely white underparts; white extending to rump-side and creating white patch behind wing.
	• In strong winds 'shearwater-flight' interchanged with fast 'side-to-side flight'; latter ⇔ Balearic Shearwater and Sooty Shearwater.
	• Even in strong winds only slightly arched wings.
note	• See also Yelkouan, Balearic and Macaronesian Shearwaters.

Balearic Shearwater *Puffinus mauretanicus*   L 37cm 14.5", WS 85cm 33.5"

all plum	• Slightly larger than Manx Shearwater and Yelkouan Shearwater with relatively heavier body than Manx.
	• Long slender bill.
	• Upperside dark brown without either black (⇔ Manx) or dark grey (⇔ Yelkouan).
	• Scaps at most with faint pale fringes ⇔ in Sooty Shearwater distinct pale fringes.
fl all plum ⇒	• *Ill-defined*, dirty-white central part of underparts. Often diffuse dark breast-band
	• In vast majority dark undertail-cov and rear-flanks connected to dark axillaries.
	• Variable in shade but both very pale and very dark ind are rare. Palest ind towards both Manx and Yelkouan. In these ind sometimes largely white underparts but *ill-defined border* with dark upperside (best seen on breast- and neck-side). Undertail-cov and rear-flanks always dark (see note).
	• Darkest ind towards Sooty but with more pale brown underwing-cov (not silvery as in Sooty). Throat and belly always slightly paler than rest of underparts. Axillaries with pale patterning ⇔ in Sooty completely dark.
	• Centre of underwing even in darkest ind still dirty-white.
	• Silhouette more elongated than in Manx and Sooty due to longer neck and bill, more slender rear-end and presence of leg projection.
	• Usually flies low with relatively long series of wing-beats and short glides; flight gives hurried impression (rarely 'shearwater-flight') ⇔ Sooty and, less so, Manx.
moult	• Ad in summer in active prim-moult (as in Yelkouan) ⇔ Manx.
notes	• Ind of breeding population on Menorca are between Balearic and Yelkouan in size and have different vocalisation, but plumage similar to Yelkouan. Status of this population as yet unclear, but it may possibly be hybrid.
	• Large part of population migrates into Atlantic Ocean after breeding season.

Shearwaters

Yelkouan Shearwater *Puffinus yelkouan*   L 32cm 12.5", WS 77cm 30.5" (see note)

all plum	• Rather broad, diffuse pale eye-ring ⇔ in Manx, even at close range, hardly visible. • Upperparts dark brown-grey, darker than Balearic, slightly paler and greyer than Manx. Only visible under very good viewing conditions, at distance upperparts appear as blackish as on Manx. • Underparts white except undertail-cov. Especially longest undertail-cov in most ind dark grey ⇔ in Manx underparts wholly white. • Sometimes pale lores ⇔ Manx and Balearic. • Normally lacking obvious pale 'curl' behind ear-coverts (characteristic for Manx) but often faintly present (in Manx 'curl' sometimes missing). • Bill slightly shorter and slimmer than in Balearic. • Steep forehead sometimes conspicuous at close range.
fl all plum ⇒	• Rather pale grey underside of prim, ill-defined and contrasting little with white underwing-cov ⇔ in Manx stronger contrast and sharper border between blackish underside of prim and white underwing-cov. • Very fast, almost fluttering wing-beats (even faster than in Balearic). Glides short ⇔ Manx. • Pale-dark border between upper- and underside more sharply defined on breast- and neck-side than in pale Balearic; pale-dark border straighter than in Manx. • Usually obvious dark axillary-patch or dark spot on front of underside of arm (sometimes also in Manx but nearly always faint). • (Very) dark brown-grey upperparts and upperwing (in ad paler at end of summer), at distance appears black and white as Manx. In Manx ad in autumn sometimes has dark brown upperside due to bleaching but no grey wash and flight-feathers always blackish. • Pale-dark border between rump and vent often rather straight ⇔ Manx has white bulge extending up to side of rump (but also present in some Yelkouan). • Often moves head up and down (like Macaronesian Shearwater) ⇔ Manx. • Silhouette less elongated than Manx with shorter, narrower and blunter hand and head. • Legs often project beyond short tail (as in Balearic) but sometimes held drawn in ⇔ in Manx no or hardly any leg projection.
moult	• Ad in summer in active prim-moult (as in Balearic) ⇔ Manx.
notes	• Ind of breeding population on Menorca between Balearic and Yelkouan in size and with different vocalisation, but plumage similar to Yelkouan. Status of this population as yet unclear, but it may possibly be hybrid. • After breeding season migrates to Black Sea, in opposite direction to Balearic.

Barolo Shearwater *Puffinus baroli*   L 27cm 1.5", WS 63cm 25"

all plum ⇒	• White face with eye standing out (eye visible against white background). In some ind more dark pattering around eye and on ear-coverts, approaching head-pattern of Boyd's Shearwater (for other differences see below). • Short, thin bill. • Rounded head with relatively steep forehead ⇔ Manx. • Legs blue-grey ⇔ in Manx pink front-side.
fl all plum ⇒	• White underwing (also axillaries) with *narrow, evenly broad*, dark-framed underwing; white normally extending well into tip of hand ⇔ Manx. Sometimes almost completely dark underside of flight-feathers and dark area near leading edge of arm. • Pale upperside of sec and inner prim creating pale band; narrow pale wing-bar along greater cov visible under good viewing conditions. • Very strong contrast between black upperparts and pure white underparts. • White area smaller but often running higher up than in Manx. • Black upperwing and upperparts, no or hardly any brown wash ⇔ in Manx (very) dark brown (but see Boyd's). • Head regularly held up. • Usually fast, somewhat 'unsteady' fluttering flight low above water (rarely high arcs ⇔ Manx); soars in strong winds often on bowed wings.
fl all plum ⇒	• Short, somewhat full body with stumpy, broad hand and bulging trailing edge of arm.

Boyd's Shearwater *Puffinus boydi*   L 29cm 11.5", WS 67cm 26.5"

all plum	• Head-side darker than in Barolo Shearwater (eye does not standout as clearly), more like Manx. Ear-coverts grey ⇔ in Barolo white. • Long tail. • Grey bill with dark tip ⇔ in Barolo normally completely dark bill.
fl all plum	• Blackish upperparts and uniform dark upperwing, often with brown-grey wash ⇔ Barolo. • Dark longest undertail-cov making tail look extra long. • Underwing with wholly dark prim and variable dark bar over cov, more or less parallel with dark leading edge.
notes	• Possibly more closely related to Audubon's Shearwater than to Barolo. • Breeds on Cape Verde Islands.

Audubon's Shearwater *Puffinus lherminieri*   L 31cm 12", WS 69cm 27"

all plum	• Long tail as in Boyd's Shearwater; tail projects beyond wing-tips when perched ⇔ in Boyd's tail- and wing-tip equal. • Narrow pale supercilium and small white spot above lores. • Upperside with brown wash as in Boyd's ⇔ Barolo Shearwater. • Dark undertail-cov as in Boyd's ⇔ Barolo. • Dark cap to underside of eye as in Boyd's ⇔ Barolo. • Grey bill with dark tip.

fl all plum note	• Slightly larger than Barolo. • Pink legs. • Rather broad dark leading and trailing edge along underwing ⇔ Barolo. • Much more similar to Boyd's than to Barolo. Breeds on south-east coast of North America; not recorded in WP.

Tropical Shearwater *Puffinus bailloni*   L 29cm 11.5", WS 67cm 26.5"

all plum ⇒	• Variable but usually large dark breast-side patch (largest breast-side patch of all smaller shearwater species). • Black crown extending down to just below eye, often creating conspicuous cap (ad with dark ear-coverts). Most resembles small Manx Shearwater. • Long bill (with deep base), wings and tail; wing-tips project somewhat beyond tail ⇔ in Barolo Shearwater tail- and wing-tips fall level. • Legs blue-grey, in ad with pink wash.
fl all plum	• Very dark upperside (in juv black, in ad dark brown) and white underparts, also undertail-cov. • Underwing white with broad dark trailing edge ⇔ in Barolo and Boyd's Shearwater narrow, in Persian Shearwater bold dark patterning on underwing.

Persian Shearwater *Puffinus persicus*   L 33cm 13", WS 74cm 29"

all plum fl all plum ⇒ note	• Upperside with conspicuous brown wash. • Long bill and long tail; tail projects beyond wing-tips when perched. • Dark underwing with long dark diagonal axillary-patch and *dark patterning on underwing-cov.* • Dark undertail-cov. • Not recorded in WP.

Storm-petrels

Most storm-petrels display white or partially white uppertail-cov. Despite being incorrect, the commonly used term for this, 'rump-patch', is also used in the accounts below.

Wilson's Storm-petrel *Oceanites oceanicus*   L 17cm 6.7", WS 40cm

fl all plum ⇒ ad/1w note	• *Long legs project beyond tail* but sometimes held drawn in. • Short, broad arm and full, long hand; paddle-shaped wings with straight trailing edge. • Yellow webbing between toes (yellow only visible at very close range). • Pale upperwing-bar distinct (usually rather short, only greater cov paler, not reaching leading-edge of wing ⇔ Leach's). • Large white 'rump-patch', extending to vent and side of undertail-cov. When seen from side, rear-body seems completely encircled by white. • Dark underwing with or without very diffuse paler (not white) band. • Tail almost straight-ended, even when fanned ⇔ in European tip rounded when fanned. • Ad moult prim from May-September; 1w from October-May. • Flight-style can resemble Red-rumped Swallow: 'forced' long soaring-flights interspersed with short series of wing-beats.

White-faced Storm-petrel *Pelagodroma marina*   L 20cm 8", WS 42cm 16.5"

all plum fl all plum ⇒ ⇒	• White underparts with exception of dark patch on breast-side. • White face and broad white supercilium, (dark) grey cap and mask. • Mainly *brown-grey* upperparts (cov more brown). • Legs very long, dark with yellow webbed toes. • Pale underwing-cov contrast strongly with black flight-feathers. • Grey uppertail-cov contrast with black tail and dark upperparts. • Legs project well beyond tail. • Characteristic feeding-flight; 'water-skiing' and 'dancing' at water surface on level held wings. • Obvious pale upperwing-bar.

White-bellied Storm-petrel *Pelagodroma grallaria*   L 20cm 8", WS 47cm 18.5"

fl all plum note	• Very similar to Black-bellied Storm-petrel (see below) but underparts below breast clean white (*incl vent*), and only undertail-cov dark. • Characteristic *Pelagodroma* flight (as in Black-bellied), see White-faced Storm-petrel. • Relatively narrow dark trailing edge to underwing, from side-view forms straight line with border between dark breast and white belly ⇔ in Black-bellied broader trailing edge and dark breast bulging towards flank, breaking straight line. • Underwing-cov pure white and sharply contrasting with dark flight-feathers ⇔ Black-bellied. • Legs projection variable from lacking to distinct, but generally more often present than in Black-bellied. • Tail square-ended (as in Black-bellied). • Broad white 'rump-patch' (as in Black-bellied). • Variable paler upperwing-cov normally forming indistinct pale wing-panel (generally paler than in Black-bellied, but much depending on wear and not a reliable feature for a lone ind). • See Black-bellied note.

Black-bellied Storm-petrel *Pelagodroma tropica*   L 20cm 8", WS 46cm 18"

fl all plum	• Very variable dark longitudinal band bisecting central underparts, when present characteristic (but often difficult to see) ⇔ in White-bellied completely white central underparts. Varies from broad and complete to entirely absent over belly (very rare); vent always dark ⇔ White-bellied.

notes	• Dark breast-sides extending in point towards flank ⇔ in White-bellied dark breast almost straight-bordered. • Pale underwing-cov contrasts with black flight-feathers. Cov on underside of hand with some dusky patterning creating indistinct border with dark flight-feathers. • See also White-bellied for further features. • This species or White-bellied Storm-petrel (see above) recorded at least once in WP.

European Storm-petrel *Hydrobates pelagicus*   L 15.5cm 6.1", WS 39cm 15.5"

fl all plum ⇒	• Variable white stripe on central part of underwing, often only visible at close range. • Small size (appearing about half of Leach's Storm-petrel under field conditions) with large, nearly rectangular white 'rump-patch', extending down to rear-flanks. • Relatively short angled wings. Wing-tips rather blunt due to relatively short p10. • Nearly uniform upperwing; faint pale upperwing-bar especially in fresh juv. • Short, almost square tail ⇔ Leach's. • Usually restless, fluttering flight with fast and shallow wing-beats, can resemble small bat. No regular arcing or long gliding ⇔ Leach's and Wilson's Storm-petrel. • Darkest storm-petrel.
ad/1w	• Ad moults prim slow, from August into winter. In 1w no prim moult in 1cy (start June 2cy).

Mediterranean Storm-petrel *Hydrobates melitensis*   L 16cm 6.3", WS 43cm 17"

all plum moult note	• As European Storm-petrel but generally larger size (longer wings) and slightly heavier bill (but much overlap). • Ad starts prim-moult in June ⇔ European ad normally in August, but variable. • Until recently regarded as doubtfully valid subspecies, now sometimes considered as a full species due to different vocalisations from European (e.g. first 2 notes of trisyllabic chatter-call flow into each other).

Leach's Storm-petrel *Oceanodroma leucorhoa*   L 20cm 8", WS 45cm 18"

all plum	• Rather long and rather slender bill ⇔ Madeiran Storm-petrel (thick) and European Storm-petrel (short). • Upperside brown-black, often with greyish wash ⇔ in European blackish (differences only visible under good viewing conditions).
ad/1w	• In ad prim moult from late autumn into winter. In 1w no prim moult in 1cy (start April 2cy).
fl all plum	• Rather evenly distinct pale upperwing-bar reaches leading-edge but often narrows towards end (in worn ad sometimes almost absent, most conspicuous in juv) ⇔ in Wilson's Storm-petrel shorter, more concentrated on middle of wing; in Madeiran weaker and shorter, not reaching leading edge. • White 'rump-patch' variable in shape and size. Usually somewhat elongated or 'V'-shaped often with *diffuse dark stripe over middle* In wind with large 'rump-patch', white extends to rear-flanks. • Relatively long, forked tail; often held slightly upwards. • In moderate to strong winds abrupt turns and accelerations on stiff wings (nighthawk-like); real travel-speed then surprisingly low. • Long, often obviously angled wings, often held somewhat arched with raised arm and hanging hand.

Swinhoe's Storm-petrel *Oceanodroma monorhis*   L 20cm 8", WS 47cm 18.5"

all plum	• Structure and size like Leach's Storm-petrel but often looks bigger due to more powerful flight style (see below). Slightly thicker bill and somewhat longer, fuller wings. • Overall browner and more uniform than Leach's with often grey wash on upperparts. Greyish head contrasts with brownish body (only visible under very good viewing conditions). • ♀ considerably larger than ♂.
ad/1w	• In ad prim moult slow, from late autumn well into spring. In 1w no prim moult in 1cy (starts April 2cy).
fl all plum ⇒	• Rump and upper tail completely dark (no white 'rump-patch').
⇒	• White basal part of prim-shaft (outer 5-6 prim), only visible from rather close range. Two other dark-rumped storm-petrels, Markham's (*O. markhami*) and Matsudaira's (*O. matsudairae*), neither of which has been recorded in WP, also show this feature. • Regularly holds wings fairly straight; wings appear to protrude straighter out of body than in Leach's, producing longer looking wings. Carpal-joint more pushed forward than in Leach's. • Flight style different from Leach's; powerful and more direct with short series of shallow wing-beats followed by longer glides. Wing-beats with deeper down-stroke than up-stroke, in Leach's the other way around. • Wing-tips slightly blunter than in Leach's. • Pale upperwing-bar well-marked and slightly broader than in Leach's, but usually less distinct, only just not reaching leading edge of wing and more yellow-brown. • Underwing with weak central paler band, continuing on hand ⇔ Leach's.

Madeiran Storm-petrel *Oceanodroma castro*   L 20cm 8", WS 45cm 18"

all plum	• Relatively strong bill with strongly hooked tip. • Often very weak contrast between sooty head and breast and slightly browner body.
fl all plum	• 'Rump-patch' *narrower* and more horse-shoe shaped than in Leach's, Wilson's Storm-petrel and European Storm-petrel, extending to undertail-cov but slightly less far than in Wilson's or European. • At most moderately developed and narrow pale bar on upperwing, fading away towards leading edge. • Longest uppertail-cov dark tipped which sometimes creates separated dark spots along white 'rump-patch' at border with tail (only visible at close range). • Holds wings only slightly angled ⇔ Leach's and European. • Uniformly dark underwing. • Relatively long, full tail. • In some ind (populations/taxa? – see note) slightly forked tail with rounded corners (often difficult to see under field conditions).

44

behav	• Often somewhat arched wings with raised arm and hanging hand, like Leach's. • Flight more stable and direct than congeners; lands relatively often on water surface. • Wings often only slightly angled, therefore looking longer ⇔ Leach's.
note	• Recently there have been proposals that within the WP four populations occur, of which some or all may deserve full (sub)species status. The populations differ from each other by breeding- and moulting-seasons, different voices and possibly subtle morphologic differences, of which the latter especially are as yet largely unclear.

Tropicbirds

Red-billed Tropicbird *Phaethon aethereus*   L 48cm 19" (excl tail-streamers) WS 105cm 41.5"

all plum	• Black mask with long black eye-stripe, extending to rear of head. • Heavy red (ad) or yellowish (imm) bill. • White with narrow black scales on upperparts.
juv	• Dark tips to tail-feathers. • Bill yellow-brown, becoming more orange with age. • Long black eye-stripe.
fl all plum	• Black tertials and inner greater cov create conspicuous marks at base of upperwing. • Black prim-cov and outer web of outer prim creates broad black wedge on outer hand. • Entirely white underside. • Fast, mechanical, stiff wing-beats interspersed with short glides.
fl ad	• Very long tail-streamers (central tail-feathers) ⇔ juv.
geog var	*P.a. indicus* (Red Sea and Persian Gulf)
ad	• Bill (red)orange with dark cutting edges. • Dark eye-stripe shorter (not reaching rear-head).

White-tailed Tropicbird *Phaethon lepturus*   L 40cm 15.5" (excl tail-streamers) WS 92cm 36"

all plum	• Structure largely like Red-billed Tropicbird but smaller size and smaller bill.
ad	• Black diagonal band over arm; upperparts uniform white ⇔ Red-billed. • Black eye-stripe just above ear-coverts ⇔ in Red-billed reaching hind-neck. • Yellow-orange bill. • Variable dark patterning on flanks.
juv	• Dark eye-stripe short, not connected on nape ⇔ Red-billed. • Upperparts coarsely marked ⇔ in Red-billed fine. • Flanks with only fine spotting or spotting totally lacking ⇔ ad.
fl all plum ⇒	• *Prim-cov white* ⇔ in Red-billed dark patterned.
fl ad ⇒	• Obvious black diagonal band over arm ⇔ Red-billed.

Gannets

Red-footed Booby *Sula sula*   L 71cm 28", WS 152cm 60"

ad ⇒	• Legs red. • White morph: white with black flight-feathers *except inner sec* and black isolated spot on prim-cov on underwing ⇔ Masked Booby. • Brown morph: cream-brown except white tail, rump and undertail-cov; black parts like white morph. • Grey bill with reddish-pink base. • Tail white ⇔ Masked.
imm	• Dark grey (white morph) or dark brown (brown morph) with paler underparts and *narrow, dark breast-band*. • Dull blue-grey to flesh-coloured bill. • Legs flesh-coloured. • Tail greyish in white morph and brown in dark morph (see ad).
fl all plum	• Faster flight than other boobies with carpal joints often distinctly pushed forward.
fl ad ⇒	• White tertials and inner sec; rest of flight-feathers black.
fl imm ⇒	• Completely dark underwing.
note	• Besides white and dark morph also complex intermediate ind, some with dark tail even in ad.

Masked Booby *Sula dactylatra*   L 81cm 32", WS 157cm 62"

all plum ⇒	• Dark around bill-base. • Grey-yellow bill (sometimes more orange-yellow).
ad	• White except black *rear-most scaps*, sec, prim, greater cov, inner median cov and tail.
juv ⇒	• Deep brown head and upperparts except *white hind-neck*. • Underparts entirely white.
fl ad	• Black hand, sec and tail.
fl imm	• Underwing-cov mainly pale ⇔ Brown Booby and Red-footed Booby imm.

Brown Booby *Sula leucogaster*   L 76cm 30", WS 145cm 57"

all plum ⇒	• Bill yellow to pink (sometimes grey); legs yellow.
ad	• Brown-black except white belly, vent and undertail-cov (and part of underwing-cov, see flight all plum). • In ad ♀ pale yellowish skin around bill; eye visible ⇔ in ad ♂ skin around bill darker blue-greyish; eye not clearly visible.
juv	• Like ad but dark parts paler grey-brown and underparts pale brown instead of white. • Grey-blue bill.

fl all plum	• Underwing strongly two-toned; dark hand and leading and trailing edge of arm with conspicuous white area on axillaries/underwing-cov. • Compared to Northern Gannet shorter wings and longer tail.
fl juv	• Upperparts (also uppertail-cov) completely dark ⇔ Northern Gannet juv.
geog var	*S.l. plotus* (Indian and Pacific Ocean)
all plum	• Upperparts more or less uniformly dark, without paler mantle, back and tail.

Northern Gannet *Morus bassanus*   L 93cm 36.5", WS 172cm 67.5"

all plum ad (sub)ad fl all plum	• Heavy dagger-shaped bill with obvious groove through upper mandible. • Mainly white except black prim and prim-cov. • Golden-yellow head and neck (most extensive in spring). • Long wings and tail. • In moderate winds, wings appear somewhat swept-back; in strong winds strongly hooked wings.
fl juv	• Entirely grey-brown with many fine pale speckles (central part of underparts, axillaries and uppertail-cov white).
fl 1s	• Like juv but underparts nearly white with dark breast-band.
fl 2w	• Wings mainly as in juv; underparts nearly white.
fl 3w	• Underparts completely white. • Ad-like head. • Upperside spotted black and white. • Sec black.
fl 4w	• Like ad with mix of black and white sec (piano pattern) and black central tail-feathers; sometimes all sec still black (see Cape Gannet).

Cape Gannet *Morus capensis*   L 85cm 33.5", WS 160cm 63"

all plum		• Smaller than Northern Gannet with slightly shorter tail.
imm		• Plumage-cycle as in Northern.
ad	⇒	• Long dark longitudinal stripe down throat (longer than Northern). • Plumage like Northern but with black sec and tail-feathers (some Northern 4w theoretically identical but in this species normally some retained dark greater cov or some white outer tail-feathers). • Golden-yellow head most extensive in autumn ⇔ in Northern in spring.
note		• Not (yet) accepted in WP. Former records appear to be no longer acceptable.

Cormorants and darters

Great Cormorant *Phalacrocorax carbo*   L 85cm 33.5"

all plum		• 14 tail-feathers. • Size very variable. ♀ often notably smaller than ♂; small ♀ *sinensis* can approach Shag in size.
ad		• Feathers of upperparts and wings have brown centres and broad black fringes.
ad s	⇒	• White thigh-patch and variable white feathering on head (from December onwards). • Reddish gape line.
juv-1w		• Normally (very) pale underparts but *flanks dark*, pale part on belly relatively narrow (see *carbo* imm) ⇔ in Double-crested Cormorant imm and Shag imm broader pale part on belly due to paler flanks. • Underparts very variable from brown to nearly white. • Juv greater cov and tertials pointed with narrow fringe around tip.
2w		• Underparts blackish without obvious blue gloss, belly spotted. • Upperparts like ad w but less glossy; crown and hind-neck with brown wash. • Uncompleted prim-moult starts again with p1, so three generations of prim present from beginning of 3cy.
fl all plum		• Small kink in neck ⇔ Shag. • Often glides between series of wing-beats ⇔ Shag and geese.
geog var		*P.c. sinensis* (Eurasia except Atlantic coast)
all plum		• Border between gular skin and feathering from gape goes straight downwards (on throat a notch of feathers is hooked forward into the gular patch ⇔ Double-crested) ⇔ Shag and *carbo*.
geog var		*P.c. maroccanus/lucidus* (north-west Africa)
ad		• White head-side, breast and upper part of belly, sharply demarcated from black remainder of underparts.
imm		• Very pale underparts (as in some *sinensis* and *carbo* imm), but ear-coverts also pale and contrasting with dark crown.
geog var		*P.c. carbo* (Atlantic coast of Europe)
all plum		• Border between feathering and gular skin is hooked forward from beginning of gape line to bottom corner of gular pouch, but less strongly than in Shag. Angle between beginning of gape line and bottom corner of gular pouch < 65° from horizontal ⇔ in *sinensis* > 73°; small overlap between 66-72°. • Larger than *sinensis* with heavier bill (especially ♂). Larger ♂ *sinensis* overlaps with small ♀ *carbo*. • Tail slightly shorter than in *sinensis* (flight silhouette more goose-like). • Often hardly any bare skin around eye ⇔ in *sinensis* sometimes conspicuous yellow 'eye-ring'. • ♂ especially has rather flat crown and angular rear-head.
ad s		• Often has larger amount of white around bill than *sinensis*; with white patch having angular border through ear-coverts ⇔ in *sinensis* white border more rounded through ear-coverts and running more parallel with the border of the gular skin.

	• White patterning on rear-side of head less extensive than in most *sinensis* creating no uninterrupted white area, but some older ♂ can show much white at beginning of breeding season.
	• Breeding plumage developed later than in *sinensis* (from end Jan, in *sinensis* from Dec).
	• In breeding season often blue-purple gloss on body ⇔ in *sinensis* more greenish. Later in summer gloss more variable and useless for identification.
1w	• Generally more white on underparts than in *sinensis*.
moult	• Slower progression than in *sinensis*.

Double-crested Cormorant *Phalacrocorax auritus* L 83cm 32.5"

all plum ⇒	• Conspicuous pale deep yellow to orange lores.
⇒	• Border between gular skin and feathering from gape *straight downwards (or even slightly bulging in direction of breast)* ⇔ Great Cormorant. No feathering protrudes forward on the chin ⇔ Great.
	• At most a narrow pale border around skin of bill base ⇔ Great.
	• Smaller size than Great with slightly more slender bill.
	• Thicker neck and fuller, rounder rear-head than Great.
	• 12 tail-feathers like Shag ⇔ in Great 14.
ad	• Deep orange gular skin around bill-base; bill grey ⇔ imm.
	• Completely deep black plumage.
ad s	• Elongated feathers on crown creating crest.
imm ⇒	• Lower mandible and (usually) cutting-edge of upper mandible yellowish to orange.
⇒	• Dark around and between legs ⇔ in Great imm at least slightly pale spotted but usually wholly pale between legs.
	• Pale, unstreaked (⇔ most Great imm) breast usually extending to *breast-sides and often reaching to above wing-bend*. Variable, underparts sometimes nearly wholly dark.
	• Bare-skinned lores, gape line and front of throat orange-yellow. Bare part of lores often extendins to above eye ⇔ Great.
	• In 2cy and 3cy breast and later upper part of belly pale(r). Darker after moult in summer.
	• Pale ear-coverts, often with diffuse dark spot (variable, sometimes wholly dark head).
behav	• Capable of perching on e.g. power line or other wire ⇔ Great.
flight	• Sometimes short glides between wing-beats (⇔ in Shag none) but less frequent than in Great.

Shag *Phalacrocorax aristotelis* L 73cm 28.5"

all plum ⇒	• *Yellow gape line* completely surrounded by feathering; border between feathering and bare skin at gape line strongly hooked forward ⇔ Great Cormorant *sinensis* (Great *carbo* in between *sinensis* and Shag).
	• Eye within feathering; feathered lores ⇔ Great.
	• Bill almost parallel (except base); hook of upper mandible does not reach below lower mandible ⇔ Great.
	• 12 tail-feathers ⇔ in Great 14.
	• Steep forehead.
ad	• Entirely dark plumage.
juv-1w ⇒	• Legs partially pale, yellowish (especially webs) ⇔ in ad and Great all plum black.
⇒	• Broad pale fringes to cov creating pale wing-panel.
	• Pale throat contrasts with dark neck ⇔ Great imm.
	• Underparts almost uniform (pale)brown, no dark breast-band ⇔ Great juv-1w.
	• Upperparts dark brown.
2w	• Body adult-like but wings (although already 2nd generation) usually still immature-looking with pale tips to cov.
2s	• Like ad s but crest very short and yellowish lower mandible.
fl all plum	• Straight neck ⇔ Great.
	• Usually very low above water surface without glides and with faster wing-beats than Great.
	• Belly rather round ('beer-belly') and thin neck. Centre of gravity more towards rear than in Great.

geog var	*P.a. desmarestii* (Mediterranean)
all plum	• Slightly smaller than *aristotelis* with longer, thinner bill.
ad	• More yellow at base of lower mandible than in *aristotelis*.
ad s	• Crest shorter than *aristotelis* or even absent.
imm	• Paler underparts than *aristotelis* (normally as pale as pale Great imm).

geog var	*P.a. riggenbachi* (north-west Africa)
all plum	• Like *desmarestii* but bill shorter and thicker like *aristotelis*.

Socotra Cormorant *Phalacrocorax nigrogularis* L 80cm 31.5"

all plum ⇒	• Obvious prim-projection ⇔ all other cormorants.
ad ⇒	• Legs, bill and bare skin around bill black.
	• Wholly black; pale spot behind eye and weak pale striping on neck and rump for a short time in summer.
juv	• Plumage resembles Shag *desmarestii* (whitish underparts).
	• Pale legs, bill and bare skin around bill.
fl all plum ⇒	• Like Shag has a thin, straight neck ⇔ Great Cormorant.
	• Long, narrow hand. Wing-tip formed by 3 outer prim ⇔ in all other cormorants by 4 outer prim.

Pygmy Cormorant *Phalacrocorax pygmeus* L 49cm 19"

all plum ⇒	• Much smaller than Great Cormorant (wing-span almost half of Great).
⇒	• Short bill.
	• Long tail.
ad s	• Head and neck (sometimes also whole underparts) with numerous white speckles.

ad w/juv	• Chestnut-brown head with white throat.
1w	• Upperside browner and less glossy than ad w (in ad greenish gloss).
	• Underparts rather pale with whitish belly and darker breast.
fl all plum	• Tail protrudes slightly further than head and neck.
	• Wing-beats notably faster than in Great.
	• Head looks relatively thick compared to neck.
note	• Little Cormorant *P. niger* (south Asia) resembles Pygmy and could possibly turn up as escape in WP. Smaller than Pygmy with slightly longer bill and tail and slightly shorter neck. In ad s deep black neck, breast and mantle (lacks brown wash) with only some white speckles; green iris (in Pygmy dark). In ad w less brown than Pygmy and well-defined white throat patch with dark underparts (in Pygmy pale throat ill-defined by paler underparts). Imm underparts darker than in Pygmy imm.

Long-tailed Cormorant *Phalacrocorax africanus*   L 53cm 21"

all plum ⇒	• Scaps and cov pale grey with dark tips, creating *large grey-spotted wing- and shoulder-patch* (in imm less clear).
	• Pale bill.
	• Size like Pygmy Cormorant but tail longer.
ad s	• Wholly dark underparts.
ad w/imm	• Pale belly (juv with wholly pale underparts).

African Darter *Anhinga rufa*   L 79cm 31"

all plum	• Structure resembles a cormorant but neck longer and more slender and long, straight bill.
ad ♂ s	• Long pale bar extending from gape line up neck-side ⇔ in ad ♀ s less distinct.
	• Dark crown and hind-neck contrasts with rufous throat and breast.
ad ♀	• Upperparts browner than in ad ♂.
ad w	• Like ad ♀ s but head and neck usually less contrasting.
juv	• Neck and breast pale ⇔ ad.
	• No white elongated scaps ⇔ ad.
fl all plum	• Short, strongly rounded wings ⇔ cormorants.
note	• Oriental Darter *A. melanogaster* (south Asia) resembles *rufa* but with less rufous neck (greyer) and less obvious pale stripe along rear-head and neck-side. Anhinga *A. anhinga* (Americas) has uniform head and neck (black in ad ♂ s, greyish in ad ♀) and more white in cov, scaps and tertials. Both Oriental Darter and Anhinga not recorded in WP.

Pelicans

White Pelican *Pelecanus onocrotalus*   L 160cm 63", WS 270cm 106"

all plum	• Legs orange-pink (in ad in breeding season reddish), more orange-yellow in imm.
	• Orange to yellow throat sack.
	• Forehead feathering ends in a point at base of upper mandible ⇔ Dalmatian Pelican.
ad	• Yellow-orange throat sack.
	• White with black flight-feathers; in breeding season with variable pink wash especially on breast and crest on rear-head.
juv-1s	• Grey-brown cov and variable amount of grey-brown on hind-neck (from 1s hind-neck nearly white).
2s-3s	• Like ad but lacks crest on rear-head and often somewhat dark centres to greater cov, rear scaps and tertials.
juv-2s(3s)	• Grey tail.
fl all plum ⇒	• Black flight-feathers (in ad with pale grey inner webs, only visible on upperside) contrast strongly with rest of plumage.
	• Legs project beyond tail ⇔ in Pink-backed and Dalmatian normally not.
fl juv-1s ⇒	• Dark bars on otherwise white underwing-cov (only imm pelican in WP with dark well-patterned underwing-cov).
	• Upperparts variably marked dark.
fl 2s-2s	• As ad but narrow dark line on underwing-cov.
notes	• For other field marks see Dalmatian.
	• American White Pelican *P. erythrorhynchos* which could occur as escape in WP resembles White but bare skin around eye much narrower (only surrounding eye) and whiter overall plumage.

Dalmatian Pelican *Pelecanus crispus*   L 170cm 70", WS 295cm 116"

all plum ⇒	• *Legs dark grey.*
	• Grey lores ⇔ in White Pelican pink.
	• Forehead feathering ends rectangularly at base of upper mandible ⇔ White.
ad ⇒	• Pale iris ⇔ White and Pink-backed Pelican.
⇒	• Long shaggy feathers on rear-head and neck.
	• Silver-grey wash over plumage.
	• Orange-red throat sack from midwinter, outside breeding less deep coloured.
juv-1s	• Upperside grey-brown (less dark than in White juv).
	• Pink throat sack.
2s	• Yellow to orange-yellow throat sack.
	• Plumage mainly like ad but at least some dark patterned cov.
fl all plum ⇒	• Pale underwing with *white central band* and *diffuse dark wing-tips* and trailing edge. Flight-feathers in imm slightly darker than in ad, upperwing rather similar to White.

Pink-backed Pelican *Pelecanus rufescens*   L 146cm 57.5", WS 250cm 98.5"

all plum ⇒	• Isolated dark loral-spot.
	• Short straight crest creating pointed rear-head.
	• Legs pale pink to orange; in west Africa yellowish.
	• Broad pale orbital-ring creating spectacled appearance in combination with dark eye but otherwise little bare skill around loral-area ⇔ White Pelican and Dalmatian Pelican.
	• When seen from below, bill relatively narrow.
	• Forehead feathering ends rectangularly at base of upper mandible (like Dalmatian) ⇔ White.
ad ⇒	• Dark half-ring at rear-side of eye.
ad s	• Rump and, to lesser extent, undertail-cov and cov pink (no pink in w).
imm	• Cov brown (paler than in White imm and darker than in Dalmatian imm); neck grey without brown ⇔ White imm.
fl all plum	• p10 obviously shorter than rest of outer prim ⇔ in White and Dalmatian length of p10 (almost) same as rest of outer prim.
	• Flight-feathers darker than in Dalmatian but not black like White. Flight-feathers in imm slightly darker than in ad.

Frigatebirds

Ascension Frigatebird *Fregata aquila*   L 91cm 36", WS 198cm 78"

all plum	• Slightly smaller than Magnificent Frigatebird with slightly more slender and tending towards grey-blue bill.
ad ♂	• Black with red throat sack (like Magnificent).
ad ♀	• Entirely dark (only completely dark frigatebird ad ♀) with slightly paler brown hind-neck and breast.
juv ⇒	• Dark, (almost) complete breast-band *evenly broad and paler (brown) than underwing* ⇔ in Magnificent juv dark breast-sides more triangular and as dark as underwing.
	• Breast-band high on breast, upper breast dark ⇔ in Magnificent lower on breast, upper breast white.
	• Head and neck completely white (also in most Magnificent juv) ⇔ in Lesser (and some Great) Frigatebird head yellow-brown.
fl all plum	• See Magnificent flight all plum.
fl juv ⇒	• Uniform white axillary stripe, see Lesser for details.

Magnificent Frigatebird *Fregata magnificens*   L 101cm 40", WS 238cm 93"

all plum	• Extremely large size with very long wings and long forked tail.
	• Long (yellow-)grey bill with large hook.
ad ♂	• Plumage wholly black with red throat which can swell up to large throat sack.
	• Purple gloss on upperparts ⇔ in Ascension Frigatebird green.
imm ♂	• Pale belly and red throat (from 4cy red throat differs from imm ♀).
ad ♀	• Dark head and whitish neck-side and breast; rest of underparts dark.
imm	• White head, breast and belly; white diamond-shaped belly-patch (sexes alike until 3cy).
fl all plum	• Characteristic with very long forked tail, very long narrow wings and long bill, as well as wing-shape: raised arm and bent-down hand with strongly pushed forward carpal (valid for all frigatebird species).
fl ad ♀ /	• White on breast at most extending into axillaries; *characteristic narrow pale lines* on axillaries
imm ⇒	(but sometimes difficult to see) ⇔ in Lesser Frigatebird ad ♀/imm and Ascension imm white extends distinctly and undisturbed into axillaries.
	• Pale arm diagonal (like in Lesser and Ascension ad ♀ and imm).

Great Frigatebird *Fregata minor*   L 93cm 36.5", WS 218cm 86"

ad ♂	• Wholly black like Ascension and Magnificent.
ad ♀	• Broad white breast extending into *grey throat*.
	• Black of belly broadly extending into white breast (white on breast broadly V-shaped).
fl imm	• Like Lesser Frigatebird but no white in axillaries. Sometimes weak pale tips to feathers of axillaries, but much less conspicuous than in Magnificent.
fl all plum	• No white on axillaries (but see flight imm).
note	• Not recorded in WP.

Lesser Frigatebird *Fregata ariel*   L 76cm 30", WS 184cm 72.5"

ad ♂ ⇒	• (Nearly) completely black with red throat sack; often *white spot on side of belly extending into axillaries* (flight). Some (older?) ind wholly black.
ad ♀	• White breast sharply demarcated from dark head.
	• Red eye-ring.
ad ♀/imm	• Pale breast distinctly extends distinctly into axillaries.
	• Pale arm diagonal (like Magnificent ad ♀/imm).
imm	• Yellow-brown head.
	• Pale breast and flanks (belly often dark spotted).
fl all plum ⇒	• Uniform white axillary stripe; front of stripe more or less parallel to leading edge (like Ascension) ⇔ in Magnificent (and Great Frigatebird) not parallel to leading edge.
	• See Magnificent flight all plum.

Herons and egrets

Eurasian Bittern *Botaurus stellaris*   L 75cm 29.5"

all plum	• Brownish with black-spotted upperside.
	• Thick neck; neck-side orange-brown.
ad	• Black cap and submoustachial-stripe.

1w	• Like ad but cap and submoustachial-stripe sometimes brownish (brown in juv). • Cap smaller than in ad, not extending into hind-neck. • Cov often paler than in ad.
moult	• Ad complete in autumn/early winter; 1w partial. Moult-limit in winter indicative of 1w.
fl all plum	• Very thick neck. • Very long toes creating long leg-projection beyond tail (only small part of tarsus projected). • Flight-feathers barred; at distance upperwing almost uniform ⇔ Purple Heron.

American Bittern *Botaurus lentiginosus* L 65cm 25.5"

all plum ⇒ ⇒	• Conspicuous pale yellow gape line to behind eye. • *Crown hardly darker than ear-coverts* ⇔ in Eurasian Bittern very dark cap. • Broad brown longitudinal stripes on breast. • Narrow supercilium; dark loral-stripe extending to upper mandible ⇔ Eurasian. • Slightly colder brown than Eurasian.
fl all plum ⇒	• *Uniform pale cov* contrast with dark flight-feathers. • Pale rufous trailing edge of arm and inner hand.

Least Bittern *Ixobrychus exilis* L 34cm 13.5"

all plum ad ♂	• Generally more rufous and more uniform than Little Bittern. • Black upperparts like Little but, when not too worn, narrow white line along scaps. • Rufous to chestnut-brown head-side and neck ⇔ in Little ad ♂ mainly grey head-side and neck-side.
ad ♀ juv-1w	• Uniform dark brown crown and upperparts; pale line at border between mantle and scaps ⇔ Little ♀. • Mantle and scaps rufous with dark anchor-pattern ⇔ in Little juv-1w dark with pale fringes. • Pale wing-panel with dark shaft-streaks.
fl all plum ⇒	•Rufous greater cov (trailing edge of pale yellowish wing-panel) and *tip of prim-cov.*

Little Bittern *Ixobrychus minutus* L 36cm 14"

ad ♂	• Uniform black upperparts ⇔ ad ♀. • Head-side and rear-side of neck with grey wash ⇔ in ad ♀ rufous-brown. • In breeding season shows (for a short period) red lores and/or bill (base).
ad ♀	• Dark upperparts with *narrow pale longitudinal stripes* ⇔ ad ♂. • Broad but weak longitudinal stripes on throat and breast ⇔ in ad ♂ almost uniform.
juv-1w	• Diffuse dark centres to lesser cov and median cov ⇔ in ad uniform pale. • Dark mantle feathers, scaps and tertials with broad rufous-brown fringes. • Well-defined longitudinal stripe on underparts; diffuse striping on head-side and neck ⇔ ad.
1w 1s	• Like ad ♀ but wings at least still juv with dark shaft-streaks in pale wing-panel. • Like ad of equivalent sex, but inner sec and often outer greater cov still brown juv feathers. 1s ♂ slightly more strongly streaked on underparts and shows less grey on side of neck than in ad ♂.

Schrenck's Bittern *Ixobrychus eurhythmus* L 35cm 14"

ad ♂ ⇒	• Vertical dark brown stripe from throat to belly. • Upperparts uniform chestnut-brown.
ad ♀ ⇒	• Numerous pale spots on mantle, scaps and cov. • Neck heavily streaked.
imm	• Moults in 1w to ad-like plumage; 1w ♀ nearly as ad ♀, 1w ♂ with spotted upperparts (like ♀-type) but uniform cov as in ad ♂.
fl all plum ⇒	• *Brown-grey sec, prim and prim-cov* creating poorly contrasting wings; underwing pale.

Dwarf Bittern *Ixobrychus sturmii* L 32cm 12.5"

ad	• Upperparts dark slaty-grey. • Underparts pale with large dark spots in vertical bars. • Legs bright orange-yellow. • Lores blue-grey to green-grey.
ad ♂ ad ♀	• Dark red-brown iris. • Yellow iris.
juv fl all plum	• Upperparts brown-grey with rufous fringes to mantle feathers, scaps and cov. • Uniform dark under- and upperwing.

Night Heron *Nycticorax nycticorax* L 61cm 24"

all plum	• Stocky body with thick neck. • Thick bill. • Legs yellow, short.
ad	• Blackish upperparts and crown.
juv	• Dark brown upperparts and upperwing with well-defined white spot at tip of each feathers. • Heavily streaked underparts (in 1w usually fainter).
1s-2w	• Early in 2cy similar to juv but paler, greyer plumage. • During 2nd part of 2cy moults into 2nd imm plumage with uniform dark grey-brown upperparts and crown and diffuse striped breast. • Pale base of lower mandible. • Legs dull yellow ⇔ in ad bright yellow.
fl all plum	• Short leg projection beyond tail . • 'Heavy body' with stiff wing-beats. • Uniform grey wings.

geog var	N.n. hoactli (North America)
all plum	• Generally slightly larger than nycticorax.
ad	• White on forehead and above eye narrower than in nycticorax. White above eye often shorter than in nycticorax, not reaching rear-side of eye.
note geog var	• Possible vagrant in WP, but part of population in WP possibly of Nearctic origin due to introductions.

Striated Heron Butorides striata   L 44cm 17.5"

all plum	• Uniform grey to blackish upperparts and blackish cap.
	• Cov with pale fringes (in juv cov with white spot on tip).
	• Isolated, pale yellow to greenish loral-stripe (bare skin).
	• Leg green-yellow (red for a short period in ad s).
	• Patterning and structure similar to Green Heron but colour pattern different.
ad	• Underparts variable from completely pale grey to almost completely rufous (rufous morph) ⇔ in Green red-brown deeper and more restricted to upper side of underparts, sharply demarcated from grey remainder of underparts.
	• Pale ear-coverts (sometimes very diffuse); in extreme rufous morph ear-coverts pale grey ⇔ Green.
	• Rufous morph (Red Sea) variable but generally much darker and more uniform than grey morph with rufous neck-side, breast and fringes to cov and dark upperparts with rufous wash. Rufous morph from subspecies of Central and South America (not recorded in WP) sometimes strongly resembles Green but underparts more uniform without obvious colour contrast between breast and rest of underparts.
	• Upperparts and wings dark grey, sometimes with greenish gloss.
juv-1w	• Dark brown-grey upperparts.
	• In juv heavily streaked neck and breast, grey to pale brown (paler than in Green juv).
	• Juv cov and prim with well-defined white spot on tips.
	• 1w sometimes already very adult-like but cov and prim still juv.
fl all plum	• Rather long leg projection beyond tail (longer than in other small herons).
	• Uniform dark upperwing ⇔ all other small herons except Night Heron.
note	• Widespread species with many subspecies in Asia, Africa and South and Central America. Only Asian subspecies occurs in WP.

Green Heron Butorides virescens   L 44cm 17.5"

all plum	• See Striated Heron all plum.
ad ⇒	• Dark, deep red-brown head-side, neck and breast (sometimes belly) sharply demarcated from grey remainder of underparts.
	• Upperparts dark grey ⇔ in Striated rufous morph upperparts often with rufous wash – in South and Central American subspecies (not recorded in WP) upperparts very similar to Green.
	• Black cap.
	• Dark grey upperparts, often with green gloss.
juv-1w	• Like Striated (see there) but head-side and neck-side deeper rufous and upperparts blackish-brown, sometimes with green gloss.
fl all plum	• See Striated.

Squacco Heron Ardeola ralloides   L 45cm 17.5"

all plum	• Grey-brown to orange-brown upperparts, in ad s also breast and upperside of belly.
ad s	• Striped crown (long crown-feathers) and hind-neck; rest of plumage unmarked.
	• Blue-grey legs and bill with black tip (short period in breeding season).
ad w	• Breast with orange-brown ground-colour ⇔ in 1w whiter.
ad w/1w	• Head and neck finely streaked ⇔ in Indian Pond Heron and Chinese Pond Heron streaking more heavy.
1w	• Ill-defined dark tip to outer prim and outer web of prim-cov (flight) ⇔ in ad w wholly white.
	• Underparts with white background.
1s	• Some ind still with distinctly striped neck and breast, disappearing later in summer and then strongly resembling ad s.
	• Prim often with dark shaft and/or outer web of prim-cov.
fl all plum	• Legs project only little beyond tail, only feet.
	• Wings (almost) white, sometimes with some patterning on cov (normally difficult to see) ⇔ in Cattle Egret wholly white wings.
	• No sharp corner in neck.

Indian Pond Heron Ardeola grayii   L 46cm 18"

all plum	• Size and structure similar to Squacco Heron but bill slightly shorter and thicker and wings shorter.
ad s ⇒	• Resembles Squacco but more distinct contrast between pale brown-yellow head and neck and dark upperparts.
	• Elongated crown-feathers wholly white ⇔ in Squacco white with dark stripes.
ad w/imm ⇒	• Sharp dark line or 'V'-shaped mark on lores with obvious yellow stripe above it ⇔ in Squacco and Chinese Pond Heron ad w/imm weak dark line at most and lores more uniform overall.
	• Upperparts cold dark grey-brown ⇔ in some Squacco as dark but often with cream-coloured or in ad tending towards purple wash.
	• Head, neck and breast heavily dark streaked, on central part of breast only narrow area unstreaked ⇔ in Squacco ad w/imm less extensively streaked, with throat and central part of breast unstreaked.
fl all plum	• Upperwing with dark diagonal bar over cov (more conspicuous than in Squacco).

Chinese Pond Heron Ardeola bacchus   L 52cm 20.5"

	• Size and structure similar to Indian Pond Heron and Squacco Heron.
	• Red-brown head and breast; back and scaps blackish.

ad w/imm	• Upperparts like Indian but darker with in ad w warm purple-brown wash.
	• Uniform dark lower elongated breast-feathers.
	• Lores pale without sharp dark patterning.
	• Extensive and bold black streaking on crown and hind-neck like in Indian.
fl all plum	• See Indian.

Cattle Egret *Bubulcus ibis*   L 47cm 18.5"

all plum ⇒	• Short yellowish bill (in imm with dark tip).
	• Legs relatively short.
ad s	• Pink-orange crown, breast-patch and elongated back-feathers.
ad w	• Ad ♂ w white with faint yellow-brown wash on crown and breast and somewhat elongated breast- and mantle feathers. Ad ♀ w completely white without elongated feathers.
1w	• Like ad ♀ w. In young juv (up to 2-3 months old) bill dark, gradually becoming yellow.
fl all plum	• Short leg projection (distinctly shorter than in Little Egret but slightly longer than in Squacco Heron); toes and part of tarsus project.
	• Flat belly and rather sharp corner in neck.
note	• Eastern Cattle Egret *B. coromandus* (possible escape in WP) in ad s has completely orange-coloured head, throat and breast, with only forehead and throat white (Cattle is white below eye). Whole plumage with slight grey hue.

Little Blue Heron *Egretta caerulea*   L 60cm 23.5"

all plum	• Rather strong bill with sharp point (bill structure in between Cattle Egret and Little Egret).
	• Legs wholly grey-green.
	• Neck shorter and thicker than in Little.
ad	• Entirely dark purple-blue.
juv ⇒	• Wholly white except dark tips to outer prim (sometimes very small).
	• Legs and bare skin on lores grey-green ⇔ other white egrets, but colour sometimes approached by Snowy Egret juv which sometimes also shows pale bill-base.
	• Grey-brown bill and dark tip.
1s	• Mix of white and dark grey feathers. Grey ad-type feathers often first appearing on upperparts, cov and tertials.
fl all plum	• More often stretched neck than other herons.
	• Long leg-projection.

Black Heron *Egretta ardesiaca*   L 51cm 20"

all plum	• Wholly slaty-black, including throat ⇔ other herons/egrets dark morph.
	• Legs relatively short; dark with yellow toes.
	• Stocky structure like Cattle Egret.
ad	• Short full crest.

Tricolored Heron *Egretta tricolor*   L 66cm 26"

all plum ⇒	• Dark grey head and neck contrast with white remainder of underparts.
	• Long neck and long slender bill.
	• Slightly larger than Little Egret.
ad	• Yellow bill with large dark tip (in ad s grey-blue).
	• Legs and toes yellow but front side often dark.
	• Mantle, breast, neck and head (except front of neck) dark blue-grey; back to rump contrasting pale brown.
imm	• Juv with red-brown head, neck and tips to cov.
	• In juv bill and legs mainly dark, becoming paler later in winter.
	• From 2cy onwards head and neck becoming mix of brown and grey.

Snowy Egret *Egretta thula*   L 59cm 23"

all plum ⇒	• *Bright-yellow lores*, concolorous with iris and toes (in Little Egret lores sometimes yellowish in spring for a few weeks, but not *bright-yellow*). In young juv lores pale grey-yellow. In short courtship period lores and toes sometimes reddish.
⇒	• Iris almost concolorous with *bright yellow lores* (except for very short courtship period and in very young juv).
	• Bare skin on lores extending over upper mandible (bare skin between feathers of forehead and upper mandible) ⇔ in Little feathers of forehead usually reach to upper mandible.
	• Generally slightly smaller than Little with slightly shorter and thinner legs (possibly useful in direct comparison). Somewhat thicker, shorter neck and slightly shorter bill than Little.
ad	• Bright yellow iris ⇔ in Little pale yellow to dull yellow.
	• Bright yellow toes (slightly extending up on tarsus ⇔ Little ad), dull yellow rear-side of tarsus and usually also tibia ⇔ Little ad.
ad s	• Full but short plumes on crown in courtship period ⇔ in Little only 2 or 3 long feathers.
	• Plumes on tertials up-curled ⇔ in Little straight.
juv	• Pale grey-yellow iris like Little but lores also pale grey-yellow (yellow like ad later in autumn) ⇔ Little.
	• Mainly yellowish legs (darker front-side only) ⇔ Little.
	• Pale base of lower mandible (like Little juv) ⇔ in ad completely black bill.

Western Reef Egret *Egretta gularis*   L 63cm 25"

| all plum ⇒ | • Longer, bulkier bill than Little Egret with *bend in culmen*; curve increases slightly towards bill-tip therefore less pointed bill-tip than in Little (but see *gularis*). |

	• Legs and bill paler than in Little but see differences per subspecies and season.
	• Iris pale grey to yellow-grey, not bright yellow ⇔ in Little more grey-yellow to yellow, latter especially in ad (but overlap, especially in imm).
	• Slightly larger and stronger-built than Little with usually distinct thicker neck (most ind of *gularis* structurally more towards Little).
	• Tibia relatively long, tarsus seems only little longer than tibia ⇔ Little.
	• Chin and throat often somewhat 'fuller' than in Little.
ad s	• 2 strongly elongated crown-feathers and elongated scaps.
	• In short courtship period legs dark and lores pink-red.
imm	• Dark morph paler than ad with less glossy plumage.
fl all plum	• Long toes.
note	• Entirely white morph rare in *gularis* but c.50% of *schistacea* (almost) wholly white.

geog var	Western Reef Egret *E.g. gularis* (west Africa)
all plum	• Often less strong bill with less bend in culmen than *schistacea*, then bill shape more like Little.
	• Dull yellow-grey lores and usually rather dark bill; ad s with almost black bill.
	• Rather dark brownish legs with yellow toes. In short courtship period black.
	• Smaller than *schistacea* and structure more like Little. Wholly white morph (rare) sometimes difficult to distinguish from Little but tibia longer and bill slightly heavier in direct comparison.

geog var	Indian Reef Egret *E.g. schistacea* (Middle East)
	• Slightly larger size than *gularis*.
ad	• Outside courtship period pale grey-yellow bill with dark tip ⇔ in *gularis* bill darker for whole year.
	• Dull yellow toes and legs in pale morph; in dark morph sometimes (much) darker.
	• Occurs in both wholly white (see note above) and wholly dark morph and numerous intermediate types; mainly white intermediate morph often with characteristic dark tips to prim and prim-cov and some dark sec, especially in imm.
fl all plum	• Shorter tarsus than *gularis* and Little.

Little Egret *Egretta garzetta*   L 60cm 23.5"

all plum	• *Grey to dull yellow* lores, except during courtship period (then reddish).
	• Almost straight culmen.
ad	• Dark bill (in w often with grey base to lower mandible).
ad s	• See Snowy Egret ad s.
juv	• Young juv sometimes still with dark toes.
imm	• Pale horn-coloured bill-base.
	• Variable but often yellowish rear-side of tarsus (can resemble Snowy but normally much less bright yellow and more diffusely bordered than in Snowy).
fl all plum	• Long leg projection beyond tail (almost entire tarsus).
note	• See also Snowy

Intermediate Egret *Egretta intermedia*   L 69cm 27"

all plum ⇒	• Heavy yellowish, relatively short bill resembles Cattle Egret (but overall much larger). Dark bill in spring for a short time.
	• Only slightly larger than Little Egret but due to structure and colour of bare skin more closely resembles Great White Egret.
	• Legs wholly black-brown; toes relatively long ⇔ in Cattle legs pale.
	• Gape line reaches to eye ⇔ Great White.
fl all plum	• Legs project far beyond tail ⇔ Cattle.

Great White Egret *Casmerodius albus*   L 92cm 36"

all plum ⇒	• Gape line reaches behind eye.
⇒	• Long orange-yellow bill; in ad in courtship period often darker to black.
	• Very long neck.
	• Dull yellow to green lores.
ad	• Legs yellowish (in w often brown to blackish, in spring sometimes reddish for a short period). Tibia often paler than tarsus.
ad s	• Elongated rear scaps and tertials (plumes); no plumes on rear-crown ⇔ Snowy Egret and Little Egret ad s.
fl all plum	• Legs project far beyond tail (nearly whole tarsus).

geog var	American Great Egret *C.a. egretta* (America)
all plum	• Smaller than *albus* (generally by approximately 12%).
ad	• Legs black (also tibia).
	• Deeper orange-yellow bill than *albus* (Europe), also in courtship period (colour difference hard to assess).

geog var	*C.a. modesta* (southern and eastern Asia)
all plum	• Smaller than *albus* with shorter tibia and more slender bill.
	• In courtship period usually red or pink-red legs and wholly black bill (sometimes also in *albus* but legs rarely wholly red).

Black-headed Heron *Ardea melanocephala* L 86cm 34"

all plum	• Slightly smaller than Grey Heron with somewhat thicker and shorter bill.
	• Legs dark grey, relatively short.
ad ⇒	• Black crown, head-side and hind-neck strongly contrasting with white throat and front of neck; lower part of neck black with white spots.
	• Uniform grey underparts, strongly contrasting with dark upperparts.
	• Upperparts darker grey than in Grey; outer greater cov, tertials and tail darker.
	• Sharply demarcated black bill-tip ⇔ in imm diffuse darker bill-tip.
	• Yellowish lores and eye-ring.
imm	• More uniform and diffusely patterned than ad with grey cap and rear-side of neck; in juv brown wash on cov.
fl all plum ⇒	• *White underwing-cov contrast* with black underside of flight-feathers.

Grey Heron *Ardea cinerea* L 90cm 35.5"

ad	• White crown; black crown-sides.
	• Pale bill (sometimes with slightly darker culmen).
ad s	• From midwinter onwards often yellow-orange bill and brown-orange legs.
1w	• Usually wholly dark upper mandible.
	• Only weak dark lateral crown-stripe (sometimes absent).
	• No black on wing-bend (prim-cov) ⇔ ad.
	• No black patterning on underparts ⇔ ad.
2w	• Like ad but crown and forehead greyish, not wholly white.
	• Dark culmen ⇔ ad.
geog var	*A.c. monicae* (coast of Mauritania)
ad	• Much paler overall than *cinerea*.
	• Side of neck very pale grey to white.
	• Upperparts pale grey with white tips to longest scaps.
	• Greater cov almost white.

Great Blue Heron *Ardea herodias* L 117cm 46"

all plum ⇒	• *Brown* leading edge of wing (marginal cov) ⇔ in Grey Heron white or largely white with some weak brown patterning.
⇒	• *Brown* tibia-feathering (in imm faint, sometimes whitish).
	• (Much) larger than Grey; ind from northern populations slightly smaller.
	• Neck longer than in Grey.
	• Bill heavier than Grey with straighter culmen (bill-shape reminiscent of White-billed Diver).
ad	• Dark pinkish neck, contrasting with white parts of head.
	• Black lateral crown-stripe narrower than in Grey. Often white supercilium.
juv-1w	• Grey-brown to grey, patchy sides of neck ⇔ in Grey all plum more uniform and grey.
	• Crown blacker and head-side whiter than in Grey imm.
	• In young juv rufous tips to (some) cov and scaps ⇔ Grey imm.
	• Dark upper mandible or culmen (like Grey).
	• Legs two-toned ⇔ most Grey imm.
2w	• Often lacking white supercilium due to broader black lateral crown-stripe than in ad which 'sags down' to eye.
	• Upper mandible obviously darker than lower mandible.
fl all plum	• Legs very long with long toes (legs project far beyond tail).
	• Broader wings than Grey; slow wing-beats.
	• Underwing-cov darker than flight-feathers ⇔ in Grey concolorous.

Purple Heron *Ardea purpurea* L 80cm 31.5"

all plum	• Long slender bill.
	• Long thin neck.
	• Legs yellowish with dark front-side of tarsus.
ad ⇒	• Well-defined black stripe along red-brown neck-side and black stripe over ear-coverts.
	• Mainly dark grey-blue upperside.
juv	• Cov and tertials with blackish centres and broad rufous-brown fringes.
	• Head diffusely brown streaked ⇔ well-defined lines in ad.
1s	• Most ind ad-like but with variable brownish upperside (part of cov, scaps and mantle). Some ind more juv-like.
	• Sec and prim brownish, retained feathers later in summer obviously worn.
	• Dark head- and neck-stripes weaker than in ad.
fl all plum	• Long toes and legs conspicuous; often upturned rear-toe.
	• Marked corner in neck.
	• Wing less arched than in Grey Heron.
	• Body moves up and down with wing-beats.
	• Underwing-cov mainly dark rufous (ad) or dark yellow-brown (imm) ⇔ in Grey dark grey.
fl ad	• Upperwing dark with little contrast ⇔ in Grey rather strong contrast between paler cov and darker flight-feathers.

Bourne's Heron *Ardea bournei* L 80cm 31.5"?

ad	• Much paler than Purple Heron with paler grey upperparts and whitish to pale brown underparts.
	• Head and neck pale brown to whitish with much fainter dark stripes than in Purple, although head-

imm	• Crown chestnut-brown. • Broad pale grey and brown-orange fringes to cov.
note	• Endemic to Cape Verde Islands.

stripes sometimes obvious but thin. Crown and rear-side of neck black.

Goliath Heron *Ardea goliath* — L 142cm 56"

all plum		• Extremely large size with heavy bill. • Upperside dark blue-grey (in juv brown spots on cov). • Legs blackish.
ad	⇒	• Black stripes on neck not reaching head; head and upperside of neck lacking black stripes ⇔ Purple Heron. • Head and neck mainly rufous-brown with white throat and front of neck. • Underparts and tibia-feathering deep chestnut.
imm		• Underparts pale with variable rufous and black patterning.
fl all plum		• Deep rufous underwing-cov, in juv still brown-grey.

Storks, ibises and flamingos

Yellow-billed Stork *Mycteria ibis* — L 100cm 39.5"

all plum	• Size like White Stork.
ad	• Long, heavy orange-yellow bill with slightly downcurved tip. • 'Face' red (bare skin). • Legs red. • Flight-feathers black. • Neck and underparts white.
ad s	• Cov with faint pink centres and white fringes.
imm	• Brownish cov with pale tips. • Bill, legs and bare parts of head weakly coloured.
fl all plum ⇒	• Resembles White but tail black.

Black Stork *Ciconia nigra* — L 96cm 38"

all plum	• Blackish head, neck, upperparts and wings. In ad purple and green gloss.
ad	• Legs and bill deep red.
juv	• Head, neck and upperparts dull black-brown. • Feathers of neck and cov with small pale tips. • Bill and legs grey-brown, often with slight reddish wash.
1w-1s	• Brownish bill, becoming reddish from 1s onwards. • Old (juv) cov brown. • Breast and head brownish with fine pale 'scales'.
2w	• Breast and head still with some brown feathers. • Legs and bill red like ad but often less bright.
flight	• Slightly shorter neck than White Stork (in silhouette often useful).
note	• Abdim's Stork *C. abdimii* (Africa) superficially resembles Black with nearly same pattern in perched ind. Abdim's slightly smaller with shorter neck and legs (short leg projection beyond tail in flight), no bright red legs and bill. In flight characteristic white wedge on back and underwing-cov with more white.

White Stork *Ciconia ciconia* — L 106cm 41.5"

ad	• Black sec and prim with green and/or purple gloss. • Iris dark brown.
juv-1s	• Legs and bill dull red, juv with dark bill-tip. • Black inner median cov. Often some isolated black in midst of white median cov, retained to halfway through 2cy. • Iris in juv grey, coming browner in 1s. • In 1s moult-limit in sec and prim; juv feathers brown, new feathers with grey wash (also in ad sec and prim with grey wash when fresh).

Marabou Stork *Leptoptilos crumeniferus* — L 145cm 57"

all plum	• Very heavy, grey-brown, pointed triangular bill.
ad	• Bare head and neck. • Upperside sooty black; cov and tertials with narrow pale fringes. • Underparts pale. • Legs long and thick, very pale greyish.
fl all plum	• Broad, strongly rounded wings with deeply indented 'fingers' like vulture. • Underwing dark with pale axillaries.

Glossy Ibis *Plegadis falcinellus* — L 60cm 23.5"

all plum		• Long downcurved bill.
ad s	⇒	• Narrow white lines, both directly above and below lores (in other plumages only very faint). • White lines part of bare skin, no feathering ⇔ White-faced Ibis (see note). • Wine-red wash especially on head and mantle.
ad w		• Fainter wine-red gloss on head and upperparts than ad s but more gloss than imm, especially on cov.
ad w/imm		• Head and neck with pale speckles.
juv/1w		• Mixture of pale brown (faded) juv feathers on head, neck and underparts and dark, weakly glossy new feathers.

55

imm	• Dull coloured with only weak brown-purple gloss on neck, upperparts and underparts; cov with only weak greenish gloss ⇔ in ad w stronger green and purple gloss on cov.
fl all plum	• Long slender neck and bill; long leg projection beyond tail (⇔ Eurasian Curlew).
note	• White-faced Ibis *P. chichi* (North America) strongly resembles Glossy and could occur as escape in WP. Former has red eye in all plum, pink bare skin around bill (bordered by narrow white line in ad s, *white line part of feathering and encircling rear-side of eye* ⇔ Glossy) and red legs in ad. In ad w and imm dull reddish bare skin around bill without pale border and dark legs (in ad w leg colour like Glossy).

Northern Bald Ibis *Geronticus eremita*   L 75cm 29.5"

all plum	• Wholly black (in ad purple and green gloss on cov).
ad	• Bare red head (crown darker).
	• Neck with elongated feathers and bare head add to 'prehistoric' appearance.
	• Legs relatively *short* and reddish.
juv	• Wholly dull brown-black (head still feathered).
fl all plum ⇒	• No leg projection beyond tail ⇔ Glossy Ibis.
	• Relatively short neck.

African Sacred Ibis *Threskiornis aethiopicus*   L 70cm 27.5"

all plum	• Heavy downcurved bill.
	• Mainly white plumage with black tertials and tips to flight-feathers (flight).
ad	• Black bare head and upper part of neck.
	• Tertials black and very long, creating fan-shaped plumes ⇔ in imm no plumes.
	• Often dirty-white plumage ⇔ imm more pure white.
imm	• Feathered dark head and hind-neck white speckled; front of neck and throat often wholly white ⇔ ad.
	• Tertials and sometimes cov with dark patterning.
fl all plum ⇒	• Wings white with complete and well-defined black trailing edge (dark tips to all flight-feathers).

Eurasian Spoonbill *Platalea leucorodia*   L 85cm 33.5"

all plum	• At long distance differs from Great White Egret by more horizontal body posture and longer bill.
ad	• Dark bill.
ad s	• Long hanging crest, often with yellow wash.
	• Brown-yellow breast patch.
	• Legs black ⇔ most imm.
ad w	• Like ad s but lacks crest and breast patch.
juv	• Dark tips to prim-cov and outer prim (flight).
	• Dark shaft of sec, prim, scaps and tertials.
	• Flesh-coloured bill.
	• Legs often rather pale greyish.
1s	• Like juv but dark feather-parts less distinct.
	• Bill with grey base and large yellow tip.
	• Legs grey.
	• Sometimes short crest.
2s	• Prim with small dark tips.
	• Shorter white crest than ad s.
	• At most faint yellow breast-patch ⇔ ad s.
	• Legs dark grey.
fl all plum ⇒	• Neck held stretched straight out and relatively short projection of legs behind tail ⇔ white egrets.

Greater Flamingo *Phoenicopterus roseus*   L 123cm 48.5"

ad ⇒	• (Pale) pink bill with relatively small black bill-tip; black not reaching corner of culmen ⇔ all other flamingos.
	• Border between black and pale on bill rounded with bulge towards bill-tip.
	• Legs uniform red-pink.
	• Usually rather light pink plumage (cov darker and deeper pink).
imm	• Brown-grey hind-neck and upperparts with dark stripes.
	• Grey bill-base with black pattern like ad.
	• Legs dark grey, later dull pink with dark knees.

Lesser Flamingo *Phoenicopterus minor*   L 85cm 33.5"

all plum ⇒	• Completely dark red bill.
	• Obvious smaller than other flamingos.
ad	• Legs wholly pink.
	• Deep pink-red upperparts.
imm	• Brown-grey hind-neck and upperparts with dark stripes.
	• Legs dark grey.

Escaped and introduced flamingos

American Flamingo *Phoenicopterus ruber*   L 120cm 47"

ad ⇒	• Border between black and pale on lower mandible variable, often rounded with bulge towards bill-base ⇔ Greater Flamingo.
	• Legs dull pink with grey wash; joints bright pink.
	• Slightly less than half of lower mandible black.
	• Plumage more orange than pink and deeply coloured ⇔ other flamingos.
imm	• Grey bill-base with black pattern like ad.

Chilean Flamingo *Phoenicopterus chilensis*   L 111cm 43.5"

ad	⇒	• Black in upper mandible reaches to underside of nostril ⇔ American Flamingo. • Distal half of bill black. • More than half of lower mandible black. • Border between black distal part and pale basal part rounded with bulge towards bill-base (like American). • Legs shorter than other flamingos, especially tibia. • Legs pale grey without pink wash; joints and toes conspicuously pink-orange.
imm		• Brown-grey hind-neck and upperparts with dark stripes. • Legs dark grey.

Grebes

Pied-billed Grebe *Podilymbus podiceps*   L 35cm 14"

all plum	⇒	• Heavy pale, almost triangular bill with *curved culmen* ⇔ in Little Grebe culmen almost straight and upper mandible very dark. • Distinctly bulkier than Little (about as Slavonian Grebe) with *elongated head-profile.* • Tail often appears as erected spike ⇔ in Little small erected tail sometimes visible. • Black stripe along base of lower mandible (except juv). • Narrow pale eye-ring.
ad s	⇒	• Whitish bill with *vertical black band* at about middle of bill. • Black throat.
ad w		• Dark crown and paler head-side ill-defined, head overall dark ⇔ in Little pale head-side, sharply demarcated by dark cap. • Breast with reddish-brown wash. • Bill duller than in ad s, often dirty yellowish.
juv-1w		• Orange neck. Head with dark stripes in juv. • Culmen slightly darker than rest of bill, remainder coloured like ad w.
fl all plum		• Dark upperwing with pale narrow trailing edge along arm.

Little Grebe *Tachybaptus ruficollis*   L 26cm 10"

all plum		• Fluffy undertail-cov. • Pale (yellow) area around gape (most conspicuous in summer plumage).
ad s		• Chestnut-brown neck-side and head-side.
w	⇒	• Pale bill ⇔ other small grebes (except Pied-billed Grebe). • Pale brown breast and neck-side.
1w		• Diffuse dark patterning on ear-coverts (often one or two dark bars) ⇔ in ad w ear-coverts uniform pale.
fl all plum		• Very variable amount of white or pale in wing. In juv-3cy variable amount of white in sec, in older ind (almost) complete dark wing. • Contrast between dark cov (incl prim-cov) and paler flight-feathers.

Great Crested Grebe *Podiceps cristatus*   L 48cm 19"

all plum	⇒	• Long, slender neck. • Pale head-side with dark stripe between gape line and eye; pale lores and supercilium ⇔ in Red-necked Grebe all plum dark lores and lacks supercilium (wholly dark face). • Short crest at rear-head creates angular head-profile.
ad		• Greater cov mainly white ⇔ in 1w mainly dark (flight).
juv-1w		• Dark stripes over ear-coverts.
1s		• Develops at most restricted head plumes.
fl all plum	⇒	• White leading-edge of arm connected with *complete white wing-base* and white sec. • Conspicuous slender and elongated structure with long, thin neck ⇔ Red-necked flight. • Head and neck often bent downwards (giving 'hump-backed' appearance) but occasionally held up for some time ⇔ Red-necked flight.

Red-necked Grebe *Podiceps grisegena*   L 43cm 13.5"

all plum	⇒	• Yellow base to bill. • Smaller than Great Crested Grebe with shorter and thicker neck.
ad s		• Pale grey cheek contrasts with black crown and red-brown neck.
ad w/imm	⇒	• *Dark lores* and front of neck ⇔ Great Crested all plum. • Dirty-grey 'mask' below dark crown ⇔ Great Crested.
juv-1w		• Dark stripes over ear-coverts, often absent by beginning of winter.
1w		• Paler bill than ad with larger yellow base. • Pale (yellowish or orange) iris ⇔ in ad dark.
fl all plum		• White leading-edge of arm isolated, no complete white wing-base as in Great Crested. Amount of white on leading-edge of arm variable and often only narrow leading edge extending up to carpal. • Darker than Great Crested with shorter, thicker and darker neck.
fl 1w		• Less white on sec than ad; often only small amount of white on leading-edge of arm and almost identical to Slavonian Grebe.
geog var		*P.g. holboellii* (eastern Asia and North America)
all plum		• Mainly as *grisegena* but obviously larger, with especially long bill (bill generally 20% longer than in *grisegena*). Size and bill-length as in Great Crested. • Head-side dark grey-brown, head therefore contrasting less (possibly only in 1w) ⇔ in *grisegena* winter plumage contrasting greyish-white head-side.
ad s		• Often more yellow on basal part of bill than in *grisegena*.

Slavonian Grebe *Podiceps auritus* L 34cm 13.5"

all plum	• Sloping forehead, flattened crown ⇔ Black-necked Grebe. • Upper- and lower mandible evenly bent towards bill-tip. • Small, white bill-tip.
ad s ⇒	• Rufous front of neck ⇔ Black-necked ad s. • No golden-yellow feathers below eye-level ⇔ Black-necked ad s.
w ⇒	• Dark crown nearly *straight-bordered* with white part of head-side; ear-coverts wholly white ⇔ Black-necked w. • Front of neck often pure white ⇔ Black-necked. • Small, pale spot on lores (sometimes also in Black-necked).
1w	• Front of neck variably dark patterned ⇔ in ad w wholly white. • Bill-base rather pale (in ad bill often dark).
fl ad s	• Ill-defined border between dark rufous breast and pale belly ⇔ in Black-necked ad s black neck sharply defined with pale belly.
fl all plum	• Pale, isolated spot on leading-edge of arm (variable and overlapping with Red-necked Grebe) and white sec (white not reaching inner prim ⇔ Black-necked). • From distance resembles Red-necked but neck much thinner. • Flight more unsteady than other grebes; continually changes from side to side (almost zigzagging flight). Regularly holds neck and head upwards ⇔ in Black-necked neck held straight forward.

Black-necked Grebe *Podiceps nigricollis* L 31cm 12"

all plum	• Straight culmen, lower mandible bent towards tip of upper mandible; bill seems uptilted. • Peaked crown, steep forehead ⇔ Slavonian Grebe.
ad s ⇒	• Completely black neck ⇔ Slavonian.
w ⇒	• Eye inside dark crown. Crown *curved bordered* with pale parts of head; ear-coverts brown-grey ⇔ in Slavonian white. • Often rather dark front of neck ⇔ Slavonian ad w.
fl ad s	• Well-defined border between dark breast and pale belly ⇔ in Slavonian ad s ill-defined.
fl all plum	• White sec extending to inner prim (not in North American subspecies *P.n. californicus*); no white on front of arm.

Hawks, vultures, eagles and allies

European Honey-buzzard *Pernis apivorus* L 55cm 21.5", WS 120cm 47cm "

all plum	• Short legs. • Very slim and long nostril.
ad	• Grey bare skin around bill (in juv yellow). • Yellow iris.
ad ♂	• Blue-grey upperside of head; upperparts usually with grey wash ⇔ ad ♀.
ad ♀	• Only lores grey.
juv ⇒	• Bare yellow skin around bill and bill-base, distal part black ⇔ ad and most other juv raptors. • In paler ind white head with dark mask characteristic. • Dark iris.
1s	• *Yellowish* bare skin around bill ⇔ ad.
fl all plum ⇒	• Dark carpal patch *oval-shaped/elongated*; also well-developed in pale ind ⇔ on most pale Common Buzzard only dark crescent on carpal joints. • Rounded tail-corners. • Soars with wings held flat and pushed forward carpal joints. • Elastic, waving wing-beats. • Base of feet level with trailing edge of arm ⇔ in all *Buteo* legs longer, base of feet more towards rear.
fl ad	• Broad dark rear-end of wing ⇔ juv. Also on upperwing distinct ⇔ Common Buzzard.
fl ad ♂ ⇒	• Distal part of flight-feathers on underwing unbarred. • Dark trailing edge to whole wing (including sec) sharply bordered ⇔ ad ♀. • Upperparts and upperwing almost uniform.
fl ad ♀	• More evenly barred underside of flight-feathers, barring usually more narrow than in ♂. • Patchy upperparts and upperwing, sec uniform dark ⇔ ad ♂. • Dark tips to prim larger than in ad ♂ and not sharply demarcated.
fl juv	• Prim completely barred up to at least p7 ⇔ *Buteos*. • Dark 'fingers', pale prim-base (often only outer prim) and relatively dark sec ⇔ ad (sometimes also in ad ♀). • Barring on underwing broader than in ad. • Paler ind with white uppertail-cov visible as contrasting white 'U' against dark tail.
fl 1s	• Mix of juv and ad-type flight-feathers.
moult	• In WP moult of prim normally restricted to p4 at most, completed in late winter in winter range.
note	• Very variable in ground-colour and pattern, especially in juv but pattern of sec, prim and tail-feathers hardly variable.
note 1s	• (Very) rare in western Europe, normally stays in summer in African winter range.

Oriental Honey-buzzard *Pernis ptilorhyncus* L 64cm 25", WS 142cm 56"

all plum ⇒ ⇒	• (Much) larger than European Honey-buzzard. • Usually pale throat bordered by dark band (characteristic when present, often absent in juv). Sometimes dark vertical throat-stripe.
ad ♂	• Dark eye ⇔ in ad ♀ pale iris. • Head and usually also upperparts with grey wash ⇔ ad ♀.
fl all plum ⇒	• No contrasting dark carpal patch (when present faint and diffuse) ⇔ European.

		• Broad wing with 6 'fingers' ⇔ in European 5 'fingers'.
		• Usually little or no patterned underwing-cov.
		• Often somewhat bulging trailing edge of arm.
		• Relatively shorter and fuller tail than European.
		• Silhouette and flight manner sometimes resembles *Aquila* eagle.
fl ad	⇒	• Rear-most dark band over middle of underwing *visible from body up to p10* ⇔ in European ad ♂ this band disappears under greater cov towards body and reaches indistinctly to p10 (in European ad ♀ band longer visible, usually disappearing just before body).
		• Broad dark trailing edge of wing ⇔ juv.
		• During autumn migration suspended moult of prim, 4-5 inner prim new ⇔ in European also but only 1-4 inner prim new.
fl ad ♂	⇒	• 2 tail-bands; very broad dark central and subterminal tail-band ⇔ European all plum.
		• Barring on flight-feathers broader and more distinct than in European.
fl ad ♀		• Conspicuous dark central tail-band and broad terminal band (similar to European ad ♂) ⇔ in European ad ♀ usually only slightly broader central tail-band(s) and narrower more diffuse terminal band than in ad ♂.
		• Barring on sec (2-3 bands) more evenly spaced between greater cov and dark trailing edge of arm ⇔ in European ad ♀ broad space between dark trailing edge of arm and barring.
fl juv		• 2 narrow central tail-bands (juv ♂) or multiple narrow tail-bands (juv ♀) ⇔ ad.
		• Barring on sec more numerous (3-4 bands) than in European juv (2-3 bands).
		• Dark 'fingers', pale prim-base and relatively dark sec ⇔ ad (sometimes also in ad ♀).
note		• Very variable: see note European.

Swallow-tailed Kite *Elanoides forficatus*   L 56cm 22", WS 129cm 50.8"

all plum	• Very characteristic with very long wings and tail, white underparts and head and black (with blue gloss) upperside and tail.
imm	• Juv with yellowish wash on head and breast, quickly fading.
fl all plum	• Very long and narrow hand and very deeply forked tail.
	• Black wings and tail contrast with white underwing-cov and body.
fl imm	• Tail less deeply forked than in ad.

Black-winged Kite *Elanus caeruleus*   L 34cm 13.5", WS 78cm 30.5"

all plum	• Mainly black cov creating black 'shoulder-patch' (in flight very conspicuous).
	• Wings reach far beyond tail (long wing-projection).
ad	• Red iris.
	• Almost white head with very faint pale grey wash on crown (at distance head looks completely white).
juv	• Yellow-brown breast and neck-side.
	• Feathers of upperparts with pale tips.
	• Grey tail.
	• Grey crown.
	• Red-brown iris.
imm	• In 2cy more like ad but scaps still with brown wash and pale tips.
fl all plum	• Black (under-side of) prim contrast strongly with very pale grey rest of underwing. Prim on upperside only slightly darker grey than sec.
	• Short tail and heavy head creating characteristic flight-silhouette.
behav	• Hovers frequently.
note	• White-tailed Kite *E. leucurus* (American species, possible escape in WP) has *much longer tail* which, when perched, reaches slightly beyond wing-tip (tail-projection ⇔ Black-winged), dark spot on prim-cov on underwing and slightly narrower black 'shoulder-patch' (not reaching base greater cov).

Black Kite *Milvus migrans*   L 53cm 21", WS 143cm 56.5"

all plum	⇒	• Dark mask ⇔ in Red Kite usually faint or absent.
		• No tail-projection ⇔ Red.
		• Relatively large bill.
ad		• Greyish head and breast with fine black longitudinal stripes merging into dark brown to dark chestnut underparts (with fine black longitudinal stripes).
		• Pale iris.
juv		• Pale longitudinal stripes or spots on underparts ⇔ ad.
		• Upperparts and head often peppered with pale spots ⇔ ad.
imm		• Paler vent and undertail-cov ⇔ ad.
		• Head gradually greyer and iris gradually paler with age; from 4cy as ad.
fl all plum		• Short legs; base of feet placed before rear-edge of arm (applies for all *Milvus* kites) ⇔ in other raptors legs longer.
		• Pale lesser cov and medium cov creating broad pale diagonal band on upperwing, contrasting with rest of rather uniform dark plumage.
		• Upperside of tail not obviously paler than upperparts ⇔ Red.
		• Under-side of hand with smaller and less conspicuous pale area than in Red.
		• 6 relatively long 'fingers' ⇔ in Red 5.
fl imm		• Pale tips to greater cov and prim-cov on upper- and underwing.
		• Often larger pale area on inner prim than in ad.
moult ad		• Inner prim moulted in breeding range, rest in winter range (moult suspended during migration) ⇔ Red.
note		• Rufous variant (most seen in Middle East) with rather strong red-brown underparts, pale head, relatively large white spot on prim-base and conspicuous dark band on underwing by dark greater cov (sometimes strongly resembling Red Kite but tail greyer). Wing-formula sometimes intermediate between Black and Red with tendency for only 5 'fingers'.

Black-eared Kite *Milvus lineatus*   L 55cm 21.5", WS 146cm 57.5"

all plum	• Ground-colour browner than Black Kite; head less grey with often larger and darker mask. • Legs and base of bill dull yellow-grey ⇔ in Black bright yellow. • Dark iris ⇔ in Black becoming paler with age in ad.
ad	• Head grey-brown, hardly contrasting with rest of body ⇔ in Black grey head and upper breast contrasting with red-brown underparts. • Underparts dark brown with yellow-brown streaks on vent and belly and rufous streaks on breast; undertail-cov pale cream-colored (some similarity to Black imm) ⇔ in Black ad belly, vent and undertail-cov uniform red-brown. • Upper breast brown without dark shaft-streaks ⇔ in Black blackish shaft-streaks on grey background.
imm	• Underparts with broad pale lines (like most Black imm) towards vent and undertail-cov almost uniform pale ⇔ in Black imm underparts more evenly patterned. • Undertail-cov with pale tips (sometimes also in Black imm).
fl all plum	• Pale base of under-side of outer prim broader, whiter and more distinct than in Black; barring on under-side of inner prim more distinct than in Black due to almost white background and sharper, narrower dark barring. • Broad hand with deeply indented 'fingers' (eagle-like); p5 long and pointed. • Short legs; base of feet placed before rear-edge of arm (applies for all *Milvus* kites) ⇔ in other raptors (except honey-buzzards) legs longer.
fl ad	• Median cov often with pale tips, in combination with paler streaking on underparts sometimes resembles Black imm.

Yellow-billed Kite *Milvus aegyptius*   L 53cm 21", WS 138cm 54.5"

ad ⇒	• Mainly like Black Kite but completely yellow bill. • Almost uniform, dark rufous underparts with fine dark striping.
imm	• Whitish head.
fl all plum	• Underparts and underwing-cov often conspicuously rufous. • Short legs; base of feet placed before rear-edge of arm (applies for all *Milvus* kites) ⇔ in other raptors (except honey-buzzards) legs longer. • Slightly more compact than Black with shorter wings and tail.
fl ad	• Pale background of both sec, prim and tail with (therefore) obvious barring.
fl imm	• Generally paler on under-side than Black with especially whitish base of prim.
note	• Central and West African *M.a. parasiticus* (possible in WP) often more strongly resembles Black than *aegyptius* but normally more uniform and like *aegyptius* with yellow bill.

Red Kite *Milvus milvus*   L 65cm 24.5", WS 152cm 60"

all plum ⇒	• Scaps, tertials and cov rather pale with *contrasting dark centres* ⇔ in Black Kite darker and more uniform upperwing and scaps. • When perched obvious tail-projection ⇔ Black.
ad	• Red-orange underparts (especially undertail-cov and vent) and underwing-cov with black longitudinal stripes (visible in flight) ⇔ in imm duller red-brown (paler buff-brown on undertail-cov and vent) with pale striping. • Grey-white head ⇔ in imm pale brown-grey. • Pale head rather sharply bordered with red-orange breast ⇔ in rufous Black ad grey head and breast merges very smoothly into rufous rest of underparts.
imm	• Generally more brown than red (⇔ ad) with pale and brown longitudinal stripes on underparts. • Rather dark iris (whitish in ad).
fl all plum	• Long, pale forked tail. • Pale inner prim and base of outer prim creating large pale area on under-side of hand (larger and whiter than in Black); upper-side of hand dark. • Broad pale diagonal band over arm, often broader and paler than in Black. • Relatively narrow hand with 5 'fingers' (see Black note and geog var). • Often soars with wings in shallow 'V', like harrier ⇔ in Black wings normally level or even slightly arched. • Conspicuous dark band on underwing formed by dark greater cov ⇔ most Black but distinct in some rufous ind. • Short legs; base of toes placed before rear-edge of arm (applies for all *Milvus* species) ⇔ in other raptors (except honey-buzzards) legs longer.
fl imm	• Pale line along tip of greater cov and prim-cov both on under- and upperwing. • Undertail-cov pale, not contrasting with underside of tail ⇔ in ad brown-red, obviously darker than underside of tail. • Dark, mainly subterminal tail-barring (in most ad only outer tail-feathers narrowly barred). • Slightly shorter and less deeply forked tail than ad.
moult ad	• Prim-moult often (almost) completed in autumn ⇔ Black.

Cape Verde Kite *Milvus fasciicauda*   L 62cm 24.5", WS 142cm 56"

all plum	• Smaller size than Red Kite with shorter and slightly rounder wings and less deeply forked tail. • Upperparts more uniform than in Red. • Underparts less bright reddish than in Red.
fl all plum	• Pale area on hand much reduced and less white (greyer) than in Red. • Central tail-feathers with normally obvious barring ⇔ Red. • Short legs; base of feet placed before rear-edge of arm (applies for all *Milvus* kites) ⇔ in other raptors (except honey-buzzards) legs longer.
note	• Endemic to Cape Verde Islands, now probably extinct.

African Fish Eagle *Haliaeetus vocifer*
L 70cm 27.5", WS 175cm 70"

all plum	• Large with short tail; *wings project beyond tail.* • Bare tarsus ⇔ in *Aquila* eagles feathered.
ad	• White head, breast, mantle, rump and tail. • Dark chestnut underparts and leading edge of arm (marginal cov and lesser cov on both upperwing and underwing).
juv	• White tail with ill-defined dark terminal tail-band. • Pale 'U' at border of breast and belly. • Diffuse paler head.
fl juv	• Pale inner web of basal part of prim creating large pale patch on underwing (upperside of prim dark). • Rump and uppertail-cov with pale spots. • Cov (especially median) with some pale patterning (creating faint pale band over cov).
behav	• Very vocal.

Pallas's Fish Eagle *Haliaeetus leucoryphus*
L 79cm 31", WS 206cm 81"

all plum	• Slightly smaller size and slightly smaller bill than White-tailed Eagle but overlap. • Bare tarsus ⇔ in *Aquila* eagles feathered.
ad imm	• Black-brown with off-white head and *tail with broad white central band.* • Dark mask. • Pale creamy underparts. • Contrast between brown lesser cov and median cov and very dark greater cov and flight-feathers. • See White-tailed Eagle for more precise ageing using moult of flight-feathers, but moult progression probably slightly less slow.
fl imm ⇒	• Underwing with *large pale patch on inner prim.* • Wholly dark under-side of tail ⇔ White-tailed. • Broad pale mid-panel on underwing (axillaries and mostly median cov).

White-tailed Eagle *Haliaeetus albicilla*
L 87cm 34", WS 220cm 86.5"

all plum (sub)ad	• Bare tarsus ⇔ in *Aquila* eagles feathered. • Completely yellow bill. • White tail. • Pale iris. • Head and breast becoming paler with age.
juv ⇒	• Pale base of lesser cov, median cov and rear greater cov; dark shaft streak and tip. • No moult (in flight evenly trailing edge of wing, as in all eagles juv).
2cy	• From spring onwards moult of inner prim and outer sec starts (new sec longer than juv ones). Tail often completely moulted in 2nd part of 2cy. Underparts, upperparts and cov very patchy. • Bill still dark.
3cy	• Mix of juv, 2nd generation and 3rd generation sec, sec-moult from 4 centres, messy appearance in combination with patchy underparts. Prim-moult attained to p6. • Bill becoming paler.
4cy 5cy imm	• Very variable but juv p10 still present in most ind. New moult-wave starts at p1 and outer sec. • Largely like ad but head still dark, often some whitish cov present and variable amount of dark in tail. • Pale lores and bill-base creating conspicuous pale spot (not in (sub)ad). Juv-4cy with dark head demarcated from pale(r) underparts. 3cy-4cy with rather pale mantle and variable amount of pale cov.
fl all plum	• Short, somewhat wedge-shaped tail. • Very broad wings with 6-7 'fingers'. • Distinctly protruding head and long neck.
fl ad	• Uniform dark underwing.
fl juv fl imm ⇒ ⇒	• Pointed sec and inner prim (like *Gyps* vultures) ⇔ *Aquila* eagles. • Pale axillary patch. • Tail-feathers with pale centres.

Bald Eagle *Haliaeetus leucocephalus*
L 79cm 31", WS 203cm 80"

all plum ad	• Bare tarsus ⇔ in *Aquila* eagles feathered. • Black-brown with sharply defined, pure white head and tail (old White-tailed ad can have very pale head but never pure white and sharply defined).
imm ⇒	• From 2cy most ind develop white belly (with some dark streaks), contrasting with dark head and dark rear-flanks, vent and undertail-cov. From 3cy underparts become darker again due to broadening of dark streaks; underparts completely dark in ad. • Whitish mantle and back (not in juv). • Cov usually with less conspicuous pale centres than in White-tailed imm. • Older imm with pale supercilium and pale ear-coverts, contrasting with dark eye-stripe. • Completely dark grey bill ⇔ in all *Aquila* eagles pale grey with dark tip. • See White-tailed for more precise ageing using moult of flight-feathers, but moult progression probably slightly less slow.
fl all plum	• Tail longer but head protrudes slightly less than in White-tailed. • Slightly narrower wing than in White-tailed with 6 'fingers' ⇔ in White-tailed 6-7.
fl imm ⇒	• Variable amount of pale grey sec and inner prim. • Pale underwing-cov creating pale bars on underwing (more distinct than in White-tailed). • Often entirely whitish axillaries. • Pale underside of tail with rather sharply demarcated dark terminal tail-band (tail-band more well-defined than in White-tailed imm but diffuser and narrower than in Golden Eagle imm).

Lammergeier *Gypaetus barbatus* L 115cm 45.5", WS 255cm 100"

ad	⇒	• Yellow-orange underparts and head.
juv-1s		• Mainly dark with pale spotted mantle and paler underparts.
		• Dark head and upperside of breast contrast with *paler underparts* ⇔ in Egyptian Vulture juv uniform dark underparts.
2s		• Starts moult of inner prim; most cov and scaps bleaching to whitish.
subad		• Mainly like ad but neck dark spotted. Ad plumage acquired after about 7-8 years.
fl all plum		• Very large with long pointed wings and tail. Imm with more rounded wings and tail, therefore more eagle-like silhouette.
		• When hanging in wind arm pushed downwards, creating characteristic silhouette.
fl ad	⇒	• Black underwing-cov contrast with dark grey underside of flight-feathers.

Egyptian Vulture *Neophron percnopterus* L 60cm 23.5", WS 162cm 64"

ad	• Mainly white plumage with black (sec and) prim and dark inner greater cov and median cov.
(sub)ad	• Yellow bare face.
imm	• Age related amount of dark brown on underparts and underwing-cov. Juv with wholly dark brown underparts and underwing-cov and creamy-brown mantle and tips to cov and tertials.
	• Juv with grey face.
	• From 2nd imm plumage onwards (end of 2cy) underside becomes less uniform with two generations prim, sec, cov and body-feathers. Gradually more pale cov on upperwing. From 3rd imm plumage onwards (end of 3cy) cov and body with more or less even mix of white and dark feathers. Sub-adult (5th-6cy) almost as adult but still with some dark cov and/or body-feathers.
fl all plum	• Long wedge-shaped tail.
	• Pale outer web on sec creating broad diffuse mid-panel on upperside of arm, also visible when perched (from 2nd generation onwards, hardly present in juv).
fl ad	• Mainly white plumage with black sec and under-side of prim (on upperwing pale band over flight-feathers caused by pale feather-centres).

Hooded Vulture *Necrosyrtes monachus* L 64cm 25", WS 172cm 68"

all plum		• Long slender bill like Egyptian Vulture.
		• Plumage completely brown-black (like Egyptian juv but larger size).
		• Entirely *pink (bare) head*; in juv brown (feathered) hind neck and rear-head.
fl all plum	⇒	• Completely brown-black with broad wings and short tail (tail much shorter than width of wing ⇔ Egyptian).
		• Legs pale, conspicuous (like Eurasian Black Vulture) ⇔ Egyptian juv.
		• Faintly paler base to all plum and prim contrast with very dark underwing-cov (underwing-cov with pale 'vulture stripe') ⇔ Egyptian juv.

Griffon Vulture *Gyps fulvus* L 102cm 40", WS 248cm 98"

all plum	• Underparts, upperparts and cov warm-brown (in most juv and when fresh in other plumages) to pale cream-coloured (in most ad and when bleached in other plumages).
ad	• Pale bill and iris.
(sub)ad	• White ruff ⇔ in juv pale brown.
	• Ad-type greater cov (from end 3cy) with rounded tips and broad pale fringes (width of pale fringes increases with age) ⇔ juv-type greater cov (up to 3cy) pointed with narrow pale fringes (pale fringes disappearing with wear from 2cy).
juv/imm	• Dark bill and iris.
	• Juv cov and scaps narrow and pointed ⇔ from 2nd generation onwards feathers broader and rounded.
	• See Eurasian Black Vulture for more precise ageing using moult of flight-feathers.
fl all plum	• Soars with wings in shallow V.
	• 6 'fingers'.
	• Bulging trailing edge of arm (more obvious in juv).
fl (sub)ad	• Broad pale area on underwing-cov (also already in some 2cy).
	• Grey inner web of flight-feathers creating barred pattern, especially on underwing.
	• Obvious wing-bar over greater cov.
fl juv	• Wholly black, pointed juv flight-feathers; trailing edge even.
	• Greater cov with very small pale tips, creating no obvious wing bar ⇔ ad.
fl imm	• For ageing using moult, see Eurasian Black Vulture imm.
	• More or less uniform yellow-brown underwing-cov, often without conspicuous pale area, but very variable and some ind like ad.

Rüppell's Vulture *Gyps rueppellii* L 90cm 35.5", WS 230cm 90.5"

all plum		• Structure like Griffon Vulture but slightly smaller size.
		• Ground-colour darker than in Griffon.
ad	⇒	• Cov and scaps with large white tips creating scaled upperside.
juv		• Rather similar to Griffon but both underparts and upperparts darker brown.
		• Underparts with conspicuous pale longitudinal stripes ⇔ in (sub)ad underparts scaled.
		• Cov and scaps with smaller and diffuser pale tips than in (sub)ad.
		• Dark ruff.
imm		• Dark bill, gradually becoming paler with age.
		• In subad tips to cov yellowish ⇔ in ad white.
		• Ruff becoming paler.
		• See Eurasian Black Vulture for more precise ageing using moult of flight-feathers.
fl all plum		• Sharply bordered white bar at front side of underwing ('vulture-stripe').
		• Pale tips to undertail-cov creating distinct spotted 'V' below underside tail.

fl ad	• Soars with wings held level ⇔ Griffon.
	• 'Vulture-stripe' in combination with 2 isolated rows of white spots on underwing-cov ⇔ in Griffon 2-3 pale connected bars on underwing-cov.
fl imm	• Upperwing with little contrast between slightly pale cov and dark flight-feathers; on underwing no contrast at all between cov and flight-feathers ⇔ Griffon.
	• Dark underwing with conspicuous 'vulture-stripe' (in Griffon 'vulture-stripe' much less contrasting). Other pale patterning on underwing less conspicuous than in ad.

African White-backed Vulture *Gyps africanus*   L 85cm 33.5", WS 220cm 86.5"

all plum	• Structure like Griffon Vulture but distinctly smaller.
	• Dark face and *black bill* (also in ad).
	• Legs very dark, especially in ad often black. In imm often dark grey but darker than in other *Gyps* vultures.
ad	• Cov very pale brown-grey (becoming increasingly paler with age).
	• White back and rump creating conspicuous pale triangular area on upperside.
	• Underparts in older ad becoming very pale to dirty-white.
juv	• Plumage strongly resembles Griffon but background slightly darker with pale streaks on cov more contrasting when fresh (later streaking worn away).
imm	• Gradually paler cov on both upper- as underwing. Pale rump/back develops gradually.
fl ad	• Largely whitish underwing-cov strongly contrasting with dark sec and prim.

Lappet-faced Vulture *Torgos tracheliotus*   L 100cm 39", WS 272cm 107"

all plum	• *Pink head* (in juv at first still brown-yellow), conspicuous at long distance in flight, with 'isolated' eye.
	• Extremely large.
	• Dark brown upperside (only slightly paler than Eurasian Black Vulture) and pale under-side with dark stripes.
imm	• See Eurasian Black Vulture for more precise ageing using moult of flight-feathers.
fl all plum	• Usually only ill-defined pale 'vulture stripe' over underwing-cov, often better developed in older ind.
fl (sub)ad	• Thighs and (rear)flank paler brownish, creating conspicuous pale areas at sides of body contrasting with dark underwing (see note).
fl imm	• Juv-type sec very pointed.
	• Underparts darker and more streaked than in ad.
note	• Nominate (not in WP) ad with almost black upperside and white thighs and (rear) flank.

Eurasian Black Vulture *Aegypius monachus*   L 105cm 41.5", WS 270cm 106"

ad	• Dark brown (some very old ind somewhat paler) with pale head, dark mask and dark grey bill.
juv	• Brown-black (still darker than ad) with black head and distal part of bill (head gradually paler with age).
	• Pink bill-base.
imm	• 1cy wholly dark; 2cy moults p1-p3; 3cy moults about half of sec and p4-p7; 4cy to 7cy subad.
fl all plum ⇒	• *Legs pale*, contrasting with dark plumage.
	• 7 'fingers'.
	• Rather straight trailing edge of arm ⇔ Griffon Vulture.
	• Usually soars with wings held level.
	• Usually wedge-shaped tail.

Short-toed Eagle *Circaetus gallicus*   L 61cm 24", WS 185cm 73"

all plum ⇒	• Only 3 dark tail-bands evenly spaced (often faint 4th visible at tail-base).
	• Large head.
	• Very short or no tail-projection.
	• Blue-grey bare skin around bill and legs (unfeathered tarsus). Tarsus sometimes yellowish.
ad	• Well-defined patterning on underparts ⇔ juv diffusely creamy-rufous patterned.
	• Head with grey wash (especially head-side) ⇔ juv/imm.
	• Ad ♀ (5cy+) with entirely dark breast; ad ♂ with dark streaked throat and breast (subad ♀ as ad ♂).
	• Underparts in ♂ less heavily marked than in ♀.
juv	• Rufous-brown head and breast-band; underparts with diffuse rufous-brown spots.
imm	• From 2cy becoming paler to nearly entirely white on underparts in 3rd-4cy.
fl all plum ⇒	• Several lines of dark spots on underwing not creating dark carpal patch ⇔ Common Buzzard.
	• Broad head-base.
	• Paler cov creating broad pale panel on upperwing (like Booted Eagle but broader and less sharply demarcated). See also flight juv.
	• Straight-cut tail corners.
fl ad	• Distinctly barred flight-feathers and dark trailing edge of sec.
fl juv	• Rather diffuse and finely barred under-side of flight-feathers, especially trailing edge ⇔ ad.
	• Pale panel on upperwing much more pronounced than in ad.
fl 2cy-3cy	• Moult-limit in prim: inner fresh, outer old ⇔ in older ind to ad more than 2 generations but later often difficult to judge in field conditions.
behav	• Hovers frequently.

Bateleur *Terathopius ecaudatus*   L 80cm 31.5", WS 170cm 67"

all plum	• (Very) short tail; in juv distinctly longer than in ad. Long wing-projection.
ad	• Pale brown-grey fore-wings (all cov, except greater cov in ad ♂).
	• Dark red upperparts and tail (scaps black).
	• Black head, greater cov and underparts.
	• Legs and bare skin around bill red.
ad ♀	• Pale band over base of sec ⇔ in ad ♂ entirely black sec.
juv	• Dark with diffuse pale brown head.

fl all plum	• Legs and bare skin around bill faintly yellow.
	• Very characteristic with bulging arm and very narrow hand in combination with (very) short tail and broad, protruding head. In ad leg projection beyond tail due to very short tail.
	• Remarkable swinging soar-flight, interspersed with series of very fast wing-beats.
fl ad	• Entirely white underwing-cov.
fl ad ♂	• Only base of outer prim pale, rest of prim and whole sec black ⇔ ad ♀.
fl ad ♀	• Paler base of flight-feathers; underwing pale with broad dark trailing edge (on upperwing broad pale band over sec and inner prim ⇔ ad ♂).
fl juv	• Pale base of flight-feathers contrast with very dark underwing-cov.
	• Pale legs conspicuous.

Western Marsh Harrier *Circus aeruginosus*   L 48cm 19", WS 126cm 50"

all plum (sub)ad ♂	• Short or no tail-projection.
	• Underparts in subad brown with pale spots on breast; in older ind becoming paler; in very old ad ♂ very pale underparts and head. Grey ground colour to flight-feathers and tail.
ad ♀	• Cream-white crown and throat divided by broad dark mask.
	• Some ad ♀ strongly resemble juv but most with rather pale rufous tail and crown (upperside of tail paler than upperside of flight-feathers ⇔ juv), some pale patterning on mantle and/or breast and large pale patch on fore-wings, formed by pale lesser cov and median cov.
	• Iris paler in older ad ♀; in young ad ♀ still rather dark.
juv	• Almost uniform dark brown plumage with brown-yellow crown and throat (similar to ad ♀), some ind with completely dark head and throat.
	• Small pale tips to cov. Sometimes strongly spotted due to large tips to all cov, remiges and tail-feathers.
1s	• Largely like juv but t1 moulted (longer than other tail-feathers and in ♂ grey).
fl (sub)ad ♂	• Black underside of outer 5 prim (only pale base) and dark trailing edge of wing contrast with grey base of remiges. In old ind dark trailing edge (almost) absent.
	• Underwing-cov in subad brown, in older ind grey and as pale as base of flight-feathers. In old ad ♂ entirely pale grey underwing (except black wing-tip).
	• Old ad ♂ often with pale rump-patch.
fl ad ♀	• In old ♀ rather strong contrast between pale underside of flight-feathers and very dark underwing-cov. Some old ind similar to 2nd-3cy ♂ but without dark trailing edge to inner prim.
note	• Dark morph ad ♂ (mainly in east of range) with entirely dark brown underparts, upperparts and upperwing contrasting strongly with pale grey tail. In flight long pale central band on underwing visible, formed by pale base of flight-feathers.

Eastern Marsh Harrier *Circus spilonotus*   L 48cm 19", WS 126cm 50"

all plum ⇒ ad ♂	• Size and structure like Western Marsh Harrier but bill often appears larger.
	• White underparts with dark streaks on breast.
	• Pale grey tail, sec and greater cov.
	• Upperparts, median cov and lesser cov boldly dark spotted, often very dense to almost uniform dark.
subad ♂	• Resembles ad ♂ but upperwing and tail almost completely barred.
	• Brown cov and upperparts.
	• 2nd cy similar to ad ♀ but underparts often still mainly dark like juv.
ad ♀ ⇒	• Plumage intermediate between Western Marsh and Hen Harrier ad ♀ with *grey ground colour* of sec and greater cov.
	• Wholly brown-streaked head with a most very weak collar, often no collar at all.
	• Underparts heavily streaked rufous-brown, often more intense rufous towards rear.
ad ♀/juv	• No well-defined dark mask ⇔ Western Marsh.
juv	• Like Western Marsh juv but less uniformly brown, with whitish face and streaked crown and hind-neck.
	• Breast streaked pale, often creating rather broad breast-band ⇔ Western Marsh juv.
fl ad ♂	• Pale grey wing with dark fingers and *dark spotted cov incl prim-cov.*
	• Underparts with clear division between dark (streaked) breast and white rest of underparts.
fl ad ♀ ⇒	• Flight-feathers and tail *grey with obvious bold barring* (tail often brown to grey-brown) ⇔ Western ad ♀ (see note).
fl juv	• Faintly barred prim and tail.
	• Often large pale patch at base of underwing ⇔ in Western Marsh small at most.
notes	• Western Marsh subad ♂ also has grey ground colour to flight-feathers (like Eastern Marsh ♀), but normally without well-marked and continuous barring and often with almost uniformly dark underparts.
	• Very old Western Marsh ♀ sometimes has paler grey-brown ground colour to flight-feathers and (rarely) some faint barring, but probably never as regular and contrasting as in Eastern Marsh.

Hen Harrier *Circus cyaneus*   L 48cm 19", WS 114cm 45"

all plum	• Tail projects beyond wing-tips ⇔ in Montagu's Harrier (almost) absent.
ad ♂	• Almost uniform grey-blue head and breast; rest of underparts white.
ad ♀	• Underparts boldly striped dark brown. Belly, vent and undertail-cov normally at least with some rufous, more triangular spots ⇔ juv.
	• Barred greater cov and sec ⇔ in juv uniform (upperwing).
	• Weak head-pattern with often rather ill-defined supercilium and only indistinct dark ear-covert patch ⇔ in juv and Montagu's ad ♀ obvious supercilium and especially darker ear-covert patch (in Montagu's ad ♀ contrasting, uniform dark patch).
juv	• Usually conspicuous pale collar like Pallid Harrier juv/ad ♀, but with obvious dark streaks in pale collar ⇔ in Pallid collar with at most fine dark spots but often uniform pale.
	• Orange-brown ground-colour of underparts ⇔ in ad ♀ whitish.
	• Usually contrast between dark breast and paler belly like Pallid ad ♀ but less well-defined.

	• Streaks on underparts gradually becoming narrower from breast towards belly; undertail-cov uniform pale ⇔ ad ♀.
	• Rather distinct head-pattern with obvious supercilium and almost uniform dark ear-coverts ⇔ in ad ♀ weaker, ear-coverts only slightly darker and finely barred.
fl all plum	• White uppertail-cov creating large white rump ⇔ in most other harriers smaller except Northern Harrier.
	• 5 'fingers' with p10 about same length as p5 ⇔ Pallid and Montagu's.
	• Broad, usually bulging arm ⇔ (Pallid and) Montagu's.
fl ad ♂	• Ad with longer wings and tail than juv.
	• Dark trailing edge of wing ⇔ Pallid ad ♂ (but see Pallid 2s ♂).
	• In subad (end 2cy to mid 3cy) still some brown feathers on upperside and weakly barred tail (see Pallid 2s ♂).
fl ♀-type	• Uniform tail ⇔ in subad ♂, Pallid and Montagu's barring on at least outer tail-feathers.
	• Ground-colour of prim evenly pale and dark barring on tip sharply demarcated ⇔ in Montagu's ♀-type ground-colour becoming darker towards feather tips and barring on tips less well-defined.
fl juv	• Mainly dark underside of arm contrasting with pale hand ⇔ in ad ♀ arm with same pale background as hand.
	• Prim narrower and more pointed than in ad ♀.
fl 1s	• Dark sec (due to broad dark and narrow pale barring) like Pallid ♀-type, but by midsummer often some sec moulted, shorter with broader pale barring. Outer prim still juv, often distinct moult-limit with fresh inner ones.
behav	• See Montagu's.
note subad ♂	• Especially in 2nd part of 2cy sometimes strongly resembles Pallid 2cy ♂ due to similar prim pattern and narrow dark trailing edge of wing. Structural differences (see all plum) and broader and more contrasting dark trailing edge of wing in Hen create best field marks.

geog var	**Northern Harrier** *C.c. hudsonius* (North America)
ad ♂	• Darker grey upperparts than Hen Harrier ad ♂ and rufous spotted underparts (resembles Montagu's Harrier ad ♂).
	• Dark tips to sec, greater cov and median cov creating rather weak dark wing-bars.
	• Generally resembles Hen subad ♂ (2s) with narrow dark tail barring (in Hen ad ♂ no barring), some brown spots on upperparts, dark head and brown patterning on breast.
ad ♀	• Underparts more finely and sharply marked than in Hen and tending to smaller and shorter streaking on central part and more distinct barring on flanks (probably only in older ind).
	• See also flight ad ♀.
juv ⇒	• Head and neck-side dark brown, *creating contrasting dark hood*.
	• Underparts almost *uniform orange*. Sometimes, especially later in winter, slightly streaked along flanks, central part of underparts unstreaked ⇔ in Hen juv normally paler and colder toned; sometimes also rather orange but usually more orange-brown and at least somewhat streaked.
	• Often conspicuous pale collar and large uniform dark ear-coverts connected with dark eye-stripe extending to bill-base. Sometimes resembles dark-headed Pallid Harrier juv.
	• Upperparts darker brown than in Hen ♀-type.
	• Pale parts both above and below eye rather narrow, above eye often rufous ⇔ in Hen ♀-type broader and often connected behind eye.
fl ad ♂ ⇒	• Black on hand mainly restricted to distal part of prim (black reaching only to prim-cov on p10) ⇔ Hen ad ♂.
	• Only 5 prim with black tips ⇔ in Hen ad ♂ 6 wholly black outer prim.
	• Broad dark trailing edge along arm (visible on both upper and underwing).
fl ad ♀	• Usually narrower barring on flight-feathers than in Hen ad ♀.
fl juv	• Underside of outer prim with 5-6 dark bars (p10 with 3-5) ⇔ in Hen ♀-type 3-5 (p10 with 3).
	• Median and lesser cov on underwing almost uniform orange (like underparts).
	• Large white rump-patch very conspicuous due to stronger contrast with very dark upperparts than in Hen ♀-type.
	• Trailing edge to inner hand often less dark than in Hen ♀-type (especially in juv ♂).

Pallid Harrier *Circus macrourus*   L 44cm 17.5", WS 110cm 43.5"

all plum	• Tail projects obviously beyond wing-tips (when perched) ⇔ Montagu's Harrier.
	• Relatively strong bill and larger head compared to Montagu's. Head especially thicker due to thicker collar than in Montagu's.
	• Long legs (sometimes more upright posture than Montagu's).
ad ♂ ⇒	• Entirely white underparts and large part of head (in subad ♂ blue-grey head contrasting with white underparts) ⇔ in Hen Harrier ad ♂ contrast between grey-blue breast and white remainder of underparts.
	• p10 and basal part of p9 pale ⇔ Hen and Montagu's ad ♂ wholly black.
	• Faint tail-barring.
ad ♀/imm	• Conspicuous pale band behind dark ear-coverts and through neck-side and hind-neck (collar), in juv often much more distinct than in ad ♀, see note.
	• Dark mask and narrow white supercilium to above eye; behind eye fainter, becoming buff ⇔ in Montagu's broad and evenly white throughout and rear-side of eye often completely encircled by white.
	• Uniform dark ear-coverts with broad elongation to base of lower mandible ⇔ in Montagu's ad ♀/juv more isolated and not reaching base of lower mandible.
	• In ad ♀ dark streaked breast, rest of underparts paler and finer striped ⇔ in Montagu's ad ♀ underparts evenly streaked. Ground-colour of underparts variable from whitish to deep rufous (like juv).
juv	• Typical head-pattern consists of very obvious and broad dark patch on ear-coverts bordered by *complete* pale collar; narrow white above and below eye; wholly dark lores and broad dark eye-stripe creating mask which separates pale parts above and below eye and reaches far towards rear-head. Juv head-pattern still obvious in 1s but supercilium often longer.

65

1s	• Neck(side) uniform dark, often without sharp streaks, contrasting with pale collar ⇔ in most Montagu's juv neck-side less dark and streaked; collar rarely distinct.
	• Underparts uniformly deep yellow-orange (in 1s paler) without streaks ⇔ Montagu's juv.
	• In juv ♂ grey-yellow iris; in juv ♀ dark iris.
	• Often still largely juv plumage in spring ⇔ most Montagu's.
1s ♂	• In 2nd part of 2cy ad ♂ features start to appear but pale brown wash over upperparts; blue-grey head and breast creating conspicuous hood.
	• Advanced ind with blue-grey head and upper breast, orange breast-band and unmarked white underparts.
2s ♂	• Like ad but still faint dark head-pattern and usually some brown feathers on upperside, in flight narrow dark trailing edge of arm.
	• Resembles Hen (sub)ad ♂ but with e.g. supercilium and pale spot below eye (in Hen uniform head) and (much) narrower dark trailing edge of arm. See also note on Hen subad ♂.
	• Distinctly barred tail ⇔ in ad only faint pale grey barring.
fl all plum	• Nearly uniform axillaries except ad ♀ (pale in juv/1s/♂, darker in ad ♀, see there) ⇔ in Montagu's ad/1s strongly barred axillaries (however Montagu's juv-1s usually has almost uniform and pale axillaries).
	• Hand relatively short (more Hen-like silhouette) ⇔ in Montagu's often long.
	• Long legs; distance between rear edge of arm and base of toes ≥ length of toes ⇔ in Montagu's distance between rear edge of arm and base of toes ≤ length of toes.
	• Wing formula often slightly different from Montagu's (which see flight all plum) but p10 = p5 indicative.
fl ad ♂ ⇒	• Very pale underside of both body and underwing and narrow black wedge-shape on wing-tips (see also Hen ad ♂).
	• Pale rump with weak *dark barring* ⇔ Hen.
fl ad ♀	• Underwing becoming gradually darker from pale leading edge through other cov to very dark sec ⇔ in Montagu's ad ♀ whole underwing evenly patterned, without obvious pale-dark contrast.
	• Uniform dark greater cov (also visible when perched) ⇔ in Montagu's ad ♀ faintly barred.
	• Axillaries with pale rounded spots on inner- and outer web, sometimes creating suggestion of barring ⇔ in Montagu's ad ♀ pale spots on axillaries larger, often connecting to create complete barring.
fl ad ♀/ imm ⇒	• Often *unmarked pale base to under-side of prim* (pale 'boomerang'), barring concentrated on central part of prim, characteristic when present. Sometimes lacks pale 'boomerang' and other type of barring occurs.
	• Inner 5-6 prim with ill-defined grey tips but in some juv ♀ darker ⇔ in Montagu's ad ♀ well-defined dark tips to all prim, in some Montagu's imm more ill-defined (when juv prim retained towards summer of 2cy).
	• Diffuse dark tips to prim (sometimes tip at most slightly darker) ⇔ in Montagu's ad ♀ and most imm larger and more demarcated.
	• Dark sec; in ad ♀ with only narrow pale barring contrasting with pale underside of hand ⇔ Montagu's ad ♀/imm (in Montagu's 1s ♀ also dark sec).
	• Axillaries and greater cov on underwing not obviously barred (mainly dark with small pale markings but in some ad ♀ larger pale spots, suggesting barring, see flight ad ♀) ⇔ in Montagu's 1s-ad ♀ strongly barred.
fl juv ⇒	• Prim barring often rather irregular and often rather broad; *no contrasting dark fingers* ⇔ in Montagu's normally finely barred and contrasting dark fingers.
	• In ♂ juv barring of prim more concentrated on central part of prim, not reaching feather-tip; in ♀ juv barring often to feather-tip.
	• Normally rather large white patch on uppertail-cov.
moult juv	• Juv plumage often retained longer than in Montagu's; in 1s up to May, normally no obvious differences from juv ⇔ in most Montagu's 1s mix of juv and 2nd generation (adult-type) feathers.
behav	• See Montagu's.
notes	• Moulting Hen ♀ can resemble both Montagu's ad ♀ and Pallid ad ♀. Conspicuous supercilium resembles Montagu's. Often dark sec, usually conspicuous pale collar and contrast between dark breast and pale belly resembles Pallid.
	• See also Montagu's when identifying ad ♀, 1s and juv.

Montagu's Harrier *Circus pygargus*   L 41cm 16", WS 109cm 43"

all plum	• Wing-tip (almost) reaches to tail-tip (when perched) ⇔ Pallid Harrier and Hen Harrier.
	• Legs relatively short; often more horizontal posture than Pallid.
(sub)ad ♂	• Narrow rufous streaks on underparts.
	• Black bar over base of sec.
ad ♀	• Eye surrounded by broad, white supercilium and half eye-ring below eye.
	• Rather faint pale head with isolated uniform dark spot on ear-coverts (reaching at most to gape line) ⇔ Pallid ad ♀.
	• Underparts evenly streaked (flight) ⇔ Pallid ad ♀.
juv ⇒	• Usually broad supercilium (also broad between eye and bill) which remains white or becomes white behind eye; rear-side of eye often completely encircled by white ⇔ Pallid juv.
	• Dark, isolated spot on ear-coverts (at most reaching gape line).
	• Streaking on neck-side and often on flanks ⇔ in Pallid juv uniform.
	• Juv ♀ with grey-yellow iris; juv ♂ with dark brown iris.
	• Underparts usually more red-brown than in Pallid juv (in Pallid more yellow-orange) but variable in both species.
fl all plum	• p10 slightly shorter than p6 ⇔ in Pallid p10 usually obviously shorter than p6, approaching p5; 4 'fingers'. p6 slightly shorter than in Pallid creating more pointed wing-tip.
	• Ad with longer wings and tail than juv.
fl ad ♂ ⇒	• Dark band at base of sec on both under- and upperwing.
	• (Especially in older ad ♂) upperwing with contrast between pale blue-grey sec, greater cov and prim-cov and darker median cov and lesser cov (together with black hand creating tri-coloured upperwing).
	• Underwing-cov and axillaries marked with red-brown spots ⇔ in Hen ad ♂ uniform white.

fl ad ♀	⇒	• Small or no paler patch on uppertail-cov ⇔ Hen ♂. • Axillaries *strongly barred* from 1s ⇔ Pallid all plum (but in some Pallid ♀ faintly barred). • Sec with broad, well-defined pale and dark bars (also distinct on upperwing) ⇔ in Pallid ad ♀ sec darker with narrower and towards body fainter and increasingly narrower pale bars. • Distinct dark trailing edge along whole wing ⇔ Pallid ad ♀. • Underwing with narrow and evenly-spaced barring on outer 5 prim (see also flight ♀-type).
fl juv	⇒	• Underwing with narrow even barring and *large dark tips (fingers) to outer 5 prim*. In ♂ outer prim sometimes unmarked. • Sometimes no but often only faintly barred axillaries ⇔ 1s and all ad (some still with uniform pale juv axillaries resembling Pallid 1s) • Dark sec up to 1s ⇔ ad.
fl 1s ♂	⇒	• Barred axillaries when moulted ⇔ in Pallid ♂uniform pale. • Appearance of ♂ field marks earlier in spring than in Pallid but dark (juv) sec retained up to autumn ⇔ Pallid 1s ♂ (see also moult 1s).
moult 1s		• Post-juv body moult in spring 2cy often well developed, sec (dark) and prim still largely juv ⇔ Pallid in spring 2cy still (almost) entirely juv. • In autumn moult not completed ⇔ in Pallid 2cy usually completed.
behav		• Often hunts slowly over a relatively small area ⇔ Pallid and Hen hunt (much) faster and over a larger area.
notes		• See Pallid when identifying ad ♀, 1s and juv. • Occurs also in (rare) dark morph. Ad ♂ uniform dark grey with dark underwing and tail, without obvious barring. Ad ♀ completely black-brown, underwing and tail barred like normal ad ♀. Juv almost black, underwing (dark sec) and underside of tail like normal juv, but prim in ♂ unmarked.

Dark Chanting-goshawk *Melierax metabates* L 51cm 20", WS 102cm 40"

all plum	• Legs long. • Short wings, long tail projects beyond wing-tip. • Slightly smaller than Northern Goshawk but in flight heavy impression due to broad wings.
ad	• Pale slaty-grey head and upperparts. • Pale underparts finely barred. • Legs and bare skin around bill red. • Completely dark central tail-feathers; outer tail-feathers pale with 3 broad dark bars.
juv	• Pale underparts finely barred brown. • Upperparts dark brown. • Legs and bare skin around bill yellowish.
fl all plum	• Broad, strongly rounded wings and long, full tail. • Blackish outer prim contrast with blue-grey rest of upperwing and pale grey rest of underwing (contrast on underwing much stronger). • Diffuse pale uppertail-cov.
fl ad	• Black wing-tips contrast with whitish central part of upperwing; front of upperwing and upperparts darker blue-grey.
fl juv	• Brown upperparts and upperwing with pale prim-flash. • Wholly barred tail.

Gabar Goshawk *Micronisus gabar* L 35cm 14", WS 70cm 27.5"

all plum	⇒	• Pale tips to sec creating, when perched, wing-bar and in flight pale trailing edge along arm ⇔ Dark Chanting-goshawk, Eurasian Sparrowhawk, Levant Sparrowhawk and Shikra. • Superficially resembles Dark Chanting-goshawk in all plumages (which see) but much smaller size (smaller than Eurasian Sparrowhawk). • White uppertail-cov, vent and undertail-cov.
ad		• Upperparts darker and deeper blue than Dark Chanting-goshawk.
fl all plum	⇒	• 3-4 evenly broad tail-bands. • Strong and *very narrow barred underwing* ⇔ Dark Chanting-goshawk, Eurasian Sparrowhawk, Levant Sparrowhawk and Shikra. • Wing-tips only diffusely darker ⇔ Dark Chanting-goshawk.
note		• Melanistic morph relatively common; has entirely dark body (also uppertail-cov); barring on sec, prim and tail-feathers like normal ind.

Northern Goshawk *Accipiter gentilis* L 61cm 24", WS 109cm 43"

all plum		• Larger with 'fuller body' than Eurasian Sparrowhawk. • Broad, rounded tail (often more visible in flight) ⇔ Eurasian Sparrowhawk. • Undertail-cov very 'full' and often extending around sides of tail (especially visible in flight) ⇔ Eurasian Sparrowhawk. • Legs thick and rather short ⇔ Eurasian Sparrowhawk. • Bill heavier than in Eurasian Sparrowhawk.
ad		• Underparts more finely barred than in Eurasian Sparrowhawk ad. • *Contrasting dark crown and mask*. Supercilium broader and longer than in Eurasian Sparrowhawk.
♀		• Size at least like Common Buzzard, distinctly larger than ♂.
ad ♀		• Upperparts brownish grey ⇔ in ♂ more bluish-grey.
juv	⇒	• Longitudinal drop-shaped marks on underparts. • Pale centres to scaps, greater cov and median cov creating diffuse pale wing-bars in flight (in northern populations distinct, in some southern populations hardly any pale centres). • Juv plumage largely retained well into 2cy.
fl all plum	⇒	• Rounded tail-corners ⇔ Eurasian Sparrowhawk. • Combination of broad, bulging arm and narrow, relatively pointed hand.

flight ad	• Distinctly protruding head and longer neck than Eurasian Sparrowhawk. • Sec, especially inner ones, *faintly or not barred* ⇔ Eurasian Sparrowhawk.
geog var	A.g. buteoides (western Siberia)
all plum ad juv	• Generally paler and larger than *gentilis* but differences strongly clinal, only most distinct ind identifiable. • Only ind with pale barring on rear-neck and upperparts and very fine barring on underparts identifiable. • Ground-colour almost white with whitish base and barring on scaps and cov.
geog var	A.g. atricapillus (North America)
ad	• Underparts very finely barred, at distance appears uniform pale grey. Some longitudinal (shaft-)streaks more obvious than barring. • Upperparts deep blue-grey ⇔ in *gentilis* more grey-brown. • Very dark crown and broad supercilium. • Tail indistinctly barred.

Eurasian Sparrowhawk *Accipiter nisus*   L 33cm 13", WS 68cm 26.5"

all plum	• ♂ smaller, ♀ larger than Common Kestrel. Large ♀ can approach small Northern Goshawk ♂ in size. • Short prim-projection < tail-projection (like in Northern Goshawk). • Long thin tarsus ⇔ Northern Goshawk.
ad ♂	• Ear-coverts and breast-sides nearly uniform orange ⇔ ad ♀. • Orange barring on underparts. • Upperside grey-blue ⇔ ad ♀. • Usually no supercilium; when present short, narrow and indistinct.
ad ♀	• Dark (brown-black to dark rufous-brown) barred underparts; ear-coverts often somewhat rufous *but finely streaked* ⇔ ad ♂. • Upperside brown-grey often with blue wash ⇔ ad ♂. • Narrow but clear supercilium.
juv	• Feathers on upperside with rufous fringes ⇔ ad. • Bold and somewhat irregular barring on underparts. • Streaked crown and ear-coverts. • Supercilium present in both sexes.
fl all plum	• Straight-cut tail corners. • Tail-base narrower than in Northern Goshawk. • Relatively slightly shorter wing than in Northern Goshawk.
fl juv	• Underwing-cov more heavily marked than in ad.

Shikra *Accipiter badius*   L 35cm 14", WS 72cm 28"

all plum ⇒	• Pale iris (rather *dark red* in ad ♂) ⇔ Levant Sparrowhawk all plum. • Generally paler than Levant Sparrowhawk all plum. • Dark vertical throat-stripe (weaker in ad) ⇔ in Levant Sparrowhawk juv throat-stripe distinct, in ad ♀ ill-defined and in ♂ absent. • Legs relatively short and thick as in Levant Sparrowhawk ⇔ Eurasian Sparrowhawk.
ad	• Bill blue-grey at base, dark on tip ⇔ in Levant Sparrowhawk completely dark both species with conspicuous yellow bare skin around bill. • Differences between sexes much reduced compared to Levant Sparrowhawk: ♀ only slightly duller and darker grey on upperparts (often brownish wash on mantle) with slightly more distinct barring on underparts than ad ♂.
ad ♂ ⇒	• Pale dove-grey upperparts; pink-orange underparts, concentrated on breast and paler than Levant Sparrowhawk ad ♂.
juv	• Underparts less heavily marked and marks paler orange-brown than in Levant Sparrowhawk with streaked upper breast continuing in heart-shaped spots on lower breast (⇔ in Eurasian Sparrowhawk all plum wholly barred underparts). • Narrow dark gular stripe ⇔ in Levant Sparrowhawk broader. • Feathers of upperparts with broad pale brown fringes.
fl all plum ⇒	• t6 with fine barring (6-8 bars), rest of tail-feathers with 5 bars (in ad ♂ central tail-feathers are unmarked). • On underwing only (small) dark tips to outer 2-5 prim (in ♀ 2-3, in ♂ 4-5), no complete dark trailing edge along hand ⇔ in Levant Sparrowhawk large dark tips to 5-6 prim and complete dark trailing edge along hand. • Relatively short wings and tail. • More rounded hand like Eurasian Sparrowhawk ⇔ Levant Sparrowhawk. • Rounded tail-corners ⇔ Eurasian Sparrowhawk.

Levant Sparrowhawk *Accipiter brevipes*   L 34cm 13.5", WS 70cm 27.5"

all plum ⇒	• *Dark iris.* • Uniform head with dark crown, ear-coverts and cheeks ⇔ in Eurasian Sparrowhawk obvious contrast between dark ear-coverts and pale cheeks. • No (or at most weak) supercilium ⇔ Eurasian ♀. • Short, thick toes ⇔ Eurasian. • Relatively long prim-projection for *Accipiter*.
ad	• Yellow bare skin around bill more distinct than in Eurasian due to darker head and bill.
ad ♂	• Pale grey-blue upperside, often slightly paler and more blue than in Eurasian. • Barring on breast finer than in Eurasian; orange-pink wash on underparts, concentrated on breast.

ad ♀	• Deep grey-brown upperparts ⇔ in Eurasian ad ♀ brown-grey. • Pale and dark rufous-brown barring on underparts evenly broad ⇔ in ad ♂ barring finer and more orange, on breast almost uniform orange.
ad ♀/juv	• Vertical throat-stripe but in ad ♀ often ill-defined.
juv	• Large dark brown drop-shaped spots in vertical rows on breast and belly; flank, vent and undertail-cov boldly barred. • Starts partial post-juv moult in winter range; flight-feathers still juv in 1st part of 2cy but upperparts, underparts and cov largely with ad-type feathers ⇔ Eurasian starts post-juv moult from April of 2cy.
fl all plum ⇒	• Rather pointed wing-tips, 4 'fingers' ⇔ in Eurasian 6 'fingers'. • Leading and trailing edge of wing more parallel-sided than in Eurasian, with straighter trailing edge to arm. • Tail-bands smaller and more numerous (4-5) than in Eurasian (3-4). In ad central tail-feathers very diffusely marked or unmarked. • Relatively longer wings and shorter tail than Eurasian. • Powerful flight with less glides than Eurasian.
fl ad ⇒	• Dark distal part of outer 4 prim contrast with rest of underwing, strongest in ♂. Dark wing-tips also easily visible on upperwing ⇔ in Eurasian upperwing almost uniform.
fl ad ♂	• Sec very diffusely barred (appears unmarked at distance) ⇔ in ad ♀/imm fine and even.
fl juv	• Bold dark patterning on flanks forms barring (on breast more streaked), like Shikra juv but in this species paler diffuse barring and undertail-cov with no or hardly any patterning.

Ageing in *Buteo*

ad	• Dark iris. • Only or mainly barred on underparts, especially belly, thighs and flanks (Long-legged Buzzard ad often lacks any patterning on underparts). In some *vulpinus* uniform dark rufous or blackish underparts at all ages).
juv	• Pale iris. • Longitudinal streaks on underparts. • Uniform plumage, no moult. • Greater cov normally with obvious pale tips.
1s	• Rather pale iris throughout whole 2cy; from July/Aug of 2cy mainly ad-like plumage (except Swainson's Hawk). • Inner prim moulted, often creating clear moult-limit due to differences in pattern and length compared to juv outer prim. • Pale tips to greater cov.
2w	• 1-4 outer prim retained juv feathers; browner, narrower hand shorter than ad-type moulted prim. • In sec often still multiple centres of shorter juv feathers retained (especially recognisable on upperside of wing by bleaching and wear).
3w	• Like ad but some ind still recognisable by some retained sec, greater cov and p(9 and) 10.
fl ad	• Broad and well-defined dark trailing edge along whole underwing. • Broad and well-defined dark terminal tail-band.
fl juv	• Diffuse terminal tail-band, usually hardly broader than other tail-bands when present. • Rather narrow and usually diffuse dark trailing edge along whole underwing, but variable and some ind approaching ad. • Pale tips to greater cov creating narrow pale wing-bar. • Slightly longer tail and more narrow wings than ad (silhouette of e.g. Common Buzzard juv sometimes resembles Marsh Harrier).

Swainson's Hawk *Buteo swainsoni*   L 49cm 19", WS 123cm 48.5"

all plum	• Usually only little wing-projection or wing-tip level with tail-tip.
ad	• In pale morph dark head and breast, white throat and forehead and variable patterned (barred) underparts with white background. • In dark morph sometimes uniform dark underparts except white throat (often also forehead pale) and white vent and undertail-cov.
imm (to 3cy)	• Somewhat pale head with usually distinct supercilium. • Underparts variably streaked ⇔ in ad barred.
ad/juv	• See 'Ageing in *Buteo*'.
fl all plum ⇒	• *Very dark underside of flight-feathers* faintly barred, in pale morph contrasts with pale cov.
⇒	• *Rather pointed wings* with p7 and p8 longest. • Rather distinct pale 'U' on uppertail-cov (when present good indication). • Narrow dark tail-barring and rather narrow terminal tail-band.
note	• Not recorded as wild in WP.

Common Buzzard *Buteo buteo*   L 53cm 21", WS 120cm 47"

all plum	• Pale breast creating ill-defined 'U'-shaped patch (in ad often more distinct than in juv); in pale ind normally absent.
2w	• Breast often heavily streaked in darker ind. • Mixture of bleached and shorter juv sec and cov (and often also body-feathers).
ad/juv	• See 'Ageing in *Buteo*' and Steppe Buzzard and Rough-legged Buzzard.
note	• Occurs in numerous colour variants; common pale type with whitish lesser cov, median cov and tail-base strongly contrasting with dark remainder of upperwing. Underwing mainly pale with strongly marked dark carpal patch. Underparts mostly white with some streaks on upper-breast and belly.
fl all plum	• Usually shallow, rather stiff and fast wing-beats ⇔ European Honey-buzzard and Rough-legged. • Tail with rather sharp corners.

geog var	*B.b. rothschildi* (Azores)
all plum	• Small size like Steppe.
ad	• Upperparts very dark brown and underparts dense and dark patterned.
juv	• Underparts pale with variable patterning on often yellowish ground-colour.

geog var	*B.b. insularum* (Canary Islands)
all plum	• Upperparts pale brown and underparts rather weakly streaked not barred (also in ad) ⇔ *buteo*.

geog var	Steppe Buzzard *B.b. vulpinus* (North Palearctic) L 44cm 17.5", WS 112cm 44"
all plum	• Smaller size than Common (small overlap).
	• Less variable and three main forms: rufous, grey-brown and black. Grey-brown form especially often very similar to Common.
	• Often rufous-orange ground-colour of tail, rufous-orange fringes to scaps and rufous barring on undertail-cov but see note.
	• Dark rufous morph all plum and black morph ad with completely uniform dark underparts.
	• Combination of rufous and grey tones in tail indicative of Steppe, but probably also of intergrade with Common.
	• Often lacks broad pale 'U' on breast but narrow pale 'U' often present ⇔ in Common broad pale 'U' often present.
ad ⇒	• Tail-feathers relatively narrow (t1 ≤ 40mm), hardly broader than juv-type ⇔ in Common ad-type much broader (t1 ≥ 48mm) than juv-type.
	• Tail-pattern variable but often narrow subterminal tail-band, rest of tail with (very) narrow dark barring with relatively large spacings, often only 5-6 bars, but more dense barring occurs ⇔ Long-legged Buzzard ad (except dark morph). In some ind completely unmarked becoming only slightly paler towards base.
	• Uniform head.
	• In most ind barring on underparts, at least on belly ⇔ Long-legged often lacks barring on underparts but sometimes some longitudinal stripes. Barring slightly finer than in Common but much overlap.
ad/juv	• See 'Ageing in *Buteo*'.
juv	• Dark longitudinal stripes on underparts like most Common juv but more evenly spread and more drop-shaped to heart-shaped; usually less distinct pale 'U' on breast ⇔ Common.
	• Thigh-feathering often uniform dark.
	• Narrow dark tail-barring narrowing or fading away towards base.
imm	• From 2cy autumn to 3cy spring underparts often intermediate between juv and ad and sometimes even still juv-like (see flight imm).
fl all plum	• Prim little barred (barring fine and mostly concentrated on distal part) and barring normally not extending further than p6 ⇔ most Common. Prim underside with pure white background.
	• Paler median cov on underwing creating pale band ⇔ most Long-legged.
	• Sec with narrow barring.
fl ad	• Barred greater cov on underwing.
fl juv	• Longitudinal stripes on underwing-cov (mainly on median cov).
fl imm	• From 2cy autumn to 3cy spring often still some outer prim and central sec retained juv feathers (see also imm).
moult	• In ad in autumn not complete. Moult suspended during migration and completed in winter range (Dec/Jan) ⇔ in Common ad moult complete in Nov, but in some (?) populations not all prim moulted in one season.
	• In juv no moult in autumn, starts at beginning of 2cy with body-moult ⇔ in Common juv body-moult in late autumn of 1cy by which time some barring could appear on underparts.
	• In autumn of 2cy prim-moult suspended with 3-5 outer prim still juv (in Common normally 2-4 prim still juv).
notes	• See Long-legged.
	• Grey-brown morph mainly occurs in western part of range, where intergrades with Common probably occur over a wide area.
	• Certain identification of grey-brown morph under field conditions outside normal range difficult. Field marks of Common and Steppe at least in Scandinavia clinal. Moreover, within range of Common ind occur with rufous tail and sometimes rufous other parts.

geog var	*B.b. menetriesi* (Middle East)
all plum	• Very similar to rufous morph of Steppe but generally larger, more rufous and with stronger contrast between pale and dark areas. Tail deep rusty.

Cape Verde Buzzard *Buteo bannermani*   L 48cm 19", WS 110cm 43.5"

all plum	• Upperparts rufous-brown with pale fringes on mantle and scaps.
	• Underparts relatively strongly dark patterned.
	• Little variation in ground-colour.
fl ad	• Underwing pattern resembles Steppe Buzzard and Long-legged Buzzard (much white at base of prim with contrasting dark trailing edge along underwing).
note	• Possibly more related to Long-legged than to Common Buzzard.

Long-legged Buzzard *Buteo rufinus*   L 56cm 22", WS 152cm 60"

all plum	• In direct comparison obviously larger than Common Buzzard (but see geog var).
	• Larger bill than Common and Steppe Buzzard.
	• Long tarsus sometimes conspicuous.
	• Long tail compared to other *Buteo*.

- Ground-colour of underparts warm yellowish to rufous-brown.

ad/1s
ad
- As in Steppe multiple and in part corresponding colour-morphs. Plumage-wise, dark rufous and dark morphs with uniform dark underparts are almost identical to Steppe of same colour-morph.
- Mantle feathers, scaps and cov with dark centres and broad rufous fringes (pale morph).
- Pale morph; pale head and breast gradually merge into dark, red-brown belly. Some very pale ind with only dark patterning on thighs (central belly pale).
- When dark belly (most ind) then almost uniform (sometimes some barring restricted to central belly) ⇔ in Steppe often (fine) barring on large part of underparts.

ad/juv
- See 'Ageing in *Buteo*'.

juv
- Pale head and breast (breast usually striped) and dark belly (resembles Rough-legged Buzzard juv but brown-yellow to rufous general impression). Sometimes central part of belly pale, only dark thigh-feathering.
- Often dark 'V'-shaped mark on rear-head (sometimes also in pale Common).

fl all plum ⇒
- Blackish carpal patch and prim-cov contrast with paler *sparsely patterned underwing-cov* (in dark type uniform dark underwing-cov) ⇔ in Steppe more contrasting pale and dark parts on underwing-cov.
- Only inner prim distinctly barred (like Steppe) but often slightly stronger marked sec than in Steppe.
- Soars/glides with arm in higher 'V'-shape than Steppe/Common but hand held more level, resulting in distinct kink between arm and hand (resembles Rough-legged).
- Longer wings than Common and Steppe, total length of wings longer than body length ⇔ in Steppe body- and wing-length almost equal.
- Flight heavier than Common with slower wing-beats.
- Narrow hand (especially in ad; sometimes Northern Goshawk-like).

fl ad ⇒
- In pale morph unbarred tail, at base almost white and gradually becoming slightly darker towards ochre-orange tail-tip; *underside of tail usually conspicuously paler than underparts*. In dark morph fine tail-barring and broader terminal tail-band. Terminal tail-band (dark morph) not obviously subterminally situated as in most Steppe
- *Uniform pale* underwing-cov ⇔ in most Steppe often pale band over median cov and barring on greater cov.
- Mantle, scaps and cov rather pale, contrasting with dark greater cov and sec.

fl imm
- Strongly marked upperwing with pale (rufous) median cov and lesser cov, dark greater cov, prim-cov and sec and conspicuous pale prim-flash.
- Barring on sec usually broader than in Steppe imm.
- Finely and densely barred tail; 2nd generation tail often still with some very fine barring.

note
- Black morph of Steppe and Long-legged most difficult to separate. Structure and differences in tail-barring (tail of Steppe finer and slightly more diffusely barred) 'best' field marks.

geog var | *B.r. cirtensis* (North Africa) | L 50cm 19.5", WS 118cm 46.5"

all plum
- Size and structure (also in flight) similar to Common (generally slightly smaller), distinctly smaller than *rufinus* but bill evenly strong.
- Relatively big head compared to *rufinus*.
- Tail extends beyond wing-tips ⇔ in Steppe Buzzard falling level.

ad
- Belly and vent including thigh-feathers usually deep orange-red (less conspicuous dark belly than in *rufinus*) but breast and head paler with rufous streaking.
- Belly obviously paler than carpal patch ⇔ in *rufinus* dark rufous belly only slightly paler than carpal patch.
- Tail bright deep orange with at most slightly paler base ⇔ in *rufinus* paler cream-orange with whitish base.

juv
- Underparts often very pale.
- In summer already rather bleached and worn due to early hatching date ⇔ *rufinus* fresher.

moult
- In all plumages distinctly earlier than in *rufinus* and thus in autumn/winter more worn and bleached than *rufinus*.

fl all plum
- (Much) smaller than *rufinus* with shorter wings, nevertheless still gives quite heavy impression.

note
- Some ind darker and more strongly patterned, including some tail-barring when can resemble Steppe and some ind hardly identifiable.

Rough-legged Buzzard *Buteo lagopus* | L 55cm 22", WS 137cm 54"

all plum
- Usually slight wing-projection ⇔ in Common Buzzard tail projects slightly beyond wing-tip.
- Feathered tarsus, long thigh feathers.

ad ♂
- Throat and upper-breast darker than belly ⇔ in ad ♀ and juv the other way around.
- Flanks barred; central part of belly paler.
- Multiple (3-4) distally situated tail-bands ⇔ ad ♀ (1-2) and juv (1).
- Sec and greater cov with distinct barring ⇔ in ad ♀ and juv almost uniform.

ad ♀
- Nearly uniform dark belly (as in juv) and paler upper-breast.

ad/juv
- See 'Ageing in *Buteo*'.

juv
- Head pale, breast with fine longitudinal streaks; uniform dark belly.
- Narrow dark eye-stripe ⇔ Common pale type.

fl all plum
- Longer wings than Common (resulting in wing-projection when perched, see all plum) with obvious kink between upheld arm and level hand.

fl ad ♂
- Underwing-cov strongly marked ⇔ in ad ♀/juv only faint.
- Usually no uniform dark carpal patch ⇔ ad ♀ and juv.

fl ad ♀
- 1-2 tail-bands; terminal band especially more well-defined than in juv.
- Usually uniform dark carpal patch as in juv.
- Faint patterned underwing-cov.

fl juv/imm
- Prim-upperside with paler basal part creating *pale prim-flash* ⇔ Common.
- Pale tail-base and uppertail-cov (longest uppertail-cov with black spot) and broad dark terminal band, ill-defined towards base.

	• Little patterned underside of flight-feathers and *restricted to feather-tips* ⇔ in Common and Long-legged Buzzard at least whole distal part of sec barred.
	• Uniform dark carpal patch contrasts strongly with pale basal part of flight-feathers (also in ad ♀).
2w	• Largely like ad of equivalent sex but with outer prim still juv and distinct moult-limit in sec.
note	• In western Europe vast majority imm (ad mainly resident or short distant migrant).
geog var	**Rough-legged Hawk** *B.l. sanctijohannis* (North America)
all plum	• Structure and size more like Common Buzzard, with shorter wings; plumage of pale morph (almost) as *lagopus* but possibly more often with some rufous on underparts and underwing-cov.
ad	• Dark morph almost completely sooty brown-black (no dark morph known in *lagopus*).
fl ad	• Dark morph has pale underside of sec, prim and tail-feathers with broad dark terminal band. In ad ♀ some contrast between dark brown underwing-cov and black carpal patch.
fl juv	• Dark morph like ad but terminal tail-band diffuse as in pale morph; upperside of tail mainly dark. Prim-flash (upperwing) conspicuous.

Greater Spotted Eagle *Aquila clanga* — L 65cm 25.5", WS 172cm 67.5"

all plum	• Brown-black general impression, some ind in all plum paler (see note '*fulvescens*'-type).
	• Gape line extending to middle under eye ⇔ Lesser Spotted Eagle and Steppe Eagle.
	• Nearly round nostril (as in Lesser Spotted).
juv ⇒	• Large pale tips to tertials, sec, greater cov and median cov and smaller on rows of lesser cov (see Lesser Spotted juv).
	• Rather pale vent and undertail-cov with rather bold dark longitudinal stripes (sometimes vent and undertail-cov uniform pale and/or whole underparts pale contrasting with dark head).
2cy	• From spring onwards moult of inner prim and outer sec (new sec longer than others). At end of year prim-moult up to p6-p7, sec mix of juv and 2nd generation. New all plum and eventually cov with pale tips so plumage generally quite similar to juv.
3cy+	• Exact ageing under field circumstances normally not possible, but often still mix of cov with pale tips or fringes. Normally no juv prim present.
imm	• When tasus feathering dark, then sometimes some white feathering at border with feet ⇔ Lesser Spotted.
fl all plum	• Prim with pale shaft and sometimes slightly paler base (imm) creating pale fan ⇔ Lesser Spotted.
	• Usually one obvious pale carpal 'comma' on under-wing (sometimes weak 2nd) ⇔ Lesser Spotted. Dark Steppe ad lacks pale carpal patch and has paler sec with dark trailing edge of arm.
	• Very broad-winged with 7 'fingers'.
	• Soars with arched hand like Lesser Spotted; sometimes resembling Grey Heron.
fl (sub)ad	• Pale carpal 'comma' distinct and from below often only mark on whole bird ⇔ in Lesser Spotted 2 less distinct carpal 'commas'.
	• Cov often (slightly) paler than flight-feathers (especially in older ad), sometimes almost as dark as Lesser Spotted.
	• Completely dark, unmarked sec and inner prim.
fl imm ⇒	• Faint and fine barring on sec and inner prim; dark bars narrower than pale ones, *barring not reaching feather-tips* ⇔ Lesser Spotted.
	• White area on uppertail-cov as in many *Aquila*; rump patchy, usually ill-defined towards back ⇔ in Lesser Spotted white patch on uppertail-cov more well marked due to normally uniform dark rump.
	• Indistinct pale window on inner prim and black wing-tips.
	• Grey wash on underside of sec and inner prim.
	• Flight-feathers slightly paler or concolorous with underwing-cov (due to moult, especially in 2nd-4cy underwing-cov sometimes seems paler).
geog var	*A.c. 'fulvescens'*-type (especially occurring in eastern part of range)
imm	• Often with entirely pale cream-coloured underparts, upperparts, head (but face normally darker) and cov, except greater cov on upper- and underwing (strongly resembles pale Tawny Eagle and Spanish Imperial Eagle juv-3cy).
fl all plum	• Flight-feathers usually wholly black (but sometimes faintly barred) ⇔ in normal type usually barred.
fl imm	• Prim-cov and greater cov on underwing inner dark, creating uniform dark band ⇔ in Tawny prim-cov and greater cov on underwing dark with pale fringes.
	• Upperwing has almost completely pale cov with ill-defined dark centres.
notes	• Besides characteristic pale type many intermediate (like more rufous) types occur and with increasing age become darker and more similar to normal type.
	• Some non-'*fulvescens*'-type ind have paler underparts but less uniform and dark cov with pale tips and typical type of barring on sec and inner prim remains.

Lesser Spotted Eagle *Aquila pomarina* — L 60cm 23.5", WS 156cm 61.5"

all plum ⇒	• Cream-yellow nape patch (juv-subad) but commonly absent; when present characteristic compared to Greater Spotted Eagle. In Steppe Eagle ad sometimes yellowish nape patch.
	• Usually contrast between dark greater cov and paler rest of cov ⇔ Greater Spotted imm.
	• Mantle and scaps darker than cov, often creating 'saddle' ⇔ in Greater Spotted mantle and scaps concolorous with cov.
	• Nearly round nostril (as in Greater Spotted).
	• Gape line reaches to just under front-side of eye.
	• Thighs not conspicuously full below ⇔ Greater Spotted and especially Steppe.
	• Short tail projects beyond wing-tip.
	• Relatively small bill and feet.
(sub)ad ⇒	• Pale iris ⇔ Greater Spotted all plum.
juv	• Pale streaking on underparts often more pronounced on breast, creating diffuse pale breast-band ⇔ in Greater Spotted, when present pale streaking sometimes more extensive around belly, rarely on breast.

imm	• Pale tips to tertials, sec and greater cov. Median cov and lesser cov with small or no spot, however some ind approach typical Greater Spotted juv with regards extent of spotting.
	• Ground-colour normally medium brown, but variable from pale brown to black-brown like Greater Spotted.
	• See Greater Spotted 2nd and 3rd+ cy for more precise ageing.
fl all plum ⇒	• Cov paler than flight-feathers, more so in ad than in imm. Paler lesser cov and median cov creating contrast with dark greater cov and flight-feathers, especially characteristic on upperwing (upperparts often again darker). In older Greater Spotted ad often also slightly paler cov but in these cases upperparts also paler (no contrast between upperparts and cov).
⇒	• Sec and inner prim barred, with pale and dark bars almost equal in width up to feather-tip ⇔ Greater Spotted (in ad usually very difficult to see). Type of barring strongly resembles Steppe but finer with 9-10 bars per feather ⇔ in Steppe 7-8.
	• Pale prim-base on upperside concentrated on inner prim, creating distinct pale spot, still visible at (some) distance ⇔ Greater Spotted.
	• Underwing with two pale carpal 'commas' of nearly same size (except very dark imm) ⇔ Greater Spotted.
	• Greater cov on underwing variably pale patterned. Some imm with extremely pale patterning, creating pale underwing-bar approaching typical imm Steppe.
	• Rather well-defined pale area on uppertail-cov.
	• Soars with arched hand like Greater Spotted.
	• Broad-winged with 6 'fingers'.
fl juv ⇒	• Pale uppertail-cov, slightly darker rump and paler back; rump and back not spotted ⇔ Greater Spotted.
	• Typically faint pale trailing-edge to wing and tail (as in Greater Spotted) ⇔ in Steppe trailing-edges broad and distinct.
	• In pale ind underwing-cov paler than underparts ⇔ in Steppe about concolorous.

Booted Eagle *Aquila pennata*   L 46cm 18", WS 125cm 49"

all plum	• Pale lower rows of lesser cov, median cov and scaps contrast with dark remainder of upperwing (pied upperwing); in pale morph more contrast on upperwing than in dark morph.
	• When perched tail projects well beyond wing-tips.
	• In dark morph almost unmarked underparts ⇔ in Common Buzzard at least sometimes pale patterning on breast.
	• Tail (almost) unbarred.
	• Feathered tarsus ⇔ all raptors of this size (except Rough-legged Buzzard).
juv	• Diffuse patterned underparts; in pale morph only diffuse brownish head and neck-side (not distinctly streaked as in 2w+).
fl all plum ⇒	• Pied patterned upperwing; pale band over cov, pale scaps (also visible when perched) and pale uppertail-cov (all morphs).
⇒	• White spot (often called 'headlights') on front-side of wing-base.
	• Straight cut tail with sharp corners.
	• Dark underside of flight-feathers with weak barring, especially in white morph. In rufous and dark morph paler background to prim and therefore more visible barring with paler base up to outer prim.
	• Pale window on inner prim.
	• In rufous and dark morph tail underside paler than underparts.
	• 6 'fingers' ⇔ Common Buzzard and European Honey-buzzard.
	• Heavy body in relation to wings.
fl juv	• Evenly pale trailing edge along wings and tail.
fl end 2cy	• Combination of moulted inner 4-5 prim and some outer sec with large white tips; rest of 'juv' trailing-edge of arm retained.
note	• Three morphs: pale, dark and rufous. In rufous morph main field marks as described above; underparts, head and cov rufous. Pale underside of tail with diffuse dark terminal band characteristic.

Golden Eagle *Aquila chrysaetos*   L 86cm 34", WS 202cm 80"

all plum	• Mainly pale (not in fresh juv and end 3cy), pointed median cov and some lesser cov, creating pale, patchy wing-panel (especially visible in flight). Southern populations (*homeyeri*) darker on both underwing-cov and upperwing-cov.
	• Short tail projects beyond wing-tips.
	• Elongated nostril.
	• Golden-yellow rear-head and hind-neck; in *homeyeri* more red-brown.
juv	• Uniform plumage without moult; earth-brown with white base to most sec and all prim (see flight imm).
end 2cy	• Largely like juv but in autumn 3-4 inner prim, some outer sec and some tail-feathers moulted. No or, at most, very few cov moulted, creating pale panel on upper-wing due to bleaching of lesser cov and median cov; greater cov dark like sec.
end 3cy	• Superficially like juv as 2nd generation tail-feathers and flight-feathers almost identical to juv-type. Prim-moult attained to p7; sec show rather even mix of juv and 2nd generation feathers with juv-type longer and browner.
	• Cov largely moulted but some central greater cov still juv. No strongly contrasting pale cov-panel (see end 2cy and end 4cy).
end 4cy	• Cov bleached and worn as in end 2cy.
	• Tail and flight-feathers (all 2nd generation) still juv-like patterned but new inner 3rd generation prim all dark ad-type which break through white band along underwing (flight).
	• Juv p10 often still retained and very worn.
subad	• From end of 5cy tail still juv-like patterned and some sec with pale base.
fl all plum	• Soars with wings in shallow 'V'.
	• Bulging arm and narrow hand, arm narrowing towards body ⇔ e.g. imperial eagles.
	• Relatively long tail; tail length equal to width of base of wing.
	• Pale cov creating distinct broad wing-panel (except fresh juv).

fl ad	• Diffuse grey tail with faint terminal band.
	• Diffuse dark trailing edge of wing.
fl imm ⇒	• White tail with broad, dark terminal band.
	• White base to (sometimes all) flight-feathers, especially much white on inner prim; in *homeyeri* less white, sometimes almost none.
note	• Above mentioned ageing indications apply for northern *chrysaetos*. Southern *homeyeri* moults faster, probably due to lack of moult-stop in winter.

Verreaux's Eagle *Aquila verreauxii*　　　　　　　L 85cm 35.5", WS 205cm 80"

ad	• When perched looks completely black with narrow white 'V'-shape on scaps.
juv	• Pied appearance with black-brown breast and face, pale brown crown gradually merging into brown back.
	• Lesser cov and median cov pale brown to pale grey.
	• Whitish thighs, vent and undertail-cov.
fl all plum ⇒	• *Very bulging centre* of arm, arm narrowing strongly towards body and towards hand.
	• Pale basal part of prim, both on under- and upperside.
fl ad	• White rump and back contrast strongly with entirely dark remainder of upperparts.
fl juv	• Pale lesser cov and median cov creating conspicuous pale panel on upperside of arm.

Bonelli's Eagle *Aquila fasciata*　　　　　　　L 59cm 23", WS 155cm 61"

all plum	• When perched tail projects obviously beyond wing-tips.
	• Legs long.
	• Medium-sized eagle, much larger than Common Buzzard with relatively heavy body.
ad	• Whitish, triangular spot on mantle (lacking in some ind).
fl all plum	• Long tail with sharp cut corners; bulging arm narrowing towards body.
	• Soars with leading edge of wing straight, level wings and up-curled 'fingers'
fl juv ⇒	• Sec and tail wholly, *evenly, thinly and sharply barred.*
	• Dark (sometimes ill-defined) border between cov and flight-feathers on underwing; prim-cov create usually dark comma-shaped carpal patch.
	• Pale, almost unmarked base of underside of outer 6 prim.
	• Rufous underwing-cov.
	• Whitish spot on lower back and rump ⇔ in ad pale spot on mantle.
	• Upperwing and upperparts almost uniformly dark with slightly paler cov than flight-feathers.
fl end 2cy	• Moulted inner prim and groups of sec with contrasting tips, creating broken trailing edge.
	• Greater cov on underwing create broad dark band.
end 3cy	• Ad-like tail (pale with dark terminal band) but flight-feathers obviously barred ⇔ ad.

Steppe Eagle *Aquila nipalensis*　　　　　　　L 70cm 27.5", WS 178cm 70"

all plum ⇒	• Gape line reaches to under middle but often to rear-side of eye.
	• Usually (diffuse) pale throat (also in some older Lesser Spotted Eagle).
	• Ground-colour variable, juv often pale yellow-brown, ad usually dark earth brown.
	• Oval nostril ⇔ in Lesser Spotted and Greater Spotted Eagle almost round.
	• Usually distinctly larger than Lesser Spotted and Greater Spotted with full thighs ⇔ Lesser Spotted.
ad	• Sometimes yellow nape patch as in Lesser Spotted imm.
juv (fl)	• Uniform plumage without moult; body varies from pale cream brown-grey to earth-brown. Underparts uniform ⇔ most Lesser Spotted juv and Greater Spotted juv). Large white tips to all remiges and tail-feathers, greater cov and prim-cov.
	• Broad white trailing-edge to wings and tail ⇔ in Lesser Spotted juv narrow to almost absent.
end 2cy (fl)	• Largely like worn juv but 3-4 inner prim, some outer sec and their corresponding greater cov and some tail-feathers moulted. Pattern of moulted feathers basically same as juv but longer and fresh with large white tips. New feathers contrast distinctly with juv feathers in which white tips almost worn off.
	• White band on underwing (but see flight imm) retained and undertail-cov and vent still pale.
end 3cy (fl)	• Combination of moderately worn 2nd generation greater cov, flight-feathers (see end 2cy) and new 3rd generation greater cov. 3rd generation greater cov, sec and tail-feathers instead of 2nd generation now distinctly different; broadly grey barred with small pale tips. Prim-moult attained to p7; sec and tail-feathers largely 2nd generation with some 3rd generation feathers.
	• White band on underwing (but see flight imm) retained and undertail-cov and vent still pale.
end 4cy (fl)	• Combination of all plum and 3rd generation or older (for pattern see end 3cy (flight)) and (patchy) white band on underwing and paler undertail-cov.
	• New sec (4th generation) with dark tips, contrasting with more uniform older sec.
	• Juv p10 often still retained and very worn.
end 5cy (fl)	• Like ad but often still some older sec without dark tips (dark trailing edge broken up).
	• Undertail-cov often still with some pale patterning.
fl all plum ⇒	• Completely barred underside of flight-feathers (in juv-3cy barring weak or sometimes even absent), also outer prim ⇔ in Lesser Spotted and Greater Spotted only sec and inner prim barred. Barring relatively coarse and consists of c.7 dark stripes on inner prim ⇔ in Lesser Spotted finer and denser.
	• Barring becomes more obvious and greyer in older ind ⇔ in Lesser Spotted and Greater Spotted less obvious in older ind.
	• Very long-winged with almost square wing-tips; p4 fingered, distinctly longer than p3 ⇔ Lesser Spotted.
	• Head often protrudes slightly further than in Lesser Spotted and Greater Spotted.
	• Soars with wings level and usually slightly arched hand.
fl ad	• Distinct barring on underside of flight-feathers and broad dark trailing edge along wing (see also flight all plum).
fl imm ⇒	• *Broad pale central band over underwing* due to pale greater cov and prim-cov but variable (sometimes absent or largely obscured). In Lesser Spotted imm sometimes narrow pale central band on underwing.
	• Uniform, cold grey-brown to cream-coloured upperparts and cov (greater cov dark as flight-feathers).

Tawny Eagle *Aquila rapax*   L 68cm 26.5", WS 173cm 68"

all plum	• Smaller size and more stocky than Steppe Eagle and imperial eagles with proportionally shorter wings and longer tail.
	• Dark scaps contrast with pale cov and mantle.
	• Very variable in ground-colour varying from dark brown (only some ad) to yellow-brown or rufous-brown (*belisarius* always pale – see note).
	• Gape line reaches to under middle of eye but is less rich yellow and less distinct than in Steppe.
	• Oval nostril.
ad	• Usually rufous to yellow-brown head, underparts, mantle and cov (in *belisarius*, see note), plumage and structure resembles Spanish Imperial Eagle juv ⇔ in Steppe normally darker and less rufous plumage.
	• Rather pale, orange to yellow iris.
	• Breast often slightly darker (diffusely streaked) than rest of underparts.
imm	• Dark iris.
	• Little plumage differences compared to ad but usually paler (and larger white tips to greater cov and sec) and often strongly demarcated dark head.
	• Juv often rufous on body and cov.
	• Ageing probably basically similar to Steppe (see there).
fl all plum ⇒	• Almost uniform pale uppertail-cov, rump and wedge on back ⇔ in all other similar *Aquila* pale area largely or wholly restricted to uppertail-cov.
	• Dark flight-feathers contrast with pale body; flight-feathers rather weakly barred ⇔ in Steppe normally distinct.
	• Dark prim-cov and greater cov with pale fringes on underwing creating black patchy border between cov and flight-feathers as in Greater Spotted Eagle '*fulvescens*'-type but in latter prim-cov and greater cov completely dark without pale fringes.
	• Paler inner prim creating broad window as in Eastern Imperial Eagle and Spanish Imperial imm.
	• Stockier than Steppe with relatively shorter wings but longer tail. Arm relatively broad, hand relatively narrow ⇔ Steppe.
fl ad	• At most narrow dark trailing edge of wing ⇔ Steppe ad broad (Steppe 3rd-4cy also lacks dark trailing edge).
fl imm	• Pale morph extremely similar to Spanish Imperial juv but in latter fine breast-streaking.
note	• Occurs in numerous subspecies and morphs; above mentioned field marks apply to pale *belisarius* (North Africa and Middle East).

Eastern Imperial Eagle *Aquila heliaca*   L 76cm 30.5", WS 190cm 75"

all plum	• When perched, tail does not project beyond wing-tips ⇔ in Golden Eagle tail projects shortly beyond wing-tips.
	• Oval nostril (as in Golden).
	• Deep massive bill, shorter than in Golden.
ad ⇒	• Whitish shoulder (variable amount of white scaps).
	• Uniformly dark with pale, yellowish rear-head and hind-neck and pale undertail-cov.
juv- ⇒	• Plumage with pale background and strong and evenly pale streaked, especially on breast,
start 3cy	upper-belly and upperparts.
	• Pale uniform thigh, vent and undertail-cov.
end 2cy (fl)	• Very similar to juv but inner 3-4 prim, some outer sec and their corresponding greater cov and prim-cov and sometimes tail-feathers moulted. Pattern of moulted feathers similar to juv-type but longer, fresh and as juv-type with large pale tips.
	• Pale trailing edge of outer wing narrow, uneven or absent. New inner prim (and corresponding prim-cov) and some central sec with whitish tips ⇔ in juv evenly broad pale trailing edge of whole wing.
end 3cy (fl)	• Still similar to juv but underparts and cov with some dark (ad-type) feathers and prim moult up to p9 (p10 still juv).
	• New inner prim (3rd generation) with grey barring and dark tips.
	• Pale trailing edge of wing narrow or absent ⇔ juv.
	• Median cov often distinctly pale.
end 4cy (fl)	• Underparts still mainly pale with dark patches (ad-type feathers moulted in) especially on breast and belly. Throat dark.
	• Most sec with dark tips, creating broken dark trailing edge.
	• Greater cov and prim-cov on underwing dark, creating dark line.
end 5cy (fl)	• Together with end 4cy most patchy plumage due to mix of imm-type pale feathers and dark ad-type. Amount of dark feathers considerably increased compared to 4cy; head and breast almost as in ad.
end 6cy (fl)	• Like ad but underside of flight-feathers paler and more distinctly barred.
	• Undertail-cov still with some pale feathers.
fl all plum	• Soars on level wings.
	• Rather rectangular wings and rather long tail ⇔ in Golden wings more rounded.
	• Short tarsus; base of feet (almost) level with trailing edge of wing as in Spanish Imperial Eagle ⇔ in other *Aquila* eagles tarsus longer.
	• (Sub)ad often soars with closed tail ⇔ imm.
	• Head often protrudes conspicuously.
	• Faint barring on underside of flight-feathers could occur in nearly all ages (except old ad); barring stops far from feather tips. In 3rd-5cy barring most prominent.
fl ad	• Uniformly blackish underparts (except undertail-cov) and underwing-cov contrast slightly with dark grey underside of flight-feathers.
	• Grey tail with rather sharply defined, broad dark terminal band.
fl imm	• Pale inner 3-4 prim create conspicuous pale window (up to 4cy), as in Spanish.
	• Very dark sec and tail-feathers contrast with rest of plumage (up to 4cy).
	• Prim-cov on underwing dark with pale fringes creating darkest cov on underwing (up to 4cy), as in Spanish.

Spanish Imperial Eagle *Aquila adalberti* L 79cm 31", WS 195cm 77"

all plum	• Slightly larger size and more stocky than Eastern Imperial Eagle.
ad ⇒	• Plumage as Eastern but with whitish leading edge of arm.
juv	• Plumage mainly rufous; underparts and upperparts less boldly streaked than in Eastern juv, on spring 2cy underparts, upperparts and cov pale yellow-brown.
imm	• Ageing basically similar to Eastern (see there).
fl all plum	• Slightly shorter, relatively broader wings than in Eastern. • Short tarsus (see Eastern).
fl imm	• Juv-3cy with *uniform* rufous to pale yellowish underparts and cov on both under- and upperwing contrasting strongly with very dark flight-feathers (resembles Tawny Eagle and Greater Spotted Eagle *'fulvescens'*-type). • Pale 3 inner prim creating conspicuous window, often more distinct than in Eastern. • Prim-cov on underwing dark with pale fringes up to 4cy (as in Eastern, see there). • Plumage development from juv to ad as in Eastern but probably faster (see there). Subad especially hardly distinguishable from Eastern in equivalent plumage.

Osprey

Osprey *Pandion haliaetus* L 56cm 22", WS 159cm 62.5"

all plum	• Pale head with very broad dark eye-stripe. • Underparts white except dark breast-band (sometimes lacking in ♂). • Upperparts dark (in ad uniform).
ad ♂	• Breast-band often faint or absent (also in some juv ♂).
ad ♀	• Usually broad breast-band.
juv	• Pale scaled upperside (pale tips to all feathers of upperside).
fl all plum	• Long narrow (hand) wings with *distinctly protruding carpal joints*. • White underparts and underwing-cov contrast with dark carpal patch and rather dark underside of flight-feathers. • Soars on somewhat bowed wings, sometimes resembling large gull.
fl juv	• Barring on sec distinct and evenly spaced ⇔ in ad barring more diffuse on distal part, creating broad diffuse trailing edge of arm. • Greater cov on underwing create regular spotted dark band ⇔ in ad more messy and variable from completely dark to white with dark centre. • Evenly barred tail (in ad diffuse terminal band).

Falcons

Lesser Kestrel *Falco naumanni* L 30cm 12", WS 68cm 26.5"

all plum ⇒	• Pale claws. • When perched tail projects only slightly beyond wing-tips ⇔ in Common Kestrel tail normally projects about half of prim-projection beyond wing-tips. • Contrasting pale throat often conspicuous (especially in ad ♂). • Small bill.
ad ♂ ⇒ ⇒	• Unmarked, rufous-brown mantle and cov except greater cov and outer median cov. • Greater cov and outer median cov blue-grey creating conspicuous band between brown arm-panel and black hand. • Underparts deep cream-coloured with faint, variable patterning. • Uniform blue-grey head except throat ⇔ in Common 1s ♂ and ad ♂ pale ear-coverts. • No malar stripe.
juv ♂	• Faint and narrowly barred tail-feathers, sometimes already with grey cast; cov more narrowly barred than in juv ♀ (juv ♀ nearly as Common). • Uppertail-cov greyish.
1s	• Moult-limit between fresh 2nd generation mantle and scaps and juv cov (also in Common 1s). Tail fresh 2nd generation.
1s ♂	• Lacks blue-grey greater cov. Unmarked ad-type mantle and scaps already present.
ad ♀	• 'V'-shaped mark on scaps and cov (especially lesser cov and median cov) ⇔ in Common more triangular shaped. • Greater cov and tertials with narrow barring ⇔ juv and Common ♀-type. • Drop-shaped longitudinal stripes on flanks; remainder of underparts thinly streaked. • Usually weak malar stripe (but often hardly different from typical Common ♀). • Feathers of upperparts, cov and tertials with narrow barring ⇔ Common. • Greyish, unmarked uppertail-cov.
ad ♀/juv	• Rather uniform head but often has conspicuous pale cheek; no or very faint dark stripe behind eye ⇔ Common.
juv	• Narrowly streaked underparts ⇔ in ad and all plumages of Common streaks broaden to spot on feather-tip. • Uppertail-cov with grey ground-colour; in some ♂ also tail-feathers already with grey showing through.
fl all plum ⇒	• p10 only slightly shorter than p9 ⇔ in Common p10 distinctly shorter than p9 and about as long as p7.
fl ad ♂	• Underparts darker than underwing. • Underwing faintly marked (sometimes unmarked) with distinct dark trailing edge of hand; diffusely demarcated along arm.
fl ad ♀	• *Broad*, ill-defined dark trailing edge along underwings, particularly broad along hand; base of hand almost uniform pale ⇔ in Common juv/ad ♀ narrower, rather sharply defined black trailing edge along underside of hand; base of underside of hand patterned and not obviously paler. • Strong contrast on upperwing due to almost uniform black hand (incl prim-cov) and pale, finely barred cov.

fl juv	• Underside of prim usually weakly barred (base unbarred), contrasting rather strongly with broad dark trailing edge and tip of hand (as in ad ♀). In juv ♀ often more strongly barred underside of prim, nearly as Common.

Common Kestrel *Falco tinnunculus* — L 34cm 13.5", WS 73cm 28.5"

ad ♂	• Cov and upperparts with variable small black subterminal spots, some ind almost unmarked. • Uniform blue-grey tail with black terminal band
ad ♀	• Greater cov barred ⇔ ad ♂, in old ad ♀ sometimes sparse. • Older ad ♀ resembles ad ♂ with greyish head and grey wash on tail but tail barred.
juv-1w	• Early moult of scaps to ad-type; in 1w ♂ combination of ad-type scaps (small black subterminal spot) and barred greater cov; 1w ♀ hardly or not separable from young ad (e.g. 2w).
1s	• Moult-limit between fresh ad-type mantle and scaps and old juv cov.
note	• For other features see Lesser Kestrel.

Alexander's Kestrel *Falco alexandri* — L 30cm 12", WS 65cm 23.5"

all plum	• Upperparts strongly dark marked. In ad ♂ from Sao Vicente upperparts as Common Kestrel ad ♂.
ad ♂	• Tail grey with narrow barring and dark terminal band. • Crown brown ⇔ in Common ad ♂ grey.
ad ♀	• As Common ad ♀.
fl all plum	• Wings rounder than in Common (as well as in other Common subspecies from the Azores and the Canary Islands).
note	• Endemic to northern Cape Verde Islands

Neglected Kestrel *Falco neglectus* — L 28cm 11", WS 60cm 23.5"

all plum	• Smaller size than Common Kestrel and Alexander's Kestrel with shorter tail (structure resembles Merlin). • Main appearance darker than Common.
ad	• Sexes almost alike (some ad ♂ with greyish tail and crown), upperparts and tail strongly and broadly barred.
note	• Endemic to southern Cape Verde Islands.

American Kestrel *Falco sparverius* — L 26cm 10", WS 56cm 22"

all plum	• Size as Merlin, structure as Common Kestrel.
ad	• Characteristic head-pattern with grey crown and 3 black vertical markings on head: 'moustache', on rear-side of ear-coverts and on neck-side.
ad ♂	• Brown upperparts with large black spots. • Uniform rufous-brown tail with broad black terminal band. • Blue-grey cov and tertials with some black spots.
ad ♀	• Strongly marked underparts resembles pattern of Merlin juv/♀ but patterning rufous. • Strongly barred rufous upperparts, cov, tertials and tail (uniform rufous uppertail-cov).
1s	• See Common 1s.
fl all plum	• Underwing with at most weak dark trailing edge (only small dark tips to outer prim) and slightly rufous ground-colour ⇔ other small falcons.
behav	• Pumps tail.

Red-footed Falcon *Falco vespertinus* — L 31cm 12", WS 70cm 27.5"

all plum	• Pale claws.
ad ♂	• Almost completely slaty-black with reddish vent and undertail-cov (at distance often looks wholly black). • Legs, bare skin around bill and orbital-ring red.
ad ♀	• Almost uniform orange underparts and crown. • Grey-blue upperparts darkly barred. • Small black mask.
ad ♀/imm	• Legs orange. • Contrasting, relatively small black mask.
juv ⇒	• Diffusely barred tertials and greater cov ⇔ in Hobby juv uniform dark. • Mantle with yellow-brown scaling. • Variable dark brown longitudinal streaks on underparts, on flanks often some barring ⇔ in Hobby juv black and usually more boldly streaked. • Vent pale cream-coloured and unstreaked ⇔ in Hobby juv darker and streaking extends to leg-feathering. • Black mask and pale brown crown; whitish forehead.
1s	• Mix of worn juv and fresh ad-type cov, mantle and scaps (in ♂ very conspicuous, in ♀ sometimes difficult to see). • Non-juv underparts; normally distinctly different from both juv and ad-type patterning. Often already ad-like but many 1s ♂ with variable amount of orange; 1s ♀ often weak white-orange with narrow teardrop-shaped longitudinal streaks; in summer becoming almost white.
fl all plum ⇒	• Except ad ♂, underwing with *strongly contrasting dark tip* ⇔ in Hobby less contrasting due to darker background of underwing. • Somewhat more bulging body compared to Hobby, especially head and breast. • Wings shorter and blunter, tail longer than in Hobby (young Hobby juv can approach structure).
fl ad ♂	• *Silvery-grey prim* contrast with dark cov and tail.
fl ad ♀ ⇒	• Almost uniform underparts and underwing-cov in combination with strongly barred flight-feathers ⇔ Hobby.
fl ad ♀/juv	• Dark trailing edge of underwing and wing-tip broader and more clear than in Hobby. Often also clear on upperwing ⇔ in Hobby all plum upperwing almost uniform.
flight juv ⇒	• Densely barred tail (see also 1s), *also distinct on upperside*. At distance uppertail paler than upperparts ⇔ Hobby.

Falcons

flight 1s	• White background of underside of flight-feathers forms contrast with buff ground-colour of underwing-cov ⇔ in Hobby juv buff ground-colour of both sec, prim and underwing-cov. • Wholly or partially still juv tail-feathers, prim and cov (in 1s ♀ new ad-type tail-feathers pale barring broader than dark barring; in juv tail-feathers pale barring narrower than, or as broad as dark barring). • Underwing-cov with dark streaks and bars ⇔ ad.
note	• For more field marks see Amur Falcon.

Amur Falcon *Falco amurensis* L 31cm 12", WS 70cm 27.5"

all plum ad ♂	• Size and structure as Red-footed Falcon. • Underparts paler than in Red-footed; head not entirely black; mask with black crown and faint malar stripe shining through. • Upperside of tail concolorous with upperparts ⇔ in Red-footed ♂ upperside of tail darker than upperparts.
ad ♀	• Hobby-like head-pattern but *crown greyer*. • Underparts white with rather bold black spotting, *on flanks turning into barring*; trousers often cream-coloured ⇔ in very pale Red-footed 1s ♀ only longitudinal stripes. • Upperparts slaty-grey with black barring. • Head not clearly paler than upperparts ⇔ Red-footed ad ♀.
1s	• Mix of worn juv and fresh ad-type cov, mantle and scaps (in ♂ very conspicuous, in ♀ sometimes difficult to see).
1s ♂	• Newly moulted ad-type t1 pale grey ⇔ in Red-footed normally very dark or black. • Underparts pale grey ⇔ in Red-footed 1s ♂ normally darker. • Often *rather broad blackish* streaks on breast ⇔ in Red-footed 1s ♂ underparts usually more uniform (often with orange spots), when streaks present then browner and fainter with some fine shaft-streaks. • 2nd generation tail-feathers often with dark subterminal bar ⇔ older generations (as in Red-footed).
1s ♀	• Largely like ad ♀ (see 1s) but flanks with teardrop-like longitudinal stripes.
juv	• Underparts, especially flanks, broadly and barred blackish (can resemble Merlin ♀/imm ⇔ in Red-footed juv with brownish patterns). • Dark grey crown (forehead sometimes conspicuously white) and colder-toned upperparts (more resembling Hobby) than in Red-footed. Mask with more pointed 'malar stripe' than in Red-footed juv. • Upperparts with blue-grey wash and with grey or whitish feather fringes ⇔ in Red-footed normally more brown wash. • Greater cov more uniform than in Red-footed juv, without obvious barring and pale edges.
fl ad ♂ ⇒	• White axillaries and underwing-cov (in Red-footed 1s ♂ sometimes whitish marginal cov (leading edge of wing).
fl ad ♀ ⇒	• Underside with white background except cream-coloured vent and undertail-cov ⇔ Red-footed. • Underwing-cov pale, thinly patterned (ghosting ad ♂). • Strongly resembles Red-footed juv but streaks on underparts bolder, turning into barring on flanks (patterning on underparts resembles Merlin ♀/imm).
fl 1s ♂	• Underwing-cov pure black-and-white patterned ⇔ in Red-footed 1s ♂ dark barring dark brown with often some red-brown and/or dark grey feathers.
fl juv/♀	• Broader dark trailing edge along wing than Red-footed juv/♀.
fl juv	• Underwing-cov with black markings on white background ⇔ in Red-footed buff ground-colour of underwing-cov.

Merlin *Falco columbarius* L 29cm 11.5", WS 62cm 24.5"

geog var	*F.c. aesalon* (northern mainland Europe)
all plum	• Rather weak head-pattern with diffuse malar stripe, dark ear-coverts and narrow but almost always prominent supercilium. • Rather long tail projects beyond wing-tips.
ad	• Narrow rufous collar.
ad ♂	• Uniform grey-blue upperparts. • Orange-brown underparts with fine black longitudinal streaks.
ad ♀	• Grey wash over upperparts ⇔ in most juv, especially ♀ more brown with very little grey wash. • Scaps and cov barred ⇔ in juv no or hardly any barring.
ad ♀/juv ⇒	• Tail with broad barring, also visible on upperside (only 5 dark tail-bands).
⇒	• Flanks darker than breast (especially visible in flight) ⇔ other small falcons. • Strongly patterned underparts, breast streaking running into broad barring, especially on flanks.
juv	• (Restricted) pale patterning on upperparts, creating no obvious barring (scaps with rounded spot on both sides of shaft) ⇔ in ad ♀ more or less complete pale band over feathers of upperparts. • Often rufous wash over whole plumage.
1s	• See Common Kestrel 1s.
fl all plum ⇒	• Wing-formula: *short p10* shorter than p7 ⇔ in all other falcons p10 longer. • Conspicuous *spotted hand* due to pale spots extending up onto outer web of prim. Broad terminal tail-band (see geog var *columbarius*).
fl ad ♂	• Very broad terminal tail-band. • Contrast between dark upperside of hand and paler rest of upperwing.
geog var	Taiga Merlin *F.c. columbarius* (North America)
all plum	• Upperparts darker than *aesalon*, also ad ♀/juv (almost) uniform dark.
ad ♂ ⇒	• Mainly as *aesalon* (underparts, especially flanks more strongly marked) but tail with broad dark subterminal band and 2 broad dark central bands (dark bars broader than pale ones); tail-tip conspicuously white ⇔ in *aesalon* at most narrow dark central tail-bands (dark bars narrower than pale ones); tail-tip pale but not conspicuous.
ad ♀/juv ⇒	• Dark tail with only 3 narrow whitish bands (dark bands about 3x broader) ⇔ in *aesalon* 4-5 broader, more buff bands (dark bands about 2x broader).

fl all plum	• Underwing darker than in *aesalon* with smaller pale spots on flight-feathers. Pale spots do not normally extend on to outer web of prim ⇔ *aesalon*.
note	• See *subaesalon*.
geog var	*F.c. subaesalon* (Iceland)
all plum	• Slightly darker and larger; juv/♀ usually with narrower pale tail-bands (darker tail) than *aesalon*. British population intermediate.
geog var	**Pallid Merlin** *F.c. pallidus* (western and central Asia)
all plum	• (Much) paler than *aesalon* with narrow shaft-streaks on underparts.
ad ♂	• 'Bleached' grey-blue tail with broad black terminal band, no narrow dark central tail-bands as often present in *aesalon*.
ad ♀/juv	• Broad pale tail-bands broader than dark ones (pale tail) ⇔ all other subspecies. • Slightly narrower, more rufous brown streaks on underparts than *aesalon* on whiter background. • Upperparts pale; pale brown and grey barred, contrasting with dark outer prim.
note geog var	• Most ind usually not possible to identify to subspecies level with certainty under field conditions (except *columbarius* and classic *pallidus*). Between *aesalon* and *pallidus* many intermediates, moreover Siberian subspecies *insignus* or intergrades between *insignus* and *aesalon* could possibly occur in WP which are paler than *aesalon* but darker than *pallidus*.

Hobby *Falco subbuteo*   L 32cm 12.5", WS 77cm 30.5"

all plum	• White throat and ear-coverts contrast strongly with dark, heavily streaked underparts and black mask. • Pale wedge on sides of head extending to behind ear-coverts towards rear-crown and dark mask ending in pointed wedge on white cheek (as in Red-footed Falcon juv, Amur Falcon juv/ad ♀ and Sooty Falcon juv) ⇔ all other falcons.
ad ⇒	• *Red-brown undertail-cov and vent*; white background of remainder of underparts.
juv	• Underparts with buff ground-colour. • Pale spots on hind-neck. • Pale tips to tail-feathers and flight-feathers (flight) ⇔ ad.
1s	• Moult-limit between fresh ad-type mantle and scaps and juv cov. • Central tail-feathers moulted, rest juv. Prim and sec completely or largely juv (wing moult starts in 2cy autumn).
fl all plum	• Dark uniform upperside with blackish hand. • Closed tail (upperside) appears uniformly dark (only inner webs clearly barred); t1-pair unbarred.
fl ad	• Dark underwing (darker than in juv). • Rather evenly patterned underwing and tail-feathers ⇔ juv.
fl juv	• Dense, well-defined and evenly patterned underwing and underside of tail without obvious contrast; underwing with *buff ground-colour* ⇔ Red-footed juv.
note	• For more field marks see Eleonora's Falcon.

Eleonora's Falcon *Falco eleonorae*   L 39cm 15.5", WS 96cm 37.5"

all plum	• In pale morph all plum and most dark morph juv-1s *white ear-coverts with rounded border and black mask* (as in large falcons with mask), white not extending to hind-neck ⇔ in Hobby, Red-footed Falcon juv, Amur Falcon juv/ad ♀ and Sooty Falcon juv mask with dark wedge on cheek and white extending to hind-neck. Some ind with small white 'hook' into black of nape-side giving a head-pattern closer to Hobby. • Relatively heavy bill; grey with dark tip ⇔ in Hobby ad wholly dark (in juv often with paler base). • When perched wing-tips fall level with tail ⇔ in Hobby usually some wing-projection. • Usually slightly protruding central tail-feathers (as in Sooty).
ad ⇒	• Pale morph: orange base colour underparts (upper-breast and throat whitish) with dark longitudinal streaks. • Dark morph: wholly black (older ind dark brown) without any contrast (see flight). • Pale morph ♂ often with dark centre to longest undertail-cov ⇔ in Hobby unmarked.
ad ♂	• Yellow orbital-ring and bare skin around bill-base. • Sooty-black upperparts and upperwing.
ad ♀	• Grey orbital-ring and bare skin around bill-base (in older ad ♀ slightly yellowish but not bright yellow as in ad ♂). • Brown-black upperparts and upperwing.
juv	• Underparts heavily streaked (heaviest in dark morph), becoming chequered along flanks. • Upperside strongly scaled (pale tips to e.g. scaps and mantle feathers). • Hind-neck uniform ⇔ in Hobby and Red-footed pale patterning on hind-neck.
juv-1s	• Tertials (and often also rear scaps) with pale barring or notched ⇔ in Hobby and Sooty only pale fringes (in 1s uniform by wear). • Undertail-cov barred (from 1s only in ♀) ⇔ in Hobby unmarked. • Uppertail nearly as in Hobby juv with barring restricted to inner web of tail-feathers. Barring finer and denser than in Hobby (closed tail looks uniformly dark) but with faint dark terminal band ⇔ Hobby juv. • Pale tips to tail-feathers and flight-feathers (flight) ⇔ ad. Pale tips to tail-feathers broader than in Hobby but in 1s lost by wear.
fl all plum	• Generally long-tailed and long-winged (in ♂ more pronounced than in ♀); imm not conspicuously long-tailed and long-winged, sometimes strongly resembling Hobby. • Conspicuously flexible wing-beats with up-stroke and down-stroke equally deep. Body moves up and down with wing-beats ⇔ in Hobby down-stroke deeper than up-stroke and body keeps still. • Head protrudes relatively far.
fl ad ⇒	• Pale morph: black underwing-cov contrast with *pale base of flight-feathers* (base of flight-feathers very faintly barred) ⇔ in Hobby all plum distinctly barred.

⇒	• Dark morph: uniform dark upperside; on underwing slight contrast between black underwing-cov and paler flight-feathers.
fl juv ⇒	• Broad dark trailing edge of underwing, more distinct than in Hobby and Peregrine Falcon juv.
	• Dark morph: *strongly patterned, dark underwing-cov contrasting with pale base of flight-feathers*; in pale morph juv almost no contrast on underwing with paler underwing-cov.
	• Almost uniform upperside but trailing edge of wing darker than rest of wing ⇔ Hobby.
	• Tail shorter than in ad ⇔ in all other falcons the other way around.
fl 1s	• Combination of juv wing (with broad dark trailing edge of underwing) and ad-like underparts and head but in dark morph underparts not yet black.
	• Old (juv) tail-feathers often with rufous wash.

Sooty Falcon *Falco concolor* L 35cm 14", WS 84cm 33"

all plum	• Yellow legs and bare skin around bill (juv develops yellow skin shortly after fledging).
	• Wings project beyond tail-tip ⇔ Eleonora's Falcon and Red-footed Falcon.
ad	• Rather dark (but variable) slaty-grey; hand gradually darker towards tip to almost black.
juv	• Resembles Hobby juv; often spotting becomes more dense on breast, creating faint breast-band.
	• Rather diffuse and rather heavily patterned underparts on buff ground-colour.
	• Head-pattern as Hobby all plum.
	• Slaty-grey upperparts ⇔ Hobby juv.
1s	• Moult-limit between fresh ad-type mantle and scaps and old juv cov.
	• Underparts not as uniform as in ad.
fl all plum	• Slightly protruding central tail-feathers (as in Eleonora's).
fl ad	• Dark grey upperside with dark tail and black hand (slight differences in dark shading only visible under good viewing conditions).
	• Underwing paler than body.
fl juv ⇒	• Barring on underside of flight-feathers and tail-feathers restricted to slightly more than basal half and *very broad dark trailing edge of underwing* and terminal tail-band.
⇒	• Dark underwing with only slightly paler underwing-cov and base of flight-feathers ⇔ Eleonora's.
	• Slight contrast between upperparts and upperwing.
	• Upperside of tail darker towards tip.

Lanner Falcon *Falco biarmicus* L 46cm 18", WS 100cm 39"

all plum	• Rather bold head-pattern with dark eye-stripe bordering complete ear-coverts and dark streak on forehead.
	• Tail projects very little or not at all beyond wing-tips ⇔ Saker Falcon.
	• Long, sharply demarcated, narrow malar stripe.
	• Variable rufous on rear crown.
ad ⇒	• Barred flanks and thighs (latter only faintly marked) ⇔ in Saker no obvious barring.
	• Obvious tail-bands on all tail-feathers (flight).
juv	• Concolorous with brown upperparts and upperwing.
	• Dark parts of head as dark as upperparts (eye difficult to see) ⇔ Saker juv.
	• Evenly patterned underparts ⇔ in Saker juv often heavier on rear-flanks.
imm	• Legs in autumn becoming already yellowish ⇔ in Saker still grey.
	• Undertail-cov uniform pale ⇔ Peregrine Falcon and Gyr Falcon.
	• Central tail-feathers with some pale spots but no distinct barring ⇔ ad
1s	• Moult-limit between fresh ad-type mantle and scaps and old juv cov.
	• Flight-feathers and tail-feathers still mainly juv.
fl all plum ⇒	• Pale vent, thighs and rear-flanks (at distance underparts appear two-toned; dark front-side, pale rear-side) ⇔ Saker.
	• Dark underwing-cov (especially in *feldeggii*) with pale spots or barring ⇔ in Saker pale longitudinal streaks.
	• Relatively dense, evenly and distinctly streaked upperside of tail ⇔ Saker, Barbary Falcon and Peregrine.
	• Large dark underwing-tip ⇔ Barbary and Peregrine.
	• Rather pointed hand ⇔ Saker.
	• Underwing-cov and underside of wing-tips dark, contrasting with paler flight-feathers (in most older *erlangeri* and *tanypterus* ad ♂ underwing-cov at most very slightly darker). Also in Saker and grey Gyr.
fl imm	• Uniform dark brown upperparts, without contrast between cov and prim (also useful when perched).

geog var	*F.b. feldeggii* (south-eastern Europe and Turkey)
ad ⇒	• Upperparts distinctly barred (sometimes barring absent).
	• Darkest form of Lanner.
	• Crown sometimes wholly dark chestnut.
fl all plum	• Broad dark band on underwing-cov.

geog var	*F.b. erlangeri* (north-west Africa)
ad	• Palest morph.
	• Upperparts uniform, unbarred; crown wholly pale buff.
	• Somewhat sandy-coloured tail (with black tail-bands), in other morph slaty-grey tail (concolorous with upperparts).
	• In ♂, especially older ind, sometimes very reduced patterning on underparts.
juv	• Strongly resembles Saker juv; focus on structure (tail projects beyond wing-tips in Saker ⇔ Lanner) and colour of vent and thighs (dark in Saker, pale in Lanner).
fl ad	• Sometimes almost uniform pale underwing, especially in older ♂.

geog var	*F.b. tanypterus* (north-east Africa and Middle East)
ad	• Much like cross between *feldeggii* and *erlangeri*, but closer to latter.
	• In ♂, especially older ind, sometimes very reduced pattering on underparts.
note	• When identifying large falcons one should be aware of possible hybrids. Hybridisation occurs especially in captivity, also with species from outside the WP, e.g. Prairie Falcon *F. mexicanus* which strongly resembles Saker. Hybrids could theoretically resemble all species.

Saker Falcon *Falco cherrug* L 51cm 20", WS 117cm 46"

all plum ⇒	• Feathers of upperparts with rufous fringes (in ad more faintly rufous than in juv) ⇔ Lanner Falcon.
	• Underparts usually heavily marked dark; dark markings more dense on thighs (usually distinctly darker than rest of underparts) ⇔ Lanner.
	• Longitudinal stripes (juv) or spots (ad) on underparts, no barring ⇔ in Lanner ad at least some barring on flanks and thighs.
	• Tail usually projects distinctly beyond wing-tips when perched, sometimes nearly as much as in Gyr Falcon (⇔ in Lanner tail projects only very little or not at all).
	• Distinct supercilium, extending to forehead.
	• Narrow, usually rather ill-defined malar stripe, usually not connecting eye, but in some ind more distinct.
	• Evenly streaked crown, without Lanner's characteristic dark stripe on forehead ⇔ in Lanner crown darker and hardly streaked.
	• Closed tail (upperside) often looks uniformly dark (mainly inner web patterned and central pair uniform).
	• Pale ear-coverts ⇔ grey Gyr.
ad	• Underparts dark spotted (⇔ in juv completely streaked), often less heavily marked than juv on breast, especially in older ind.
juv	• Underparts dark streaked, often bold (especially on rear-flanks) making underparts as a whole dark.
	• Dark parts of head paler than upperparts (eye conspicuous) ⇔ Lanner juv.
imm	• Legs grey ⇔ Lanner and Peregrine Falcon imm.
	• Undertail-cov unmarked ⇔ Peregrine and Gyr.
1s	• See Lanner 1s.
fl all plum ⇒	• Upperwing with contrast between brown cov and dark flight-feathers (resembles Common Kestrel).
	• Dark underwing-cov with pale streaks (in some dark ind almost uniform dark underwing-cov) ⇔ in Lanner (especially *feldeggii*) pale spots or barring.
	• Basal part of prim underside not or faintly barred ⇔ most Lanners.
	• Wing-tips slightly broader than in Lanner.
	• Pale barring on tail-feathers mainly on inner web, t1-pair unmarked.
fl juv	• t2-t6 variable but often with *circular pale spots* on inner web, not creating clear barring ⇔ Lanner ad and some juv.
note	• *F.c. 'saceroides'*-type occurs especially in European breeding populations; resembles Lanner or Gyr by having more greyish upperparts with somewhat barred mantle, cov, tail and flanks. Saker features of this type are structure (tail projects beyond wing-tips), rufous feather-fringes on upperparts and more streaked than barred underwing-cov. See also note in Lanner.

Gyr Falcon *Falco rusticolus* L 58cm 23", WS 121cm 47.5"

all plum	• When perched tail projects well beyond wing-tip (≥ 50% of prim-projection) ⇔ in Peregrine Falcon tail-projection c.10% of prim-projection.
	• Barred upperside of closed tail (in white morph; especially ad sometimes with unmarked white tail) ⇔ in Saker Falcon uniform central tail-feathers.
	• (Rather) weak malar stripe (usually lacking in white morph).
	• Rather dark, streaked ear-coverts (not in white morph). In juv sometimes whole head-side dark without obvious malar stripe.
ad ⇒	• Upperparts, cov and tertials grey, even and strongly barred ⇔ in Peregrine, Lanner Falcon ad *feldeggii* and *'saceroides'*-type of Saker barring less evenly spaced.
	• Flanks barred ⇔ in imm longitudinal streaks on underparts.
juv/imm	• Legs grey (as in Saker imm) ⇔ Peregrine and Lanner.
juv/imm grey morph	• *Pale oval mark on* dark flank- and thigh-feathers ⇔ in Saker uniform dark.
	• Pale speckles on mantle feathers, tertials and cov, not creating complete barring ⇔ ad.
	• Rather cold-brown upperparts ⇔ Saker juv.
	• Longitudinal streaks on underparts, *also on undertail-cov* ⇔ in Peregrine imm undertail-cov barred.
	• Rather dark ear-coverts (not in white morph).
juv/imm white morph	• Dark centres to mantle feathers, scaps, lesser cov and median cov with white fringes; larger feathers also with visible white base, creating mosaic pattern.
	• Underparts white with fine dark longitudinal streaks.
	• Tail with fine dark barring.
1s	• See Lanner 1s.
fl all plum	• Grey morph with distinct contrast between dark patterned underwing-cov (especially greater cov and median cov) and pale underside of flight-feathers (as in Saker and Lanner).
	• Broad, more or less rounded hand.
	• Pale bases on upperside of outer prim contrast with dark tips (very variable; frequently in paler ind, absent in dark juv).
fl ad	• Barred upperparts and tail (see ad).
fl juv ⇒	• Distinct and finely barred upperside of tail (at a distance upperside of tail appears slightly paler than upperparts).

Peregrine Falcon *Falco peregrinus* L 45cm 17.5", WS 102cm 40"

all plum ⇒	• Broad malar stripe usually strongly rounded on underside ⇔ other large falcons (except *madens* and Barbary Falcon).

81

ad ♂	• Finely barred underparts, upper-breast sometimes nearly unmarked.
ad ♀	• Rather bold barred underparts (♀ obviously larger than ♂).
juv ⇒	• Flanks with *triangular spots*; middle of underparts paler and only longitudinally streaked ⇔ Saker Falcon and Lanner Falcon.
⇒	• Barred undertail-cov (also in grey Gyr Falcon ad, sometimes also in dark Eleonora's Falcon juv-1s) ⇔ in other large falcons juv undertail-cov streaked (Gyr juv) or unmarked (Lanner and Saker).
imm	• Legs grey-yellow to green-yellow ⇔ in other large falcons imm legs up to 1s grey except Lanner.
1s	• See Lanner 1s.
fl all plum ⇒	• Rump and uppertail-cov palest part of upperside (as in Barbary).
	• Underwing evenly patterned (underwing-cov barred) without contrast between underwing-cov and flight-feathers (underside of flight-feathers evenly barred) ⇔ in Saker and Lanner e.g. underwing-cov distinctly darker than flight-feathers (underside of flight-feathers only faintly barred at base).
	• Dark tail-bands broader towards tip of tail (as in Barbary).

geog var	Tundra Peregrine Falcon *F.p. calidus* (arctic Siberia)
all plum	• Paler than *peregrinus* with longer wings and tail.
	• Generally obviously larger than *peregrinus* from western and central European populations, but size similar to *peregrinus* from north-eastern European and Siberian populations. These ind also paler than European ind.
ad	• Upperparts paler grey and underparts almost unmarked (looks uniform at distance) but large clinal area, only ind from heart of range recognisable.
	• Ad moults only small part of inner prim after breeding. Complete moult in winter range with last prim in Jan ⇔ *peregrinus* moults all prim after breeding.
juv	• Pale (fore)crown and head-side.
	• Paler more brown-grey upperparts than *peregrinus* with more obvious pale fringes on feathers on upperparts, resembling Saker but fringes not rufous.
	• Malar stripe relatively narrow and relatively large, uniform pale cheek.
	• Differs from both Lanner and Saker by patterning of underparts (narrow rufous-brown longitudinal stripes, flanks with small triangular spots, see also juv in main text of Peregrine Falcon).
	• Differs from Lanner e.g. by absence of dark forehead-stripe and from Saker by short tail-projection.
	• Undertail-cov narrowly barred to almost unmarked ⇔ in *peregrinus* broadly barred; in Lanner and Saker unmarked pale.
fl ad	• Dark top of hand contrasts strongly with pale remainder of plumage.
fl juv	• No obvious contrast between underwing-cov and basal part of flight-feathers ⇔ in Lanner and Saker strong contrast.

geog var	*F.p. tundrinus* (arctic North America and Greenland)
all plum	• Very similar to *calidus* incl moult; ind outside normal range not identifiable with certainty.
	• Generally smaller than *calidus*.
ad	• Underparts often warmer coloured and dark parts of head blacker, more obviously contrasting with mantle than in *calidus*.
juv	• Often more warm coloured overall than *calidus*.

geog var	Mediterranean Peregrine Falcon *F.p. brookei* (e.g. Middle East)
all plum	• Smaller size with very dark head (also cheek largely dark).
	• Breast with rufous ground-colour.
juv	• Very boldly patterned underparts ⇔ Barbary juv.

Cape Verde Falcon *Falco madens*   L 47cm 18.5", WS 112cm 44"

all plum	• Underparts with buff ground-colour.
ad ⇒	• Crown, nape and mantle with brown to rufous patterning or wash (only 'peregrine' with rufous-brown upperparts and wash on dark parts of head).
	• Underparts with buff ground-colour.
	• Ad ♀ browner overall than ad ♂, less rufous.
	• Extensive dark hood covering whole cheek.
	• Rufous tones in plumage similar to Barbary Falcon but much larger size.

Barbary Falcon *Falco pelegrinoides*   L 37cm 14.5", WS 87cm34"

all plum	• Resembles in most respects Peregrine Falcon.
ad ⇒	• Rufous rear-crown and large, rufous, uniform nape-patch, sometimes extending to ear-coverts. Especially in western part of range (Morocco) much less distinct, where some ind appear intermediate between Barbary and Peregrine.
	• Underparts finely barred on rufous ground-colour.
	• Upperparts paler than Peregrine (much paler than subspecies of Peregrine *brookei* which overlaps in range).
juv	• Less and thinner longitudinal streaks on underparts than Peregrine.
	• Brown-yellow wash on underparts.
	• Directly after fledging grey bare skin around bill starts becoming yellow ⇔ Peregrine *brookei*.
	• Combination of yellow eye-ring/bare skin around bill and longitudinal stripes on underparts ⇔ Peregrine imm.
	• Large, pale and unstreaked ear-coverts.
	• Supercilium becomes more obvious towards hind-neck, head-pattern resembles Lanner Falcon but malar stripe much broader.
1s	• See Lanner 1s.

fl ad	• Dark tail-bands becoming broader towards tail-tip; rump and base of tail paler than distal part of tail ⇔ Lanner.
	• Pale underparts and underwing with small dark 'comma' on carpal joints ⇔ in Peregrine no or very faint comma.
	• Rufous wash on underwing-cov ⇔ Peregrine.
fl juv	• Rufous underwing-cov creating 2-toned underwing.

Rails

Water Rail *Rallus aquaticus* L 24cm 9.5"

all plum	• Legs flesh-coloured.
ad ⇒	• *Long* slightly down-curved, mainly red bill with dark culmen and tip.
	• Black and white barred flanks and vent; undertail-cov uniform buff.
	• Blue-grey head-side and central part of breast and belly.
juv	• Boldly patterned head with supercilium, eye-stripe and dark crown.
	• Barring on flanks extends on to breast-sides.
	• Sometimes shorter bill than ad.
1w	• Cream-coloured supercilium.
	• Whitish throat.
1s	• Like ad but underparts with variable amount of brown feathers and fresh blue-grey feathers with white fringes.
	• Wings still juv and more worn than in ad.

Spotted Crake *Porzana porzana* L 21cm 8.5"

all plum	• Underparts strongly white barred and spotted (especially breast).
	• Narrow *pale bars across tertials*.
	• Undertail-cov uniform buff (vent and flanks barred) ⇔ Little Crake and Baillon's Crake.
	• Feathers of upperparts with black centres and white fringes on outer-web (creating evenly streaked upperparts) ⇔ other rails and crakes except Sora.
juv-1w	• Dull coloured bill ⇔ ad (in ad w also less bright coloured bill with dark tip).
	• Breast brown ⇔ in ad w brown-grey.
	• Vent and rear-flanks spotted ⇔ ad.
	• In 1w mixture of juv- and ad-type body-feathers (juv-type brown with pale tips; ad-type brown with well-defined white bar).
	• No moult-limit in scaps or tertials ⇔ in ad in autumn often mix of old and new feathers, most obvious on scaps and tertials.
	• Ear-coverts nearly uniform brown ⇔ in ad w brown-grey.
	• Pale throat ⇔ in ad w usually greyish.

Sora *Porzana carolina* L 20cm 8"

all plum ⇒	• Yellow bill.
⇒	• *Uniform black tertial-centres* ⇔ in Spotted Crake pale cross-bars.
	• No pale speckles on head and breast ⇔ Spotted.
	• Upperparts as in Spotted.
	• Undertail-cov and central part of vent uniform whitish, paler and more distinct than in Spotted.
	• Brown crown with black median crown-stripe.
	• Deep bill-base (higher than in Spotted).
ad ⇒	• Black face and black stripe over central part of throat and breast.
juv ⇒	• Breast *uniform yellow-brown*.
1w	• After post-juv moult nearly as ad but black of face less deep and hardly extending towards throat.
1s	• Tertials and greater cov often still (partial), creating moult-limit against fresh scaps and median cov.
	• Wings still juv and more worn than in ad.

Little Crake *Porzana parva* L 18cm 7.1"

all plum ⇒	• *Long prim-projection* c.75-100% with at least 5 prim-tips beyond tertials ⇔ Baillon's Crake.
ad ⇒	• Green-yellow bill with *red base* (red base sometimes difficult to see and sometimes nearly absent in imm).
	• Brown upperparts, paler brown than in Baillon's.
	• Pale patterning on mantle and scaps not all dark encircled ⇔ Baillon's.
	• Pale inner webs of tertials, together with pale stripes on upperparts, often creates continuous pale line ⇔ in Baillon's less contrasting.
	• Legs greenish.
	• Rather long pointed tail ⇔ in Baillon's shorter and blunter.
ad	• Only undertail-cov and vent barred, barring not reaching behind legs ⇔ Baillon's.
ad ♂	• Deep grey-blue underparts and head.
ad ♀ ⇒	• Underparts salmon-coloured, belly often paler.
	• Dull blue supercilium.
juv	• Largely barred underparts but breast and central part of belly often unmarked ⇔ in Baillon's juv underparts strongly patterned.
	• Dark eye often conspicuous against often very pale head-side.
	• Blackish middle-crown ⇔ in Baillon's juv crown mainly brown.
	• Dark spot on ear-coverts ⇔ in Baillon's juv ear-coverts with only diffuse darker area.
	• Yellow-greenish bill, sometimes already with characteristic red base.
1s	• Wings often still juv and more worn than in ad.

Baillon's Crake *Porzana pusilla*   L 17cm 6.7"

all plum	⇒	• Short prim-projection c.30% with very short spacings between prim-tips ⇔ Little Crake. • White patterning on mantle, scaps and cov surrounded by black ⇔ in Little ad mainly unbordered white patterning and white restricted to mantle and scaps. • Cov with white spots ⇔ in Little (almost) none. • Upperparts dark brown. • Legs vary from green, pale brown to dark grey.
ad/1s	⇒	• Barring on undertail-cov extending on to belly, behind legs ⇔ Little ad. • Greenish bill (without red bill-base). • Blue-grey underparts, usually darker than in Little ad. • Deep rufous-brown upperparts. • Black streaked crown on red-brown ground-colour.
♀		• Strongly resembles and sometimes indistinguishable from ♂ (⇔ Little), but with slightly paler grey underparts and often slightly paler throat. Possibly more often isolated brown patch on ear-coverts and crown only indistinctly streaked.
juv		• Barred undertail-cov and flanks to breast-sides. • Dull green bill. • Faint supercilium.
1s		• Wings still juv and more worn than in ad.
geog var		*P.p. pusilla* (southern Russia to eastern Asia)
all plum		• Broad brown eye-stripe connected to brown of upperparts (in European race *intermedia*, possibly especially ♀, sometimes with isolated brown patch on ear-coverts). • Underparts less deep blue, more (dark) grey. ♂ with paler throat (like *intermedia* ♀) and ♀ (much) paler on underparts than *intermedia* ♂. • Upperparts slightly paler brown.
juv		• Underparts often conspicuously pale with only weak barring on flanks (as a whole more similar to Little juv).

Striped Crake *Aenigmatolimnas marginalis*   L 20cm 8"

all plum	• Relatively thick bill and extremely long toes.
ad	• Upperparts and wings finely pale streaked.
ad ♂	• Rufous flanks, vent and undertail-cov without obvious barring.
ad ♀	• Underparts mainly greyish ⇔ ad ♂.
imm	• Upperparts and breast uniform brown; throat, belly and undertail-cov white.

Corncrake *Crex crex*   L 24cm 9.5"

all plum		• Barred flanks, vent and undertail-cov (in juv diffuse).
ad		• Dark centres to all feathers of upperparts creating bold dark bars on upperparts (centres of rear-most scaps and tertials especially conspicuous). • Blue-grey supercilium and often throat.
juv		• Supercilium pale brown. • Centres of scaps and tertials less black and more diffusely bordered by pale fringe than in ad.
fl all plum	⇒	• Almost *uniform red-brown* upperwing, brightest on cov (also often visible when perched). • Long, thick neck stretches far out. • Legs pale; legs project beyond tail.

African Crake *Crecopsis egregia*   L 22cm 8.5"

all plum	• Pale supercilium. • Size and structure similar to Spotted Crake but tail shorter (projects at most slightly beyond wing-tips). • Upperparts brown with black centres to all feathers (as in Corncrake); no white patterning on upperparts. • Belly up to undertail-cov boldly barred.
ad	• Red bill-base, eye-ring and iris. • Grey breast sharply demarcated from barred belly. • Dark crown forms capped appearance.
juv	• Brown breast ill-defined with barred belly ⇔ ad. • Bill and eye dark ⇔ ad.

Common Moorhen *Gallinula chloropus*   L 29cm 11.5"

all plum	• White undertail-cov with black central stripe. • White broken flank-streak.
ad	• Red shield and bill with yellow tip.
juv	• Grey-brown (upperparts darker than underparts) with whitish throat and middle of breast.
1w	• Brown wash on underparts and head. • Dull coloured bill and shield.
1s	• In northern and central Europe most ind still with brown wash on breast, short narrow flank-streak, often central part of underparts and throat whitish and variable amount of old bleached and worn feathers. In southern Europe usually as ad.

Lesser Moorhen *Gallinula angulata*   L 24cm 9.5"

all plum	• Resembles Common Moorhen but considerably smaller size.
ad	• Plumage as Common but *wholly yellow bill* with only small, pointed shield.

| imm | • Legs slightly more yellow than in Common and no red on tibia ⇔ Common.
• Dull yellow bill ⇔ in Common imm dark.
• Underparts pale with warm yellow-brown breast. |

Allen's Gallinule *Porphyrio alleni* L 27cm 10.5"

all plum	⇒	• Legs red(dish).
	⇒	• Blue-green outer webs to flight-feathers.
		• Heavy, triangular bill.
ad	⇒	• Black stripe over centre of white undertail-cov (as in Common Moorhen) ⇔ American Purple Gallinule.
		• Red bill.
		• Glossy green upperparts.
		• Deep purple-blue underparts.
juv	⇒	• Mantle feathers, scaps, tertials and cov dark with broad pale fringes, creating boldly scaled upperside.
		• Dark bill.
		• Head and underparts uniform pale yellow-brown.
		• Legs dull red.

American Purple Gallinule *Porphyrio martinica* L 33cm 13"

all plum	⇒	• Legs long and yellow.
		• Uniform white undertail-cov and vent.
ad	⇒	• Red bill with yellow tip and light blue shield.
		• Deep purple-blue underparts.
		• Almost uniform green upperparts.
1w		• Brown neck, becoming purple-blue.
		• Green wash on brownish upperparts.
		• Dark bill; colours of ad gradually coming through.

Western Swamp-hen *Porphyrio porphyrio* L 47cm 18.5"

all plum	⇒	• Very large size, similar to Black Grouse.
		• Legs red.
		• Heavy red or reddish bill with large shield.
		• Uniform, white undertail-cov.
ad	⇒	• Deep purple-blue upperparts and underparts *without green*.
juv		• More faintly coloured than ad.
		• Black patterning on bill.

African Swamp-hen *Porphyrio madagascariensis* L 47cm 18.5"

| all plum | | • See Western Swamp-hen all plum. |
| ad | ⇒ | • *Green mantle*, back, scaps and tertials contrasting with blue underparts and wings. |

Grey-headed Swamp-hen *Porphyrio poliocephalus* L 43cm 17"

all plum		• See Western Swamp-hen all plum.
ad	⇒	• Greyish head (imm with only grey wash on head), sometimes only grey on forehead.
		• Pale blue breast and green-blue cov and tertials contrasting with purple-blue belly and upperparts.
		• Scaps and wings almost concolorous ⇔ African Swamp-hen.
note		• Ind with black- or bronze-coloured upperparts belong to (sub)species from Southern Hemisphere.

geog var		*P.p. caspius* (Turkey and around Caspian Sea)
ad		• Usually distinct grey head.
note		• This subspecies sometimes lumped with *seistanicus*.

| geog var | | *P.p. seistanicus* (western Asia) |
| all plum | | • Like *caspius* but smaller and less often with obvious grey head. |

Common Coot *Fulica atra* L 39cm 15.5"

ad		• Completely sooty black plumage except for narrow pale trailing edge to sec.
		• White bill and shield, with sharp wedge of black feathers between the two.
		• Legs greenish with lobes on front toes.
juv		• Whitish spot on lores and diffuse pale underparts and front-side of neck.
1w		• As ad but dark subterminal spot on bill.
1s		• Tarsus grey-yellow ⇔ in ad bright yellow, orange or reddish.
fl all plum		• Pale trailing edge to sec.

American Coot *Fulica americana* L 39cm 15.5"

ad	⇒	• *White outer-edge of undertail-cov* creating white streak along tail-sides (sometimes surprisingly difficult to see).
	⇒	• Bill has almost straight, vertical border with head, no protruding feathering on lores ⇔ Common Coot and Red-knobbed Coot.
		• Small *dark red spot* on upperside of shield (shield smaller than in Common and Red-knobbed).
		• Dark subterminal spot on bill.
		• Some contrast between black head and neck and slightly paler flanks ⇔ in Common no contrast.
juv		• As Common juv but very diffusely patterned head; throat and front-side of breast greyish ⇔ in

1w	Common juv bold head-pattern.
	• As ad but in autumn dull red shield still lacking.
	• Underparts greyish ⇔ in ad darker.
fl all plum	• Pale trailing edge along arm as in Common.
note	• Hybrid Common Moorhen x Common Coot can sometimes resemble American Coot due to white on undertail-cov and usually absence of pale flank stripe. Structure and size usually more like Common Coot than Common Moorhen but with yellow to orange bill and brown wash on upperparts.

Red-knobbed Coot *Fulica cristata*   L 41cm 16"

all plum ⇒	• Lore ends blunt-tipped on bill (no sharp black wedge as in Common Coot).
	• Bill-tip ill-defined pale blue.
	• Triangular head-profile with pointed head (in Common flatter crown).
	• Highest part of back often lies behind middle of body.
ad s	• Dark red knobs on upperside of shield (in ad w often hardly visible).
1w	• Lacks knobs; shield narrower than in ad.
fl all plum	• No pale trailing edge to sec ⇔ Common.

Cranes

Common Crane *Grus grus*   L 107cm 42"

all plum	• Bill length ≥ head length (but see juv-1w) ⇔ Demoiselle Crane.
	• Complete or partially pale bill.
	• Dark tips to greater cov, usually some median cov and tertials ⇔ Demoiselle.
ad	• Tertials hang down to (almost) vertical.
	• Red patch on crown.
ad s	• Brownish wash over upperparts.
ad w	• Upperparts mainly grey.
juv-1w	• No black on neck and brownish head.
	• Tertials shorter and hang down less far than in ad.
	• Brown tips to cov.
	• Often shorter bill than ad.
1s	• Black on neck developing, rather diffusely, not sharply defined.
	• Grey upperparts ⇔ in ad s brownish.
	• Tertials as juv-1w, sometimes somewhat longer.
	• New cov with black marks (sometimes mix of juv and 2nd generation cov and tertials); multiple rows of cov with dark tips ⇔ ad.
2w	• As ad but multiple rows of cov with dark tips and sometimes still some old brown cov and tertials.
	• Tertials often slightly shorter than in ad but obviously longer than in 1s.
	• Bill not yet completely pale.
fl all plum	• White spot on prim-cov contrasts with dark rest of hand ⇔ Demoiselle.
	• Marked contrast between pale cov and black flight-feathers ⇔ in Demoiselle more diffusely bordered.

Sandhill Crane *Grus canadensis*   L 92cm 36"

ad ⇒	• Mainly grey with in summer brown on underparts and mantle; some cov with brown centres.
	• Red fore-crown ⇔ in juv-1s still greyish.
juv	• Large rufous spots on mantle, scaps, tertials and cov.
	• Rufous head as in Common Crane.
1s	• Part of brown juv plumage retained, often creating messy pattern on body and cov.
	• Crown and forehead almost bare but not yet red as in ad.
fl all plum	• Pale base to flight-feathers creating pale band, especially in southern populations.
	• Faint contrast between cov and flight-feathers and narrow dark trailing edge along whole wing.

Siberian Crane *Grus leucogeranus*   L 130cm 51"

ad	• White plumage except black hand (prim-cov white).
(sub)ad	• Red (bare) face and dark red bill.
	• Legs reddish.
juv	• Head, hind-neck and upperparts cream-brown; cov with cream-brown centre.
1s-2w	• Variable amount of cream-brown on neck and upperside (bare parts as in ad).
note	• No recent sightings in WP.

Demoiselle Crane *Grus virgo*   L 95cm 37.5"

all plum ⇒	• Short bill, Bill length ⇔ head length.
ad	• Black of neck extends to centre of breast ⇔ Common Crane.
	• Tertials only slightly curved (less strongly curved than in Common).
	• Uniform pale grey upperside ⇔ in Common ad s darker upperside, often patchy and with brownish wash (Common ad w normally paler grey on upperside).
juv-1w	• Dark parts of head greyish, not black as in ad.
	• Tertials shorter than in ad and almost straight ⇔ Common all plum.
	• Lacks white ear-tufts.
fl all plum	• Contrast between dark hand and pale cov less marked than in Common.
	• Hand shorter than in Common.
fl ad	• Elongated breast-feathers often hang down in point.

Bustards and buttonquails

Little Bustard *Tetrax tetrax*
L 43cm 17"

all plum	• By far smallest bustard, only slightly larger than Common Coot.
	• Rather short bill.
ad ♂	• p7 conspicuously short.
	• In winter as ♀ with slightly less dense patterning on underparts.
ad ♂ s	• Black-and-white neck and breast. Face grey-blue.
ad ♀	• Fine and sharply patterned upperparts and breast.
juv-1s	• Greater cov and median cov with yellow-brown ground-colour and fine dark barring ⇔ in ad greater cov almost wholly white.
	• Tail-feathers narrow and pointed; without obvious white tips ⇔ ad.
	• ♂ develops no black on neck in 1s.
fl all plu ⇒	• White flight-feathers with large black tips to outer 4 prim and small tips to other prim.
	• Black prim-cov creating dark crescent on upperwing.
fl juv-1s	• Outer prim short, narrow and pointed and diffusely barred to tip.

Denham's Bustard *Neotis denhami*
L 80cm 31.5"

all plum ⇒	• White tips to cov (large on inner median cov and greater cov) creating multiple wing-bars, varying in width (in juv less distinct).
	• *Rufous hind-neck*, extending towards breast-sides (in juv less distinct).
	• Black lateral crown-stripe and eye-stripe; white supercilium.
	• Uniform, dark brown upperparts.
fl all plum ⇒	• Boldly patterned upperwing with multiple wing-bars, varying in width, and white prim-base.

Nubian Bustard *Neotis nuba*
L 60cm 23.5"

all plum	• Rufous upperparts with diffuse dark spots.
	• Black throat patch and broad black lateral crown-stripe.
	• Deep rufous breast-sides.
	• Grey neck.
	• Whitish head-side.
fl all plum ⇒	• Rufous cov contrast with black sec and white base of prim.

Macqueen's Bustard *Chlamydotis macqueenii*
L 60cm 23.5"

ad ⇒	• Black patterning on (rear-side) of crown centre ⇔ in Houbara Bustard no patterning.
	• Tail narrow and diffusely barred ⇔ in Houbara broader, darker barring.
	• Upperparts sandy-coloured (usually without rufous-brown wash as in Houbara).
	• Dark patterning on upperside 'V'-shaped without patterning in between (creating separated spots) ⇔ Houbara. Cov with isolated dark spots.
	• Black, vertical stripe on breast interrupted by white ⇔ Houbara.
fl all plum	• See Houbara.
fl juv-1s	• See Houbara.

Houbara Bustard *Chlamydotis undulata*
L 60cm 23.5"

all plum	• Relatively pale warm sandy-brown upperparts ⇔ in Macqueen's Bustard upperparts more grey sandy-brown.
ad ⇒	• Uniform pale crown ⇔ Macqueen's.
⇒	• Rather bold and well-marked upperparts (creating barring) *with vermiculations in between* ⇔ Macqueen's.
	• Tail broadly dark barred ⇔ Macqueen's.
	• Cov without obvious isolated dark spots but with dense vermiculations ⇔ Macqueen's.
fl all plum ⇒	• Black hand with large white spot on basal part of outer prim.
fl juv-1s	• Outer prim short, narrow and pointed with diffusely pale patterning in tip.
geog var	*C.u. fuertaventurae* (Fuerteventura and Lanzarote)
ad	• Like *undulata* but upperside (also cov) darker with bolder dark patterning.
	• Tail-barring more distinct than in *undulata*.
	• Crown-sides often darker (creating dark lateral crown-stripe).

Arabian Bustard *Ardeotis arabs*
L 80cm 31.5"

all plum	• Grey neck with very fine dark barring (at distance neck looks uniform grey).
	• Black lateral crown-stripe extending to rear-head creating short crest; white supercilium.
	• Pale tips to cov, larger on median cov and greater cov.
	• Brown upperparts.
fl all plum	• Sec and inner prim finely barred white, creating numerous narrow wing-bars.

Great Bustard *Otis tarda*
L ad ♂ 97cm 38", ad ♀ 80cm 31.5"

ad ♂ s	• Long white 'moustache' (absent in winter).
	• Rufous-brown neck/breast-band (in w rufous-brown restricted to neck-side). Width of band grows with age (at maximum width from 6cy).
ad ♂	• Grey-blue head and upper part of neck; neck thick, especially in s.
	• Broad white band over median cov and greater cov ⇔ ♀.
imm ♂	• Resembles ad ♀ (size between ad ♂ and ♀) but developing rufous-brown neck/breast-band and sometimes short white 'moustache'; some younger ind in w difficult to distinguish from ad ♀ when

♀	size comparison not possible. • Obviously smaller than ad ♂ in direct comparison with narrower neck. • White in wing almost restricted to greater cov, pale band over cov usually hardly visible when perched (also in young imm ♂). • Head and neck with grey-blue wash; in s neck often with rufous wash but no complete rufous-brown breast-band.
fl all plum ⇒	• Contrasting pale band over middle of wing (greater cov and median cov), in ♀ and ♂ imm only on greater cov, pale band narrower than in ad ♂. • Black sec; prim with diffuse grey base. • Deep chest.
flight juv-1s	• Outer prim short, narrow and pointed.

Small Buttonquail *Turnix sylvaticus* L 16cm 6.3"

all plum ad ⇒	• Lacks hind-toe. • Rows of dark spots on flanks. • Orange breast, white throat (♀ more brightly coloured and patterned than ♂). • Pale fringes to mantle-feathers and scaps.
fl all plum	• Dark flight-feathers contrast with pale cov.

Painted-snipes, oystercatchers, stilts, crab-plover and thick-knees

Greater Painted-snipe *Rostratula benghalensis* L 24cm 9.5"

all plum	• Large eye surrounded by pale mask. • Dark upperparts and breast, sharply demarcated from white underparts. • Pale shoulder-stripe extending over breast-sides towards underparts. • Bill decurved. • Pale median crown-stripe.
ad ♂/juv	• Pale patterning in centre of cov ⇔ ad ♀.
ad ♀ ⇒	• Red-brown neck ⇔ in ad ♂ dark brown (ad ♀ much deeper coloured than ad ♂, as in phalaropes and Dotterel). • Cov almost uniformly dark.
juv	• As ad ♂ but breast paler and not sharply demarcated from white underparts.
fl all plum	• Rail-like with legs projecting beyond tail and broad wings. • Flight-feathers barred pale.

Oystercatcher *Haematopus ostralegus* L 42cm 16.5"

ad w/imm juv-1w	• White stripe across throat. • Black bill-tip. • Very dark brown upperparts.
1w	• Like ad w but terminal tail-band narrower than in ad.
1s	• Distinct contrast between brown (juv) cov and black new ones.
imm	• Legs and eye dark red to dull red (bright red usually develops as late as 4cy onwards).

Black-winged Stilt *Himantopus himantopus* L 34cm 13.5"

all plum	• Extremely long, pink-red legs. • Long thin, straight bill. • Very variable amount of dark on crown and hind-neck from completely white to completely black (ind with maximum amount of black often ad ♀ but generally not sex-related).
ad ♂	• Deep black upperside. • Sometimes pink wash on underparts.
ad ♀	• Dark brown upperside.
juv-1w	• Narrow pale fringes to feathers of upperside.
1s	• Wing still largely juv, browner than in ad. Often moult-limit between old brown and new black feathers.
fl juv-1w ⇒	• Narrow white trailing edge along arm and inner part of hand ⇔ ad.
note	• Black-necked Stilt *H. mexicanus* could occur as escape in WP. Resembles Black-winged but normally has isolated white spot above eye and in all ind sharply defined black on crown and hindneck connected to black mantle. In some Black-winged (mostly ad ♂) also much black on crown and hind-neck but less sharply defined and isolated from black mantle by white collar.

Pied Avocet *Recurvirostra avosetta* L 42cm 16.5"

ad ♂	• Bill longer and slightly less up-curved than in ad ♀.
juv	• As ad but variable brown patterning on upperparts, scaps and tertials (bill shorter than in ad).
1w	• Crown dark brown ⇔ in ad black.
1s	• Wings still juv, browner than in ad. In some ind retained worn partially brown tertials and some cov.
behav	• Capable of prolonged swimming in deep water.

Crab-plover *Dromas ardeola* L 41cm 16"

all plum	• Very heavy, black bill. • Legs long, blue-grey. • Large size.
ad	• Mainly white plumage with black central part of upperparts and black flight-feathers.
juv	• Upperparts dark-grey instead of black; crown, hind-neck and tertials grey instead of white.
1s	• Crown and hind-neck streaked grey. • Prim still juv, browner than in ad.

Stone-curlew *Burhinus oedicnemus* L 42cm 16.5"

all plum	• Large yellow eye. • Long tail projects beyond wing-tips. • Yellow-brown upperparts with narrow black streaks. • Legs and bill-base yellow. • Somewhat diffuse black submoustachial-stripe.
ad ⇒	• White stripe on cov bordered by narrow black stripes above and below ⇔ in juv-1w dark borders are weaker and a lot less obvious.
juv	• Wing-pattern of ad with black and white lines less distinct; greater cov with more distinct white tips than in ad, creating more obvious wing-bar below black-and-white pattern.
1s	• Wings (including prim) largely juv. Moult-limit best visible in greater cov with outer narrower, more pointed and dark with pale tips than inner ad-type feathers (pale with dark diagonal mark).
fl all plum	• White subterminal spots on black hand (resembling 'mirrors' in large gulls) and white spot on base of inner prim (in juv-1w often lacking); arm with pale bars. • White underwing with dark trailing edge and dark spot on prim-cov.

Senegal Thick-knee *Burhinus senegalensis* L 36cm 14"

all plum	• Legs long (longer than in Stone-curlew).
ad ⇒	• Heavy, almost completely black bill (in Stone-curlew less heavy and obviously 2-coloured). • *Very broad grey band* over cov bordered by black fringe ⇔ in Stone-curlew narrow white-and-black bar over cov. • Eye broadly encircled by white inner and black outer line; bolder head-pattern than in Stone-curlew. • Obvious black submoustachial-stripe.
1s	• See Stone-curlew 1s.
fl all plum	• Hand as in Stone-curlew but 'mirror' larger. • Arm with very broad pale band ⇔ Stone-curlew.

Coursers and pratincoles

Egyptian Plover *Pluvianus aegyptius* L 20cm 8"

all plum	• Very broad black eye-stripe, extending in black band through hind-neck and over central part of upperparts; crown black. • Grey-blue cov, tertials and scaps. • Broad white supercilium. • Legs short; blue-grey.
ad	• Black breast-stripe; buff underparts.
juv	• Breast-stripe very faint; underparts only slightly buffish.
1w-1s	• Like ad but prim more worn, especially in 2cy.
fl all plum	• Pied patterned wings mainly white with black band over base of flight-feathers and black leading edge of hand; leading edge of arm grey-blue.

Cream-coloured Courser *Cursorius cursor* L 21cm 8.5"

all plum	• Short, pointed, somewhat downcurved bill. • Broad pale supercilium and long dark eye-stripe extending to hind-neck; lores uniform pale.
ad	• Uniform deep cream-colored upperside.
1w	• Often some juv cov and tertials retained, cov with dark mark, tertials with narrow dark striping. Post-juv moult very variable (early born hatchlings often moult almost completely to ad before winter; late born hatchlings in autumn still mainly in juvenile plumage). • Head-pattern less pronounced than in ad. • Juv prim with broad pale fringes around tips.
fl all plum ⇒	• Uniform black underwing. • Uniform black hand (upperwing).

Temminck's Courser *Cursorius temminckii* L 19cm 7.7"

all plum	• Structure and head-pattern as in Cream-coloured Courser but slightly smaller and upperparts much darker. • Legs grey ⇔ in Cream-coloured yellowish.
ad ⇒	• Rear-crown rufous ⇔ in Cream-coloured blue-grey.
⇒	• Breast brown, turning into rufous belly, sharply demarcated from white rest of underparts ⇔ Cream-coloured.

Collared Pratincole *Glareola pratincola* L 26cm 10"

all plum	• Often horizontal posture ⇔ in Black-winged Pratincole normally more upright. • Long, almost straight nail of middle toe ⇔ in Black-winged short nails.
ad	• Wing- and tail-tips sometimes level but *tail often projects slightly beyond wing-tip*. • Crown not much darker than rest of upperside ⇔ Black-winged. • (Obvious) contrast between pale cov and dark flight-feathers (but e.g. depending on light situation).
ad s	• Bill (at base) up to ± 40% red (extending beyond throat-feathering and below nostril) Black-winged and Oriental Pratincole.
ad w	• Rather marked dark throat-streaks ⇔ Black-winged.
juv	• Mid-brown ground-colour of upperparts. • Tail shorter than in ad. • Dark subterminal mark on mantle feathers and cov and pale tips (as in Black-winged and Oriental juv).
1w	• Shorter juvenile tail than ad.

1s	• Pale fringes on feathers of upperparts and wing.
moult	• When moult completed like ad (most ind). In some ind retained juv inner sec, some cov and/or tertials.
	• Both ad and 1cy moult completely in autumn with moult suspended during migration (September-November). Ad start earlier (from July) and up to p7 moulted before suspension during migration. 1cy start from Aug and replace up to p5 until migration. Moult completed in winter range.
fl all plum ⇒	• White trailing edge.
	• Rufous underwing-cov (sometimes surprisingly difficult to see) as in Oriental.
	• Sec becoming paler outwards ⇔ Black-winged and Oriental.
	• Rather long tail due to strongly elongated outer tail-feathers.
note	• See Black-winged and Oriental for other features.

Oriental Pratincole *Glareola maldivarum*   L 25cm 10"

all plum ⇒	• Short, shallow forked tail reaches halfway to projected prim-tips, also in juv ⇔ Collared Pratincole and Black-winged Pratincole juv.
	• Legs long (as in Black-winged) ⇔ in Collared slightly shorter.
	• Elongated oval nostril ⇔ in Collared more elongated. Difference between both species often very small.
	• Pale half eye-ring often thickens at rear end ⇔ Black-winged and Collared.
ad	• Red on bill rather variable but always less than in Collared, sometimes even none in ad w. Red on lower mandible level with end of throat-feathering at most.
ad s	• Upperparts darker than in Collared, in between Black-winged and Collared but judgment of paleness of upperparts in all three pratincole species strongly depends on light and viewing conditions.
	• Breast, upper-belly and flanks warm orange-coloured ⇔ Black-winged and Collared, however Collared is sometimes pale orange on these parts.
	• Broad black surround of throat, especially vertical part.
	• Dark crown and rear-head.
ad w	• Dark throat-patch surround retained much more than in Collared ad w.
juv	• See Collared juv.
1w	• As Collared 1w (which see) but often better defined dark throat surrounding.
1s	• See Collared 1s.
moult	• Mainly like Collared, see there.
fl all plum ⇒	• *Short tail* with small, *diagonal* black tip to t6 *(black tip much smaller than white base)* ⇔ in Collared black tip of t6 extends over whole elongation and is only slightly shorter than white base (best judged on spread tail or from below).
	• No obvious white trailing edge of wing (sometimes very narrow fringe).
	• Inner prim without distinct contrast between inner- and outer web ⇔ in Collared pale inner web at tip.
	• Rufous underwing-cov as in Collared.

Black-winged Pratincole *Glareola nordmanni*   L 26cm 10"

all plum	• Often stands conspicuously upright, sometimes with long stretched neck and slender body ⇔ Collared Pratincole.
	• Legs slightly longer than in Collared.
	• Generally runs more than Collared.
ad	• Wing-projection beyond tail (as in Oriental Pratincole) ⇔ in Collared tail often projects beyond wing-tips.
	• Upperside darker and colder brown than in Collared.
	• Faint contrast between cov and prim ⇔ in Collared often stronger.
	• Crown often slightly darker than hind-neck ⇔ in Collared rear-crown normally palest part of upperside.
	• Underparts whiter than in Collared.
ad s	• Only gape line red; red not reaching end of throat-feathering and not reaching nostril ⇔ Collared.
	• Much black on and above lores ⇔ Collared.
	• White half eye-ring does not usually reach to front side of eye ⇔ Collared.
	• Breast relatively pale with only weak buff wash ⇔ in Collared breast and fore-flanks often darker.
ad w	• As Collared ad w but usually at most slightly darker stripes on throat.
juv	• Dark ground-colour of upperparts (⇔ Collared) but often difficult to judge.
	• For other field marks see Collared juv.
1w	• See Collared 1w.
1s	• See Collared 1s.
moult	• Like Collared, see there.
fl all plum ⇒	• Very dark, not rufous underwing-cov, *slightly darker than underside of remiges* ⇔ Collared and Oriental. At distance and under difficult circumstances underwing looks dark in all 3 pratincole species.
	• No pale trailing edge of wing (sometimes very narrow in juv-1w).
	• Rather short tail.
	• Almost entirely dark flight-feathers (as in Oriental) ⇔ Collared.

Plovers

Little Ringed Plover *Charadrius dubius*   L 16.5cm 6.5"

all plum	⇒	• Fine, dark bill.
		• Elongated rear-end and tail often project obviously beyond wing-tips ⇔ Ringed Plover.
		• Almost no prim-projection due to long tertials which nearly reach tail-tip ⇔ Ringed.
ad	⇒	• Yellow eye-ring.
		• Legs grey-brown to flesh-coloured.
		• Lower side of dark mask usually ends angled on rear-side of ear-coverts ⇔ Ringed.
ad s	⇒	• Pale fringe behind black band on forehead.
		• Breast-band usually narrow.

ad ♀ s	• Brown ear-coverts (in ♂ black).
ad w	• Dark parts of head and breast-band brown.
juv ⇒	• Rather uniform head, without (obvious) supercilium and diffuse *yellow-brown* patch on forehead.
	• Breast-band usually broken in middle.
	• Narrow pale brown eye-ring.
	• Legs often orange (as in Ringed all plum).
1w	• Like ad w, but some ind recognisable by retained juv-type cov/tertials with dark subterminal fringes.
1s	• Prim strongly worn.
fl all plum ⇒	• Nearly uniform upperwing (very narrow wing-bar; in juv sometimes slightly more distinct).
	• White tail-sides and white tis to t2-t6; becoming larger from t2 towards t6.

Ringed Plover *Charadrius hiaticula*   L 18cm 7.1"

all plum	• Breast-band complete (sometimes broken in middle in imm), broad based on breast-sides and varying in width (normally broader than in Little Ringed Plover and Semipalmated Plover all plum).
	• Broad supercilium behind eye.
	• Legs orange.
ad s	• Two-toned bill (orange basal part, black tip); bill all dark in w.
ad ♀	• Like ad ♂ but dark parts of head and breast-band (partially) brown.
ad w	• As ad s but bill only paler at base; forehead and supercilium not pure white (see geog var).
juv-1w	• Pale fringes to feathers of upperparts and wings.
	• Dark bill.
	• Legs dull orange (sometimes with greenish wash).
	• Breast-band narrower than in ad.
	• White supercilium and patch on forehead ⇔ Little Ringed juv.
1s	• See Little Ringed 1s. *Tundrae* 1s not recognisable due to complete post-juv moult.
fl all plum	• Obvious, broad wing-bar.
	• White tail-sides and white tips to t2-t6 (tail-pattern almost as Little Ringed).

geog var	*C.h. tundrae* (northern Europe to north-western Siberia)
ad	• Slightly smaller than *hiaticula* with slightly darker upperparts.
moult	• Unlike *hiaticula*, develops distinct winter plumage (black parts, e.g. breast-band and parts of head browner than in *hiaticula* in winter). In spring fresher and darker than *hiaticula* due to body moult to summer plumage (in *hiaticula* no spring moult). Border between both subspecies not well known, intermediates occur and show partial body moult in spring and 'intermediate winter plumage'.

Semipalmated Plover *Charadrius semipalmatus*   L 17cm 6.7"

all plum ⇒	• Black loral-stripe reaches bill above gape line (*gape line lies in white area*) ⇔ Ringed Plover (in ad ♂ s usually no difference with Ringed).
	• Narrow yellowish eye-ring, in breeding season broader (in Ringed in breeding season sometimes yellow eye-ring too but very narrow).
	• Short, usually conspicuously stumpy bill.
	• Semipalmations between front-toes, conspicuous between middle and outer (in Ringed sometimes small semipalmation between inner and middle toe). Only visible at very close range.
	• Relatively small, round head.
	• Breast-band generally narrower than in Ringed.
ad s ⇒	• Short indistinct supercilium behind eye (*often absent in ad ♀ s*) and white spot on forehead not reaching eye (broken supercilium) ⇔ in Ringed ad s obvious supercilium and patch on forehead longer, ending in point below eye.
ad w	• Clearly recognisable winter plumage (as Ringed *tundrae* ⇔ Ringed *hiaticula*); upperparts uniform (unlike 1w), black parts of summer plumage (breast-band and parts of head) brown.
	• All dark bill (like Ringed w).
juv	• See Ringed juv.
juv-1s/ad w	• Supercilium short but broad and usually thickens at rear-side of eye ⇔ most Ringed all plum.
	• Legs usually 2-toned; dark grey front-side and pale, orange rear-side ⇔ in Ringed imm usually more uniform and legs yellower.
1s	• See Little Ringed 1s.
fl all plum	• Obvious wing-bar but slightly smaller than in Ringed.
	• Prim-cov on underwing almost unmarked white, like rest of underwing ⇔ in Ringed grey centre creating dark crescent on underwing.

Killdeer *Charadrius vociferus*   L 25cm 10"

all plum	• Double breast-band.
	• Long tail (projection).
	• Red-brown tail-base and rump.
	• Relatively long pointed bill.
ad w	• From late winter onwards rufous fringes to feathers of upperparts, cov and tertials; in 1w normally broader and paler with slightly more distinct dark subterminal line but differences with ad w often very small.
1w	• Sometimes obvious moult-limit between fresh scaps and old juv cov. Juv cov with narrow pale fringes (see also ad w).
1s	• Prim and normally some outer tail-feathers still juv and rather worn.
fl all plum	• Broad white wing-bar.

Kittlitz's Plover *Charadrius pecuarius*   L 15cm 5.9"

all plum ⇒	• Supercilium (in ad s white, in other plumages yellow-brown) connected with pale collar.
	• Legs very long and dark.
	• Slender, rather long and dark bill.
	• (Indistinct) pale eye-ring.
	• Dark lesser cov creating dark 'shoulder patch' (as in Sanderling).
	• No or only faint mark on breast-side, almost always less distinct than in Kentish Plover.
ad	• Rather broad, pale fringes to mantle feathers, scaps and cov.
ad s	• Black eye-stripe and band over forehead (in ♀ some brown intermix).
	• Orange-pink breast and upper part of belly.
ad w	• Weakly patterned head with dark mask and crown.
1w	• Like ad w but fringes to feathers of upperparts narrow.
1s	• Prim and normally some outer tail-feathers still juv and rather worn.
fl all plum ⇒	• Toes project completely beyond tail ⇔ Kentish.
	• Dark underside of arm ⇔ other small plovers.
	• Rather distinct wing-bar, broadening over inner-hand and ending abruptly (similar to Caspian Plover).
	• Much white on outer edge of tail (t3-t6 whitish).

Three-banded Plover *Charadrius tricollaris*   L 17cm 6.7"

all plum ⇒	• Long tail (tail projects beyond wing-tips).
ad	• Double black breast-band.
	• Grey head-side.
	• Red eye-ring.
	• Supercilium extends from forehead to rear-crown.
	• Uniform dark brown upperparts.
	• Red bill with black tip.
fl all plum	• White trailing edge on arm, narrow wing-bar.

Kentish Plover *Charadrius alexandrinus*   L 16cm 6.3"

all plum ⇒	• Legs (very) dark to black.
	• Dark breast-side patch, no complete breast-band.
	• Whitish to pale brown collar ⇔ in some plumages of Mongolian/Lesser Sand Plover (especially Lesser Sand ♀ -type) and Greater Sand Plover pale but rufous collar.
	• Obviously smaller than Ringed Plover.
	• Relatively large head.
ad ♂ s	• Rufous-brown rear-crown, black fore-crown; forehead white.
	• Black eye-stripe.
	• Black stripe on breast-side.
ad w/ad ♀ s	• Like washed out ad ♂ s (breast-side patch and ear-coverts less well defined or mixed with brown). In ad ♀ s crown at most slightly browner, concolorous with upperparts.
1s	• Prim still juv and worn. 1s ♂ without chestnut crown.
fl all plum	• Tail with completely white outer edge and rectangular dark centre.
	• Obvious wing-bar.

Lesser Sand Plover *Charadrius mongolus*   L 18cm 7.1"

all plum	• Legs (very) dark grey ⇔ Greater Sand Plover. Sometimes with green or yellow wash (especially in juv), then as Greater.
	• Relatively shorter and especially blunter tipped bill than Greater; bill length ⇔ length bill-base to rear-side eye (some Lesser and Greater *columbinus* overlap in bill length).
	• Lesser smaller than Greater with rounder head. Hardly any larger than Ringed Plover, Kentish Plover-like jizz. Mongolian Plover sometimes not clearly smaller than Greater.
	• Stands more upright with larger part of body before legs than Greater.
	• Legs longer than in Ringed but shorter, especially tibia, than in Greater. However impression of leg-length under field conditions often dubious, some ind appear longer legged than some Greater.
	• Usually no more than 3 steps in one run ⇔ in Greater often more than 9.
w	• Large dark breast-side patch, sometimes creating complete band as in some Greater ad w. No reliable plumage differences with Greater w, except that Mongolian often retains grey-brown patches on flank (see Mongolian all plum).
	• Dark ear-coverts usually almost straight bordered with white cheek ⇔ most Greater w.
juv	• As ad w but relatively broad pale fringes to mantle feathers, scaps, cov and tertials.
1s	• As ad s but summer plumage develops later in summer and less complete (Greater 1s nearly as ad w). Prim and part of scaps still juv and usually distinctly worn, cov fresher ⇔ in ad s cov worn and scaps fresher.
fl all plum	• No or very little leg projection beyond tail (in Lesser more often than in Mongolian) ⇔ in Greater obvious leg projection.
	• Prim-cov on underwing often create broad dark crescent, characteristic when present. In Greater crescent usually narrower and less dark.
	• Wing-bar distinct and evenly broad over inner hand (difference with Greater under field conditions hardly usable, see Greater flight).
	• See further flight all plum in both Mongolian and Lesser.
moult	• Moult towards winter plumage takes place in winter range from late August; complete summer plumage retained until late summer (often also in Greater *crassirostris* and *leschenaultii*). Greater *columbinus* usually moults earlier, in breeding range.
	• Summer plumage develops later in spring than in Greater (in Greater *columbinus* from February, in *crassirostris* and *leschenaultii* from March and in Mongolian/Lesser from April).

note	• Prim-moult from August to December/January ⇔ in Greater *columbinus* beginning of July to September. Greater *leschenaultii* and *crassirostris* start prim-moult in breeding range in July, stop moult during migration and continue in winter range up to December. • Polytypical species (5 subspecies), for identification usually gathered in two groups/species: Lesser (*atrifrons*-group 3 subspecies) and Mongolian (*mongolus*-group 2 subspecies).
geog var	**Lesser Sand Plover** (*atrifrons*-group): *C.m pamirensis, C.m. atrifrons, C.m schaeferi* (Central Asia)
all plum ⇒	• Completely white unmarked flanks ⇔ Mongolian. • Longer bill (slender, rather pointed and often at most slightly bulging near tip ⇔ Mongolian); longer tarsus but shorter wings than Mongolian. *Schaeferi* with generally longest and thickest bill and *pamirensis* with generally most slender and most pointed bill. • In some ind bill structure nearly as small-billed Greater *columbinus*. • Usually only slightly larger than Ringed Plover ⇔ Mongolian larger and often hardly smaller than small Greater.
ad ♂ s	• No black line between white throat and breast-band ⇔ Mongolian ad s. • From spring to summer black forehead; uniform black in *atrifrons*; in *pamirensis* and *schaeferi* usually small white spots on black forehead (from summer white forehead patch as in Mongolian). • Orange breast-band ⇔ in Mongolian darker and more reddish. • Sometimes some orange spots on upperparts (small in Greater) ⇔ Mongolian. • Clear differences between sexes, see Mongolian ad s.
ad ♀ s	• Yellow-brown forehead. • Orange neck-side broadly extending through nape ⇔ in Mongolian usually narrower and normally not reaching nape.
ad w/juv	• Patch on breast-sides relatively small and pale ⇔ in Mongolian broader, darker and often creating complete breast-band.
juv	• Pale fringes to mantle feathers, scaps, tertials and cov often deeper buff than in Mongolian juv.
1w	• Breast-side and collar pale orange-brown ⇔ in Mongolian pale brown-grey, without warmer wash.
fl all plum	• Narrow dark band over rump and uppertail-cov (white sides of uppertail-cov) ⇔ in Mongolian broad band (uppertail-cov entirely dark). • Tail-feathers not obviously darker than upperparts ⇔ in Mongolian darker.
geog var	**Mongolian Plover** (*mongolus*-group): *C.m. mongolus, C.m stegmanni* (eastern Asia)
all plum ⇒	• *Brown-grey patches on flanks*, often continuing to up to rear-flanks ⇔ in Lesser unmarked flanks. In Greater ad s regular and in Lesser ad s sometimes orange spots along flank but concolorous with breast-band, never grey-brown as in Mongolian. • Blunter and shorter bill but longer wings (sometimes with obvious prim-projection) than Lesser. Tip of bill slightly swollen and ending (rather) bluntly (but variable); distal bulging over less than half of bill length ⇔ Greater (see also Lesser).
ad ♂ s	• Dark orange-reddish breast-band, on breast-sides *merged with grey brown spots* (characteristic grey brown spots continue along rest of flank). Later in summer breast-band paler orange as in Lesser. • Usually white forehead patch (small in *stegmanni*) and black line between white throat and breast-band.
ad ♀ s	• Usually differs little from ad s ♂ but dark parts of head browner and narrower breast-band ⇔ in Greater ad s and Lesser ad s more obvious difference between sexes. • Upperparts usually slightly darker than in Greater and Lesser, often with dark grey wash (latter ⇔ Greater).
ad w/juv	• See Lesser.
juv	• See Lesser.
fl all plum	• Broad dark band over uppertail-cov (uppertail-cov almost completely dark ⇔ Lesser and Greater). • Tail-feathers darker than uppertail-cov (as in Greater) ⇔ in Lesser tail-feathers hardly darker than uppertail-cov.

Greater Sand Plover *Charadrius leschenaultii*　　　　　　　　　　　　　　L 21cm 8.5"

all plum ⇒	• Long bill, characteristic when obviously long-billed ⇔ Mongolian/Lesser Sand Plover. Some *columbinus* with relatively short bill, bill length than nearly as in Lesser. • Culmen curves rather gently towards bill-tip, bill pointed ⇔ Mongolian/Lesser. • (Weak) bulging on bill often over about half of bill length ⇔ in Mongolian/Lesser less than half. • Legs rather dark, normally with greenish wash; long tibia gives long-legged impression. Rarely blackish legs ⇔ in Mongolian/ Lesser regular. • Larger than Lesser but sometimes hardly different from Mongolian, with usually angular head due to flattened crown, Grey Plover-like jizz. • When feeding sometimes quickly covers large distance, with normally more than 9 steps in one run (see Mongolian/Lesser). • Relatively large eye in middle of head-side. • Bill length ≥ distance from bill-base to rear-side of eye (bill length rather variable; in all subspecies relatively short-billed ind occur, irrespective of sex).
w/juv	• See Mongolian/Lesser.
juv	• See Mongolian/Lesser.
1s	• Summer plumage not or at most slightly developed. Most ind like worn ad w with some fresh winter-type feathers.
moult	• See Mongolian/Lesser.
fl all plum	• Wing-bar widens over inner-hand ⇔ Mongolian/Lesser. • Dark, rather ill-defined tail-band (as in Mongolian) ⇔ in Lesser tail becomes a little darker towards tip. • Legs usually project obviously beyond tail (but see *columbinus*). • Narrow grey band over rump and uppertail-cov as in Lesser ⇔ Mongolian.

Plovers

note ad s	• From July, colour of upperparts and breast-band subject to bleaching and moult, subspecies identification then often difficult. • All subspecies sometimes show dark line above breast-band, in *columbinus* probably rarely, in *crassirostris* and *leschenaultii* regular.
geog var	**Anatolian Sand Plover** *C.l. columbinus* (western Asia)
all plum	• Slender bill with little or no gonys-angle (and small bulging on distal part of culmen). • Smallest subspecies with smallest bill and shortest legs and wings.
ad s	• Light-brown upperparts with much rufous patterning ⇔ especially in *leschenaultii* usually little or no rufous patterning on upperparts; in *crassirostris* very variable. • Often broad orange breast-band continuing patchily along flank (as in Mongolian but less grey-brown) ⇔ *crassirostris* and *leschenaultii*.
ad ♂ s	• Usually little black on head (in extreme cases extensive black mask), sometimes faint patterned.
ad ♀ s	• Much more faint patterned than ad ♂ with vague (or no) mask and vague incomplete breast-band.
fl all plum	• Legs usually project only a little beyond tail ⇔ in *crassirostris* and *leschenaultii* obvious leg projection.
geog var	*C.l. crassirostris* (western to central Asia)
all plum	• Largest subspecies with longest bill (usually more slender than in *leschenaultii*), legs and wings resulting in obvious prim-projection.
ad ♂ s	• Breast-band broader than in *leschenaultii* but narrower and darker red-orange than in *columbinus* with often isolated rufous spot(s) on fore-flanks off wing-bend ⇔ Mongolian/Lesser. • Generally more well-marked head-pattern than most *columbinus* (as in *leschenaultii*, also resembles Mongolian/Lesser). • Breast-band darker than in most *columbinus* ad s (as in *leschenaultii*).
geog var	*C.l. leschenaultii* (central Asia east from *crassirostris*)
all plum	• Intermediate between *columbinus* and *crassirostris* in bill-, leg- and wing-length.
ad ♂ s	• Generally more well-marked head-pattern than most *columbinus* ad s (as in *crassirostris* and Mongolian/Lesser). • Narrow orange breast-band; fore-flanks usually unmarked ⇔ *crassirostris*. • Upperparts generally darker and browner than in *columbinus* ad s with less or no rufous patterning but much variation in all subspecies. • Breast-band darker red-orange than in most *columbinus* ad s (as in *crassirostris*).

Caspian Plover *Charadrius asiaticus*   L 20cm 8"

all plum ⇒	• Elongated rear-end due to long wings and often long wing-projection but prim-projection short due to long tertials. • Dark crown and eye-stripe strongly contrasting with large white patch on forehead, broad white supercilium and white throat. • Long legs with long tibia; dark grey to yellowish. • Rather long, thin bill. • Complete, brown breast-band (in ad ♂ brown-orange).
ad ♀ s/ad w	• Uniform brown upperparts (with grey wash) and breast-band (in older ♀ slightly rufous, as washed out ad ♂) ⇔ ad ♂ s.
juv/1w	• As ad w but with broad pale fringes and dark centres to all feathers on upperparts. 1w like juv but mantle-feathers and scaps moulted; cov still juv but pattern often difficult to detect due to abrasion.
1s	• Like worn ad w with some summer-type feathers on underparts. Moult-limit in cov. Prim worn.
fl all plum ⇒	• Rather narrow wing-bar over arm, broadening on inner prim *and ending abruptly halfway across hand*. • Long pointed wings. • Legs project beyond tail: toes completely exposed.

Oriental Plover *Charadrius veredus*   L 24cm 9.5"

all plum	• Resembles Caspian Plover (except white-headed ad ♂ s), but longer, yellow-orange legs; structure similar to Caspian.
ad ♂ s	• Pale head with darker crown and hind-neck (head often completely white in late summer), gradually merging into orange-brown breast which is bordered by black band below.
ad ♀/ad ♂ w	• Underparts whitish, breast with only faint brown wash ⇔ in Caspian ad ♀ breast is distinctly darker.
ad w	• Dark crown and ear-coverts; neck-side paler but overall very similar to Caspian. Supercilium less sharply demarcated than in Caspian. • Feathers of upperparts with narrow indistinct rufous fringes ⇔ in Caspian paler, more conspicuous and often broader fringes.
1s	• Differs from ad s probably in same way as Caspian 1s.
fl all plum	• Hardly any wing-bar and completely blackish underwing.

Eurasian Dotterel *Charadrius morinellus*   L 22cm 8.5"

all plum ⇒	• Characteristic narrow white breast-band. • Very conspicuous supercilium, on rear-head (almost) connected. • Legs green-yellowish.
ad s	• Red-orange belly (central part blackish); white vent and undertail-cov. • Upperparts grey-brown with buffish feather-fringes. • Ad ♂ s much less vividly coloured than ad ♀ s.
w	• Breast and flanks brown-grey; central part of underparts white.
juv-1w	• Upperside with dark feather centres and well-defined pale fringes (1w with mix of juv and ad-type feathers) ⇔ in ad w paler feather centres with diffuse brown-yellow fringes.

1s fl all plum ⇒	• Like worn ad w with some summer-type feathers. Moult-limit in cov. Prim heavily worn. • Uniform dark under- and upperwing (no wing-bar). • Conspicuous white shaft on p10. • Leg do not project beyond tail.

American Golden Plover *Pluvialis dominica*   L 26cm 10"

all plum ⇒	• Long prim-projection (c.100%) with 4-5 prim-tips behind tertials; long wing-projection (prim-projection longer than bill ⇔ Pacific Golden Plover but see note in Pacific), creating elongated rear-end. • Tertials relatively short but variable (in ad s sometimes long), see Pacific. • Relatively long tibia (slightly longer than in European Golden Plover but less so than in Pacific). • Slightly longer bill than in European (in Pacific obviously longer). • Legs little variable, dark grey to blackish ⇔ in Pacific usually paler, indicative when pale lead-grey (especially in imm); in European variable from grey-brown to blackish. • Size as or only slightly smaller than European ⇔ Pacific usually obviously smaller than European. • Often slight bulging on distal part of upper mandible (normally less obvious than in Pacific) ⇔ in European no bulging.
ad s	• White breast-side patch large and conspicuous, ending on black flank (resembles Grey Plover) ⇔ in Pacific ad s less large and extends down in black and white barred flank. • Underparts entirely black (especially in ad ♂; in ad ♀ often pale patterning on e.g. cheek and undertail-cov). • Undertail-cov wholly black (♂) or nearly so (♀). • Upperparts with bolder patterning than in European (as in Pacific). Usually larger amount of black in centre of scaps than in Pacific. • Moults relatively late into winter plumage (usually much later than European). Black and white chequered flanks in moult to winter plumage, but markings large and rounded ⇔ in Pacific ad s narrow barring; in late moulting European unpatterned white flanks.
ad w/juv-1w	• No yellow on underparts (general appearance grey, sometimes also in European) ⇔ Pacific. • Conspicuous, whitish supercilium and often dark cap. • Dark ear-coverts and dark area directly before eye often creating dark mask ⇔ Pacific. • Often somewhat contrasting dark triangle on upperparts due to black centres to mantle feathers (as in Pacific) ⇔ European. • Pale nape contrasts with dark crown and upperparts ⇔ Pacific. • Feathers of upperside grey-brown with small whitish to yellowish spots.
ad w	• Often with little notched tertials and/or cov. • Underparts obviously whiter than in juv-1w; grey breast-band.
juv	• Often some contrast between dark grey scaps and slightly paler grey cov. • Underparts strongly but diffusely patterned (mainly barred ⇔ Grey and grey European) on greyish ground-colour ⇔ in ad w more weakly patterned on whitish background. • Central part of upper-belly sometimes almost uniform white, contrasting with patterned breast and darker lower-belly ⇔ Pacific. • Uniform 'white bow' on forehead, directly above bill, as in Pacific ⇔ Grey and most European (in some European rather obvious too).
1s	• Variable but usually relatively fresh winter plumage-type with some summer-type cov, mantle feathers and scaps; no complete summer plumage. Sometimes still some worn juv feathers. Underparts variable from hardly any black patterning to rarely largely black (as in Pacific). • Summer-type feathers obtained later than in ad s, in end of summer fresher. Ind with relatively fresh summer-type in early winter indicative of 1s. • Prim worn juv feathers, often dull brown compared to ad.
note juv	• Grey Plover juv sometimes confusing but in Grey upperparts with much stronger notches and breast has well-defined dark streaks/speckles on white background, often creating breast-band (in American more diffusely patterned on grey background, not creating breast-band). Only fine longitudinal stripes on whiter flanks ⇔ in American juv flanks barred and darker.
fl all plum	• Grey axillaries and undertail-cov (as in Pacific). • Short leg-projection ⇔ Pacific. • Weak wing-bar (as in Pacific) ⇔ European. • Narrow, long wings, as in Pacific ⇔ in European broader, more triangular. • p10 longer than p9 ⇔ in Pacific almost same or slightly longer (only useful in extremes).

Pacific Golden Plover *Pluvialis fulva*   L 23cm 9"

all plum	• Long tertials often *nearly reaching tail-tip* ⇔ American Golden Plover and European Golden Plover. In some American ad s long tertials reaching to halfway along tail. • Legs long due to long tibia; usually rather large part of tibia visible (in American slightly shorter tibia) ⇔ in European only small part of tibia visible. • Longer bill than in European with bulging on distal part of upper mandible (as in many American but bulging often less distinct) ⇔ in European more pointed bill without bulging. • Smaller and more slender than European. • Often short prim-projection (≤ 40%) with 2-3 prim-tips beyond tertials (see note); rather short wing-projection (bill longer than wing-projection but see note) ⇔ American. • Legs often pale lead-grey (mostly in imm, in ad s dark), usually paler than in European and American.
ad s ⇒	• White flank with black band over central flank-feathers (creating black and white chequered flank), sometimes hidden behind black belly feathers or overhanging wing. • Undertail-cov white with some dark markings (♀) or, in well marked ♂, mainly black patterned. • Pale notches in feathers of upperside larger than in European ad s (as in American). • White on breast-sides slightly broadening and extending to black and white barred flank (see American ad s).

	• ♀ moults upperside more complete to summer plumage than American ♀ (often nearly all cov and tertials summer plumage-type ⇔ American ♀).
	• Moults generally later into winter plumage than European.
ad w	• Supercilium conspicuous, usually with obvious yellowish wash.
	• Background of underparts obviously whiter than in juv-1w; grey breast-band. Breast brownish mixed with bright yellow.
	• Often with little notched tertials and/or cov.
	• Belly usually unpatterned ⇔ juv (as in all golden plovers ad w).
juv	• Feathers of upperside with large, bright yellow notches.
	• Underparts as in American juv but *with at least some yellow*.
	• Underparts more barred than in European juv on more greyish ground-colour.
	• Usually obvious dark vertical spot on lores; in American less obvious; in European none or indistinct.
	• Obvious dark spot on ear-coverts ⇔ in American usually slightly less marked, in European usually indistinct.
	• Flanks and belly well-marked on greyish ground-colour ⇔ in ad w more weakly marked on whitish background.
	• Supercilium conspicuous but less distinct than in American (overlap with European).
	• Malar stripe area very fine streaked (only visible at close range) ⇔ in European usually more obvious.
	• Uniform 'white bow' on forehead, directly above bill (as in Pacific) ⇔ most European (in some European rather obvious too).
1s	• See American 1s.
fl all plum	• Obvious leg projection (often toes project completely) ⇔ American.
	• p9 and p10 almost same length or p10 slightly longer ⇔ American (see there).
	• See American for rest of flight field marks.
note	• Ind belonging to (some?) populations from far eastern Siberia (unlikely in WP) with notably longer prim-projection, approaching American in extent!

European Golden Plover *Pluvialis apricaria*   L 27cm 10.5"

all plum	• Rather long prim-projection (c.70%) with 4 prim-tips beyond tertials; prim reach beyond tail.
	• Short tibia.
	• Bill ends rather evenly in narrow point ⇔ American Golden Plover and Pacific Golden Plover.
	• Tertials and scaps finer (denser) and less deeply notched than in American and Pacific.
ad s ⇒	• Variable black underparts; flanks unpatterned white.
	• Ind from southern populations (southern Scandinavia) develop no complete summer plumage; cov especially usually winter plumage-type, distinctly worn.
juv	• Flanks and belly well-spotted on greyish ground-colour ⇔ ad w more weakly marked with more obvious breast-streaking on whitish background, creating obvious breast-band.
	• Feathers of upperside sharper, finer and more evenly notched than in ad w.
1s	• Nearly as ad s (rarely no development to summer plumage) but prim and tail-feathers old and worn ⇔ in American and Pacific rarely well-developed summer plumage.
fl all plum	• White axillaries and underwing-cov.
note	• See American and Pacific for other features.

Grey Plover *Pluvialis squatarola*   L 28cm 11"

all plum ⇒	• Vent and undertail-cov unpatterned white.
	• Strong bill.
	• Legs thick, usually blackish ⇔ in European Golden Plover usually grey-brown to grey.
	• Small hind toe ⇔ in other similar plovers absent.
ad s ⇒	• Belly and flanks entirely black, vent and undertail-cov white; white on breast-sides widens strongly towards middle of breast.
ad ♂	• In summer plumage pure black and white and often almost white crown; tail white with narrow black bars.
ad ♀	• In summer plumage browner on upperparts than ♂ and darkly marked crown, underparts rarely wholly black; tail with broader dark bars than in ad ♂.
ad w	• Upperparts, tertials and cov rather plain ⇔ in 1w tertials and cov notched (upperparts already moulted into ad-type).
juv	• Upperside strongly and deeply notched and with buffish wash ⇔ ad w.
1s	• No real summer plumage, often yellow-brown on upperside; underparts and flanks patchy black ⇔ European.
	• Prim and tail-feathers old and worn.
fl all plum ⇒	• Black axillaries.
	• Black prim-cov on upperwing.
	• Broad wing-bar.
	• Pale rump.
note	• See 'note juv' in account of American Golden Plover.

Spur-winged Lapwing *Vanellus spinosus*   L 27cm 10.5"

ad	• Breast and belly black; vent and undertail-cov white; head-side and neck-side white.
	• Almost uniform brown upperparts.
	• Crown black and vertical black band from throat towards breast.
	• Legs and bill black.
1w	• Like ad but crown and cov with pale feather-tips/fringes, later worn off.
1s	• Flight-feathers old and worn.
fl all plum	• Black sec and hand bordered by pale 'Woodpigeon-band'; arm brown as upperparts.
	• Broad black tail-band.
	• Underwing-cov white; flight-feathers black.

Black-headed Lapwing *Vanellus tectus*   L 24cm 9.5"

ad	• Black neck and ear-coverts and black crown with long Northern Lapwing-like crest. • Black neck and black patchy band over central part of underparts on to belly; remainder of underparts pale. • Legs and bill red with black bill-tip; red spot on lores. • Brown upperparts. • Yellow iris.
1w	• See Spur-winged Lapwing 1w.
1s	• See Spur-winged 1s.

Red-wattled Lapwing *Vanellus indicus*   L 33cm 13"

ad	• Red bill with black tip. • Red line (bare skin) above lores. • Legs long, yellow. • Black crown, throat and central part of breast. • Black band over middle of (white) tail.
1w	• See Spur-winged Lapwing 1w.
1s	• See Spur-winged 1s.
fl all plum	• Brown cov and white 'Woodpigeon-band' over greater cov. • Black hand and sec. • Legs project shortly beyond tail (only toes).

Sociable Lapwing *Vanellus gregarius*   L 29cm 11.5"

all plum ⇒	• Characteristic head-pattern: conspicuous eye-stripe, very long broad supercilium and dark contrasting crown. • Legs dark.
ad s	• Black belly-patch, becoming red-brown towards vent (in ♀ patch smaller). • Brown-grey upperparts, neck and breast.
ad w	• Brown scaled breast; white belly, but sometimes still dark belly-feathers present in autumn. • Mantle feathers and scaps with rather broad pale fringes (see juv-1w). Tertials pale grey-brown ⇔ in juv-1w rather dark brown.
juv-1w	• Mantle feathers and scaps with broad pale fringes as in ad w, but also with narrow dark *subterminal fringes* ⇔ ad w. • Breast more streaked than in ad w, remainder of underparts white.
1s	• Summer plumage developed later than ad (up to April). Some cov (especially lesser cov) and sometimes other parts still juv. • Flight-feathers old and worn.
fl all plum ⇒	• *White sec*; black hand. • White tail with broad, black band (not extending to outer tail-feathers). • Legs project slightly beyond tail.

White-tailed Lapwing *Vanellus leucurus*   L 28cm 11"

all plum ⇒	• Legs very long, deep yellow. • Almost uniform head with diffuse pale supercilium and forehead; no eye-stripe. • Relatively long bill. • Entirely white tail.
ad	• Upperside uniform brown-grey.
juv	• Mantle feathers, scaps, cov and tertials with conspicuous black subterminal spot, creating spotted upperside. • Dark patterning on tips of tail-feathers, later worn off.
1s	• Prim and tail-feathers old and worn. Sometimes still some dark patterning on tip of t6.
fl all plum	• Mainly black hand; broad white band over middle of wing with isolated black alula. • Brown arm with narrow black line separating white central band. • Very long leg projection beyond tail.

Northern Lapwing *Vanellus vanellus*   L 30cm 12"

ad ♂ s	• Complete black breast, throat, lores and forehead; white cheeks.
ad ♀ s	• Variable amount of white on middle of black breast, throat, lores and forehead; pale parts of head not pure white ⇔ ad ♂ s .
ad w	• Pale around bill and on throat (similar to some ad ♀ s). Rear-head cream-coloured. • Pale tips to cov and scaps. • Long crest ⇔ juv.
juv-1w	• In juv short crest ⇔ from 1w long. • Narrow pale, somewhat notched fringes on all feathers of upperside ⇔ in ad w more uneven and broader pale tips to cov and scaps. • Breast-band narrow and dark brown ⇔ in ad black.
1s	• Prim old and worn juv feathers.
fl ad ♂	• Large white spot on tips of outer 3 prim (only small weak dark tip); white tip extending over whole width of feather ⇔ ad ♀.
fl ad ♀	• White spot on outer 3 prim smaller and lying more subterminal due to larger dark tip. White spot does not extend over whole breadth of feather but bordered by dark fringe along inner web ⇔ ad ♂.
fl juv-1w	• Hand notably more narrow than in ad.

97

Sandpipers and allies

Ageing of *Calidris* **in spring**

1s	• Summer plumage often less developed with relatively large amount of worn winter-type feathers compared to ad. • Juv prim (variable per species, often only inner or only outer retained) and often part of tail-feathers retained into spring, often more worn, narrower and more pointed than in ad at same time of year. Prim moult from April onwards ⇔ ad moult prim from Sept onwards. • Exceptions to above are mentioned in species accounts.

Great Knot *Calidris tenuirostris*
L 27cm 10.5"

all plum	⇒	• Blackish, patchy breast-band (strongest in ad s; weakest in ad w), strongly contrasting with white rest of underparts.
	⇒	• Long prim-projection (c.80-100%) and obvious wing-projection ⇔ Red Knot.
		• Bill length > length of head ⇔ Red.
		• Flanks spotted ⇔ in Red barred.
		• Loral stripe often almost vertical ⇔ Red.
		• Size as Ruff ♀.
ad s	⇒	• Large black spots along flanks, see also all plum.
		• Scaps largely deep rufous with narrow black shaft-streak.
ad w		• Rather broad pale fringes to all feathers of upperside (broader than in Red ad w).
1w/ad w		• Breast dark patterned.
		• Crown, hind-neck and neck rather boldly dark streaked ⇔ Red ad w.
1w		• Like ad w, but (often obvious) moult-limit between newly moulted mantle and scaps and retains juv cov.
juv	⇒	• *Narrow, well-defined anchor-pattern on scaps and cov* with grey centres; well-defined white fringes on cov.
1w		• See Dunlin 1w.
1s		• See 'Ageing of *Calidris* in spring'.
fl all plum	⇒	• Almost unpatterned white rump/uppertail-cov (some dark spots in summer plumage).
		• Uniform dark grey tail emphasises contrast with pale rump/uppertail-cov.
		• Narrow wing-bar (narrower than in Red).
		• Underwing whitish, paler than in Red.
		• Wings longer and narrower than in Red (rather distinct in direct comparison).

Red Knot *Calidris canutus*
L 24cm 9.5"

all plum		• Distinctly larger than other *Calidris* except Great Knot.
		• Legs greenish to black.
		• Long prim-projection (c.60-100%).
		• Supercilium broadening behind eye.
ad s	⇒	• Rather pale pink-red underparts (vent and undertail-cov white); feathers of upperside mainly grey with black and rufous patterning.
		• Rufous scaps with black shaft-streak and 2 horizontal black lines, during summer scaps become almost black as in many other *Calidris*.
w		• Breast and flanks to undertail-cov rather strongly marked.
		• Feathers of upperside uniform grey-brown with narrow black shaft-streak.
juv	⇒	• Narrow, dark subterminal band on all cov and feathers of upperparts.
		• Upperparts and wings nearly grey ⇔ in ad w grey-brown.
		• Yellowish wash on breast.
1w		• See Dunlin 1w.
1s		• See 'Ageing of *Calidris* in spring'.
fl all plum	⇒	• Pale, streaked rump-area without dark bar on middle ⇔ most other *Calidris*.
		• Obvious wing-bar.
		• Underwing greyish (axillaries and median cov/lesser cov spotted grey).
geog var		*C.c islandica* (northern Greenland and arctic Canada).
		• Slightly shorter bill than in Siberian population (*canutus*).
ad s		• Upperparts paler than *canutus* with narrower black markings on upperparts; orange-pink inner- and outer webs on scaps larger and squarer.
		• Underparts paler pink-orange in fresh plumage.
moult		• Prim-moult in ad later than in *canutus* with outer prim sometimes retained into mid-winter.

Sanderling *Calidris alba*
L 19cm 7.7"

all plum	⇒	• No rear toe.
		• Broad white line along lower edge of closed wing (large white tip on all greater cov).
		• Relatively thick, straight bill.
ad s	⇒	• Strong (rufous) patterning *in* dark centres of scaps, inner greater cov and to lesser extent in tertials (⇔ Red-necked Stint ad s).
		• Densely patterned breast, creating breast-band.
		• Pale spot below eye.
		• Streaked ear-coverts ⇔ Red-necked Stint.
ad w/juv		• Dark lesser cov creating dark wing-bend.
1w		• See Dunlin 1w.

juv	⇒	• Almost star-shaped dark centres to mantle feathers and scaps creating *strong black and pale grey patterned upperparts*.
1s		• See 'Ageing of *Calidris* in spring'.
		• Ind which return to north in 2cy often in complete summer plumage. Prim-moult highly variable from completed in spring to all prim still juv at end of summer ⇔ most other *Calidris*.
fl all plum	⇒	• Broad wing-bar; *Calidris* with broadest and most contrasting wing-bar.
		• Uniform white underwing ⇔ in other *Calidris* at least lesser cov create dark bar.
note ad s		• In spring often almost no rufous patterning on upperside and breast due to broad white fringes on fresh feathers covering rufous colour; so-called 'white summer plumage'.
note		• Due to highly variable summer plumage sometimes rather similar to Red-necked Stint, Semipalmated Sandpiper, Western Sandpiper and Baird's Sandpiper but combination of structure and exact feather-patterns characteristic.

Semipalmated Sandpiper *Calidris pusilla*   L 15.5cm 6.1"

all plum	• Thick bill with deep base and lateral thickening at tip (visible when viewed from the front); usually shorter than in Western Sandpiper but much variation in both species, extremes (long-billed Semipalmated ♀ and short-billed Western ♂) overlap.
	• Short prim-projection (c.10-30%) with 1-3 prim-tips beyond tertials (shorter than in Little Stint and Red-necked Stint).
	• Dark grey to blackish tertial-centres with pale, not deep rufous fringes.
	• Webs between front toes as in Western (most distinct between middle and outer toe but usually difficult to see).
	• Generally slightly larger and more compact than Little Stint with slightly longer legs.
	• Tail-tip often projects slightly beyond wing-tips ⇔ in Little Stint the other way around (there is some overlap, so this feature is only useful in extreme cases).
ad s	• Dense and sharply spotted breast and *some streaks along flanks* (latter sometimes absent) ⇔ Little Stint.
	• Mantle feathers and scaps with large, somewhat pointed and elongated black centres and yellow-brown fringes (often creating broad pale and dark streaks).
	• Crown, ear-coverts and hind-neck (heavily) streaked (later in summer less streaked). Dark ear-coverts often more conspicuously framed by paler surroundings than in Little Stint
	• Pale 'V'-shape on mantle and/or scaps absent or very ill-defined.
	• Overall colour of upperparts very variable from very pale brown-grey without warm colours to warm rufous-brown. By late summer warm colours normally almost worn away even in the brightest ind.
	• Often moults later into winter plumage than Western; upperparts with mix of grey winter-feathers and black summer-feathers and breast-band less densely patterned ⇔ Western in September almost in complete winter plumage.
ad w	• Grey feathers of upperparts with very narrow dark shaft-streak ⇔ Little Stint ad w and 1w with moulted upperparts.
	• Faint breast-side pattern, usually not creating complete breast-band.
juv	• Patterning on feathers of upperparts and wings dominated by even (on lower scaps slightly asymmetric) anchor-pattern especially on scaps ⇔ in Little Stint juv scaps with large dark centres; slightly or not at all anchor-patterned.
	• Upperside and cov with almost uniform ground-colour ⇔ in Red-necked Stint juv contrast between rather dark mantle and scaps and pale grey cov.
	• Strongly streaked, dark crown; sharply demarcated from distinct supercilium ⇔ Red-necked Stint juv and Western juv. No obvious 'split supercilium'.
	• Dark ear-coverts sometimes conspicuous.
	• Breast-side pattern rather well-defined on brown-greyish ground-colour (often with fine streaks up to middle of breast ⇔ in Little Stint juv and Red-necked Stint juv streaks restricted to breast-sides) ⇔ in Little Stint juv diffuse patterning on warmer ground-colour; in Red-necked Stint juv diffuse patterning on variable ground-colour from grey to peach-coloured.
	• Pale 'V' on mantle weak or absent.
1w	• See Dunlin 1w.
	• Winter-type feathers of upperparts with very narrow shaft-streaks ⇔ in Little Stint broad, especially in 1w.
1s	• See 'Ageing of *Calidris* in spring'.
	• Some ind develop complete summer-plumage with all prim moulted as in ad, these ind indistinguishable from ad.
fl all plum	• Narrow wing-bar.

Western Sandpiper *Calidris mauri*   L 16cm 6.3"

all plum		• (Fairly) long bill with (suggestion of) downwards kink on distal part; culmen almost straight, lower mandible bends towards upper mandible (similar to bill structure of Dunlin but base slightly thicker and culmen straighter). Sometimes rather short and straight. Tip sideways thickened (visible on front view).
		• Very short prim-projection (c.20%) with (1) 2-3 prim-tips behind tertials.
		• Webs between front toes (generally slightly larger than in Semipalmated Sandpiper but difficult to see).
		• Supercilium in front of eye often conspicuously broad (especially in juv).
		• Head sometimes distinctly large, often giving top-heavy impression.
ad s	⇒	• Breast peppered with *arrowhead-shaped spots*, thinner arrowhead-shaped spots or thin stripes extending along flanks to vent.
	⇒	• Scaps with *brown-orange base* and black centres ⇔ in Semipalmated only rufous fringes.
		• Grey cov contrast with brown-orange scaps.
		• Rufous crown and ear-coverts (sometimes also in Semipalmated).
w		• Pale grey feathers of upperparts with very narrow black shaft-streak.
		• Breast with sharp dark streaks, usually creating complete breast-band ⇔ other stints w (in Little Stint w often breast-band formed by diffuse streaks).

99

juv	⇒	• Upper scaps with *black centres and deep rufous fringes*, strongly contrasting with grey centres to lower scaps and cov and whitish fringes to grey feathers ⇔ Semipalmated juv.
		• Well-marked and pointed anchor-pattern on lower scaps.
		• Head rather weakly patterned with only middle of crown strongly streaked, fading away towards crown-sides; ear-coverts pale.
		• Breast-sides well-marked and finely streaked on yellow-brown ground-colour; middle of breast unpatterned white.
		• Often pale breast-sides (extending above wing-bend).
		• Pale 'V' on mantle and scaps usually ill-defined.
		• Tertial-centres rather pale grey, concolorous with cov.
		• Moults from August towards 1w, generally earlier than Semipalmated.
1w		• See Dunlin 1w.
1s		• See 'Ageing of *Calidris* in spring'.
fl all plum		• Rather narrow wing-bar.

Red-necked Stint *Calidris ruficollis*   L 15cm 5.9"

all plum		• Bill short and rather thick, becoming thinner towards tip ⇔ in Semipalmated Sandpiper thicker bill with deeper base and usually thickening at tip (but variable in both species). Slightly shorter and thicker than in Little Stint.
		• Legs sometimes conspicuously short.
		• Relatively long prim-projection for stint (as in Little).
		• Relatively larger head compared to Little.
		• Tail-feathers short, except central pair (t1). T1 projects farther than in Little.
ad s	⇒	• Uniform, red-orange ear-coverts, upper breast and usually also throat, bordered on underside by *band of black speckles on white background*.
		• From summer contrast between mainly dark mantle and scaps and paler grey cov (in fresh spring plumage contrast less distinct or absent).
		• From summer scaps (and usually some cov) with large dark centres and deep rufous fringes, creating dark blocks on upperside (in fresh spring plumage whole upperside with broad pale grey fringes).
		• Tertial-fringes pale grey to pale cream-coloured (sometimes one rufous tertial-fringe) ⇔ in Little conspicuous rufous fringes but lower one of longest tertials often greyish.
		• Supercilium narrow and not obviously 'split' ⇔ Little ad s.
ad w		• Lores very dark (darkest part of head) often extending over ear-coverts, creating diffuse mask.
		• Diffuse grey breast-side pattern, almost without obvious streaks and not creating complete breast-band.
		• Feathers of upperparts grey with dark shafts and sometimes small dark centres (latter probably only in 1w).
juv	⇒	• Scaps with conspicuously contrasting *white 'V'-shaped tips*, usually much more distinct than in Little juv. In Semipalmated Sandpiper juv pale tips and fringes to almost all scaps and cov.
		• Rather strong contrast between rather *dark mantle and upper scaps and pale grey lower scaps and cov* ⇔ Semipalmated Sandpiper and Little juv. Mantle feathers and upper scaps with pale rufous fringes; lower scaps and cov grey and without obvious rufous fringes (sometimes only weak rufous tips).
		• Breast-side pattern *ill-defined* on grey brown ground-colour often with weak peach-coloured wash (at strongest resembles colour of Curlew Sandpiper juv) ⇔ Little juv.
		• Lower scaps usually with anchor-pattern or subterminal dark spot ⇔ Little juv.
		• Mantle-'V' weak or almost absent.
		• Tertial-centres dark grey as in Semipalmated Sandpiper ⇔ in Little black.
		• Tertial-patterning as in ad s (but no deep rufous fringes).
		• Usually faint head-pattern with diffusely bordered dark crown; middle of crown darker than sides. Supercilium often broken directly before eye ⇔ Little juv and Semipalmated Sandpiper juv.
		• Sometimes short 'split supercilium' but rarely as distinct as in Little ⇔ in Semipalmated Sandpiper juv very short at most.
1w		• See Dunlin 1w.
1s		• See 'Ageing of *Calidris* in spring'.
		• Some ind develop complete summer plumage as in ad, have all prim moulted and are thus indistinguishable from ad.
fl all plum		• See Little.

Little Stint *Calidris minuta*   L 14.5cm 5.7"

all plum		• Prim-projection c.30-50% with normally 2-3 prim-tips beyond tertials; usually obvious wing-projection beyond tail.
		• Rather short, almost straight bill.
		• Legs dark.
		• 'Split supercilium'; most conspicuous in juv, least in winter plumage.
ad s		• Pale throat and central part of upper breast (rarely whole breast red-brown).
		• Red-brown ear-coverts faintly streaked ⇔ in Red-necked Stint uniform red-orange.
		• Dark centres to scaps and tertials; tertials with rufous fringes (sometimes one grey fringe).
		• Rufous-brown upperparts without (strong) colour-contrast between mantle/scaps and cov.
		• Mantle-'V' sometimes indistinct cream-coloured but usually more obvious than in other stints.
w		• Brown-grey feathers of upperparts with dark shaft-streaks and rather small dark centre at base (latter especially distinct in 1w).
		• Dark loral-spot separated from eye ⇔ Red-necked w.
		• Well-marked breast-side pattern for a 'Eurasian stint', often creating complete breast-band.
juv	⇒	• Obvious mantle-'V' and rather obvious scaps-'V'.
	⇒	• Nearly entirely black centres to scaps *without distinct anchor-pattern* (in some ind rather large grey base and rather obvious anchor-pattern) ⇔ Semipalmated Sandpiper juv and Red-necked juv.

⇒	• Deep-rufous fringes to mantle feathers, scaps, tertials and usually also cov ⇔ Red-necked juv and Semipalmated Sandpiper juv (some Semipalmated Sandpiper juv with rather deep rufous fringes).
	• Rather *well-defined breast-side pattern* on rufous ground-colour ⇔ in Red-necked juv diffuse breast-side pattern on usually greyer ground-colour; in Semipalmated Sandpiper juv well-defined breast-pattern on greyish ground-colour.
1w	• See Dunlin 1w.
1s	• Most ind develop complete summer plumage as in ad, have all prim moulted and are thus indistinguishable from ad. Some ind retain juv (distinctly worn) inner prim which contrast with fresh outer prim.
fl all plum	• Obvious wing-bar.
	• Middle-grey tail-sides ⇔ in Temminck's Stint white.

Temminck's Stint *Calidris temminckii*   L 14.5cm 5.7"

all plum	⇒	• Legs grey-green, sometimes yellow to orange.
		• Long tail usually projects beyond wing-tips but often not very conspicuous.
		• Completely diffusely streaked to almost uniform breast-band.
		• Faintly patterned head; supercilium indistinct or absent.
		• Short prim-projection (in ad often absent due to long tertials).
		• No mantle- and scaps-'V'.
		• Eye-ring usually conspicuous and (almost) complete.
ad s		• Variable amount of summer type-scaps with dark bases or black, more or less 'U'-shaped centres and large diffuse rufous tips split by black shaft-streak (upperside not completely covered by summer-type feathers).
ad w/1w	⇒	• Uniform grey head and breast (creating breast-band) and slightly paler throat.
		• Feathers of upperparts grey-brown with weak dark shaft-streak.
juv	⇒	• Feathers of upperparts and cov grey-brown evenly scaled with narrow, dark, subterminal line and buff fringes.
		• Faintly streaked crown.
1w		• See Dunlin 1w.
1s		• Retains juv (distinctly worn) inner prim which contrast with fresh outer.
fl all plum	⇒	• White t5 and t6 (t4 almost white), creating white outer edge of tail (also often visible when bird perched).

Long-toed Stint *Calidris subminuta*   L 14.5cm 5.7"

all plum	⇒	• Supercilium ending *broadly and abruptly before bill* (not reaching bill); dark lores and dark forehead connected before bill-base.
		• Legs pale, yellow-green to grey-green; rather long, especially tibia.
		• Loral-stripe often narrowing strongly below large pale loral-spot (especially in juv, in ad s sometimes not) ⇔ in Least Sandpiper evenly broad loral-stripe over whole length.
		• Prim-projection very short or absent.
		• Pale base of lower mandible, sometimes also basal part of upper mandible (in w usually entirely dark bill).
		• Middle toe and tarsus longer than bill ⇔ Least.
		• Thin bill ending in narrow tip.
		• Usually conspicuously long neck when alert (sometimes also in Least Sandpiper).
ad s	⇒	• Feathers of upperparts with black centres and very broad, pale orange fringes (especially scaps and tertials), at distance cinnamon impression.
		• Breast finely streaked on whitish to orange ground-colour ⇔ Least Sandpiper ad s.
ad s/juv		• Cov with black centres *extending to feather-tips*, with buff (juv) to deep rufous fringes (ad s). Dark centres extending to feather-tips gives *upperparts (especially mantle) streaked impression* ⇔ in Least Sandpiper more scalloped impression.
		• Supercilium broadening strongly before eye.
w		• Brown-grey feathers on upperside and sharply demarcated dark centres to cov and scaps (in some ind only rear-most scaps and inner greater cov) ⇔ in Least Sandpiper w dark centres normally smaller and more faint (only diffuse broad shaft-streaks).
		• Dark crown contrasts with paler hind-neck (only a useful difference from Least Sandpiper in obvious cases).
		• Neck-side and breast-sides rather strongly streaked ⇔ Least Sandpiper w.
juv	⇒	• Scaps with white tip on outer web (as in Least Sandpiper but more obvious).
		• Very brightly patterned upperparts with very obvious mantle-'V'.
		• Breast-sides finely streaked on brown ground-colour and (just) not creating breast-band (centre of breast unpatterned).
1w		• See Dunlin 1w.
1s		• See 'Ageing of *Calidris* in spring'. Outer prim old and worn.
fl all plum	⇒	• Toes project clearly beyond tail ⇔ Least Sandpiper and other *Calidris*.
		• Darkest underwing of all small stints (dark lesser and median cov, prim-cov and underside of hand).
		• Weak wing-bar.

Least Sandpiper *Calidris minutilla*   L 14cm 5.5"

all plum	• Legs rather pale, greenish to yellowish.
	• Prim-projection very short or completely lacking.
	• Head-pattern dominated by broad and long dark loral-stripe (loral-stripe normally hardly narrowing below large pale loral-spot ⇔ Long-toed Stint).
	• Supercilium usually extends to bill ⇔ in Long-toed Stint dark forehead to bill.
	• Slightly downcurved bill ending in narrow tip.

ad s ⇒
- Middle toe, tarsus and bill all about of same length.
- Steep forehead ⇔ in Long-toed Stint less conspicuous.
- Breast with dark triangular spots on brown ground-colour, creating complete band. Brown breast (nearly) concolorous with mantle ⇔ all similar species.
- Upperside rather dark due to large black centres to mantle feathers and scaps. Scaps and cov with weak rufous and grey fringes.
- Rather obvious mantle-'V', often disappearing due to wear.

ad s/juv
- Greater cov and sometimes some tertial-fringes with somewhat wavy fringes; in well-marked ind (normally only in ad s) somewhat notched (when present characteristic) ⇔ other Calidris.

w
- Poorly contrasting, grey-brown head with ill-defined supercilium (resembles Temminck's Stint w).
- Breast rather diffusely streaked but creating complete breast-band ⇔ in Temminck's Stint breast uniform.
- Feathers of upperparts and cov dark grey-brown with dark shaft-streak; slightly broader shaft-streak on mantle feathers and lower scaps and sometimes larger dark centres to upper scaps (in 1w larger dark scaps-centres than ad w) ⇔ Long-toed Stint w.
- Poorly contrasting, grey-brown head with ill-defined supercilium (resembles Temminck's Stint w).
- Breast rather diffusely streaked but creating complete breast-band ⇔ in Temminck's Stint breast uniform.

juv ⇒
- Lower scaps with black centres reaching to feather tips but less distinct than in Long-toed Stint.
- Scaps with white tip on outer web, creating rather obvious scaps-'V' (also in Long-toed Stint).
- Deep-rufous fringes to scaps and cov (rufous-brown overall impression), sometimes cov distinctly less rufous-coloured than scaps.
- Dominant dark lores and well-defined pale spot ('pushed in' loral-stripe as in e.g. Baird's Sandpiper and Long-toed Stint) but loral-stripe usually continues rather broadly at loral-spot ⇔ Long-toed Stint (see also all plum).
- 'Split supercilium' sometimes present but short ⇔ in Little Stint and Long-toed Stint usually longer.

1w
- See Dunlin 1w.

1s
- See 'Ageing of Calidris in spring'.
- Some ind develop complete summer plumage as in ad, have all prim moulted and are thus indistinguishable from ad.

fl all plum
- Rather narrow wing-bar.
- Rather dark underside of hand.

White-rumped Sandpiper *Calidris fuscicollis*   L 19cm 7.5"

all plum ⇒
⇒
⇒
- Obvious broad supercilium; eye seems 'pushed up' from below in supercilium.
- Long prim-projection (c.80-100%) and large wing-projection.
- White uppertail-cov and part of rump.
- Whole breast densely and sharply streaked/spotted, usually some streaks extending to flanks.
- Often pale(r) base of lower mandible.
- Bill slightly downcurved with somewhat stumpy tip.
- Legs dark, in some ind rather pale brown.
- Relatively long toes.

ad s ⇒
- In spring/summer strongly streaked/spotted crown, throat and especially ear-coverts and breast; patterning often extending to flanks with arrowhead-shaped spots (less streaked later in summer).
- Black centres to mantle feathers and scaps (scaps with pale base) with rufous fringes on upper scaps; later in summer fringes of upper scaps more yellow-brown.
- Early moult to winter plumage (from July). In August head and mantle/scaps often already winter plumage with conspicuous greyish head.
- When fresh, weak mantle-'V'.

juv
- Obvious mantle-'V' and scaps-'V'.
- Rufous fringes to mantle feathers and upper scaps; lower scaps and cov with buffish fringes and conspicuous white 'V'-shaped tip.
- Rufous wash on crown (sometimes also on ear-coverts).
- Tertials blackish, often becoming slightly greyer towards edge; whitish to rufous tertial-fringes.
- Nearly uniform grey rear-head.

1w
- See Dunlin 1w.

(1)w
- Grey feathers of upperparts with dark shaft-streak. In 1w scaps with broader diffuse dark shaft-streak (as in Little Stint 1w) than in ad.
- Fine streaking along flanks.

1s
- See 'Ageing of Calidris in spring'.
- Some ind develop complete summer plumage as in ad, have all prim moulted and are thus indistinguishable from ad. Others retain part or all prim until autumn, retained prim then obviously worn.

fl all plum
- Unpatterned white uppertail-cov and part of rump creating rectangular white area.
- Rather weak wing-bar.

Baird's Sandpiper *Calidris bairdii*   L 19cm 7.5"

all plum ⇒
- Very long prim-projection (c.100%) and large wing-projection.
- Conspicuous and well-defined pale spot above lores, on underside 'pushed' in dark loral-stripe (usually most obvious in juv).
- Only slightly cdownurved (sometimes entirely straight) dark bill with narrow tip.
- Often characteristic yellow-brown overall impression.

ad s
- Mantle feathers and especially scaps with large dark, often somewhat rectangular centres on greyish ground-colour; upperside strongly black chequered.
- Usually has a rather ill-defined head-pattern with brown wash and usually rather indistinct but long supercilium.
- Breast diffusely and finely streaked on brown ground-colour, creating complete breast-band.

w		• Grey-brown feathers of upperparts with yellow-brown wash and rather broad dark shaft-streak; sometimes upperparts grey.
		• Breast finely streaked on pale brown ground-colour.
juv	⇒	• Upperside dominated by pale scaled pattern; all feathers with broad, yellow-brown to whitish fringes, usually without complete crossing by dark shaft ⇔ e.g. Curlew Sandpiper juv.
		• Breast (sometimes also ear-coverts) peppered with well-defined dark spots, creating complete patterned breast-band.
		• Cov and scaps with yellow-brown base and usually rather slight anchor-pattern; sometimes rather distinct anchor-pattern on scaps.
		• Moults into 1w in winter range.
1w		• See Dunlin 1w, but normally no 1w-plumage in WP (normally migrates in juv plumage).
1s		• See White-rumped Sandpiper 1s.
fl all plum	⇒	• Relatively dark tail/rump-area due to only narrow pale tail-sides and narrow pale rump-sides.
		• Narrow wing-bar.

Pectoral Sandpiper *Calidris melanotos*   L 22.5cm 8.5"

all plum	⇒	• Breast densely streaked, *finishing abruptly* on upper belly (in ad ♂'s breast somewhat scaled), *ending in slight point in middle*.
		• Legs pale, green to yellow-orange.
		• ♂ larger than ♀ almost without overlap.
		• Pale bill-base (both mandibles).
		• 'Split supercilium'; most obvious in juv, least obvious in winter plumage.
ad s		• Rather obvious mantle-'V' ⇔ in juv both mantle- and scaps-'V' with distinct white on outer-edge of scaps.
		• Feathers of upperside with dark centres and faint rufous to whitish fringes (rufous fringes especially on upper scaps and tertials).
		• Elongated, pointed scaps and rear-most greater cov, as in Sharp-tailed Sandpiper (in juv less conspicuous).
w		• Resembles weakly patterned, grey ad s; little difference between summer and winter plumage ⇔ Sharp-tailed.
		• Breast more diffusely streaked than in ad s on greyer ground-colour.
juv		• Strongly patterned and coloured upperside with white mantle-'V' and scaps-'V'; scaps with white outer-edge and shorter and more pointed than in ad in autumn.
		• Tertial-fringes concolorous with or more rufous than crown ⇔ Sharp-tailed.
		• Prim-projection long (70-100%), often shorter in ad due to longer tertials.
1w		• See Dunlin 1w, but normally no 1w-plumage in WP (normally migrates in juv plumage).
1s		• See 'Ageing of *Calidris* in spring'.
		• Some ind develop complete summer plumage as in ad, have all prim moulted and are thus indistinguishable from ad.
fl all plum		• (Very) weak wing-bar.
		• Dark prim-cov on underwing (as on Sharp-tailed) ⇔ Ruff.

Sharp-tailed Sandpiper *Calidris acuminata*   L 21.5cm 8.5"

all plum	⇒	• Dark, rufous cap conspicuous and especially contrasting behind eye with broad supercilium (least obvious in ad s) ⇔ Pectoral Sandpiper.
		• Legs grey-green.
		• Tertial-fringes less deep rufous than crown ⇔ in Pectoral the other way around.
		• Eye-ring relatively thick and conspicuous.
		• Supercilium prominent and widens behind eye ⇔ in Pectoral less prominent.
		• Pale bill-base, as in Pectoral but pale part usually smaller, sometimes entirely dark bill.
		• Prim-projection rather long, as in Pectoral (in ad often shorter due to long tertials).
		• Slightly longer-legged and shorter-billed than Pectoral.
		• Shape of scaps as in Pectoral ⇔ most other *Calidris*.
ad s	⇒	• 'V'-shaped spots on breast, *extending over flanks to undertail-cov*.
		• Rather obvious mantle-'V', scaps-'V' absent or weaker.
		• Feathers of upperside with dark centres and broad buffish to rufous fringes (rufous fringes especially on upper scaps and tertials).
		• When moulting to winter plumage somewhat patchy with rather obvious differences between winter- and summer-feathers (in Pectoral ad s moulting to winter plumage less obvious differences).
w		• Resembles greyish ad s with less contrasting rufous crown, fine streaks or spots on breast and weak patterning on flanks.
juv	⇒	• Orange, uniform centre of breast (breast-sides and throat streaked).
	⇒	• Streaked vent (sometimes also faint streaking in Pectoral juv).
		• Pale throat and ear-coverts; lores rather faintly patterned.
		• Head and upperside nearly as in ad s but slightly broader fringes on cov and tertials.
1w		• See Dunlin 1w, but normally no 1w-plumage in WP (normally migrates in juv plumage).
1s		• See Pectoral 1s.
fl all plum	⇒	• Obvious longitudinal streaks on pale rump-sides (only *Calidris* with these streaks in combination with dark centre of rump).
		• Weak wing-bar.

Curlew Sandpiper *Calidris ferruginea*   L 20cm 8"

all plum	⇒	• Bill c.1.5 x head length and evenly curved from distal half.
		• Obvious supercilium (except in ad s).
		• Legs black; tibia especially relatively long.

Sandpipers and allies

ad s	⇒	• Rather long prim-projection (c.60-80%) and wings obviously reach beyond tail (⇔ Dunlin).
		• Dark reddish underparts (darker than in Red Knot).
		• Mantle- and scaps-pattern similar to Red Knot ad s but often with broader black markings: rufous bases, dark bar-shape patterning and grey tips (creating pied rufous-black-grey pattern). Mantle and scaps contrast with pale grey cov.
ad w	⇒	• Feathers of upperparts and cov almost uniform pale grey with very narrow, dark shaft-streak.
juv	⇒	• Usually rather indistinct anchor-pattern on scaps and cov *but obvious white fringes creating scaled pattern on feathers of upperparts and cov.* Anchor-pattern evenly on cov to mantle feathers.
		• Peach-coloured breast-sides, faintly streaked.
		• In autumn in WP complete juv plumage normally retained.
1w		• See Dunlin 1w, but usually no 1w-plumage in WP (normally migrates in juv plumage).
1s		• See 'Ageing of *Calidris* in spring'. Most ind retain complete winter plumage throughout summer.
fl all plum	⇒	• White, unpatterned uppertail-cov/rump.
		• Obvious wing-bar.

Stilt Sandpiper *Calidris himantopus*   L 21cm 8.5"

all plum	⇒	• Legs very long for *Calidris*; yellow to yellow-green.
	⇒	• Nearly straight bill with deep base (often slightly curved on distal part). Bill length 1.5 x head-length.
		• Prim-projection c.50-80% with 2-3 prim-tips beyond tertials and large wing-projection (as in Curlew Sandpiper).
		• Distinct supercilium.
ad s	⇒	• Completely and strongly barred underparts.
		• Rufous ear-coverts and crown.
ad w	⇒	• Densely spotted throat and breast, extending to flanks and some spots onto belly (sometimes whole underparts evenly spotted).
		• Undertail-cov strongly spotted, suggestion of barring.
		• Pale grey upperparts; scaps with very narrow dark shaft-streak.
juv-1w		• Grey centres to cov with narrow anchor-pattern due to narrow dark shaft-streak.
		• Juv mantle feathers dark with rufous fringes contrasting with paler scaps and cov with whitish to buffish fringes (early moult to 1w; 1w with grey ad w-type mantle and scaps).
		• Breast densely marked and some ('V'-shaped) markings on flanks ⇔ Curlew Sandpiper juv.
		• Juv cov and tertials show strong resemblance to those of Curlew Sandpiper juv.
1w		• See Dunlin 1w.
1s		• Like ad s but contrast between old and worn inner and fresh outer prim.
fl all plum	⇒	• *Weak wing-bar* ⇔ Curlew Sandpiper.
	⇒	• Legs project well beyond tail for *Calidris* (toes entirely projected).
		• White uppertail-cov (slightly patterned), in ad s stronger marked, then less obviously pale.
		• Dark underside of prim contrast with white underwing-cov.

Purple Sandpiper *Calidris maritima*   L 20.5cm 8"

all plum	⇒	• Pale spot above lores conspicuous due to mainly dark uniform head (absent in worn summer plumage).
	⇒	• Legs relatively short, yellow-orange, in summer more greenish.
		• Orange bill-base. Bill-structure about as in Dunlin but thicker with deeper base.
		• Long tail often projects beyond wing-tips.
		• Long prim-projection due to very short tertials.
		• Strongly patterned breast and flanks, extending to undertail-cov.
		• Feathers of upperparts dark with narrow pale fringes; in ad s and juv faint rufous fringes to upper scaps and mantle feathers.
ad s		• Throat and breast heavily spotted.
		• Summer-type feathers on upperside with grey and rufous tips side by side.
		• Streaked rufous crown and ear-coverts.
ad w		• Nearly uniform dark grey head and breast.
		• Flanks diffusely streaked.
juv-1w		• Well-defined whitish fringes to juv cov ⇔ in ad w inconspicuous narrow fringes.
		• Throat and breast streaked (more well-defined than in ad).
		• In juv crown often rufous as in ad s.
1w		• See Dunlin 1w.
1s		• See 'Ageing of *Calidris* in spring'.
fl all plum	⇒	• Hand on underside nearly entirely dark.
		• Wing-bar conspicuous due to dark upperside of wing. Wing-bar broadens towards body, due to increasing amount of white on inner sec (white on inner sec unique among *Calidris* in WP).
		• White rump-sides slightly patterned ⇔ most other *Calidris*.

Dunlin *Calidris alpina*   L 19cm 7.7"

all plum		• Bill length 1-1.5 x head-length; basal half of bill straight, distal half downcurved.
ad s	⇒	• Black belly(-patch).
		• Rufous mantle feathers and scaps with relatively small, black, elongated centres.
ad w		• Brown-grey feathers of upperside with narrow dark shaft-streak on mantle feathers and scaps, slightly broader on cov.
		• Rather uniform head-side.
juv	⇒	• Patchy black belly.
		• Obvious mantle-'V'.
		• Moults early towards 1w (starting with scaps).
1w		• Like ad w, but (often obvious) moult-limit between newly moulted mantle feathers and scaps and still juv cov.

1s	• See 'Ageing of *Calidris* in spring'. Most ind develop full summer-plumage with worn, juv prim.
fl all plum	• Obvious, broad wing-bar.
	• Broad, white rump-sides.

geog var	*C.a. alpina* (northern Scandinavia and north-western Asia)
all plum	• Long bill.
ad s	• Very white breast and flanks.
	• Large black uniform belly patch.

geog var	*C.a. schinzii* (southern Scandinavia, Iceland, Britain)
all plum	• Small size with rather short bill (bill-length as head-length).
ad s	• Black belly patch relatively small and not uniformly black as in other subspecies (does not apply when worn).
	• Breast with relatively broad black streaks.
	• Relatively dull rufous fringes to scaps and mantle feathers (early moult towards summer plumage probably (partly) responsible for more worn and bleached summer plumage than in other subspecies at same time of year).
	• Ear-coverts and neck-side deeper cream-coloured than in *alpina* and *arctica*.
	• Ground-colour of underparts buffish ⇔ in other subspecies whiter.

geog var	*C.a. arctica* (northern Greenland)
all plum	• Together with *schinzii* smallest subspecies with shortest bill (bill-length ≤ head-length). Bill of *arctica* generally shortest and almost straight.
ad s	• Very white breast.
	• Dark belly patch smaller than in *alpina*.
	• Relatively narrow and pale brown-yellow fringes to feathers of upperparts when fresh.

geog var	*C.a. hudsonia* (North America)
all plum	• Long bill with deep base.
ad s	• Similar to *sakhalina* but upperparts deeper brown, not orange, black centres to scaps slightly larger and black belly-patch smaller.
	• Fine flank streaking extending to vent.
w	• Extensive *fine* streaks on underparts; on flanks especially extending at least to legs. Sometimes weakly present in other subspecies (except *sakhalina*) but not extending to legs.
1w	• Often dark, especially on breast (in strongest case creating obvious breast-band).
	• Often dark lores ⇔ other subspecies.

geog var	*C.a. sakhalina* (north-eastern Siberia)
all plum	• Largest subspecies together with *hudsonia*.
	• Long bill but generally slightly shorter than in *hudsonia*.
ad s	• Head-side, neck-side and breast white with only very small black speckles or streaks.
	• Large black belly-patch contrasts strongly with white background of remainder of underparts.
	• Bright brown-orange crown, mantle and scaps.
	• Relatively small black centres to scaps; rear-most scaps almost without darker centres.

Broad-billed Sandpiper *Limicola falcinellus* L 16.5cm 6.5"

all plum ⇒	• Conspicuous complete broad dark loral-stripe (more marked than in all *Calidris*).
	• Tip of bill (distal quarter) abruptly hooked. Bill longer than head-length with deep base.
	• 'Double' supercilium (supercilium and pale lateral crown-stripe), less distinct in winter.
	• Upperside rather streaked due to pale fringes along both inner- and outer edge of all feathers.
	• Prim-projection short c.30%, with 2-3 prim-tips beyond tertials.
	• Legs rather short and dark, often somewhat green-brown.
ad s ⇒	• Mantle feathers, scaps, cov and tertials with dark centre; in spring with well-marked white and buff fringes (at distance looks like pale wash over upperparts), worn off later in summer and upperparts become very dark.
	• Breast peppered with triangular spots, extending along flanks towards undertail-cov.
	• Rather distinct mantle- and scaps-'V'.
ad w	• Dark lesser cov creating dark wing-bend (as in Sanderling w).
	• Grey (rather pale) feathers of upperparts with broad dark shaft-streaks.
juv	• As ad s but breast markings not triangular and not extending along flanks. Breast in general less dark than in ad s.
	• Distinct, sharp mantle- and scaps-'V'.
	• Mantle feathers, upper scaps and tertials with rufous fringes ⇔ in ad s whitish.
1w	• See Dunlin 1w, but normally no 1w-plumage in WP (normally migrates in juv plumage).
1s	• See 'Ageing of *Calidris* in spring'.
fl all plum	• Dark lesser cov creating dark wing-bend (as in Sanderling w).
	• White outer-edge of tail.
	• Narrow wing-bar.
	• Rather narrow, white rump-sides.

| geog var | *L.f. sibirica (*eastern Siberia) |
| ad s | • Often only slightly different from *falcinellus* but generally more rufous ear-coverts, breast more rufous and more densely dark spotted, paler head with more narrow lateral crown-stripe and broader pale frings to feathers of upperparts. |

Buff-breasted Sandpiper *Tryngites subruficollis*   L 20cm 8"

all plum ⇒	• Dark streaked crown; rest of head unmarked with conspicuous large eye.
	• Strongly scaled mantle, scaps and cov.
	• Prim-projection c.70% (in ad shorter), wing-tip reaches to tail-tip or slight wing-projection.
	• Legs brown-yellow to yellow-orange, sometimes green-yellow.
	• Underparts warm brown-yellow; some dark speckles restricted to breast-sides (resembles Ruff juv).
	• Head-feathering extends conspicuously further on lower mandible than on upper mandible (⇔ e.g. Ruff).
ad	• Black centres to feathers on upperparts with broad pale fringes (but see 1s).
juv	• Dark centres to mantle feathers and most rear scaps with whitish fringes; paler centres to scaps and cov with narrow, well-defined pale fringes and weak anchor-pattern; overall dense and finely scaled impression ⇔ ad.
	• Cov and scaps often with subterminal black line.
1s	• Most ind indistinguishable from ad; ind with moult-limit in scaps or moult-limit between scaps and cov before July (scaps fresh, broadly fringed, cov old with narrow, often whitish fringes) perhaps indicative of this age.
fl all plum ⇒	• White underwing with dark trailing edge and dark tips to prim-cov, *creating dark crescent on carpal joints*.
⇒	• No wing-bar; almost uniform upperwing.
	• Rump mostly dark brownish (only narrow pale rump-sides) ⇔ Ruff.
behav	• Feeds with very quick movements.

Ruff *Philomachus pugnax*   L ♂ 31cm 12", ♀ 24cm 9.5"

all plum	• Legs grey-green to orange.
	• ♂ considerably larger than ♀.
	• Prim-projection very short or absent ⇔ Pectoral Sandpiper, Sharp-tailed Sandpiper and Buff-breasted Sandpiper.
ad ♀ s	• Black centres and pale fringes to feathers of upperparts; cov, scaps and tertials distinctly barred ⇔ juv.
	• Variable amount of dark spots on breast.
ad w	• As ad ♀ s but breast uniform brown-grey and no or only some barred feathers.
	• ♂ often with paler underparts, occasionally white throughout.
juv ⇒	• Upperparts *strongly and evenly scaled*.
	• No pale mantle- or scaps-'V'.
1s	• Often difficult to judge; inner lesser cov and median cov sometimes still juv; worn, brown with dark tips.
1s ♀	• Moult-limit in prim, outer 2 new, rest old (in 1s ♂ prim moult completed).
behav	• Feeds quietly, 'purposefully' ⇔ most *Calidris* and Buff-breasted Sandpiper.
fl all plum	• Entirely white underwing (also prim-cov ⇔ Buff-breasted Sandpiper, Pectoral Sandpiper and Sharp-tailed Sandpiper).
	• Much white on sides of rump, creating long oval-shaped spots on either side of dark central stripe.

Jack Snipe *Lymnocryptes minimus*   L 19cm 7.5"

all plum ⇒	• 'Double supercilium' (supercilium and pale lateral crown-stripe).
⇒	• Only longitudinal stripes on flanks, no flank barring.
	• Dark eye-stripe and stripe over ear-coverts coming together behind eye.
	• Small size with relatively short bill.
	• No pale median crown-stripe ⇔ all other small snipes.
	• Very obvious long mantle- and shoulder-stripe contrast with very dark mantle and scaps.
fl all plum	• Rather broad white trailing edge along arm.
	• Dark, pointed tail.
	• Flight-feathers paler than prim-cov and greater cov (some contrast visible under good viewing conditions) ⇔ all other small snipes.
	• Broad pale bands over underwing-cov as in Common Snipe.
behav	• Takes flight only just in front of disturber and lands quickly again.

Common Snipe *Gallinago gallinago*   L 27cm 10.5"

all plum	• Long bill ≥ 2 x head-length.
	• White unpatterned belly.
	• Supercilium only slightly bulging between eye and bill (see Wilson's Snipe and Pintail Snipe).
	• Supercilium cream-coloured, darker than (whitish) stripe over ear-coverts ⇔ all small snipes in WP except Wilson's.
	• Tertials barred: dark bands broadening towards tip ⇔ most other congeners except Wilson's.
ad/juv	• Ad end of summer (partially) worn ⇔ juv uniform fresh (moult of cov in August-September).
	• Mainly dark scaps with broad golden-coloured fringes on outer webs ⇔ in juv often paler (with well-developed brown patterning) and slightly narrower and whiter fringes on outer webs.
	• Ad undergo prim moult in autumn ⇔ juv.
juv-1w ⇒	• Tertials dark with well-defined, narrow deep rufous bars and narrow pale fringe around tip ⇔ in ad pale patterning broader and dark patterning more diffuse (rendering tertials as a whole paler) and more grey-brown and rather broad pale fringe around tip.
	• Median cov with narrow pale fringe around tip (quickly worn off) and dark subterminal band ⇔ in ad relatively large, well-defined and straight-bordered white tip cut through by dark shaft.
	• Tail-feathers with brown-orange distal part, slightly pale tip and no dark shaft in tip ⇔ in ad distal part also brown-orange but tip whitish and dark shaft in tip.
note juv-1w	• Above-mentioned (except tertial-pattern) strongly variable and normally difficult to see under field conditions. See also moult. From November onwards tertials, median cov and tail-feathers normally all moulted to ad-type and ageing using these feather-groups not possible.
1w	• Prim more worn than in ad but differences often small.

1s	• Often distinct moult-limit in cov ⇔ ad.
fl all plum ⇒	• Obvious white trailing edge of arm, broadening towards body (in juv-type sec more narrow).
moult	• Ad undergo prim moult in autumn ⇔ juv.
	• Ad start from July onwards with moult of cov, tertials and tail-feathers ⇔ juv moult later and slower with often only some new ad-type cov, tertials and tail-feathers in autumn.
note	• For other field marks see Wilson's, Pintail and Great Snipe.

Wilson's Snipe *Gallinago delicata*   L 26cm 10"

all plum ⇒	• Outer tail-feathers generally more narrow and even of width, and with ends more angular (but some overlap with Common Snipe: ≤ 9mm ⇔ in Common ≥ 10mm. Outer tail-feather bulging on inner web.
	• Outer tail-feathers generally with more numerous and well-defined dark bars (4-5) and with narrower white bands than in Common (usually 3, sometimes 2-5 dark bars). Dark bars often more diagonal compared to shaft. Dark and pale bars about same width, or dark ones wider ⇔ in Common barring normally diffuse and especially in distal part of feather pale bands broader.
	• Axillaries heavily barred with broader black than white bands ⇔ in Common often broader white than black bands, but rarely measurements for Common overlap with Wilson's.
	• 14-18 tail-feathers (normally 16) ⇔ in Common normally 14 but can have 12-18.
	• Upperparts often lack distinct warm-brown tones; centre to mantle feathers (very) dark, sometimes almost lacking patterning (occasionally recalling Jack Snipe). Head often warmer brown and contrasting with rest of plumage ⇔ in Common.
	• Lateral crown-stripes often solidly black ⇔ in Common often with brown patterning.
	• Well-defined and broad barring on breast-sides and flanks (dark and pale bars almost of equal width), sharply demarcated against white background ⇔ in Common often more diffuse, narrower and set against yellow-brown ground colour.
	• Generally 'colder' coloured with brown on underparts concentrated on (upper-)breast (much variation in both Common and Wilson's in ground colour due to factors such as bleaching and wear – see note).
	• Rather even and straight tertial-barring (dark bars becoming broader towards tip as in Common). Patterning usually fading away slightly towards base ⇔ in Common usually irregular and more 'V'-shaped pale patterning on tertials, not fading away towards base. Much overlap and note differences in tertial pattern between juv and ad (see Common juv-1w).
	• Pale outer edge to scaps often narrower (especially on rear scaps) and whiter than in Common, but in Common juv-1w also narrower and whiter.
	• Generally shorter bill than in Common (especially in population from eastern part of North America). In all snipe species ♂ with shorter bill than ♀.
	• Loral-stripe often rather narrow, supercilium very broad and 'bulging' before eye (pattern resembles Pintail Snipe).
juv-1w	• See Common juv-1w.
1w	• See Common 1w.
1s	• See Common 1s.
fl all plum	• Underwing-cov have strong dark markings without distinct broader pale bars (as in Pintail and Great Snipe) ⇔ Common.
⇒	
⇒	• Smaller pale tips to sec (< 2 mm) creating narrower pale trailing edge to arm than in Common (> 3.5 mm). Pale trailing edge to arm as narrow as pale bar along greater cov ⇔ in Common trailing edge of arm (much) broader.
	• Often has pale tips to prim-cov as in Pintail and Great (but less distinct), creating narrow wing-bar ⇔ Common.
voice	• Call very similar to Common, flight-call may be slightly more dry than Common. 'Drumming' display using tail-feathers increasing in volume like Common, but notes much fuller and much less dry and mechanic, rather reminiscent of song of Tengmalm's Owl.
note ⇒	• Some geographic and rather marked individual variation in nearly all features; most of features mentioned above fall within range of variability of Common, also dependent upon age (see Common juv-1w). Strongest pointers: pattern and shape of outer tail-feathers, narrow pale trailing edge to arm, pattern of underwing-cov, pattern of axillaries.

Great Snipe *Gallinago media*   L 28cm 11"

all plum ⇒	• Large and complete white tips to all cov; dark shaft not crossing through white tip ⇔ Common Snipe (in Great juv smaller white tip, sometimes dark shaft crosses through white tip).
⇒	• Underparts heavily barred, especially along flanks and incl thigh-feathering ⇔ Common.
	• Narrow, dark loral-stripe and very broad supercilium before eye (head-pattern more like Pintail Snipe than Common).
	• Rather ill-defined dark stripe over ear-coverts ⇔ in Common usually rather distinct.
	• Supercilium usually narrows directly behind eye.
	• Bill length ⇔ 2 x head-length, usually shorter than in Common.
	• Mantle and scaps with broad pale outer edges (nearly as in Common).
	• Legs slightly longer than in Common.
ad	• Outer 3 pairs of tail-feathers white almost without patterning ⇔ juv.
juv	• Only a little dark patterning at tail-base; on flying up much more white visible in tail than in Common.
	• Belly almost unmarked ⇔ ad.
ad/juv	• Ad in early autumn worn ⇔ juv fresh.
1s	• Most ind indistinguishable from ad, some ind with some worn retained juv cov which then strongly contrast with rest.
fl all plum	• Heavy body (sometimes resembling Eurasian Woodcock).
	• Underwing densely barred (as Pintail Snipe and Wilson's Snipe), looks uniformly dark grey under field conditions.
	• 2 narrow but distinct white wing-bars over both arm and hand, *especially conspicuous on prim-cov.*

	• Rather narrow white trailing edge on arm.
	• Broad, usually more rounded wings than Common.
voice	• Flight-call shorter and less rasping than Common's (or not rasping at all).
behav	• Takes flight only just in front of disturber and lands quickly again ⇔ Common nearly always flies far when disturbed.

Pintail Snipe *Gallinago stenura*   L 25cm 10"

all plum ⇒	• 24-28 tail-feathers (usually 26), of which outer 7-9 pair consist of spiky feathers (characteristic but very difficult to see under field conditions).
	• Generally shorter bill (c.1.5 x head-length ⇔ Common Snipe ≥ 2 x head-length), wings and tail than Common but heavier body (weight generally distinct heavier than in Common with only slight overlap).
	• Supercilium before eye very broad (broader than eye) and nearly angularly set off against lateral crown-stripe. Supercilium usually concolorous with pale stripe over ear-coverts ⇔ Common.
	• Greater cov and sometimes tertials paler than in Common with broader pale bands than dark ones ⇔ in Common the other way around.
	• Scaps with rather evenly broad fringes on both inner and outer web but very variable, some more towards Common ⇔ in Common fringes on outer web broad, on inner web narrow of even absent.
	• Lesser and median cov with broader pale fringes than in Common, creating pale panel.
	• Narrow loral-stripe and narrow dark stripe over ear-coverts making head-side pale ⇔ in Common broader and head-side darker.
	• Short tail reaches only slightly beyond wing-tips, giving impression of stumpy rear-end ⇔ Common.
	• Upperparts more evenly patterned than in Common.
	• At least inner 6 greater cov and all median cov distinctly barred ⇔ in Common only inner 2-3 greater cov distinctly barred. In Common median cov with more spot-like markings.
	• Tertials evenly barred; dark barring rather even and narrow, hardly broadening towards tip and less wavy or 'V'-shaped than in most Common.
	• White, unpatterned belly, as in Common but unpatterned part smaller in area.
	• Relatively ill-defined patterned head-side.
	• Supercilium narrows usually directly behind eye.
ad/juv	• Ad in early autumn worn ⇔ juv fresh.
	• Mainly dark scaps with broad golden-coloured fringes ⇔ in juv paler (with well-marked brown patterning), narrower and more contrasting white fringes on outer web. Narrow white fringes on greater cov and tertials ⇔ in ad absent.
ad	• Upper scaps with somewhat Common-like pattern: golden-coloured fringes on outer webs and very narrow pale fringes on inner webs. Lower scaps normally with more evenly pale fringes ⇔ Common.
1s	• Often distinct moult-limit in cov ⇔ ad.
	• (Part of) prim still juv and worn.
fl all plum	• Strongly barred underwing-cov, without larger white areas (as in Swinhoe's Snipe, Wilson's Snipe and Great Snipe).
	• Very narrow pale trailing edge of wing ⇔ in Common broader and whiter.
	• Upperwing with rather strong contrast between pale brown cov (creating pale wing-panel) and dark sec, prim and prim-cov.
	• Rather broad, rounded hand ⇔ Common.
	• More leg projection beyond tail than Common and Swinhoe's due to shorter tail (toes project almost completely).
	• Hardly any white in outer tail-feathers.
note	• Under field conditions very difficult or impossible to distinguish from Swinhoe's (see Swinhoe's for differences).
voice	• Flight-call shorter and less rasping than Common's (or not rasping at all).

Swinhoe's Snipe *Gallinago megala*   L 28cm 11"

all plum ⇒	• 18-26 tail-feathers (usually 20), outer tail-feathers (normally 6 pairs) narrow and increasingly narrowing outwards ⇔ in Pintail Snipe outer (often 8 pairs) all of same breadth and very narrow (about as narrow as outer pair of Swinhoe's).
	• For more features see Pintail all plum.
ad/juv	• Ad in early autumn worn ⇔ juv fresh.
	• Mainly dark scaps with broad rich buff fringes ⇔ in juv paler (with extensive brown patterning) and narrower and usually contrasting white fringes on outer webs (sometimes fringe on outer web concolorous with inner web ⇔ in Pintail rarely).
1s	• Probably as in Pintail (see there).
voice	• Flight-call similar to Pintail but lower pitched and less regular repeated.
	Field marks mentioned below overlap at least partially with Pintail; combination indicative of Swinhoe's:
	• Generally larger and heavier than Pintail and Common Snipe.
	• Head-pattern very like Pintail.
	• Generally longer tail than Pintail but relatively shorter than in Common.
	• 3-4 broad dark bars on greater cov.
	• Flanks often rather heavily barred.
fl all plum	• (Nearly) no leg projection beyond tail ⇔ Pintail.
	• Very narrow whitish trailing edge to wing.
	• Underwing completely and heavily barred (as in Pintail).
	• Outer tail-feathers barred ⇔ in Pintail almost uniformly dark.
	• Purer white in tail (outer tail-feathers and tips of central tail-feathers) than in Pintail.
note	• Bill generally slightly longer than in Pintail but variation and overlap too large to use as reliable field mark.

Short-billed Dowitcher, Long-billed Dowitcher and Asiatic Dowitcher

all plum	• Supercilium and dark loral-stripe conspicuous.
	• Legs dark grey-green, in juv paler green-yellow.
	• Slightly larger than Common Redshank.
	• Long bill with paler basal half ⇔ in Asian Dowitcher completely dark bill.
	• No or very short prim-projection.
fl all plum	• Pale tips to sec and inner prim, creating somewhat Common Redshank-like pale trailing edge of wing.
	• Narrow wing-bar.

Short-billed Dowitcher *Limnodromus griseus*   L 27cm 10.5"

all plum	• See introduction to Short-billed Dowitcher, Long-billed Dowitcher and Asiatic Dowitcher.
	• Bill generally shorter than in Long-billed Dowitcher; in short-billed ind (♂) bill length < 2x head-length ⇔ most Long-billed (especially ♀).
	• Very small prim-projection ⇔ in Long-billed usually none.
	• Black tail-bars not much broader than white ones ⇔ Long-billed (but more variation than in Long-billed). In eastern North American *griseus* tail-pattern probably overlaps with Long-billed. In central North American *hendersoni* probably most white in tail, when present characteristic difference with Long-billed.
	• Tail-barring often irregular ⇔ most Long-billed.
ad/1s	• Wing-tips level with or extending slightly beyond tail.
ad s	• Patchy pattern on underparts more evenly spread than in Long-billed, also thighs spotted ⇔ Long-billed.
	• Feathers of upperparts well marked, with grey, white and rufous fringes and tips.
	• Mainly black spots on underparts (no obvious barring on breast-sides ⇔ Long-billed), without well-defined white tips.
	• Pale 'tiger-stripes' on mantle (especially in *hendersoni*).
	• Summer plumage acquired considerably later than in Long-billed (from May).
ad w	• Grey breast(-sides) often mixed with pale patterning; grey not extending down to upper belly ⇔ Long-billed ad w.
	• Small black speckles on breast ⇔ in Long-billed ad w normally unmarked.
	• Grey feathers of upperparts (generally paler than in Long-billed) with narrow dark shaft-streaks and often more obvious pale fringes than in most Long-billed.
juv-1w ⇒	• Buff patterning *in* dark centres to tertials, inner greater cov and inner median cov ⇔ Long-billed juv.
	• Very dark crown with fine rufous streaks; no grey patterning on rear-crown ⇔ in Long-billed juv-1w often grey rear-crown and hind-neck.
	• Warm cream-coloured wash on breast ⇔ in Long-billed juv more greyish.
	• Supercilium longer than in Long-billed juv-1w.
	• Breast-sides, vent and undertail-cov with dark, rounded spots (ghosting pattern of ad s) ⇔ in Long-billed juv usually more heavily patterned with larger spots and bars.
	• Broad dark loral-stripe contrasts strongly with supercilium (in Long-billed also often broad dark loral-stripe but contrast less with supercilium).
	• Both juv scaps and cov distinctly pointed ⇔ ad-type feathers rounded.
1s	• Variable but usually incomplete summer plumage, sometimes hardly any summer feathers ⇔ Long-billed 1s nearly as ad s.
	• Often moult-limit in prim with outer new, rest juv. Other ind retain all juv prim until first complete autumn moult.
fl all plum	• Legs project slightly beyond tail (only part of toes), as in Long-billed.
voice	• Call quickly repeated, low pitched, slightly nasal and *two- or three syllabic*, rather similar to Turnstone ⇔ Long-billed.

geog var	*L.g. griseus* (eastern North America)
ad s	• Rather evenly spread, dense patterning on whole underparts (especially heavily barred on flanks), orange breast and upper belly; white background of belly, vent and undertail-cov.
	• Usually greyish head.
	• Feathers of upperparts with rather narrow rufous fringes.

geog var	*L.g. hendersoni* (central North America)
ad s	• Patterning almost restricted to flanks and breast-sides; vent finely spotted. Also vent and undertail-cov orange (as in Long-billed ad s).
	• Feathers of upperparts with broad rufous-red fringes.

geog var	*L.g caurinus* (western North America)
all plum	• Often obvious prim-projection ⇔ in Long-billed lacking.
ad s	• Upperside strongly patterned, e.g. obvious pale tips to scaps and tertials as in Long-billed.
	• Dark patterning on underparts as in *griseus* but belly, vent and undertail-cov variable orange-coloured.
note	• Not recorded and least likely of 3 subspecies to occur in WP.

Long-billed Dowitcher *Limnodromus scolopaceus*   L 29cm 11.5"

all plum	• See introduction to Short-billed Dowitcher, Long-billed Dowitcher and Asiatic Dowitcher.
	• Long bill. In very long-billed ind (♀ with bill length > 2 x head-length) probably no overlap with Short-billed Dowitcher.
	• Black tail-bars broader than pale ones ⇔ most Short-billed.
ad	• Wing-tips fall at most level with tail-tip (no wing-projection) ⇔ most Short-billed.
	• Prim-projection very short or absent.

Sandpipers and allies

ad s	⇒	• In fresh plumage (April-May) conspicuous white tips to scaps and tertials (also in western subspecies of Short-billed *caurinus*).
	⇒	• Breast-sides more strongly patterned than rest of underparts ⇔ Short-billed ad s.
		• Underparts in fresh plumage with black subterminal markings and white tips; black-white-orange scaled underparts.
		• Central tail-feathers often with rufous background ⇔ in Short-billed ad s white background.
		• Underparts entirely reddish (by end of summer more orange, as in Short-billed ad s) with colouring up to undertail-cov ⇔ Short-billed ad s (although due to moult Long-billed often shows whitish vent by late summer, as in Short-billed ad s).
		• Rather faintly marked head ⇔ Short-billed ad s.
ad w		• Usually uniform grey breast extending to upper part of belly, rather sharply demarcated from rest of underparts ⇔ Short-billed ad w.
		• Grey feathers of upperparts with narrow, dark shaft-streaks.
juv-1w	⇒	• Scaps with large dark centres and narrow rufous notched fringes, contrasting with grey cov ⇔ Short-billed juv.
	⇒	• Completely dark tertial-centres with pale fringes of even width ⇔ Short-billed juv-1w.
		• Both juv scaps and cov distinctly pointed ⇔ ad-type feathers rounded.
		• Greyish rear-crown and hind-neck and rather obvious but short supercilium; crown only slightly darker than hind-neck ⇔ in Short-billed juv-1w stronger head-pattern with especially very dark crown (without grey) reaching hind-neck and longer and more distinct supercilium.
1s		• Summer plumage sometimes less developed than in ad, other ind as ad. Generally summer plumage much more well-developed than in Short-billed 1s.
		• Often moult-limit in prim with outer new, rest juv. Other ind retain all juv prim until first complete autumn moult.
fl all plum		• As Short-billed but projection of legs beyond tail slightly longer, toes more often entirely projected.
voice		• Call a short, rather high-pitched *single note* 'keek', often repeated every 2-3 sec ⇔ Short-billed.
behav		• Prefers freshwater habitat ⇔ Short-billed often in saltwater habitat.

Asiatic Dowitcher *Limnodromus semipalmatus*   L 35cm 14"

all plum		• See introduction to Short-billed Dowitcher, Long-billed Dowitcher and Asiatic Dowitcher.
		• Completely dark, straight bill with deep base (in juv flesh-coloured bill-base for a short time).
		• Very broad, *dark loral-stripe*, running from bill to eye.
		• Legs dark ⇔ Short-billed Dowitcher and Long-billed Dowitcher.
		• No or very short prim-projection ⇔ in Bar-tailed Godwit long.
		• More resembles small Bar-tailed Godwit (with which they frequently associate) than Short-billed or Long-billed.
ad s	⇒	• Feathers of upperparts with dark centres and narrow, *evenly broad*, whitish and orange-red fringes ⇔ Bar-tailed Godwit ad s and Short-billed and Long-billed ad s/juv.
		• Head and breast deep rufous-red; vent and undertail-cov whiter with dark bars.
		• Whitish supercilium conspicuous (less conspicuous in other plumages).
		• Pale spot under bill-base.
ad w		• Feathers of upperparts with entirely dark uniform centres and narrow pale fringes.
		• Strongly patterned breast, sharply demarcated from white belly.
		• Flank barring to undertail-cov ⇔ Bar-tailed Godwit ad ♀ s/ad w.
juv		• Like ad w with yellow-brown ground-colour on breast and yellow-brown fringes to scaps, greater cov and tertials.
		• Flesh-coloured bill-base.
fl all plum		• Virtually unpatterned white underwing-cov (looking uniformly white from distance) ⇔ in Bar-tailed Godwit faintly or well-patterned.
		• White background of rump and uppertail-cov but indistinct due to dark barring ⇔ in Short-billed and Long-billed conspicuous white wedge.
		• Grey tail faintly barred or unbarred.
		• Paler sec and inner prim contrast with dark outer prim and prim-cov (as in Short-billed and Long-billed but less strong) ⇔ Bar-tailed Godwit.
behav		• Feeds in typical dowitcher manner: vertical boring when wading in (deep) water.
note		• Not recorded in WP, but possible vagrant.

Eurasian Woodcock *Scolopax rusticola*   L 36cm 14"

all plum	⇒	• Dark bars on rear-crown; front part of crown and forehead unmarked.
		• Underparts finely barred on yellow-brown ground-colour.
		• Narrow, dark rufous stripe on breast-side.
1w		• Chestnut tips to prim-cov broader than, but concolorous with rest of barring on prim-cov ⇔ in ad narrower and paler than rest of barring, creating narrow stripe over hand.
		• Underside of tail-feathers with relatively narrow and grey tips ⇔ in ad broad white tips creating broad white terminal band.
		• Later in autumn, outer prim slightly more worn than in ad.
1s		• Characteristic pattern of juv-type prim-cov still useful (see 1w).
		• Prim obviously worn.
		• Sometimes still some juv tail-feathers retained with different pattern than ad-type (see 1w).
fl all plum	⇒	• All flight-feathers strongly rufous notched, creating well-marked outer-wing ⇔ all other snipes.
		• Broad dark subterminal tail-band.
		• Broad rounded wings.
fl 1w		• Sec and cov with broader chestnut barring/notching than in ad; upperwing for a while more chestnut than black ⇔ in ad more black than chestnut.

American Woodcock *Scolopax minor* L 28cm 11"

all plum ⇒	• Like Eurasian Woodcock but smaller size and at least *some grey scaps*.
⇒	• Prim-projection (almost) absent ⇔ in Eurasian ± 80%.
	• Very faintly barred or unbarred underparts with orange-brown ground-colour.
fl all plum	• Very broad rounded hand with obvious 'fingers' (3 strongly narrowed outer prim).
	• Uniform and unbarred upper- and underside of flight-feathers.
	• Underwing-cov orange-brown.

Black-tailed Godwit *Limosa limosa* L 41cm 16"

all plum ⇒	• Supercilium only distinct between eye and bill.
	• Long tibia ⇔ Bar-tailed Godwit.
	• Pale, orange basal part of bill and black tip.
ad s	• Neck and breast orange. Underparts black barred ⇔ Bar-tailed ad s.
w	• Almost uniform brown-grey upperparts ⇔ Bar-tailed w.
	• Breast uniformly pale brown-grey; belly white.
juv	• Uniform, rufous-brown breast.
	• Greater cov and tertials only notched on distal part.
1s	• Summer plumage often less developed. Ind which summer in winter range acquire hardly any summer-type feathers.
	• Retained juv prim heavily worn.
fl all plum ⇒	• Very broad wing-bar.
	• White uppertail-cov and base of tail creating rectangular white block.
	• White underwing with sharp dark leading and trailing edge.
	• Long leg projection beyond tail.
note	• For other features see *islandica*.

geog var	**Icelandic Black-tailed Godwit** *L.l. islandica* (Iceland)
all plum	• Legs and bill slightly shorter than in *limosa* (♀ larger than ♂ with longer bill and legs).
ad s	• Strong colour-contrast between mainly red-brown mantle and scaps and mostly *fresh pale grey cov* (resembles Bar-tailed) ⇔ *limosa*.
	• Upperside densely marked with summer-type feathers with red-brown patterning; often some tertials and cov summer-type with broader and deeper red-brown patterning ⇔ in *limosa* narrower, paler rufous patterning and at least some uniformly grey brown winter-type feathers; sometimes some inner cov summer-type.
	• Head and underparts deeper red-brown than in most *limosa* (some *limosa* coloured as *islandica*) and both black barring and red-brown patterning on underparts reaches further down, sometimes to vent (especially in ♂). Upper breast later in spring *without black patterning* (see moult) ⇔ in *limosa* black barring on underparts reaching to breast.
juv	• Strongly rufous neck and breast.
	• Boldly marked scaps (between those of *limosa* juv and Bar-tailed juv).
moult ⇒	• Spring moult complex and more complete than in *limosa*; in limosa most cov and some tertials and scaps retained (grey-brown winter-type feathers).
	• Ad moults later into winter plumage than *limosa*; in August sometimes still complete summer plumage.

Hudsonian Godwit *Limosa haemastica* L 39cm 15.5"

all plum ⇒	• Rather long prim-projection (c.70%) with 3-4 (sometimes 2 as in Black-tailed Godwit) prim-tips beyond tertials and *distinct wing-projection* ⇔ Black-tailed.
	• Supercilium broad (broader than in Black-tailed) and pure white. As in Black-tailed concentrated between eye and bill but often more distinct behind eye.
	• Slightly upturned bill.
	• Legs shorter than in Black-tailed.
ad ♂ s ⇒	• Greyish neck. Underparts dark chestnut; upperparts blocked black.
ad ♀ s	• Underparts with only some dark chestnut spots.
w	• Brown-grey upperparts (often more grey than in Black-tailed).
	• Grey breast sharply demarcated from white belly ⇔ Black-tailed w.
juv	• Grey-brown breast and neck (instead of warm orange-brown in Black-tailed) and grey cov.
	• Head and underparts greyish, lacking warm colouration ⇔ Black-tailed juv.
	• No obvious pale fringes and tips to scaps and tertials; upperwing and scaps more uniform than in Black-tailed juv.
	• Patterning on distal part of greater cov, scaps and tertials less distinct, notches less deeply cut than in Black-tailed.
	• Crown darker than in Black-tailed juv, contrasting more strongly with supercilium.
fl all plum ⇒	• Black underwing-cov.
	• Short, relatively narrow wing-bar, concentrated on mid-wing ⇔ in Black-tailed longer and broader.
	• Leg projection beyond tail slightly shorter than in Black-tailed, only toes. In Black-tailed also part of tarsus.

Bar-tailed Godwit *Limosa lapponica* L 39cm 15.5"

all plum ⇒	• Long supercilium, also distinct behind eye ⇔ Black-tailed Godwit.
	• Barred tail ⇔ Black-tailed.
	• Rather long prim-projection (c.70%) ⇔ Black-tailed.
	• Mantle and hind-neck streaked black ⇔ Black-tailed.
	• Legs relatively short ⇔ Black-tailed.
	• Slightly upturned bill.

ad ♂ s ⇒	• Underparts entirely deep orange-red with dark patterning restricted to sides of breast and flanks ⇔ Black-tailed *islandica* ad ♂ s.
ad ♀ s	• Pale underparts with creamy wash on breast and along flanks.
	• Feathers of upperparts with dark centres and buff fringes ⇔ w.
w	• Grey-brown feathers of upperparts with broad dark shaft-streaks ⇔ in Black-tailed w nearly uniform upperparts.
	• Some scaps and tertials faintly notched.
juv ⇒	• All scaps, greater cov and tertials evenly notched ⇔ Black-tailed juv.
	• Underparts pale buff and faintly patterned.
1s	• Summer plumage often less developed with retained juv feathers heavily worn. Summer-type feathers in both ♂ and ♀ paler than in ad of same sex.
	• Retained juv prim heavily worn.
fl all plum ⇒	• Weak wing-bar (only on hand somewhat more obvious) ⇔ Black-tailed.
	• White wedge on back and pale underwing-cov.
	• Very short leg projection beyond tail (only part of toes).
	• Underwing-cov slightly spotted.

Little Curlew *Numenius minutus*   L 30cm 12"

all plum ⇒	• Smallest curlew by far, only a little larger than European Golden Plover.
	• Underparts hardly patterned.
	• Bill much shorter than in Eurasian Whimbrel (< 2 x head-length) and only slightly curved.
	• Dark spot on lores, directly before eye (no loral-stripe).
	• Dark crown with very narrow pale median crown-stripe.
	• Large conspicuous eye, obviously due to pale lores.
	• Buffish ground-colour of neck and flanks ⇔ Eurasian Whimbrel.
	• Wing-tips reach (almost) to tail-tip (⇔ in Upland Sandpiper long tail projects beyond wing-tips).
	• Flank unbarred or faintly barred.
	• Orange basal half of lower mandible.
	• Thin neck and small head.
	• Legs grey (⇔ in Upland Sandpiper yellowish).
	• Dark wing-bend often with pale spot in front on breast-sides.
1w	• Tertials finely notched ⇔ ad.
	• Fringes of feathers generally less warm yellow-brown than in ad, becoming almost white later in autumn.
	• Tips to outer prim narrower and more pointed than in ad.
1s	• Some ind moult completely in winter and thus in spring as ad, other ind retain (part of) prim which then are heavily worn.
fl all plum ⇒	• Rump and uppertail-cov strongly patterned but slightly paler (with grey wash) than mantle.
	• Uniform dark flight-feathers contrast with paler cov.
note	• Eskimo Curlew *N. borealis* (North America, but almost certainly extinct) somewhat resembles Little but larger and with e.g. broader and longer loral-stripe, longer prim-projection and large wing-projection, weaker head-pattern, flanks strongly patterned with Y-shaped markings, chestnut-brown underwing and no colour-contrast between rump and mantle.

Eurasian Whimbrel *Numenius phaeopus*   L 42cm 16.5"

all plum	• Relatively short bill, basal half straight (in some Eurasian Curlew juv ♂ very short bill); base of lower mandible hardly any paler ⇔ Eurasian Curlew.
	• Distinct pale median crown-stripe ⇔ in Eurasian Curlew sometimes very narrow pale median crown-stripe.
	• Distinct eye- and loral-stripe (in Eurasian Curlew sometimes also rather obvious).
	• Usually slightly darker, colder-brown upperparts than Eurasian Curlew.
	• Legs slightly shorter than in Eurasian Curlew.
	• Scaps grey notched, usually not creating obvious pale lines ⇔ Eurasian Curlew.
1w	• In autumn fresher and more contrasting plumage than ad (but differences often small).
1s	• Moult-limit in cov and prim ⇔ ad.
	• Rare in WP, most ind spend summer in winter range.
fl all plum	• Rather uniform upperwing ⇔ in Eurasian Curlew usually a little contrast between paler sec and inner prim and darker outer prim.
	• Usually no leg projection beyond tail ⇔ in Eurasian Curlew usually slightly.
moult	• Ad moults completely in winter range. 1w moults partially in winter, prim only from May on. Ind with prim-moult in summer are 2cy.
geog var	*N.p. variegatus* (Siberia)
all plum	• Can resemble *hudsonicus* by often having some patterning on rump. Some 1w have extensive patterning on rump but most ind show variable amount of plain white. Rest of plumage as Eurasian.
geog var	*N.p. alboaxillaris* (steppe north of Caspian Sea)
all plum	• Paler than *phaeopus* with mainly whitish background.
	• Fringes to feathers of upperside pale cream-coloured, paler than in *phaeopus*.
	• Dark lateral crown-stripe less distinct than in *phaeopus*.
	• Underparts finely streaked (breast densely streaked); bars restricted to flanks.
fl all plum	• Underwing-cov and axillaries white, (almost) unpatterned.
note	• Status unclear; possible extremely rare or even extinct.

Hudsonian Whimbrel *Numenius hudsonicus*
L 44cm 17.5"

all plum	• As Eurasian Whimbrel but paler head and (much) more contrasting pattern (ear-coverts often pale). • Median crown-stripe slightly broader than in *Eurasian*. • Often with slightly yellow-browner ground-colour than Eurasian. • Breast often more faintly marked and flanks more finely streaked than in Eurasian.
1w	• See Eurasian 1w.
1s	• See Eurasian 1s.
fl all plum ⇒	• Back, rump and uppertail-cov dark patterned, concolorous with mantle ⇔ in Eurasian unpatterned white. • Underwing, axillaries and flanks strongly and densely barred on *warm, yellow-brown ground-colour* ⇔ in Eurasian more finely marked on white background.
moult	• See Eurasian moult.

Slender-billed Curlew *Numenius tenuirostris*
L 39cm 15.5"

all plum ⇒	• Short, thin bill (usually wholly dark, sometimes base of lower mandible slightly paler in imm), from distal half rather slightly downcurved. Bill length about 1.5 x head-length.
⇒	• Legs blackish ⇔ Eurasian Whimbrel and Eurasian Curlew grey. • Normally distinctly smaller than Eurasian and slightly smaller than Eurasian Whimbrel but in all curlew species ♀ sometimes notably larger than ♂; large Slender-billed ♀ may be almost the size of small Eurasian ♂. • Dark loral-stripe sometimes more distinct than in Eurasian Whimbrel, crown often rather dark (capped appearance), supercilium often distinct. • Whitish background to whole plumage.
1w-ad ⇒	• Streaks on breast gradually turning to oval or heart-shaped spots on belly. • Upperparts rather faintly and evenly patterned; lacks large dark centres to mantle feathers and scaps as in other curlew species (but see juv). • Upperparts cold brown without yellow.
juv	• More yellow-brown fringes to feathers of upperparts than in ad. • Scaps with large, blackish centres, contrasting with paler and finely marked cov. • No large spots on underparts; breast, upper-belly and flanks faintly streaked. • Pale base of lower mandible.
1s	• Cov mainly juv (pale and worn), contrasting with dark scaps. • Prim, most tertials and tail-feathers retained juv feathers, distinctly worn.
fl all plum ⇒	• Underside of prim almost *uniformly dark*, creating dark underside of hand ⇔ in Eurasian Whimbrel and Eurasian underside of outer prim barred.
⇒	• White tail with only some broad bars, tail paler than arm ⇔ other curlew species. • Uniform white underwing-cov and axillaries (as in Eurasian *orientalis* and Eurasian Whimbrel *alboaxillaris*). • Very dark outer 4-5 prim and prim-cov contrast with pale inner flight-feathers. • Narrow wings.
behav	• Feeds in plover-like manner. • Often stands more upright than Eurasian Whimbrel and Eurasian with more stretched neck.
note	• No definite records for more than a decade; now possibly extinct.

Eurasian Curlew *Numenius arquata*
L 52cm 20.5"

all plum	• Evenly downcurved, long to very long bill (♀ with longer bill than ♂); pale base to lower mandible. • Scaps with cream-coloured notches and fringes, normally creating obvious pale bands ⇔ Eurasian Whimbrel. • Little contrast between upperparts and underparts (*arquata*) ⇔ Eurasian Whimbrel.
ad	• Tertials with dark bars, more streaked than in juv.
juv	• Often difficult to distinguish from ad but tertials often with deeply cut notching. • Sometimes very short bill in juv ♂.
1s	• Retained juv prim distinctly worn.
fl all plum	• Some contrast between black outer prim and prim-cov and paler sec and inner prim ⇔ Eurasian Whimbrel. • Usually some projection of legs beyond tail ⇔ in Eurasian Whimbrel usually none.
geog var	*N.a. orientalis* (Asia)
all plum	• Underparts with narrow stripes without fine bars ⇔ *arquata*. • Uniform white underwing-cov (also axillaries and lesser cov) but in some *arquata* only very little patterning. Probably wholly clinal from strongly patterned in extreme west of distribution (i.e. Ireland) to unpatterned towards east. • Paler upperparts and underparts with more narrow longitudinal stripes on whiter ground-colour than *arquata*. • Bill generally longer than in *arquata*.

Upland Sandpiper *Bartramia longicauda*
L 31cm 12"

all plum ⇒	• Long tail projects well beyond wing-tips.
⇒	• Large conspicuous eye; no eye-stripe. • Pale, short and straight bill (bill-length as head-length) with dark culmen and tip. • Legs green-yellow. • Dark crown with narrow pale median crown-stripe. • Slender neck.
ad	• Feathers of upperside with dark centres and broad buff fringes, without contrast between upperparts and cov ⇔ juv.

juv	• Median cov and lesser cov with pale internal markings and evenly pale fringes ⇔ in ad notched.
	• Scaps with large dark centres and narrow pale fringes, contrasting with slightly paler cov.
	• Narrow (scaled) patterning on flanks ⇔ in ad broad blocks on flanks.
1w	• Mix of (worn) juv and (fresh) ad-type cov, tertials and tail-feathers.
1s	• Retained juv prim distinctly worn.
fl all plum ⇒	• Long tail with pale outer-side.
	• Strongly and finely barred axillaries and underwing-cov.
	• Pale shaft of p10 conspicuous due to dark remainder of hand.
	• Upperwing with obvious contrast between dark hand and paler arm.

Terek Sandpiper *Xenus cinereous* L 23.5cm 9.5"

all plum ⇒	• Characteristic head-profile with *steep forehead* and high, rounded crown.
	• Rather long, slightly upcurved bill.
	• Dark wing-bend (marginal cov and lesser cov).
	• Legs relatively short, yellow to orange (in juv dull yellow).
	• Grey, uniform tail.
	• Faint supercilium.
	• Grey impression at distance.
ad s ⇒	• Black upper scaps creating black band on almost uniform brown-grey upperparts.
w	• Only little black patterning on scaps (sometimes entirely absent). Moult-timing very variable.
juv-1w	• Not obviously different from ad but uniform fresh plumage (in ad wholly or partially worn), tips to scaps and tertials with very small dark patches and very narrow pale fringes along tips (later in winter worn off and under field conditions like ad w).
1s	• Very variable; some ind moult completely and are then indistinguishable from ad s, other ind retain variable amount of (worn) juv cov and inner prim. Ind which summer in winter range often develop no summer plumage at all.
fl all plum ⇒	• White on sec and inner prim creating Common Redshank-like wing-pattern, but area of white less broad than in Common Redshank and lacks white wedge on back.
	• Legs hardly or do not project beyond tail.
behav	• Typical foraging gait: runs with head low.

Common Sandpiper *Actitis hypoleucos* L 19cm 7.5"

all plum ⇒	• White of underparts extending up between wing-bend and breast-sides creating white peak in front of wing.
⇒	• Long tail projects beyond wing-tips.
ad s	• Well-defined black patterning on centres of mantle feathers, scaps and cov; tertials black barred.
	• Breast-side patch streaked ⇔ juv.
juv	• Cov with narrow white-yellowish fringes; no well-defined black spots on upperparts.
	• Breast-side patch uniform.
1s	• Upperparts often more grey than in ad s and cov all worn winter-type ⇔ in ad s mix of old and new cov.
	• Often outer sec and inner prim retained juv feathers, heavily worn.
fl all plum	• Rather broad wing-bar.
	• Flies with series of shallow, very fast wing-beats low over water surface.
behav	• Moves rear body almost constantly up and down.
note	• For other field marks see Spotted Sandpiper.

Spotted Sandpiper *Actitis macularius* L 19cm 7.5"

all plum	• Legs yellow or at least yellowish ⇔ in Common Sandpiper rarely yellowish.
	• Pale, brown-yellow to orange (ad s) bill with dark tip.
	• Rather obvious supercilium ⇔ most Common.
	• Tail shorter than in Common, tail-projection beyond wing-tips short (sometimes none). Tail-projection ≤ half of bill length ⇔ in Common tail-projection ≥ half of bill length.
	• Less white in outer-tail and tips of tail-feathers than in most Common, but variable, in some Common also less white.
ad s ⇒	• Underparts thrush-like spotted; some spots retained well into autumn (November). Some Common ad s with fine spotting on underparts, but creating regular and straight lines.
ad w	• Uniform upperside with indistinct pale bars on lesser cov and median cov.
ad w/juv-1w	• Dark breast-side uniform (unstreaked) and not connected on centre of breast ⇔ in Common slightly patterned with dark shaft-streaks and almost connected.
	• Grey brown upperside (juv usually greyer) ⇔ Common.
juv-1w ⇒	• Tertials unmarked, or only marked on tip ⇔ in Common rather distinct and evenly spread notching over whole length of tertials.
	• Cov with only dark subterminal fringes, creating partially 'isolated' bars ⇔ in Common more messy and densely barred cov due to often double dark mark on each feather.
	• Patterning on cov much better developed than patterning on upperparts ⇔ in Common cov and upperparts differ less.
1s	• Cov all worn winter-type ⇔ in ad s mix of old and new cov.
	• Spots on underparts smaller and less numerous than in ad s.
	• Some prim retained juv feathers, heavily worn.
fl all plum ⇒	• Obvious wing-bar but narrows over arm towards body, *not reaching body* ⇔ in Common evenly broad over whole arm and reaching body.
	• Inner sec with rather even small white tips ⇔ in Common white strongly broadening towards body.
	• One dark bar over underwing-cov ⇔ in Common often variable second bar at base of greater cov of underwing.

Green Sandpiper *Tringa ochropus*   L 22cm 8.5"

all plum	⇒	• Dark breast sharply demarcated from white upper-belly ⇔ Solitary Sandpiper and Wood Sandpiper.
		• Supercilium only between eye and bill; supercilium connected with eye-ring.
		• Long tertials, short prim-projection (prim-projection 20-50%); wing-tips reach tail-tip or slightly beyond.
		• Legs green-grey.
		• Slightly paler basal part of bill.
ad	⇒	• Blackish upperparts and sparse and small whitish notches/spots on scaps and tertials; cov almost without notches/spots ⇔ Wood.
juv		• More evenly patterned than ad with notches/spots on all feathers of upperside and yellowish instead of whitish in ad.
		• Upperparts more brownish than in ad.
1s		• Flight-feathers old and worn.
		• Summer plumage less developed with often only some summer-type cov (other cov old and without notching).
fl all plum	⇒	• Wholly *black underwing*.
		• Unpatterned white uppertail-cov.
		• 3 broad dark bars on upperside of tail, concentrated on distal part ⇔ in Wood finer, more even and more numerous bars.

Solitary Sandpiper *Tringa solitaria*   L 21.5cm 8.5"

all plum	⇒	• Long prim-projection (c.60-90%, with 3-4 prim-tips beyond tertials), in ad s prim-projection shorter due to longer tertials; obvious wing-projection.
	⇒	• Eye-ring more distinct than supercilium, creating strong spectacled-effect (supercilium sometimes completely absent) ⇔ Green Sandpiper. *Eye-ring often thickened behind eye and ending in point.*
		• Often paler basal half of bill than Green, sometimes pale yellow-green.
		• Sides of vent often slightly marked ⇔ Green.
		• Slightly smaller and more slender than Green.
		• Leg-colour usually as in Green but often slightly greener. Sometimes yellow(brown)ish ⇔ Green.
ad s		• As Green but generally more notches/spots on feathers of upperside.
		• Fore-flanks often distinctly barred ⇔ in Green diffuse scaled pattern.
ad w		• Mainly as ad s but upperparts with less white spots.
juv		• Mainly as ad but upperside browner and feathers with whitish notches/spots.
1s		• Summer plumage less developed and inner flight-feathers old and worn.
fl all plum	⇒	• Black rump and central tail-feathers; uppertail-cov strongly barred.
	⇒	• t6 barred ⇔ in Green t6 uniform white (underside of closed tail barred ⇔ Green).
		• Uniform dark underwing (as in Green but slightly paler).
		• Leg projection beyond tail almost as long as tail-length ⇔ in Green shorter.
		• Narrower, longer and more pointed wings than Green.
geog var		*T.s. solitaria* (eastern North America)
all plum		• Upperparts very dark.
		• Loral-stripe distinct and unbroken black ⇔ *cinnamomea*.
juv		• Pale spots on upperparts white.
geog var		*T.s. cinnamomea* (north-western North America, winter range overlaps partially with *solitaria*)
all plum		• Generally slightly larger than *solitaria*.
		• Upperparts slightly paler and greyer than in *solitaria*.
		• Loral-stripe weaker than in *solitaria* due to fine pale flecking in loral-stripe.
juv		• Pale spots on upperparts cream-coloured ⇔ *solitaria*.
note		• *Cinnamomea* not recorded in WP.

Grey-tailed Tattler *Tringa brevipes*   L 25cm 10"

all plum		• Head dominated by dark lores and conspicuous supercilium (as in Wandering Tattler).
		• Legs relatively short; yellow.
		• Long prim-projection (100%, 4 prim-tips behind tertials), wing-tips reach to or slightly beyond tail-tip ⇔ Wandering.
		• Supercilium rather clear behind eye and connected on forehead ⇔ Wandering.
		• Pale basal part of bill (usually both mandibles but sometimes entirely dark upper mandible) ⇔ Wandering.
		• Dark brown-grey upperside (Wandering often darker).
ad s	⇒	• Barred breast and flanks; belly and undertail-cov uniform white ⇔ Wandering.
		• Narrow pale fringes to feathers of upperparts (pale fringes quickly disappearing with wear) ⇔ in Wandering uniform.
ad w	⇒	• Little or no grey wash along flanks; belly broadly white ⇔ Wandering.
		• Diffuse dark breast-band, concolorous with upperparts.
		• Uniform grey upperparts.
juv		• As ad w with small notches on cov, tertials and tail-feathers.
fl all plum	⇒	• Uppertail-cov with narrow pale fringes, creating barring ⇔ in Wandering uniform uppertail-cov.
		• Upperside (almost uniform) dark grey.
		• Very narrow wing-bar.

Wandering Tattler *Tringa incanus*   L 26cm 10"

all plum	⇒	• Long prim-projection (± 100%, 5 prim-tips visible) and long wing-projection.
		• Nostril lies in long groove; groove consists of more than half of upper mandible ⇔ Grey-tailed Tattler (difficult to judge under field conditions).

- Legs short, yellow.
- Supercilium only distinct between eye and bill (behind eye very narrow and faint; in ad s sometimes more obvious behind eye).
- Slightly darker on upperparts than Grey-tailed.
- Pale bill-base restricted to lower mandible ⇔ Grey-tailed.
- Pale eye-ring conspicuous and thick (more distinct than in Grey-tailed; less obvious in ad s).

ad s ⇒
- Densely barred breast, belly, flanks and undertail-cov; vent usually more weakly or unpatterned ⇔ Grey-tailed.
- Upperparts almost uniform.

ad w ⇒
- Dark grey breast and broad grey band along flanks; only central part of belly white ⇔ Grey-tailed.

juv
- Like ad w with very small notches (smaller than in Grey-tailed juv) on cov and tertials.

fl all plum
- Very short, very narrow wing-bar, only along outer greater cov and inner prim-cov (wing-bar only visible under good viewing conditions).
- Black underwing-cov contrast with paler underside of flight-feathers ⇔ Grey-tailed.

note
- Not recorded in WP.

Spotted Redshank *Tringa erythropus*   L 31cm 12"

all plum ⇒
- Red basal part of lower mandible; *upper mandible entirely dark* ⇔ Common Redshank.
- Bill much longer than head-length ⇔ Common.
- Uppertail-cov strongly and evenly barred.
- Legs red except in ad s, then usually blackish.

ad w/imm ⇒
- Strong contrast between dark eye/loral-stripe and short conspicuous supercilium (supercilium mainly before eye).
- Obviously barred ⇔ Common.

ad w
- Grey feathers of upperside with small white notches and narrow white fringes ⇔ 1w.

juv ⇒
- Rather dark underparts (when fresh with cream-coloured wash), *heavily and evenly barred to undertail-cov.*
- Upperside with dark ground-colour and large yellowish to white notches on feathers.

1w
- Underparts from October almost unpatterned as in ad w but wings as juv.

1s
- Most ind nearly as ad s, but some retained winter-type feathers on upperparts and underparts.
- Prim old and brown.

fl all plum
- Upperwing with pale contrast between paler sec and inner prim and black outer-edge of hand. Underwing uniform white like Common.
- White wedge on back.
- Legs project far beyond tail ⇔ Greenshank and Common.

Greater Yellowlegs *Tringa melanoleuca*   L 36cm 14"

all plum
- Two-toned bill; basal part (± 30%) dull green-grey, rest dark ⇔ in Lesser Yellowlegs dark bill (sometimes slightly paler bill-base).
- Bill-structure as in Greenshank but slightly more slender, as long as tarsus and 1.5 x head-length ⇔ Lesser.
- Neck-side and breast sharply streaked ⇔ in Lesser juv/w diffusely streaked or almost uniform.
- Prim-projection c.50-80%, wing-projection rather short (usually shorter than in Lesser) ⇔ in Greenshank short prim-projection.
- Legs yellow to orange (as in Lesser).
- Head not obviously paler than upperparts ⇔ Greenshank.

ad s ⇒
- *Underparts strongly barred* (at least flanks, lower breast and upper belly marked) ⇔ Lesser.
- Upperside as Lesser but summer plumage better developed (upperside often with large proportion of summer-type feathers) ⇔ Lesser. 1s with moderate amount of summer-type feathers and in this respect like Lesser ad s.

ad w
- Feathers of upperparts evenly and sharply notched ⇔ Lesser.

juv
- Feathers of upperparts with large, whitish to cream-coloured notches.

1s
- Summer plumage not well developed (as in Lesser ad s); flanks with narrower barring than in ad s.
- Juv prim (dull dark brown) completely retained until at least end of May ⇔ in ad s glossy black.

fl all plum ⇒
- No white wedge on back ⇔ Greenshank.
- White uppertail-cov and lower part of rump contrast with barred tail and dark upperwing.
- Leg projection beyond tail larger than in Greenshank and Wood Sandpiper.

Greenshank *Tringa nebularia*   L 32cm 12.5"

all plum
- Relatively strong bill, slightly upcurved.
- Legs grey-green to yellow-green.

ad s ⇒
- Upperparts with variable amount of, nearly entirely black summer-type feathers, *creating blackish lines on upperparts.*

ad w
- Grey scaps, cov and tertials finely notched. Feathers of upperside longer and more rounded than juv-type feathers (like in most larger shorebirds).

juv
- Upperside darker than in ad with narrow pale even fringes on cov and feathers of upperparts or with obvious notches.

1s
- Most ind summering in Europe like ad s but with often less amount of summer-type scaps and often more summer-type cov. All prim or at least inner prim old and worn. Other ind in mainly winter plumage.

fl all plum
- Uniform upperwing.
- Broad white wedge on back.
- Pale, almost unmarked tail ⇔ Spotted Redshank and Common Redshank.

note
- See further references in Marsh Sandpiper and Greater Yellowlegs.

Lesser Yellowlegs *Tringa flavipes* — L 27cm 10.5"

all plum ⇒	• Long prim-projection (80-100%), large wing-projection (wing-projection often larger than in Greater Yellowlegs). • Legs long; yellow, sometimes orange. • Short distinct supercilium between eye and bill, not or only slightly extending behind eye ⇔ Wood Sandpiper. • Slightly larger than Wood Sandpiper (thus much smaller than Greater). • Usually hardly any patterning on flanks visible (hidden under wings; in ad s often fine, well-defined black markings on side of vent). • Bill-length nearly as head-length ⇔ Greater. • Bill-feathering extending (nearly) up to nostril ⇔ in Greater nostril lies slightly further up bill, bill-feathering not reaching nostril.
ad s	• Variable amount of summer-type feathers with large, deeply cut notches. • Tertials strongly notched, looking like barring ⇔ other small *Tringa*. • Finely streaked head-side, neck and breast. Patterning often slightly extending onto flanks and sometimes onto rear-side of vent as in Greater but in Greater more boldly marked and central part of underparts patterned.
w ⇒	• Upperside only slightly marked, sometimes almost uniform grey ⇔ e.g. Greater all plum. • Greater cov and tertials rather faintly notched.
juv juv/(1)w	• Feathers of upperside with well-defined whitish notches. • Diffusely patterned grey breast(-band) ⇔ in Greater all plum sharply streaked.
1s	• As ad s but summer plumage often less advanced and inner sec old, outer fresh (moulted in winter).
fl all plum	• White uppertail-cov and lower part of rump contrast with barred tail and dark, almost uniform upperwing. • Leg projection beyond tail larger than in Greenshank and Wood Sandpiper.

Willet *Tringa semipalmata* — L 38cm 15"

all plum ⇒	• Legs thick, blue-grey. • Strong two-toned bill; blue-grey (both Western and Eastern) to pinkish (some winter plumage Eastern) basal part, black tip with deep base (bill superficially resembles that of Greenshank). • Webs between toes.
ad s	• Grey to brown-grey upperparts with variable amount of black barred summer-type feathers (see geog var). • Streaked breast gradually progresses into barred flank on yellow-brown ground-colour (see geog var).
ad w	• Uniform grey to brown-grey upperparts. • White underparts with diffuse grey breast-sides and flanks.
1w	• Brown-grey upperside with faint subterminal dark patterning on cov and usually rather weak notches on tertials and inner greater cov (see geog var). • Underparts as in ad w.
1s	• Often part of (worn) juv cov retained • Juv prim retained to summer, then heavily worn.
fl all plum ⇒ ⇒	• *Very broad wing-bar*, accentuated by black hand. • Underwing pattern: black cov, broad white bar over flight-feathers and black trailing edge on hand.
geog var	**Eastern Willet** *T.s. semipalmata* (eastern North America)
all plum	• Slightly thicker bill than in Western. • Slightly smaller and more compact build with shorter rear end than in Western. • Slightly shorter legs than in Western.
ad w/1w	• Upperparts brown-grey with slightly contrasting darker scaps ⇔ in Western upperparts pure grey without darker scaps.
ad s/1s 1w	• Much more summer-type feathers than in Western. • Stronger pattern of scaps, cov and tertials than in Western.
geog var	**Western Willet** *T.s. inornata* (western interior North America, part of population winters along east coast)
ad s/1s	• Less strongly marked breast and flanks and more greyish ground-colour than in Eastern s.
ad w/1w	• Cold-grey upperparts ⇔ Eastern.
note	• At least some records in WP concern Western.

Marsh Sandpiper *Tringa stagnatilis* — L 23.5cm 9"

all plum	• Long straight, especially slender bill. • Nearly *uniform pale lores* (in ad s often diffusely grey) and supercilium extending to behind eye ⇔ all similar species. • Legs very long; grey-green.
ad s ⇒	• Upperparts with *black spots not creating dark bands*, tertials with black barring ⇔ Greenshank ad s. • Flanks with some dark 'V'-shaped spots.
ad w/imm	• Dark cap ⇔ Greenshank. • Upperparts in ad w very pale grey ⇔ in Greenshank darker grey-brown.
juv-1w ⇒	• Narrow dark forehead-wedge (fore-crown) in combination with lack of loral-stripe creating broad white area above lores. • Throat and central part of breast unpatterned, creating pale vertical area in front view ⇔ in Greenshank and Wood Sandpiper central part of breast patterned (except in Greenshank ad w). • Strong contrast between dark upperparts and uniform, bright white underparts. • Pale mantle-stripes sometimes conspicuous; flanks unpatterned ⇔ ad s. • Feathers of upperside strongly marked; notching on greater cov and tertials gradually more extensive towards tips.

1s
- Early moult towards 1w, from August.
- Some like ad s but all prim or at least inner ones old and worn and summer plumage less developed, other ind in mainly winter plumage.

fl all plum ⇒
⇒
- Long leg projection beyond tail ⇔ Greenshank.
- Underwing with dark spot on base of hand ⇔ other *Tringa* waders.
- Sec slightly paler than rest of upperwing ⇔ Greenshank.
- Narrow white wedge on back ⇔ in Greenshank broad.
- Tail with diffuse, narrow greyish bars on whole t1-t3 and on outer web of t4-t6. Closed tail looks pale grey, spread tail in flight looks almost white.

Wood Sandpiper *Tringa glareola*   L 20cm 8"

all plum ⇒
- Long supercilium reaches far behind eye, in ad s often less clear behind eye.
- Legs yellow-green, sometimes yellow.
- Breast-patterning fades gradually into unpatterned belly ⇔ in Green Sandpiper sharply defined.
- Barred flanks, sometimes invisible under wing.
- Prim-projection (very) short.

ad
- In s large proportion of upperside consists of bold whitish notches, in winter plumage notches smaller.

juv
- Multiple rows of yellow spots on mantle feathers and well-notched scaps, cov and tertials (somewhat reminiscent of golden plovers).

1s
- Summer plumage less developed with often less summer-type cov (other cov old and with less contrasting notching). (Inner) flight-feathers old and worn.

fl all plum ⇒
- Rather pale underwing ⇔ Green and Solitary Sandpiper.
- White rump and uppertail-cov.
- Finely barred tail ⇔ Green.
- Slight contrast between pale arm and dark upperside of hand.

Common Redshank *Tringa totanus*   L 25cm 10"

ad ⇒
- Legs bright red.
- Red basal part of bill, dark tip.
- Weak supercilium, mainly between eye and bill; pale eye-ring and dark loral-stripe most conspicuous parts on head.

ad s
- Streaked breast, patterning becomes weaker towards flanks.

ad w
- Uniform grey-brown upperparts; breast diffusely grey-brown.

juv
- Dull-red to green-grey bill-base.
- Legs orange, sometimes yellowish.
- Underparts rather densely marked with longitudinal stripes, especially on breast.
- Faint supercilium.
- Feathers of upperside with many fine yellow-brown to whitish notches.

1s
- Like ad s, but prim and (when still present) tertials and median cov more worn.

fl all plum ⇒
- White sec and white tips to inner prim creating large white area on rear-side of wings.
- White wedge on back; finely barred tail.

geog var
T.t. robusta (Iceland)

all plum
- Slightly larger than *totanus*.

ad s
- Both underparts and upperparts with more rufous wash than in *totanus*.
- Underparts with large dark spots.
- Upperside often with large proportion of summer-type feathers (c.70%) ⇔ in *totanus* only c.30%.

w
- Darker and more diffusely marked than *totanus*.

Ruddy Turnstone *Arenaria interpres*   L 22cm 8.5"

all plum
- Short, relatively thick pointed bill.
- Very broad black breast-band; rest of underparts white.
- Legs short and thick; orange.

ad s
- Whitish head with well-defined black lines connected with breast-band; e.g. eye-stripe and submoustachial-stripe.
- Upperside rufous with black lower scaps (upper scaps and cov rufous) and mantle. In ♂ summer plumage much better developed than in ♀.

ad w
- Dark feathers of upperside with broad diffuse brown fringes; upper scaps rufous, lower scaps with white fringes.

juv
- Narrow pale fringes to cov, tertials and mantle feathers; scaps with whitish fringes.

1s
- Variable amount of (worn) juv cov and body-feathers; summer plumage not well developed. Ind which summer in winter range develop no or only very restricted summer plumage.
- Outer prim old and worn.
- Complete first ad w-plumage appears as early as late summer ⇔ ad s.

fl all plum
- Pied patterned upperside with broad white wing-bar, broad white rump/back, white bar along wing-base and white tail-base.

geog var
A.i. morinella (southern arctic Canada)

ad s
- Mantle, scaps, tertials and cov almost uniform chestnut ⇔ in *interpres* with dark patterning, most obvious in tertials.
- Crown more narrowly streaked than in *interpres*, sometimes also completely white (especially in ♂).

Wilson's Phalarope *Phalaropus tricolor*   L 21cm 8.5"

all plum	• Legs yellowish (except ad s, then usually blackish).
	• Slender dark bill slightly longer than head-length; bill longer than in Red Phalarope and Red-necked Phalarope.
	• Longer neck than Red-necked and Red.
ad ♀ s	• Upperparts deeply coloured and patterned with broad black stripe over head-side and neck-side to mantle. Pale grey crown, white hind-neck and grey mantle and scaps
	• Upperparts strongly two-toned (grey and dark rufous) ⇔ in ad ♂ s almost uniformly dark.
ad ♂ s	• Variable; pied ind with pale forehead merging into darker rear-crown, rufous patch on neck-side, narrow black line through neck-side and whitish patch on rear-neck. Mantle and scaps hardly any paler than rest of upperparts. Other ind very almost unpatterned and duller, like dark winter plumage.
ad w/1w ⇒	• *Grey crown and mask* ⇔ in Red and Red-necked blackish.
juv	• Moults early (in August) into 1w (as in Red ⇔ Red-necked).
1w	• Uniform pale grey mantle feathers and scaps; dark cov and tertials with broad pale, buffish fringes, becoming whitish later.
1s	• Some ind undergo complete post-juv moult and develop complete summer plumage in spring (thus inseparable from ad s). Some ind in active prim moult in spring and develop no or restricted summer plumage.
fl all plum ⇒	• Uniform dark grey upperwing without obvious wing-bar.
	• Whitish rump and uppertail-cov contrast with dark wings and tail.
	• Legs project beyond tail ⇔ Red and Red-necked.

Red-necked Phalarope *Phalaropus lobatus*   L 18cm 7.1"

all plum ⇒	• Thin, dark bill; bill length as head-length.
	• Legs relatively short, dark grey.
ad s	• Dark grey head (in ad ♀ s dark grey face, in ad ♂ s greyish with pale loral-spot or complete supercilium) with brown-orange neck-side, white throat and dark grey breast; ♀ more deeply coloured and more boldly patterned than ♂.
ad s/juv	• Pale golden-yellow mantle- and scap-stripe ⇔ Red Phalarope.
w	• Medium-grey upperparts (darker feather centres than in Red w creating striped upperside) with pale fringes to scaps ⇔ in Red w uniform grey upperparts and in imm only narrow pale mantle-stripes.
juv	• Small white spot in front of wing-bend (sometimes hidden under wing-bend).
	• Juv plumage retained until late autumn; upperside dark with broad pale 'V'-shape on mantle and scaps.
w/juv	• Pale head and neck with dark crown, hind-neck and mask (as in Red w/juv).
1s	• Many ind that return to breeding area undergo complete post-juv moult and develop complete summer plumage in spring (thus inseparable from ad s). Ind which summer in winter range retain part of juv plumage, e.g. prim and develop no or restricted summer plumage, these ind sometimes return to breeding area.
fl all plum	• *Calidris*-like rump-patterning: dark central bar on rump, white rump-sides (as in Red).
	• Dark bar on underwing-cov (lesser cov) ⇔ Red.
	• Narrow but well-defined wing-bar (narrower than in Red).

Red Phalarope *Phalaropus fulicarius*   L 21cm 8.5"

all plum	• Legs relatively short, grey to yellow-brown ⇔ Red-necked Phalarope.
	• Relatively stout bill with usually pale base.
	• Viewed from above bill-tip rather broad, spatula-shaped ⇔ Red-necked and Wilson's Phalarope.
ad s	• Underparts red-orange; ♀ more deeply coloured and patterned than ♂ with black crown and front of head. ♂ usually with variable amount of white on central part of underparts, (much) weaker head-pattern and more evenly streaked upperparts (some ♂ almost as ad w).
	• Large white mask.
ad w	• Ad moulting towards winter plumage differs from 1w by e.g. orange spots on underparts and (when present) old *worn* cov and *worn* dark tertials.
	• Uniform pale grey mantle feathers (with very narrow dark shaft-streaks).
	• When winter plumage completed all cov, scaps and tertials grey ⇔ in 1w tertials still juv, almost black.
	• Yellow at bill-base often deeper and more sharply demarcated than in 1w.
juv-1w ⇒	• Moults early into 1w (from September); in autumn mix of very dark juv tertials (⇔ in ad pale grey like upperparts) and pale grey ad w-type mantle-feathers and scaps ⇔ Red-necked juv.
	• Diffuse rufous breast (sides).
	• No obvious pale 'V'-shape on mantle and scaps ⇔ Red-necked juv.
	• Crown with white patterning during ongoing post-juv moult ⇔ Red-necked juv wholly dark (due to later post-juv moult).
1s	• Moult not fully known, but plumage development probably as in Red-necked 1s.
fl all plum ⇒	• Rather dark wings with broad wing-bar over arm, *strongly broadening at inner arm, inner 2 sec almost completely white* ⇔ Sanderling flight.
	• Pale, almost uniform/unpatterned underwing (like Sanderling) ⇔ Red-necked.
	• *Calidris*-like rump-patterning: dark central bar on rump, white rump-sides (as in Red-necked).
	• Long tail ⇔ Sanderling flight.
fl w	• Pale upperparts contrast with dark wings.
note	• Also known as Grey Phalarope.

Skuas

Ageing of skuas

Ageing of skuas is often difficult, except in ad and most juv plumages. During the summer immatures regularly wander northwards from their winter range in the Southern Hemisphere, and all age classes are regularly recorded in the WP, sometimes reaching as far north as their breeding range. The underwing-cov and axillaries are the last feather-group to change to ad-type in the 3rd or 4cy; so completely dark underwing-cov point to ad except in dark morph and intermediate-type Arctic Skuas and in the darkest Pomarine Skuas, in which the underwing-cov and axillaries are already completely dark in juv plumage.

Pomarine Skua *Stercorarius pomarinus* L 46cm 18" (excl elongated central tail-feathers), WS 120cm 47

all plum ⇒	• Rather heavy, two-toned bill. Strongest two-toned in juv; in older ind sometimes weakly present but nevertheless good distinction from older ind of other species which all show completely dark bill.
(sub)ad s ⇒	• Pale morph with very dark flanks and breast-band, *chequered bordered* with white belly.
⇒	• In pale morph breast-band dark with pale scales (in ad ♂ breast-band sometimes almost absent) ⇔ in Arctic Skua ad pale morph paler and uniform (in Arctic 2s often also patchy or scaled breast-band but rest of underparts are then usually also patterned).
	• In pale morph usually clear yellow hind-neck and neck-side (deeper yellow than in Arctic ad s).
	• In pale morph dark cap connected to bill and extending down under lower mandible, cap well-defined ⇔ Arctic (sub)ad s.
	• Black-brown upperparts, breast-band, axillaries and undertail-cov.
	• Some ind retain some winter plumage features (barring on upperparts and/or underparts) until summer ⇔ Arctic.
(sub)ad w	• Barred uppertail-cov and undertail-cov (sometimes also rump, back and mantle) and cap ill-defined, applies for pale morph. Dark morph (sub)ad w differs usually only slightly from (sub)ad s.
	• Central tail-feathers shorter than in ad s.
juv	• Ground-colour rather cold, dark grey-brown to black-brown, sometimes warmer yellow-brown; underparts barred.
	• Rather uniform (usually) dark head with at most weak barring ⇔ Arctic juv.
	• Rarely diffuse pale spot on rear-head as in most Arctic.
	• Mantle-patterning rather weak, yellow-brown, creating 'V'-shaped markings.
	• Legs pale with dark feet, base of feet often pale.
(fl) 1s	• Combination of uniform upperwing (without pale feather-tips), ghost of cap and pale head-side, slightly elongated central tail-feathers, pale markings on tarsus and eventual moult of sec and/or prim.
	• Flanks barred (as in Arctic and Long-tailed Skua 1s).
	• Underwing-cov, axillaries and undertail-cov strongly barred as in juv except in darkest ind.
	• Tarsus pale-dark marked, sometimes completely pale; feet dark, including on base.
(fl) 2s	• Like 1s but central tail-feathers longer, head-pattern almost like ad s and greater cov on underwing uniformly dark (rest of underwing-cov still with pale pattering but less regular and less extensive than in 1s).
	• Tarsus pale only at base or pale-dark marked.
fl all plum	• Steady flight with heavy body and broad wing-base. Even in strong wind normally continues with wing-beats, rarely uses 'shearwater-flight' or long periods of gliding.
	• Lacks in some plumages pale prim-patch, e.g. in ad dark morph, or only pale shafts in most ad ⇔ Arctic.
	• See Arctic all plum for flight in strong wind.
fl juv/imm	• By far most common type has dark head and underparts and contrasting pale barred uppertail-cov, undertail-cov and underwing-cov ⇔ in Arctic dark type uppertail-cov, undertail-cov and underwing-cov dark.
	• Double white patch on underside of hand (on prim-cov small, on prim-base large); sometimes also in ad ⇔ in Arctic sometime weakly present and only visible at close range.
	• Rounded central tail-feathers, slightly or not longer than other tail-feathers ⇔ Arctic juv and Long-tailed juv.
	• Uppertail-cov palest part of upperparts (with well-marked barring) ⇔ in Arctic juv/imm uppertail-cov slightly or not paler than upperparts.
	• Underwing-cov paler than underparts ⇔ in Arctic the other way round (but most Long-tailed similar).
	• Evenly black and whitish barred uppertail-cov and undertail-cov; 'zebra-stripes' (as Long-tailed but uppertail-cov paler due to broader white bands).
behav	• Parasites conspicuously aggressively; attacks victim directly ⇔ Arctic attacks less directly and generally aims at food of victim.
note	• In ad, dark morph scarce (about 10%), intermediate morph very rare. Juv little variable in ground-colour ⇔ Arctic and Long-tailed juv.

Arctic Skua *Stercorarius parasiticus* L 40cm 15.5" (excl tail-streamers) WS 113cm 44.5"

all plum	• Rather slender bill with slight gonys-angle.
	• Relatively small-headed (sometime obvious).
(sub)ad s ⇒	• Breast-band (of pale morph) paler than in Pomarine Skua (sub)ad s and less or often not chequered. Breast-band rather ill-defined and usually fades away towards edge ⇔ Pomarine sub)ad s.
	• Pale spot on forehead directly above bill-base (sometimes absent) ⇔ Pomarine.
	• (Almost) completely dark bill ⇔ Pomarine.
	• Cap becomes gradually slightly paler towards forehead ⇔ Pomarine and Long-tailed Skua.
	• Pale morph with dark, not blackish upperparts ⇔ in Pomarine blackish.
	• Dark cap usually hardly extending to below bill (see Pomarine).
(sub)ad w	• See Pomarine (sub)ad w. Barring on uppertail-cov and undertail-cov less well-marked than in Pomarine (sub)ad w.
juv ⇒	• Small pale tips to outer prim, extending over both webs ⇔ Pomarine and Long-tailed.

	• Yellow-brown to orange-brown rear-head and hind-neck, *often creating warm-coloured collar* ⇔ in Pomarine no collar, in Long-tailed (yellow-)greyish.
	• Very variable with head and underparts from pale warm yellow-brown or rufous-brown with yellow to orange-brownish ⇔ Long-tailed juv.
	• Upperparts with rufous wash ⇔ Long-tailed juv.
	• Head and upper-breast with longitudinal stripes ⇔ in Pomarine uniform, spotted or barred, in Long-tailed (almost) uniform.
	• Two-toned bill but less strongly contrasting than in Pomarine all plum.
	• Legs pale with dark feet, base of feet often pale.
(fl) 1s	• Combination of uniform upperwing (without pale feather-tips), ghost of cap and pale head-side in pale and intermediate type, slightly elongated and pointed central tail-feathers, pale markings on tarsus and eventual moult of sec and/or prim.
	• Flanks barred (as in Pomarine and Long-tailed 1s).
	• Underwing-cov, axillaries and undertail-cov strongly patterned as in juv except in dark and intermediate type (see introduction).
	• Tarsus pale-dark marked, sometimes completely pale; feet dark, including on base.
(fl) 2s	• Central tail-feathers longer than in 1s, head-pattern and underparts almost ad s but underwing-cov still with extensive pale patterning in pale type.
	• In pale type patchy breast-band, resembling Pomarine ad s.
	• Tarsus pale only at base or pale-dark marked.
fl all plum	• Pale prim-patch conspicuous (except in some ad of dark morph), in juv sometimes also on upperwing ⇔ in Pomarine and Long-tailed lacking in some plumages, in Pomarine never on upperwing.
	• In strong winds uses 'shearwater-flight', at distance similar to shearwaters but wings more strongly arched ⇔ shearwaters (except Sooty Shearwater which often has somewhat arched wings). In 'shearwater-flight' arcs flatter than in shearwaters, applies also for Pomarine and Long-tailed.
	• Greater cov on underwing very long and often reaching tip of inner sec ⇔ in Pomarine and Long-tailed slightly shorter, normally not reaching tip of inner sec.
fl juv	• Rump/uppertail-cov not obviously paler than rest of upperparts ⇔ Long-tailed and Pomarine juv.
	• Both undertail-cov and uppertail-cov not so regularly barred, barring more wavy than in Long-tailed and Pomarine and on brown-yellow ground-colour ⇔ in Long-tailed and Pomarine whitish.
	• Relatively large pale area at tail-base on paler ind, often entire basal half pale with broad dark terminal band ⇔ in Long-tailed and Pomarine amount of pale at tail-base restricted.
	• Slightly elongated, pointed central tail-feathers.
	• Lesser cov and marginal cov rather pale, creating pale leading edge of wing ⇔ in Pomarine never, in Long-tailed sometimes.
behav	• See Pomarine.

Long-tailed Skua *Stercorarius longicaudus*   L 37cm 14.5" (excl tail-streamers), WS 106cm 41.5"

all plum ⇒	• Rather stumpy, relatively short bill; bill-tip sharply hooked. Elevation on culmen consists of nearly half of upper mandible ⇔ in Arctic Skua elevation on culmen lies more towards bill-tip and consists of less than half of upper mandible.
	• Nostril before distal half of bill; distance between point of bill-feathering and beginning of nostril smaller than distance between end of nostril to bill-tip ⇔ in Arctic and Pomarine Skua the other way round
	• Tarsus pale in many ad ⇔ in Arctic and Pomarine ad complete dark.
	• Relatively small head can give dove-like impression.
(sub)ad s	• Mantle, scaps, cov and tertials paler than prim ⇔ Arctic and Pomarine.
	• Diffuse dark, grey-brown belly and flanks.
	• No breast-band (very pale Arctic also often lacks breast-band).
	• Strongly elongated central tail-feathers, about as long as body but sometimes broken off, especially in autumn.
	• Lower side of cap almost straight ⇔ Arctic and Pomarine (sub)ad s.
(sub)ad w	• See Pomarine (sub)ad w.
juv ⇒	• Cold (grey)brown overall; *no warm-brown.*
⇒	• In most ind uniform pale area on lower breast/upper belly (but see note juv).
	• Bill two-toned with more black on tip than in Arctic (nearly whole distal half black) ⇔ on Arctic black more restricted to tip.
	• Evenly barred uppertail-cov and undertail-cov on whitish background (in very dark ind uppertail-cov almost dark); 'zebra-stripes' as in Pomarine ⇔ in Arctic usually more diffuse 'zebra-stripes' on yellow-brown ground-colour.
	• Head and breast normally almost uniformly brown-grey (but ground-colour very variable) ⇔ in Arctic usually sharply streaked.
	• Often pale collar ⇔ in Arctic and Pomarine rarely distinct.
	• Whitish scaled on mantle (even on dark ind), straighter and more strongly contrasting than in Arctic.
	• Round tips to outer prim with or without very narrow pale tips ⇔ in Arctic pointed prim with usually obvious pale tip, split by dark shaft.
	• Pale tips to central tail-feathers (t1).
	• Pale tarsus and base of feet (in older ind including ad feet completely dark but tarsus remains pale or pale-marked, see all plum).
fl juv	• Underwing-cov strongly almost black-and-white barred ⇔ in Arctic less strongly barred and background brown-yellow.
(fl) 1s	• Combination of uniform upperparts and upperwing (without pale feather-tips), ghost of cap and pale head-side, elongated central tail-feathers often like 2 very narrow spikes, dark base of feet (only tarsus pale, see juv) and eventual moult of sec and/or prim.
	• Flanks barred (as in Arctic and Pomarine 1s).
	• Underwing-cov, axillaries and uppertail-cov strongly patterned as in juv.

(fl)2s	• Like ad s but axillaries and underwing-cov with pale patterning.
	• Elongated central tail-feathers often shorter than in ad s.
note juv	• Occurs in different morphs (unlike ad); colour and patterning of especially underparts and head can strongly vary from entirely black-brown to almost white. Upperparts and upperwing vary little.
fl all plum	• Conspicuous narrow wings.
	• Much gliding and from moderate winds upwards 'shearwater-flight'.
	• Drop-shaped body with full breast and narrow, pointed rear-body.
	• Wing-beats shallower than in Arctic, wings often hardly below body.
	• Only p9 and p10 with white shafts (often difficult to judge because other shafts sometimes appear white too) ⇔ in Arctic white shaft on (p5-)p8-p10, in Pomarine at least on p5-p10.
	• See Arctic all plum for flight in strong winds.
fl ad ⇒	• No white prim-base.
	• Rather strong contrast between cov (pale) and flight-feathers (dark) ⇔ other skuas ad.
	• Dark grey underwing ⇔ in other skuas ad blackish.
fl juv	• Well-marked and evenly barred *uppertail-cov, paler than upperparts* (also in Pomarine juv) ⇔ Arctic juv.
	• Central tail-feathers obviously elongated, with rounded and pale tips (from 1s with pointed tips as in Arctic all plum) ⇔ in Arctic more pointed central tail-feathers, usually without pale tips.
	• Evenly and strongly marked underwing-cov creating uniformly pale underwing at distance (in some dark morph juv dark underwing-cov).
	• Relatively little white on underside of prim.
geog var	*S.l. pallescens* (North America and Greenland)
ad	• Underparts slightly paler than in *longicaudus*, pale part reaches further towards vent.
juv	• Pale morph probably regularly with pale spot on base of hand of upperwing (as in some Arctic juv) ⇔ *longicaudus* juv.

Great Skua *Stercorarius skua* L 55cm 21.5", WS 139cm 54.5"

all plum	• Heavy bill with marked gonys-angle.
	• Rufous-brown (juv) to yellow-brown ((sub)ad) general impression ⇔ South Polar Skua.
	• Dark cap (in juv often obscure).
	• Legs uniformly dark ⇔ dark Pomarine Skua.
ad	• Pale spotted breast, flanks, upperparts (especially hind-neck) and most cov (latter ⇔ South Polar all plum).
	• Paler ear-coverts ⇔ juv.
	• Darker area around eye and forehead creating mask.
	• Underparts yellow-brown spotted ⇔ juv.
juv ⇒	• Uniform underparts ⇔ ad, Pomarine imm, pale Arctic Skua imm and Long-tailed Skua imm.
	• Diffuse dark head, especially face, creating no cap or mask ⇔ ad.
	• Usually rather distinct two-toned bill ⇔ ad.
	• Pale orange-brownish subterminal markings on mantle feathers, scaps and cov but sometimes almost absent, then nearly uniform dark and very difficult to distinguish from dark South Polar juv or ind from Brown Skua-complex.
	• Underparts often with rufous-brown wash ⇔ South Polar all plum.
fl all plum ⇒	• White base on all prim creating large pale patch on hand, also on upperwing. Only in minority of Arctic and rarely in Long-tailed white prim-spot on upperwing present; in Pomarine lacking.
⇒	• Heavy body with broad long arm and relatively short triangular hand characteristic.
	• Usually conspicuous 'beer-belly'.
	• Parasites less persistently and movements during persecutions less abrupt than other skuas.
moult	• Juv moult prim from March-August, ad from August-April. In overlap time (August) ad starts with replacement of p1, while prim-moult well advanced in juv/2cy (up to p9/p10 replaced). In 3rd and 4cy intermediate moult-schedules.

South Polar Skua *Stercorarius maccormicki* L 53cm 21", WS 132cm 52"

all plum ⇒	• Cov nearly always uniformly dark (except some paler shaft-streaks), variably contrasting with rest of body depending on colour-morph and/or age.
	• Very variable, from cold pale brown-grey to cold dark brown, not conspicuously rufous-brown as most Great Skua.
	• No cap or dark spot around eye (see Great).
	• Usually paler hind-neck than Great due to very fine pale shaft-streaks. In paler ind rather marked contrast between pale hind-neck and dark upperparts.
	• Slightly less heavy build than Great with smaller head, bill and legs (see note).
	• Most ind have pale 'nose-band' (feathers just before base of upper mandible) in spring due to wear (before moult of head-feathers) ⇔ in Great sometimes present in late summer.
(sub)ad	• In dark morph pale streaked mantle feathers; scaps and neck-feathers with fine pale shaft-streaks; cov hardly marked ⇔ in Great ad strongly pale streaked mantle feathers, scaps and at least some cov, neck and head (in Great at distance these parts appear almost uniformly yellow-brown).
	• Underparts faintly spotted or uniform ⇔ in Great ad strongly spotted and streaked.
juv/imm	• Dark with grey-brown head, neck and breast often extending to mantle and rest of underparts; paler parts contrast with uniform dark cov. Probably no distinct pale morph in juv-2cy.
	• In very dark juv only paler neck with fine pale shaft-streaks (under field conditions very difficult to distinguish from some dark Great juv and Brown Skua-complex).
	• Often two-toned bill ⇔ most Great juv.
	• Tarsus often with pale parts ⇔ ad.
fl all plum	• Very dark underwing (underwing-cov and axillaries blackish) contrasts with paler underparts.
	• Pale prim-base generally smaller than in Great; c.20% of upperside of hand (in both Great and South Polar imm with smaller patch on hand).

	• In flight sometimes resembles Pomarine Skua due to smaller head and slightly longer, more wedge-shaped tail but differences in proportions compared to Great often very slight.
moult	• Juv moult prim in July-January, ad in April-September. In 3rd and 4cy intermediate moult-schedules (see Great). (Sub)ad in autumn at end of moult and (largely) fresh ⇔ Great.
notes	• Ad occurs in 2-3 colour-morphs, juv only in one (dark). The opposite occurs in Great; Great juv variable (usually divided into paler and darker morph) but only one ad colour-morph.
	• ♀ larger than ♂, with heavier bill, also in Great.
	• More study is needed for a better insight into variation of South Polar and Brown, as well as Great (especially juv/imm); above-mentioned field marks give an indication at most. Very dark ind are possibly not distinguishable under field conditions.

Brown Skua *Stercorarius antarcticus* L 54cm 21.5", WS 137cm 54"

all plum	• Most similar to dark Great Skua with long, heavy bill.
	• *antarcticus* (Falkland Islands and south-east Argentina) slightly smaller with more slender build than Great; *lonnbergi* (Antarctic) larger with very heavy bill.
	• Prim-projection often shorter than in South Polar Skua with prim often hardly extending beyond tail.
	• Almost uniform dark cov as in South Polar ⇔ Great.
	• In *lonnbergi* head more uniform and darker.
	• Legs longer than in South Polar.
ad	• Usually rather strong pale patterned neck, neck-side, mantle and scaps. Rest of upperparts not or less obviously patterned – *lonnbergi* generally with slightly less pale markings.
	• In *antarcitus* dark head with usually ill-defined dark cap.
imm	• More uniformly dark than ad with very fine pale streaks on neck.
	• Uniform dark brown underparts.
	• Crown not darker than rest of head.
	• Tarsus often with pale parts ⇔ ad.
fl	• Very dark underwing-cov as in South Polar.
moult	• Basically similar to South Polar.
note	• Field identification and status in WP as yet unclear (probably only immature are potential vagrants). With help of DNA analysis it has been discovered that small number of records in Britain can be attributed to either Brown Skua or South Polar Skua.

Gulls

Ivory Gull *Pagophila eburnea* L 44cm 17.5"

all plum	• Legs black and short.
	• Green-grey bill with orange-yellow tip (bill colour in ad better developed than in 1w).
ad	• Entirely uniform white (albino or leucistic Common with e.g. longer and paler legs).
1w	• Dark around bill and often eye (dark face).
	• Small dark spots on tips of sec, prim and tail-feathers; irregular and variable in amount on cov, scaps, uppertail-cov and prim-cov (underwing-cov unpatterned).
note	• After moult in 2cy normally not separable from ad, but ind with any dark patterning around bill probably 2w.

Sabine's Gull *Xema sabini* L 33cm 13"

all plum		• Relatively short but rather big bill.
		• When perched slender, elongated rear-end.
ad		• Black bill with yellow tip.
		• Ad summer-hood retained late into autumn (summer-hood without pale eye-ring).
		• Grey upperside rather dark as in Common Gull.
juv	⇒	• Dark crown, rear-head and neck-side, distinctive at distance (flight).
		• Grey-brown upperside with narrow pale feather-tips (scaled upperside).
1s		• From May mainly as ad s but only partial dark summer-hood and often some dark markings on tail and tertials.
		• White tips to outer prim smaller than in ad.
2w		• As ad w but smaller white tips to outer prim (in autumn usually worn off).
		• Early in autumn (August) already winter-head ⇔ ad retain summer-hood longer (up to September).
fl all plum		• Black outer-edge of hand creating broad black wedge ⇔ in Kittiwake 1w more narrow.
		• Diffuse dark band on underside of arm.
		• Upperparts concolorous with cov ⇔ in Kittiwake 1w pale grey upperparts contrasting with dark wing pattern. In certain lighting conditions and distance, Kittiwake 1w may show dark and paler parts of arm which appear to merge into each other, thus looking surprisingly similar to Sabine's.
		• Dark cov-panel broad, rounded towards rear and strongly contrasting with bright white sec ⇔ Kittiwake 1w
		• Large amount of white on sec and inner prim creating large white triangle on rear-side of upperwing.
moult		• Complete moult in winter, prim-moult up to April; only body-moult end of summer (opposite of other gulls in WP).

Kittiwake *Rissa tridactyla* L 40cm 15.5"

all plum	⇒	• Legs short and dark (sometimes orange).
		• Short but rather heavy bill.
ad w		• Faintly bordered dark spot behind ear-coverts.
juv-1w	⇒	• Dark collar, disappearing from beginning of 2cy.
1s		• Plumage like 1w but usually strongly bleached and worn.
2w	⇒	• Subterminal marking on p5 ⇔ ad.
		• Dark outer web of p10.

fl all plum ⇒	• Often still some dark patterning on culmen.
	• White underwing with small black tip.
	• Relatively bulging body and narrow hand.
flight ad	• Upperwing two-toned, arm darker than hand.
	• Tip of p7-p10 completely black (subterminal bar over tip p6) creating well-defined entirely black tip of hand.
flight 1w ⇒	• *Pure white sec and inner prim* creating strong contrast with dark diagonal band over arm and dark outer side of hand ⇔ in Little Gull 1w less strong contrast due to darker sec and inner prim.
	• Dark outer side of hand narrower than in Little Gull 1w; pale part of upperwing reaches from carpal joints almost to leading edge ⇔ Little Gull.

Slender-billed Gull *Chroicocephalus genei*   L 40cm 15.5"

all plum ⇒	• Pale iris (darker in juv and ad in breeding season).
	• Long bill, sloping forehead and long neck creating typical 'long-nosed effect'.
	• Long legs.
	• Long neck.
	• Larger than Black-headed Gull (especially ♂).
	• In ad pale grey upperside, slightly paler than in Black-headed.
	• Prim-projection relatively short: c.100%; relatively short wing-projection about same as length of visible part of tail ⇔ in all similar species prim-projection and wing-projection longer.
	• Bill-feathering extending on to upper mandible (creating long gape-line) and ending somewhat rounded ⇔ in Black-headed extending less far and ending more pointed.
ad s ⇒	• White uniform head.
	• Usually orange to pinkish wash on underparts (can occur in all 'black-headed' gulls).
ad w/imm	• White head with usually only small diffuse spot on rear-side of ear-coverts.
juv-1w ⇒	• Pale bill with small dark tip (juv) or without dark tip (from 1w).
	• Juv scaps with pale brown centres, paler than in Black-headed.
	• Legs yellow-orange, paler than in Black-headed juv-1w.
1s	• As juv but paler and more uniform, dark parts bleached (usually much more strongly bleached than Black-headed 1s).
2w-2s	• As ad, often still with some dark markings on tertials, tail-feathers and sometimes cov.
fl all plum	• Long neck conspicuous.
	• Rather long, somewhat rounded tail.
	• Long, broad wings.
	• Broad white leading edge of hand, slightly broader than in Black-headed.
	• Sometimes conspicuously slow wing-beats.
fl juv-1w ⇒	• White leading edge of hand uniform up to carpal joints; no dark pattering on alula and prim-cov (⇔ Black-headed juv-1w), sometimes very small patterning on outer prim-cov.
	• Rather weak band on sec and diagonal band on arm.

Bonaparte's Gull *Chroicocephalus philadelphia*   L 33cm 13"

all plum ⇒	• Legs *pale orange-pink* (especially in imm) ⇔ in Black-headed Gull rather dark flesh-coloured (imm) to dark red (ad).
⇒	• Thin black bill; in imm sometimes slightly paler bill-base (lower mandible) ⇔ in Black-headed longer with orange to red base and dark tip (in Black-headed ad s wholly dark red).
	• In direct comparison with Black-headed obviously smaller.
	• Short tarsus (sometimes striking in direct comparison with Black-headed).
ad s	• Deep-black summer-hood. Summer-hood retained longer than in Black-headed (often into September).
	• Legs orange-red.
ad/1w	• Upperside slightly darker than in Black-headed.
	• Usually faint grey neck-side, breast-sides and hind-neck (sometimes also slightly in Black-headed).
1w	• Darker brown centres of juv feathers of upperside than in Black-headed.
1s	• As 1w but dark patterning more faint; sometimes partial summer-hood but much less often develops complete summer-hood than Black-headed 1s.
	• Centres of cov and tertials darker, creating more strongly contrasting band than in Black-headed 1w-1s.
2w	• Sometimes still recognisable by dark markings on prim-cov and/or tail ⇔ Black-headed 2w as ad w.
fl all plum ⇒	• Both upper- and underwing with narrow black line along trailing edge of hand. Conspicuous white underside of hand with sharp black trailing edge (in 1w-1s dark trailing edge along whole wing).
	• Broad, white leading edge of hand; outer 4 prim with much white (generally slightly more white than in Black-headed).
fl 1w-1s ⇒	• Narrow, well-defined dark trailing edge along whole wing.
⇒	• Dark fringes to *outer prim-cov*; inner prim-cov unpatterned ⇔ in Black-headed 1w-1s dark fringes to inner prim-cov and outer prim-cov unpatterned.

Black-headed Gull *Chroicocephalus ridibundus*   L 37cm 14.5"

all plum	• Red (ad) to grey-brown (imm) bill with dark tip (in ad s no dark tip).
	• Legs dark red (ad) to orange (imm).
ad s ⇒	• *Dark brown* summer-hood, at distance looks black ⇔ all other dark-headed gulls black, except Brown-headed Gull.
1w	• Upperparts grey as in ad but tertials and cov (except outer median cov and greater cov) brown.
1s	• Combination of mainly (worn) juv wings (cov partial moulted), grey upperside and sometimes complete summer-hood.
fl all plum ⇒	• Dark underside of hand and white wedge on outer edge.
note	• For other features see Mediterranean Gull, Slender-billed Gull and Bonaparte's Gull.

Brown-headed Gull *Chroicocephalus brunnicephalus* L 42cm 16.5"

all plum ⇒	• Large bill (red in ad, yellow-orange in imm) with sharply demarcated dark, somewhat drooping tip and weak gonys-angle.
	• Pale iris (from 2cy, as in Grey-headed Gull).
	• Larger than Black-headed Gull.
	• Head-pattern in all plumages nearly as Black-headed.
	• Head-shape resembles Grey-headed.
	• Upperside slightly darker than in Black-headed.
ad s	• Brown summer-hood, paler than in Black-headed ad s.
fl all plum	• Broad wings as in Grey-headed.
	• Pale underwing ⇔ Grey-headed.
fl ad	• Large black wing-tips with 2 large mirrors (on p9 and p10), sometimes small 3rd mirror on p8.
	• Black hand with angular border and white leading edge of hand ⇔ in Grey-headed border rounded.
fl juv-1w	• Usually broad, dark tail-band.
	• Black outer prim; rest of prim with white basal and black distal part.

Grey-headed Gull *Chroicocephalus cirrocephalus* L 41cm 16"

all plum	• Rather large long bill.
	• Long neck and slightly sloping forehead creating somewhat Slender-billed Gull-like head-profile.
	• Legs long.
	• Medium-grey upperside, darker than in Black-headed (not in juv).
ad s	• Grey summer-hood, bordered towards neck by dark grey ring (moulting Black-headed ad in spring can approach this pattern).
ad	• Pale iris (from 2nd part of 2cy).
ad w/juv-1w	• Weak head-pattern with small dark spot behind ear-coverts.
	• Visible prim-tips completely black.
fl all plum ⇒	• Uniform dark grey underwing.
	• Outer 2-3 prim completely black.
fl ad ⇒	• Large black wing-tips (broadest on outer prim) roundly bordered with white central part of hand.
	• White central part of hand stands out as large white crescent nearly vertical on wing-length.
	• 2 large mirrors (as in Brown-headed Gull).
fl juv-2w	• (Very) narrow dark tail-band, not reaching t6.
	• Short white leading edge of hand.
	• Faint arm diagonal.
	• Mirrors from 2nd part of 2cy.

Little Gull *Hydrocoloeus minutus* L 26cm 10"

all plum	• Distinctly smaller (c.30%) than Black-headed Gull.
	• Short, slender, dark bill.
	• Relatively short prim-projection.
ad s	• Black hood extending to hind-neck (like Mediterranean Gull ad s).
	• No pale eye-ring ⇔ all black-headed gulls ad s (except Sabine's Gull).
ad w/imm	• Dark crown (sometimes almost absent).
2s	• Development of summer-hood variable.
fl ad ⇒	• Somewhat rounded wing-tips; *white trailing edge of even width along whole wing* ⇔ Ross's Gull.
	• Dark to blackish underwing (underwing-cov paler).
fl imm	• Pale underwing-cov ⇔ ad.
fl juv-1w ⇒	• All prim-cov dark (also inner) or with dark patterning ⇔ in all similar species juv-1w inner or outer prim-cov white.
	• Dark 'V' on upperwing due to dark band over cov and dark outer prim.
	• Diffuse dark band on sec ⇔ in Ross's and Kittiwake white sec.
	• Wings noticeably more pointed than in ad.
fl 2w/2s	• Variable amount of dark patterning on tip of outer prim.
	• Underwing-cov paler than in ad.

Ross's Gull *Hydrocoloeus rosea* L 31cm 12"

all plum	• Very small slender black bill.
	• Small rounded dove-like head.
	• No dark crown ⇔ Little Gull.
	• Often conspicuously short-legged.
ad s/1s	• Narrow dark ring around whole neck.
ad w/imm ⇒	• Eye conspicuous, surrounded by small dark mask or dark spot before eye; eye looks extremely big at distance.
	• Faint grey breast-sides, sometimes forming weak broken breast-band.
1w	• Visible prim-tips of closed wing look black-white-black, especially p5-p7 ⇔ in Little dark tips larger, creating more solid dark wing-tip.
	• Strong contrast between pale grey mantle and scaps and very dark tertials, median cov and lesser cov.
fl all plum ⇒	• Long wedge-shaped tail (especially central tail-feathers elongated).
⇒	• White axillaries creating conspicuous triangle, sharply demarcated from grey underwing-cov.
	• Pointed wings ⇔ Little ad.
fl (sub)ad ⇒	• Broad white trailing edge of wing, narrowing on inner prim, not extending to outer prim ⇔ Little.
	• Black outer edge of p10.
fl 1w ⇒	• Completely white sec and inner prim ⇔ in Little 1w diffuse dark band on sec.
	• White on hand extending into wing-tip due to partial white outer-webs, creating white wedge ⇔ in Little 1w all prim with white inner web and dark outer web.

- Well-defined narrow dark trailing edge along outer 6-7 prim.
- Dark diagonal band over arm 'connected' over back/rump ⇔ in Little 1w usually broken by grey back/rump.
- Only dark tips to central tail-feathers, no complete tail-band.

Laughing Gull *Larus atricilla*   L 39cm 15.5"

all plum	• Long bill with obvious gonys-angle; longer and bigger than in Franklin's Gull.
	• Long wings; very long wing-projection beyond tail.
	• Conspicuous broad broken eye-ring (as also in Franklins).
	• Legs dark, black to dark chestnut (dark red in ad s ⇔ in Franklin's ad s bright red).
1w-ad	• Dark grey upperside (together with Franklin's only small gull in WP with this colour).
ad	• Small white tips to outer prim (sometimes entirely worn off by end of summer).
ad s	• Black summer-hood extending to neck and on to upper-breast.
	• Dark red bill with black subterminal band.
ad w	• Mainly white head with diffuse dark spot on ear-coverts and diffuse connection over crown (resembles head-pattern of Mediterranean Gull ad w).
	• Dark bill with very difficult to see dark red tip.
1w ⇒	• Dark grey to brown-grey breast, neck-side and flanks.
	• Dark grey mantle and scaps, as in Franklin's 1w ⇔ all other gulls of this size.
	• Head with some dark patterning behind eye and over rear-crown as in ad (about same as in Mediterranean w).
	• Highly variable in extension of post-juv moult, some ind with already moulted cov and tertials.
1s	• As bleached 1w with sometimes partial summer-hood. From mid 2cy cov, inner prim and tail-feathers moulting to ad-type.
2w/2s	• As ad w but no or small white tips to prim and often grey neck- and breast-sides. 2s like ad s but no white prim-tips present in spring.
fl all plum ⇒	• Dark underside of outer-hand.
fl ad ⇒	• Underwing-cov pale grey, strongly contrasting with *dark underside of wing-tips*.
⇒	• Large black wing-tips without mirrors and (very) small white tips to outer prim.
	• Dark grey mantle and upperwing with broad white trailing edge along sec and inner prim.
fl 1w	• Rather dark underwing with black hand and very dark axillaries creating broad diagonal band on base of underwing; rather faint dark lines along underwing-cov.
	• Rather broad white trailing edge of arm.
	• Distinct contrast between black sec and paler greater cov ⇔ in Franklin's none.
	• 2 rather faint pale lines over greater cov and median cov.
	• Broad, black terminal tail-band contrasts with white basal part of tail and uppertail-cov.
	• Grey mantle and brown upperside of arm with some grey cov.
fl 2w-2s	• Like ad w but still black prim-cov and no or small white tips to prim.

Franklin's Gull *Larus pipixcan*   L 34cm 13.5"

all plum ⇒	• Dark grey upperside in combination with small size charcteristic (in size slightly smaller than Black-headed Gull).
	• Very broad broken eye-ring, normally broader than in Laughing Gull. Upper and lower crescent behind eye almost connected ⇔ in Laughing more obviously separated.
	• Often rather thick but not long bill.
	• Legs rather short.
ad s	• Black head with striking white broken eye-ring.
	• Red bill and legs.
(sub)ad ⇒	• Large white tips to prim ⇔ Laughing.
1w	• Dark grey mantle and scaps; dark brown cov.
	• Broad pale fringes to tertials.
	• White underparts (sometimes grey wash on breast-sides) ⇔ in Laughing 1w grey breast and flanks.
	• Entirely dark bill.
1w/1s ⇒	• Complete moult to 1s starts in February; tail-feathers and inner prim moulted first.
ad w/imm ⇒	• Well-developed half-hood behind eye. 1w somewhat streaked on crown and ear-coverts.
	• Dark bill (often lacking red tip in ad w ⇔ Laughing).
imm	• After 1s-moult (from May) very ad-like but with small white prim-tip.
	• In 2w large white prim-tip but more black on tip of hand than ad w.
fl ad ⇒	• Very broad white trailing edge of arm, narrower along hand.
⇒	• Little black in wing-tips, black separated by white band from grey remainder of upperwing ⇔ in Laughing more black on underside of hand.
	• Medium-grey upperside.
	• Grey central tail-feathers, often difficult to see.
fl 1w ⇒	• Pale underwing with dark, rather well-defined dark wing-tips ⇔ Laughing.
	• Broad pale trailing edge of arm.
	• Rather narrow tail-band, not reaching t6 (sometimes not even reaching t5).
	• Brown-grey upperwing (little contrast ⇔ Laughing); grey mantle.
	• Inner prim creating weak pale window ⇔ in Laughing all prim uniform dark.
fl 1s/2w	• As ad w with large black wing-tips (also sharply demarcated on underwing) and small white tips to outer prim (rarely no complete moult from 1w to 1s).
notes	• Complete moult in both spring and autumn; from 1s/2w nearly as ad.
	• Some 1s and 2s may resemble Laughing ad s with combination of black hood and Laughing-like wing-pattern.

Relict Gull *Larus relictus*   L 45cm 17.5"

all plum	• Structure and size resembles Mediterranean Gull but bill thicker and shorter, often conspicuous full protruding breast and small rounded head, adding to rather strange jizz.
	• Legs often conspicuously long, in imm dark brown, in ad dark red.
ad	• Pale grey upperside similar to Black-headed Gull.
ad s	• Black cap with very broad white broken eye-ring (resembling Franklin's Gull).
ad w	• Pale head with fine dark spots. Sometimes weak dark ear-spot.
behav	• Gait: conspicuous fast steps, often looking as though walking on tip-toes.
1w	• Small well-defined dark tips to cov forming rather strong spotted upperside of wing.
	• White head with dark streaked collar.
	• Tertials dark with large white tips.
1s	• Like 1w but paler due to bleaching and wear. Early moult of cov, when upperwing becomes quickly more uniform.
2w	• Like ad w but smaller white tips to outer prim and lacks long tongues of ad (hand pattern similar to Common Gull ad). Sometimes still dark tertial-centres.
flight ad	• 2 large mirrors. Long tongues on p6-p8 cutting deeply into black, sometimes very similar to Mediterranean 2w-2s.
flight 1w	• White unmarked underwing (as in Mediterranean 1w).
	• Greater cov forming conspicuous pale band on upperwing (as in Mediterranean 1w).
	• Rather narrow tail-band, often not reaching t6.

Mediterranean Gull *Larus melanocephalus*   L 38cm 15"

all plum		• White, broken eye-ring.
		• Deep bill with rather obvious gonys-angle.
		• Legs relatively long.
ad s	⇒	• Deep-red bill with dark subterminal band or spot.
	⇒	• Entirely white prim.
		• Deep-black summer-hood extending to neck (when relaxed shape of hood can appear nearly as in Black-headed Gull).
		• White broken eye-ring more distinct than in Black-headed.
		• Legs dull red.
ad w	⇒	• Dark mask behind eye with usually weak connection over rear-head (also in imm w).
		• Red bill with dark subterminal spot.
		• Legs dark red.
juv		• Upperside dark brown, strongly scaled by pale fringes; bases of feathers rather pale, becoming darker towards tip ⇔ in Common Gull juv feather centres even and less dark with scaled pattern less contrasting.
		• Pale, diffuse brown-grey head with obvious white 'eye-lids'.
1w		• Pale grey mantle, scaps and greater cov; juv (dark) median cov, lesser cov and tertials.
		• Completely dark bill.
		• Head-pattern as in ad w but usually larger mask.
1s		• As 1w but dark parts bleached; rarely with partial summer-hood.
juv-2w	⇒	• Legs dark ⇔ other small gulls.
2w/2s		• Variable dark patterning on visible prim-tips, otherwise as ad.
		• In 2w dull orange bill-base with dark tip.
fl ad		• White upper- and underwing with translucent flight-feathers.
fl 1w	⇒	• White underwing-cov, axillaries and flanks ⇔ Common 1w.
	⇒	• Contrasting broad pale central band (greater cov) and inner prim on upperwing.
		• Large pale tongue on inner web of prim (also outer prim) ⇔ in Common 1w almost uniformly dark hand.
		• Dark band on sec.
		• Pale upperparts.
fl 2w/2s		• As ad w with some (variable) black patterning on outer prim.

Audouin's Gull *Larus audouinii*   L 48cm 19"

all plum	⇒	• Legs rather long, *dark green-grey*.
	⇒	• Dark eye (dark red in ad).
		• Low sloping forehead.
		• Pale blue-grey upperside (after 1s).
		• Strong bill with obvious gonys-angle and evenly curved distal part of culmen; bill-tip same level as underside of gonys.
		• Bill-feathering extends far up bill, creating long gape-line.
ad	⇒	• Dark red bill (at distance appears completely dark).
	⇒	• Little contrast between pale grey upperside and white head. *Grey of upperside extends over breast and neck-side.*
		• Small white tips to p6-p10 (worn off by end of summer).
juv-1w	⇒	• Dark greater cov *without obvious patterning*, in flight creating broad dark band.
		• Rapid moult progression, by end of 1cy often already grey upperparts with only small dark centres to mantle feathers and scaps.
		• In juv boldly scaled upperparts.
		• In juv diffuse pale area around bill-base and fore-crown, rest of head uniform.
2w/2s		• White head.
		• White tail with narrow dark subterminal band.
		• Ad-like bill but paler red.
3w-3s		• Like ad but prim-cov with dark markings and very small or no white tips to outer prim.
fl all plum		• Relatively narrow wings with relatively long arm.

	• Often glides over long distances.
	• Body looks slender.
fl ad ⇒	• One mirror on p10, only on inner web ⇔ other large gulls.
	• Large, triangular black wing-tips, strongly contrasting with very pale grey upperwing.
	• Narrow pale trailing edge of arm ⇔ in other large gulls broader.
fl juv-1w ⇒	• Broad pale band along greater cov on underwing; narrow, well-defined dark lines along cov and prim-cov on underwing.
⇒	• Entirely black upperside of tail (with white fringes) contrasts with uniform white 'U' on uppertail-cov. Underside of tail grey with broad dark terminal band.
	• Dark flight-feathers; no obvious pale window on inner prim ⇔ e.g. Herring Gull and Common Gull juv-1w.
	• Dark spot on rear-flanks.
fl 2w/2s	• Pale upperside of arm with dark band on sec and dark hand resembling Mediterranean Gull 1w.
	• Narrow dark subterminal tail-band.

Pallas's Gull *Larus ichthyaetus*   L 63cm 25"

all plum	• *Long, sloping forehead*; characteristic head-profile in combination with long bill.
	• Rather broad broken eye-ring ⇔ other large gulls.
	• Heavy long bill with thickening of distal part due to large gonys-angle.
	• (Except juv) pale grey mantle and upperwing.
	• When swimming lies high on water, often striking in group of mixed gulls.
ad	• Orange-yellow bill with reddish distal part and black subterminal band.
	• Large white tips to outer prim ⇔ in 2w/3s white tip smaller.
	• Legs yellow.
ad w	• Head-pattern as in 1w.
juv	• Distinctly scaled on mantle and scaps due to broad whitish feather-fringes.
juv-1w ⇒	• Brown patterning on hind-neck extending to breast-sides
1w	• Rather faint mask over ear-coverts and rear-head (resembling head-pattern of Mediterranean Gull and Laughing Gull ad w/imm).
	• Grey-brown bill with large black tip.
	• Legs greyish to green-yellow.
	• Post-juv moult often already advanced by mid-winter, with many ad-type cov and often some tertials.
2w	• Already ad-like but no large pale visible prim-tips.
	• Narrow black terminal tail-band.
	• Often still dark patterning on lesser cov.
	• Yellow bill with black subterminal band (no red on bill ⇔ ad).
fl ad	• Almost completely white hand with little black on wing-tips; subterminal black marking on p6-p10 and large white tip. Both mirrors (on p9 and p10) melted with white tip.
fl 1w ⇒	• Broad, very sharply demarcated dark tail-band; rest of tail, uppertail-cov and lower part of rump unpatterned white.
	• Pale grey median cov and greater cov contrast with dark lesser cov and sec.
	• White underwing with black outer-hand and fine dark lines along axillaries (greater cov, median cov) and prim-cov.
	• Pale inner webs of inner prim creating well-defined barred pattern.
fl 2w/2s	• Dark outer prim, prim-cov and alula-area creating 3 separated dark areas (only distal part of mentioned feather-groups dark) ⇔ in other large gulls imm more connected dark outer-hand.
	• Narrow well-defined dark tail-band.
	• Very pale underwing with dark outer-hand.
	• 2 mirrors (p9 and p10).
	• Dark leading edge of arm (lesser cov).
notes	• Despite large size, plumage-cycle of this species corresponds with small '3-year gulls'.
	• Also known as Great Black-headed Gull.

Sooty Gull *Larus hemprichii*   L 44cm 17.5"

all plum ⇒	• Long, rather heavy, *two-toned bill* (dull yellow with black subterminal band and red tip in ad; grey with black tip in imm).
	• Only narrow half eye-ring above eye ⇔ White-eyed Gull.
	• Larger size than White-eyed with relatively larger head.
ad	• Dark brown-grey upperside ⇔ White-eyed paler and pure grey.
	• Legs yellow.
	• Dark grey breast-band almost concolorous with upperparts ⇔ White-eyed.
	• Sooty brown-black hood, extending down to neck and breast ⇔ in White-eyed pure black.
ad w	• As ad s but hood paler brown.
1w ⇒	• Cov with pale fringes and tips creating multiple broad wing-bars ⇔ White-eyed 1w.
	• Brown-grey head slightly paler than upperparts ⇔ in White-eyed 1w black-brown.
2w	• As 1w but uniform cov as in ad.
fl all plum	• Broad hand.
	• Narrow white trailing edge of arm, broadest in ad.
	• Very dark underwing with some contrast between dark underwing-cov and paler sec and inner prim.
fl 1w ⇒	• Tail with broad black terminal band; uppertail-cov and lower part of rump completely white; white rump-area broader than black tail-band ⇔ in White-eyed 1w the other way round.
	• 2 rather obvious white wing-bars along median cov and greater cov ⇔ in White-eyed 1w wing-bars much fainter.
	• Broad white trailing edge along arm.
	• Distinct contrast between pale arm and dark hand ⇔ White-eyed 1w.

White-eyed Gull *Larus leucophthalmus*   L 41cm 16"

all plum	• Very long, slender bill. • Obvious white broken eye-ring ⇔ Sooty Gull. • Narrow (brown-)grey ridge along flanks, often only visible in flight.
ad ⇒	• Pale grey breast-band paler than mantle ⇔ Sooty ad. • Brown-grey upperside. • Red bill with black tip. • Black hood, extending to neck and breast. • Legs yellow.
ad w	• Similar to ad s but hood with white spots/stripes.
1w ⇒	• Dark bill with slightly paler base ⇔ Sooty 1w. • White belly, vent and undertail-cov. • Dark grey-brown mantle, scaps, head and breast.
2w	• As ad w but hood less developed and still dark grey bill.
fl all plum ⇒	• Pale marginal cov; *narrow pale leading edge on wings* ⇔ in Sooty dark leading edge on wings. • Pointed hand ⇔ Sooty. • Almost uniform dark underwing ⇔ Sooty all plum.
fl 1w	• *Completely black tail* contrasts with white outer uppertail-cov ('U'-shaped white patch); central uppertail-cov grey ⇔ in Sooty uppertail-cov completely white. • Some contrast between pale brown cov and dark hand. • Narrow white trailing edge of arm.
fl 2w	• Narrow tail-band as in Sooty but more grey upperside and obvious head-pattern.

Common Gull *Larus canus*   L 43cm 17"

all plum	• Dark eye; in some lighting conditions iris sometimes looks paler (genuinely pale-eyed ind rare but see geog var). • Rather slender bill.
ad	• Upperside darker than in Black-headed Gull and most Herring Gull (Kodak greyscale 5.0-6.5). • Legs yellow-green.
1w	• Legs and bill flesh-coloured to green-grey (bill with dark tip).
2w	• Small or no white tips on visible prim-tips. • Usually still faint dark patterning on tertial-bases. • Broad dark bill-band (bill-pattern nearly as Ring-billed Gull 2w). • Legs often more greenish than in ad w.
fl all plum	• Silhouette differs from large gulls by relatively longer tail and shorter neck.
fl ad ⇒	• Large mirrors which, together with relatively large amount of black on wing-tips, create a conspicuous pattern.
fl 2w	• Small mirrors ⇔ ad. • Large amount of black in hand. • Black outer prim-cov. • Sometimes with dark markings on tip of tail-feathers (rarely creating complete tail-band as in typical Ring-billed 2w but see geog var).
fl 1w	• Broad black terminal tail-band; almost uniform white uppertail-cov and rest of tail (but see geog var). • Greater cov creating dark grey band on upperwing (see Ring-billed and Mediterranean Gull).
note	• For other features see Ring-billed, Mediterranean, Bonaparte's Gull and Audouin's Gull.

geog var	**Short-billed Gull** *L.c. brachyrhynchos* (northern and western North America)
all plum	• Relatively small rounded head, large eye and short fine bill. • Small size compared with *kamtschatschensis* which otherwise resembles it in all plumages.
ad	• Large grey tongue with white tip on p8 extending beyond base of mirror on p9 (see note *heinei* ad). • p5 with 'W'-shaped mark extending over whole width and sometimes dark mark on p4. • White tip on grey tongue of p5-p8 together with mirror on p9 and p10 create distinct and undisturbed 'string of pearls'. • Grey inner web of p9 extends over almost half of visible part of feather. • Generally slightly darker upperside than *canus*, Kodak greyscale 5.5-7.5, tending more towards blue-grey than *kamtschatschensis*. • Rather pale brown-yellow iris.
ad w	• Hind-neck and breast-side rather heavily and diffusely dark spotted, rest of head almost unmarked ⇔ in *canus* ad w dark spots sharper and more regularly spread over head, hind-neck and breast-side. • Bill with at most weak dark subterminal mark.
1w	• Very like *kamtschatschensis* 1w (see below) but underparts almost uniform grey-brown, becoming more grey later in winter. • Broad dark tail-band and strongly barred upper- and undertail-cov. • Large part of juv plumage retained until late in winter (and often into summer). Retained juv cov in summer strongly worn and bleached ⇔ in *canus* cov normally moulted and thus more fresh.
2w	• Often looks more immature than *canus* and *heinei* due to often still extensive dark patterning on hind-neck and breast-side, dark spot on base of tertials and dark patterning on tail-tip, often creating more or less complete tail-band.
fl ad	• Dark white tips to inner 4 prim creating broad trailing edge to inner hand, hardly narrower than along sec ⇔ in *canus*, *heinei* and some *kamtschatschensis* white trailing edge strongly narrowing on inner hand due to small white tips on p1-p4.
fl 1w	• *Largely dark tail* with pale stripes cutting into black on outer webs of basal part of outer tail-feathers, creating striped pattern. Tail-band poorly defined. This tail-pattern sometimes occurrs in *kamtschatschensis* 1w and possibly in *heinei* 1w, but normally in these two the tail-band contrasts with pale base.

Gulls

- Uppertail-cov and undertail-cov strongly barred.
- Axillaries and underwing-cov strongly patterned with dark centres to lesser cov and median cov ⇔ in *kamtschatschensis* cov with dark fringes and paler centres.

geog var	*L.c. heinei* (western and central Asia)
all plum	• Generally larger than *canus*.
ad	• Upperside slightly darker than in *canus*, Kodak greyscale 6.0-8.0.
	• Some ind with white tip on p8 as in *brachyrhynchos* but not combined with complete black band over p5.
ad w	• Generally more obvious bill-band than in *canus* (in combination with size resembles Ring-billed but upperside much darker).
note geog var	• Field marks strongly clinal; identification under field conditions outside normal range very difficult or impossible, but 1w with tail-pattern as *kamtschatschensis* probably belongs to this taxon.

geog var	Kamtchatka Gull *L.c. kamtschatschensis* (eastern Asia)
all plum	• Relatively strong and long bill.
	• Large size and immature plumages can resemble Ring-billed.
ad	• Upperside darkest within Common Gull complex, Kodak greyscale 6.0-9.0.
	• Rather pale brown-yellow iris, often paler than in *brachyrhynchos*.
ad w	• Bill often distinctly yellow and as in *brachyrhynchos* almost without dark subterminal patterning. Sometimes weak orange tip to lower mandible.
	• Dark patterning often concentrated on hind-neck, creating dark shawl.
1w	• Uppertail-cov and undertail-cov respectively strongly patterned and barred.
	• Broad dark tail-band and diffuse dark remainder of tail; from base onwards pale stripes cut into dark parts, creating striped pattern as in *brachyrhynchos* but tail-base with more white and tail-band normally more well-defined.
	• Underparts strongly and densely patterned brown (less uniform than in *brachyrhynchos* 1w).
	• Large part of juv plumage retained late into winter with only grey mantle and grey scaps appearing.
	• Head and hind-neck patterned, hind-neck almost uniformly dark.
	• Bill often distinctly pink (with dark tip).
2w ⇒	• 2nd generation cov weak grey-brown, intermediate between juv and ad-type and contrasting with ad-type grey scaps and mantle ⇔ in all other Common Gull taxa 2w cov ad-type and thus concolorous with scaps and mantle.
	• Tertials with dark base as in *brachyrhynchos* (sometimes also in *canus* and *heinei*, possibly only in latter).
	• Resembles advanced *canus* 1w.
fl ad	• Wing-pattern often similar to *canus*, but pattern approaching *brachyrhynchos* occurs regularly.
fl 1w	• Axillaries and underwing-cov strongly patterned.
fl 2w	• Tail and sec with dark patterning as in *brachyrhynchos* (sometimes also in *canus* and *heinei*, possibly only in latter).
note	• Not recorded in WP.

Ring-billed Gull *Larus delawarensis*   L 45cm 17.5"

all plum	• Bill heavier (especially thicker) than in Common Gull with stronger gonys-angle.
	• (Except juv) pale grey upperside (about as in Black-headed Gull).
	• Narrow pale tertial-fringes/tips (in ad-type tertials sometimes with rather large white tips) ⇔ Common all plum.
	• Legs relatively long, often conspicuous among Common Gulls.
ad	• Pale iris.
	• Broad dark sharply demarcated subterminal bill-band (in Common ad w/imm also obvious but normally narrower and more diffuse).
	• Rather small white tips on visible prim.
	• Legs and bill green to yellow (sometimes orange).
ad w	• Heavy head markings especially on rear-head and hind-neck ⇔ in Common head markings usually more evenly spread.
1w ⇒	• Upperparts pale scaled, usually worn off and/or moulted after December but new 2nd generation feathers again with pale tips.
⇒	• Moult often more advanced than in Common; in latter half of winter often already some uniform grey 2nd generation cov and tertials (when present characteristic).
	• Legs and bill-base pinkish (in 1s often already with yellowish wash).
	• (Rather) strongly spotted head, neck and breast; on breast-sides well-defined 'V'-shaped spots.
	• Greater cov usually faintly and diffusely barred ⇔ in Common 1w uniform (in Herring Gull strongly barred).
	• Dark tertials with narrow, pale fringes ⇔ in Common 1w broader.
	• Lesser cov and median cov sharply patterned/marked with pointed dark centres ⇔ in Common 1w more faintly marked with rounder centres.
	• Pink bill with black tip, extreme bill-tip pale (often very small, sometimes absent) ⇔ in Common 1w wholly dark bill-tip.
2w	• Rather dark iris (from beginning of 3cy rather pale).
	• No or very small white tips to outer prim.
	• One or more tertials with dark base.
	• Legs and bill green-yellow to grey-green, bill sometimes still pink.
fl ad	• Rather large amount of black on wing-tips.
	• 1-2 mirrors, smaller and (when 2) more obviously separated than in Common.
	• Black wing-tips with somewhat rounded border and grey inner hand ⇔ in Common ad usually more angular bordered with grey cutting more deeply into black.

fl 1w	⇒	• Broad dark subterminal tail-band, sometimes very broad and ill-defined towards tail-base. A number of ind with pale line over width of dark tail-band, tail-band then splits into 2 bands (in 1s pale line in dark tail-band usually absent).
	⇒	• Pale central band (greater cov) on upperwing contrasts with dark sec and outer prim; inner prim creating very pale window. Upperwing more like Mediterranean Gull 1w than Common 1w.
		• Upperside of arm (median cov and lesser cov) gives heavily spotted impression due to more well-marked spots on paler background than in Common 1w.
		• Rather well-defined dark lines along tips of underwing-cov ⇔ in Common 1w fainter, in Mediterranean 1w uniform white underwing.
fl 2w		• Subterminal tail-band usually fainter or broken on central tail-feathers.
		• Black outer hand (p6-p10) and dark patterning on outer prim-cov and alula.
		• Usually very small mirror on p10 ⇔ in Common 2w large mirror on p10 and usually also on p9.
		• Dark band on sec usually broken, consisting of well-marked dark spots; band on sec sometimes absent ⇔ in Common 2w no dark band on sec.

Ageing of large gulls

The ageing features mentioned below are only indicative; individual variation in moult strategy and feather patterns, especially between 2s and 4w is very large. Some ind in this plumage-range cannot be aged safely; these birds are best referred to as e.g. '3s-type'.

The typical plumages used in this book (juv-1w-1s-2w etc) are often difficult to define in large gulls due to rather slow changes (almost continuous moult; only in northern regions in mid-winter is there often a short moult-stop). In addition, not every species or individual follows this order; for instance most northern (sub)species which winter at a relatively northern latitude retain an almost complete juv plumage into spring of 2cy, through which '1w-plumage' will develop in spring and '1s-plumage' will be largely omitted (e.g. in Glaucous-winged Gull). By contrast, ind from southern (sub)species start much earlier with their post-juv moult and are often in '1w-plumage' by the autumn of their 1cy. Taxa from the Lesser Black-backed Gull-complex (especially *fuscus, intermedius* and *heuglini*) have a much faster progression to ad plumage.

juv	• Completely dark bill (in some species paler base developed in 1cy).
	• Pointed outer prim.
	• 1st generation mantle feathers and scaps with large dark centres and pale fringes, notched or unnotched.
	• Underparts vary from slightly marked (e.g. Caspian Gull) to entirely uniform dark (e.g. American Herring Gull and Thayer's Gull).
	• Tail with narrow terminal band (e.g. Yellow-legged Gull) to entirely dark (e.g. American Herring, Thayer's and some Lesser-Black-backed Gulls).
	• Generally the darkest and most uniform plumage (latter except ad).
1w	As juv except:
	• Juv mantle feathers and scaps completely or partially replaced by 2nd generation feathers. 2nd generation mantle feathers and scaps less dark and in most species with single or double anchor-pattern (different generations often also visible in different stages of wear). In most northern species or (sub)species first 2nd generation mantle feathers and scaps obtained only in 2nd part of winter (e.g. Thayer's and Herring Gull *argentatus*) while southern (sub) species have all mantle feathers and scaps renewed as early as September (e.g. Yellow-legged).
	• Most species develop paler bill-base (in Glaucous Gull and most American Herring pale bill with black tip).
	• Tail as in juv (Baltic starts with moult of tail).
	• Wings as in juv, except some Caspian, Lesser Black-backed *intermedius* and most Yellow-legged in which cov-moult starts in 1cy.
	• Most species develop paler head and underparts than juv due to wear and bleaching (also by moult).
1s	• Retained juv feathers often strongly bleached and worn, making species-specific patterns difficult to judge.
	• All species show moult of cov, normally starting with median cov (some ind as late as 2nd part of 2cy), and most start from May/June with prim-moult (earlier than in ad). Baltic, some Lesser Black-backed *intermedius* and some Heuglin's Gull are more advanced than other species (see above).
	• Head and underparts normally paler than in juv-1w but large interspecific variation.
	• Tail in most species still partially juv (in most species tail moult starts from May/June). In some species already completely new tail (most Baltic and some Heuglin's).
	• Pale bill-base gradually more obvious, sometimes yellowish with black tip (Glaucous-winged Gull retains entirely dark bill).
	• Pale-eyed species develop pale iris from this age onwards.
2w	• New prim with rounded tips, in some species already small mirror on p10 ⇔ juv prim.
	• Fresh plumage with usually 3rd generation mantle feathers and scaps which indicate what the ad-type colour will be (sometimes immature grey-colour paler than species-specific ad-type colour). Smaller species already very ad-like.
	• Usually entirely ad-type mantle feathers and scaps creating 'clean' upperparts which contrast with older (worn and browner) 2nd generation cov.
	• Completely 2nd generation greater cov and in some species already 3rd generation greater cov. 2nd generation feathers (much) more 'complex' and less regularly patterned than in juv (except some Yellow-legged). 3rd generation feathers nearly as ad-type.
	• Completely 2nd generation tail, usually with narrower tail-band than juv; however some Herring have more black in new tail than in juv tail. Other species (e.g. Lesser Black-backed and Heuglin's) can show (almost) entirely white 2nd generation (possibly 3rd generation) tail or some wholly white feathers.
	• Pale bill with dark tip (very variable, in some species or ind earlier or later).
2s	• Usually mix of bleached and worn 2w and ad-type feathers. Lesser Black-backed and Heuglin's often look largely adult-like.
	• Bill gradually becomes yellowish but dark subterminal spot retained.

3w	• Ad-type leg-colour starts to appear.
	• Very variable in almost all species; most ad-like with still some marked or diffuse brown cov and tertials and usually still dark markings on tips of tail-feathers.
	• New prim (in most species 3rd generation) with (small) white tips.
	• Bill (almost) as in ad but most still show dark subterminal mark. Dark subterminal bill-mark can also occur in (older) ad in winter.
	• Sometimes very difficult to distinguish from advanced 2w (see above).
	• Baltic and some *intermedius* similar to ad while in Herring and Great Black-backed Gull still obvious 'immature markings' on tail-feathers, cov and tertials.
3s	• Like ad with usually some bleached cov (greater cov), sometimes still dark base to tertials and in some species some dark markings on tips of tail-feathers.
	• Bill and leg colour as in ad.
4w	• Like ad but in some species still dark patterning on prim-cov and dark subterminal marking on bill. Dark subterminal bill-pattern can also occur in (older) ad.
	• New prim (in most species 4th generation) show obvious white tips.
4s	• Body moult in spring (at least head and neck) leads to fully ad plumage in all species.
ad	• Some ind still show dark patterning on prim-cov even when fully ad (e.g. in Herring and Baraba Gull, probably only ♀) and dark subterminal bill-markings (e.g. Caspian and Herring) in winter.

Identification of large gulls

Large individual and geographical variation and the often great influence on appearance due to wear, bleaching and moult makes the identification of large gulls a great challenge. The critical observer should leave some ind unidentified. Due to the continued progression of knowledge of the identification of large gulls the field marks presented here may only represent provisional characteristics. This is especially true for the Asian (sub)species.

Lesser Black-backed Gull *Larus fuscus*   L 54cm 21"

all plum	• Long wings; long wing-projection (longer than in Great Black-backed Gull, Herring Gull *argenteus* and most Yellow-legged Gull).
ad	• Small white tips to outer prim, usually worn away by late summer.
	• Usually 2 mirrors: large one on p10 (sometimes merging with white tip) and small one on p9; latter normally absent in *intermedius* (see geog var).
ad w	• Heavy head streaking extending to neck and upper-breast.
juv	• Clear white forehead directly before bill, later in autumn spreads to lores and crown ⇔ Herring juv. Not useful from 1w onwards.
juv-1w	• Tertials usually completely dark with narrow pale fringes around tips, usually covering whole distal part, often small notches at tip.
	• Outer greater cov almost entirely dark, with rather faint notches towards inner wing; in very pale ind barring continues on greater cov as on Herring juv-1w.
	• Entirely black bill.
	• Pale underparts with rather sharp brown patterning ⇔ more diffuse in most Herring juv-1w.
1s	• Very variable, but greater cov usually fresh (2nd generation) and strongly marked (*graellsii*).
2s	• Contrast between brown (old) cov and uniform dark grey upperparts (*graellsii*) but very variable.
3w-4w	• Variable but mainly ad-like with some signs of immaturity. Combine points under all plum and ad with relevant 3w-4w points under 'Ageing of large gulls'. 4w normally indistinguishable from ad.
fl all plum	• Can adopt 'shearwater-flight' in strong winds at sea, resembling skua or even shearwater (at sea plumage of 1w also responsible for skua similarity) but all large gulls make some wing-beats in descending arch unlike skuas and shearwaters.
fl ad	• Small white tips to outer prim.
fl 1w ⇒	• Inner prim slightly or not paler at all than outer ⇔ Herring 1w.
	• Broad, uniform black tail-band, ill-defined towards tail-base, contrasting with pale uppertail-cov.
moult ad	• Starts prim-moult in June and continues, normally without stopping, to p10 in November/December.
note moult	• In imm, moult is extremely variable in both timing and in which feather-groups are moulted, and this has consequences for the appearance of some ind. Choice of wintering area is probably an important factor in extent of winter moult and thus appearance of ind in spring. Wintering further south means more extensive winter moult; this explains partial differences in appearance between different subspecies which choose different wintering areas (*graellsii* south-western Europe, almost no winter moult; *intermedius* north-western Africa, partial winter moult and *fuscus* (southern and eastern Africa, extensive winter moult).
geog var	*L.f. graellsii* (western Europe)
ad	• Grey upperside (Kodak greyscale 9.0-12.0) which clearly contrasts with black wing-tips ⇔ *intermedius*.
	• Approximately half of ind with 2 mirrors (on p9 and p10).
geog var	*L.f. intermedius* (north-western Europe)
all plum	• Slimmer and more elongated than *graellsii*.
	• Generally smaller size and less heavy bill than *graellsii*.
ad	• Dark grey to blackish upperside (Kodak greyscale 11.0-14.0, darkest ind in north-western Norway), slightly contrasting with black wing-tips (can show brown wash as in *fuscus*). Some of most northern ind probably not safely separable from *fuscus*.
	• Further as described under *graellsii* but mirror on p10 probably never merges with white tip.
	• Small proportion of ind with 2nd mirror on p9.
moult	• Imm moult generally faster but later in year than *graellsii*; 1cy in late autumn often still almost juv ⇔ *graellsii*. In spring of 2cy more developed than *graellsii*.
	• Some ind with completely new tail (2nd generation) in 1s ⇔ *graellsii*.
note	• In many respects intermediate between *fuscus* and *graellsii*, especially moult strategy. Separation of ind from northern populations and *fuscus* often impossible.

geog var	Baltic Gull *L.f. fuscus* (north-eastern Europe)
all plum	• Generally smaller than *graellsii* and *intermedius* (although ♂ sometimes as big as Herring *argenteus* ♀).
	• Long prim-projection due to relatively long wings.
	• Relatively slender bill (probably especially in ♀). In some ♂ bill as heavy as other large gulls.
ad	• Black-brown upperside (Kodak greyscale 13.0-17.0), no or very little contrast between upperwing and wing-tips, generally even darker than Great Black-backed (but some *intermedius* overlap).
	• Well-marked 'step' between large white tips to p1-p4 and (very) small white tips to p5-p10; p5 (often 1st prim-tip beyond tertials) with small white tips ⇔ in *graellsii* step to smaller white tip from p6 and tips becoming gradually smaller towards wing-tip.
	• Very small white tips to outer 6 prim, almost worn off from beginning of summer.
	• Some ind with 2nd mirror on p9 (probably especially in ♂).
ad moult	• Prim-moult normally starts in August, usually only with p1 and p2, moult then suspended and finished in wintering area (central and eastern Africa). In Europe in autumn almost completely old hand and no active cov-moult.
ad w	• Whiter head than *graellsii*/*intermedius* with less head-streaking, especially concentrated behind eye and on neck-side (up to September/October no head-streaking at all).
	• More than half of scaps black-brown (also in *intermedius* subad).
juv	• Feathers of upperparts with whitish fringes, strongly contrasting with dark, black-brown centres (less typical ind similar to typical *graellsii* and *intermedius*). See note juv.
	• Generally whiter head and upperparts with well-defined dark patterning ⇔ in *graellsii* and *intermedius* generally more diffuse on underparts.
	• Greater cov with dark base, narrow pale fringe and usually faint notched tip ⇔ in Heuglin's Gull juv normally broader pale fringe and stronger notched tip.
	• Post-juvenile moult (scaps) sometimes starts from August but generally later than *graellsii* and *intermedius* juv-1w; some ind migrate to wintering areas in complete juv plumage.
	• Undertail-cov usually less strongly marked than in *graellsii* and *intermedius*.
	• Upperparts generally warmer brown than in *graellsii* and *intermedius*.
note juv	• All above-mentioned field marks for juv are true for typical ind. *Many ind differ from these field marks* and are more like *graellsii* and *intermedius* juv. In addition, within *graellsii* ind similar to typical *fuscus* juv occur regularly. At present there are no definite field marks for juv, not even in combination.
1s ⇒	• In majority of cases 1w moult most or even all prim, fresh wings in 1s ⇔ *graellsii* and *intermedius* (some *intermedius* moult at least part of prim in 1w). Some ind with complete 2nd generation prim start a new moult during the course of the summer, resulting in *3rd generation inner prim*. Occasionally a new moult begins before the first is completed. Some ind strongly retarded in moult and have very worn juv prim and cov.
	• Mix of old brown (2nd generation) cov and scaps and fresh black (3rd generation) cov and scaps; no barred cov (also in some *intermedius*) ⇔ *graellsii* normally moults cov for first time in June, fresh 2nd generation feathers in 1s.
	• Completely new (2nd generation) tail. Often pale patterning on dark tail-band, sometimes one or more entirely white tail-feathers (as in Heuglin's and some *intermedius*) ⇔ *graellsii*.
	• Head and underparts almost uniform white; some patterning on ear-coverts, neck-side and flanks.
	• Pale grey-brown to greyish bill with dark tip ⇔ in *graellsii* and *intermedius* usually more uniformly dark bill.
	• 3rd generation (ad-type) feathers sometimes paler than later generation ad-type feathers; grey instead of black.
2s	• Usually very ad-like, including yellow iris.
	• Suspended moult of prim: p1 to p6-p9 fresh (3rd generation), outer older (2nd generation) but still relatively fresh and moult-limit often not obvious. Similar moult pattern also noted in *intermedius* but in these moult-limit often more obvious due to older 2nd generation outer prim.
	• Usually broken tail-band with some entirely white tail-feathers ⇔ in 2s *graellsii* in spring complete tail-band. From July onwards above-mentioned pattern can occur in *graellsii* and *intermedius* with entirely white 3rd generation tail-feathers. Tail-pattern of some *intermedius* as in *fuscus*.
	• 2nd generation p10 sometimes already with mirror.
imm	• Plumage cycles pass faster than in other large gulls, e.g. 2s already very ad-like ⇔ *graellsii* and *intermedius* 2s (some *intermedius* from northern populations almost identical).
fl juv-1w	• Underwing-cov paler than in *graellsii* and *intermedius* at this age, often 2 pale bars on underwing-cov.
note ⇒	• Identification of *fuscus* outside normal range appears almost impossible with at least some Norwegian *intermedius* almost identical to *fuscus*, including moult strategy; the exception is probably 1s with complete set of 2nd generation prim.

Heuglin's Gull *Larus heuglini*		L 62cm 24.5"
all plum	• Bill very variable from long and rather slender to long and heavier; structure sometimes recalls Caspian Gull (possibly ♀), others (possibly ♂) with heavier long bill with obvious gonys-angle and thickening at distal part, making bill-tip seemingly droop.	
	• Sometimes subtle structural differences with Lesser Black-backed Gull *graellsii*: longer bill, longer wings resulting in longer prim-projection, longer legs, relatively small head and longer and more slender neck (structure overall tending towards Caspian).	
ad	• Dark grey upperside (Kodak greyscale 9.0-10.0), as in Lesser Black-backed *graellsii*.	
	• Very small white tips to outer prim-tips. p5 still with small white tip as on Lesser Black-backed *fuscus* (p1-p4 with large white tips).	
	• Iris sometimes rather dark (at close range dark spots in iris visible) but regularly pale yellow; however often slightly duller than in other taxa of Lesser Black-backed complex.	
	• Legs variable. When yellow then often paler than yellow on bill. In winter sometimes pink.	
ad w	• Few and fine head-streaks, neck especially often boldly patterned.	
juv	• Greater cov with dark bases and usually large pale tips creating strongly two-toned greater cov (inner greater cov usually with more patterning than in Baltic and Caspian); median cov and lesser cov with broad pale fringes contrasting with dark bases of greater cov.	

	• Tertials rather weakly notched but generally more so than in subspecies of Lesser Black-backed juv.
	• Dark centres to feathers of upperparts and wings but not so blackish as in most Baltic juv. Usually still dark shaft-streaks visible in dark centres of scaps.
	• Underparts more diffusely patterned than in Baltic juv, more similar to Lesser Black-backed *graellsii/intermedius* or underparts even recalling Herring juv.
	• Upperside paler than in Baltic, generally more dull brown ⇔ in Baltic chocolate-brown.
1w/1s	• White head, at most very slightly patterned.
	• Underparts with often very restricted brown patterning on breast-sides and along flanks, remainder uniformly white (strongly resembling Caspian 1w).
1s	• State of cov-moult in June very variable from completely juv to completely 2nd generation; usually rather even mix of 2 generations (completely 2nd generation cov characteristic); juv cov often still rather fresh ⇔ in Caspian 1s (until June) cov still usually largely juv and worn.
	• Upperside with ad-type mantle feathers showing through, scaps and cov with variable amount of ad-grey and often obvious dark shaft-streaks (Caspian-like) ⇔ in Lesser Black-backed *graellsii* usually distinct anchor-pattern on cov and scaps but many Lesser Black-backed *intermedius* show only dark shaft-streaks.
	• Underparts and head almost white with strong streaking on neck-side and breast-sides.
	• Some ind start moult of prim, sec and tail-feathers in winter range, by June some inner prim already new (probably rarely more than 4).
	• Tail probably in most ind 2nd generation, in some ind partially moulted (generation difference often difficult to see but in juv tail-feathers white tips worn off and basal part rather evenly barred; 2nd generation tail-feathers with white tips and more finer and complex patterning). Possibly a small number of ind retain completely juv tail. Often one or more almost completely white tail-feathers (sometimes also in Baltic) ⇔ Lesser Black-backed *intermedius/graellsii* (in *intermedius* quite often completely new uniform tail).
	• 2nd generation tertials greyish with large white tips.
	• Bill in typical ind dull yellow to pink with large black tip.
	• Usually obvious dark narrow stripe directly behind eye (normally also present in Caspian).
2s	• Upperside usually almost completely ad-like, sometimes still rather large amount of brownish cov.
	• Eye still very dark.
	• Tail completely white or still some black markings.
	• Sometimes still juv outer prim (rare combination with rest of ad-like plumage).
3w-4w	• Variable but mainly ad-like with some signs of immaturity. Combine points under all plum and ad (moult) with relevant 3w-4w points under 'Ageing of large gulls'. 4w normally indistinguishable from ad.
fl ad	• Much black in hand; black subterminal markings from p3 or p4 onwards (in Lesser Black-backed *graellsii* normally from p4 or p5 onwards).
	• p8, p9 and p10 almost entirely black up to prim-cov ⇔ in Lesser Black-backed *graellsii* only p9 and p10, p8 with grey base.
	• One rather small mirror on p10 (relatively far from white prim-tip); often also very small mirror on p9.
	• Often pale marking between grey of centre and black of subterminal patterning in tip of (p3) p4-p7 ⇔ subspecies of Lesser Black-backed Gull.
fl juv-1s	• Inner prim usually hardly any paler than outer ⇔ Caspian, Herring and Armenian Gull.
	• Dark terminal tail-band generally narrower than in subspecies of Lesser Black-backed complex (except some Lesser Black-backed *intermedius*) but very variable, sometimes tail almost completely black. When narrow terminal tail-band present, then area above tail-band often with dense, narrow dark barring.
	• Underwing-cov often conspicuously pale (especially median cov and greater cov) and finely barred; generally palest underwing in Lesser Black-backed complex (sometimes however underwing-cov dark).
	• Uppertail-cov and rump white, (nearly) without patterning.
	• Greater cov at base usually dark; together with dark sec creating 2 dark wing bars, especially on outer edge of arm.
	• Significant proportion of ind have moulted sec in 1s (2nd generation sec glossy blackish, juv sec duller and brown) ⇔ in Caspian all sec still juv.
moult ad ⇒	• From June onwards some inner prim; by September most ind have replaced p1, p2 and p3 (sometimes up to p5). Rest of moult takes place in wintering area *up to March* ⇔ other large gulls, except Baltic and some Lesser Black-backed *intermedius*.
	• Normally hardly any moult of body feathers in autumn (still completely white head).
note juv	• Above-mentioned field marks are based on 'typical' ind; there are numerous exceptions and at present there are no characteristic differences from subspecies of Lesser Black-backed juv.
note geog var	• '*taimyrensis*', formally regarded as subspecies of Heuglin's but now considered hybrid population between *heuglini* and Vega Gull *L. vegae* of north-eastern Siberia.
all plum	• Paler grey upperside than *heuglini*, nearly as Armenian ad or Herring *argentatus*.
	• Larger than *heuglini*.
	• Legs yellow to pink.
ad	• Grey base of p8 visible behind prim-cov ⇔ in *heuglini* p8 dark down to prim-cov.
	• Rather large mirror on p9 ⇔ in *heuglini* small or absent.
	• Outer prim-tips with more white than in Vega and *heuglini*.
ad w	• Heavy head streaking ⇔ *heuglini*.
1w	• Similar to *heuglini* 1w but underparts generally darker.
fl all plum	• See *heuglini*.

Herring Gull *Larus argentatus*   L 60cm 23.5"

all plum	• Legs flesh-coloured (sometimes yellow, see note '*omissus*').
ad	• 2 mirrors and rather large white tips to outer prim.
juv-1w ⇒	• Tertials usually distinctly notched.
	• Rather slight contrast between upperparts, wings, underparts and head ⇔ Lesser Black-backed Gull.

- Densely and diffusely spotted underparts, patterning evenly spread ⇔ in Lesser Black-backed and Great Black-backed Gull 1w sharper and especially in Great Black-backed patterning more or less concentrated on central part of underparts.
- Greater cov barred (as in most large gulls) but dark barring not or only slightly broader towards edge of wing ⇔ e.g. Yellow-legged, Lesser Black-backed, Caspian Gull and Heuglin's Gull.

1s
- Like juv but usually strongly bleached; late start of cov-moult, usually simultaneous with moult of inner prim (May) ⇔ Lesser Black-backed *graellsii* starts cov-moult earlier (*intermedius* much earlier).

2w
- Upperside often mix of 2nd generation feathers with dark patterning and ad-type grey feathers.
- Cov and tertials all 2nd generation with more fine and irregular patterning than in juv-type.
- Often pale(r) iris.

3w-4w
- Variable but mainly ad-like with some signs of immaturity. Combine points under all plum and ad with relevant 3w-4w points under 'Ageing of large gulls'.

fl juv-1w
- Inner prim obviously paler than outer, creating pale window.

fl 2w
- Wings often still superficially similar to juv-1w with inner prim and uppertail-cov often (still) paler.

note
- See also references in Yellow-legged, Caspian, Lesser Black-backed and Great Black-backed.

geog var   *L.a. argentatus* (Scandinavia and Baltic) [versus *L.a. argenteus* (western Europe)]

all plum
- Larger with longer extremities (wings, legs and bill) than *argenteus*.
- Legs often deeper pink than in *argenteus*.

(sub)ad
- Upperside slightly darker than in *argenteus* (especially in ind from northern Scandinavia). Kodak greyscale 5.0-7.0 in *argentatus*, 4.0-5.0 in *argenteus*.
- Relatively little black on wing-tips. Variable but commonest hand pattern in most northern ind: p10 like in Caspian; on p9 tongue reaches mirror (Thayer's-pattern) ⇔ *argenteus* and most Caspian. In many others hand pattern overlaps with Caspian.
- p5 usually with small dark marking near tip, often creating narrow band ⇔ in Yellow-legged and Caspian normally broad band over p5.

ad w
- Often heavy head- and breast-streaking, sometimes creating barring on breast as in Glaucous Gull (see also American Herring Gull ad w).
- Often dark subterminal bill-marking.

1w
- Scandinavian ind especially can show relatively large amount of white in tail-band, sometimes strongly resembling Great Black-backed 1w but pale patterning in dark tail-band narrower than dark patterning.
- A small number of ind in autumn/early winter in western Europe show strikingly fresh plumage; little or no 2nd generation scaps and Lesser Black-backed-like tertials and cov- pattern (evenly narrow fringes with or without only weak notching).
- Usually more well marked (more contrastingly patterned) than typical *argenteus*.
- Broad white outer fringe on tail ⇔ *argenteus*.
- Tips to visible prim often with obvious pale fringes but very variable ⇔ in *argenteus* only pale tips.

2w
- In some ind mirror on 2nd generation p10 already present ⇔ in *argenteus* none.

note geog var
- Above-mentioned field marks especially true for typical ind from northern Scandinavian population, however there are many intermediate types due to large clinal area between both forms and also considerable differences between Baltic and northern Scandinavia populations (see below).

note '*omissus*'
- 'Yellow-legged' Herring Gulls occurs regularly within populations of *argentatus* in northern Norway and the eastern part of the Baltic Sea; Baltic population named *omissus*. Ind from Norwegian population bulky with dark upperside (darkest ind as dark as Yellow-legged), relatively little black on wing-tips (but variable) and almost no black on p5 ⇔ Yellow-legged. Ind from Baltic population with dark subterminal band on p5 but pale upperside and long tongue on outer prim ⇔ Yellow-legged.

Yellow-legged Gull *Larus michahellis*   L 57cm 22.5"

all plum
- Heavy, blunt-ended bill (with strongly curved hook) and marked gonys-angle.
- Long wing-projection ⇔ Herring Gull *argenteus* (*argentatus* often also long-winged).
- Legs long.
- Throat, neck-side and breast looks full.
- Relatively large head with relatively steep forehead, flat crown and angular rear-head.

ad
- Colour of upperside between Herring *argenteus* and Lesser Black-backed Gull *graellsii* (Kodak greyscale 6.0-7.0).
- From autumn onwards almost no head-streaking; in July/August some head streaking ⇔ Herring.
- Legs bright yellow.
- Deep orange-yellow bill with red gonys spot, often extending to upper mandible ⇔ in Herring not extending on upper mandible.
- Relatively small white tips to visible prim-tips.
- Complete (usually broad) subterminal black band on p5 (as on Caspian Gull flight ad). In Herring *argenteus* sometimes narrow subterminal bar on p5; in *argentatus* often present.

ad w
- Like ad s but dark around eye and often some fine patterning behind eye (creating eye-stripe).
- Sometimes dark subterminal bill-mark (more often in 4s).

juv-1w ⇒
- In 1cy usually moults at least some cov (2nd generation cov with well-defined diamond-shaped centres) which distinctly differ from juv cov ⇔ in Herring 1w clear contrast between 2nd generation mantle feathers and scaps and all juv cov.
- Juv strongly resembles Lesser Black-backed juv but when fresh juv-type mantle feathers and scaps generally warmer brown and fringes to mantle feathers, scaps and cov broader and often cream-coloured ⇔ in Lesser Black-backed fringes narrower and whitish.
- Some dark patterning around and directly behind eye, creating mask (resembles ad w).
- Dark tertials with pale fringes around tips, regularly weakly notched (fringe normally not extending to base) and usually on one tertial pale subterminal spot ('nail'); in many Lesser Black-backed similar pattern.
- Black bill contrasts with white forehead; in 2cy sometimes slightly paler bill-base, rarely in 1cy.

	• Inner greater cov boldly barred/notched, in most ind becoming more uniform towards edge of wing to almost entirely dark without barring/notching ⇔ in Lesser Black-backed less obvious difference in patterning between inner and outer greater cov.
	• Some dark patterning around and directly behind eye, creating mask (resembles ad w).
	• Centre of breast, belly and vent often almost unpatterned, contrasting with dark upper-breast.
	• Outer prim dark brown ⇔ in Lesser Black-backed black.
	• 2nd generation scaps with relatively narrow but well-defined double anchor shaped pattern on greyish ground-colour (also occurs frequently in Herring) ⇔ in Lesser Black-backed often more diffuse anchor-pattern.
	• Plumage more contrasting than in Herring juv-1w; upperparts usually deeper chocolate-brown than in most Herring *argenteus* 1w.
1s	• Variable but wing usually still looking relative young with strongly contrasting, dark and sharply barred or blotched cov and scaps ⇔ in Herring 1s more diffusely marked.
	• Strongly patterned 2nd generation lesser cov and median cov with large, contrasting dark centres.
	• 2nd generation greater cov often boldly barred.
	• 2nd generation tertials often with very dark base and boldly barred patterning on tips.
	• Head pale with dark mask.
	• Often still wholly dark bill.
2w	• Mainly as 1s but upperside (largely) uniform grey.
	• Often still rather dark bill.
	• Often mix of boldly patterned 2nd generation cov and uniform grey 3rd generation cov; scaps often uniform grey (3rd generation).
2s-3w	• Dark markings on wings (before tertials); tail more sharply demarcated and darker than in Herring.
3w-4w	• Variable but mainly ad-like with some signs of immaturity. Combine points under all plum and ad with relevant 3w-4w points under 'Ageing of large gulls'.
fl ad	• Rather large amount of black on wing-tips with usually 2 mirrors, normally obviously separated from white prim-tip. In (eastern) variant tip of p10 merges into mirror, creating completely white tip as in many ind of western population of Caspian.
	• Grey tongue on p10 and p9 relatively short (when viewing the underwing), usually not reaching distal half of prim ⇔ most Herring.
fl 1w ⇒	• White tail-base, uppertail-cov and rump strongly contrast with well-defined, blackish terminal tail-band uppertail-cov with dark heart-shaped spot. Overall very similar to, and overlapping with, Caspian 1w.
	• Small pale window on inner hand (sometimes difficult to see) consisting of paler inner web of inner prim only ⇔ in Herring much more obvious, in Lesser Black-backed absent.
	• Undertail-cov and vent white with just some spots, no obvious barring as in most Herring.
	• Upperwing with dark band on sec and (sometimes) greater cov, contrasting with paler cov-panel and mantle ⇔ in most Lesser Black-backed 1w cov not distinctly paler.
	• Usually dark underwing; especially cov and axillaries have rather sharply defined dark patterning with paler bars ⇔ in Herring 1w more uniform and diffuse underwing.
fl 2w	• Rather narrow dark terminal tail-band ⇔ in Herring 2w often broad and diffuse.
	• Heavily and sharply marked underwing-cov and axillaries.
fl 3w	• Usually shows the remains of a dark tail-band, concentrated on inner tail-feathers ⇔ in Herring 3w often little, irregular and faint tail patterning.
	• Often just one small mirror (as in many Herring) ⇔ in Caspian large mirror on p10 and small one on p9.
moult	• Moults in all plumages earlier than Herring; in ad prim-moult completed from autumn to beginning of winter ⇔ in Herring and Lesser Black-backed still growing outer prim at that time.
note '*omissus*'	• 'Yellow-legged' Herring Gulls occur regularly within populations of *argentatus* in northern Norway and eastern part of Baltic (see note under Herring Gull).
geog var	*L.m. atlantis* (Azores. Ind from Canary Islands, Madeira and west coast of Morocco intermediate between *atlantis* and *michahellis* but probably more closely related to latter).
all plum	• Shorter tarsus, larger feet, heavier bill and broader wings than *michahellis*.
ad	• Upperside darker than in *michahellis* (Kodak greyscale 7.0-8.0); darkest ind in Azores.
(sub)ad w ⇒	• From end of summer whole head strongly but finely streaked creating characteristic dark hood; in 2s-3w very extensive. In ind from Canary Islands, Madeira and west coast of Morocco much less obvious.
	• Very pale yellow to whitish iris ⇔ in *michahellis* deeper yellow.
juv-1w	• Very dark upperparts (pale notching restricted) and underparts can recall American Herring Gull.
	• Dark front side of tarsus, *often retained to 2cy* ⇔ in *michahellis*, Herring and Lesser Black-backed only in juv.
1s	• Underparts strongly dark patterned.
	• Still dark front side of tarsus.
	• Bill wholly dark.
	• Often already very pale iris ⇔ *michahellis* and Lesser Black-backed.
2w ⇒	• Still very dark patterned head with already distinct pale iris forms conspicuous combination (rarely found in other taxa).
	• Underparts still strongly dark patterned.
	• Often still almost entirely black bill.
fl all plum	• Broad wings, especially arm.
fl ad	• Usually only one mirror and a lot of black in hand, p4 often with dark subterminal band.
fl juv-1w	• Broader dark terminal tail-band than *michahellis* (tail- and uppertail-cov pattern strongly resembles Lesser Black-backed).
	• Inner prim hardly any paler (upperwing nearly as Lesser Black-backed).
	• Very dark greater cov creating 2nd dark band (in *michahellis* usually less distinct).

Armenian Gull Larus armenicus   L 54cm 21.5"

all plum	⇒	• Heavy and especially blunt bill with large gonys-angle; in ♀ often noticeably shorter bill than ♂.
		• Iris varies from rather pale to completely dark, probably rarely or never obviously pale.
		• Legs yellow (from about 2s on).
		• Sexual differences sometimes rather distinct; in ♀ rather high crown, round head-shape and short bill. In ♂ flatter forehead, more angular head-shape and longer bill (resembling Yellow-legged Gull).
ad	⇒	• Deep yellow bill with black subterminal band (some ind lose band in summer) ⇔ see also Caspian ad w.
		• Large red gonys spot can extend to upper mandible (commoner in Yellow-legged) and often pale tip.
		• Rather dark blue-grey upperside (slightly darker than in Yellow-legged, Kodak greyscale 7.0-8.5).
1w		• Plumage similar to Yellow-legged but greater cov strongly and evenly barred; dark bars narrower than pale bars (more like Herring Gull 1w).
		• Pale head often without obvious dark mask ⇔ Yellow-legged 1w.
		• Strongly patterned underparts, especially flanks, breast-sides and neck-side (flanks often also barred).
2w		• Resembles Yellow-legged 2w but head whiter, almost without dark mask.
3w-4w		• Variable but mainly ad-like with some signs of immaturity. Combine points under all plum and ad with relevant 3w-4w points under 'Ageing of large gulls'.
fl ad		• Much black in wing-tips (outer 3 prim almost completely black up to prim-cov), no obvious tongue on inner web of p9 and p10 ⇔ Baraba Gull.
		• Underside of flight-feathers creating conspicuous dark band (as in Lesser Black-backed Gull) ⇔ in Yellow-legged and Caspian Gull much weaker.
		• One mirror on p10, distinctly separated from white prim-tip (sometimes small mirror on p9).
		• White trailing edge of wing narrows strongly on inner prim ⇔ Yellow-legged and Caspian.
fl 1w		• Distinct pale window on inner prim ⇔ all congeners.
		• Relatively narrow, sharply demarcated tail-band, similar to tail-band of Yellow-legged.
		• Dark sec create one bar over arm ⇔ Yellow-legged and Caspian have two dark bars over arm and greater cov.
		• Relatively pale grey-brown underwing (as in Caspian).
2w		• Pale underwing ⇔ in most Yellow-legged darker.
moult		• Ad start early (April/May) with prim-moult. 1w start early with cov-moult (in winter and spring already many 2nd generation cov). Moult strategy resembles that of Yellow-legged.

Caspian Gull Larus cachinnans   L 62cm 24.5"

all plum		• Dark iris, some ad with paler iris (but possibly never as pale as in Herring Gull).
		• Usually long rather slender bill and no marked gonys-angle. Some ♂ with bill as heavy as Yellow-legged.
		• Ventral area often bulging ⇔ Yellow-legged and Herring.
		• Much size difference between ♀ and ♂ (♂ often larger than Herring argentatus; ♀ often smaller than Herring argentatus).
		• Relatively small head with rather flat crown and sometimes knob on forehead.
		• 'Rangy' look due to long wing-projection, long legs and (often conspicuously) long neck.
(sub)ad		• Upperside paler than Yellow-legged (Kodak greyscale 5.0-6.5) nearly as Herring argentatus or even argentatus.
		• In winter legs pale yellowish, often with pink or green wash; toes and webs pink in winter; in summer often bright yellow as in Yellow-legged.
		• Neck-side and breast-sides often finely and sharply streaked, creating obvious collar.
		• Yellow bill (often pale green-yellow in winter and subad) with red gonys-spot which sometimes extends to upper mandible (latter more often in Yellow-legged, very rare in Herring).
ad w		• Uniform white head and fine dark streaks on hind-neck and neck-sides.
		• Small black subterminal spot, mainly on upper mandible; spot smaller than in Armenian ad w but overlap in bill-pattern of both species probably not exceptional (in subad bill-pattern as on 'normal' Armenian ad).
		• Faded yellow-green bill with pale orange gonys-spot restricted to lower mandible.
juv-1w	⇒	• In juv upperparts paler and often more grey-brown (colour can resemble Common Gull juv) than in Yellow-legged juv.
	⇒	• Greater cov dark at base and paler near tip, creating diffuse wing-bar.
		• Tertials dark with broad pale, sickle-shaped tips, usually not sharply demarcated (recalls tertial-pattern of Common Gull 1w).
		• Cov usually with no well-defined barring/notching, but rather uniformly dark with narrow pale fringes. Especially inner greater cov with irregular pale patterning.
		• Bill not as black as on Yellow-legged and Herring; in 1w usually with pinkish base.
		• Middle of breast uniform white.
		• Legs pale flesh-coloured.
1w		• Mantle and scaps tew with some dark diamond-shaped spots and usually narrow anchor-pattern (usually no well-defined double anchor-pattern). Whole of mantle and scaps contrast strongly with dark cov.
		• Often some mainly grey new cov ⇔ Herring.
1w-2w		• Uniform white head contrasts strongly with fine-streaked hind-neck and spotted neck-side and breast-sides.
1s		• Grey mantle feathers and scaps with narrow dark centres (usually only shaft-streak) contrast with dark cov (cov often strongly bleached).
		• Bill rather pale, usually grey-brown with dark subterminal band and pale tip.
		• New tertials have uniform dark base and fairly uniform white tip ⇔ in Yellow-legged tip boldly barred.
2w		• Underparts during winter usually become completely white.
		• Neck usually with typical fine streaking (see 1w-2w).
		• New p10 (2nd generation) with mirror (sometimes present in Herring, rarely in Yellow-legged).
		• Iris dark ⇔ most Yellow-legged and Herring 2w.
3w		• Neck and breast-sides strongly streaked, creating conspicuous marked collar against wholly white head.
		• Dark spot at base of grey tertials (also in some Yellow-legged 3w and American Herring 3w) ⇔ Herring 3w.
3w-4w		• Variable but mainly ad-like with some signs of immaturity. Combine points under all plum and ad with relevant 3w-4w points under 'Ageing of large gulls'.
fl ad	⇒	• Little black in wing-tips with long grey-white tongue on p9 and p10 'cutting' deeply into black of distal part of prim (in many Herring argentatus similar pattern) ⇔ Yellow-legged.

fl 1w	• 2 mirrors, on p9 and p10; mirror on p10 often merges with tip, by which wholly white tip arises (as also often in Herring *argentatus*). • Complete subterminal band over p5 and dark marking on p4 as in Yellow-legged ⇔ Herring *argenteus* (in many Herring *argentatus* also marking on p5, sometimes creating evenly broad band as on Caspian and Yellow-legged). • On underwing hardly any contrast between sec and underwing-cov ⇔ in Yellow-legged rather obvious contrast between grey sec and white underwing-cov. • Broad white trailing edge on arm ⇔ in Herring and Yellow-legged narrower. • Pale underwing-cov with only a few dark lines and unmarked white base of axillaries (more strongly marked and not rare). • Relatively pale underside of outer prim ⇔ Yellow-legged 1w. • Pale window on inner hand consists of pale inner prim, often almost as obvious as in Herring 1w but darker outer webs creating fan of bars; some ind darker and more like Yellow-legged 1w. • Whitish tail-base and white, almost unpatterned rump. • Sparsely marked white tail-base, uppertail cov and rump strongly contrasting with rather well-defined, blackish terminal tail-band; uppertail cov with dark heart-shaped spot. Overall very similar to, and overlapping with, Yellow-legged 1w. • Often pale mark in dark outer web of inner prim ⇔ Yellow-legged 1w.
fl 2w	• Almost entirely white underwing-cov. • Small mirror on p10.
behav ⇒	• Both long call and threatening behaviour with half open wings (also in *barabensis* and Heuglin's Gull) ⇔ Herring and Yellow-legged.

geog var	**Baraba Gull** *L.c. barabensis* (central Asia)
all plum	• Iris rather dark, reminiscent of variation in *cachinnans*. • Bill-structure resembles *cachinnans* but normally shorter and thicker; in ♂ often considerable gonys-angle.
ad	• Upperside darker than Yellow-legged (like Armenian, Kodak greyscale 7.0-8.5) but paler than most Lesser Black-backed Gull (*graellsii*). • Completely white head from February ⇔ in Heuglin's Gull winter streaking. • In spring prim more worn than in Heuglin's (Heuglin's very fresh in spring). • No active moult in early spring ⇔ Heuglin's still in moult (tertials and outer prim). • Legs deep yellow.
juv-1w	• Mantle and cov strongly and boldly patterned with large dark markings ⇔ most other eastern (sub)species 1w, except Armenian. • Greater cov and tertials similar to *cachinnans* but often more patterned with broad pale and dark bands. • Pale, almost unmarked centre of underparts.
fl ad	• Much black in hand with relatively large amount of black on p5 and usually black marking on p4, sometimes even on p3. • Rather long tongue on outer prim resembles *cachinnans* ⇔ Armenian and *'taimyrensis'*. • Basal half of underside of p8 grey ⇔ in Heuglin's only 10-15% grey at base. • One (p10) or 2 mirrors (p9 and p10).
moult	• Ad start rather early (May) with prim-moult. 1w start with cov-moult in winter, often later but more extensive than in *cachinnans* and Yellow-legged. Cov-moult often complete in spring ⇔ *cachinnans*.

American Herring Gull *Larus smithsonianus*   L 61cm 24"

all plum	• Larger than Herring Gull *argenteus*, more like Herring *argentatus* but often even more bulky impression. • Relatively long bill with narrow base, sometimes giving impression of slightly drooping tip. • Legs pink, sometimes with reddish wash (latter from 3cy onwards).
ad	• In considerable amount of ind from eastern North America different patterns of p5-p10 from Herring *argenteus* and less from Herring *argentatus*. In general relatively little black on wing-tips with grey tongues 'cutting' deeply into the black. Black concentrated on feather tips (resembling Caspian Gull). • Most common pattern per feather: p10 with broad and long grey tongue ending more or less *rectangularly*, in combination with black border between white mirror and tip; p9 with small mirror (sometimes absent) not extending on to outer web, and grey base (black not extending to prim-cov); p8 with black outer web extending in *narrow 'tooth' along outer edge of outer web ('bayonet')*; p7 like p8 but 'bayonet' shorter; p6 with 'W'-pattern and sharp tip to outer web (short 'bayonet'); p5 with complete bar, often *symmetrical 'W'-shaped*. Intergrade *argenteus/argentatus* can approach above-mentioned characters but combination of patterns of p5, p6 and p10 characteristic. • Pale upperside (Kodak greyscale mostly 4.0-4.5) ⇔ in Herring *argentatus* mostly 5.0-6.0. Combination of size like Herring *argentatus* and colour of or paler than Herring *argenteus* indicative. • Rather small red gonys-patch.
ad w	• Often heavy dark patterning on head and hind-neck, extending to neck-side and breast more than normal in Herring *argenteus* but many Herring *argentatus* almost identical. • Often denser dark patterning around eye, in most marked cases almost creating a mask. • Often pale yellow bill (sometimes with green wash) with small orange/red and small dark spot on gonys (as on many Herring *argentatus*).
juv-1w ⇒	• Densely dark patterned vent, undertail-cov, rump and uppertail-cov with many dark bars, in which dark bars are broader than pale ones; longest undertail-cov mainly dark with restricted pale patterning ⇔ Herring, Lesser Black-backed Gull and Great Black-backed Gull 1w.
⇒	• *(Almost) uniform* (deep) brown to brown-grey underparts and upper part of mantle and hind-neck, retained well into 2cy (underparts later mix with grey feathers) ⇔ Herring 1w. • Almost entirely dark tail; basal part of t4-t6 often slightly marked (when perched exact pattern difficult to judge). • General colouration deeper brown than in Herring 1w. Ground-colour of pale parts of vent, undertail-cov, rump and uppertail-cov pale brown to pale grey-brown ⇔ in Herring, Lesser Black-backed and Great Black-backed 1w ground-colour white.

- Basal part of bill pale from 2cy (often earlier), usually wholly pinkish with well-defined black tip (resembles Glaucous Gull 1w).
- Dark tertials, usually pale-fringed at tip and faintly notched, darker and more uniform than in Herring 1w (resembles tertial-patterning of Lesser Black-backed 1w and especially Yellow-legged Gull 1w).
- 2nd generation scaps with very variable pattern, sometimes not different from variation within Herring but ground-colour often browner. Scaps often with more Caspian-like pattern (broad dark shaft-streaks, at most ill-defined anchor-pattern), rare in Herring 1w. Often shows multiple 'types' of scaps, probably due to rather slow moult ⇔ in Herring 1w 2nd generation scaps evenly patterned and obviously of one generation.
- Cov less strongly notched than in Herring 1w, often fading away on greater cov, creating dark uniform base. Some ind with almost entirely dark outer greater cov; then underparts also very dark ⇔ Lesser Black-backed 1w.
- Sometimes contrasting paler head due to dark breast, neck-side and hind-neck, resembles Yellow-legged 1w but neck-side and hind-neck often uniform brown.
- Post-juv moult usually starts late, often still some juv scaps present well into 2cy (like in Herring *argentatus* 1w). Timing of post-juv moult mostly dependent on degree of latitude of hatching area; European vagrants probably from northern origin, moult strategy comparable with that of Herring *argentatus*.

1s
- Like 1w but paler and thus less conspicuous.
- Sometimes uniform white head, contrasting with dark neck-side and mantle, resembling Caspian.

2w ⇒
- Nearly uniformly dark hind-neck and upper part of mantle (as in 1w), usually connected through neck-side with variable dark underparts.
- Underparts often still largely dark but less solid than in 1w.
- Tail still almost entirely black (in Herring 2w tail often darker than in 1w). Uppertail-cov/rump at beginning of winter often still as 1w, later in winter gradually whiter.
- Usually still strongly and finely barred undertail-cov and vent, sometimes diffuser. Often *entirely dark centre of undertail-cov* ⇔ Herring 2w.
- Wings often still juv-like brown but 2nd generation cov more ill-defined and more finely patterned; dark greater cov often creating broad dark band. Some ind with mix of ad-grey median cov, greater cov and tertials.
- Upperparts often still mainly brown with usually only some grey ad-type feathers ⇔ Herring 2w. However very variable, other ind with much grey in mantle and scaps and much more similar to Herring 2w.
- Scaps very variable but Caspian-like pattern characteristic (even on 2nd generation in 1w).
- 2nd generation tertials largely dark with narrow pale fringes, bases often almost as dark as prim ⇔ in Herring usually barred but sometimes also completely dark with pale fringes.
- Median cov sometimes forming conspicuous pale band.

3w
- Most ind still look rather young, similar to Herring 2w but inner prim with ad-grey colouration (grey-brown in 2w).
- Ad-like tertials often with well-defined blackish spot ('ink spot') at base ⇔ when tertial-spot present in Herring 3w then usually browner and more diffuse.
- Usually still much black in tail (flight).
- Head, hind-neck and breast often strongly dark patterned ⇔ in most Herring imm less so.
- Usually small to very small white tips to outer prim.

4w
- Tertials often with well-defined blackish 'ink spot' at base (like 3w) but rest of plumage (almost) entirely ad-like.

fl ad
- Underside of hand often shows little black (on underside black concentrated on prim-tip); often row of white markings present between black outer edge and long grey tongue (pale tip on tongue) ⇔ Herring *argenteus* (but Herring *argentatus* can show similar pattern).

fl 1w ⇒
- Rump/uppertail-cov generally dark (strongly and finely patterned/marked), not or only slightly contrasting with upperparts ⇔ Herring 1w and Lesser Black-backed 1w.
- Almost completely black tail ((t4) t5-t6 usually with fine pale spotting at base) contrasting with paler, strongly and densely patterned rump/uppertail-cov (some Herring approach or even match this pattern completely).
- Axillaries and underwing-cov uniform deep brown (also in some Herring).
- Large pale window on inner prim but slightly duller and browner than in Herring (also in 2w).

fl 2w
- Black tail contrasts with very pale uppertail-cov/rump (but some 2w resemble 1w due to still dark uppertail-cov/rump). In Herring 2w often largely black tail but with paler base.

fl 3w
- Combination of ad-grey inner prim and still very dark centres to (some) sec ⇔ in Herring 3w at most diffuse brown patterning on sec.
- Well-defined blackish patterning on tail-feathers, sometimes tail still largely black (sometimes resembling Ring-billed Gull 2w).
- Often long pale tongue on outer prim ⇔ in Herring subad outer prim largely black.

fl 4w
- Dark prim-cov and ad plumage indicative of this age; sometimes still well-defined dark centres to sec and tertials ('ink spot') ⇔ Herring 4w.

Glaucous-winged Gull *Larus glaucescens*   L 63cm 25"

all plum ⇒
- Visible prim-tips (nearly) *concolorous with tertials*; brownish in imm, greyish in (sub)ad.
- Dark iris.
- Small eye placed relatively high on head and sometimes conspicuous thick loral feathering, creating typical weird facial impression.
- Relatively short prim-projection; short wing-projection with 2-3 visible prim-tips beyond tail.
- Heavy build with relatively small head but bulky bill. Size variable between Herring Gull (♀) and Great Black-backed Gull (♂).
- Tips of sec often visible under greater cov (in most large gulls completely concealed by greater cov).
- Legs rather short; (dark) pink, in juv-1w sometimes dark pink-brown.

Gulls

ad	⇒	• Grey visible prim-tips (nearly) concolorous with mantle and upperwing.

ad ⇒ • Grey visible prim-tips (nearly) concolorous with mantle and upperwing.
• Grey colour of upperside darker than in Thayer's Gull and Glaucous Gull ad (about as in Herring *argentatus*) but variable with western North American populations generally paler and eastern Asian populations darker; Kodak greyscale 4.0-7.5.
• Rather large white tips to outer prim.
• Orbital-ring and gape-line pinkish.

ad w • Head and neck very diffusely spotted, not sharply streaked. At close range *very fine barring* visible.
• Bill pale yellow, often with small dark subterminal spot.

juv-1w ⇒ • Entirely black bill ⇔ Glaucous and Iceland Gull (but in some Kumlien's Gulls and most Thayer's also entirely dark).
⇒ • Visible prim-tips medium brown, (nearly) concolorous with tertials.
⇒ • Underparts uniform dark grey-brown, at close range sometimes *fine barring visible (fine barring also in later plumages on head and breast)*.
• Whole of bird uniformly coloured without conspicuous pale or dark patterning; fresh juv often more well-marked and then very like Thayer's juv but in latter e.g. prim darker than tertials with distinct contrast between dark outer webs and pale inner webs.
• Tertials only finely patterned on tips, rest uniformly dark (as in Thayer's juv-1w) ⇔ in Glaucous 1w barred throughout.
• Visible prim-tips with pale fringes on both webs (as in Kumlien's) ⇔ in Thayer's juv-1w pale fringe more restricted to tip.
• Greater cov with uniform base and fine patterning near tip, sometimes faint barring on tip.
• Tail almost uniform grey-brown.
• Post-juv moult starts very late, in spring normally only some 2nd generation scaps.

1s • Like juv but worn and bleached, therefore usually very uniform; mantle and scaps forming almost uniform grey upperparts.

2w-3w • Very uniform brown-grey cov, almost unpatterned.
• Most 2w with diffuse patchy underparts, hardly contrasting with upperside.
• Mantle and scaps uniform grey (ad-type).
• Bill becoming paler on base and culmen (sometimes still entirely dark bill).
• 3w with small white tips to outer prim.
• Most 3w with pale bill and dark subterminal mark.
• Most 3w often with dark patterning on tail (or even uniform grey-brown like in younger plumages).

subad (3w-5w) • Very variable with ad-like plumage but immaturity often visible by extensive dark bill markings, sometimes dark patterning on tail, relatively small mirror on p10 and relatively small white tips to outer prim. Combine points under all plum and ad with relevant 3w-4w points under 'Ageing of large gulls'.

fl all plum • Heavy body and broad wings often conspicuous.
fl ad • One large mirror on p10, usually small one mirror on p9 and sometimes one on p8 or all outer prim with subterminal white spot, creating weak 'string of pearls'.
• Top of hand largely grey; white on tips of outer 5 prim restricted to extreme tip and small mirror ⇔ in Kumlien's ad large amount of white on tips and often completely white tips to outer 5 prim.
• Broad white trailing edge of arm.

fl 1w • Nearly whole plumage diffuse pale brown, like dark washed-out Glaucous 1w. Tail and sec darkest part of plumage.

fl 2w-3w • Rather dark, uniform upper-tail contrasts slightly with paler uppertail-cov and rump.
note • Identification complicated by regular hybridisation, especially with Western Gull *L. occidentalis* and American Herring Gull. In these hybrids visible prim-tips darker than tertials and contrast between dark outer webs and pale inner webs on tips of outer prim. First generation hybrid Western x Glaucous-winged 1w in 1cy often with mix of juv and 2nd generation scaps due to influence of early post-juv moult of Western. In hybrid Glaucous x Glaucous-winged from 2cy pale bill-base, paler iris; in (sub)ad pale outer prim-tips (paler than tertials) in which grey restricted to tip of p6. Hybrid Glaucous x (American) Herring ad ('Nelson's Gull') can resemble Glaucous-winged but usually with prim-tips darker than tertials, pale iris and paler upperside.

Thayer's Gull *Larus thayeri*   L 59cm 23'

all plum • (Rather) dark iris.
• Rather long bill (but shorter than in Herring Gull) with relatively slender and parallel base ⇔ in Kumlien's Gull shorter and not especially slender-based.
• Herring-like structure (⇔ most Kumlien's) but with rather flat forehead, rounded crown and often somewhat square rear-head.
• Bill-feathering extends relatively far on upper mandible.
• Well-marked size difference between ♂ and ♀.

ad • Visible prim-tips on underside almost white.
• Colour of upperside slightly darker than in Iceland Gull and Kumlien's (Kodak greyscale 4.5-5.5), about as in Herring *argenteus* but deeper blue.
• Legs deep dark pink.
• Tertials with large white tips.
• Variable but often large white tips to outer prim.
• Bill often somewhat green-yellow in winter.
• Eye-colour variable, usually rather dark (rarely as pale as in Herring).
• Orbital-ring in summer purple.

ad w • Heavy breast- and neck spotting diffusely set off against somewhat rufous-brown wash.
• Winter head markings retained late into spring (due to late body moult in nearly all plumages).

juv-1w • Nearly uniform dark earth-brown underparts; underparts darker than upperparts.
• Juv scaps with spade-shaped dark centres and broad pale fringes, at least some retained until late winter. Whole of upperparts rather pale, cold brown-grey.

- Uniform dark tertial-centres with well-defined small notches at tips ⇔ in Kumlien's often almost same pattern but dark tertial-centres paler towards tip.
- Visible prim-tips darker than tertials and cov ⇔ in dark Kumlien's concolorous with tertials and cov.
- Diffuse dark mask.
- Densely patterned undertail-cov, resembles American Herring Gull 1w.
- Narrow pale fringes and tips along both webs of visible prim-tips; at distance only tip seems pale ⇔ in Kumlien's 1w broader, complete pale fringe around prim-tip.
- Often already ad-like leg colour, deeper pink than in other large gulls 1w.

2w
- Cov and tertials and often large part of scaps uniform grey-brown; cov and tertials with only faint patterning at tip (resembles Glaucous-winged Gull 2w but these more uniform).
- Underparts largely dark, grey-brown spotted.
- Rather dark outer prim with pale tip and fringe.

3w-4w
- Variable but mainly ad-like with some signs of immaturity. Combine points under all plum and ad with relevant 3w-4w points under 'Ageing of large gulls'.

fl ad
- Prim-pattern very variable. Most commonly occurring pattern: outer 6 prim with dark subterminal patterning (often except p10; p5 with narrow subterminal band) and dark patterning on (mainly) outer web; long pale tongue on 5 outer prim.
- Most ind with black running up outer edge of p9 (not broken by mirror) ⇔ Kumlien's.

fl juv-1w ⇒
- Pale inner webs *of all prim* creating fan of pale bars on spread wing (in less spread wing large pale window on inner hand) ⇔ in (American) Herring 1w completely dark outer prim.
- ⇒ Round dark spots on prim-tips, especially on inner ⇔ in dark Kumlien's subterminal band on (inner) prim-tip.
- Underwing pale brown with narrow dark sharply demarcated trailing edge of hand.
- Rather dark sec-bar, broken by pale inner webs (also in 2w) ⇔ in many Kumlien's less contrastingly dark and in (American) Herring 1w still darker and more uniform.
- Tail, uppertail-cov and rump rather dark, resembles pattern of American Herring 1w but outer 3 tail-feathers barred at base and tail-band less black, making upperside as a whole less contrasting. In some dark Kumlien's 1w also dark tail-band but with fine pale patterning.

fl 2w
- Uniform grey-brown plumage with dark tail and hand; dark tail contrasts with white uppertail-cov and rump.

fl 3w
- Hand still looks 'young' but mirror on at least p10 ⇔ 2w.
- Still extensive dark tail-band.
- Underwing-cov still with relatively large amount of patterning.

Iceland Gull *Larus glaucoides* L 56cm 22"

all plum ⇒
- Long prim-projection, rather short bill; wing-projection longer than bill ⇔ Glaucous Gull.
- Rounded head.
- Common Gull-like structure ⇔ Glaucous.

(sub)ad
- Legs deep pink.

ad w
- Rather heavy head-, neck- and breast-streaking but usually less so than in Glaucous ad w.

juv-1w
- Bill-pattern very variable, usually rather dark with paler base, in some ind completely dark bill. Sometimes however similar to Glaucous 1w but rarely with sharply demarcated dark tip.
- Plumage often rather cold cream grey-brown ⇔ Glaucous juv-1w.

1s
- Like bleached 1w; bill with obvious dark tip ⇔ leucistic/albino Herring Gull with different structure, e.g. longer bill and shorter wing-projection.

2w
- More patchily patterned (sometimes with rather dark markings) than in 1w. Sometimes dark wash on prim (like Kumlien's Gull imm).
- Pale iris.

2w-3w
- Usually *greenish wash* on bill ⇔ Glaucous all plum.

3w-4w
- Variable but mainly ad-like with some signs of immaturity. Combine points under all plum and ad with relevant 3w-4w points under 'Ageing of large gulls'.

note
- See also references in Kumlien's and Thayer's Gull.

---

geog var Kumlien's Gull *L.g. kumlieni* (north-eastern Canada) L 57cm 22.5"

all plum
- Structure and size nearly as Iceland Gull but prim-projection generally slightly shorter, head often slightly more square and especially bill slightly heavier.

ad ⇒
- Variable area of grey to black on visible prim-tips, grey usually extending far on to distal part of outer prim.
- Large white tips to outer prim.
- Sometimes rather dark iris (as in Thayer's Gull).
- Legs deep pink.
- Pale upperside as in Iceland (Kodak greyscale 3.0-4.0).

ad w
- Rather sparse head streaking.

juv-1w
- Diffuse dark centres and especially outer-webs of visible prim-tips; in pale ind only dark wash on both sides of shaft, in darker ind completely dark with pale fringe around tip ⇔ in strongly marked Iceland 1w sometimes rather well-defined patterning on projected prim-tips with occasionally some diffuse patterning when fresh.
- Tertial-pattern variable from almost uniform dark centre with weak, often diffuse notching along fringe and tip to irregularly barred. Most ind with rather dark base and dark wavy pattern on brown-grey ground-colour ⇔ in Iceland normally rather strong barring on white background.
- Distal part of tail diffusely streaked, creating dark subterminal band.
- Bill often all dark ⇔ most Iceland.
- Often slightly colder brown-grey overall than Iceland.

1w-2w ⇒
- Outer 4-5 prim darker than rest of wing with pale fringes ⇔ Iceland.

2w
- Brown-grey prim and tail; Mantle and scaps normally ad-grey.
- Often still much black on bill-tip ⇔ most Iceland.

3w
- Upperparts ad-grey but still some brownish cov.

141

	• Grey-brown wash on outer prim.
	• Dark subterminal bill-band.
fl ad	• Grey patterning on outer web of p8, p9 and p10; subterminal grey spot on p6, p7-p9; tip of p10 all white; small number of ind with dark marking on p5.
fl 1w	• Outer prim as dark as or slightly darker than prim-cov.
	• Uniform tail-band.
	• Sec often darker than in Iceland.
	• Often well-defined dark tips to prim-cov ⇔ in Thayer's juv-1w more diffuse or less contrasting due to overall darker prim cov.
fl 2w	• Broad, dark terminal tail-band contrasts with white uppertail-cov.
fl 3w	• Tail like 2w but paler.
note	• See also Thayer's.

Glaucous Gull *Larus hyperboreus*   L 65cm 25.5"

all plum ⇒	• Wing-projection shorter than bill length ⇔ in Iceland Gull longer. Relatively short prim-projection.
	• Legs pink.
	• Large angular head with somewhat flattened forehead.
ad w	• Very bold head-streaking up to neck and upper breast. Often winter plumage retained until March.
juv-1w ⇒	• Bright pink-orange bill with sharply demarcated black tip.
	• Plumage warm cream-brown (see Iceland 1w).
1s	• Like bleached 1w ⇔ leucistic/albino Herring Gull generally smaller, with usually longer wing-projection and slightly shorter bill.
2w	• Untidy plumage with irregular pattern of dark markings on white background (sometimes mainly white).
	• Pale iris.
	• Dark subterminal bill-band, often not sharply demarcated.
3w-4w	• Similar to ad w but dark markings extending far down to breast and patchy upperside. Combine points at all plum and ad w with relevant 3w-4w points at 'Ageing of large gulls'.
subad	• Similar to ad w but dark markings extending far down to breast and patchy upperside.
fl all plum	• Relatively short (especially hand) broad and somewhat rounded wings.
	• Obvious pale hand, on underwing translucent, in 1w contrasts with darker underwing-cov (also in Iceland).
	• Heavy head and breast often conspicuous ⇔ Iceland.
note	• Hybrid Glaucous x (American) Herring Gull ('Nelson's Gull') occurs regularly; these ind are intermediate but often more similar to Glaucous (ind more similar to (American) Herring are probably overlooked). In 1w bill-pattern often like Glaucous and diffuse grey-brown outer prim.

Slaty-backed Gull *Larus schistisagus*   L 63cm 25"

all plum	• Often conspicuously thick and heavy bill (especially in ♂).
	• Legs orange-pink, in (sub) ad conspicuously 'bubble-gum' pink.
	• Prim-projection relatively short and wing-tips reach only a little beyond tail-tip as in Great Black-backed ⇔ Lesser Black-backed.
	• Tips of sec often visible under greater cov (as in Glaucous-winged and Cape Gulls) ⇔ other large gulls.
	• Eye placed high and relatively far back on head-side, as in Glaucous-winged.
ad	• Upperside slightly variable dark grey-blue, 'blue' cast often conspicuous. Kodak greyscale around 12, extremes 10-14, similar to Lesser Black-backed *graellsii*.
	• Very pale, almost white iris.
	• Much white on tertial- and sec-tips, also conspicuous when sitting.
ad w	• Variable amount of head- and breast streaking, often concentrated around eye and creating vague mask.
1w	• Generally rather uniform grey-brown, resembling extremely dark Glaucous-winged 1w. Some ind from mid-winter onwards already pale due to bleaching of juv feathers.
	• More or less uniform dark bases to otherwise virtually unpatterned greater cov.
	• Tertials dark with only paler tips.
	• Underparts rather uniform, diffusely patterned dark grey-brown.
	• 2nd generation scaps and mantle feathers greyish with dark shaft-streaks or triangular marks.
2w	• Often still rather young appearance; wings only finely mottled brown-grey, at distance appearing uniform. Some ind with more adult-type blue-grey.
	• Mantle and scaps variable from uniform ad-type grey-blue to pale brown-grey with dark shaft-streaks (no anchor-pattern).
	• Pale iris from this age onwards, but in many ind still dark.
3w	• Often still some dark streaks on belly.
	• Bill pale pink-yellow.
3w-4w	• Variable but mainly ad-like with some signs of immaturity. Combine points under all plum and ad with relevant 3w-4w points under 'Ageing of large gulls'.
fl all plum	• Dark tips to outer prim creating darkest area on underwing and often contrasting with relatively pale rest of underwing.
fl (sub)ad ⇒	• White subterminal marking on p(5)6-p8, creating conspicuous 'string of pearls'. Only 'black-backed gull' with subterminal white in all outer prim.
	• Very broad white trailing edge of arm and inner hand.
	• Underwing relatively pale for 'black-backed gull' with contrasting black tips to outer prim.
	• 2 mirrors (p9, p10); on p9 small, sometimes lacking, then 'string of pearls' broken up.
fl 1w	• Dark tail, pale patterning only at base of outer tail-feathers.
	• Rump and uppertail-cov diffusely and densely patterned; in combination with dark tail can resemble Thayer's Gull 1w.
	• Dark underwing-cov contrast with pale underside of sec and prim and with dark tips to outer prim.
fl 2w	• Pale brown-grey upperwing, tail still largely still dark, contrasting with almost white uppertail-cov.
	• Underwing pale, contrasting with dark tips to outer prim.

Great Black-backed Gull *Larus marinus*   L 70cm 27.5"

all plum	• Long, deep bill with large gonys-angle.
	• Legs relatively long, flesh-coloured to pink.
	• Relatively short wing-projection ≤ half prim-projection.
	• Dark eye; in (sub) ad slightly paler but not as pale as in Lesser Black-backed Gull.
ad	• Large white tips to outer prim ⇔ Lesser Black-backed.
	• Upperside very dark grey, Kodak greyscale 13.5-15.5; slight contrast between black wing-tip and rest of wing.
ad w	• Completely white head ⇔ Lesser Black-backed ad w.
1w	• Tertials with pale patterning in dark centre.
	• Flanks more strongly and sharply patterned than rest of underparts ⇔ Herring *argentatus* 1w.
	• Greater cov and median cov with much white and narrow dark barring (dark bars narrower than pale bars).
	• Pale head with variable but no heavy patterning.
	• Black bill (from 2cy with paler base).
2w	• Usually mainly like 1w but pattern on tertials and cov finer; pale bill-basc.
3w	• Still looks relatively young with brownish cov and relatively large areas of dark patterning in tail compared to other 3w large gulls.
4w	• Variable but mainly ad-like with some signs of immaturity. Combine points under all plum and ad with relevant 4w points under 'Ageing of large gulls'.
fl ad	• 2 large mirrors, mirror on p10 forming complete large white tip; mirror on p9 sometimes merges into white tip. Sometimes 3rd small mirror on p8.
fl 1w	• Usually multiple narrow and one broad(er) dark terminal tail-band (some Herring *argentatus* 1w with almost identical pattern).
	• Relatively pale upperwing.
	• Distinct pale window on inner prim.

Kelp Gull *Larus dominicanus*   L 63cm 25"

geog var	**Cape Gull** *L.d. vetula* (southern Africa)
all plum	• Size about as Herring Gull (♂ slightly larger) but structure more like Great Black-backed Gull with very heavy bill (with large sagging gonys-angle), *short prim-projection (only 4 prim-tips beyond tertials) and short wing-projection.*
	• Tip of sec often visible under greater cov (in most large gulls completely concealed by greater cov except in Glaucous-winged Gull and Slaty-backed Gull).
	• Often rather flattened forehead.
	• Legs thick compared to Lesser Black-backed Gull.
ad	• Colour of upperside similar to dark Lesser Black-backed *intermedius* and Great Black-backed.
	• Dark iris (in South American form *dominicanus* often pale).
	• Legs dull yellow-grey to green-grey.
	• Large white tips to tertials and rear-most scaps (large white tips to sec Lesser Black-backed).
	• Relatively large white tips to outer prim.
ad w	• Usually uniform white head, sometimes sparse fine head streaking.
1w	• Plumage largely similar to Lesser Black-backed 1w but underparts sometimes darker.
	• Legs rather dark brownish.
imm	• All plumages from 1s to ad reminiscent of Lesser Black-backed of equivalent age.
fl ad	• Broad white fringe along arm and inner hand.
	• White markings between grey tongue and black subterminal marking on p5-p7 (white tip on tongue) ⇔ in Lesser Black-backed none.
	• 1(-2) mirrors (mirror on p10 often merge into white tip).
fl 1w	• Nearly completely black tail (sometimes sparse pale patterning at base).
	• Uppertail-cov white with dark patterning.
	• Inner prim dark with only slightly paler inner webs (similar to Lesser Black-backed 1w).
note moult	• Species of Southern Hemisphere: imm moult prim from December-March; ad from February-June. In ind remaining in WP, moult-timing approaches that of Northern Hemisphere gulls (e.g. ind from Mauritania finish prim moult in December/January).

Terns and skimmers

Black Noddy *Anous minutus*   L 33cm 13"

all plum ⇒	• Very slender, long bill with faint gonys-angle in middle ⇔ Brown Noddy.
ad	• Completely black (strongly worn 1s brownish on cov) except white forehead and crown, rather well-defined with dark grey rear-head.
	• Forehead and crown white ⇔ Brown.
juv	• Like ad with white forehead and crown ⇔ Brown juv.
	• Mantle feathers and scaps with narrow, well-defined pale tips ⇔ Brown.
	• Cov and tertials with very narrow pale fringes, in some cases absent.
fl all plum	• Black under- and upperwing, lacking contrast.
	• Tail dark grey.
	• Strongly rounded, spatula-shaped tail (as in Brown) ⇔ all *Sterna* and *Chlidonias* terns.
note	• Not recorded in WP.

Brown Noddy *Anous stolidus*   L 41cm 16"

all plum ⇒	• Rather heavy and long bill (nearly as long as head-length ⇔ in Black Noddy longer) with gonys-angle on distal half.
ad	• Pale forehead, gradually merging into grey-brown rear-head, only white just before bill-base.

juv		• Nearly entirely dark brown (strongly worn 1s pale brownish on cov). • Crooked border between white forehead and black lores ⇔ in Black straight. • Narrow dark band over bill-base ⇔ in Black white forehead to bill-base. • Rather dark, white speckled forehead. • Mantle feathers and scaps with broad, diffuse pale tips. • Cov and tertials narrow with well-defined pale fringes.
fl all plum		• Strong rounded, spatula-shaped tail (as in Black) ⇔ all *Sterna* and *Chlidonias* terns.
fl ad		• Some contrast between cov and dark rest of upperwing. • Pale underwing-cov.

Aleutian Tern *Onychoprion aleutica*   L 30cm 12"

ad s		• Black cap with sharply demarcated white forehead and black eye/loral-stripe connected to black bill (head-pattern resembles Bridled Tern and Sooty Tern). • No contrast between grey underparts and upperparts.
ad		• Legs and bill completely black.
juv	⇒	• Large dark centres to mantle feathers, scaps, tertials and inner greater cov with deep rufous fringes. • Diffuse rufous breast-sides creating almost complete breast-band. • Uniform, warm ochre-coloured neck-side. • Common Tern juv-like head-pattern.
fl all plum	⇒	• Pattern of underside of hand: dark grey trailing edge of arm and broad trailing edge along outer 5 prim; paler inner sec creating pale window, no dark trailing edge.
fl ad		• White rump and tail contrast strongly with grey mantle (in ad w less contrast due to greyer rump and tail). • Dark grey upperwing with dark prim-wedge (outer 5 prim) and paler window on inner prim.
fl juv-1w		• Dark mantle and leading edge of arm contrast with paler grey trailing edge of arm, hand, rump and tail.

Sooty Tern *Onychoprion fuscata*   L 43cm 17"

all plum		• Slightly larger than Bridled Tern, about as Sandwich Tern.
ad s	⇒	• Black cap with large white triangular patch on forehead extending to above eye (patch larger than in Bridled, see there). • Completely deep black upperparts ⇔ Bridled. • Black loral-stripe narrow and connected to bill low at base of upper mandible. • Tail (dark with pale outer-side) slightly shorter than in Bridled (tail sometimes projects only slightly or not at all beyond wing-tips).
ad w		• Like ad s but pale spotted hind-neck (at distance may appear to have pale collar as in Bridled but upperparts completely deep black).
imm		• Very dark brown upperside with small white spots on feathers of upperparts, tertials, cov and uppertail-cov, forming white stripes on wings. • Completely dark head, throat, breast and upper belly, ill-defined by whiter under belly, vent and undertail-cov. • Imm plumage retained for 3-5 years, in subad at least still dark breast.
fl all plum		• Dark underside of tail and flight-feathers ⇔ Bridled. • Long wings. • Powerful, sometimes resembling skua.
fl ad		• White underwing-cov and underparts.
fl juv		• Grey underwing-cov with often diffuse pale band on middle of underwing.

Bridled Tern *Onychoprion anaethetus*   L 40cm 15.5

ad s	⇒	• Black cap separated by *pale grey hind-neck*; mantle darker grey, sometimes with brownish wash ⇔ Sooty Tern.
	⇒	• White patch on forehead extending to behind eye, *forming supercilium* ⇔ Sooty. • Broad loral-stripe reaches bill over whole base of upper mandible ⇔ Sooty. • Tail often projects beyond wing-tips ⇔ Sooty. • In *melanoptera* (see geog var) much white in tail ⇔ Sooty.
ad w		• Like ad s but cap dull dark brown and more white on forehead.
juv		• Cap and loral pattern like ad but more faint grey-brown (usually conspicuous broad dark loral-stripe). • Rather pale mantle feathers and scaps with narrow subterminal dark bands and white tips. • Cov and tertials with white tips, which together with mantle feathers create rather scaled upperside but white quickly worn away. Sometimes pale scales very weakly developed.
fl all plum	⇒	• Pale base of prim on underwing, creating diffuse dark trailing edge of hand ⇔ in Sooty prim completely dark.
fl ad s		• Blackish upperwing contrasts slightly with somewhat paler rump and tail. Upperwing contrasts strongly with pale grey hind-neck. • White underwing with broad, diffuse black trailing edge.

geog var	*O.a. melanoptera* (Atlantic Ocean) [compared with *O.a. antarctica* (Red Sea and Persian Gulf, south to Madagascar)]
all plum	• When perched mainly white tail (t6 completely white; t5 and t4 white with grey tip; t1-t4 grey with white base; dark parts in tail usually not visible) ⇔ in *antarctica* mainly grey tail with only white basal half of t6.
ad s	• Slightly broader pale hind-neck than *antarctica*.
fl ad	• More white on underside of prim and more white in outer side of tail than *antarctica*.

Little Tern *Sternula albifrons*   L 23cm 9"

all plum ⇒	• Much smaller than other terns, except Saunders's Tern, Least Tern and *Chlidonias* terns.
	• Relatively large head and bill.
ad s	• Well-defined white forehead in dark cap; lores black.
	• Yellow bill with black tip.
	• Very dark narrow prim-wedge formed by outer 2 (3) old prim (very rarely one, see Least).
ad w	• White forehead larger than in ad s and ill-defined; lores pale.
	• Black bill.
	• Narrow dark leading edge of arm.
juv	• Mantle feathers, scaps and tertials with large dark 'V'-shaped markings on greyish ground-colour (about as on Sandwich Tern and Roseate Tern juv).
	• Legs pale, yellowish.
1w/1s	• After juv-type upperparts and cov moulted similar to ad w but dark leading edge of arm broader.
2s	• Like ad s but broader dark prim-wedge with 3 old prim and fainter head-pattern due to white-flecked crown.
	• Often greyish wash on rump and uppertail-cov but always distinctly paler than rest of upperparts ⇔ Saunders's and Least.
fl all plum	• Narrow wings and tail. Flight fast and surprisingly powerful.
fl ad s	• Rather broad but faint trailing edge on underside of hand.
	• Very dark outer 2 (3) prim creating *conspicuous dark outer side of hand*.
	• Rather distinct contrast between grey mantle and white rump and tail (central tail-feathers sometimes greyish) ⇔ Saunders's and Least.
fl juv-1w	• Dark outer side of hand contrasts with white sec (later in autumn sec becoming slightly greyish). Wings show some resemblance to Arctic Tern juv but outer side of hand darker and lacks dark tip to outer prim.
	• Narrow dark leading edge of wing (as in ad w).

Least Tern *Sternula antillarum*   L 22cm 8.5"

all plum	• Slightly smaller and with slightly shorter legs than Little Tern.
ad	• Often grey wash on breast-sides, sometimes on whole underparts.
ad s	• White patch on forehead usually smaller than in Little, rarely extending behind eye.
juv-1w	• Like Little but dark markings on mantle feathers more 'U'-shaped than 'V'-shaped.
	• Upperparts with yellow-brown wash.
	• Broader dark mark on wing-bend than in Little.
fl ad ⇒	• Grey rump and tail (but at least outer web of t6 white) concolorous with mantle ⇔ Little.
	• Very narrow dark prim-wedge, formed by 1-2 (sometimes 3) old prim ⇔ in Little ad s rarely one old prim in Northern Hemisphere.
	• Pattern of underside of hand like Little.

Saunders's Tern *Sternula saundersi*   L 23cm 9"

ad	• Underparts with faint grey wash.
	• Outer tail-feathers not strongly elongated as in some Little and Least Tern.
ad s ⇒	• White patch on forehead smaller than in Little, more rectangular and not extending to above eye (eye within black cap, not within loral-stripe as in Little).
	• Loral-stripe broader than in Little.
	• Blackish prim-wedge formed by 3-5 outer old prim (also shaft often black ⇔ Little).
	• Slightly paler grey upperparts than Little; upperparts contrast strongly with more black outer prim.
	• Legs short and olive-coloured ⇔ in Little more orange-yellow.
	• Bill orange-yellow with diffuse dark tip ⇔ in Little ad s more yellow with sharply demarcated black tip.
ad w	• Upperparts darker (from August) than in ad s and Little ad.
fl ad ⇒	• No colour difference between grey mantle, rump and tail (but t6 white), as in Least.
	• Pattern of underside of hand as in Little.
fl 1w	• Like Little 1w but sec creating more obvious dark band later in year.

Gull-billed Tern *Gelochelidon nilotica*   L 38cm 15"

all plum ⇒	• Heavy black bill with usually distinct gonys-angle (in juv often grey-brown base).
	• Legs black and long with clearly visible tibia ⇔ Sandwich Tern. Sometimes resembles gull.
	• Rounded crown.
ad s ⇒	• Black cap with *straight border* from bill to rear-side of ear-coverts.
	• When moulting to winter plumage, crown becomes evenly paler over whole length ⇔ in Sandwich only forehead white spotted at first.
ad w	• White head (also crown) with dark mask through eye and over ear-coverts (sometimes about that of Forster's Tern ad w/imm but less uniform).
juv-1w ⇒	• Only faintly darker tertials and patterning on upperwing (flight); head with faint dark mask ⇔ all congeners.
	• Upperparts almost uniform.
	• Pale grey-brown base to lower mandible.
1s	• Like ad w but part of sec and outer prim dark and heavily worn.
2s	• Like ad s but outer prim darker, creating dark prim-wedge.
fl all plum	• Pattern of underside of hand: conspicuous dark trailing edge (not reaching inner 2-3 prim) becoming broader towards outside; rather ill-defined due to indentations of paler outer webs. *Dark trailing edge of hand also often distinct on upperwing* ⇔ Sandwich.
	• Calm, steady (not very tern-like) flight with almost slowed-down wing-beats.
	• Normally flies with closed tail ⇔ Sandwich.
fl ad ⇒	• Upperside uniform grey; almost no colour difference between upperwing, rump, uppertail-cov and tail.
	• Dark prim-wedge at end of summer faint (in 2s stronger) ⇔ Sandwich.
fl juv-1w	• Faint pale brown patterned upper arm, darker sec-bar and terminal tail-band.

145

Caspian Tern *Hydroprogne caspia*   L 52cm 20.5"

all plum ⇒	• Very heavy (orange-)red bill with subterminal dark spot.
ad	• Early moult towards summer plumage (in February).
ad w	• Black cap with small white speckles, more extensive on forehead; forehead looks grey at distance.
juv	• Cap nearly as in ad w but black patterning on yellow-brown ground-colour ⇔ in ad white background.
	• (As in most terns juv) very variable patterning on upperparts but usually more faintly marked than in other terns juv, sometimes almost unpatterned.
1w	• Like ad w but tail still juv (dark tail-feathers with pale tips).
1s	• Winter head and usually distinct border between dark worn juv-type feathers and paler ad-type ones (on tail and wings).
2s	• Like ad s but dark prim-wedge and pale spots in dark cap.
imm	• Bill duller red than in ad and without paler tip.
fl all plum ⇒	• Pattern of underside of hand: dark outer 6 prim forming *dark tip of hand*, gradually becoming paler on inner prim.
	• Flight conspicuously stable for tern.
	• Top heavy: heavy head protrudes further than short tail ⇔ Royal Tern.
fl ad	• In summer in Northern Hemisphere no obvious dark prim-wedge (but distinct in 2s which strongly resembles ad in other respects).
fl juv	• Underwing pattern as in ad.
	• Tail becomes gradually darker towards tip.
fl 1s	• Largely dark tail and dark band on sec.
note 1s	• Rare in summer in Europe, normally remains in winter range.

Whiskered Tern *Chlidonias hybrida*   L 26cm 10"

all plum	• Legs relatively long.
	• Relatively strong bill (in ♂ longer than in ♀).
	• Tail-feathers with rounded tips (as in other *Chlidonias* terns ⇔ *Sterna* terns).
ad s	• All prim silvery grey with diffuse dark tips (no prim-wedge); in 1s and 2s dark prim-wedge.
	• Broad white band below cap ⇔ in Arctic Tern less obvious narrow white stripe under cap.
	• Dark grey underparts to belly, sharply demarcated from white vent and undertail-cov.
ad w	• Dark rear-crown and ear-coverts creating broad mask; crown almost entirely finely white spotted; under-side of mask almost straight ⇔ in White-winged Black Tern cap more uniform grey and with distinct dark ear-patch.
	• Pale grey upperside (paler than in s).
juv-1w ⇒	• Mantle feathers, scaps and tertials with large dark centres, brown-yellow bases and pale tips, creating *strong dark spotted upperparts* with brown-yellow wash contrasting with pale grey cov (⇔ in White-winged Black juv more uniform dark upperparts).
	• Cap ill-defined, often extending to above eye and broadly running through neck and with small ear-patch ⇔ in White-winged Black and Black Tern cap more sharply bordered, narrowing on neck and with larger, especially in White-winged Black, more angular ear-patch.
	• Narrow (usually only faint) dark trailing edge of wing with dark marginal cov.
	• Sometimes brown patch on breast-sides (paler and smaller than in Black juv).
	• Often moults early (from August) to 1w, but very variable. In autumn no prim-moult ⇔ ad w in autumn.
1s	• Like ad w but outer flight-feathers darker. Underparts often with some dark spots. Moult progression very variable; some ind develop already almost complete summer plumage but differ from ad s by multiple generations of prim and often some pale spots on underparts and dark spots on cov.
2s	• Like ad s but outer prim darker and underparts with some pale spots (at least in the field probably almost inseparable from advanced 1s).
fl ad s ⇒	• *Upperparts and upperside of tail uniform grey* ⇔ in Common Tern distinct contrast between grey mantle and back and white rump, uppertail-cov and tail.
	• Obvious contrast between dark underparts and pale underwing-cov ⇔ Common.
	• Grey cov contrast slightly with paler flight-feathers.
fl ad w	• Faint dark sec-bar, rest of upperwing very pale silvery-grey.
	• In autumn dark prim-wedge arises which disappears again in 2nd part of winter (outer prim moulted in November/December).
	• Usually very faint patch on breast-sides but sometimes rather distinct.
fl juv-1w	• Grey upperwing with dark band on sec. Lesser cov usually a little darker than rest of cov, usually forming only faint dark leading edge of arm ⇔ in Black and White-winged Black (and also Common imm) more sharply bordered and more contrasting dark leading edge of arm.
	• Rather weakly developed pale tail-sides, in between White-winged Black juv-1w and Black Tern juv-1w.
note 1s	• Rare in summer in WP, normally stays in winter range.

Black Tern *Chlidonias niger*   L 24cm 9.5"

all plum	• Legs dark (sometimes reddish).
	• All tail-feathers with rounded tips (as in other *Chlidonias* terns ⇔ *Sterna* terns).
ad s	• Uniform grey upperside contrasts with blackish head and underparts to belly (vent and undertail-cov white).
ad w/imm ⇒	• Dark patch on breast-sides (in juv most distinct); rest of underparts white.
	• Uniform black crown extends from front side of eye to over whole ear-coverts.
	• White half-ring behind eye.
juv	• Dark grey-brown mantle, becoming slightly paler towards rear; scaps and tertials with large faint brown tips; upperside darker than in ad s.
1s	• Resembles ad w but outer flight-feathers darker and more worn.
	• Upperside rather messy with different generations of cov and obvious dark lesser cov-bar ⇔ in ad w more uniform grey and lesser cov only slightly darker.

	• Underparts often with some dark spots.
	• Prim moult advanced to completed ⇔ in ad about half of prim replaced by end of summer.
2s	• Strongly resembles ad s but broad dark prim-wedge and darker sec.
fl ad s	• Pale underwing contrasts strongly with dark grey underparts ⇔ White-winged Black Tern ad s.
	• Pale grey upperside; slightly paler fore-side of wings, rump and tail.
fl ad w/juv	• Upperparts concolorous with upperwing.
fl juv	• Rather dark grey upperwing, rump and tail.
	• Mantle and scaps slightly darker than upperwing.
note 1s	• Rare in summer in Europe, normally stays in winter range.

American Black Tern *Chlidonias surinamensis* $\qquad$ L 23cm 9.1"

all plum	• Generally slightly smaller than Black Tern but great overlap.
ad s ⇒	• Uniform and deep black head, breast and belly strongly contrasting with white vent, resembles White-winged Black ad s.
	• Black head merging into dark grey mantle ⇔ in Black Tern black head and grey mantle more sharply bordered.
	• Upperwing often slightly paler than in Black (sometimes resembling White-winged Black ad s).
ad s moult	• Underparts with generally evenly scattered white spots from throat to belly (as in White-winged Black, but in some more like Black) ⇔ in Black moult starts on head, followed by underparts starting from breast.
	• Moults later into winter plumage than Black (but rather variable in Black with some ind still in almost complete summer plumage late in autumn).
ad w	• Crown paler than spot on ear-coverts.
	• Weak grey flanks.
	• Upperparts often darker than in Black.
juv-1w ⇒	• Crown with white speckles or uniform pale grey; *crown paler than spot on ear-coverts* (head-pattern more like White-winged Black) ⇔ in Black uniformly black.
	• Normally large dark patch on breast-sides connected with *brown-grey flanks* (see note) ⇔ in Black flanks white.
	• Upperparts darker and more uniform than in Black; rump hardly any paler than upperside of tail (uppertail-cov slightly but more distinctly paler).
1s ⇒	• Crown uniform pale grey; crown paler than patch on ear-coverts (as in juv-1w).
	• Upperparts darker than in Black 1s (as in juv-1w).
	• Prim moult advanced to completed ⇔ in ad and Black ad about half of prim replaced by end of summer.
	• For other field marks see Black 1s.
fl all plum	• Dark lesser cov on pale underwing often creating dark band on leading edge of underwing ⇔ in Black underwing-cov almost uniform pale grey.
fl ad s	• Black underparts strongly contrasting with pale underwing.
	• Often paler cov which contrast with darker upperparts ⇔ in Black very little contrast.
fl ad w/ imm	• Upperwing almost uniformly dark with rather weakly contrasting carpal bar ⇔ in Black cov rather pale contrasting with dark carpal bar.
	• Underwing with darker leading edge ⇔ in Black uniform whitish.
note	• In certain stages of moult Black ad plumage somewhat similar to American Black juv/1w, incl dark flanks. Therefore correct ageing is essential. Ad has at least 2 generations of prim and lacks fine juv-pattern of pale tips and dark subterminal marks on cov and scaps.

White-winged Black Tern *Chlidonias leucopterus* $\qquad$ L 22cm 8.5"

all plum	• Slightly shorter bill than in Black Tern with slightly stronger culmen.
	• Legs reddish (sometimes also in Black).
	• Legs slightly longer than in Black.
	• Smaller webbing between toes than Black.
	• All tail-feathers with rounded tips (as in other *Chlidonias* terns ⇔ *Sterna* terns).
ad	• Rather pale outer edge of hand (characteristic especially in non-ad s).
ad s	• Whitish cov (especially lesser cov and median cov) contrast strongly with underparts and upperparts.
	• Head and underparts to belly entirely deep black ⇔ Black (American Black Tern ad s also with deep black underparts).
	• Mantle and scaps dark grey contrasting with pale cov ⇔ in Black pale grey mantle and scaps (without obvious contrast between mantle, scaps and cov).
ad w/juv ⇒	• Usually much white behind and above eye, often creating supercilium; in ad w black isolated ear-patch ⇔ Black ad w/juv.
⇒	• Unmarked white breast-sides (sometimes very faint brown smudge) ⇔ in Black ad w/juv distinct dark patch on breast-sides.
	• Ear-patch angular ⇔ in Black rounded and broadly connected to dark crown.
	• More white on forehead than in Black (in ad w crown streaked ⇔ in Black more uniformly dark).
	• More white on rear-head than in Black (strongly narrowing black on neck).
	• In ad w upperparts paler than in Black ad w.
juv ⇒	• Diffuse dark brown centres to mantle feathers, scaps and back creating distinct dark 'saddle' ⇔ in Black 'saddle' inconspicuous and broad pale fringes on rear scaps; in Whiskered Tern feathers with marked black centres, creating patchy pattern.
	• Often rather distinct dark wing-bend (flight) ⇔ in Whiskered narrow or almost absent.
1s	• Like ad w but outer flight-feathers darker and worn.
	• Underparts sometimes with some dark spots.
	• Rump grey.
2s	• Resembles ad s but black parts duller, often some pale spots on underwing-cov, broader dark prim-wedge (at least 4 old prim) and dark sec (flight).
fl all plum ⇒	• White rump and uppertail-cov; in juv-1s uppertail-cov grey ⇔ Black.
	• More compact build with broader wings and shorter tail than Black.

fl ad s	⇒	• Completely black underwing-cov contrast with pale underside of flight-feathers. In ad moulting to winter plumage patchy black ⇔ Black all plum.
	⇒	• Almost white fore-side of arm; hand pale grey.
		• Narrow dark prim-wedge, formed by 1-3 outer prim (in 2s at least 4) ⇔ in Black 4-6.
fl ad w		• Pale grey upperside.
		• Regularly retains some dark underwing-cov, when present characteristic compared to Black.
fl ad w/ imm		• Very pale grey tail with *broad white outer sides*.
fl juv		• Dark 'saddle' contrasts strongly with pale upperwing and rump.
note 1s		• Rare in summer in Europe, normally stays in winter range.
		• Some ind possibly with plumage like 2s (see Whiskered 1s and 2s).

Sandwich Tern *Thalasseus sandvicensis*   L 40cm 15.5"

all plum	⇒	• Slender black bill with small yellow tip (in very young ind grey-brown).
		• Legs black, rather short.
		• Rectangular rear-head due to short crest.
		• Fresh (visible) prim-tips with broad white fringes along inner webs and tips (but see account of Cabot's Tern below).
ad	⇒	• Pale grey upperside.
		• Black bill with yellow tip.
ad s		• Short shaggy crest on rear-head.
juv-1w		• In juv mantle feathers and scaps with well-defined black 'V'-shaped marks, from end of summer uniform pale grey.
		• Somewhat wavy pale fringes to mainly dark greater cov and tertials ⇔ large pale-billed terns.
		• Bill of 1cy often not fully grown until late in autumn, shorter and relatively thick bill can then resemble Gull-billed Tern.
1s		• Like ad w but flight-feathers darker and heavily worn.
fl all plum		• Pattern of underside of hand: narrow weak dark trailing edge, formed by small dark tips of outer 5-6 prim.
fl ad		• Pale grey upperside contrasts with white rump and tail.
		• From summer onwards broad dark prim-wedge, in autumn very conspicuous.
fl imm		• Juv tail-feathers with rather sharply demarcated dark tips, forming faint tail-band (in most other larger terns more diffuse tail-band).
		• No dark wing-bend.
note 1s		• Rare in summer in western Europe, does not normally occur further north than Mediterranean.

Cabot's Tern *Thalasseus acuflavida*   L 38cm 15'

all plum		• Very similar overall to Sandwich but slightly smaller size and slightly shorter, deeper-based bill with more obvious gonys-angle.
ad	⇒	• White fringes on inner webs of visible prim-tips narrower, lacking completely on outer prim towards tips (applies only for fresh prim) ⇔ in Sandwich broader and running around tips of outer prim.
		• Yellow bill-tip generally slightly larger.
		• In mid-winter prim-moult not yet completed, outer prim old and very dark ⇔ in Sandwich prim-moult normally completed. In some ind during breeding season still sometimes old (very dark) outer prim.
		• Often rather dark spot on base of tertials and sec (in fright creating dark sec-bar) ⇔ in Sandwich at most vaguely present, but normally not at all.
1w	⇒	• Tertials with large dark centres and large white tips ⇔ in Sandwich complex dark pattern of notches and wavy bars especially on outer (shortest) tertials.
		• Cov largely plain grey, dark markings only on rear greater cov and median cov ⇔ in Sandwich most cov with sharp 'V'-shaped marking.
		• Scaps often with only narrow dark subterminal markings, some ind (almost) without ⇔ in Sandwich well-defined 'V'-shaped marking on scaps.
		• Bill often variable grey-yellowish or deeper orange-yellow ⇔ in Sandwich often completely dark but ind with variable amount of yellow in bill often occur.
		• Juv prim and tail-feathers retained until spring ⇔ in most Sandwich only outer prim and outer tail-feathers retained (obvious moult-limit).
		• Post-juv moult less advanced than in Sandwich; in mid-winter often still largely juv cov and tertials ⇔ Sandwich.
		• 2cy in spring still retains winter head with contrasting white forehead and solid black rear-head.
1w/ad w		• Rear-head uniform black ⇔ in Sandwich with fine spots. Uniform white forehead from nestling onwards ⇔ in Sandwich juv-1w whole crown, including forehead dark.
		• Rear-crown feathers longer than in Sandwich, creating longer crest.
geog var		**Cayenne Tern** *T.a. eurygnatha* (Central and South America)
ad		• Dull yellow to dull orange bill; Central American populations with more grey-yellow bill and dark base. Sometimes almost completely dark bill as in Sandwich or Cabot's but yellow tip diffusely demarcated.
		• Prim-pattern between Sandwich and *acuflavida* with broad white fringes on inner prim and progressively thinner fringes on outer prim.
		• Ind with completely pale bill often retain dark nasal grove (sometimes visible in other 'orange-billed terns' too).
		• Crest longer than in *acuflavida*.
		• Upperparts slightly darker than in *acuflavida*.
note		• Ind from South American populations have longest crest, longest bill with strongest tendency to orange colour and largest size sometimes strongly resemble Elegant Tern, but bill probably never completely bright orange-red.
		• Not recorded with certainty in WP.

Elegant Tern *Thalasseus elegans*   L 43cm 17"

all plum	• Bill usually long (≥ head-length), although bill-length varies notably between sexes as in most other terns; in Elegant, ♂ up to 20% longer billed than ♀. Bill tapers towards tip, culmen evenly bend towards tip. Lower mandible slightly bent downwards from weak gonys-angle onwards (gonys-angle in middle or before), creates impression of drooping bill-tip ⇔ in Lesser Crested Tern bill generally shorter, lower mandible usually straight (almost without gonys-angle) and culmen less gradual, bending more strongly towards tip. • Reddish-orange bill, tip paler. In juv and some ad (mostly ♀ and ad w) more orange ⇔ in Lesser Crested almost uniform yellow-orange (judgement of colour best in neutral light; in glaring sunlight Lesser Crested can appear to have paler tip).
ad ⇒	• Usually long, often *drooping* crest to hind-neck. • Upperside slightly paler than in Lesser Crested, similar to Sandwich Tern. • Often pink wash on underparts, especially in spring but sometimes also at other times ⇔ other 'orange-billed terns'. • Dark centred sec (in flight creating dark sec-bar).
ad s	• Rather narrow white loral line ⇔ in Lesser Crested ad s often broader.
ad w/imm ⇒	• Black mask/rear crown without obvious white half-ring (as on Lesser Crested) or spot (as on Royal Tern) behind eye.
juv-1w	• Relatively ill-defined patterned upperside.
fl ad	• Pattern of underside of hand: broad, short, rather sharply demarcated trailing edge, formed by dark tips of outer 5-6 prim only ⇔ in Lesser Crested narrower and longer trailing edge along hand. • White rump and tail contrast (slightly) with pale grey mantle ⇔ most Lesser Crested.
fl juv-1w	• Similar to Royal flight juv but patterning on upperwing fainter. • In 1w-1s small white tips to t4-t5 ⇔ Lesser Crested 1w-1s.
note	• See also Cayenne Tern.

Royal Tern *Thalasseus maxima*   L 45cm 17.5"

all plum	• Large size sometimes resembles Caspian Tern but in direct comparison distinctly smaller (size as Common Gull). • Bill-tip often slightly paler than rest of bill and somewhat translucent. • Often holds bill slightly upwards. • Legs relatively long compared to Lesser Crested Tern.
ad	• Heavy bill with deep base (see geog var), structure between Caspian and Lesser Crested. • Very pale grey upperside; rump paler than mantle and back, looks white at distance. • Legs black, sometimes with orange spots.
ad s	• Closed cap lost very early (in breeding season).
ad w ⇒	• Least black on head of all larger terns; dark mask with black spot before eye and white area directly behind eye; eye in mask visible at distance, also in Lesser Crested but often less distinct ⇔ Elegant Tern.
imm	• About half of juv with orange legs, rest orange spotted or completely black. With increasing age amount of ind with black legs increases to almost 100% (see also ad).
fl all plum	• Head and tail protrude almost equal distance, therefore tail seems longer than in Caspian.
fl ad	• White tail and rump contrast slightly with pale grey mantle. • Pattern of underside of hand: outer 5-7 prim with dark tips creating ill-defined rather broad trailing edge, slightly broadening towards outer side. • In autumn obvious dark prim-wedge.
fl juv-1w	• Pied patterned upperwing with 3 dark bars over arm: sec-bar, greater cov-bar and wing-bend (lesser cov) separated by very pale grey. In 1w greater cov-bar becomes paler.
fl 2s	• Summer head like in ad s but dark prim-wedge and band on sec (also often rather distinct in ad s, so ageing after moult in 2cy probably impossible).
geog var	*T.m. maxima* (North and Central America)
ad	• Heavy uniform orange to red bill with rather obvious curved culmen and gonys-angle.
geog var	*T.m. albididorsalis* (western Africa)
ad	• Bill slightly paler orange (*more yellow towards tip*), lacking red and less heavy than in *maxima* with flatter culmen and less obvious gonys-angle. Bill-structure more similar to Lesser Crested, colour identical to Lesser Crested ⇔ *maxima*. • Upperparts slightly paler than in *maxima*, paler than in Sandwich Tern. • Tail slightly longer than in *maxima*.

Great Crested Tern *Thalasseus bergii*   L 46cm 18"

all plum ad s ⇒	• Heavy, (cold) grey-yellow bill with deep base, in ad s slightly more orange-yellow. • Black cap ends just before upper mandible; *lores completely white*. • Rather large shaggy crest on rear-head.
ad w	• Rather faint bordered dark ear-coverts and rear-crown due to numerous white speckles. • Small pale spot behind eye.
juv-1w	• Strongly and darkly patterned, when moulting towards 1w pied patterned with dark grey and dark brown. • Cap better developed than in other yellow-billed terns juv-1w.
fl all plum	• Conspicuous long wings usually held strongly angled. • Waving foraging flight can resemble Montagu's Harrier. • Inner prim with conspicuous pale tips.
fl ad	• Pattern of underside of hand: usually rather faint bordered, broad dark trailing edge, formed by dark tips of outer 6-7 prim.

fl ad s	⇒	• Upperwing (from February) with 'paradoxical' contrast between pale prim and slightly darker rest of upperwing; from end of summer less contrast due to wear.
fl juv-1w		• Dark upperwing with pale arm panel and 2 pale wing-bars along median cov and greater cov.
fl 1s		• Variable but normally more messy on upperside than ad w and strongly contrasting dark outer prim and inner sec.
fl 2s		• Like ad s but often some remnants of imm plumage like dark tip to some tail-feathers or some dark sec.
geog var		*T.b. velox* (Red Sea, Persian Gulf and northern part of Indian Ocean)
ad	⇒	• Dark grey upperside similar to Lesser Black-backed Gull *graellsii*.
		• Faint contrast between dark mantle, paler rump and slightly darker tail.
geog var		*T.b. thalassina* (eastern Africa)
ad		• Much paler on upperside than *velox*, similar to Lesser Crested Tern.

Lesser Crested Tern *Thalasseus bengalensis* L 36cm 14"

all plum	⇒	• Rather heavy bill (with especially relatively deep base), very weak gonys-angle lays in or behind middle; bill uniform yellow-orange (yellow in winter, sometimes almost red in spring). See Elegant Tern for more details on bill structure.
		• Size and structure as Sandwich Tern but bill-base slightly deeper.
ad		• Upperparts paler than in Great Crested Tern *velox* but darker than in Sandwich, Royal Tern and Elegant. The subspecies occurring in Europe (*emigrata*, breeds in Mediterranean off Libya) is slightly paler on upperside than *bengalensis* (Red Sea) and *torresii* (Persian Gulf) and only slightly darker than Sandwich.
ad s		• Shaggy crest, ending somewhat rectangularly on rear-head.
		• Outer prim relatively pale, at beginning of summer often almost as pale as upperparts (becoming darker later in year).
ad w/imm	⇒	• Rear-crown and crest uniform black, *lacking white speckling* ⇔ Royal.
		• Pale spot behind eye (usually smaller than in Royal) ⇔ in Elegant ad w/imm usually no obvious pale spot behind eye.
fl all plum		• Bill usually held almost horizontally ⇔ Sandwich more often holds bill downwards.
fl ad	⇒	• Grey rump and tail, usually *almost without contrast with upperparts* (but sometimes rump paler than upperparts).
		• Pattern of underside of hand: rather narrow, well-defined trailing edge, formed by rather small black tips of outer 6-7 prim.
		• Somewhat two-toned upperwing (pale inner prim and prim-cov contrast slightly with cov).
fl juv-1w		• Like Royal juv but prim darker and less strongly patterned on upperwing.
fl 2w		• Sometimes slightly darker patterning on tail-feathers and sec.
note		• See also Elegant.

Forster's Tern *Sterna forsteri* L 34cm 13.5"

all plum		• Rather strong bill with deep base and weak gonys-angle.
		• Rounded crown sometimes conspicuous.
		• Legs relatively long.
ad		• Pale grey upperside recalls Roseate Tern and Sandwich Tern.
ad s	⇒	• White underparts ⇔ Common Tern ad s.
	⇒	• Tail projects beyond wing-tips ⇔ Common.
		• Bill bright pale orange-red with large black tip.
		• Rather broad white loral line under cap due to wavy border with cap ⇔ in Common and Arctic Tern narrow straight line.
ad w/imm	⇒	• Somewhat oval uniform black mask, rather sharply demarcated from white or grey (rear-)head/hindneck. Gull-billed Tern ad w/imm may approach this pattern but mask (almost) never uniform and well-defined.
		• Wing-bend slightly or not at all darker ⇔ many other terns ad w/imm.
1w		• Like ad w with dark tertial-centres and dark (visible) prim-tips.
1s		• Like 1w but moult of cov and inner prim (outer prim darker). Crown often with dark spotting and bill-base red.
		• Base of tertials darker.
2w		• Like ad w but in most ind outer prim old and dark ⇔ in ad prim-moult complete from October.
2s		• Similar to ad s but dark outer prim and active moult of inner prim.
		• Often white flecking on fore-crown and some retained cov with brownish centres (lesser cov and median cov).
fl all plum		• From 1w onwards contrast between grey mantle, white part of rump and uppertail-cov and grey tail.
		• Dark *inner-side* of elongated outer tail-feathers (in 1w only dark tip) ⇔ in Common dark outer-side.
		• Pattern of under-side of hand: broad trailing edge, formed by large dark tips of outer 6-7 prim (somewhat reminiscent of pattern of Common and Gull-billed but broader).
		• Underwing nowhere distinctly translucent ⇔ Common and Arctic.
fl ad s	⇒	• Upperwing uniform silver-grey; (as in Arctic) no dark prim-wedge (see 2w).
fl 1w		• Pale centres to prim (only tip darker) ⇔ in Sandwich 1w outer prim evenly rather dark.
fl 2w		• Rather obvious dark prim-wedge in late autumn indicative of this age.

Common Tern *Sterna hirundo* L 36cm 14"

all plum	• Obvious pale half eye-ring below eye ⇔ weak or absent in Arctic Tern all plum.
	• Tail-tip reaches at most to wing-tips.
ad s	• Orange-red bill with black tip (sometimes lacks black tip, especially at end of summer).

ad w	• From September bill black (with very small pale tip).
	• Forehead white, rest of cap retained.
	• Dark wing-bend due to dark lesser cov.
	• Underparts white.
juv ⇒	• Broad black wing-bend, also obvious when perched.
	• Pale reddish bill-base ⇔ Arctic juv.
	• Mantle feathers, scaps and tertials with large black, slightly angular markings, often also on cov.
	• Pale brown wash over upperparts, later (August-September) grey mantle with white scales.
imm	• Features of 1s and 2s mentioned below are indicative at most; it is not possible to age most ind with certainty in the field.
1s	• Dark wing-bend, sec and outer prim.
	• Rump greyish.
	• Cap usually at most slightly developed as in ad w.
	• Unknown proportion of ind already close to ad s but outer prim darker, often largely dark bill and white speckled forehead (so strongly resembling 2s). These ind sometimes called 'portlandica-type' although this term also applies for other tern species in (well-advanced) 1s plumage. See also 2s.
2s	• Under field conditions often not possible to age with certainty but 2(often active) moult centres in prim (in ad s one moult centre and not active in midsummer), cap not complete (paler forehead) and mix of white and grey feathers on underparts. Some ind more closely resemble 1s than ad s.
fl all plum	• Pattern of underside of hand: broad, somewhat ill-defined dark trailing edge, formed by dark tips of outer 5-7 prim.
fl ad s	• From mid-summer onwards obvious dark prim-wedge.
fl imm	• Dark wing-bend prominent (but also in some ad w).
note 1s	• Scarce in summer in Europe, most ind remain in winter range.
geog var	*S.h. longipennis* (Asia)
ad	• Upperside and underparts darker than in *hirundo*, about as in Arctic.
	• Usually outer tail-feathers project slightly beyond wing-tips ⇔ in *hirundo* they do not.
	• Bill generally slightly shorter than in *hirundo*. In summer completely black, or slightly red at base (amount of red on bill gradually decreases towards east of range).
	• Legs dark chestnut (at distance legs and bill look black).

Arctic Tern *Sterna paradisaea*   L 36cm 14"

all plum	• Legs very short (sometimes looks almost leg-less) ⇔ Common Tern.
	• No obvious pale half eye-ring below eye ⇔ Common.
	• More compact, shorter body than Common with often fuller breast.
	• Relatively short bill.
ad	• Tail projects beyond wing-tips (outer tail-feathers can be shorter for various reasons).
ad s ⇒	• One generation prim, *no dark prim-wedge* (see moult).
⇒	• Underparts rather dark (nearly concolorous with upperparts). Grey of underparts extending to ear-coverts. Rather narrow white line just under cap (conspicuous in mixed group of perched terns).
	• Dark red bill, normally without black tip, sometimes becoming darker towards tip.
	• Legs blood-red.
	• Black cap 'pinched in' on hind-neck, extending less far towards mantle than in Common.
ad w	• Dark cap with ill-defined white forehead.
	• Underparts white.
	• Bill black.
juv-1w	• Rather weak darker leading edge of arm, usually much less distinct than in Common juv-1w.
	• Usually completely black bill (sometimes orange base of lower mandible) ⇔ Common juv-1w.
	• Cap deeper black and extends slightly further down than in Common juv-1w (white on underside of eye-lid weak or absent ⇔ Common).
	• White on inner webs of projected prim extends far into feather-tip, often visible when perched like sharply demarcated white hook ⇔ in Common white on inner webs not normally visible when perched due to larger dark feather-tips and white more weakly bordered.
	• Small dark markings on upperside on cold grey-brown ground-colour.
1s	• Like ad w; all prim fresh ⇔ Common 1s.
2s	• Resembles ad s but forehead often white, dark leading edge of arm and underparts dark spotted (not uniform grey as in ad s).
fl all plum ⇒	• Pattern of underside of hand: long, narrow, well-defined dark trailing edge formed by small dark tips of outer 6-8 prim.
	• Uniform snowy-white underwing.
	• Sometimes conspicuously translucent flight-feathers (in Common only inner prim).
	• Flight-style usually different from Common: upwards stroke quick, downwards beat slow resulting in more soaring flight.
	• Longer tail and slightly shorter wings than Common creating more Swallow-like jizz.
fl juv-1w ⇒	• Completely white sec ⇔ all similar terns imm.
⇒	• Pale prim with ad-like well-defined dark trailing edge on upperside of hand ⇔ in Common imm uniform dark grey upperside of hand.
	• Narrow dark wing-bend (lesser cov); rest of cov silvery grey.
	• White rump and uppertail-cov ⇔ in Common juv-1w grey rump.
	• Long tail.
fl 1s	• All prim 2nd generation (no dark prim-wedge).
moult ⇒	• Moults all prim quickly in winter (no separated moult waves ⇔ many other terns), *never obvious dark prim-wedge*.
note 1s	• Scarce in summer in Europe, normally stays in winter range.

White-cheeked Tern *Sterna repressa*   L 33cm 13"

all plum	⇒	• Long, evenly slender bill (usually with slightly drooped tip).
	⇒	• Grey rump.
ad		• Long tail streamers extend beyond wing-tips.
ad s		• Upperparts uniform grey; underparts nearly concolorous with upperparts.
		• Dull red bill with dark tip or wholly dark upper mandible. Dark bill-tip usually larger than in Common but similar to some Common from eastern populations (see Common *longipennis*), which also have darker underparts.
		• Rather broad white stripe over ear-coverts.
		• Tail-projection slightly beyond wing-tips (as in eastern populations of Common).
ad w		• Cap slightly more extensive towards forehead than in Common ad w, in some ind completely dark forehead.
juv		• Dark upperside (dark patterned centres to mantle feathers, scaps, tertials and cov) contrasts with slightly paler visible prim-tips ⇔ Common.
		• Very dark wing-bend (as in Common imm) up to 1s (in ad w also faint dark wing-bend).
		• Yellow-brown wash over upperparts as in Common juv.
fl all plum	⇒	• Pale central band (pale greater cov and median cov) on underwing, grey lesser cov and almost complete dark trailing edge of wing.
		• Grey tail and rump contrast slightly with paler mantle and upperwing.
		• Pattern of underside of hand: broad, ill-defined but complete trailing edge formed by dark flight-feathers.
fl ad s		• Silver-grey upperwing with (from spring to beginning of summer) pale inner and silver-grey outer prim.
fl juv-1w		• Hand silver-grey (upperside of hand paler than arm ⇔ Common).
		• Dark greyish tail.
fl 1s-2s		• Old, very dark outer prim creating dark prim-wedge.
		• In 2s ad s-like cap but white line before bill-base.
		• In 2w/2s underparts dark spotted, sometimes also in 1s.

Roseate Tern *Sterna dougallii*   L 34cm 13.5"

all plum		• Well-defined white fringes to inner webs and tips of (visible) prim, as in Sandwich Tern nominate.
		• Long bill (in juv shorter).
ad	⇒	• Black bill; in ad red base in (late) summer, often 'S'-shaped bordered by dark distal part, normally most black on lower mandible ⇔ in Common normally most black on upper mandible.
		• Very pale upperparts and completely white underparts.
ad s	⇒	• Very long outer tail-feathers reaching far beyond wing-tips (outer tail-feathers replaced at end of summer and temporarily absent or shorter).
		• Underparts white, often with pink wash.
		• Legs bright pale orange-red.
ad w		• Very long outer tail-feathers (growing from September onwards).
		• Faint dark wing-bend.
juv		• Completely dark cap, also on forehead (in 1w pale forehead) ⇔ Common and Arctic Tern juv.
		• Black 'V'-shaped patterning on mantle feathers, tertials and outer greater cov on very pale grey to pale buff ground-colour, resembling Sandwich Tern.
		• Cap on under-side (on ear-coverts) wavy, creating small dark pointed 'ear' ⇔ in Sandwich juv straight.
		• Completely dark bill.
		• Early moult into 1w, then uniform pale grey upperside.
1s		• Like ad w but broad dark prim-wedge (outer prim dark and worn); outer tail-feathers normally almost as long as in ad.
fl all plum	⇒	• Short wings and distinctly *faster* and stiffer wing-beats than Common and Arctic, resembling Little Tern.
		• Underwing almost uniform white.
fl ad	⇒	• Pattern of underside of hand: (almost) no dark trailing edge.
		• Gradually darker prim-wedge formed by 2 to (at most) 5 (usually 3) prim already conspicuous from spring on, also often visible when perched (Little-like).
		• Very pale mantle without contrast with rump and tail ⇔ Common and Arctic.
		• Whole rear-side of underwing translucent against pale background.
		• Completely white tail (also outer tail-feathers ⇔ Common and Arctic).
		• Very long outer tail-feathers (when present) very flexible, usually moving up and down with wing-beats.
fl juv-1w		• Hand becoming slightly darker towards outside, rest of upperwing very pale.
		• Very pale underwing, but dark inner webs of outer prim creating dark bar-pattern on underside of wing-tips.
		• Usually obvious dark wing-bend but not uniformly dark as in Common.
		• Very pale tail.
		• Sec pale, slightly paler than in Common juv-1w but not as white as on Arctic.
behav		• Dives from relatively high altitude directly in water, like Sandwich ⇔ Common and Arctic. Remains longer in water after dive than Common and Arctic.
note 1s		• Very rare in summer in Europe, normally stays in winter range.

African Skimmer *Rynchops flavirostris*   L 41cm 16"

all plum		• Heavy orange-red bill (with yellowish tip); lower mandible distinctly longer than upper mandible.
		• Long wings resulting in long wing-projection.
ad		• White forehead, ear-coverts, neck and underparts.
		• Deep black crown, hind-neck and upperparts.
juv		• Bill dark with yellow base.
		• Pattern as in ad but black parts dark grey.

- Legs yellow ⇔ in ad reddish.

fl all plum • Narrow white trailing edge along sec and inner prim.

note • Black Skimmer *Rynchops niger* (not recorded in WP) resembles African but with heavier bill with *black tip* and *broad white trailing edge* of arm, narrowing on inner prim.

Auks

Common Guillemot *Uria aalge* L 42cm 16.5"

all plum ⇒ • Diffusely streaked flanks (in arctic *hyperborea* strongest).

ad s • 'Bridled' type (with white eye-ring and white line behind eye) rare in south, becoming more common towards north.

ad • Often moults from October onwards into summer plumage; complete summer plumage from November ⇔ 1w.

w • White head-side and dark eye-stripe (white extending to behind eye) as in Razorbill w.

1w • Moults later than ad into summer plumage (1s); winter plumage in February or later strong indication of 1w.
- In 2cy more brownish prim than ad.
- In late summer, young with shorter bill than ad(w) and darker head-side, in combination resembling Brünnich's Guillemot ad(w).

fl all plum • Dark axillaries and often also axillary-stripe connected with dark band on middle of underwing; underwing, together with streaked flanks, looks dirty at distance ⇔ in Razorbill underwing and flanks uniform white.
- Short tail; legs project beyond tail (legs often slightly held up) ⇔ in Razorbill legs indistinct.
- Rather little white on sides of rump ⇔ Razorbill and Brünnich's.

geog var *U.a albionis* (western Europe)

all plum • Dark brown upperparts; in *hyperborea* (arctic Norway, Spitsbergen) and *aalge* (northern Europe) very dark brown to black upperparts.

Brünnich's Guillemot *Uria lomvia* L 42cm 16.5"

all plum • White stripe above cutting-edge of basal part of upper mandible, in summer slightly more distinct than in winter (Common Guillemot or Razorbill with small fish in bill also sometimes appear to have this and sometimes in Common real very narrow line present).
- Slightly shorter and thicker bill than Common; culmen rather strongly curved towards bill-tip (but see 1w) ⇔ in Common culmen more slightly curved and smoother over whole bill length.
- Distance between tip of feathering of upper mandible and gape > distance between tip of feathering of upper mandible and bill-tip ⇔ in Common the other way around.
- Legs yellow-grey, paler than in Common.
- Unmarked white flanks, as in Razorbill (but in summer plumage sometimes some dark streaks on rear-flank) ⇔ Common (but in some Common *aalge* very weakly developed).
- Slight gonys-angle present ⇔ in Common none.
- Upperparts blacker than in Common (especially southern *albionis*), nearly as Razorbill but head and neck with brown gloss (latter only visible under very good viewing conditions).
- Often pale bill-tip.
- Often somewhat 'Great Northern Diver-like bump' on forehead.

ad s ⇒ • White of underparts running in sharp tip into black of upper-breast ⇔ in Common more rounded border between white underparts and black parts on breast.

w • Even in complete winter plumage entirely dark ear-coverts and rear-side of head-side, *creating dark cap without pale area behind eye* ⇔ Razorbill and Common ad w/1w. Moulting Razorbill and Common ad in autumn can also show complete dark cap at certain stage between winter and summer plumage.
- Broad dark neck-side to (almost) complete dark throat-stripe (often also present in Common when moulting from winter to summer plumage) ⇔ Razorbill.

w • Like ad w but bill still short.

all plum • Slightly more stocky build with more bulging body than Common (especially due to shorter, thick hind-neck).
- Weak dark axillaries and often mid-panel on underwing, at distance looks white (in between Razorbill and Common). In fact axillary-feathers with only dark centres.
- Short tail; legs project beyond tail (like Commmon) ⇔ Razorbill.
- Rather much white on side of rump, as in Razorbill ⇔ Common.

moult • Moults notably later than Razorbill and Common, into both winter plumage as summer plumage (see Common).

Razorbill *Alca torda* L 40cm 15.5"

all plum • Rather short deep bill.
- Unpatterned white flanks.
- Pure black upperparts.
- Long, pointed tail.

ad • White vertical stripe over bill.
- White head-side and dark eye-stripe (white extending to behind eye) as in Common Guillemot w.

w • Bill smaller than in ad (without white vertical stripe), culmen strongly curved ⇔ Brünnich's Guillemot.

all plum ⇒ • Entirely white underwing-cov and axillaries ⇔ Common Guillemot.
- Tail longer than in Brünnich's Guillemot and Common Guillemot.
- Rather much white on sides of vent, as on Brünnich's Guillemot ⇔ Common Guillemot.
- No projection of legs beyond tail ⇔ Atlantic Guillemot and Brünnich's Guillemot.
- Head often held slightly up or moving up and down (Like Red-throated Diver).

ad w/1w • Dark crown extends further down than in Common Guillemot ad w/1w (but less far than in Brünnich's Guillemot ad w/1w).

Black Guillemot *Cepphus grylle* L 35cm 14

ad	• Legs bright red.
	• Uniform white wing panel.
ad s	• Sooty black with large white oval on arm (and white underwing-cov).
ad w	• White rump, uppertail-cov, underparts and majority of head (but darker patterning on crown and neck-side present).
	• Barred mantle feathers and scaps.
fl all plum	• White underwing-cov conspicuous.
	• Belly conspicuously bulging ('beer belly' profile).
	• Head often help up.
	• Even ind in continuous flight often give the impression of looking to land at every moment.
fl ad	• Uniform white patch on arm.
fl ad w	• White rump and uppertail-cov contrast with black tail.
(fl) 1w	• White patch on arm with some dark patterning ⇔ ad w.
	• Rump and/or uppertail-cov usually slightly patterned ⇔ in ad w nearly white.
(fl) 1s	• Like ad s but white patch on arm as in 1w (in Icelandic *islandicus* ad s usually some dark patterning o white patch on arm).
geog var	*C.g. mandtii* (whole arctic of northern Canada to north-eastern Siberia)
w	• Upperparts and scaps with much more white than in more southern subspecies like *arctica* and *grylle*.
	• Small dark loral-spot.

Long-billed Murrelet *Brachyramphus perdix* L 25cm 10

all plum ⇒	• Rather long slender bill.
	• Narrow white eye-ring.
ad s	• Completely dark black-brown, pale scaled; throat paler.
w	• Dark grey upperparts, white underparts (1w with dark mottling on underparts).
	• Pale scaps creating pale stripe on upperside (as in Marbled Murrelet *B. marmoratus*, not recorded in WP).
	• Dark upperside of head with almost straight border with white ear-coverts and neck/breast-side ⇔ in Marbled pale lores and beginning of pale collar and dark breast-side.
	• Often some pale patterning on dark hind-neck but not creating distinct white collar as in Marbled.
1w	• Dark scaling on white underparts ⇔ in ad w unmarked white.
fl all plum	• Often some pale patterning on black underwing-cov ⇔ in Marbled all dark.

Ancient Murrelet *Synthliboramphus antiquus* L 25cm 1C

all plum ⇒	• Upperparts and flanks grey; rest of underparts white.
	• Pale pinkish bill.
	• Mainly dark head; rear-side of ear-coverts pale.
	• Steep forehead and flattened crown.
	• Size about as Puffin.
ad s ⇒	• Black throat and broad patchy pale stripe behind eye.
ad w	• Throat white; no pale stripe behind eye.
fl all plum	• Pale underwing-cov separated from white underparts by dark flanks.

Little Auk *Alle alle* L 20cm 8

all plum ⇒	• Very small size.
	• Short stumpy bill.
	• White fringes to scaps creating small pale stripes on upperside.
ad s	• Black head and breast.
ad w/1w	• Pale fore-side of neck, throat and rear-side of ear-coverts.
fl all plum ⇒	• Blackish underwing (with difficult to see pale stripe in middle).
	• Pale trailing edge of arm ⇔ Puffin.
	• Very fast wing-beats, sometimes resembling sandpiper.
	• When flying far out at sea quite often changes direction; closer to coast usually flies more in a straight line

Crested Auklet *Aethia cristatella* L 26cm 1

all plum	• Completely dull black upperparts and dark grey underparts.
	• Thick short bill.
ad ⇒	• Long strongly curled-forward crest on forehead.
	• Narrow long pale stripe from eye to hind-neck.
ad s	• Red bill with yellow tip (in ad w smaller, more yellow bill).
juv	• Bill smaller and dark, later on more yellowish; no pale stripe on head and short crest.
fl all plum	• Legs project distinctly beyond tail.

Parakeet Auklet *Aethia psittacula* L 25cm 1

ad	• Grey-black upperparts and head; pale underparts but breast and flanks dark spotted ⇔ in Crested Auklet underparts dark.
	• Narrow, long pale stripe from rear of eye to hind-neck (in Crested smaller and shorter).
	• Strange-shaped thick, orange-red bill.

Atlantic Puffin *Fratercula arctica* L 31cm 1

all plum ⇒	• Narrow but sharply demarcated dark breast-band (often still visible in flight at some distance).
	• Legs orange-red.

ad s	• Nearly white head-side.
	• Large bright coloured, triangular bill.
ad w	• Dark grey head-side with blackish face.
	• Bill smaller (narrower at base) and duller coloured than in ad s.
1w	• Like ad w but bill smaller.
fl all plum	• No white trailing edge of arm ⇔ Razorbill, Little Auk, Brünnich's Guillemot and Common Guillemot.
	• Rather dark underwing; appears uniformly dark at distance, when closer paler areas on middle of arm and prim-cov visible.
	• Broad dark axillary line connected with dark rear-flanks.
	• Dumpy silhouette.
fl ad w/1w⇒	• *Large dark head* and narrow black breast-band characteristic.

Tufted Puffin *Fratercula cirrhata*   L 38cm 15"

all plum	• Completely dark; in ad s deep black with white face and long yellow crest on rear-head.
ad s	• Huge, mainly red bill.
ad w	• Completely brown-black with smaller bill than in ad s.
juv	• Relatively small yellowish bill.
	• Plumage dull brown-black with slightly paler underparts.

Sandgrouse

Lichtenstein's Sandgrouse *Pterocles lichtensteinii*   L 24cm 9.5"

all plum	• Large eye with pale ring, thicker on front side.
	• Short tail.
ad ♂ ⇒	• Two black breast-stripes with *uniform orange areas in between*.
	• Two vertical head-stripes; one above eye and one on forehead.
	• Completely finely barred.
ad ♀	• Completely very finely barred, especially on upperparts.
fl all plum ⇒	• Rather dark, *little contrast* on underwing.
	• Upperwing with black hand and pale arm.

Crowned Sandgrouse *Pterocles coronatus*   L 27cm 10.5"

all plum	• Yellow-orange throat patch running over ear-coverts (as in Spotted Sandgrouse).
	• Short tail like Lichtenstein's Sandgrouse.
ad ♂ ⇒	• Vertical black stripe before bill-base.
	• Brown-grey cov and scaps with pale tips.
	• Underparts uniformly sandy-coloured.
ad ♀	• Finely spotted underparts.
fl all plum	• Contrasting under- and upperwing: pale underwing-cov (except black greater cov and prim-cov) contrast with black flight-feathers; completely black upperside of sec, prim and prim-cov.
	• Short tail.

Spotted Sandgrouse *Pterocles senegallus*   L 31cm 12"

all plum	• Yellow-orange throat patch running over ear-coverts, more obviously bordered than in Crowned Sandgrouse.
	• Narrow dark longitudinal stripe from belly to undertail-cov.
	• In general, palest, most sandy-coloured sandgrouse in WP.
ad ♂	• Grey-blue head, neck and breast (except yellow-orange throat patch).
	• Cov and tertials with grey bases, creating wing-bars.
ad ♀	• Dark speckled crown, cov, upperparts and breast on sandy ground-colour.
fl all plum ⇒	• Upperwing (*also hand* ⇔ other sandgrouse) mainly sandy-coloured with dark trailing edge.
	• Pale underwing-cov; black sec and slightly paler prim with darker tips (no dark leading edge on underwing ⇔ Pin-tailed Sandgrouse).

Chestnut-bellied Sandgrouse *Pterocles exustus*   L 31cm 12"

all plum	• Large blackish to red-brown belly patch as in Black-bellied Sandgrouse.
	• Narrow, black stripe on breast.
ad ♂	• Diffusely marked, yellow-brown head.
	• Narrow, well-defined black tips to scaps and cov.
ad ♀	• Similar to Black-bellied ♀ but belly patch dull black-brown, not deep black. No black throat-stripe and central tail-feathers elongated.
fl all plum ⇒	• Completely blackish underwing.
	• Completely black hand and yellow-orange patterned arm with black trailing edge.
	• Elongated central tail-feathers.

Black-bellied Sandgrouse *Pterocles orientalis*   L 33cm 13"

all plum ⇒	• Large black belly patch (belly and vent completely black).
	• Narrow black breast-stripe.
	• Largest sandgrouse.
ad ♂	• Black throat-stripe below orange throat patch; rest of head and breast blue-grey.
	• Feathers of upperparts and cov with large orange tips; upperside completely orange spotted.
ad ♀	• Horizontal black throat-stripe.
	• Speckled and streaked crown, breast and upperside.
	• Orange lower edge of closed wing (orange tips to greater cov).

| fl all plum ⇒ | • Strong contrast between white underwing-cov and axillaries and black sec, prim and belly.
• Completely black hand and yellow-orange marked arm with black trailing edge.
• Looks thickset, also caused by short tail. |

Pin-tailed Sandgrouse *Pterocles alchata*   L 30cm 12"

all plum ⇒	• Black eye-stripe. • White belly, vent and undertail-cov. • Strongly elongated central tail-feathers.
ad ♂	• 2 narrow breast-stripes. • Black throat patch.
ad ♀	• 3 narrow breast-stripes. • Multiple rows of narrow whitish wing-bars.
fl all plum ⇒ ⇒	• White underwing-cov contrast with *black leading and trailing edge of underwing*. • Dark breast contrasts with white underparts. • Rather dark (grey) upperside of hand.
geog var	*P.a caudacutus* (North Africa and Middle East)
all plum	• Paler than *alchata* (Iberian Peninsula) with paler brown breast(-band).
ad ♂	• Pale line on cov white instead of yellow.
ad	• Outer greater cov and median cov white to yellow-brown, instead of rufous-brown in *alchata*.

Pallas's Sandgrouse *Syrrhaptes paradoxus*   L 30cm 12"

ad ⇒	• Black belly patch (smaller than in Black-bellied Sandgrouse).
ad ♂	• Orange head with diffuse grey rear-crown, ear-coverts, neck and breast. • Little marked cov (only black spot on bases of greater cov and median cov). • Barred upperparts. • Diffuse breast-stripe (consisting of numerous small streaks).
ad ♀	• Streaked crown, ear-coverts and neck-side ⇔ ad ♂. • Cov completely patterned ⇔ ad ♂. • Horizontal black throat-stripe.
fl ad ⇒	• Elongated outer prim and central tail-feathers. • Underwing almost completely pale with narrow black trailing edge along sec and inner prim. • Pale upperwing with pale brown arm and grey hand.

Pigeons

Rock Dove *Columba livia*   L 33cm 13"

ad	• 2 black wing bars. • Pale grey mantle contrasts with dark blue-grey hind-neck.
fl all plum	• Small white rump-patch. • Narrow dark terminal tail-band. • Pale underwing with sharply demarcated dark trailing edge.
note	• Within populations of Feral Pigeon's ind occur which are (almost) identical to wild Rock. Identification of wild Rock outside normal range and/or habitat therefore almost impossible.
note geog var	• In Middle East multiple subspecies with grey rump and back (no contrasting white rump-patch) and paler grey upperparts.

Stock Dove *Columba oenas*   L 30cm 12"

all plum ⇒	• Black spot at base of inner greater cov and tertials. • Dark eye. • Mantle concolorous with head ⇔ in e.g. Rock Dove mantle paler.
ad	• Greenish neck-side patch. • ♂ with often pure blue-grey upperparts; ♀ slightly more brown-grey, but only in extremes useful.
juv	• No greenish neck-side patch (all juv pigeons lack neck-side patch). • Dark bill.
1s	• Like ad but many ind still with some retained juv tail-feathers, sec and cov, these shorter (tail-feathers narrower), browner and more worn than ad-type feathers. Post-juv prim-moult highly variable and sometimes not completed by spring.
fl all plum	• Dark blue-grey upperwing (base of sec and inner prim blue-grey) with broad, black rear- and leading edge of hand. • Dark grey underwing with black trailing edge.

Yellow-eyed Stock Dove *Columba eversmanni*   L 27cm 10.5"

ad ⇒	• Yellow-orange iris and broad yellow eye-ring. • Greenish neck-side patch.
juv	• No greenish neck-side patch (all juv pigeons lack neck-side patch).
1s	• See Stock Dove but in some ind juv prim retained up to July.
fl all plum	• Pale rump-patch. • Uppertail-cov darker than mantle ⇔ in Stock uppertail-cov paler than mantle.

Woodpigeon *Columba palumbus*   L 40cm 15.5"

| ad ⇒ | • White neck-side patch. |
| juv | • Uniform head without pattern on neck-side (all juv pigeons lack neck-side patch). |

Pigeons

1s
- Dark bill and iris.
- See Stock Dove but even more variable.
- Prim moult from one centre ⇔ in ad from 2.

fl all plum ⇒
- Broad white band on centre of upperwing creating border between black hand and grey arm; broad black band at tip of tail bordered by narrow pale band in centre of tail.
- Rather uniform dark grey underwing.

Trocaz Pigeon *Columba trocaz* — L 43cm 17"

ad
- Like large dark Woodpigeon with somewhat diffuse pale grey neck-side patch (no well-defined white neck-side patch as in Woodpigeon).

fl ad
- Pale central band on upperwing indistinct and diffuse ⇔ Woodpigeon.
- Pale central band on tail (on both upper and underside) broad and conspicuous, more distinct than pale band on upperwing ⇔ in Woodpigeon the other way round.

note
- Only occurs on Madeira.

Bolle's Pigeon *Columba bollii* — L 38cm 15"

ad
- Resembles Trocaz Pigeon but smaller and greenish instead of pale grey neck-side patch.
- Breast pink-purple.
- Orange iris; red orbital-ring.

fl ad ⇒
- Dark tail base ⇔ Trocaz.
- Pale central band on upperwing narrow and diffuse (as in Trocaz) ⇔ Woodpigeon.
- Pale central band on tail (on both upperside and underside) more distinct than central band on upperwing ⇔ in Woodpigeon central band on upperwing more distinct than pale central band on tail.

note
- Bolle's (Canary Islands) and Trocaz (Madeira) geographically separated.

Laurel Pigeon *Columba junoniae* — L 42cm 16.5"

ad
- Very dark uniform wings.
- Completely pale tail with *broad white terminal band*.
- Dark purple-orange underparts.
- Green neck-side patch.
- Bill-tip paler than in Bolle's Pigeon.

fl all plum
- Characteristic, slow Eurasian Jay-like flight.

fl ad
- Very dark wings contrast strongly with pale grey-blue tail with broad white terminal band.

African Collared Dove *Streptopelia risoria* — L 29cm 11.5"

all plum ⇒
- Shorter tail than Collared Dove; tail projects beyond wing-tips ≤ prim-projection.
- Vent and undertail-cov pure white; underparts two-toned ⇔ Collared.
- Tail very dark, creating stronger contrast with white tips on t2-t6 than in Collared.
- Upperparts and head slightly warmer purple-brown than in Collared.

ad
- Black collar slightly broader than in Collared ⇔ in juv none.

note
- Introduced morph of African (known as 'Barbary Dove') breeds on Balearic Islands and could occur as escape in rest of WP; is paler on upperparts and head and with usually slightly longer wings and tail.

Collared Dove *Streptopelia decaocto* — L 32cm 12.5"

all plum
- Nearly uniform cream-grey upperparts and slightly paler greyish underparts.

ad
- Single black band around rear half of collar ⇔ in juv none.

uv
- Like ad but black collar weak or absent.

1s
- Some ind retain one or more juv sec which is shorter and more worn than ad-type.

fl all plum
- Dark hand contrasts with rest of plumage.
- Broad white terminal tail-band.

note
- For other field marks see African Collared Dove.

Turtle Dove *Streptopelia turtur* — L 28cm 11"

ad
- Scaps and cov with broad orange fringes.
- Whitish belly, purple breast and grey neck.
- White-surrounded black streaks on neck-side.
- Brownish wash on rump and uppertail-cov.

juv ⇒
- Pattern of cov and tertials much duller than ad with *obvious, black shaft streaks* ⇔ ad.

s
- See Collared Dove.

fl all plum
- Dark underwing-cov contrast with pale belly ⇔ in Collared underwing-cov paler than underparts.
- White outer side of tail; broad at corners, becoming narrower towards centre.

note
- For other field marks see Oriental Turtle Dove.

Oriental Turtle Dove *Streptopelia orientalis* — L 33cm 13"

all plum
- Darker and larger (heavier) than Turtle Dove with more Woodpigeon-like jizz.
- In *orientalis* purple-brown underparts *extending to vent, undertail-cov greyish*; in *meena* underparts brown-orange with coloured part reaching less far and *fading towards cream on vent and undertail-cov* ⇔ in Turtle rather sharp border between purple-pink breast and flanks and *pure white belly, vent and undertail-cov*.
- *Little bare skin surrounding eye, often restricted to in front of eye only* ⇔ in Turtle extensive diamond-shaped bare skin around eye.
- Variable pale fringes and tips to outer median cov and greater cov *creating diffuse wing-bars*.
- From 1w onwards, 5-6 narrow black bars in neck-side patch separated by greyish bars ⇔ in Turtle 3-4

157

broad black bars separated by white bars.
- Grey crown contrasts with brownish hind-neck (more obvious in *orientalis*) ⇔ in Turtle crown and hind-neck usually grey, but some ♀ Turtle have brownish hind-neck.
- Rump dark blue-grey, in *orientalis* also uppertail-cov ⇔ in Turtle only back blue-grey, rump and uppertail-cov brown-grey with buff fringes.
- Pale grey to white terminal tail-band (in *meena* white, see geog var) ⇔ in Turtle white.
- Prim-projection almost equal to projection of tail beyond wing-tips (longest prim about level with longest uppertail-cov) ⇔ in Turtle prim-projection distinctly longer than projection of tail beyond wing-tips (longest prim behind longest uppertail-cov).
- Often relatively short prim-projection with 5-6 prim-tips beyond tertial-tips (p8-p10 of equal length, or p8 a very slightly shorter); projected prim as a whole looks triangular ⇔ in Turtle 6-7 prim-tips project beyond tertials (p9-p10 of equal length, p8 slightly shorter); and projected prim as a whole often looks narrower and more elongated.

geog var	*S.o. meena* (central and western Asia, west to Urals)
all plum	• Paler and smaller than *orientalis* with broader, paler rufous fringes to cov, whitish vent, undertail-cov and terminal tail-band; in many respects intermediate between Turtle and *orientalis*.
juv	• Moults possibly later than *orientalis*; at beginning of winter often still mix of juv- and ad-type cov and tertials (*orientalis* more advanced with hardly any juv cov and tertials).
note geog var	• Above-mentioned (general) features mainly based on *orientalis*, most features less pronounced in *meena*.

Laughing Dove *Streptopelia senegalensis* — L 25cm 10"

all plum	• Short prim-projection. • Long tail.
ad	• Rufous breast-band with sharply demarcated black spots. • Blue-grey outer cov creating broad band along lower edge of closed wing. • Uniform mantle and scaps ⇔ Turtle.
fl all plum ⇒	• Large white tail-corner on outer tail-feathers extending almost to base (t6 80% white); black base of outer tail-feathers, forming no complete dark band ⇔ turtle doves. • Dark underwing-cov ⇔ Collared Dove. • Blue-grey (cov) panel on upperwing.

Namaqua Dove *Oena capensis* — L 23cm 9" (incl ta

all plum ⇒	• Very small size with *very long wedge-shaped tail*. • 3 horizontal bars on back; black-white-black (in ♂ more obvious than in ad ♀ and juv).
ad ♂	• Black face and breast.
ad ♀	• Uniform upperside; no black parts on head.
juv	• Large pale tips to scaps and cov.
fl all plum	• Rufous upperside of hand and rufous underwing. • Black axillaries.

Mourning Dove *Zenaida macroura* — L 30cm 12

all plum	• Small size; very long, pointed tail with white tips to outer tail-feathers. • Large black spot on tertials and inner cov. • Small dark spot on ear-coverts. • Grey-brown upperside with weak grey wash on hind-neck and crown. • Deep pink legs. • Blue-grey eye-ring. • Grey brown head and upperparts.
1w	• In autumn moult-limit in prim and sometimes in cov ⇔ ad. • Dark spot on ear-coverts sometimes weak or absent ⇔ ad.

Mousebirds

Blue-naped Mousebird *Colius macrourus* — L 32cm 12.5" (incl ta

ad	• Mainly cream-brown with extremely long tail (especially central tail-feathers). • Full crest on rear-head. • Pale blue spot on rear-head (below crest). • Red orbital ring, lores and frontal shield.

Parakeets

Ring-necked Parakeet *Psittacula krameri* — L 41cm 1

all plum ⇒	• Bright grass-green. • Rather small red bill
ad	• Very long, pointed tail. • Almost completely green with darker flight-feathers and green-blue central tail-feathers.
ad ♂	• Narrow black collar, tinged pinkish at rear (collar acquired in 3rd cy) ⇔ in ad ♀/imm no collar.
note	• Introduced and locally common in some towns and cities.

Monk Parakeet *Myiopsitta monachus* — L 28cm 1

ad	• Pale grey forehead, throat and breast; rest of underparts dull yellow-green. • Bright green upperparts and rear of head.

- Dark blue flight-feathers.
- Introduced.

Cuckoos

Jacobin Cuckoo *Clamator jacobinus*   L 31cm 12"

all plum
- Structure like Great Spotted Cuckoo but smaller size.
- Completely dark upperparts, crown and tail (tail-feathers with white tips).
- White spot on prim-base.
- Pale underparts with fine dark streaks on throat and breast.

all plum
- Underwing-cov pale as on Great Spotted.

Great Spotted Cuckoo *Clamator glandarius*   L 37cm 14.5"

all plum ⇒
- White tips to cov, tertials and scaps creating strong pattern.
- Long, strongly rounded tail.
- Somewhat spiky crest.

ad
- Completely pale grey ear-coverts and crown contrast with dark hind-neck.
- Dark grey upperparts.

juv ⇒
- Blackish cap and upperparts ⇔ ad.
- Small white tips to cov, tertials and scaps.
- Rufous prim (with dark tips).

1s
- Dark cap with variable amount of (ad) grey; dull grey crown and dark ear-coverts.
- Black-brown upperside.
- Prim faint rufous-brown when still retained juv feathers (but see note 1s).

ad
- Completely greyish, strongly patterned upperwing.

juv ⇒
- Rufous prim creating conspicuous rufous hand ⇔ ad.
- Marked contrast between upperparts (blackish) and underparts (white).
- Hand more rounded than in ad.

note 1s
- Variable in moult progression depending on hatching date (ind from southern populations months older than ind from northern populations). Early hatched ind more ad-like with e.g. new ad-type prim.

Didric Cuckoo *Chrysococcyx caprius*   L 18cm 7.1"

all plum
- Very small (smaller than Common Starling).
- Broad supercilium broken above eye.
- Red eye-ring.

ad ♂
- Greenish upperparts, hind-neck, ear-coverts and crown.
- Underparts white; flanks strongly barred.
- Pale patterning on outer cov and pale barring on sec.

ad ♀
- Upperparts and head mainly brownish with dull green wash.
- Underparts nearly completely barred.
- Cream-coloured ground-colour of throat and breast.

juv
- Like ad ♀ but upperparts wholly red-brown and finely dark barred.
- Bill red.

all plum
- Strongly barred underwing-cov ⇔ Klaas's Cuckoo (see note).

note
- Klaas's Cuckoo *C. klaas* (not recorded in WP) with same structure as Didric but upperparts uniform bright green (ad ♂) or almost uniform brownish (ad ♀). Very narrow supercilium only behind eye and only finely barred flanks. Underwing-cov unpatterned white.

Common Cuckoo *Cuculus canorus*   L 34cm 13.5"

ad
- Blue-grey upperside, head and breast.
- Finely barred lower breast and belly.

ad ♀
- Breast and head usually not entirely grey (as in ad ♂) but broken by variable amount of patterning on brownish ground-colour.
- In brown morph completely rufous-brown barred upperparts (⇔ juv), cov and flight-feathers.

juv ⇒
- White patch on rear-head ⇔ ad.
- Completely barred underparts and head-side.
- White tips to cov, scaps and tertials ⇔ ad ♀ brown morph.
- Barring on cov and flight-feathers as in ad ♀ brown morph but slightly darker red-brown.
- Dark-brown iris ⇔ in ad (incl brown morph ♀) pale orange-yellow.

1s
- Some ind still with some retained sec, these shorter, with brown patterning and more worn than uniform ad-type feathers.

note
- See Oriental Cuckoo for more field marks.

Oriental Cuckoo *Cuculus optatus*   L 32cm 12.5"

plum
- Slightly smaller overall and with slightly shorter tail and relatively slightly larger head than Common Cuckoo.
- Barring on underparts often slightly deeper black, broader, more sharply defined and with slightly larger spacings than in Common.
- Broad barring on vent and undertail-cov characteristic but very variable, often not different from Common. Barring sometimes completely absent (sometimes also in Common). Common with broad barring on undertail-cov rare.
- Vent and undertail-cov deep yellow-brown, often extending up onto belly and underwing-cov ⇔ in Common weak yellowish belly and underwing-cov on white background (sometimes yellowish colour is absent).

		• Upperside (mantle, scaps and tertials) slightly darker than in Common, therefore contrasting slightly more with pale head and breast.
		• Marginal cov of hand (feathers on outer side of wing-bend, usually concealed under alula) with some broad dark bars especially on distal part ⇔ in Common completely narrow and regularly barred. In some Common streaked only on inner side and uniform white on outer side (normally not visible under field conditions).
ad ♀		• Like in Common, brown morph ♀ occurs; generally more strongly barred with well-defined and regula barring especially on mantle, rump and uppertail-cov ⇔ Common.
juv-1w		• Tail more faintly patterned than in Common with more 'V'-shaped dark barring on paler background.
		• Breast and belly more heavily marked than in Common with broad dark markings; vent and undertail-cov usually almost unpatterned (see note in all plum).
		• Only very narrow pale fringes around tips of prim ⇔ Common juv-1w.
1s		• See Common 1s.
fl ad		• Broad, central white band on underwing, broadening on to hand and extending far into wing-tips ⇔ in Common narrower and narrowing on hand, sometimes extending into wing-tip to p7/p8.
		• Lesser cov and prim-cov on underwing pale and almost unmarked, often creating 2nd pale band on underwing ⇔ in Common lesser cov darker and strongly barred, not distinctly paler than rest of underwing-cov.
		• Ground-colour of underwing-cov often weak yellow-brown ⇔ in Common white.
		• White barring on outer prim broad and ending rectangularly ⇔ in Common often narrowing towards shaft but variable and sometimes not different. Normally only visible in the hand or on very good flight photographs but sometimes also visible when perched with wings hanging down.
voice	⇒	• Song very different from Common: 6-8 quickly repeated 'pu-pu' notes, with all syllables of same length and pitch (timbre reminiscent of song of Eurasian Hoopoe).
note		• Above-mentioned features apply for typical ind. All features very variable and possibly completely overlap with Common.

Black-billed Cuckoo *Coccyzus erythrophthalmus*   L 29cm 11.

all plum	⇒	• Dark bill.
		• Deep dark brown upperparts ⇔ in Yellow-billed Cuckoo slightly paler grey brown.
		• Outer tail-feathers not distinctly darker than rest of tail ⇔ in Yellow-billed outer tail-feathers black.
ad	⇒	• Grey underside of tail with black subterminal patterning and *small white tips to tail-feathers*.
		• Red orbital-ring.
1w	⇒	• Grey underside of tail without black subterminal patterning and *no or very small white tips to tail-feather*
		• Yellowish orbital-ring.
		• Faint cream-coloured undertail-cov ⇔ in Yellow-billed white.
note		• See also Yellow-billed.

Yellow-billed Cuckoo *Coccyzus americanus*   L 31cm 1

all plum	⇒	• Yellow lower mandible and base of upper mandible (not in young juv).
		• Rather obvious red-brown outer webs of many prim ⇔ in Black-billed Cuckoo faint red-brown.
		• Complete white underparts including throat contrast strongly with dark neck-side ⇔ in Black-billed cream-coloured throat.
		• Strong bill ⇔ in Black-billed smaller, more slender.
		• Grey brown upperparts.
		• Yellow orbital-ring.
ad		• Black underside of tail with *large white tips to tail-feathers*.
1w		• Yellow orbital-ring.
		• Dark grey underside of tail with *large, faintly bordered white tips to tail-feathers*.

Senegal Coucal *Centropus senegalensis*   L 38cm

all plum	• Red-brown upperparts (barred in juv).
	• Long, full black tail, strongly rounded.
	• Heavy black bill.
	• Pale underparts.
	• Cap and hind-neck black.
fl all plum	• Very short, broad red-brown wings with white underwing-cov.

Asian Koel *Eudynamys scolopaceus*   L 42cm 16

all plum	• Size about as Western Jackdaw, long broad tail.
	• Thick pale bill; culmen strongly downcurved down.
	• Bright red eye.
	• Legs thick and (brown-)grey.
ad ♂	• Wholly black with strong blue gloss.
1w ♂	• Mix of ad-type black and juv-type brown feathers.
♀	• Very strongly patterned; upperparts brown with white spots, underparts white with dark streaks and spe
	• Strongly barred tail.

Barn owls

Barn Owl *Tyto alba*   L 36cm

ad	⇒	• Almost heart-shaped pale facial disc and black eye.
		• Variable amount of blue-grey feathers on upperparts with fine white speckles.
		• Long wing-projection.

uv-1w
- Legs relatively long.
- All flight-feathers of one generation ⇔ in 2cy+ more generations.
- Barring on 1st generation tail-feathers more obvious than in ad (but see also geog var).

geog var
Pale-breasted Barn Owl e.g. *T.a. alba* (southern and western Europe, including Britain) and *T.a. erlangeri* (Middle East, Arabia). Features below apply at least for *alba*.

all plum
- Underparts completely white or with yellow-brown around breast; *with or without very few black spots* ⇔ *guttata*.
- White leg-feathering.
- Upperside yellow-brown ⇔ in *guttata* normally deeper orange-brown.
- Upperside with ≤ 40% grey (often pale grey).
- Alula with much white on outer-web ⇔ *guttata*.
- Often some dark smudgeing of face restricted to around eyes ⇔ in *guttata* normally more extensive.
- Pale grey prim tips.

ad ♂
- Often completely white underparts and facial disc.

ad ♀
- Often slightly darker than ad ♂ with some dark speckles on underparts; sometimes cream-coloured on breast and darker brown-grey on neck.

all plum
- Underwing very pale with at most faint dark barring on underside of outer prim and underside of tail-feathers (sometimes almost absent); carpal patch (almost) absent ⇔ *guttata*.

geog var
Dark-breasted Barn Owl *T.a. guttata* (mainland of Europe except southern Europe)

all plum
- Upperside with ≥ 60% grey (often dark grey). Crown often entirely grey.
- Underparts vary from mainly white with only brown-orange breast (rare, only in ♂) to completely dark brown-orange (most ♀) and anything in between; variable amount of dark spots always present ⇔ *alba*.
- Buff leg-feathering ⇔ in *alba* white.
- Variable but normally brown-orange upperside and outer webs of flight-feathers ⇔ in *alba* and *erlangeri* upperside and outer webs more brown-yellow.
- Medium to dark grey prim tips.

all plum
- Underwing pale with faint dark carpal patch and slightly darker underwing-cov.
- Dark barring on underside of outer prim and underside of tail-feathers often rather distinct ⇔ *alba*.

geog var
T.a. schmitzi (Madeira)

all plum
- Rather small size with strong tarsus and toes. Lower part of tarsus and toes unfeathered.
- Underparts yellow, paler than in *gracilirostris*. Upperparts bluish-grey.

geog var
T.a gracilirostris (Fuerteventura and Lanzarote; *alba* on western Canary Islands)

all plum
- Small size with relatively long tarsus and toes.
- Underparts yellow (♂) to brown-yellow (♀) like *guttata*, darker than in *schmitzi*. Upperparts bluish-grey.

Cape Verde Barn Owl *Tyto detorta*   L 38cm 15"

ad
- Darker and deeper orange-coloured on underparts than Barn Owl *guttata*.
- Upperparts dark grey with fine pale spots surrounded by black.

Owls

Striated Scops Owl *Otus brucei*   L 21cm 8.5"

ad ⇒
- Underparts with only very slight white bars and head almost lacks white speckling ⇔ Eurasian Scops Owl.
- Short prim-projection c.80% (100% in Eurasian); wing-tips reach at most to tail-tip ⇔ in Eurasian slight wing-projection.
- Cov almost uniform with narrow dark shaft-streaks ⇔ in Eurasian diffuse pale barring on cov.
- Leg feathering extends to base of toes ⇔ in Eurasian toes unfeathered.
- Dark streaked underparts with only very fine barring ⇔ in Eurasian obvious pale barring as dark longitudinal stripes on underparts.
- Rear-neck with little or no white patterning ⇔ in Eurasian pale spotting on rear-neck.
- Tail-barring on upperside usually less clear towards tip ⇔ in Eurasian more regular and evenly barred.
- Yellow-brown stripe along scaps ⇔ in Eurasian white or yellow-brown (depending on colour morph).

juv ⇒
- Underparts barred ⇔ in Eurasian juv streaked underparts.

note
- Mainly greyish plumage, confusion only possible with grey morph of Eurasian.

Eurasian Scops Owl *Otus scops*   L 20cm 6.3"

all plum ⇒
- Underparts and crown finely dark streaked and *densely white spotted and barred* ⇔ in Striated Scops Owl no white patterning.
- Smaller than Little Owl.
- Broad, somewhat stumpy ear-tufts; when ear-tufts down then angular head ⇔ Little.

juv
- Very similar to ad but wing- and tail-feathers worn.

notes
- Occurs in brown, grey and intermediate morph.
- See also Striated.

Snowy Owl *Bubo scandiaca*   L 59cm 23"

all plum ⇒
- Very large size, plumage with white background and yellow iris.
- Smaller than ♀.

ad ♂
- Almost completely white, often some black markings on tertials and scaps (younger ad with more patterning).

ad ♀	• Underparts with fine black barring.
	• Feathers of upperside regularly black patterned with triangular markings.
1w ⇒	• Dark spot on neck-side/breast-sides, remains of juv (mesoptile) plumage (retained to late in 2cy).
	• Patterning of cov, tertials and flight-feathers less black and slightly diffuser than in ad.
	• Tertials with mottling on tips.
	• Unpatterned facial disc contrasts strongly with dark patterned rest of head.
1w ♂	• Resembles ad ♀/imm ♀ but feathers of mantle and scaps finely barred with narrower somewhat 'V'-shaped markings ⇔ in ad ♀/imm ♀ broader, more triangular markings and in ad ♀ blacker marking
	• Crown and side of head moderately marked ⇔ 1w ♀.
imm	• From 2w black markings become gradually smaller and more well-defined (fully ad from 4cy).

Eurasian Eagle Owl *Bubo bubo* L 66cm 26

all plum (sub)ad ⇒	• Very large size.
	• *Underparts warm cream-brown* with heavy longitudinal stripes and fine barring ⇔ other large owls
	• Ear-tufts long, often hanging almost horizontally.
	• Red-orange iris.
1w	• All flight-feathers of one generation ⇔ in 2cy+ more generations.
fl all plum	• Strongly barred flight-feathers, barring consists of narrow dark stripes ⇔ in other large owls broad dark barring.
note	• Great Horned Owl *B. virginianus* (recorded as escape in WP) with dark barring on underparts and more vertical ear-tufts.

Pharaoh Eagle Owl *Bubo ascalaphus* L 59cm 2?

ad ⇒	• Sides of facial disc *dark bordered* ⇔ Eurasian Eagle Owl.
	• Smaller than Eurasian with longer legs and shorter tail.
	• Usually pale sandy-coloured but variable in colour and patterning, some ind almost equally coloured to European subspecies of Eurasian.
	• Ear-tufts shorter than in Eurasian.
	• Yellow-orange iris.
	• Strongly spotted breast; rest of underparts finely barred (some ind almost uniform on underparts exce breast, see *desertorum*).
fl all plum	• Barring on underside of flight-feathers faint or almost absent.
geog var	*B.a. desertorum* (Arabia)
ad	• Like *ascalaphus* but generally paler (pale and dark ind occur in both *ascalaphus* and *desertorum*).
	• Breast streaked (⇔ *ascalaphus*); rest of underparts almost uniform.
note geog var	• *desertorum* inhabits more desert-like areas; validity of this subspecies doubtful.

Brown Fish Owl *Bubo zeylonensis* L 54cm 21.

all plum	• Legs yellow-grey, almost unfeathered ⇔ Eurasian Eagle Owl.
	• Slightly smaller than Eurasian Eagle.
ad ⇒	• Scaps with entirely white outer webs creating conspicuous shoulder stripe.
	• Ear-tufts short and broad, positioned on rear-side of head; head looks square.
	• Head-pattern very faint; face not or only slightly dark bordered.
	• Crown with dense and well-defined streaking.
	• Yellow iris.
	• Underparts finely streaked (just shaft-streaks) and very finely barred (applies for WP subspecies *semenov*
1w	• All flight-feathers of one generation ⇔ in 2cy+ more generations.
fl ad	• Strongly and heavily barred flight-feathers (as in *Strix* species) ⇔ Eurasian Eagle.

Northern Hawk Owl *Surnia ulula* L 39cm 15.

all plum 1w-ad	• Fierce yellow eye.
	• Long tail.
	• Mainly white scaps creating broad pale shoulder-band.
	• Rear-side of face broadly black bordered.
	• Finely barred underparts.
1w	• Narrow rounded tail-feathers ⇔ in ad broader and usually more rounded.
	• Upperparts with brown wash ⇔ ad.
	• All flight-feathers of one generation ⇔ in 2cy+ more generations.
	• Sometimes retained part of juv (mesoptile) plumage on breast, creating diffuse dark breast-band ⇔ a
	• Tertials diffusely patterned ⇔ in ad more obviously well-defined white.
	• Upperside of tail-feathers faintly white barred ⇔ in ad more distinct.
fl 1w-ad	• Sec, prim and underside tail completely and regularly barred.
geog var	*S.u. caparoch* (North America)
1w-ad	• Darker than Eurasian subspecies; feathers of upperside blacker with smaller white spots.
	• Crown dark with small white spots.
	• Dark barring on underparts broader than in Eurasian subspecies.

Eurasian Pygmy Owl *Glaucidium passerinum* L 17cm 6

ad	• Very small size.
	• Short supercilium only above eye ⇔ Little Owl.
	• Relatively long tail; tail projects distinctly beyond wing-tips.
	• Rather square head, sometimes with upturned crown-side creating kind of ear-tufts.

1w	• Relatively small, yellow eye. • Underparts mainly streaked but flanks and upper breast barred. • Often some contrast between dark brown (juv) flight-feathers and dark grey upperparts and scaps, becoming more brown again later in winter ⇔ in ad greyish. • Outer prim relatively narrow and pointed and often obviously worn ⇔ ad. • Tertials except longest almost without paler tip ⇔ in ad well-defined white tip.
fl all plum	• Scaps and mantle feathers with small diffuse pale tips ⇔ in ad tips whiter and creating some barring. • Underwing with strongly contrasting barring on flight-feathers; underwing-cov uniformly pale.

Little Owl *Athene noctua*   L 25cm 10"

all plum	• Broad rounded head with flattened crown. • Yellow iris. • Base colour of upperparts dark grey-brown. • Only heavy longitudinal stripes on underparts ⇔ Eurasian Pygmy Owl and Tengmalm's Owl.
ad juv-1w	• (Retained) sec and p10 with pointed tips ⇔ in ad rounded. • Juv tail-feathers with 4-5 cream-coloured bands ⇔ in ad-type 3 whitish.
fl ad note	• Underwing with completely and uniformly barred flight-feathers ⇔ Tengmalm's. • Many subspecies known; the forms *lilith*, *saharae*, *glaux* and *indigena* (see below) are often treated as a full species, Lilith's Owl.

geog var	*A.n. lilith* (Middle East)
all plum	• Much paler than European subspecies; entirely sandy-coloured. • Upperparts with large white spots. • Underparts with pale brown streaks. • Tail-barring (3) broad and irregular. • Facial disk ill-defined.

geog var	*A.n. saharae* (deserts of Arabia and Sahara)
all plum	• Similar to *lilith* but smaller and even paler. • Upperparts with smaller and less numerous pale spots than *lilith*. • Underparts with narrow brown streaks. • Facial disk conspicuously whitish. • Tail-barring (4) narrow and regular.

geog var	*A.n. glaux* (North Africa)
all plum	• Similar in colour to *indigena*, darker than *lilith* and *saharae* but paler and browner than *noctua*. • Underparts quite heavily streaked, approaching *noctua*. • Tail-barring narrow but regular.

geog var	*A.n. indigena* (south-eastern Europe to northern Middle East)
all plum	• Like *glaux* but upperparts darker and more rufous with small but dense pale spotting. • Underparts dense and diffusely streaked. • Tail-barring very narrow, often irregular and incomplete.

Tawny Owl *Strix aluco*   L 40cm 15.5"

ad		• Large thick head with black eye. • Short wings, tail projects slightly beyond wing-tips ⇔ in Long-eared Owl no tail-projection beyond wing-tips but wing projects beyond tail; in Ural Owl long tail projects far beyond wing-tips. • 2 white vertical crown-stripes (running between eyes ⇔ Ural).
1w l ad note	⇒	• All flight-feathers of one generation ⇔ in 2cy+ more generations. • Heavily barred flight-feathers and dark carpal patch on underwing ⇔ Long-eared. • In western Europe to Mediterranean occurs both in red-brown and grey morph (subspecies *sylvatica*); central European *aluco* larger and less deep red-brown than red-brown morph of *sylvatica*.

geog var	*S.a. mauritanica* (North Africa)
all plum	• Dark grey-brown. • Strongly marked with fine dense barring on underparts and upperparts.

Hume's Owl *Strix butleri*   L 31cm 12"

all plum	⇒	• Yellow-brown breast with only very diffuse barring. • Yellow-orange iris. • Almost uniformly greyish upperside.
all plum		• Both upper- and underwing similar to Tawny Owl but underparts (almost) unmarked ⇔ Tawny.

Ural Owl *Strix uralensis*   L 55cm 21.5"

ad	⇒	• Like giant grey Tawny Owl with long tail. • On underparts only longitudinal stripes ⇔ in Tawny longitudinal stripes with bars. • Large black eye. • No white stripes on forehead as in Tawny but white crown-stripes present.
1w all plum		• All flight-feathers of one generation ⇔ in 2cy+ more generations. • Flight-feathers entirely barred with broad dark bars; also underwing strongly barred. • Evenly barred tail ⇔ Great Grey Owl.

geog var	*S.u. macroura* (central Europe)
all plum	• Larger than *uralensis* (European Russia and western Siberia) and *liturata* (Scandinavia) with especially longer tail.
	• Variable; some ind slightly more strongly marked on underparts and on facial disc than *liturata* and especially than paler *uralensis*.
note	• Variable melanistic morph occurs relatively frequently in this taxon.

Great Grey Owl *Strix nebulosa*   L 64cm 25"

ad ⇒	• 2 broad white curved bars between eyes creating white cross.
	• Large size with long tail.
	• Relatively small eye with yellow iris.
	• Mainly grey plumage.
	• Facial disc with dark rings like annual rings of tree.
1w	• All flight-feathers of one generation ⇔ in 2cy+ more generations.
fl all plum ⇒	• Rather long tail with *broad dark terminal band*.
	• Pale basal part of prim creating pale prim-flash.
	• Flight-feathers completely barred with broad dark bars, on underwing barring rather faint ⇔ Ural Owl.

Long-eared Owl *Asio otus*   L 34cm 13.5"

all plum ⇒	• Only dark 'shadow' above and under eye (creating vertical dark lines on facial disc) ⇔ Short-eared Owl.
	• Red-orange iris (sometimes orange-yellow) ⇔ Short-eared.
ad ⇒	• Ear-tufts long (ear-tufts can be held down).
	• Strongly marked underparts with bold longitudinal stripes and some bars; ind from northern population sometimes lack barring on underparts (in Short-eared no bars on underparts).
	• Projected prim-tips concolorous with tertials ⇔ in Short-eared distinctly darker than tertials.
1w	• All flight-feathers of one generation ⇔ in 2cy+ often more generations sec.
fl all plum	• Pale underwing with black carpal patch and obvious barring restricted to distal part of outer prim ⇔ Tawny Owl.
	• Tail-feathers and upperside of flight-feathers finely barred ⇔ Short-eared.
note	• Ind from northern Europe greyer than ind from western Europe.

Short-eared Owl *Asio flammeus*   L 37cm 14.5"

all plum ⇒	• Underparts with only narrow longitudinal stripes ⇔ Long-eared Owl.
⇒	• Eye in dark area; black 'mascara' around whole eye ⇔ Long-eared.
	• Streaking on underparts heavy on breast, finer on rest of underparts ⇔ in Long-eared evenly distributed over underparts.
	• Pale yellow iris ⇔ Long-eared.
ad ♂	• Pale grey face ⇔ in ad ♀ more cream-coloured.
1w	• Tertials bleached and worn from November followed by rest of plumage during winter ⇔ in ad fresh plumage in winter.
fl all plum ⇒	• Pale underwing with dark tips to outer prim ⇔ in Long-eared fine barring to tips of outer prim and tips of outer prim pale.
	• Pale trailing edge of wing (only distinct on upperside).
	• Upperside of hand with conspicuous pale spot at base.
	• Regular, broad and well-defined barred upper-tail ⇔ Long-eared.

Marsh Owl *Asio capensis*   L 33cm 13"

all plum ⇒	• Uniform dark brown upperparts, cov and breast (rest of underparts greyish).
	• Pale face conspicuous due to very dark rest of head. Dark eye.
1w	• Tertials and rear scaps with pale barring and white tips ⇔ in ad uniform dark.
fl all plum ⇒	• White trailing edge of arm conspicuous due to dark upperwing.
⇒	• Mainly dark central tail-feathers 'interrupt' tail-barring.
	• Underwing with all flight-feathers on distal part barred (wing-tips as in Short-eared Owl).
	• Upperwing with almost completely dark sec and large pale prim-spot on both upper- as underwing (upperside of hand resembles that of Short-eared).
	• Broad, almost rectangular hand.

Tengmalm's Owl *Aegolius funereus*   L 25cm 10"

ad	• Large square head with whitish facial disc.
	• Only slightly larger than Little Owl but looks distinctly bulkier.
	• Yellow iris.
	• Diffusely dark chequered underparts.
juv	• Underparts and head almost completely black-brown.
1w	• All flight-feathers of one generation ⇔ in 2cy+ more generations.
fl ad	• Underwing with rather strongly barred sec but fainter barred prim; underwing-cov uniform pale.
	• Mainly dark upperwing with white spot on sec, prim and cov.

Nightjars

Nubian Nightjar *Caprimulgus nubicus*   L 22cm 8."

all plum ⇒	• Small, not much larger than Common Starling.
	• Tail projects slightly beyond wing-tips.
	• Large white spot on outer prim, often also visible when perched.

fl all plum ⇒	• Rufous collar.
	• Resembles mostly small Red-necked Nightjar with short tail.
	• Rufous underwing with black distal part of hand.
	• Rufous patterning on sec, inner prim and prim-cov.
	• Large, very conspicuous white spot on outer prim (white spot about in middle of prim as in Common Nighthawk ⇔ other nightjars in WP).
	• t5 and t6 with large white tip.
	• Relatively short tail and rounded wing-tips.
	• In ad ♂ more white on hand and tail than ad ♀.
note	• WP *tamaricis* is greyer and smaller than nominate *nubicus*, with narrowly streaked crown.

European Nightjar *Caprimulgus europeus*   L 26cm 10"

ad	• Dark marginal and lesser cov creating dark wing-bend.
	• Large white tips to lower row of lesser cov creating broad wing-bar, rest of cov with smaller pale tips, greater cov almost without.
juv	• Almost like ad ♀, but fresh plumage late summer ⇔ ad ♀ worn.
	• Tail-feathers pointed to rounded ⇔ in ad square-ended.
1w	• In both 1w and ad 2 generations of prim and tail-feathers (suspended moult, completed in winter range). Ageing by moult stage impossible (but see juv) ⇔ Red-necked Nightjar.
fl ad ♂	• Obvious white spot on distal part of outer prim (p8-p10) and white tips to outer tail-feathers.
fl ad ♀	• No distinct white spot on outer prim and tail-feathers.
note	• For more field marks, see Red-necked.

Red-necked Nightjar *Caprimulgus ruficollis*   L 32cm 12.5"

all plum ⇒	• Long tail; tail-projection beyond wing-tips 50% of prim-projection ⇔ in European Nightjar max 30% of prim-projection.
⇒	• Pale tips to all cov of same size; upperwing with multiple even but usually faint wing-bars ⇔ European.
	• Rufous collar, rufous patterning around eye, on throat, along scaps and on cov.
	• Broad white, vertical throat-stripe.
	• White submoustachial-stripe longer and more obvious than in European.
	• Larger and both paler grey and more rufous than European with relatively larger head.
	• Marginal and lesser cov not darker than rest of upperside of arm ⇔ European.
ad	• In both ♀ and ♂ p8-p10 with white spot (but in ♀ smaller and diffusely bordered), slightly larger than in European ad ♂.
juv-1w	• Almost like ad ♀; most ♂ with small white spot on outer prim, most ♀ with buffish spot. Fresh plumage late summer ⇔ ad ♀ worn.
	• Tail-feathers pointed to rounded ⇔ in ad square-ended.
1w	• All juv tail-feathers and flight-feathers retained ⇔ in ad 2 generations of prim and tail-feathers (suspended moult, completed in winter range).
fl all plum	• Pale spots on cov creating wing-bars on arm.
geog var	*C.r. desertorum* (north-eastern Morocco [*ruficollis* in rest of Morocco], northern Algeria and northern Tunisia)
all plum	• Ground-colour paler and greyer than in *ruficollis*.
	• Rufous patterning on prim broader and creating distinct and even barring ⇔ in *ruficollis* rufous patterning weak and irregular.
	• Smaller black streaking on crown, scaps and cov than in *ruficollis* (on scaps restricted to shaft-streaks).
	• Rufous collar more uniform, broader and deeper coloured than in *ruficollis*.
	• Rufous parts on head-side and throat deeper coloured than in *ruficollis* and almost uniform.
	• Underparts finer and less patterned than in *ruficollis*.

Egyptian Nightjar *Caprimulgus aegyptius*   L 24cm 9.5"

all plum ⇒	• Mainly pale grey-brown; *no broad dark median crown-stripe* as in other nightjars in WP (see note).
	• Relatively unmarked (no contrasting patterns), looks uniformly sandy at distance. Cov with cream-coloured tips.
	• Rather short tail-projection beyond wing-tips.
fl all plum ⇒	• Dark upperside of hand contrasts with pale rest of wing and upperparts.
	• No obvious white spot on prim and outer side of tail.
	• Pale underparts.
	• Underside of prim obviously pale barred.
note	• European *unwini* (Asia) paler, greyer and more finely patterned than *europeus* and therefore can resemble Egyptian. Unlike Egyptian, *unwini* has, like in *europeus*, e.g. dark crown centre, dark wing-bend (marginal cov and lesser cov) and white wing-bar over lesser cov.
geog var	*C.a saharae* (North Africa and Nile Delta)
all plum	• Smaller than *aegypius*.
	• Background slightly more pink-yellow or orange-yellow than more greyish in *aegypius*.
note geog var	• Border between breeding range of *saharae* and *aegypius* in Egypt probably well-defined, with *saharae* in whole Nile Delta but *aegypius* only in Suez Canal area. Aegypius widespread in Egypt in winter.

Common Nighthawk *Chordeiles minor*   L 24cm 9.5"

all plum ⇒	• Wing-tips beyond tail-tip or wing-tips and tail-tip falling level ⇔ in *Caprimulgus* nightjars tail-tip beyond wing-tips.
	• Underparts strongly and finely barred *on whitish background*.

ad	• Dark brown-grey upperparts.
juv-1w	• Broad, horizontal throat-stripe (sometimes also present in 1w but normally indistinct).
fl all plum ⇒	• Pale tips to flight-feathers (in flight creating pale trailing edge along wing).
	• Large white spot on *basal part* of outer 4 prim creating broad dark cross-band (also often visible when perched); in ad/1w ♀ slightly smaller and spots not pure white.
	• Forked tail.
	• Very dark upperside of sec, prim and prim-cov contrast with paler cov.
	• Narrow pointed wings.
fl ad ♂	• White subterminal tail-band; in other plumages no white in tail.
note	• Regularly active in daylight during migration.

Swifts

White-throated Needletail *Hirundapus caudacutus*   L 20cm 7.9

all plum ⇒	• White undertail-cov and vent, extending narrowly onto flanks (white horse-shoe shaped).
	• Large size, only slightly smaller than Alpine Swift but fuller bodied.
	• Diffuse paler back and rump (in juv hardly present).
	• Well-defined white throat-patch.
	• Small white patch on forehead (in juv hardly present).
	• White inner webs to tertials.
fl all plum	• Broad long hand.
	• Very short straight-ended tail.
	• Often fast, powerful flight with series of powerful wing-beats interspersed with relatively long glides.

Chimney Swift *Chaetura pelagica*   L 14cm 5.5

all plum	• Small; size as House Martin but different structure (see flight all plum).
	• Diffuse pale throat, forehead and upper breast; more or less conspicuous dark mask.
fl all plum ⇒	• *Very short arm and full long hand* creating characteristic silhouette, also due to cigar-shape body. Wings narrow near body.
	• Straight-ended tail with rounded corners (tail-feathers with small 'spikes' but only visible at close range).
	• Combination of structure and manner of flying can resemble bat.

Alpine Swift *Apus melba*   L 22cm 8.5

all plum ⇒	• Well-defined large white belly-patch and white throat-patch (latter sometimes difficult to see); white belly-patch exactly below whole wing base (dark breast-band separates white belly- and throat patch).
	• Uniform brown upperside (upperside distinctly paler than in Common Swift).
juv	• In autumn uniformly fresh, no moult ⇔ ad.
	• Pale fringes on tertials and cov slightly broader than in ad. In ad often restricted to small pale tips.
	• Outer tail-feathers with straight outer-edge ⇔ in ad outer-edge curved inwards.
1s	• Worn wings and tail; cov with mix of worn juv and more fresh ad-type feathers.
fl all plum ⇒	• Large size with very long pointed wings.
	• Relatively short tail.

Cape Verde Swift *Apus alexandri*   L 14cm 5.5

all plum	• Plumage resembles Plain Swift but smaller with shorter and more rounded wings and shorter, less forked tail.
	• Slightly paler than Plain, more dark grey-brown; throat hardly paler than rest of plumage.

Plain Swift *Apus unicolor*   L 15cm 5.9

all plum	• Upperside black-brown, a fraction paler than Common *apus*.
fl all plum	• Narrower and more pointed wings than Common.
	• Very faint small pale (not white) throat-patch with some pale scales below patch to upper-breast (latter difficult to see).
	• Slim bodied.
	• Tail fork deeper than in Common.

Common Swift *Apus apus*   L 17.5cm 6.9

ad	• Brown-black with off-white throat patch.
juv	• Like ad but pale throat-patch larger, paler and extending to forehead.
	• Pale fringes to cov.
	• Underparts often faintly scaled.
	• In autumn uniformly fresh, no moult ⇔ ad.
1s	• Worn brownish juv wings, prim pointed.
fl all plum	• Uniform brown-black upperwing (in some 1s distinctly brown).
	• Very pointed wings.
	• Under good viewing conditions contrast between black underwing-cov and paler underside of flight-feathers.
note	• See also Pallid Swift and Pacific Swift.
	• Proportion of 1s inds remain in winter range.
geog var	*A.a. pekinensis* (Asia)
all plum	• Large pale throat-patch as in Pallid, *extending to forehead* but more strongly contrasting with dark underparts and rear-head than in Pallid.

fl all plum
- Upperwing resembles that of Pallid due to pale panel created by paler sec and greater cov contrasting with dark upperparts.
- Dark saddle sometimes more strongly contrasting than in *brehmorum* of Pallid.
- Underparts dark (slightly paler than in *apus* but darker than in Pallid); ad lacks obvious scaling on underparts, rump and uppertail-cov (juv with fine pale scales on underparts, only visible at very close range). Upper- and undertail-cov paler than in *apus*.

note geog var
- *Apus* and *pekinensis* gradually merge over broad zone; above-mentioned features only useful for typical *pekinensis*, ind from western part of distribution and integration zone probably not separable from *apus*.

Pallid Swift *Apus pallidus*   L 17cm 6.7"

all plum ⇒
- Feathers on underparts with *pale base* and rather obvious pale fringes around each feather-tip (latter also in Common Swift juv) ⇔ Common including *pekinensis*.

⇒
- Relatively *pale head* contrasts with darker body and mantle ⇔ Common.
- Scaling often most distinct on central part of underparts ⇔ in Common, incl *pekinensis*, often more contrast in feathers of vent and undertail-cov.
- In good viewing conditions distinctly paler and browner than Common (but paler Common does occur, especially juv in late autumn).
- Dark mask conspicuous due to pale head (*pale area behind eye*), pale throat and forehead.
- Slightly larger but *more ill-defined paler throat patch* than in Common (Common juv also has larger pale throat patch, but this has a more well-defined border with the dark rest of head).

ad
- In July/Aug moult of inner prim up to p4 ⇔ in most Common ad no moult in summer range, but sometimes p1-p2 moulted.

juv
- In autumn uniformly fresh, no moult ⇔ ad.

fl all plum ⇒
- Pale underwing with pale greater cov *and median cov* and only lesser cov dark, creating narrow dark leading edge; median cov on underwing with white tips ⇔ in Common only paler greater cov; median cov and lesser cov creating broad dark panel.
- Size as Common but looks slightly thicker due to fuller (rear-)body and head, broader wings and shorter tail.
- Dark back and mantle contrast with paler rump, head and upperside of sec and greater cov.
- Tail shorter and less deeply forked than in Common with only slight difference in length between outer 2 tail-feathers (t4 and t5) ⇔ in Common distinct difference in length between t4 and t5 meaning tail is longer and more deeply forked (except in young juv).
- Paler undertail-cov and vent contrast with dark belly.
- Hand slightly broader than in Common, wing-tips sometimes appear more rounded.
- Tail-feathers, especially inner webs, relatively pale and translucent against light background.
- Dark outer prim creating dark prim-wedge, especially visible on underwing ⇔ Common.
- Pale greater cov creating pale panel on upperwing ⇔ in Common almost uniform (in juv pale fringes to cov).
- Sometimes paler prim-cov which break dark leading edge of wing.

geog var   *A.p. brehmorum* (Canary Islands and western part of Mediterranean)

all plum
- Like *pallidus* but generally slightly darker and slightly less contrasting.
- Underparts more greyish than in *pallidus*.

fl all plum
- Dark saddle often indistinct.

geog var   *A.p. illyricus* (Balkans)

all plum
- Darker than *pallidus*, *brehmorum* and even Common juv with less contrast in wing.
- Dark saddle contrasts with paler rump (more obvious than in *brehmorum*).

note
- Plumage of Common *pekinensis* (possible vagrant in western Europe) resembles Pallid (see Common geog var) but structure as Common, more slender and slightly longer and more deeply forked tail.

Pacific Swift *Apus pacificus*   L 19cm 7.5"

all plum ⇒
- Fine but distinct whitish-scaled underparts.
- Larger than Pallid Swift and Common Swift, much larger than White-rumped Swift.
- Rather large weakly bordered pale throat-patch.
- Almost rectangular (somewhat horse-shoe shaped) white rump-patch sometimes running slightly onto rear-flanks.

juv
- In autumn uniformly fresh, no moult ⇔ ad.

fl all plum ⇒
- Tail more fish-tail shaped with sharper (instead of more rounded) angle between central tail-feathers than in Common. When spread tail rather 'full' (⇔ White-rumped) and longer than in Common with deeper fork.
- Long, strongly sickle shaped wings.
- Thicker, slightly more protruding head than in Common.
- Underwing with weaker contrast between paler basal part of flight-feathers and dark (median) cov than in Common.
- Underwing-cov with relatively large pale tips (especially on median cov).

juv
- Like ad but narrow pale trailing edge along sec and inner prim.

note
- Partially leucistic Common occur with only white rump. Different structure and pale scales on underparts are necessary for positive identification in WP.

White-rumped Swift *Apus caffer*   L 15cm 5.9"

all plum
- Rather half-moon shaped, narrow white rump-patch, not extending onto rear-flanks.
- Large white throat-patch rather sharply demarcated from dark remainder of underparts.
- Narrow pale supercilium.
- Upperparts with dark blue gloss ⇔ other swifts.

imm fl all plum	• Pale fringes to cov ⇔ ad. • Long tail often held closed for prolonged periods and then looks like narrow spike. • Narrow, pale trailing edge of arm (difficult to see). • Very narrow, pointed wings.

Little Swift *Apus affinis*   L 13cm 5.1

all plum ⇒	• Almost straight-ended tail with *paler grey inner webs* of tail-feathers. • Small, at most very slightly larger than House Martin. • Large white throat-patch rather sharply demarcated from dark rest of underparts. • Rectangular (almost square) white rump-patch, extending onto rear-flanks.
fl all plum	• Underside of flight-feathers translucent against pale background and contrasting with dark underwing-cov. • Broad hand; arm very short and often slightly narrowing.

African Palm Swift *Cypsiurus parvus*   L 17cm 6.7

all plum ⇒	• Whole plumage grey-brown. • Smaller than Common Swift.
fl all plum ⇒	• Very long, deeply forked tail. • Very pointed wings. • Very fast flight; glides with wing held down.

Kingfishers

White-throated Kingfisher *Halcyon smyrnensis*   L 28cm 16

all plum ⇒	• Brown head, mantle and underparts except breast. • Pale blue upperparts and tail. • Throat and breast white (in juv finely dark scaled). • Large size.
ad	• Heavy orange-red bill.
juv	• Dull red-brown bill.
fl all plum	• Pale prim with dark tips (especially conspicuous on underwing).

Grey-headed Kingfisher *Halcyon leucocephala*   L 23cm 1

all plum	• Pale grey head, mantle and breast (in juv finely dark scaled and streaked). • Belly, vent and undertail-cov red-orange (in juv dull orange). • Back, scaps and cov black. • Tail and rump blue.
ad	• Heavy orange-red bill.
juv	• Dull red-brown bill.
fl all plum	• Pale blue prim-base (especially conspicuous on underwing).

Common Kingfisher *Alcedo atthis*   L 18cm 7.1

all plum	• Pale blue bar on upperparts extending from mantle to uppertail-cov often most conspicuous part at distance and in flight.
ad ♂	• Completely black upper- and lower mandible or small orange base to lower mandible.
ad ♀	• Reddish basal part of lower mandible > 50%.
juv	• Extreme bill-tip pale.
	• Legs dark ⇔ in ad bright red-orange.
1s	• Like ad but wings worn.

Pied Kingfisher *Ceryle rudis*   L 26cm 1

ad	• Upperparts boldly barred black and white.
ad ♂	• Double black breast-band.
ad ♀	• Single black breast-band.
fl ad	• White base of prim creating large white prim-spot.

Belted Kingfisher *Ceryle alcyon*   L 32cm 12.

all plum	• Blue-grey head with white spot on lores. • Completely blue-grey upperparts. • Very large size (largest kingfisher in WP).
♂	• Some blue-grey breast-band.
♀	• Like ♂ but double breast-band; both grey and rufous one. Rufous breast-band extends onto flank.
1w	• Grey breast-band with brown patterning. • Flanks with brownish marks (in ♂ grey from 1s onwards).

Bee-eaters, rollers and hoopoes

Little Green Bee-eater *Merops orientalis*   L 23cm

all plum	• Notably smaller than Blue-cheeked Bee-eater.
geog var	*M.o. cleopatra* (Egypt)
ad	• Greenish head; broad dark line between throat and breast. • Strongly elongated central tail-feathers but shorter than in Blue-cheeked (in *cyanophrys* much shorter

geog var	*M.o. cyanophrys* (Middle East)	
ad	• Blue forehead and throat with faint dark border between throat and breast and moderate elongated central tail-feathers.	
fl	• In both subspecies red underwing-cov as in Blue-cheeked but dark trailing edge broadening on arm as in European Bee-eater.	

Blue-cheeked Bee-eater *Merops persicus*   L 30cm 12"

all plum	• Slightly larger than European Bee-eater with slightly longer bill.
ad	• Longer elongated central tail-feathers than in European.
juv	• Throat and ear-coverts completely brown-orange.
	• No elongated central tail-feathers.
fl all plum	• Completely red-orange underwing (also underwing-cov ⇔ European) with dark trailing edge along whole wing; trailing edge not broadening on arm ⇔ European and Little Green Bee-eater.

geog var	*M.p. persicus* (Asia)
ad	• Blue-white supercilium and ear-coverts.
	• Yellow chin, red throat.
	• Elongation of central tail-feathers ≤ tail length.

geog var	*M.p. chrysocercus* (Africa)
ad	• Elongation of central tail-feathers ≥ tail length.
	• More narrow blue supercilium and no white under black eye-stripe ⇔ *persicus*.
note geog var	• Elongated central tail-feathers longer in ♂ than in ♀ in all subspecies.

European Bee-eater *Merops apiaster*   L 27cm 10.5"

all plum ⇒	• Well-defined yellow throat.
	• Pale scaps creating pale band on upperside.
	• Black eye-stripe widens on ear-coverts ⇔ in Blue-cheeked Bee-eater of even width.
ad ♂	• Majority of greater cov and median cov red-brown, creating uniform wing panel.
ad ♀	• Usually only some greater cov and median cov red-brown, less vivid coloured and less uniform; red-brown wing panel smaller, duller and more faintly bordered than in ad ♂.
juv	• Greenish upperparts, paler scaps contrast with darker cov; crown red-brown ⇔ Blue-cheeked juv.
1s	• Like ad but prim-cov worn (contrastingly dark against neighbouring feathers) ⇔ in ad bright-green like rest of hand.
fl all plum ⇒	• Reddish wash on underside sec, underwing-cov greyish ⇔ Blue-cheeked.
	• Black trailing edge of wing broader on sec than on prim ⇔ in Blue-cheeked trailing edge of wing of even width.

European Roller *Coracias garrulus*   L 31cm 12"

all plum	• Brown mantle, back, tertials and scaps.
	• Green-blue head, underparts and cov.
juv	• Like dull coloured ad.
	• Pale grey tips to prim.
	• Lacks purple gloss on upperside of e.g. sec ⇔ ad.
1s	• Like ad but juv prim worn and less deep black than in ad.
	• Pale bill-base.
fl all plum	• Black flight-feathers contrast with pale cov.

Abyssinian Roller *Coracias abyssinicus*   L 29cm 11.5" (excl tail-steamers)

ad ⇒	• Resembles European but with *strongly elongated outer tail-feathers*.
juv	• No elongated outer tail-feathers, resembles European (but see flight).
fl all plum ⇒	• Purple gloss on upperside of prim ⇔ in European prim blackish but underside with purple gloss.
	• No contrasting dark alula as in European.

Indian Roller *Coracias benghalensis*   L 32cm 12.5"

all plum	• Upperparts, neck and breast brown (not so deep rufous-brown as in European Roller).
	• Pale throat due to fine white stripes extending to breast.
	• Blue crown.
fl all plum ⇒	• Pale blue central part of outer prim creating conspicuous pale prim-spot.

Broad-billed Roller *Eurystomus glaucurus*   L 28cm 11"

ad ⇒	• Uniformly purple head and underparts except blue undertail-cov.
⇒	• Yellow bill.
	• Rufous-brown upperparts.
fl all plum	• Uniformly dark blue hand and rear-side of arm, contrasting with brown cov.

Eurasian Hoopoe *Upupa epops*   L 27cm 10.5"

all plum	• Black and white pied wings, back and rump.
	• Head and underparts pink-brown; mantle often slightly darker grey-brown.
	• Full long crest with black tip on every feather.
	• Long downcurved bill.
	• White bar over black tail.

juv-1w	• Tertials with frayed, white outer-edges and fringes not extending around feather-tips ⇔ in ad broader, well-marked, often still slightly coloured outer-edges extending around feather-tips. • White part in outer tail-feather (t5) with uneven or diffuse border with black part in feather-tip, especially on outer web ⇔ in ad even and well-defined border. • Outer prim-tip with pale fringe ⇔ in ad none.
1s	• Prim still juv; browner, more worn and narrower than ad-type feathers. • When juv t5 still present, see juv-1w for pattern.

Woodpeckers

Wryneck *Jynx torquilla* L 17cm 6.7"

all plum	• Upperparts with *dark middle bar* extending from crown to back. • Upperside with tree-bark like pattern. • Long dark eye-stripe. • Underparts barred but middle of belly almost unpatterned. • Long, somewhat diffusely barred tail. • Thick woodpecker legs with 2 front toes and 2 hind toes.
1w	• Prim-cov narrow and pointed; pale spot on top cut through by shaft making 2 spots ⇔ in ad broader, rounder and pale spot restricted to outer web.
behav	• Forages mainly on ground.

Northern Flicker *Colaptes auratus* L 32cm 12.5"

all plum	• Very characteristic with brown mantle, back and fine black barred cov. • Whitish underparts (with cream-coloured wash) and black rounded spots. • Broad black crescent on middle of breast. • Grey-blue hind-neck and crown and red nape-patch. • Brown face and throat.
ad ♂	• Black submoustachial-stripe (ad ♀ lacks submoustachial-stripe).
fl all plum ⇒	• Rump white. • Bright yellow underwing.

Grey-headed Woodpecker *Picus canus* L 28cm 11'

all plum ⇒	• Rather dark, usually red-brown iris ⇔ in Green Woodpecker almost white.
ad ⇒	• Grey head with black lores and narrow black submoustachial-stripe ⇔ in Green completely black 'bandit-mask' connected to submoustachial-stripe. • Faintly barred tail (t1 most obvious), outer tail-feathers unpatterned ⇔ in Green normally obviously barred outer tail-feathers (especially t5). • Only undertail-cov faintly barred ⇔ Green.
ad ♂	• Red spot on forehead.
ad ♀	• Grey crown without red.
juv	• Nearly as ad; underparts unpatterned ⇔ Green. • Yellow rump and uppertail-cov as in Green.
behav	• Drums much more often than Green.

Green Woodpecker *Picus viridis* L 33cm 13"

all plum	• Black 'bandit-mask' (see juv). • Completely red cap to hind-neck.
ad	• Barred rear-flanks, vent and undertail-cov (sometimes weak) ⇔ Grey-headed Woodpecker.
♂	• Submoustachial-stripe with red centre (also in juv ♂).
♀	• Completely black submoustachial-stripe.
juv	• Underparts and head-side completely dark spotted. • Mantle, scaps and cov with white speckles. • 'Bandit-mask' faintly developed.
fl all plum	• Conspicuous yellow rump and uppertail-cov. • Barred outer tail-feathers ⇔ in Grey-headed uniform (also visible when perched).

Iberian Green Woodpecker *Picus sharpei* L 32cm 12.5

ad ⇒	• No 'bandit-mask' as in Green Woodpecker; grey around eye, lores darker (see also Levaillant's Green Woodpecker). Sometimes faint green-grey supercilium. • Throat, breast and ear-coverts greyish ⇔ Green. • Sometimes pale line between submoustachial-stripe and mask, especially in ♀ (as on Levaillant's). • Upperside duller green than in Green. • Crown and submoustachial-stripe (latter only in ♂) paler orange-red instead of pure red in Green.
ad ♂	• Submoustachial-stripe almost completely red (♀ with completely black submoustachial-stripe) ⇔ in Green red submoustachial-stripe surrounded by black.
juv	• Spots on head and underparts less dark than in Green.

Levaillant's Green Woodpecker *Picus vaillantii* L 32cm 12.5

all plum	• No 'bandit-mask' (⇔ Green) but grey on lores (as in Iberian Green Woodpecker), • Always completely black submoustachial-stripe (in Iberian ad ♂ almost completely red).
ad ⇒	• Narrow, pale stripe directly above submoustachial-stripe.
ad ♀ ⇒	• Dark grey somewhat streaked crown, red only on rear-head.
behav	• Drums much more often than Green.

note
- Endemic to the Atlas mountains (Morocco, Algeria and north-western Tunisia) where Green does not occur.

Black Woodpecker *Dryocopus martius* L 43cm 17"

all plum
- Completely black plumage with pale bill.
♂
- Completely red cap (also in juv ♂).
♀
- Red spot on rear-crown.
juv
- Throat dark grey.
- In first weeks after fledging iris not whitish (as in ad) but blue-grey.
fl all plum
- Head usually held up.
behav
- Drumming rather slow and long.

Yellow-bellied Sapsucker *Sphyrapicus varius* L 22cm 8.5"

all plum
- Large white shoulder-patch as in Great Spotted Woodpecker but more towards wing-bend; lesser cov, median cov and most greater cov white; scaps black ⇔ Great Spotted Woodpecker.
- Yellowish belly (most extensive in ad ♂).
- Barred flanks and mantle, in ♀ denser and slightly more messily patterned, in juv-1w very diffusely patterned.

ad
- Head-pattern resembles Three-toed Woodpecker but broad dark breast-band and red crown in both sexes; red throat in ♂, in ♀ white. In some ad ♀ crown (almost) black.
- In ad ♀ black parts of head less deep than in ad ♂ with fine white patterning; yellow part on underparts smaller, restricted to faint patch on belly.

juv-1w
- Much more weakly patterned than in ad and black parts not uniform, some ind already with reddish crown and in some ♂ also throat.
- Crown diffusely pale streaked.
- Underparts diffusely streaked and barred.

Great Spotted Woodpecker *Dendrocopos major* L 25cm 10"

all plum ⇒
- Red undertail-cov and vent rather sharply demarcated from whitish rest of underparts.
- Black line on under-side of ear-coverts connected with black hind-neck.
- Tertials unmarked or with rounded spot on base ⇔ in Middle Spotted Woodpecker rather faint but evenly barred.

ad ♂
- Red spot on rear-head.
ad ♀
- Black crown and hind-neck.
uv
- Red cap with black lateral crown-stripes ⇔ Middle Spotted ad (in Middle Spotted juv faint red cap with black streaking).
- Undertail-cov and vent pale reddish.
- All tail-feathers pointed ⇔ in ad only central ones.

s
- Prim-cov, greater cov, sec and tertials retained juv feathers, more worn and browner than fresher moulted prim.

note
- See Middle Spotted and Syrian Woodpecker for more field marks.

geog var
D.m. major (northern Europe and western Siberia)

all plum
- Larger than *pinetorum* (western and central Europe).
- Bill relatively short, broad at base and lower mandible more abruptly curved towards tip than in *pinetorum* (almost recalls bill-shape of White-billed Diver).
- Generally more white on tail-side (t4 and t5 with black barring distinctly narrower than white bars).

geog var
D.m. numidus (Tunisia and Algeria)

all plum
- Bill long and slender.
ad ⇒
- Broad, patchy black breast-band, in centre mixed with red.

Syrian Woodpecker *Dendrocopos syriacus* L 24cm 9.5"

all plum ⇒
- Black line on rear-side of ear-coverts absent or broken, not extending to black hind-neck (see note).
ad ⇒
- (Much) less white in tail than Great Spotted: only some white notches on outer webs of t5-t6 (t4 lacks white) ⇔ in Great Spotted t5-t6 mainly white with black markings.
- Flanks often with faint longitudinal stripes.
- Fewer but larger white markings on prim creating only 3 white bars on closed wing ⇔ in Great Spotted 4.
- (More) white above and before eye than in Great Spotted.
- Larger and whiter patch on forehead than in Great Spotted.
- Pink-red undertail-cov, rather faintly bordered ⇔ Great Spotted.
- Upperparts sooty-black ⇔ in Great Spotted glossy.

ad ♂
- Large red patch on rear-crown, larger than in Great Spotted.
ad ♀
- Completely black crown and hind-neck (as in Great Spotted ♀).
juv
- Rather faint reddish breast-band.
- Red crown, rest of head-pattern as in ad.
- Longitudinal stripes on flanks.
- All tail-feathers pointed ⇔ in ad only central ones.

s
- See Great Spotted 1s.
note
- Great Spotted juv with often broken black line on rear-side of ear-coverts (see all plum), line sometimes entirely missing.
- Sometimes hybridises with Great Spotted where range overlaps.

Middle Spotted Woodpecker *Dendrocopos medius* L 21cm 8.5

all plum	⇒	• Completely white head-side; eye conspicuous. • Relatively small bill. • Black line on rear-side of ear-coverts broken, not extending to black hind-neck. • About 3 inner greater cov and median cov with white tips ⇔ in Great Spotted at most only inner one.
ad	⇒	• Red crown *without black lateral crown-stripes* ⇔ e.g. Great Spotted juv. • Pink-red undertail-cov, faintly bordered by rest of underparts. • Longitudinal stripes on underparts, especially flanks (in ♂ broader and sharper than in ♀). • Moustachial-stripe reaches not to bill.
ad ♂		• Red crown sharply demarcated from black hind-neck.
ad ♀		• Red crown on rear-head, ill-defined with black hind-neck.
juv		• Like ad ♀ but weaker dull red cap.
1s		• See Greater Spotted 1s.

White-backed Woodpecker *Dendrocopos leucotos* L 27cm 10.5

all plum	⇒	• White back and *rump*, visible especially in flight (see geog var).
	⇒	• Large white tips to median cov and greater cov creating extra wing-bars (in addition to those over flight-feathers) ⇔ other spotted woodpeckers. • Largest spotted woodpecker. • Black line on rear-side of ear-coverts broken, not extending to black hind-neck. • Moustachial-stripe reaches to bill ⇔ Middle Spotted Woodpecker. • Tertials strongly barred ⇔ other large pied woodpeckers.
ad		• Red undertail-cov, vent and belly with reddish wash and diffuse longitudinal stripes.
ad ♂		• Completely red crown with black lateral crown-stripe.
ad ♀		• Black crown.
juv		• Red-black spotted crown (in juv ♂ more red than in juv ♀)
1s		• See Great Spotted 1s.
behav		• Drumming fast and short, distinctly quickening near end.
geog var		Lilford's Woodpecker *D.l. lilfordi* (southern and eastern Europe)
all plum		• Much darker than *leucotus* with black barred back, rump and flanks.

Lesser Spotted Woodpecker *Dendrocopos minor* L 15.5cm 6.1

all plum	⇒	• Size as House Sparrow. • No red or reddish undertail-cov ⇔ all other spotted woodpeckers. • Small bill. • Black and white barred tertials and back (together with wings whole upperside strongly and evenly barred). • Black line on rear-side of ear-coverts short, creating large white area on head-side. • Ear-coverts often cream-coloured. • Tail-feathers, including central ones, not strongly pointed.
ad ♂		• Red crown (including in juv).
ad ♀		• Black crown.
juv		• White tips to outer prim ⇔ ad. • Neck-side and undertail-cov buffish.
1s		• See Great Spotted Woodpecker 1s.

Three-toed Woodpecker *Picoides tridactylus* L 23cm

all plum	⇒	• Mainly *barred underparts* (only spotted woodpecker with barred underparts). • Black ear-coverts and rear-crown. • Dark head-side with white stripe above and under ear-coverts. • Narrow wing-bars over flight-feathers. • Relatively long slender bill.
ad ♂		• Yellow median crown-stripe.
ad ♀		• White-black streaked crown (no yellow on crown).
juv ♂		• Yellow spot on front of crown.
juv ♀		• Often small yellow patch on forehead ⇔ ad ♀.
behav		• Slow drum, single ticks (almost) countable (resembles short version of drum of Black Woodpecker).
geog var		*P.t. tridactylus* (northern Europe including northern Poland)
ad		• Nearly unpatterned white band along centre of upperparts. • Flanks obviously barred but less heavy than in *alpinus*. • Outer tail-feathers white with black barring ⇔ *alpinus*.
geog var		*P.t. alpinus* (central Europe)
		• Heavier barred flanks than *tridactyla*. • Outer tail-feathers black with white markings ⇔ *tridactyla*. • Central part of upperparts usually less white than in *tridactyla* (especially ind from Alps?) but very variable with ind from south-eastern Europe often as white on central part of upperparts as *tridactyla*.

PASSERINES

New World flycatchers

Acadian Flycatcher *Empidonax virescens*   L 14.5cm 5.7"

all plum	• Long prim-projection c.100% ⇔ in most other *Empidonax* shorter.
	• Rather well-defined pale throat ⇔ in most other *Empidonax* more diffuse paler throat.
	• Narrow pale eye-ring ⇔ in most other *Empidonax* broad.
	• Completely yellow lower mandible.
	• Green upperparts.
	• Legs dark grey ⇔ in Alder Flycatcher black.
	• Greyish throat and breast; rest of underparts yellowish.
1w	• Wing-bars dirty-white ⇔ in ad white.
voice ⇒	• Call: loud and sharp 'peek' or 'pwe-eest', higher pitched than in other *Empidonax*.
note	• All plumage features apply for fresh autumn ind.

Alder Flycatcher *Empidonax alnorum*   L 14.5cm 5.7"

all plum	• Rather short prim-projection for flycatcher (80-100%).
	• Eye-ring rather broad and distinct.
	• Grey-green upperparts.
	• Completely yellow lower mandible.
	• Faint yellow underparts with diffuse grey-spotted breast-sides.
	• Crown slightly streaked.
1w	• Wing-bars dirty-white ⇔ in ad white.
voice ⇒	• Call: monotone, flat and short 'pip'.
notes	• All plumage features apply for fresh autumn ind.
	• Almost identical to Willow Flycatcher *E. traillii* (not recorded in WP) which has shorter prim-projection, dark tip to lower mandible, slightly more green-grey upperparts, narrower tail, slightly larger bill, more uniform breast-sides, narrower eye-ring and more uniform crown. Call: very different from Alder: 'wheet', not unlike call of Barn Swallow.

Least Flycatcher *Empidonax minimus*   L 13.5cm 5.3"

all plum	• Short prim-projection (± 70%).
	• Small with relatively short tail and wings.
	• Eye-ring broad, often broader at front- and rear-sides.
	• Greenish upperparts.
	• Bill rather small; yellow lower mandible, often with dark tip.
1w	• Wing-bars dirty-yellow ⇔ in ad white.
voice	• Call: sharp and short 'pwit'.
note	• All plumage features apply for fresh autumn ind.

Eastern Phoebe *Sayornis phoebe*   L 18cm 7.1"

all plum ⇒	• Dark head almost without patterning; paler throat.
	• Whitish underparts with brown wash on breast-sides (in 1w yellowish belly).
	• Large size with long dark tail (shrike-like jizz).
	• Dark brown upperparts.
	• Rather short prim-projection c.70%.
1w	• Underparts yellowish ⇔ in ad white.
	• Whitish tips to median cov and greater cov ⇔ in ad diffuse grey-brown tips.
behav	• Pumps tail.

Fork-tailed Flycatcher *Tyrannus savana*   L 25cm 10" (ad m 38 cm 15" incl tail)

all plum	• Wholly white-grey-black with extremely long forked black tail.
all plum	• Grey upperparts, black cap contrasts strongly with broad white neck-side and underparts.
	• White underwing-cov.
note	• South American species which has been recorded along whole Atlantic coast of North America; one record in WP; October 2002 in southern Spain.

Vireos

White-eyed Vireo *Vireo griseus*   L 13cm 5.1"

all plum	• Greyish neck-sides and yellow flanks to vent.
	• 2 white wing-bars contrast strongly with very dark median cov.
	• Conspicuous yellow eye-ring and supercilium.
	• Upperparts greenish with in ad greyish hind-neck and greenish crown.
ad	• Whitish iris.
1w	• Iris rather dark, becoming paler later in winter.
	• Head more greyish than in ad with at most weak greenish crown.

Yellow-throated Vireo *Vireo flavifrons*   L 14cm 5.5"

all plum	• Yellow throat and breast; rest of underparts white.
	• Yellow supercilium connected with yellow eye-ring.
	• 2 white wing-bars over median cov and greater cov.

173

- Brown-green cap, ear-coverts and mantle.
- Thick bill.
- Well-defined white fringes to tertials.

Philadelphia Vireo *Vireo philadelphicus* L 13.5cm 5.3

all plum ⇒	• Underparts entirely yellowish, most extensive on breast and throat ⇔ Red-eyed Vireo.
	• Much smaller than Red-eyed with shorter tail and smaller bill.
	• Dark grey-blue crown without distinct lateral crown-stripe; short eye-stripe forming darkest and most conspicuous part of head; whitish supercilium narrow but conspicuous.
	• Greater cov with pale fringes, creating pale wing-panel ⇔ in Red-eyed none.
	• Upperparts green-grey.
	• Tail-projection beyond wing-tips ≤ prim-projection ⇔ in Red-eyed ≥ prim-projection.
	• Wholly dark eye.
1w	• Often moult-limit in greater cov.
fl all plum	• Yellowish underwing-cov ⇔ in Red-eyed pale green-grey.

Red-eyed Vireo *Vireo olivaceus* L 15.5cm 6.1

all plum ⇒	• Broad whitish supercilium with conspicuous dark lateral crown-stripe and blue-grey crown.
	• Strong bill with hook.
	• Dark eye-stripe.
	• Upperparts uniform brown-green.
	• Whitish to cream-coloured underparts; undertail-cov and vent yellowish.
	• Legs thick, blue-grey.
	• Relatively large head.
ad	• Red iris.
1w	• Brown iris.
	• Moult-limit in greater cov, but often inconspicuous. Sometimes all greater cov still juv with weak pale yellowish fringes (ad-type almost uniform as upperparts). Regularly some or all tertials moulted.

Old World orioles

Eurasian Golden Oriole *Oriolus oriolus* L 24cm 9.5

ad ♂	• Vivid yellow body, black wings and tail with yellow terminal band.
	• Central tail-feathers deeply black ⇔ in ad ♀ with ♂-like plumage grey-green.
1s ♂-2s ♂/ ad ♀ (♀-type)	• Green-yellow upperparts.
	• Flanks yellowish with narrow diffuse streaking, rest of underparts whitish.
	• Faint dark lores (in 2s ♂ more black).
	• Black-brown wings, especially tertials and greater cov (in 2s ♂ deeper black).
	• Some ad ♀ with exceptional yellow upper- and underparts and therefore superficially like ad ♂ but lores grey and central tail-feathers grey-green.
1s-2s ♂	• Often large white or yellow tips on prim-cov ⇔ most ad ♀ (some 1s ♂ with small tips and some ad ♀ with large tips, see note).
1w	• Dark bill and iris ⇔ in ad ♀ reddish.
	• Small yellowish tips to median cov (when retained).
	• Underparts with rather broad dark streaking ⇔ in ♀-type very fine.
fl all plum	• Long, dark upperwing contrasts with pale body.
	• Bright yellow corners on tail-tip.
	• Pale tip of prim-cov creating obvious pale spot on base of hand.
	• Strongly undulating flight.
moult	• All ages undergo complete spring moult in winter range (but some ind retain some old sec).
note	• Large variation in size and shape of pale tips on prim-cov in ♀-type. Ageing in ♀-type in both autumn and spring is not possible with certainty, except 2cy ♀ which has very small tips to prim-cov in spring. Ad ♀ sometimes identical to both 1s ♂ and 2s ♂ but lores normally pale grey instead of dark grey to blackish.

Shrikes

Rosy-patched Shrike *Rhodophoneus cruentus* L 23cm

all plum	• Long brown strongly rounded tail with broad white terminal band (white especially visible on underside).
	• Upperparts uniform brown with pink-red rump patch.
ad ♂	• Pink-red throat extending downwards in narrowing band over central part of breast; rest of underparts pale pink-brown.
ad ♀	• Like ad ♂ but with white throat encircled by black collar.

Black-crowned Tchagra *Tchagra senegalus* L 23cm

all plum ⇒	• Large red-brown wing-panel; tertials and lower scaps with large dark centres.
	• Black crown and eye-stripe; broad cream-coloured supercilium.
	• Shrike-like structure with strong bill and long strongly rounded tail.
	• Upperparts grey-brown; underparts grey.

Brown Shrike *Lanius cristatus* L 19cm 7.

all plum ⇒	• Dark brown tail contrasts only slightly or not at all with faint red-brown rump and uppertail-cov ⇔ isabelline shrikes.
⇒	• Rather short prim-projection (c.60%) with usually only 5-6 prim-tips beyond tertials ⇔ Red-backed Shrike

- Narrow, long tail (due to narrow tail-feathers) with t6 normally ≥ 25 % shorter than visible part of tail ⇔ in Red-backed and isabelline t6 ≤ 20% shorter than visible part of tail.
- Nearly uniform brown upperparts and crown (in eastern subspecies *lucionensis* more grey-brown mantle and grey crown) ⇔ Red-backed 1w.
- No white prim-spot (sometimes very small).
- Relatively large head. Usually strongly bill with deep base and strong curved culmen ⇔ in all congeners less heavy.
- p1 relatively long; p2 relatively short, falls level with p6 ⇔ Red-backed and isabelline shrikes (except 'Chinese Shrike').
- Pale throat contrasts with cream-coloured breast and flanks.

ad ♂
- Mask well-defined to bill.
- Broad, well-defined supercilium above broad and complete mask. Supercilium extending broadly over bill, creating white forehead.

ad ♀
- Often very like ad ♂ but flanks and breast (faintly) scaled. Often mask not as deep black and crown slightly less deep brown than in ad ♂. Fresh ad ♀ in autumn sometimes faintly dark scaled on flanks.

juv-1w ⇒
- Upperparts in 1w almost uniform dark brown ⇔ in Red-backed ♀/1w greyish rump and hind-neck.
- Dark spot on lores directly before eye ⇔ in Red-backed often pale sickle-shaped spot directly before eye, in isabelline often pale lores.
- Mask usually well-developed and already blackish.
- Underparts with obvious barring on breast-sides and flanks (nearly as in Red-backed ♀/1w) on somewhat coloured background ⇔ Red-backed ♀/1w.
- Juv feathers with indistinct dark subterminal markings due to dark ground-colour ⇔ isabelline shrikes and Red-backed juv-1w.
- Narrow pale outer-side of tail (p6 with pale fringe) but not pure white as in Red-backed.
- In juv strongly marked upperparts, therefore resembling Red-backed juv-1w but see e.g. structure (all plum). 1w more uniform on upperparts.

1s
- Like ad (complete moult in winter).

moult ad
- Complex; most ind undergo 2nd (almost) complete moult in winter.

isabelline shrike complex (including Red-tailed Shrike and Daurian Shrike)

all plum ⇒
- Rufous-brown rump, uppertail-cov and tail often contrast with more grey-brown upperparts (in Daurian Shrike sometimes at most slight colour difference between upperside of tail and upperparts) ⇔ in Red-backed Shrike upperparts deeper rufous-brown than tail.

⇒
- Underside of tail rufous-cinnamon ⇔ Red-backed.
- 3 emarginations on outer web of prim (p3-p5) ⇔ in Red-backed 2 (p3-p4).
- Prim-projection shorter than in Red-backed with 6-7 (sometimes 5) prim-tips beyond tertials (7-8 in Red-backed) but longer than in Brown Shrike.
- No pale tail-sides ⇔ Red-backed.
- Pale spot at base of prim (in 1w sometimes indistinct, in 'Chinese Shrike' usually absent) ⇔ Red-backed and Brown.
- Relatively strong bill with high base ⇔ Red-backed.
- Tail-tip slightly more rounded than in Red-backed but t6 shorter in relation to visible part of tail, to a similar extent as in Red-backed (see Red-backed and Brown all plum).

ad ♀
- Mask less well-marked than in ad ♂ and often pale lores.
- Breast-sides and flanks often with fine scales.

1w
- Uniform rufous-brown to grey-brown upperparts (sometimes still some patterning present, especially on crown and uppertail-cov) ⇔ in Red-backed mantle and scaps more rufous-brown than tail and strongly scaled. Colour of upperparts sometimes difficult to judge, strongly dependent on light/viewing conditions.
- Relatively faintly scaled on breast-sides and flanks (but variable, see Red-tailed Shrike 1w) ⇔ in Red-backed 1w scaling more distinct and more numerous.
- Dark scaled crown ⇔ ad (but see 1s).
- Mask usually faint and almost only behind eye.
- Pale pinkish bill-base.
- Dark subterminal fringes to juv tertials and greater cov (as in Brown and Red-backed) but in most Daurian feathers completely dark centres. In ad-type feathers completely dark centres.

1s
- Most ind with some retained juv inner prim, otherwise (almost) like ad.
- Up to autumn of 2nd cy sometimes still shows some dark spots on forecrown and/or crown-sides.

note
- Some ind, especially 1w but even ad ♂, not identifiable with certainty due to intermediate field marks between Daurian Shrike and Red-tailed Shrike.

Red-tailed Shrike *Lanius phoenicuroides*   L 17cm 6.7"

all plum ⇒
- See introduction to isabelline shrike complex.
- Almost white underparts (especially throat and underside of ear-coverts) with faint salmon-coloured wash on flanks and breast-sides when fresh (sometimes underparts completely white) ⇔ Daurian Shrike.

ad
- Usually distinct but variable white prim-spot (as in Daurian ad).
- In early autumn variable moult strategy but normally only partially moulted and largely worn; some ind from late September onwards completely moulted and uniformly fresh.

ad ♂ ⇒
- Brown crown and rear-head (often deep chestnut-brown) merge into grey-brown to brown-grey (sometimes pure grey) upperparts. Obvious colour contrast between chestnut-brown crown and brown-grey mantle characteristic but variable, sometimes only crown paler and not distinctly rufous.
- Well-defined and complete mask, usually extending narrowly over forehead ⇔ in Daurian rarely.
- (Usually broad) white supercilium, usually extending to rear-side of mask.
- Deep rufous rump, uppertail-cov and tail contrast with mantle and back. Tail becomes darker towards tip, as in Daurian.
- Usually completely black bill which together with mask creates continuous dark line (sometimes paler base of lower mandible).

ad ♀	• Colour of upperparts and underparts as in ad ♂ (including variation), but upperparts often with more grey wash. • Supercilium white as in ad ♂. • Flanks and breast variably scaled (some ind hardly scaled, others nearly as Red-backed Shrike ad ♀). • Mask and supercilium fainter than in ad ♂ (lores especially diffusely dark or completely pale). • Tail less deep rufous than in ad ♂.
1w	• Usually stronger head-pattern than Daurian with rather conspicuous dark mask (lacking brown wash) and white supercilium. • Upperparts dark earth-brown, sometimes with more rufous crown; in general darker than Daurian. • Barring on underparts dark brown to black, sometimes almost as extensive as in Red-backed 1w (as in Brown Shrike) ⇔ Daurian 1w (in some Daurian 1w rather heavy dark barring on underparts but then in combination with extensive orange on throat, breast and flanks). • Fine dark barring on crown and uppertail-cov ⇔ in most Daurian 1w almost none. • Dark subterminal line on cov and tertials usually broader than in Daurian. • Centre of (juv) median cov whitish ⇔ in Daurian often rufous wash to whitish centres of (juv) median cov. • In general more like Red-backed juv and sometimes Brown juv (which see) than Daurian.
note	• 'karelini'-type (which is often regarded as a morph but is possibly a valid subspecies) has completely (pale) grey upperparts and crown and often whiter underparts (ad ♂ and ad ♀); in addition, 'pure' intermediate types occur.

Daurian Shrike *Lanius isabellinus* L 17cm 6.7"

ad	⇒	• See introduction to isabelline shrike complex. • Whole underparts more or less warm cream-coloured (characteristic when deep orange) ⇔ Red-tailed Shrike. • Upperparts, hind-neck and crown pale sandy-coloured with rufous wash to pale grey; crown and upperparts almost uniform coloured but hind-neck and crown often slightly warmer. • Relatively little contrast between upperparts and paler warm buff underparts ⇔ Red-tailed. • Base of lower mandible pale, usually grey-brown (in ad ♂ sometimes completely black) ⇔ in most Red-tailed completely black. • In early autumn variable moult strategy from only partially moulted and largely worn to completely moulted and uniformly fresh.
ad ♂		• Rather faintly bordered, short, not pure white supercilium ⇔ Red-tailed. • Well-defined and complete mask but usually narrower than in Red-tailed and rarely extending over forehead. • Wings and tail as in Red-tailed ad ♂.
ad ♀		• Upperparts sandy-coloured brown-grey to grey. • Supercilium short, cream-coloured. • Mask often does not extend to bill. • Sometimes faint scaling on flanks and breast-sides but not as extensive as in some Red-tailed ♀.
ad ♀/1w		• Supercilium, underside of ear-coverts and sides of throat with rufous wash ⇔ in Red-tailed whitish.
1w	⇒	• Underparts, especially flanks, with cream-coloured to deep orange wash (latter characteristic but often paler than in ad). Characteristic when underside of ear-coverts coloured. • Upperparts sandy-brown, about as in ad (but less greyish as in some ad); not deep brown ⇔ Red-tailed 1w. • Mask brownish (often indistinct) normally with rufous-brown wash (head-pattern in general fainter and more uniform than in Red-tailed 1w). • Supercilium, underside of ear-coverts and throat cream-coloured to orange ⇔ in Red-tailed whitish. • Usually faint barring on breast-sides and flanks; pale brown to red-brown barring on orange flanks characteristic.
geog var		'Chinese Shrike' *L.i. arenarius* (eastern part of range)
all plum		• Pale dirty cream-coloured upperparts, hind-neck and crown (similar to Daurian Shrike but paler and more uniform). Crown not or only slightly deeper coloured than upperparts. • Supercilium diffuse or absent. • Cream-coloured underparts as in Daurian but often duller and less warm. • Tail pale rufous (not deep rufous) and not or only slightly gradually darker towards tip ⇔ Daurian and Red-tailed Shrike. • Slightly shorter wings (with 5 prim-tips beyond tertials) and relatively longer tail than Daurian and Red-tailed. • Pale flesh-coloured base of lower mandible. • p2 shorter than in Daurian and Red-tailed; p2 falls level with p6 (in Daurian and Red-tailed p2 falls between p5 and p6). • At most small prim-spot; absent in ♀ and 1w.
ad		• Dark brown to black mask fading away between eye and bill (pale lores, often even in ad ♂). • Dark brown-greyish prim and tertial-centres, contrasting little with upperparts ⇔ in Daurian and Red-tailed black prim and tertial-centres. • Fringes to cov and tertials cream-coloured (in Daurian and Red-tailed fringes paler). • Little difference between ad ♂ and ad ♀; in ad ♀ less dark mask and sometimes faintly scaled on underparts; pale prim-spot absent. • In early autumn already completely moulted and fresh.
1w		• Very similar to Daurian 1w but with more uniform and paler, especially on upperparts. • Underparts very faintly and finely scaled.
notes		• Validity of this taxon doubtful. Recent research has revealed a continuous cline form Daurian into Chinese, so maybe Chinese is best regarded as an eastern form of Daurian. • Mid-winter records of Daurian in the Middle East possibly refer to this taxon.

ed-backed Shrike *Lanius collurio*   L 17cm 6.7"

all plum
- (Fairly) long prim-projection (80-100%) with 6-7 (8) prim-tips beyond tertials.
- 2 emarginations on outer web of prim (p3-p4) ⇔ in all congeners 3 (p3-p5).
- Tail almost straight-ended, only t6 obviously shorter than other tail-feathers (max 20% shorter than visible part of tail)

ad ♂ ⇒
- Grey crown, hind-neck and rump contrast strongly with red-brown mantle and scaps (mantle sometimes greyish, especially in autumn due to wear, then similar to *kobylini*, see geog var).
- Basal part of outer tail-feathers with much white, creating white corners at base of tail.
- Black mask.
- Whitish underparts with pink wash.

ad ♀
- (Faint) grey (rear-)crown and rump contrast with chestnut-brown mantle and scaps. In others (possibly 1s ♀) also red-brown crown and uppertail-cov and only grey wash on hind-neck.
- Underparts (heavily) dark scaled.
- White outer-edge on t6.

juv-1w
- Dark scaled rufous-brown upperparts (sometimes more greyish). Hind-neck greyish. Upperparts warmer brown than upperside of tail ⇔ isabelline shrikes.
- Whitish underparts dark scaled (only faint cream-coloured or brown wash on flanks).
- White outer-side of tail.
- Usually somewhat grey hind-neck and uppertail-cov ⇔ isabelline shrikes and Brown Shrike.
- Rufous centres to tertials and cov.
- Sometimes rufous-brown upperside of tail as on isabelline shrikes.

s
- Like ad (complete moult in winter).

ote
- See also isabelline shrikes.

eog var   *L.c. 'kobylini'* (between Black Sea and Caspian Sea)

ad ♂
- Mantle less deep chestnut than in *collurio*, upper part of mantle grey like crown (but part of population in western Europe similar in this respect).
- Underparts slightly deeper reddish-pink.
- Larger proportion of population with small pale prim-spot than in *collurio*.
- Crown very variable from paler grey to darker blue-grey in comparison with *collurio*.

ad ♀
- Upperparts darker and warmer brown than in *collurio*.
- Underparts with deeper ground-colour than in *collurio* and only weak barring; barring sometimes almost absent.

ote
- Validity of this taxon questionable and possibly outcome of gene-flow from isabelline shrike.
- Very variable and only typical ind identifiable; ind identical to *collurio* occur within range of *'kobylini'*.

ong-tailed Shrike *Lanius schach*   L 25cm 10"

ll plum ⇒
- Grey crown, hind-neck and mantle *gradually merging* into deep buff scaps, back, rump and uppertail-cov.
- Deep buff flanks and undertail-cov.
- Size as Great Grey Shrike but very long strongly rounded tail.
- Usually rather small pale prim-spot.
- Narrow supercilium above mask but often very diffuse, sometimes absent.
- Thick bill.
- Narrow pale outer-edge of tail.

ad
- Broad mask extending over forehead, especially in ♂ (often also in 1w ♂); otherwise sexes almost alike.

1w
- Greater cov with pale tips, forming wing-bar.
- Underparts often scaled, probably especially in 1w ♀.

esser Grey Shrike *Lanius minor*   L 20cm 7.9"

all plum ⇒
- Long prim-projection ≥ 100% ⇔ Great Grey Shrike.
⇒
- Short thick bill with evenly curved culmen.
- No white line between grey scaps and black wings ⇔ Great.
- White base of prim creating large, almost rectangular spot (⇔ in Great and Southern Grey Shrike smaller and strongly narrowing on outer prim); no white at base of sec.
- No supercilium, as in some subspecies of Southern.
- Much white in tail-sides, broadening especially at base (as in Great *homeyeri*) ⇔ in Great *excubitor* white widens on distal part of tail. Closed tail seen from below mainly white (⇔ Southern and Great *excubitor*).
- Tail almost straight-ended.
- Pinkish wash on underparts (more distinct in ad ♂).

ad ♂ ⇒
- Black forehead and forepart of crown. In fresh autumn plumage forehead often mottled grey, see ad ♀.

ad ♀
- Blackish forehead extending less high than in ad ♂ (less than depth of bill ⇔ ♂) and less deep black (often mottled grey in spring/summer).

juv-1w
- Juv with dark scaled upperparts and crown (underparts normally almost unmarked), in 1w upperparts more uniform.
- Pale fringes and tips to greater cov and tertials.
- Mask smaller than in ad.

s
- (Almost) like ad. Some ind with some retained juv wing-feathers.

reat Grey Shrike *Lanius excubitor*   L 24cm 9.5"

all plum
- Long rounded tail.
- Relatively slender bill.
- White in tail-sides broadening on distal part (*excubitor*) ⇔ Lesser Grey Shrike.

- Short prim-projection c.50% with 3-4 prim-tips beyond tertials.
- Distinct white spot at base of prim, narrowing towards outer wing and white often extending to base of sec (in Scandinavian populations less obvious or not extending at all) ⇔ Lesser and Steppe Grey Shrike.
- In Scandinavian populations upperparts slightly darker and often very faintly scaled on underparts ⇔ ind from central Europe.
- Except juv, grey upperparts with narrow white shoulder-stripe ⇔ in Lesser no shoulder-stripe.
- White tips to sec and longest tertials.
- Pale grey, sometimes pale brown-grey underparts.
- Very diffuse supercilium.

	• (Faintly) scaled underparts in fresh plumage, present late into winter (especially in 1w and ad ♀).
juv-1w	• Ground-colour of underparts in autumn often weak cream-coloured, becoming whiter later in winter.
	• Faintly scaled underparts as in many ad; almost uniform upperparts, scaps and crown ⇔ Lesser juv.
1w ⇒	• Greater cov with pale tips, creating wing-bar ⇔ ad.
1s	• Prim old and grey or brown and at least some outer (white-tipped) greater cov retained, often contrasting with other fresh cov.

geog var	*L.e. homeyeri* (eastern Europe to central Asia)
all plum ⇒	• Much white in wing; white basal half to flight-feathers creating large white wing-panel (in flight long broad wing-bar *over whole wing-length* ⇔ in Steppe white restricted to prim).
	• Large white tips to sec and inner prim.
⇒	• Broad white tail-base; t6 (and usually also t5) completely white. White widens towards base, resembling tail pattern of Red-backed Shrike ad ♂, Steppe and Lesser ⇔ in *excubitor* base of t6 black, but in some (eastern?) *excubitor* t6 wholly white to base.
	• White uppertail-cov and rump ⇔ *excubitor*.
	• Upperparts pale grey, paler than in *excubitor*.
	• Usually narrow supercilium above whole mask, slightly more distinct than in *excubitor*.
	• Slightly longer tail and wings than *excubitor*.

geog var	*L.e. sibericus* (central and eastern Siberia)
all plum	• Underparts distinctly scaled (fainter in some ad ♂).
	• White rump (as in *homeyeri*) ⇔ *excubitor*.
	• Only prim with white base (creating relatively small white spot), no white on base of sec (like e.g. in Southern and northern populations of *excubitor*).
	• Mask relatively small.
ad	• Upperparts (except rump) rather dark grey, usually with brown wash.
	• Underparts greyish ⇔ in *excubitor* almost pure white.
1w	• Upperparts with distinct brown wash.
	• Underparts densely scaled, often with brown wash on flanks.
	• Greater cov and median cov with pale brown tips ⇔ in *excubitor* 1w more whitish.
note 1w	• Imm field marks retained longer than in *excubitor*; pale lores and bill-base until late in 2cy.

Southern Grey Shrike *Lanius meridionalis*   L 24cm 9.

all plum	• Stronger bill than Great Grey Shrike.
	• Mask widens on ear-coverts and reaches to below eye.
	• Legs longer than in Great. Toes and feet as a whole strong ⇔ Great.
	• Tail relatively narrow.
ad ⇒	• Narrow but well-defined supercilium extending from bill to rear-side of eye.
⇒	• Rather dark underparts with orange-pink wash (similar to Lesser Grey Shrike); throat contrastingly white.
	• Lead-grey upperparts, darker than in Great.
	• Small prim-spot but lacks white at base of sec, especially visible in flight (Great sometimes also lacks white at base of sec, especially in northern populations).
	• ♀ often with slightly smaller prim-patch and slightly greyer lores but much overlap with ♂, only useful in extremes.
1w	• Uniform underparts as in ad ⇔ Great 1w scaled on underparts.
	• Rather large white tips to sec.
	• Upperparts often paler than in ad.
1s	• Like ad s but moult-limit in prim, with outer prim fresh, rest of prim old (juv) or all prim juv (in Great (*excubitor*, *homeyeri* and *sibericus*) all prim juv).
note	• African subspecies mentioned below possibly best treated together as distinct polytypic species 'Desert Grey Shrike' with *meridionalis* as separate monotypic species.

geog var	Desert Grey Shrike *L.m. elegans* (Sahara to southern Egypt)
ad	• Rather pale grey upperparts, underparts pale grey.
	• Very faint supercilium.
	• White outer webs to sec connected with large prim-spot (as in Steppe Grey Shrike but underparts whiter and prim-projection shorter). Sometimes some white at base of sec.

geog var	*L.m. koenigi* (Canary Islands)
ad	• No or very weak supercilium.
	• Upperparts rather dark grey, only slightly paler than in *meridionalis*.
	• Underparts pale grey ⇔ *meridionalis*.
	• Rather small white prim-spot.

geog var	*L.m. algeriensis* (coastline of north-western Africa)
ad	• No supercilium and broad black mask. • Strong bill with conspicuous hook. • Rather large white prim-spot. • Upperparts rather dark grey, underparts pale grey ⇔ *elegans*.
note	• Towards east of range larger prim-spot, whiter underparts and more white on scaps (becoming more similar to neighbouring *elegans*).
geog var	**Levant Grey Shrike** *L.m. aucheri* (Middle East, Arabia and southern Iran)
ad	• Large black mask extending slightly over forehead (but much less than in Lesser ad). • No supercilium. • Flanks extensively grey.

Steppe Grey Shrike *Lanius pallidirostris*   L 23cm 9"

all plum ⇒	• Very large white prim-spot, sharply demarcated from entirely black base of sec (feature only visible in flight). Sometimes some white at base of sec but if present often not visible when perched.
⇒	• Pale grey to pale grey-brown crown and upperparts. • Underparts pale grey with in autumn cream-coloured wash, little contrast with upperparts ⇔ Great Grey Shrike and Southern Grey Shrike. • Long prim-projection c.80%, longer than in Great and Southern but shorter than in Lesser Grey Shrike. Wing-tip normally extends beyond uppertail-cov. • Bill thicker than in Great (between Lesser and Great). • Tarsus relatively long (longer than in Great). Thick toes, strong feet ⇔ Great. • Much white in tail-sides (t6 and often also t5 wholly white), distinctly broadening at both base and tip and creating diamond-shaped black tail-centre (about as in Great *homeyeri* ⇔ Great *excubitor*). In some (eastern?) *excubitor* t6 wholly white to base. • Tail narrower and less fan-shaped than in Great.
ad	• Sec and tertials completely black ⇔ 1w. • Often with wholly black bill and narrow black loral-stripe in summer (♂?), also in 1s.
1w	• Large white tips to greater cov creating complete wing-bar. • Tertials and sec with relatively broad pale fringes and/or tips ⇔ in Great and Southern 1w narrower. • Black mask slightly fainter than in ad. • Pale lores (sometimes also in Great 1w). • Pale grey-brown bill with dark tip (sometimes also in Great 1w). • Not scaled on underparts ⇔ Great 1w.
1s	• Like ad s but moult-limit in prim; outer prim fresh, remaining prim old (juv) ⇔ in Great 1s (*excubitor*, *homeyeri* and *sibericus*) all prim juv.

Grey-backed Fiscal *Lanius excubitoroides*   L 25cm 10"

all plum ⇒	• Tail white only at base of outer tail-feathers; distal part of tail completely black. • Structure like Great Grey Shrike but patterning more like Lesser Grey Shrike; larger than Great with stronger bill.
ad ⇒	• Scaps black ⇔ all congeners. • Mask as in Lesser (completely black forehead) but with supercilium behind eye. • Underparts white. • Large white prim-spot as in Lesser.
juv	• Like ad but mantle barred and mask not extending over forehead.

Woodchat Shrike *Lanius senator*   L 18cm 7.1"

all plum ad/1s	• Long prim-projection ≥ 100%. • Brown-red crown and hind-neck. • White scaps creating conspicuous white spot. • Dark mantle and back; pale rump and uppertail-cov. • Black forehead. • From spring onwards feathers of wings one generation with pale fringes; fringes disappear due to wear in summer (see 1s).
ad ♂	• Mask consists of completely black forehead, often small pale loral-spot. • Dark brown-red crown and hind-neck. • Mantle completely black. • Little or no pale parts around eye. • Wings deeper black and with more narrow fringes to tertials and greater cov than ad ♀.
ad ♀	• Dark grey mantle ⇔ in ad ♂ black. • Crown and hind-neck paler red-brown than in ad ♂. • Large pale loral-spot. • Whitish eye-ring and narrow supercilium. • Broad pale fringes to tertials and greater cov.
juv-1w ⇒	• Whitish base of prim usually create large prim-spot which extend diffusely towards distal part of prim. • Pale centres to scaps and median cov (sometimes also pale spot in centre of greater cov). • Grey-brown upperparts (in 1w uniform). • Broad pale outer-side of tail (broader than in Red-backed Shrike 1w). • Faintly bordered pale rump (flight). • Whitish underparts with dark scaled pattern. Scaled pattern often more dense on breast-sides.
1s	• Like ad of equivalent sex (♀ often very weakly patterned) but prim-cov, outer sec and sometimes other parts in wing old and brown, contrasting with fresh, deep black greater cov and tertials.

geog var	**Balearic Woodchat Shrike** *L.s. badius* (Balearic Islands, Corsica and Sardinia)
all plum ⇒ ⇒	• No white prim-spot (sometimes very small, not reaching beyond longest prim-cov). • Bill normally stronger than in *senator*. • Prim-tips less evenly spaced than in *senator* (p2 level with p5 ⇔ in *senator* p2 almost level with p6).
ad	• Black on forehead slightly narrower than in *senator*. • Red-brown rear-head slightly paler than in *senator*. • Wings often deeper black than in *senator* (especially in ad ♂) • Narrower white shoulder-patch than in *senator*. • Uppertail-cov more grey than white ⇔ *senator*.
juv-1w	• No pale creamy prim-spot (sometimes also seemingly absent in *senator*).
note	• *L.s. rutilans* (Portugal) somewhat intermediate between Balearic and *senator* with smaller white prim-spot and paler rear-crown as in Balearic.
geog var	*L.s. niloticus* (from Middle East eastwards)
all plum	• Larger white prim-patch than *senator*.
ad	• Much white in basal part of outer tail-feathers (also white base of t1 extending behind uppertail-cov ⇔ *senator*).
1w	• Post-juv (and also post-breeding ad) moult often more advanced than in *senator*. • Prim-patch much more well-bordered than in *senator*. • Pale base to tail-feathers often already visible (also in juv). • Generally greyer overall, less red-brown than *senator*.

Masked Shrike *Lanius nubicus*   L 17.5cm 6.9

all plum	• Smaller and more slender build than Woodchat Shrike with longer tail. • Relatively slender bill. • Large white prim-spot. • Prim-projection c.80%. • Long black tail with evenly broad white outer-edge.
ad ⇒	• Large white patch on forehead connected with supercilium (sometimes on 1w completely white). • Broad black mask. • Large white shoulder-patch as in Woodchat.
ad ♂	• Deep black upperparts. • Orange band along breast-sides and flanks.
ad ♀	• Dark grey upperparts. • Cream-coloured flanks and breast-sides but less deeply coloured than in ad ♂. • Lores often pale.
juv-1w ⇒ ⇒	• Large white prim-spot well-defined ⇔ in Woodchat juv-1w ill-defined. • Whitish to pale grey fringes to greater cov and tertials ⇔ in Woodchat cream-coloured to rufous. • Rump concolorous with upperparts ⇔ in Woodchat juv-1w whitish. • Post-juv moult starts late; often as late as October paler forehead and first white scaps appear. • Scaled, greyish upperparts (Woodchat *niloticus* juv-1w also greyish on upperparts). • Large pale centres to scaps and median cov (like Woodchat juv-1w).
1s	• (Almost) like ad. Most ind with some retained juv wing- and tail-feathers.
behav	• Often holds tail downwards and flicks it up and down ⇔ Woodchat.

Crows

Eurasian Jay *Garrulus glandarius*   L 34cm 13.

all plum	• Blue-black barred prim-cov, alula and outer greater cov. • Broad black malar stripe. • Pink-brown hind-neck, mantle, back and majority of underparts. • White rump (flight) ⇔ Spotted Nutcracker. • Dark streaked crown. • Black tail.
1w-1s	• Barring of blue wing-feathers (prim-cov, alula and outer greater cov) irregular in width ⇔ in ad regula
geog var	*G.g. cervicalis* (North Africa)
all plum	• Completely uniform black crown. • White face. • Deep red-brown upperparts.
geog var	*G.g. atricapillus* (Middle East)
all plum	• Black crown; white forehead. • Almost white face.

Siberian Jay *Perisoreus infaustus*   L 28cm 1

all plum	• Brown-grey with orange rump, tail-feathers (except t1) and prim-cov. • Diffuse dark cap. • Small bill with conspicuous pale feathering above upper mandible.
1w-1s	• Wings still largely juv, but slight differences with ad.

Iberian Magpie *Cyanopica cooki*   L 33cm 13"

all plum	• Black cap, sharply demarcated from white throat and neck-side.
	• Pinkish-brown body with azure-blue upperwings and tail.
1w-1s	• Most ind with moult-limit in flight-feathers with outer prim and inner sec fresh, rest old.
note	• Formerly considered conspecific with Azure-winged Magpie (*C. cyanus*) of east Asia.

Eurasian Magpie *Pica pica*   L 46cm 18"

all plum	• White belly, rest of underparts black. White scaps, rest of upperparts black with blue gloss.
	• Long, strongly rounded tail. ♂ with longer tail than ♀.
1w-1s	• White in prim extends less than in ad; larger dark tips to prim and less well-defined ⇔ in ad white extend almost to tip of prim.
	• Retained juv tail-feathers, prim, tertials and greater cov more worn and less glossy than new ad-type feathers. Moult-limit most obvious in 2cy.

Maghreb Magpie *Pica mauritanica*   L 40cm 15.5"

all plum	• Like Eurasian Magpie but with blue spot behind eye (skin); however hint of blue spot behind eye sometimes occurs in ind from populations of Eurasian in southern Spain.
	• More black on prim than Eurasian.
	• Slightly longer tail than Eurasian.

Spotted Nutcracker *Nucifraga caryocatactes*   L 34cm 13.5"

all plum	• Dark brown with large white spots on majority of underparts and upperparts.
	• Uniform dark crown.
1w-1s	• Like ad but prim, tail-feathers, tertials and greater cov still all juv; especially tertials, greater cov and prim-tips browner, greater cov with frayed white tips ⇔ in ad glossy, deep black wings and greater cov with or without small well-defined white tips. In *caryocatactes* often 2 generations of greater cov
	• Pale tips to inner prim and outer sec (in ad very small pale tips at most).
fl all plum	• Dark with white undertail-cov.
	• White terminal tail-band.
	• At distance contrast between dark crown and pale underparts and head.
	• 2-3 'mirrors' on underwing (white oval patch on central part of inner prim.

geog var	**Slender-billed Nutcracker** *N.c. macrorhynchos* (Siberia) compared to *N.c. caryocatactes* (central Europe, Scandinavia to European Russia)
all plum	• Longer slender bill but overlap.
	• White terminal tail-band generally broader.

Alpine Chough *Pyrrhocorax graculus*   L 37cm 14.5"

all plum ⇒	• Bill-feathering on upper mandible extends further than on lower mandible ⇔ in Red-billed Chough equally as far.
⇒	• Tail projects distinctly beyond wing-tips ⇔ in Red-billed wing- and tail-tip fall about level.
	• Short (pale yellow) bill, length about half head-length. Only culmen distinctly curved.
	• Legs short, reddish as in Red-billed (browner in younger ind).
fl all plum	• Long tail longer than breadth of wing ⇔ Red-billed.
	• Under certain lighting conditions underwing-cov appear obviously darker than flight-feathers (as in Red-billed).
	• 5 'fingers', generally less deeply indented than in Red-billed and somewhat rounded wing-tips ⇔ Red-billed.

Red-billed Chough *Pyrrhocorax pyrrhocorax*   L 39cm 15.5"

all plum	• Larger size than Alpine Chough.
ad	• Red bill.
juv	• Dull orange-yellow downcurved bill shorter than in ad but longer than half head-length ⇔ Alpine.
1w-1s	• Retained juv tail-feathers, prim, tertials and greater cov more worn and less glossy than new body-feathers and eventual moulted lesser cov.
fl all plum ⇒	• Broad wings, breadth of wing ≥ tail length ⇔ in Alpine longer tail.
	• 6 long 'fingers' and square wing-tips ⇔ Alpine.
note	• For other features see Alpine.

Western Jackdaw *Corvus monedula*   L 32cm 12.5"

all plum ⇒	• Short bill.
ad	• Grey rear-head and hind-neck.
	• Pale grey iris.
juv	• Eye darker grey than in ad.
1w-1s	• Brown wash over prim and tail-feathers, contrasting with glossy black body-feathers and lesser cov.
	• Central tail-feathers narrower and slightly more pointed than in ad.
fl all plum	• Relatively pointed wing-tips.

geog var	*C.m. spermologus* (southern and western Europe)
ad	• Rear-head and hind-neck almost uniform greyish (no hint of paler band through neck-side).
	• Underparts and upperparts dark, hardly contrasting with wings ⇔ *monedula*.
	• Slightly heavier bill than *monedula* and *soemmerringii*.

geog var	*C.m. monedula* (Scandinavia and eastern Europe)
ad	• Paler rear-head and hind-neck than *spermologus* and variable pale grey band through neck-side. • Mantle, scaps and especially underparts slightly paler grey than in *spermologus* due to faint paler feather-fringes, contrasting with deep black crown, throat and wings.
geog var	*C.m. soemmerringii* (from eastern Europe eastwards)
ad	• Even paler rear-head and hind-neck than in *monedula* and distinct whitish band through neck-side broadening on hind-neck. • Upperparts and underparts as on *spermologus*, darker than in *monedula*.
note geog var	• Large overlap zones between all three subspecies with ind showing intermediate features.

Daurian Jackdaw *Corvus dauuricus* L 34cm 13.5

all plum	• Completely dark eye ⇔ Western Jackdaw ad. • Structure like Western.
ad	• Cream-white underparts (except breast, throat and undertail-cov) and neck-side extending through neck (superficially as in Hooded Crow but mantle black).
1w/1s ⇒	• Completely dark plumage (⇔ ad), *deep black throat* contrasts with rest of plumage. • *Fine pale streaks on ear-coverts* variable with age, from completely absent in young ind in autumn to distinctly streaked later in winter. • Weak ad pattern (dark grey rather than cream-white) shows through in some 1s. • For general features for 1w, see Western 1w.
note	• Juv plumage (shortly worn) remarkable in being quite similar to ad but pale parts darker cream-coloured and dark parts brownish to dark grey. Juv very unlikely in WP.

House Crow *Corvus splendens* L 43cm 17

all plum	• Relatively small head with long heavy bill. • Rather long tail-projection beyond wing-tips. • Pale grey(brown) neck-side, gradually merging towards breast, contrasting with black throat and central part of breast. • Underparts variable but usually distinctly paler than upperparts. • Slightly smaller than Carrion Crow but distinctly larger than Western Jackdaw.
fl all plum	• Somewhat rolling flight; wings narrowing at base.

Rook *Corvus frugilegus* L 45cm 17.5

all plum	• Rather evenly and faintly curved culmen towards tip (important in imm) ⇔ Carrion Crow all plum. • Long frayed thigh-feathering. • Groove along cutting edge of upper- and lower mandible broad at base, but strongly narrowing from middle towards bill-tip (important in imm) ⇔ in Carrion Crow evenly broad over whole length. • Tip of p2 falls between tip of p5 and p6 ⇔ in Carrion Crow between tip of p6 and p7. • Steep forehead, angular crown.
imm	• Still no distinct pale bare bill-base well into 2cy. • Brown wash over prim and tail-feathers ⇔ ad. • Gape-line visible ⇔ in Carrion Crow covered by feathering. • Bill-feathering to almost halfway on culmen (similar to Carrion Crow).
fl all plum	• Somewhat wedge-shaped tail ⇔ Carrion Crow flight all plum.

Carrion Crow *Corvus corone* L 47cm 18.5

all plum	• Plain black all over. • Stumpy bill ⇔ Rook. • Square tail ⇔ Rook. • Bill-feathering to halfway on culmen ⇔ Common Raven.
1w-1s	• See Western Jackdaw 1w-1s.

Hooded Crow *Corvus cornix* L 48cm 19

all plum	• Structure like Carrion Crow.
ad	• Black head, breast, wings and tail. • Hind-neck, mantle, back and scaps grey; underparts grey except breast.
juv	• Like ad but grey underparts and upperparts with brown wash; lesser cov and median cov dark grey instead of black.
1w-1s	• Brown wash over flight-feathers.
geog var	*C.c. sharpii* (south-eastern Europe)
all plum	• Like *cornix* but slightly smaller with smaller bill and grey parts generally slightly paler. In Cyprus and Middle East even smaller and paler, often regarded as separated subspecies (*pallescens*).
note	• Hybridises over small area with Carrion (e.g. Dutch Wadden Islands). Pale hybrids resemble Hooded bu especially vent, undertail-cov and uppertail-cov darker. Dark hybrids often show paler grey neck and mantle and variable dark grey underparts.

Pied Crow *Corvus albus* L 46cm 1

all plum	• Relatively long bill.
ad	• White upper-breast and belly connected with white band over mantle; pattern resembles Daurian Jackdaw but white not extending to hind-neck.

fl ad	• Size as Carrion Crow. • Rather long rounded tail.

Brown-necked Raven *Corvus ruficollis* L 52cm 20.5"

all plum	• More slender bill than in Common Raven. • Slightly smaller than Common. • Tail projects obviously beyond wing-tips ⇔ in Common wing- and tail-tip almost level. • More slender head due to less rough beard than in Common. • Bill-feathering less prominent than in Common. • Brown neck and mantle (also often in Carrion Crow juv).
1w-1s	• Brown wash over flight-feathers.
1 all plum ⇒	• Underside of flight-feathers relatively pale, contrasting with black underwing-cov. • More slender head and neck than in Common. • Tail less diamond-shaped but central tail-feathers often protrude slightly.
behav	• In flight regularly holds bill slightly downwards ⇔ Common.
note	• Brown neck and mantle difficult to see and Common with wear or bleaching can also show brownish hind-neck.

Common Raven *Corvus corax* L 60cm 23.5"

all plum	• Obviously larger than Carrion Crow. • Very heavy, deep bill; bill-feathering extending clearly beyond basal half of culmen ⇔ Carrion Crow. • Long throat-feathers somewhat hanging down.
1w-1s	• See Western Jackdaw 1w-1s.
1 all plum	• Relatively long wedge-shaped tail. • Protruding head. • Relatively narrow hand compared to arm.
note	• For more features see Brown-necked Raven.
geog var	*C.c. tingitanus* (Canary Islands and North Africa)
all plum ad	• Small with relatively short tail (no tail-projection). • Less purple gloss than other taxa but more oily blue-green.

Fan-tailed Raven *Corvus rhipidurus* L 49cm 19"

all plum	• Heavy bill like Common Raven, heavier than in Brown-necked Raven. • Obvious wing-projection beyond tail. • Only slightly larger than Carrion Crow.
1w-1s	• Brown wash over flight-feathers.
1 all plum	• Extremely broad wings and short tail creating characteristic flight-silhouette.

Kinglets

Ruby-crowned Kinglet *Regulus calendula* L 10.5cm 14.1"

all plum	• Like Goldcrest but uniform head without streaks and greyer upperparts. • Eye-ring strongly thickened in front of and behind eye, disappearing above and below eye. • Dark base of sec narrower than in Goldcrest and evenly broad. • More conspicuous green fringes to sec, prim and tail-feathers than in Goldcrest.
ad ♂	• Red crown-patch ⇔ imm/ad ♀.

Goldcrest *Regulus regulus* L 9cm 3.5"

all plum	• No eye-stripe but broad pale eye-ring; eye very conspicuous. • Brown-green upperparts; almost uniform dirty grey-brown underparts ⇔ *Phylloscopus* warblers. • Narrow moustachial-stripe (like elongated gape-line). • 'V'-shaped wing-bar exaggerated by pale base of prim. • 'Shadow' below wing-bar over greater cov (dark base of sec) broader and darker than in Yellow-browed Warbler.
ad	• Black lateral crown-stripe.
ad ♂/1w ♂	• Median crown-stripe mix of yellow and orange (orange sometimes difficult to see).
ad ♀/1w ♀	• Yellow median crown-stripe.
juv	• Uniform greyish head; no median- or lateral crown-stripe. • Pale bill ⇔ in ad dark.
1w-1s	• Pointed tail-feathers ⇔ in ad rounded. • In 1s old prim without green edges.

Azores Kinglet *Regulus azoricus* L 9cm 3.5"

geog var	*R.a. azoricus* (Sao Miguel, Azores)
all plum	• Resembles Goldcrest but upperparts darker green.
geog var	*R.a. inermis* (western Azores)
all plum	• Underparts darker than in *azoricus*.
geog var	*R.a. sanctaemariae* (Santa Maria, Azores)
all plum	• Much paler than other races, upperparts pale yellow-green, underparts whitish.

Canary Islands Kinglet *Regulus teneriffae*   L 9.5cm 3.7"

ad	⇒	• Black lateral crown-stripe on forehead connected, as in Firecrest ⇔ Goldcrest.

- Black lateral crown-stripe on forehead connected, as in Firecrest ⇔ Goldcrest.
- Longer bill than Goldcrest and Firecrest.
- Tertials with pale fringes around tips, not obviously thickened ⇔ in Goldcrest pale spots on tips of tertials.
- Short wings resulting in short prim-projection.
- Underparts somewhat rufous.
- No eye-stripe and no supercilium, as in Goldcrest.
- Wing-pattern as in Firecrest.

Firecrest *Regulus ignicapilla*   L 9.5cm 3.7"

all plum	⇒	• Broad white supercilium and black mask ⇔ Goldcrest.
	⇒	• Bronze-coloured neck-side and moss-green upperparts ⇔ Goldcrest.
		• Wing-pattern as in Goldcrest but dark patch at base of sec smaller.
ad		• Black lateral crown-stripe on forehead connected ⇔ Goldcrest.
ad ♂/1w ♂		• Median crown-stripe bright orange (sometimes with some yellow).
ad ♀/1w ♀		• Median crown-stripe orange-yellow, sometimes deeper orange. Difference with ♂ small but orange less bright.
juv		• Greyish head-side with rather faint to distinct broad supercilium, but dark mask ⇔ *Phylloscopus* warblers.
		• Pale bill.
1w-1s		• See Goldcrest 1w-1s.
note juv		• Some juv with obvious supercilium surprisingly similar to Yellow-browed Warbler but head-pattern differs with dark mask, dark moustachial-stripe and pale spot below eye; dark base on sec broader than in Yellow-browed Warbler.

Madeira Firecrest *Regulus madeirensis*   L 9.5cm 3.7"

ad		• Longer bill than in Goldcrest and Firecrest.

- Longer bill than in Goldcrest and Firecrest.
- More black in wing; greater cov largely black and broad dark 'shadow' under wing-bar (dark base of sec).
- Short supercilium, hardly extending behind eye; more grey on rear of head-side than in Firecrest.

Penduline tits

Penduline Tit *Remiz pendulinus*   L 11cm 4.3"

all plum	⇒	• Very pointed bill.
		• Pale brown to grey fringes to sec, prim and tertials creating large pale wing-panel.
ad		• Deep red-brown mantle, scaps and cov.
		• Rufous band above black mask (often absent in western populations).
ad ♂		• Large black mask, extending broadly over forehead (in 1w-1s ♂ slightly smaller) ⇔ in ad ♀ smaller and narrower mask, only extending narrowly over forehead.
		• Rufous spots on underparts creating form of breast-band (often absent in western populations).
juv		• Uniform greyish head.
		• Red-brown greater cov and median cov contrast with paler upperparts and rest of wing.
		• Uniform grey-white underparts.
		• Yellow bill, becoming darker later.
1w		• Like ad but prim more worn and often moult-limit in greater cov and tail-feathers (or tail-feathers actively moulting).
		• (Rear-)crown cream-coloured, hardly contrasting with brown mantle ⇔ in ad, especially ♂, grey rear crown contrasting distinctly with mantle.
1s		• Some ind with variable number of retained juv prim and greater cov (see 1w); others resemble ad (ind from southern populations normally undergo complete post-juv moult).

geog var		*R.p. macronyx* (central Asia)
ad	⇒	• Completely blackish head, like helmet.

geog var		*R.p. coronatus* (central and eastern Asia)
ad		• Black mask connected with black rear-head; often only pale spot on fore-crown.

geog var		*R.p. caspius* (western Asia)
ad	⇒	• Rufous forehead and crown(sides), sometimes extending to mantle.
		• Broad pale fringes to tertials, sec and tail-feathers.

Tits

Tenerife Blue Tit *Cyanistes teneriffae*   L 11cm 4.3"

ad		• No wing-bar.
		• Almost black eye-stripe and crown; narrow supercilium.
		• Broad black line through hind-neck and along throat.
		• Thick bill.
note		• Endemic to Tenerife and La Gomera.

Gran Canaria Blue Tit *Cyanistes hedwigii* L 11cm 4.3"

ad	• Like Tenerife Blue Tit but with very broad eye-stripe and line through hind-neck and along throat.
	• Broad supercilium.
	• Very thick bill.
note	• Endemic to Gran Canaria.

Palma Blue Tit *Cyanistes palmensis* L 11cm 4.3"

ad	• Central part of underparts whitish.
	• Upperparts blue-grey, sometimes with green wash.
	• Narrow wing-bar and small pale tips to tertials.
	• Narrow dark belly-stripe.
	• Relatively long tarsus.
note	• Endemic to La Palma.

Hierro Blue Tit *Cyanistes ombriosus* L 11cm 4.3"

ad	• Mantle grey to grey-green. Scaps grey-green.
	• Underparts deep green-yellow.
	• Only faint wing-bar, sometimes completely lacking as in Tenerife Blue Tit.
	• Obvious dark belly-stripe.
	• Relatively long tarsus.
note	• Endemic to Hierro.

Ultramarine Blue Tit *Cyanistes ultramarinus* L 11cm 4.3"

ad	• Dark blue upperparts.
	• Dark blue to blackish crown.
	• Dark belly-stripe faint to distinct.
	• Distinct wing-bars and pale tertial-tips.
	• Underparts deep yellow.
note	• Found in north-west Africa and on Fuerteventura and Lanzarote; birds on the Canary Islands have a thicker bill.

European Blue Tit *Cyanistes caeruleus* L 11.5cm 4.5"

ad	⇒	• Well-patterned head with blue crown, long eye-stripe, long supercilium and white ear-coverts and cheeks.
		• Greenish upperparts.
		• One wing-bar; pale tips to tertials.
		• Blue tail without white sides.
		• Dull yellow underparts.
1w-1s		• Prim and prim-cov still juv, in 2cy worn, often moult-limit in cov and sometimes in tail.
ad ♂		• Broad dark collar ⇔ in ad ♀ slightly smaller. Much overlap, only useful in extremes.
		• Vivid-blue wings and crown ⇔ in ad ♀ slightly duller blue.
juv		• Yellow wash on ear-coverts.

Azure Tit *Cyanistes cyanus* L 12.5cm 4.9"

ad	⇒	• Almost completely white greater cov creating broad wing-bar.
		• Completely white crown.
		• Long dark blue tail with large white corners and edges.
		• Large white tips to tertials and sec.
		• Underparts completely white.
		• Upperparts grey-blue.
1w-1s		• See European Blue Tit.
note		• Hybrid Azure x European Blue ('Pleske's Tit') sometimes rather similar to Azure but with less white in tail, usually yellow wash on part of underparts and no pure white crown. Hybridises in south of range with Yellow-breasted Tit *C. flavipectus,* producing offspring identical to 'Pleske's Tit'.

Great Tit *Parus major* L 14cm 5.5"

all plum	• White sides to tail.
	• One wing-bar ⇔ Coal Tit.
ad	• White rear-side of head/ear-coverts.
	• Black crown.
ad ♂	• Broad black band along central part of whole underparts (especially broad between legs) ⇔ ad ♀.
	• Broad black band through neck-side ⇔ in ad ♀ smaller.
ad ♀	• Narrow black band along central part of underparts reaching down to legs.
juv	• Duller coloured than ad.
	• Yellowish ear-coverts.
1w-1s	• See European Blue Tit.

Crested Tit *Lophophanes cristatus* L 11.5cm 4.5"

all plum	• Black and white spotted crown, extending into pointed crest on rear-head (in juv shorter, more rounded crest).
	• Upperparts, wings and tail uniform brown.
	• White head with well-defined black patterning; black throat-patch, eye-stripe and rear-edge of ear-coverts.
	• Underparts pale with warm-brown wash on flanks, vent and undertail-cov.
1w-1s	• See European Blue Tit.

Coal Tit *Periparus ater*   L 10.5cm 4.1

ad	⇒	• 2 whitish wing-bars ⇔ in Great Tit one, only over greater cov.
	⇒	• White nape-patch.
		• Greyish upperparts.
		• Dirty grey-brown underparts.
		• Large white spot on ear-coverts.
		• Black crown.
		• Relatively large head.
1w-1s		• See European Blue Tit.

geog var	*P.a. britannicus* (Britain and Iberia)
ad	• Brown-grey upperparts.

geog var	*P.a. hibernicus* (Ireland)
ad	• When fresh has pale yellow central underparts and ear-coverts.
	• Upperparts with olive tinge.

geog var	*P.a. ledouci* (Algeria and Tunisia)
ad	• Yellowish underparts and ear-coverts.
	• Greenish upperparts.

geog var	*P.a. cypriotes* (Cyprus)
ad	• Much black on head, reaching to mantle and upper part of breast. Relatively small white patches on nape and on sides of head.
	• Upperparts earth-brown to green-brown.
	• Underparts from cream-brown on breast to deep warm-brown on undertail-cov.
	• Median cov with pale brown tips.

Sombre Tit *Poecile lugubris*   L 13.5cm 5.3

ad	⇒	• White on head-side rather narrow, like *sharp triangle*.
		• Black cap extending to below eye and straight-bordered with white ear-coverts.
		• Large black throat-patch, sharply demarcated from pale breast.
		• Rather long tail.
		• Grey brown upperparts.
		• Dirty-white underparts (no brown wash on flanks).
1w-1s		• See European Blue Tit.

geog var	*P.l. anatoliae* (Turkey and Middle East)
all plum	• Grey upperparts.

Willow Tit *Poecile montana*   L 12.5cm 4.9

ad	⇒	• Pale wing-panel due to broad pale fringes along sec and tertials ⇔ in Marsh Tit poorly developed at most.
		• White ear-coverts extending far towards rear ⇔ Marsh.
		• Black bill with at most weak pale cutting edge ⇔ Marsh.
		• Slightly rounded tail with t6 rather obviously shorter than rest of tail-feathers ⇔ Marsh (only useful in extreme examples due to overlap).
		• Throat-patch relatively large and ill-defined ⇔ Marsh (only useful in extreme examples due to overlap).
1w-1s		• See European Blue Tit.
voice	⇒	• Song: a series of descending whistling notes, 'dju, dju, dju' ⇔ Marsh.
		• Call: typically sounds like 'zi zi daah daah daah', later notes drawn-out and very nasal ⇔ Marsh.

geog var	*P.m. borealis* (northern Europe)
ad	• Greyish upperparts.
	• Very pale underparts with only weak brown-grey wash on flanks.
	• Small black bib.

geog var	*P.m. kleinschmidti* (Britain)
ad	• Upperparts browner than in *rhenana* (western Europe).
	• Rufous-brown flanks but less pinkish than in *rhenana*.

geog var	*P.m. montana* (Alps)
ad	⇒	• Flanks pink-brown.
		• Larger than other subspecies with slightly shorter tail.

Marsh Tit *Poecile palustris*   L 12cm 4.

ad	• Pale spot at base of upper mandible, just above cutting edge ⇔ in Willow Tit none. Both species sometimes with pale cutting edges.
	• Pale area below cap divided between rather well-defined faint brown neck-side (extending up from breast-sides) and whitish ear-coverts ⇔ in Willow both ear-coverts and neck-side whitish. Sometimes neck-side very weakly and diffuse brown-grey towards rear.

- Normally rather uniformly brown wings, but sometimes narrow pale fringes to sec and tertials, rarely creating wing panel ⇔ Willow Tit.
  - t6 often just slightly shorter than other tail-feathers ⇔ Willow (see Willow account).
  - Throat-patch small and well defined ⇔ Willow (see Willow account).

w-1s
- See European Blue Tit.

voice ⇒
- Song: rather variable but often fast rattle. Sometimes reminiscent to song of Western Bonelli's Warbler.
- Call: typically includes sharp 'pit-chou' (quick and steep falling in pitch), often 'pit-chou dee-dee-dee-dee', latter much faster and less nasal than in Willow.

Siberian Tit *Poecile cinctus*   L 13.5cm 5.3"

ad ⇒
- Dark grey-brown cap with diffuse dark eye-stripe (mask).
- Rufous-brown upperparts.
- Orange-brown flanks.
- Large pale grey wing-panel over sec.
- Rather large throat-patch (larger than in Willow Tit) merging patchily into pale breast.
- Rather long tail.

w-1s
- See European Blue Tit.

Parrotbills

Bearded Tit *Panurus biarmicus*   L 14.5cm 5.7"

all plum
- Long, strongly rounded, mainly brown tail.
- White outer webs to prim and prim-cov (prim-cov black in 1w) creating broad white band over closed wing.

ad ♂
- Grey-blue head with long vertical malar stripe ⇔ ♀/1w.
- Black undertail-cov.

ad ♀
- Combination of dull yellowish bill and pale lores ⇔ in ♂ bright yellow-orange bill.
- Brown head with greyish head-side and throat.

1w ♂
- Black mantle and back.
- Pale bill (like ad); black loral-stripe.

1w ♀
- Dark bill; black loral-stripe.

Larks

Juvenile larks

nearly all species juv moult completely into adult plumage shortly after fledging. Juv feathers in some species are either strongly patterned with pale fringes or tips and dark subterminal line; in other species almost no differences between adult and juv plumage.

Kordofan Bush-lark *Mirafra cordofanica*   L 15cm 5.9"

all plum ⇒
- Structure like Dunn's Lark but *head rectangular due to short crest on rear-head*.
- Pale bill with strongly curved culmen and straight lower mandible as in Dunn's but bill more slender.
- No prim-projection.

ad ⇒
- Upperparts nearly uniform *warm yellow-brown* with only faint dark streaking on mantle and scaps; faint pale fringes to tertials ⇔ Dunn's.
- 'Open face' without dark stripes; eye conspicuous.
- Faint supercilium and submoustachial-stripe.

Chestnut-headed Sparrow-lark *Eremopterix signatus*   L 11cm 4.3"

all plum
- Structure like Black-crowned Sparrow-lark.

ad ♂ ⇒
- Upperparts darker and more rufous-brown than in Black-crowned with pale fringes to mantle feathers and scaps ⇔ in Black-crowned almost uniform more brown-grey upperparts.
- Head-pattern resembles Black-crowned but dark parts mainly chestnut-brown not black (sometimes brownish in Black-crowned); forehead blackish, *centre of crown white* ⇔ Black-crowned.
- Only central part of underparts black; breast-sides and whole flanks broadly white.
- Cov and tertials with darker centres than in Black-crowned.

ad ♀
- Like Black-crowned ad ♀ but darker upperparts grey-brown; underparts greyish, diffuse dark streaks extending onto belly ⇔ in Black-crowned ad ♀ breast yellow-brown, remainder of underparts unpatterned white.

all plum ⇒
- Black underwing-cov contrast with paler underside of flight-feathers (as on Black-crowned).

Black-crowned Sparrow-lark *Eremopterix nigriceps*   L 12cm 4.7"

all plum
- Thick, pale grey-brown bill with curved culmen (and downwards-bowed cutting edge).
- No prim-projection.

ad ♂
- Pied plumage: black underparts in combination with grey brown upperparts; head black-and-white marked with large white spot on ear-coverts.

ad ♀/1w
- Upperparts almost uniform sandy-brown.
- Crown and ear-coverts faintly streaked.
- Slightly darker centres to median cov, greater cov and tertials creates slight contrast between closed wing and upperparts.
- Whitish underparts with faintly streaked breast.

all plum ⇒
- Black underwing-cov contrast with paler underside of flight-feathers (like Black Lark ♀).
- Black tail, except central tail-feathers (as on Dunn's Lark); tail looks dark when seen from below.

geog var	*E.n. nigriceps* (Cape Verde Islands)
ad ♂	• Rufous upperparts. • Large white patch on forehead. • Uniform grey hind-neck.
geog var	*E.n. albifrons* (North Africa)
ad ♂	• Like *nigriceps* but upperparts less deep rufous and patch on forehead slightly larger.
geog var	*E.n. melanauchen* (eastern Africa and Middle East)
ad ♂	• Upperparts rather dark grey-brown with mainly black hind-neck extending to mantle. • Patch on forehead relatively small.
ad ♀	• Slightly darker than *nigriceps* and *albifrons*.

Dunn's Lark *Eremalauda dunni* L 14.5cm 5.?

all plum ⇒	• Very short prim-projection (when fresh sometimes none). • Large pale bill with strongly curved culmen (in *dunni* smaller).
fl all plum ⇒	• Dark tail (except central tail-feathers) ⇔ other 'desert larks'; tail looks dark when seen from below, underside of closed tail pale with dark sides (and pale outer-edge).
geog var	*E.d. eremodites* (Middle East)
ad ⇒	• Faintly and diffusely streaked upperparts, neck, crown and (sometimes) breast ⇔ other 'desert larks' (almost) unstreaked. • Smaller than Desert Lark. • Rather strong head-pattern; broad pale eye-ring with dark lower border and distinct 'mascara-tear'.
fl all plum ⇒	• Dark tips to outer prim (as in Bar-tailed Lark).
geog var	*E.d. dunni* (Sahara)
all plum ad	• Considerably smaller than *eremodites* with slightly shorter bill. • Generally paler and more rufous than *eremodites*. • Head-pattern weak; pale eye-ring with only faint darker lower edge, lacks distinct 'mascara-tear' ⇔ *eremodites*. • Streaking on crown, hind-neck and upperparts red-brown, streaking often faint ⇔ in *eremodites* streaking dark brown and rather strong. • Feathers of upperparts with broad orange-brown fringes ⇔ in *eremodites* pinkish-grey. • Dark tips to outer prim less contrasting than in *eremodites*. Often little contrast with tertials ⇔ in *eremodites* obvious contrast.

Bar-tailed Lark *Ammomanes cinctura* L 13.5cm 5.

all plum ⇒	• *Small, rather stumpy pale bill* with only culmen slightly darker ⇔ Desert Lark. • Smaller and more compact than Desert. • Short prim-projection c.30% with 2-3 prim-tips beyond tertials.
ad	• Very dark visible prim-tips contrast strongly with orange tertials and rest of wing. • Grey-brown upperparts; rufous fringes to sec and tertials. • Underparts usually whiter than in Desert.
fl all plum ⇒	• Narrow and *well-defined black terminal tail-band*, also visible from below. • Dark tips to prim (more obvious on outer prim).

Desert Lark *Ammomanes deserti* L 16cm 6

all plum ⇒	• Yellow-orange lower mandible with dark tip; upper mandible largely dark ⇔ Bar-tailed Lark. • Heavy long bill. • Relatively long prim-projection c.50% with 3-4 prim-tips beyond tertials.
ad	• Uniform upperparts (sandy-coloured to very dark grey, see note geog var) and underparts. • Diffuse dark tertial-centres with rather broad, paler fringes ⇔ in Bar-tailed no conspicuous dark centres. • Visible prim-tips darker than rest of wing.
fl all plum ⇒	• Broad, dark, *diffuse* terminal tail-band. • Both upper- and underwing almost uniform, gradually becoming slightly darker on hand.
note geog var	• Occurs within relatively restricted area in multiple subspecies with mainly only very slight differences size, colour of underparts and upperparts and bill-structure. Colour of plumage always strongly related to colour of habitat. Identification in most cases very difficult. Below are some subspecies possibly recognisable in the field.
geog var	*A.d. payni* and *A.d. algeriensis* (north-western Africa)
ad	• Upperparts, crown, breast and flanks deep rufous-brown (*payni* slightly darker and greyer than *algeriensis* with darker, less rufous head and breast). • Long, slim bill. • Tail rufous at base (especially in *algeriensis*).
geog var	*A.d. deserti* (mainly Egypt and Sudan)
ad	• Upperparts grey-brown, contrasting with rufous rump and uppertail-cov.

jeog var   *A.d. isabellinus* (Egypt and Middle East east of Israel)
ad   • Upperparts sandy-coloured with rufous wash, hardly contrasting with rump and uppertail-cov.

eog var   *A.d. annae* (lava desert in Jordan)
ad ⇒   • Upperparts and underparts mainly black-brown.
     • Throat and undertail-cov slightly paler.
     • Faint rufous rump and uppertail-cov.

oopoe Lark *Alaemon alaudipes*   L 21cm 8.5"

ll plum   • Large size with long downcurved bill.
     • Long legs and tail.
     • Black eye- and moustachial-stripe.
     • Breast diffusely streaked; rest of underparts uniform white.
     • Upperparts brown-grey to rufous (latter in rufous subspecies, e.g. *boavistae* of Cape Verde Islands).
all plum   • Very characteristic pattern with broad white wing-bar, black hand and white trailing edge of wing. White underwing-cov contrast strongly with black hand.
ehav   • Walks and runs over long distances.

upont's Lark *Chersophilus duponti*   L 17.5cm 6.9"

ll plum ⇒   • Rather long, slender bill with evenly downcurved culmen (lower mandible also slightly downcurved).
d ⇒   • Feathers of upperparts with dark centres and well-defined pale fringes, creating strongly scaled impression ⇔ Crested Lark.
     • Supercilium and (pale) median crown-stripe rather distinct; dark lateral crown-stripe.
     • Breast broadly marked with fine well-defined streaks.
all plum   • White outer-side of tail; no white in wing.

eog var   *C.d. margaritae* (North Africa, except in the north-west where *duponti* occurs)
d   • Like *duponti* but (dark) brown replaced by somewhat rufous yellow-brown.
     • Bill longer than in *duponti*.

hick-billed Lark *Ramphocoris clotbey*   L 17.5cm 6.9"

l plum ⇒   • Very heavy pale grey to pinkish bill.
     • Long prim-projection c.100%.
     • Legs grey.
d   • Faint rufous lesser cov; dark centres to median cov and greater cov.
     • Brown-grey upperparts, hind-neck and crown.
d ♂ ⇒   • Underparts strongly patterned with *large black spots* on white background.
     • Black head-side with white spot on ear-coverts and broad white eye-ring.
d ♀   • Faintly patterned head-side with dark loral-stripe and ill-defined pale spot on ear-coverts.
     • Variable amount of black spots on white underparts (spots smaller than in ad ♂).
all plum ⇒   • *Broad white trailing edge of wing* (broadest at corner of flight-feathers, strongly narrowing on outer prim).
     • Blackish bases to flight-feathers, on underwing creating broad dark band.

alandra Lark *Melanocorypha calandra*   L 19cm 7.5"

l plum   • Tail-projection beyond wing-tips ≥ 40% of prim-projection.
     • Long prim-projection, longer than in Bimaculated Lark with 4 prim-tips beyond tertials.
     • Rather ill-defined head-pattern (but sometimes as well-defined as in Bimaculated).
d ⇒   • Large black spots on side of breast and at least some streaks on breast-sides; extensive streaks on breast diagnostic difference with Bimaculated.
all plum   • Very dark underwing.
     • Broad white trailing edge along sec, smaller along inner prim.
     • White tail-side (e.g. t6 completely white).
     • Upperwing with strong contrast between pale cov and blackish flight-feathers.
     • Rather broad, angular wing-tips.
ote   • See Bimaculated for more features.

maculated Lark *Melanocorypha bimaculata*   L 17.5cm 6.9"

l plum ⇒   • Very short tail-projection beyond wing-tips (about 1cm); < 50% of prim-projection.
     • Long prim-projection c.80% with 3-4 prim-tips beyond tertials.
     • Bill length/height-ratio larger than in Calandra Lark.
     • Pale bill with usually well-defined dark culmen (sometimes also in Calandra) ⇔ in Calandra dark culmen usually ill-defined.
     • Culmen curves strongly towards bill-tip ⇔ in Calandra more evenly curved.
     • Black patch on breast-sides rather narrow and usually creating complete horizontal breast-stripe ⇔ in Calandra usually broader patch on breast-sides, not connecting on centre of breast.
     • Long white supercilium very distinctive and reaches to end of ear-coverts ⇔ in Calandra less obvious but still distinct and slightly shorter.
     • Little or no breast(-side) streaking ⇔ Calandra.
     • White half eye-ring (under eye) with well-defined dark border with ear-coverts below that ⇔ in Calandra more ill-defined pattern.
     • Rather narrow, well-defined loral-stripe ⇔ in Calandra often fainter.
     • Mantle feathers and scaps often sharply streaked with black shaft-streaks and pale inner webs; feathers of upperparts almost as strongly patterned as greater cov and median cov ⇔ in Calandra

	mantle and scaps often less strongly streaked.
	• Rather well-defined, usually rufous-brown ear-coverts.
	• Hind-neck often slightly paler than mantle and crown ⇔ in Calandra no colour difference.
fl all plum ⇒	• White terminal band on short tail (not on t1).
	• No white trailing edge of arm.
	• Underwing-cov uniform brown, not blackish as on Calandra (but underside of flight-feathers blackish, forming some contrast on underwing ⇔ Calandra).
	• Less contrasting upperwing ⇔ in Calandra contrast between dark flight-feathers and paler cov.

White-winged Lark *Melanocorypha leucoptera*   L 18cm 7.1

ad ⇒	• Brown-orange lesser cov and prim-cov creating broad coloured wing-bend. In ad ♂ more obvious tha in ad ♀.
	• Pale grey bill.
	• Streaked breast and flanks; rest of underparts white.
	• Broad white surround of eye; eye conspicuous.
	• Long prim-projection c.100%.
	• Rufous uppertail-cov.
ad ♂	• Brown-orange crown and ear-coverts.
ad ♀	• Grey-brown dark streaked crown.
fl all plum ⇒	• Very broad white trailing edge of arm and inner hand. Sec almost completely white.
⇒	• Black base of sec and black hand creating conspicuous black band on white underwing.
	• Broad white sides of tail.
note	• Mongolian Lark *M. mongolica* (recorded as escape in the Netherlands) resembles White-winged but with large black breast-patch, black prim-cov, long supercilium to hind-neck and more uniformly patterned with larger uniform rufous and white parts.

Black Lark *Melanocorypha yeltoniensis*   L 19.5cm 7.

all plum ⇒	• Thickset and large; size almost as Common Starling.
	• Legs grey to black (in juv sometimes dark grey-brown) ⇔ in other large larks paler.
	• Long prim-projection c.100%.
	• Bill pale grey.
ad ♂ s	• Dull black; upperparts with variable amount of white scales (pale fringes to mantle feathers and scaps see note) and *conspicuous pale bill*.
ad ♀	• Heavy, somewhat triangular patterning on breast creating faint breast-band in fresh autumn plumage. In spring often creating large patch on breast-sides like in Bimaculated Lark and Calandra Lark.
	• Rump and upperparts grey-brown and rather strongly patterned (colour of upperparts dependent on wear, see note).
	• White outer web on all prim and at least t6.
	• Brown patterning on dark tertial-centres; broad pale fringes to tertials, greater cov and median cov (worn away from spring onwards).
	• Whitish belly; flanks with some dark spotting.
fl ad ♀ ⇒	• Black underwing-cov contrast with paler flight-feathers and whitish underparts.
	• Paler rump contrasts slightly with dark tail.
note	• Broad pale feather-fringes wearing off towards summer when ad ♂ becomes almost entirely black a ad ♀ noticeably darker than in fresh yellow-brown autumn plumage.

Greater Short-toed Lark *Calandrella brachydactyla*   L 15cm 5.

all plum ⇒	• No or very short prim-projection.
⇒	• Underparts pale; variable patterning on breast-sides.
	• Broad, long supercilium.
	• Median cov with large dark centres creating dark wing-bar, strongly contrasting with pale lesser cov (when visible) ⇔ in Lesser Short-toed Lark smaller dark centres, less strong contrast.
	• Pointed pale bill.
	• Usually rufous crown (mainly in European *brachydactyla*, sometimes in other subspecies).
	• 2 conspicuous dark bands over scaps (less so or absent in *longipennis*, see geog var).
	• Narrow but swell-defined (dark) eye-stripe behind eye.
	• Almost uniform ear-coverts ⇔ in Lesser Short-toed streaked.
	• 'Mascara-tear' ill-defined or absent ⇔ Skylark.
ad ♂	• Conspicuous dark spot on neck-side extending to breast-sides.
fl all plum	• No white trailing edge of wing ⇔ Skylark.
	• Pale lesser cov creating pale wing-bend.
voice	• Call: rather low-pitched and dry rolling 'drrit' or 'drut-drut'.

geog var	*C.b. longipennis* (Asia)
all plum	• Sandy-coloured upperparts with narrow streaks on mantle and scaps (narrower than in *brachydactyl.*).
	• Bill smaller than in *brachydactyla*.
	• Crown concolorous with upperparts.
note geog var	• Identification of *longipennis* and other even more subtle subspecies complicated by large individual variation within every subspecies.

Hume's Short-toed Lark *Calandrella acutirostris*   L 14cm 5.

ad	• Bill pointed and generally 10% longer than in Greater Short-toed Lark.
	• Longest 4 prim (p2-p5) all of about same length ⇔ in Greater 3 longest prim (p2-p4) of same length p5 much shorter.

- Little white on outer tail-feathers, only outer web and tip of t6 white; underside of closed tail does not look entirely white ⇔ in Greater t6 almost white; underside of tail completely white.
- Long yellow-brown bill with distinct dark culmen and tip ⇔ in Greater bill shorter and more pinkish without obvious dark culmen and bill-tip.
- Head-pattern fainter than in Greater with only faintly streaked crown, eye-stripe almost absent, supercilium less obvious between eye and bill but loral-stripe slightly more distinct than in Greater.
- Some contrast between grey mantle and rufous rump and uppertail-cov.
- Cream-coloured wash over whole breast; rest of underparts and throat pure white ⇔ in Greater usually only cream-coloured wash on breast-sides.
- Centre of median cov less contrasting than in Greater.

voice ⇒ • Call: less dry and especially longer and more rolling than in Greater. Also a very diferrent almost whistling 'piweep'.

esser Short-toed Lark *Calandrella rufescens*   L 14cm 5.5"

all plum ⇒ • Prim-projection c.40% with 3-4 prim-tips visible beyond tertials.
- Thick, usually rather stumpy bill.

ad ⇒ • Variable breast pattern (individual and geographical) but usually *complete and broad band of evenly fine stripes*.
- Fine flank streaking within *cream-coloured band along flanks* (no flank streaking on white background) ⇔ Skylark and Greater Short-toed Lark (in Greater flank streaking often completely lacking).
- Median cov with dark centres but normally restricted to broad shaft-streak and not strongly contrasting with rest of wing ⇔ in Greater strongly contrasting dark median cov.
- Streaked ear-coverts and finely streaked crown creates rather stripy head ⇔ Short-toed.
- Indistinct supercilium (in western forms more obvious).
- Upperparts heavily streaked, similar to Skylark.
- Smaller than Skylark but large overlap in size with Greater.

all plum • No pale trailing edge of arm (as on Greater ⇔ Skylark).
oice • Call: dry, drawn-out 'drrrrt', drier and longer rolling than call of Greater, at end almost bouncing.

sian Short-toed Lark *Calandrella cheleensis*   L 14cm 5.5"

ll plum • Very like Lesser Short-toed Lark, but generally larger and paler.
- More white in tail than Lesser (t6 almost completely white).
- Paler and slightly thicker bill than Lesser.
- Ear-coverts often at most very slightly streaked ⇔ Lesser.

eog var *C.c. niethammeri* (Turkey)

d • Sandy to cream-coloured upperparts.
- Streaking on mantle and scaps very narrow and well-defined.
- Streaking on breast narrower and sometimes slightly more diffuse than in Lesser.

eog var *C.c. persica* (southern Iran, winters in Arabia and possibly Israel)

l plum • Slightly more rufous than *niethammeri* with usually pink wash on rump.
ote geog var • True taxonomic status of the different subspecies within the Lesser Short-toed Lark complex is still unclear.
- Features mentioned under *niethammeri* ad probably also apply to taxa outside WP.

ested Lark *Galerida cristata*   L 18cm 7.1"

l plum ⇒ • Long pointed crest ⇔ in Skylark shorter, more stumpy crest.
- Long, slightly downcurved pointed bill (but in most north-western populations bill shorter and almost straight) ⇔ Skylark.
- Short prim-projection about 20% ⇔ Skylark.
- Slightly rufous outer tail-feathers.

all plum • No white in wings.
- Rufous underwing-cov.
te • For differences with Thekla Lark, see below.
ote geog var • Occurs in numerous subspecies which differ mainly by colour of plumage and bill structure; due to large individual variation, field identification virtually impossible but northern populations have shorter bill.

aghreb Lark *Galerida macrorhyncha*   L 19cm 7.5"

plum ⇒ • Large size, *long bill* with deep base.
- Weakly streaked upperparts warm pale brown-yellow, sometimes with pinkish wash.
- Underparts cream-coloured with fine grey streaks on breast.

og var *G.m. randonii* (high altitudes of Algeria and Morocco)

plum • Breast heavily and darkly streaked ⇔ *macrorhyncha*.
- Upperparts more heavily streaked than in *macrorhyncha*.
- Bill longer than in *macrorhyncha* (longest bill in Crested Lark complex).
te • Patchy distributed throughout north-west Africa and overlapping with Crested but occupies drier areas, with *randonii* in Morocco especially along High Atlas and in south-east Morocco, and *macrorhyncha* south of *randonii* and in lower sandy desert-like areas up to Mauritania.

Thekla Lark *Galerida theklae*   L 16cm 6.3

all plum	⇒	• Short bill with both upper- and lower mandible curving towards tip; lower edge of lower mandible somewhat curved upwards but occasionally almost straight ⇔ in Crested Lark longer, sometimes very long bill with sometimes almost straight but usually downcurved lower mandible (but in most north-western populations bill shorter and lower edge of lower mandible almost straight).
ad		• Greyish rump contrasts with cinnamon-coloured uppertail-cov and outer tail-feathers ⇔ in Crested at most very slight colour contrast between rump and uppertail-cov.
		• Broad whitish eye-ring ⇔ in Crested more cream-coloured and therefore less conspicuous.
		• No prim-projection ⇔ in Crested often (very) short.
		• p1 often slightly longer than prim-cov (sometimes shorter) ⇔ in Crested always shorter.
		• Shorter, fuller and less pointed crest than Crested.
		• Whitish supercilium short and broad and does not reach far behind eye ⇔ in Crested cream-coloured long and narrow.
		• White area under ear-coverts sometimes creates band on neck-side, sometimes also in Crested but more diffuse.
		• Short, thick, well-defiined chequered breast streaks, often becoming more distinct towards sides ⇔ in Crested narrow, sometimes more diffuse streaking, more concentrated in centre.
		• Population of Iberian Peninsula often with conspicuously darker and more rufous-brown upperparts than Crested (in North Africa slightly paler and head-pattern less well marked).
		• Dark tertial-centres with rather well-defined pale fringes ⇔ in Crested paler tertial-centres with diffuser paler fringes.
		• Rather rufous outer tail-feathers ⇔ in Crested slightly less rufous pale brown (flight).
fl all plum		• Grey to sandy-coloured underwing-cov ⇔ in Crested rufous.
		• Outer tail-feathers more rufous than underwing-cov, in Crested the other way around.
behav		• Often perches in trees and bushes ⇔ Crested rarely.
geog var		*G.t. ruficolor* (Morocco; central and high Atlas and central western coastal plain)
all plum		• Feathers of upperparts with dark centres and contrasting pale grey-brown to normally rufous-brown fringes (generally paler, more rufous and more contrasting than *theklae*).
geog var		*G.t. carolinae* (Sahara margins of eastern Morocco, Algeria, Tunisia to Libya and possibly north-western Egypt)
all plum		• Upperparts mainly rufous to cinnamon, centres of feathers dark rufous.
		• Streaking on breast brown-rufous on almost white background.

Woodlark *Lullula arborea*   L 14.5cm 5.

all plum		• Slender bill.
		• Prim-projection c.50%.
		• Short tail.
		• Emarginations on outer webs of prim deeply cut in, sometimes conspicuous.
ad	⇒	• Very dark prim-cov and alula with *large pale tips* creating pied pale-dark pattern (also visible in flight)
	⇒	• Long supercilium connected on hind-neck.
		• Rufous-brown unstreaked ear-coverts completely pale-framed.
		• Finely streaked whitish breast, ill-defined extending to flanks.
fl all plum		• Rounded wings.
		• Pale tips to tail-feathers (except central pair).
		• t6 with diffuse, faint paler outer web and tip.
		• Pale central band over underwing-cov (pale greater cov).
		• Lacks pale trailing edge on wing.

Skylark *Alauda arvensis*   L 17cm 6

all plum	⇒	• Prim-projection ≥ 50% with relatively large distance between visible prim-tips ⇔ Crested Lark and Greater Short-toed Lark.
		• Slender and rather short bill.
		• Relatively long tail.
ad		• Finely spotted/streaked breast; streaking usually extending diffusely onto flanks.
		• Yellow-orange bill-base.
fl all plum		• Broad white trailing edge of wing along sec and inner prim (in juv somewhat pale brown and narrower trailing edge of wing than ad but by autumn as ad).
		• White outer tail-feathers.
		• Relatively narrow wings.

Oriental Skylark *Alauda gulgula*   L 15cm 5.

all plum	⇒	• Very short prim-projection but in spring often longer due to heavily worn tertials.
	⇒	• Slender long bill with more pointed tip than in Skylark (resembles Crested Lark).
ad	⇒	• Large, *uniformly pale loral area* ⇔ in Skylark usually narrow loral-stripe or dark spot on lores directly before eye.
		• When fresh, weak rufescent outer web of flight-feathers, forming indistinct rufous wing-panel.
		• Narrow breast streaks, at most faintly extending along flanks (but usually no flank streaks).
		• Broad supercilium extending rather far behind eye and ending in a point ⇔ Skylark.
		• Underparts usually completely cream to sandy-coloured ⇔ in Skylark white belly, vent and undertail-cov.
		• Usually (almost) uniform whitish throat ⇔ Skylark.
		• Rufous ear-coverts.

l all plum	• Diffuse rufous trailing edge along sec and inner prim. • Short tail and wings resembles Wood.
voice ⇒	• Call: rather loud, dry, buzzing and penetrating 'brreez', often repeated a few times.

aso Lark *Alauda razae*   L 12.5cm 4.9"

all plum	• No or short prim-projection when tertials worn, short tail with pale outer side. • Strong bill; legs relatively long and thick.
ad	• Upperparts heavily streaked on greyish ground-colour. • Only upper-breast and breast-sides finely streaked. • ♂ larger size with larger bill than ♀.
ote	• Endemic to Raso (Cape Verde Islands).

orned Lark *Eremophila alpestris*   L 17.5cm 6.9"

geog var	Shore Lark *E.a. flava* (northern Europe)
d	• Yellowish head with black lores and downcurved black bar on ear-coverts. • Black band over throat and upper-breast. • Grey-brown feathers of upperparts with narrow shaft-streaks. • Usually rather rufous rump.
d ♂ s	• Uniform rufous-brown to pink-brown crown and hind-neck. • Relatively long horns.
d ♀ s all plum	• Streaked dull brown crown and neck-side. • Pale underwing.
eog var	Atlas Horned Lark *E.a. altas* (Atlas mountains in Morocco)
d	• Conspicuous reddish-cinnamon crown and hind-neck contrasting with rather pale grey upperparts. • Broad black mask and breast-band; mask sometimes connected to breast-band by narrow line.
eog var	American Horned Lark *E.a. alpestris* (Arctic north-eastern Canada)
ll plum	• Slightly larger than *flava* with longer and especially more pointed bill. • Outer tail-feathers more pointed than in *flava*, resulting in slightly notched tail.
d	• Upperparts (including rump and uppertail-cov), median cov and lesser cov more uniform and more rufous than in *flava* ⇔ in *flava* contrast between rufous lesser cov and brown median cov. • Upperparts darker than in *flava* with heavier and darker streaking. • Breast below breast-band usually obviously streaked ⇔ *flava*. • Pale area on ear-coverts narrow (narrower than dark band on front side of ear-coverts) ⇔ in *flava* broader than dark band on front side of ear-coverts. • Contrast between rufous flanks and pure white belly ⇔ in *flava* less contrast. • Crown slightly darker than in *flava* due to extensive dark streaking. • Pale tips to median cov and greater cov smaller than in *flava*; wing-bars less distinct. • Yellow parts on head deeper yellow than in *flava*.
eog var	Caucasian Horned Lark *E.a. penicillata* (mountains of south-east Europe to Middle East)
d ⇒	• Black on ear-coverts broadly connected to broad breast-band ⇔ *alpestris* and *flava*. • Whitish throat and face. • Crown and hind-neck nearly concolorous with upperparts ⇔ in *alpestris* and *flava* crown and hind-neck more or less rufous.

mminck's Lark *Eremophila bilopha*   L 14.5cm 5.7"

d ⇒	• Rufous upperparts; tertials and cov often somewhat deeper coloured. • Black ear-coverts not connected to breast-band (as in Shore Lark *flava*). • No yellow on head ⇔ Shore.
v	• Almost uniformly rufous upperparts, head and breast (timing of post-juv moult very variable with this plumage sometimes retained longer than in most other larks; see 'Juvenile larks').

Swallows and martins

nded Martin *Riparia cincta*   L 15cm 16"

l plum ⇒	• Underparts white with dark breast-band; dark stripe over central part of belly connected with breast-band.
⇒	• Well-defined short white supercilium to above eye. • White throat sharply demarcated from dark head. • Much larger than Sand Martin.
all plum ⇒	• Long tail with rounded tail-corners; no tail-fork. • Pale underwing-cov.

own-throated Martin *Riparia paludicola*   L 12cm 4.7"

plum ⇒	• *Diffuse* sandy-brown throat and upper-breast; rest of underparts white ⇔ in Rock Martin and Crag Martin dark vent and undertail-cov.
all plum	• Dark underwing-cov contrast with paler flight-feathers (as also in Sand, Rock and Crag). • Very slightly forked tail. • Upperparts medium-brown with paler rump and uppertail-cov. • Relatively short wings.

193

Swallows and martins

Sand Martin *Riparia riparia*   L 13cm 5.1

all plum ⇒	• White underparts with broad brown breast-band.
	• Dark brown upperparts and wings.
	• Pale throat and neck-side.
juv-1w	• Throat and neck-side darker than in ad.
	• Pale fringes to cov and tertials.
fl all plum ⇒	• Very dark underwing-cov contrast slightly with underside of flight-feathers (as on Pale Sand Martin, Brown-throated Sand Martin, Rock Martin and Crag Martin) ⇔ House Martin and Barn Swallow.

Pale Sand Martin *Riparia diluta*   L 13cm 5.1

all plum	• Smaller size than Sand Martin.
ad	• Upperparts grey-brown to mouse-grey (paler than Sand, resembles Rock Martin).
	• Pale head in which dark eye and lores create slight mask ⇔ Sand.
	• Ear-coverts paler than in Sand, weakly bordered with white throat ⇔ in Sand sharp border between dark ear-coverts and white throat.
	• Breast-band usually narrow, more ill-defined and more grey-brown than in Sand. Centre paler and more weakly bordered at lower edge.
	• Rear-side of tarsus feathered over whole length ⇔ in Sand only at corner with rear toe.
	• Tail very slightly forked ⇔ in Sand slightly deeper fork.
juv	• Fringes to cov, tertials and undertail-cov variable but regularly rich rufous ⇔ in Sand also variable but rarely rufous.
fl all plum	• Underwing-cov paler than in Sand, not strongly contrasting with rest of underwing.
notes	• Sand *shelleyi* (Egypt) is, as Pale Sand, smaller than Sand *riparia* and paler grey-brown on upperparts (colour between Pale Sand and Sand); in *shelleyi* narrow but sharply demarcated breast-band.
	• Status in WP unclear.

Tree Swallow *Tachycineta bicolor*   L 14.5cm 5.

all plum	• Upperparts with extensive blue-green gloss, especially in ad ♂ ⇔ in House Martin weak purple-blue.
ad ♂	• Upperparts and head with strong blue-green gloss.
ad ♀	• Upperparts and head dark grey-brown with variable amount of blue-green gloss.
juv-1w	• Resembles Sand Martin but (darker) grey-brown and much weaker breast-band *narrower in middle*; breast-band sometimes absent.
fl all plum	• Slightly forked tail.
	• Broad triangular wings can recall Crag Martin.
	• Very dark underwing ⇔ House Martin.
	• Underwing more uniform than in Sand Martin, no obvious contrast between underwing-cov and underside of flight-feathers.
fl ad ⇒	• Resembles House Martin but with completely dark upperparts (no white rump).
moult	• Complete moult often almost finished before autumn migration ⇔ other swallows moult completely in winter range.

Purple Martin *Progne subis*   L 20cm

all plum	• Large size with large head and relatively strong bill (culmen strongly curved).
	• Slightly forked tail.
ad ♂	• Completely blackish with strong purple gloss.
ad ♀	• Undertail-cov with large dark centres.
	• Crown and upperparts with purple gloss.
1w/1s ♀/ad ♀	• Dirty white underparts with dark spots (breast slightly darker).
	• Upperparts and head dark brown with paler forehead and neck-side.
1w/1s ♀	• Dirty white underparts with fine longitudinal stripes.
	• Undertail-cov with narrow shaft-streaks ⇔ ad ♀.
1s ♂	• Like ad ♀ but stronger gloss on crown and variable amount of dark purple glossy feathers on head, upperparts and underparts.
1s ♀	• Like ad ♀ but browner on upperparts and undertail-cov with fine dark shaft-streaks.

Crag Martin *Ptynoprogne rupestris*   L 14.5cm 5.

all plum	• Larger and more thickset than Sand Martin.
ad	• Faint dark stripes on throat ⇔ in 1w and Rock Martin none.
juv-1w	• Well-defined pale fringes to cov and tertials.
	• Very few or no dark throat-stripes ⇔ ad.
1s	• Prim still juv and distinctly worn.
fl all plum ⇒	• Dark underwing-cov, diffusely bordered with paler belly.
	• Undertail-cov darker than rump.
	• Pale spots on t2-t5.
	• Dark underwing-cov and axillaries contrast with paler underside of flight-feathers and pale belly.
	• Broad arm creates triangular wing-shape.

Pale Crag Martin *Ptynoprogne obsoleta*   L 12.5cm 4

all plum ⇒	• Much paler and more obviously grey on upperparts than Crag Martin.
	• Smaller than Crag, hardly any larger than House Martin or Sand Martin.
	• Pale throat; no dark streaks on throat ⇔ Crag.
	• Broad pale tips to dark undertail-cov ⇔ in Crag much diffuser.
juv-1w	• Well-defined pale fringes to cov and tertials.
1s	• Prim still juv and distinctly worn.

194

all plum	• Underside with same contrast as in Crag but less strong (underwing-cov paler but always distinctly darker than belly and base of flight-feathers). • Smaller pale spots on tail than Crag, often difficult to see on upperside of tail. • Upperwing with some contrast between pale sec and slightly darker prim.
eog var	*P.o. presaharica* (southern Morocco and Algeria)
l plum	• Slightly larger than *obsoleta* (Middle East). • Underparts slightly darker than in *obsoleta* with obvious warm wash.

arn Swallow *Hirundo rustica*   L 18cm 7.1"

l plum	• Dark upperside. • Broad dark breast-band. • White to slightly cream-coloured underparts (*rustica*). • All tail-feathers with pale spots on central part (only visible on underside); in flight creates central tail-band.
d	• Dark red throat and forehead. • Strongly elongated outer tail-feathers (in ♂ ± 3x longer than inner tail-feathers; in ♀ ± 2x longer than inner tail-feathers).
v-1w	• Buff-coloured throat and forehead. • No or only faint pale fringes to feathers of upperparts and wings (but see *erythogaster*) ⇔ other swallows and martins juv. • Shallow forked tail (outer tail-feathers not strongly elongated) ⇔ ad.
all plum	• See Red-rumped Swallow.
eog var	*H.r. savignii* (Egypt)
plum d	• Smaller than *rustica*. • Underparts and underwing-cov are deep brown-orange (pale markings on tail are pale rufous to brown-orange).
eog var	American Barn Swallow *H.r. erythrogaster* (North America)
plum	• Red of breast continues into breast-band; only very narrow black-blue breast-band retained, often broken on middle of breast ⇔ *rustica*. • Dark patch on sides of vent larger than in *rustica*. • Underparts and underwing-cov orange (also in some *rustica* and nearly all *savignii* and *transitiva* but in these more brown than orange). • Outer tail-feathers (t6) shorter than in *rustica*.
v-1w te geog var	• Obvious cream-coloured fringes to cov ⇔ *rustica*. • Ind with darker rufous-brown to pink-brown underparts occur in all European populations, resembling *savignii* but often more like *transitiva* (Lebanon and Israel, integration zone in Balkans). Identification of *transitiva* in western Europe not possible at present.

hiopian Swallow *Hirundo aethiopica*   L 13cm 5.1"

plum ⇒	• Resembles Barn Swallow but smaller; underparts entirely white with narrow broken breast-band. • Tail relatively short; outer tail-feathers in ad only slightly elongated. • Rufous patch on forehead; cream-coloured throat.
ad	• White markings on tail as in Barn.

re-tailed Swallow *Hirundo smithii*   L 17.5cm 6.9"

plum	• Structure and size like Barn Swallow but elongated outer tail-feathers much longer in ad (when perched appear as long as prim-projection). • Upperparts dark with strong blue gloss. • Brown-red crown (in imm brown). • Underparts including throat white. Dark patches on rear-flanks and breast-sides.
all plum	• Blue gloss over whole upper wing ⇔ in Barn only over cov. • Much white on central part of tail.

use Martin *Delichon urbicum*   L 14.5cm 5.7"

⇒	• Black upperparts (with blue gloss) and upper wing and large white rump-patch. • Black cap sharply demarcated from white throat. • Completely white underparts.
-1w	• Pale underparts somewhat 'dirty', especially on flanks, throat and undertail-cov. • Pale tips to tertials, sec and prim. • Lacks blue gloss (see ad). • Somewhat paler ear-coverts.

d-rumped Swallow *Cecropis daurica*   L 17cm 6.7"

og var	*C.d. rufula* (southern Europe to western Asia)
plum ⇒ ⇒	• Pale cream-coloured underparts, except well-defined black undertail-cov and underside of tail ⇔ Barn Swallow. • Pale head-side exaggerates dark eye; dark crown. • Upperside with large rufous (or two-toned rufous/white) rump-patch and rufous collar (but see geog var). • Strongly elongated outer tail-feathers but generally shorter than in Barn.

juv-1w	• Faint streaked underparts on faint rufous ground-colour.
	• Head-side cream-brown ⇔ ad.
	• Pale tips to cov and tertials.
	• Wings browner than in ad.
fl all plum	• When foraging often long glides ⇔ Barn.
	• Rather pale underwing without strong contrast between pale underwing-cov and dark flight-feathers in Barn sharp border between pale underwing-cov and blackish flight-feathers.
	• In some ind pale spot on central part of t6 (especially in ♀).
fl juv	• Whitish rump and shorter tail than ad (can resemble House Martin).
geog var	*C.d. daurica* (central Asia)
all plum	• Slightly more deeply forked tail than *rufula*.
	• Slightly larger than *rufula*.
ad	• Underparts and neck-side completely finely dark streaked on whiter ground-colour than in *rufula*.
	• Broad dark band divides hind-neck, connecting dark crown to dark upperparts; no complete rufous collar ⇔ *rufula* (sometimes narrow dark connection between crown and mantle in *rufula*).
note	• Possible in WP.

Cliff Swallow *Petrochelidon pyrrhonota* L 14cm 5.

all plum	• Throat dark, only slightly paler than crown; head generally dark.
	• Pale collar and patch on forehead.
fl all plum	• Very pale cream-coloured underparts except *dark spots on undertail-cov, large red throat patch and dark breast patch*.
	• Large rufous rump-patch, towards rear sharply bordered, towards uppertail-cov more faintly bordered
	• Stocky, with short straight-ended tail and broad wing base.
	• Grey (juv) or rufous and grey (ad) collar and faint cream-coloured longitudinal stripes on mantle; rest upperparts and upperwing black.
	• Dark underwing and throat contrast with pale underparts.

Bulbuls

Common Bulbul *Pycnonotus barbatus* L 20cm 7

ad	• No pale eye-ring ⇔ White-spectacled Bulbul.
	• White undertail-cov ⇔ White-spectacled.
	• Completely black-brown upperparts.
	• Dirty grey breast and belly.
	• Black throat.
behav	• Very vocal.

White-eared Bulbul *Pycnonotus leucotis* L 19.5cm 7

all plum	• Like White-spectacled Bulbul (including yellow undertail-cov) but slightly smaller and with large white spot on head-side.
	• White tips to tail-feathers creating pale tail-band.
	• Both upperparts and underparts slightly paler than White-spectacled.

White-spectacled Bulbul *Pycnonotus xanthopygos* L 20.5cm 8

ad	• (Almost) complete pale eye-ring.
	• Yellow undertail-cov.
	• Pale grey bill-base.
	• Rest of plumage as in Common Bulbul.

Red-vented Bulbul *Pycnonotus cafer* L 20cm 7

all plum	• Black head and upper-breast with brown ear-coverts. Small crest creating angular rear-head.
	• Red undertail-cov.
	• White uppertail-cov
	• Black tail with white terminal band.
ad	• Upperparts, lower-breast and flanks strongly scaled due to pale fringes of dark feathers. Due to wear pale fringes disappearing and whole fore-part of bird (incl head, upperparts, breast and flanks) becoming uniformly dark. Belly whitish.

Bush warblers

Cetti's Warbler *Cettia cetti* L 13.5cm

all plum ⇒ ⇒	• Very short wings and short prim-projection (wing hardly reaching tail base).
	• Conspicuous pale half eye-ring below eye; narrow whitish supercilium.
	• Head-side and breast with grey wash.
	• Uniform chestnut upperparts.
	• Dirty white underparts but flanks brownish; vent brown (concolorous with upperparts), undertail-cov with faint pale tips.
	• Rather long tail containing only 10 feathers.
geog var	*C.c. albiventris* (central Asia)
all plum	• Larger than *cetti*.

- Upperparts paler than *cetti* (and *orientalis*), hardly any rufous but more olive-brown; underparts whiter.
- Supercilium often more obvious than in *cetti*.

ote geog var
- *C.c. orientalis* occurs in Middle East and western Asia. Intermediate between *cetti* and *albiventris* and differences clinal. Field identification of *orientalis* and *albiventris* outside normal range not possible.

Long-tailed tits

ong-tailed Tit *Aegithalos caudatus*   L 14cm 5.5"

ll plum
av
- Small size with very long, strongly rounded tail with white outer-sides.
- Central tail-feathers short (almost half length of t2 and t3).

ote geog var
- Most subspecies merge into each other by clinal zone; ind from these zones show intermediate features.

eog var *A.c. caudatus* (north-east Europe)

d
- Pure snowy-white head sharply demarcated by black hind-neck and mantle.
- Often almost white underparts, only flanks with bright pinkish wash.
- Often whitish scaps with faint pinkish wash (in more eastern populations almost white).
- Often broad white fringes to sec and tertials (tertials often almost white but sometimes dark with only white fringes).

ote
- In many white-headed ind in winter in western Europe underparts and scaps dirty pink like *europaeus*, white head diffuse and often not sharply bordered with dark hind-neck and white of head not pure snowy-white, representing variation in *europaeus* or intergrade with *caudatus*

eog var *A.c. europaeus* (central Europe)

d
- Broad but rather diffuse black lateral crown-stripe.
- Whitish underparts with pink wash on belly, vent and undertail-cov.
- Scaps deep pink.

eog var *A.c. rosaceus* (western Europe)

d
- Like *europaeus* but lateral crown-stripe broader and centre of crown spotted.
- Narrow streaked breast-band.
- Ear-coverts darker than in *europaeus*.
- Underparts slightly darker than in *europaeus*.

eog var *A.c. irbii* (southern part of Iberian Peninsula)

d
- Grey scaps and sides of mantle (central part of mantle black).
- Broad black lateral crown-stripe.
- Underparts diffusely streaked.
- Ear-coverts streaked (head generally darker than *europaeus*).

eog var *A.c. tephronotus* (eastern Turkey)

- Grey scaps and mantle (only central part of mantle blackish).
- Black throat-patch. Relatively short tail.
- Diffuse streaked underparts.
- Ear-coverts streaked.

og var *A.c. siculus* (Sicily)

- Upperparts greyish like *tephronotus*, almost lacking pink except rump. Dark band over upper mantle present ⇔ *tephronotus*.
- Lateral crown-stripe dark brown.
- Sometimes vague dark patch on throat.

Babblers

q Babbler *Turdoides altirostris*   L 22cm 8.5"

plum ⇒
- Uniform grey-brown underparts, flanks more rufous ⇔ Common Babbler.
- Finely dark streaked mantle, hind-neck and crown; underparts unstreaked ⇔ Common.
- Legs darkish flesh-coloured.

te
- Range overlaps for small part with Common.

ghan Babbler *Turdoides huttoni*   L 23cm 9"

og var *T.h. salvadori* (south Iraq, Kuwait and south-west Iran)

plum
- Generally paler grey-brown than other babblers in WP.
- Upperparts, hind-neck and crown heavily streaked.
- Legs yellow. Slender bill.
- On underparts only breast-sides and flanks finely streaked.

te
- Range overlaps for small part with Iraq Babbler.

abian Babbler *Turdoides squamiceps*   L 27cm 10.5"

plum
- Grey-brown almost unstreaked upperparts; finely spotted crown, hind-neck and mantle.
- Whitish throat and breast; breast finely spotted.
- Pale basal part of bill.

- Grey brown wash on underparts.
- Very long tail.

Fulvous Babbler *Turdoides fulva*   L 25cm 1

all plum ⇒
- Rufous-brown underparts; pale throat.
- Uniform deep brown upperparts.
- Dark eye.
- Black bill with small yellow base.

Phylloscopus warblers

- Supercilium conspicuous to very conspicuous.
- Eye-stripe conspicuous in most species (except in bonelli's warblers).
- Many species with 1 or 2 usually obvious wing-bars.
- Upperparts unpatterned.
- Tail-tip slightly notched.
- Pale ear-coverts.
- Often very lively and difficult to observe, especially the smaller species.

Eastern Crowned Warbler *Phylloscopus coronatus*   L 12cm 4.

all plum ⇒
⇒
- Resembles Arctic Warbler but with pure white underparts and *often yellowish undertail-cov.*
- Strong head-pattern, with very broad dark eye-stripe, dark crown-sides and *pale median crown-strip* which fades away towards forehead (not reaching bill).
- Often contrast between green mantle and grey hind-neck.
- Strong bill with entirely pale lower mandible ⇔ in Arctic often dark tip.
- Supercilium broad and slightly two-toned, yellowish before eye, white at rear.
- Prim-projection shorter than in Arctic, about 70%.
- When fresh, often 2 narrow wing-bars.
- Upperparts and fringes of flight-feathers yellow-green.
- Legs dark but toes often flesh-coloured.

voice
- Call: short 'pjew', slightly reminiscent to 'pink' call of Common Chaffinch.

behav
- Moves relatively calmly for a *Phylloscopus* and without 'wing-flicking'.

Green Warbler *Phylloscopus nitidus*   L 10.5cm 4

all plum ⇒
- Supercilium, ear-coverts, eye-ring and underparts yellowish; breast contrasts with whiter belly; when fresh whole underparts yellowish (western Turkish population almost without yellow on underparts) ⇔ Greenish Warbler.
- Supercilium reaches bill, not extending over forehead ⇔ Greenish (see Arctic Warbler and Two-barred Greenish Warbler).
- Pink-yellow lower mandible sometimes with dark tip ⇔ in Greenish no dark tip.
- Wing-bar broader and ends more abruptly than in Greenish. 2nd wing-bar on median cov more often present than in Greenish (in fresh plumage probably always). Wing-bars sometimes approach pattern Two-barred Greenish.
- Supercilium often slightly longer than in Greenish.
- Upperparts and crown deep yellow-green, when worn more grey-green. Crown often less contrasting dark than in Greenish.
- Lores variable, some ind with only loral-spot like Greenish, others with loral-stripe like Two-barred Green
- Legs usually slightly paler than in Greenish.
- Prim-projection generally slightly longer than in Greenish, 60-80%.

moult
- See Greenish.

behav
- Usually sings for prolonged periods from one place ⇔ Greenish.
- Bill often held slightly upwards (as in Greenish and Two-barred Greenish).

voice
- Call: rather similar to Greenish but more sparrow-like and often tending towards trisyllabic call of Two-barred Greenish.

Two-barred Greenish Warbler *Phylloscopus plumbeitarsus*   L 10.5cm 4

all plum ⇒
- *Evenly broad* wing-bar over *6-7 greater cov*, longer and broader than in Greenish Warbler and Arctic Warbler; greater cov wing-bar consists of large pale tips to outer webs and small white tips to inner webs. When fresh distinct 2nd wing-bar on medium cov.
- Distinct loral-stripe as in Arctic but sometimes fading away slightly towards bill ⇔ in Greenish usual only loral-spot.
- Prim-projection 60-80% (generally longer than in Greenish, especially in eastern populations) ⇔ in Arctic longer.
- Supercilium somewhat cream-coloured, long and broad behind eye and sometimes slightly less disti between eye and bill. Does not extend over forehead (as in Arctic and Green Warbler) ⇔ Greenish.
- Legs dark grey-brown to grey; rear-side paler (usually slightly paler than in Greenish).
- Upperparts and crown relatively dark (darker than in Arctic and Greenish), often creating capped effe as in Greenish, exaggerating contrast with supercilium.
- Usually completely orange-yellow lower mandible (rarely with dark tip).
- Ear-coverts often slightly spotted as in Arctic ⇔ in most Greenish unpatterned.
- Underparts slightly whiter than in Greenish (thus obviously whiter than in Arctic).
- Tertials almost uniform (only narrow greenish fringes) ⇔ in Hume's Leaf Warbler, Yellow-browed Warbler and Pallas's Leaf Warbler obvious whitish fringes.

behav
- Bill often held slightly upwards (as in Green and Greenish).

voice
- Call: like Greenish (and more so like Green) but clearly trisyllabic.

Phylloscopus warblers

Greenish Warbler *Phylloscopus trochiloides*   L 10cm 3.9"

all plum
- Pale feathering at base of upper mandible creating narrow but conspicuous pale stripe over bill-base ⇔ Arctic and Two-barred Greenish Warbler.
- Long pale yellow supercilium, broader above and behind eye ⇔ in Arctic Warbler narrower, staying almost even in width.
- Obvious dark eye-stripe; loral-stripe becoming fainter towards bill. Usually only dark loral-spot directly before eye ⇔ Arctic.
- Prim-projection 55-65%, usually shorter than in Willow Warbler, always shorter than in Arctic.
- Usually one (very) narrow and rather short narrowing wing-bar (over 4-5 greater cov), ill-defined and fading away on inner greater cov (sometimes 2nd weak wing-bar over median cov in fresh plumage) ⇔ Two-barred Greenish.
- Legs usually dark grey-brown.
- Upperparts grey-green, more greyish when worn.
- Underparts whitish, sometimes with weak yellowish wash.
- Orange-yellow lower mandible, sometimes with dark tip.
- Rather dark (rear-)crown and conspicuous supercilium often creating capped effect.
- Ear-coverts diffusely spotted ⇔ in Arctic usually obviously spotted.

moult
- Ad moults partially in late summer, body and sometimes some tertials; possible visible moult-limit in autumn in tertials, prim worn ⇔ 1w in autumn uniform fresh.
- Ad moult flight-feathers in winter.

voice
- Call: rather loud, disyllabic 'tsi-leet', reminicent of Pied or White Wagtails, rapidly rising and falling in pitch.

behav
- Bill often held slightly upwards (as in Green and Two-barred Greenish).

Arctic Warbler *Phylloscopus borealis*   L 12.5cm 4.9"

all plum
- Conspicuous but relatively *narrow* supercilium, not extending onto forehead; (in Green Warbler supercilium extends to bill, in Two-barred Greenish Warbler supercilium usually does not reach fore-crown as in Arctic) ⇔ in Greenish Warbler extends over bill.
- Very long prim-projection 70-90%.
- p1 slightly or not at all longer than prim-cov; *only 3 emarginations* on outer web of prim (p3-p5; p6 lacks emargination) ⇔ in Greenish, Green and Two-barred Greenish p1 distinctly longer than prim-cov and 4 emarginations on outer web (p3-p6; on p6 sometimes faint).
- Rather short and usually rather narrow wing-bar (over outer 3-6 greater cov), ending abruptly on inner; in fresh plumage often faint 2nd over median cov. Wing-bar over greater cov consists of pale tips to outer webs (no pale tips to inner webs), usually creating chequered wing-bar ⇔ in Greenish, Green and Two-barred Greenish pale tip extends on to inner web (normally only visible on very good pictures or in the hand).
- Conspicuous eye-stripe also on lores forming distinct stripe and extending to bill; together with supercilium creating well-defined loral pattern ⇔ in Greenish only dark spot before eye (Green and Two-barred Greenish intermediate).
- Legs pale brown to pinkish, toes often yellowish in autumn (paler than in Greenish), but variable, sometimes dark.
- Strong bill with slightly deeper base. Lower mandible pale flesh-coloured with dark tip, normally dark tip over half of lower mandible ⇔ Greenish, Green and Two-barred Greenish.
- Ear-coverts with fan of pale and dark stripes ⇔ most Greenish, Green and Two-barred Greenish (in Two-barred Greenish sometimes rather strongly marked ear-coverts too).
- Faint darker lateral crown-stripes due to slightly paler centre of crown ⇔ Greenish, Green and Two-barred Greenish have darker crowns and thus lack darker lateral crown-stripes.
- Slightly bulkier than Greenish with larger head.
- Very diffuse grey streaking on underparts, especially breast and flanks; underparts darker than in Greenish, Green and Two-barred Greenish (usually less conspicuous in autumn). In ind from western part of range underparts often almost white as in congeners.
- Upperparts greenish, more greyish when worn.
- Often looks rather short tailed, possibly due to long wings (tail-projection beyond wing-tip not much longer than prim-projection).
- Prim-cov as a whole create pointed triangle ⇔ in Greenish, Green and Two-barred Greenish shorter and more blunt.

moult
- Ad moults partially (usually only some tertials and tail-feathers) in late summer; somewhat worn in autumn (often difficult to see) or moult-limit in tertials ⇔ 1w in autumn uniform fresh (sometimes t1 moulted).
- Ad moults flight-feathers in winter.

voice
- Call: rather loud, short very metalic 'tsrick', often repeated every 3-5 sec (single-toned 'tzit' call is known from Two-barred Greenish and Greenish, but much less metallic).

Pallas's Leaf Warbler *Phylloscopus proregulus*   L 9.5cm 3.7"

all plum ⇒
⇒
- Very strong head-pattern with very broad and long supercilium and distinct median crown-stripe (supercilium and median crown-stripe often slightly deeper yellow between eye and bill ⇔ Yellow-browed Warbler).
- Yellowish rump-patch.
- Broad and long dark eye-stripe, more distinct than in all congeners.
- Almost completely dark bill (only pale base of lower mandible) ⇔ in most Yellow-browed larger pale bill-base.
- Underparts whiter than in Yellow-browed.
- 2 broad yellow wing-bars (in Yellow-browed more whitish).
- Distinct whitish fringes around tips of tertials (as in Yellow-browed).
- Tarsus often dark ⇔ Yellow-browed.
- Relatively short tail.

Phylloscopus warblers

Yellow-browed Warbler *Phylloscopus inornatus*   L 10cm 3.9"

all plum	• Very conspicuous pale yellowish supercilium extending to hind-neck.
	• 2 broad wing-bars concolorous with supercilium; broad dark 'shadow' (dark base of sec) under greater cov.
	• Contrastingly patterned tertials with dark centres and broad whitish fringes.
	• Usually faint paler middle of crown (never as pale and well-defined as in Pallas's Leaf Warbler).
	• Legs usually pale ⇔ in most Hume's Leaf Warbler rather dark.
	• Upperparts and crown usually rather dark greenish.
1w	• When worn in late winter, more greyish with fainter supercilium and wing-bars, colour nearly as in fresher ad Hume's at same time of year.
voice	• Call: high pitched, penetrating disyllabic 'tsoe-ie', second phrase rising in pitch.

Hume's Leaf Warbler *Phylloscopus humei*   L 10cm 3.9"

all plum	• Dark 'shadow' under greater cov (dark base of sec) *narrower and less distinct* than in Yellow-browed Warbler. Sometimes almost absent.
	• Rather broad whitish wing-bar over greater cov, less distinct 2nd wing-bar over median cov (2nd wing-bar sometimes completely absent).
	• Supercilium *extends into sharp point* at rear of head, fainter between eye and bill, sometimes more cream-coloured ⇔ in Yellow-browed supercilium rather even in distinctness over whole length.
	• Upperparts usually rather pale grey-greenish ⇔ in Yellow-browed darker moss-green.
	• Brown-grey crown with at most faint greenish wash ⇔ in Yellow-browed normally distinctly green on crown, (when fresh) without grey wash.
	• Legs dark, sometimes paler grey-brown.
	• Usually rather faint loral-stripe ⇔ Yellow-browed.
	• Dark bill, often with pale base and cutting edges. Variable, paler billed ind overlapping with Yellow-browed.
	• Centre of median cov, greater cov and tertials slightly paler than in Yellow-browed (dark grey instead of black).
	• Slightly paler, less spotted ear-coverts than in Yellow-browed.
	• Generally slightly shorter bill than in Yellow-browed.
	• Underparts usually with somewhat brown-greyish wash, less whitish than in most Yellow-browed.
	• Sometimes faint paler centre of crown (as in some Yellow-browed) ⇔ other *Phylloscopus*.
voice	• Call: variable (more variable than Yellow-browed) but generally shorter and lower-pitched than Yellow-browed. At least 3 main call types: 1) nasal and rather flat 'weest'; 2) often nasal, clearly disyllabic 'tu-wéé' with stress on second note, slightly similar to call of Greenish Warbler but lower-pitched, less sharp and less explosive; and 3) less frequently a Common Chiffchaff-like, almost monosyllabic 'hu-ee'

Radde's Warbler *Phylloscopus schwarzi*   L 12cm 4.7"

all plum ⇒	• Supercilium normally two-toned; above lores broad, cream-coloured and diffusely bordered (often extending over bill ⇔ Dusky Warbler); above and behind eye whitish and reaching very far back to above rear-side of ear-coverts.
	• *Legs orange* to flesh-coloured (sometimes darker) ⇔ in Dusky often darker.
	• Relatively thick, often stumpy bill often with distinctly curved culmen ⇔ in Dusky bill more pointed. In some ind bill has more slender tip and straighter culmen, but bill still noticeably short.
	• Broad dark eye-stripe (only slightly smaller than diameter of eye).
	• Yellow-brown underparts, especially flanks and undertail-cov (in 1w usually deeper and warmer coloured than in ad).
	• Upperparts green-brown ⇔ in Dusky more pure brown to grey-brown.
	• Relatively large paler part on upper mandible ⇔ in Dusky dark upper mandible with usually only cutting-edge of upper mandible paler. Bill paler overall than in Dusky.
	• Spotted ear-coverts.
	• Dark lateral crown-stripe, especially above and behind eye ⇔ Dusky.
	• 4 deep emarginations on outer web of prim (p3-p6), emargination on p3 far towards base (as in Dusky
	• Usually somewhat rounded tail ⇔ most other *Phylloscopus*.
voice	• Call: rather full, sometimes disyllabic 'djuk' or 'tuk-tjuk' without 's'-sound ⇔ Dusky. Sometimes reminicent of call of Tree Sparrow.

Dusky Warbler *Phylloscopus fuscatus*   L 11.5cm 4.5"

all plum	• Long distinct whitish supercilium well-defined above lores (*ending sharply and narrowly before bill*, not extending over bill ⇔ Radde's Warbler). Supercilium not distinctly two-toned; when two-toned, supercilium is whiter above lores and eye ⇔ Radde's.
	• Long prominent dark eye-stripe extending sharply to bill (as in Radde's).
	• Legs dark to rather pale (but usually darker than in Radde's), often with faint pink wash ⇔ Common Chiffchaff northern (sub)species and Plain Leaf Warbler.
	• Pointed bill with pale basal part of lower mandible, sometimes completely dark (contrast between pale and dark parts often larger than in Radde's). Bill overall darker than in Radde's.
	• Normally almost no colour difference between flanks and undertail-cov ⇔ Radde's.
	• Undertail-cov usually paler and less warmly coloured than in Radde's but sometimes deep cinnamon-coloured.
	• Upperparts as in Radde's but generally more pure brown, towards winter more grey-brown.
	• 4 deep emarginations on outer web of prim (p3-p6), see Radde's.
	• Dark lateral crown-stripe sometimes rather distinct, especially above lores ⇔ in Radde's more distinct behind eye.
voice	• Call: reminiscent of call of Lesser Whitethroat or Blackcap, but normally in a more irregular series and with obvious 's'-sound. Obviously drier, higher-pitched and more ticking than call of Radde's.

Western Bonelli's Warbler *Phylloscopus bonelli* L 11cm 4.3"

all plum
- Milky-white underparts conspicuous (also in Eastern Bonelli's Warbler).
- All wing-feathers (except upper tertials and often greater cov) with pale green fringes, contrasting with *dark tertials with broad, usually pale grey fringes.*
- Complete pale eye-ring (sometimes broken at rear).
- Usually faint head-pattern with pale lores and ear-coverts and rather faint supercilium.
- Yellow-green rump contrasts with dark tail, often difficult to see (also in Eastern).
- Prim-projection c.70% with large spacings between outer prim-tips (tips of p4, p5 and p6); as in Eastern, Wood Warbler and Willow Warbler.
- Mantle and scaps often somewhat warm brown-green (but regularly greyer) ⇔ on Eastern cold (green-)grey.
- Legs and bill rather pale grey-brown.

behav
- Often confiding (like Eastern).
- Whirling foraging flight along branches (like Eastern).

moult
- Ad moults partially (body and tertials) in late summer, in autumn contrast between old wings and fresh tertials ⇔ 1w in autumn uniform fresh (sometimes t1 moulted).
- Ad moults flight-feathers in winter.
- Some ind in spring with distinctly worn wings, probably 1s which has not completed winter moult.

voice
- Call: Spotted Redshank-like 'tshuweet', but with Willow Warbler-like sound ⇔ Eastern.

note
- Song: full rattle ⇔ Eastern (see Eastern account). Call often mixed in song.
- For further features, see Eastern.

Eastern Bonelli's Warbler *Phylloscopus orientalis* L 11.5cm 4.5"

all plum
- Greater cov with pale grey fringes, creating (often isolated) pale grey wing-panel ⇔ in Western Bonelli's Warbler often at least some greater cov with greenish fringes to greater cov contrasting with rest of wing.
- Complete eye-ring often very broad, more conspicuous than in Western.
- Head-pattern similar to Western but *ear-coverts often darker* and more regularly shows faint, diffuse dark loral-spot.
- Cold green-grey upperparts ⇔ in Western normally warmer with more brownish wash, especially on crown.
- Legs with little variation: dark grey-brown to blackish ⇔ in Western more variable from pale brown to dark.
- Visible part of p1 ≤ distance between tip of prim-cov and tip of alula ⇔ in Western visible part of p1 ≥ distance between tip of prim-cov and tip of alula.
- Blackish tertials contrast with broad pale grey fringes (also pale grey fringe to longest tertial); contrast stronger than in Western ⇔ in Western often greenish outer fringe to longest tertial.
- Grey-yellow rump contrasts with dark tail, often more obvious than in Western.
- Sec, prim and tail-feathers with green-grey fringes, generally slightly greyer than in Western.
- p2 often longer than p6, often falling between p5 and p6 ⇔ in Western p2 level with or slightly shorter than p6.
- Often only 3 emarginations on outer web of prim ⇔ 4 in Western.
- Prim-projection ± 80%, slightly longer than in Western.
- Pale lower mandible ⇔ on grey Common Chiffchaff northern (sub)species entirely dark bill or only paler base.
- Tail sometimes slightly shorter-looking than in Western.
- Dirty whitish supercilium ⇔ in Western brighter yellowish to white.
- Underwing-cov and axillaries pale yellow ⇔ in Western bright yellow.
- Bill generally slightly shorter and finer than in Western.

behav
- See Western

moult
- See Western.

voice
- Call: 'tsiep' or 'tjup' sometimes reminicent to certain call-type of Common Crossbill but less full ⇔ Western.

note
- Song: dry, rather flat rattle, often contains more than 10 notes ⇔ in Western slightly fuller and often less than 10 notes per sequence.
- Above-mentioned plumage differences with Western at most indicative and probably not diagnostic.

Wood Warbler *Phylloscopus sibilatrix* L 12cm 4.7"

⇒ - Very long prim-projection ≥ 100% (prim-projection > tail-projection beyond wing-tip).
⇒ - Yellow breast and throat contrast with pure white remainder of underparts (sometimes no yellow on breast).
- Long dark eye-stripe and long yellow supercilium extending to above rear-side of ear-coverts.
- Bright green to brown- or grey-green upperparts.
- Dark tertials with pale grey-yellow fringes contrast with rest of dark wing.
- Fringes of sec, prim and greater cov distinctly yellow-green.
- Legs often pale yellow-brown.
- Only 2 or 3 emarginations on outer web of prim.
- p1 not distinctly longer than prim-cov ⇔ all *Phylloscopus* in WP except Arctic Warbler.
- Yellow fringes at base of tail-feathers creating pale tail-corners at base of closed tail.

ault
- Ad moults partially in late summer; prim, sec and greater cov old in autumn ⇔ 1w in autumn uniform fresh (sometimes t1 moulted).

te
- Some ind lack yellow on underparts and therefore slightly resemble bonelli's warblers; distinct head-pattern with broad eye-stripe and supercilium and very long prim-projection are most important differences from bonelli's warblers.

Plain Leaf Warbler *Phylloscopus neglectus*   L 9.5cm 3.?

all plum	• Short tail, shortest tail of all *Phylloscopus*. Small size and relatively large head can resemble Goldcrest
	• Fringes of remiges with some green at most (*often no green at all* as in Caucasian Chiffchaff) ⇔ in Siberian Chiffchaff green always present.
	• Short prim-projection < 50%.
	• Upperparts almost uniform cold grey-brown.
	• Underparts whitish but flanks and undertail-cov brownish.
	• Diffuse, rather short but broad white to cream-coloured supercilium extending to halfway above ear-coverts. Especially conspicuous above lore.
	• Narrow dark eye-stripe and often conspicuous white eye-ring.
	• Legs dark.
	• Spotted ear-coverts ⇔ all Common Chiffchaff northern (sub)species.
1w	• Yellow wash on underparts and supercilium.
voice	• Call: very different from closest relatives, a sparrow-like, 'drep-drep-drep' reminiscent of quiet and low-pitched calls at start of song given by Common Chiffchaff *collybita* and *abietinus*.

Common Chiffchaff *Phylloscopus collybita*   L 11cm 4.

all plum	• Dark legs, in palest case dark grey-brown.
	• Prim-projection c.60%.
	• Pale eye-ring, broken before and behind eye; lower half conspicuous.
	• Uniform ear-coverts ⇔ Willow Warbler.
	• 4 emarginations on outer web of prim (p3-p6) ⇔ in Willow Warbler three (p3-p5).
	• Fine, usually rather dark bill (usually ill-defined pale base of lower mandible and pale cutting edges) ⇔ on Willow Warbler slightly stronger bill with deeper base and pale basal half of lower mandible.
1w	• Often moult-limit in greater cov with at most some inner greater cov moulted.
1s	• In contrast to many other *Phylloscopus* prim still juv and worn; often 2 generations of tail-feathers, t1 fresh and sometimes moult-limit in greater cov ⇔ in ad all feathers relatively fresh without clear differences between generations.
behav	• Continually flicks tail downwards during foraging ⇔ in Willow Warbler less persisting.
geog var	*P.c. collybita* (western and central Europe, east to eastern Europe)
all plum	• Short supercilium narrowing and fading away behind eye.
	• Yellow-brown flanks and breast-sides ⇔ most other (sub)species, except Canary Islands Chiffchaff.
	• Upperparts almost uniform brown (rump and uppertail-cov with at most faint green wash ⇔ *abietinus* and *tristis*).
voice	• Call: almost monosyllabic, rising in pitch: 'wuiet' with more stress on later part than in Willow Warbler
note geog var	• Identification of south-eastern (sub)species highly difficult (and in many cases impossible) due to insufficient knowledge and existence of possible overlap-zones between different (sub)species. Ind from these zones sometimes referred to as e.g.: *brevirostris* (mainly Turkey), *caucasicus* (mainly Armenia) and *menzbieri* (mainly Iran) but validity of (some of) these subspecies as yet unclear.
geog var	*P.c. abietinus* (central and northern Scandinavia, eastern Europe east of *collybita*, east to Urals)
all plum	• Upperparts paler and greyer than in *collybita* with faint brown-green wash. Rump and uppertail-cov often conspicuously greenish ⇔ *collybita* and *tristis*. Unknown proportion of population like *collybita*.
	• Underparts paler than in *collybita* with only faint brown-grey wash on flanks; breast with only faint yellow wash ⇔ *collybita*.
	• Grey wash on crown and hind-neck.
	• Slightly more obvious (whiter) longer supercilium than *collybita*.
	• Slightly paler yellow-green fringes to sec, prim and tail-feathers than in *collybita*.
	• Slightly longer wings than *collybita* resulting in slightly longer prim-projection.
voice	• Similar to *collybita*.
geog var	Siberian Chiffchaff *P.c. tristis* (Siberia from Urals eastwards)
all plum	• Upperparts (except rump and uppertail-cov) grey-brown to dark rufous-brown without green. Rump a uppertail-cov sometimes with dark green wash.
	• Rather pale underparts without yellow; breast-sides and rear-flanks buff-brown. Ind from heart of distribution deep buff-brown.
	• Legs and bill black (cutting edges of bill and extreme base often paler).
	• Warm brownish ear-coverts.
	• More obvious and longer supercilium and eye-stripe than in *collybita*. Supercilium usually more disti behind eye and buff (without yellow).
	• When fresh (autumn), relatively broad pale fringes to tertials and sec. Tertials with contrasting blackish centres.
	• Faint greenish fringes to sec, prim and tail-feathers.
	• Marginal underwing-cov (leading edge of underwing) pale yellow ⇔ in *collybita* and *abietinus* deep yell
	• Alula often contrastingly dark.
	• Sometimes dark lateral crown-stripe.
	• Often faint to rather obvious wing-bar over greater cov.
	• Bill smaller and straighter than *collybita* and *abietinus* (with at most very slightly curved culmen, sometimes looking almost upcurved).
voice	• Call: almost single-toned, clear but thin 'íéééhp', higher-pitched than in *collybita* and *abietinus*, at m slightly rising in pitch at end. In ad in breeding range often slightly descending at end.
	• Song: very different from *collybita* and *abietinus*, faster, fuller, more varied in sound and notes more flowing into each other.

notes
- '*fulvescens*'-type is western *tristis*. Plumage differs from *tristis* by whiter underparts (occasionally with some yellow), some green on upperparts (especially scaps) and sometimes some yellow in parts of supercilium. Legs sometimes dark brown with paler toes. Voice as *tristis*.
- Origin of 'grey-and-white' ind occurring in western Europe in late autumn as yet unclear. Unknown proportion of these ind concern grey *abietinus* but others possibly grey variant of '*fulvescens*', often referred to as '*naevia*'; origin and validity of '*naevia*' unknown.
- Populations breeding in Middle East call like *tristis* but sing like *collybita/abietinus*.

berian Chiffchaff *Phylloscopus ibericus*   L 11.5cm 4.5"

all plum
- Plumage and structure in many respects between Willow Warbler and Common Chiffchaff; upperparts deeper green than Common *collybita* (sometimes even resembling Wood Warbler).
- Underparts generally paler than in Common with (weak brown-)yellow breast and often almost white rest of underparts; undertail-cov often yellow ⇔ in Common breast yellow-brown, often creating faint breast-band.
- Supercilium long, broad and distinct, often yellowish above lores.
- Half eye-ring below eye narrower and less conspicuous than in Common.
- Long, especially fine bill (sometimes culmen slightly pinched in at base rendering it longer-looking than in Common).
- Long tail.
- Prim-projection longer than in Common, c.70% ⇔ in Common c.60%.
- Legs longer and usually slightly paler than in Common (especially rear-side of tarsus).
- Wing-tips often more pointed than in Common with p3 and p4 of same length but p5 distinctly shorter, when present characteristic (in some ind, including most 1w, p5 = p3-p4 as in Common).
- In autumn (probably especially in 1w) breast and undertail-cov bright yellow.

1s
voice
- Post-juv moult more extensive than in Common 1s; many 2cy with new outer prim (p1-p6) ⇔ Common 1s.
- Call: nasal *descending,* sometimes reminiscent of call of Eurasian Bullfinch ⇔ Common *collybita* and *abietinus*.
- Song: a series of whistles of different pitches, normally in threes; e.g. 'weet-weet-weet, wuut-wuut-wuut' followed by short trill (trill not audible from distance). Duration of one song-burst less than 4 sec ⇔ in Common considerable longer.

anary Islands Chiffchaff *Phylloscopus canariensis*   L 11.5cm 4.5"

all plum
- Short prim-projection < 50%.
- Upperparts dark brown.
- Legs sometimes rather pale.
- Underparts relatively dark with rufous-brown wash on flanks.
- Relatively long, slightly rounded tail.

voice
ote
- Song: more explosive and varied than in Common, somewhat reminiscent of song of Cetti's Warbler.
- Endemic to Canary Islands.

aucasian Chiffchaff *Phylloscopus lorenzii*   L 10.5cm 4.1"

all plum ⇒
- Upperparts and crown deep rufous-brown; no green-yellow on rump and *whitish fringes to sec, prim and tail-feathers* ⇔ all Common Chiffchaff northern (sub)species.
- Well-defined, long and narrow eye-stripe.
- Long bright whitish supercilium very conspicuous, brightest and broadest between eye and bill and extending over bill (on most Common northern (sub)species supercilium behind eye whiter than between eye and bill).
- Short prim-projection c.50%.
- Lower part of eye-ring often more distinct than in Common northern (sub)species.
- Breast-sides and flanks rather dark brownish, contrasting with white belly.
- Relatively long tail.
- Pale base of lower mandible.
- Prim and tail-feathers dark with slightly paler brown fringes, usually creating rather strong colour contrast with paler (upperparts and) underparts.
- Fine, slender and rather short bill.
- Legs very dark with bright yellow soles ⇔ Dusky Warbler.
- Tertial-centres almost concolorous with upperparts and without conspicuous pale fringes ⇔ all Common northern (sub)species.

ote
oice
- Head-pattern resembles that of Dusky Warbler but behaviour (like Common) and call very different.
- Song very similar to Common *collybita* and *abietinus*, but sometimes slightly higher pitched; call reminiscent of Siberian Chiffchaff.

illow Warbler *Phylloscopus trochilus*   L 12cm 4.7"

d ⇒
- Long prim-projection c.80-100%.
- Legs rather pale, usually flesh-coloured; toes also pale ⇔ Common Chiffchaff (but sometimes legs completely dark as Common Chiffchaff).
- Long whitish supercilium, longer and more distinct than in Common Chiffchaff *collybita*.
- Dark eye-stripe prominent.
- Yellowish wash on throat and breast, often creating breast-band (but very variable from almost completely white to completely yellowish) ⇔ on Common Chiffchaff more brownish wash with faint yellow streaks on underparts.
- Upperparts usually greenish, sometimes completely grey; see geographic variation.
- Yellowish basal half of lower mandible rather sharply demarcated from dark tip ⇔ on Common Chiffchaff more grey-brown and more diffusely bordered.

	• 3 emarginations on outer web of prim (p3-p5) ⇔ in Common Chiffchaff 4 (and many other *Phylloscopus*) (p3-p6).
	• Usually spotted ear-coverts ⇔ Common Chiffchaff.
1w	• Almost completely uniform yellowish underparts, sometimes resembling Icterine Warbler.
	• In autumn prim and tail-feather tips slightly worn ⇔ in ad very fresh with obvious pale tips.
moult	• Ad moults completely in both autumn and spring (1w moults partially in autumn).
voice	• Call: disyllabic, rising in pitch: 'hu-weet' ⇔ in Common *collybita* and *abietinus* more monosyllabic.
geog var	*P.t. acredula* (northern and eastern Europe east to central Siberia)
ad	• Generally greyer on upperparts and whiter on underparts than *trochilus* (often almost lacking green and yellow) but many ind identical to *trochilus*.
geog var	*P.t. yakutensis* (Siberia south and east of *acredula*)
ad	• Upperparts brown-grey.
	• Underparts conspicuously white.
note	• Variation of especially *acredula* large; some ind very similar to *yakutensis*, therefore identification of *yakutensis* outside normal range very difficult.

Sylvia warblers

- No (distinct) supercilium.
- In many species dark head contrasting with pale throat.
- Long to very long tail with usually conspicuous white outer-side on at least t6.
- Legs relatively thick; in most species strong bill and relatively large head.
- Many southern species with orange to bright-red orbital-ring.
- In most species obvious sexual dimorphism.

Marmora's Warbler and Balearic Warbler

all plum	• Structure resembles Dartford Warbler (applies especially to Balearic) but tail slightly shorter. Marmora's approaches Sardinian Warbler in structure.
	• Upperparts paler than in Dartford.
	• Little white in tail-sides; t6 with narrow white outer-edge and tip, t5 with small white tip (almost identical to Dartford).
	• Very short prim-projection c.30-40%.
	• Well-defined, evenly broad white outer-edge of alula (see Dartford).
	• Orange to red orbital-ring (broad in ad in spring).
	• Pink to orange-red bill-base with small dark tip (dark tip sometimes almost absent).
	• Legs orange ⇔ Dartford.
ad	• Iris deep brown-orange.
ad ♂/1s ♂⇒	• Both upperparts and *underparts blue-grey*; central part of underparts paler.
	• Faint blackish lores (also in 1w ♂) ⇔ ♀ and Dartford all plum.
1w ♂/ad ♀	• Like ad ♂ s but more brown-grey than blue-grey on upperparts; underparts slightly paler but breast and flanks almost uniform grey.
1w ♀	• Upperparts with distinct brown wash and brown fringes to greater cov and tertials.
	• Underparts pale, without distinct dark breast and flanks ⇔ 1w ♂.
	• Sometimes difficult to distinguish from Dartford 1w ♀ but pale throat contrasts with rest of underparts, lacks pink-brown tone, lores dark and bill with smaller dark tip.
	• Colour contrast between greyish hind-neck and crown and brownish mantle ⇔ Dartford.
1w	• Prim usually distinctly worn.
1s	• Like ad of equivalent sex but fresh tertials contrast with old brown wings.
juv-1s	• Iris brown (darker than in ad).
juv-1w	• Dark lores concolorous with ear-coverts ⇔ Dartford.

Marmora's Warbler *Sylvia sarda*   L 12.5cm 4.

all plum	• See introduction to Marmora's Warbler and Balearic Warbler.
	• Structure between Dartford Warbler and Sardinian Warbler (distance between wing- and tail-tip usually shorter than wing length ⇔ Balearic Warbler and Dartford).
ad ♂/1s ♂	• Lores usually darker than in ad ♀, sometimes not distinct and sexing then not possible.
ad	• From almost uniform blue-grey (♀ with slightly paler underparts).
	• Pale pinkish bill-base.
	• Bill shorter than in Balearic.
juv-1w	• Legs dark grey-brown ⇔ in Balearic all plum paler orange.
	• Can strongly resemble Sardinian juv-1w but e.g. pinkish bill-base (grey in Sardinian).
voice ⇒	• Call: sharp, short, loud and rasping 'treck-treck' (reminiscent of call of European Stonechat) ⇔ Balearic and Dartford.

Balearic Warbler *Sylvia balearica*   L 12cm 4.

all plum	• See introduction to Marmora's Warbler and Balearic Warbler.
	• Legs paler and more orange than in Marmora's Warbler.
	• Longer, more slender bill with more yellow-orange base to both lower and upper mandible than in Marmora's. Dark tip to lower mandible generally smaller than in Marmora's.
	• Structure similar to Dartford Warbler (distance between wing- and tail-tip about the same as wing-length ⇔ Marmora's).
ad	• Paler underparts (*pale throat contrasts with dark side of head*) ⇔ Marmora's (Marmora's in fresh

autumn plumage sometimes with slightly paler throat).
- Flanks often with brownish wash ⇔ Marmora's.

voice ⇒ • Call: short 'tsrek', lower pitched, less sharp and more nasal than call of Marmora's.

Dartford Warbler *Sylvia undata*   L 12.5cm 4.9"

all plum
- (Very) long tail with little white in tail-sides; t6 with narrow white outer-edge and tip, t5 with small white tip (Marmora's Warbler and Balearic Warbler almost identical).
- Very short prim-projection c.30-40%.
- At least slightly red-orange on throat/breast (least in 1w ♀) ⇔ Marmora's and Balearic.
- Pale orange-yellow lower mandible with large, sharply demarcated dark tip.
- Red orbital-ring.
- White outer-edge to alula broader, less well-defined and broadening towards tip slightly more than in Marmora's and Balearic.

ad ⇒
- Fine white speckles on throat.
- Bright red iris (also in many 1s).
- Broad red orbital-ring in spring.

ad ♂/ ⇒
ad ♂ s
- Wine-red underparts.
- Dark grey upperparts.

ad ♂ w/ad ♀
- Like faint coloured ad ♂ s with white spots on underparts.
- Upperparts with brown wash.

juv-1w
1w
- Often pale lores ⇔ Marmora's and Balearic.
- Iris darker than in ad, more red-brown.
- Underparts paler, more pink-brown than in ad with white spots (pink-brown more extensive in 1w ♂ but sexing usually difficult in 1w). Always slightly pink-brown on underparts ⇔ Marmora's and Balearic all plum.
- Upperparts usually with more brown wash in ♀ (but see geographic variation).

1w/1s
- Prim and prim-cov usually distinctly worn.

voice
- Call: long, low-pitched, unclear rattling 'djurrr' or 'djurrr, drrr-drrr' (call often interweaved in short stuttering song) ⇔ Marmora's and Balearic.

geog var   *S.u. dartfordiensis* (north-western France and southern England)

ad
- Upperparts with earth-brown wash ⇔ *undata*.
- Underparts dark chestnut, less white on belly and vent than in *undata* and almost no grey on rear-flanks.

Tristram's Warbler *Sylvia deserticola*   L 12cm 4.7"

all plum ⇒
- Blue-grey head including lores (in ad and 1s uniform, in 1w ♀ often partially hidden under brown feather-tips).

⇒
- Conspicuous white eye-ring.
- Rufous wing-panel (in summer sometimes almost worn away).
- Long tail (resembling Dartford Warbler, Marmora's Warbler and Balearic Warbler) but slightly shorter and with much more white in sides.
- Rather short prim-projection c.50%.
- Legs pink-orange.
- Much white in tail-sides, pattern similar to Spectacled Warbler.

ad
- Plumage colours resemble Dartford (dark blue-grey upperparts and brown-red underparts) but with distinct white eye-ring, large and bright rufous wing-panel and faint whitish submoustachial-stripe.
- Central part of belly white.
- Submoustachial-stripe diffuse, not pure white ⇔ Subalpine Warbler.

ad ♂/ad ♂
- Upperparts and head uniform deep blue-grey (in winter upperparts with brown wash).
- Underparts uniform deep terracotta with white belly patch (in winter underparts paler).

ad ♀
- Like ad ♂ but more faint and paler coloured; some pale ind (especially in winter) can resemble Spectacled ad ♂ but flanks are always darker brown-red, lacks distinct dark lores and does not have pure white throat.

1w
- Iris dull brown (red-brown in ad).
- In general paler coloured than ad.

1w ♀
- Some ind very similar to Spectacled due to occasional virtual absence of rufous on underparts. Differs from Spectacled 1w in: at least some rufous on rear-flanks, breast-sides and/or malar area; upperparts often show a mix of brown and grey feathers (in Spectacled more uniform grey-brown); rufous wing-panel smaller and more diffusely bordered than in Spectacled with greater cov and tertials paler sandy; uniform grey head including lores; dark centres to greater cov often visible (usually not visible in Spectacled); dark tertial-centres broader and tertial-tips evenly spaced (unevenly spaced in Spectacled with shorter distance between middle and longest); and whitish fringes to prim-cov (in Spectacled rufous).

1s
- Prim and prim-cov juv, usually distinctly worn.

behav
- Often holds tail upwards as in Dartford, Marmora's and Balearic.

voice
- Call: clearly different from Spectacled, sparrow-like, thick 'tseck' or 'tsrack', sometimes connected to stuttering rattle.

Spectacled Warbler *Sylvia conspicillata*   L 12.5cm 4.9"

all plum ⇒
- Large *uniform* rufous wing-panel (sec, tertials and greater cov), normally no black parts of greater cov visible ⇔ Common Whitethroat.

⇒
- Very short prim-projection c.30% with 4-5 prim-tips visible.
- Strongly contrasting black tertial-centres, especially shortest and middle tertials with narrow *pointed* centres.

		• Throat conspicuously white; rest of underparts varying from greyish to salmon-coloured.
		• Conspicuous white eye-ring, broken on front- and rear-side (in 1w ♀ sometimes almost absent).
		• Small size, only slightly larger than Willow Warbler.
		• Fine, pointed bill ⇔ Common Whitethroat.
		• Legs often conspicuously pale pinkish.
		• Long dark tail with distinct pale outer-side; t6 almost completely white, t(4-)5 with white tip; tail contrasts with paler upperparts ⇔ Common Whitethroat.
		• Usually pale base to upper mandible including base of culmen ⇔ in Common Whitethroat dark upper mandible except cutting edges.
♂	⇒	• *Blackish lores*, forehead and area around eye.
		• Grey-blue crown and ear-coverts, more distinctly bluish than in Common Whitethroat.
♀		• Brown-grey to grey head and upperparts (greyer than Common Whitethroat ♀ *communis*); lores often paler or concolorous with rest of head ⇔ ♂.
juv-1s		• Iris dark (in ad slightly paler red-brown).
1w/1s		• Often 2 generations of tertials (active tertial-moult in autumn) ⇔ Common Whitethroat 1w.
1s		• Prim and prim-cov juv, usually distinctly worn.
		• Head-pattern in ♂ less developed than in ad.
behav		• Moves tail 'nervously' ⇔ Common Whitethroat.
voice		• Call: long, rather clear rattle, often with very short, barely audible interruptions.

Subalpine Warbler *Sylvia cantillans* L 12.5cm 4.9

all plum	⇒	• Brown, usually sandy-coloured (♀ -type) to whitish tertial-fringes, not deep rufous as in Common Whitethroat and Spectacled Warbler.
		• Prim-projection 70-90% with 6-7 prim-tips beyond tertials.
		• Blue-grey uppertail-cov and rump (usually more distinct in ad than in imm).
		• Little contrast between tail and upperparts ⇔ Spectacled.
		• Relatively little white in tail (t6 mainly white, t5 with white tip at most) ⇔ in congeners tail with more white and stronger contrast between black and white.
		• Legs in most imm dark (grey-)brown; often more orange in ad.
		• Short, relatively fine bill.
ad		• Iris dark orange (often browner in ad ♀).
ad ♂/1s ♂		• Dark grey-blue upperparts and head (in 1s ♂ sometimes brownish forehead).
		• Orange-red, brown-red or pink-red breast to almost whole underparts (see geog var).
		• White submoustachial-stripe conspicuous.
ad ♀		• In spring like very faint coloured ad ♂, often with grey-blue head (but browner forehead) and pale underparts, sometimes with pinkish wash (usually only on breast).
		• Some older ad ♀ more deeply coloured, nearly as 1s ♂ but eye-ring whitish.
juv-1s		• Brownish iris (in 1s ♂ iris colour often as in ad).
1s		• Like ad of equivalent sex but usually distinct moult-limit in greater cov (especially conspicuous in ♂); prim and prim-cov worn; alula fresh. Sometimes entire wing still old.
ad ♀ w/ 1s ♀/1w		• Faint grey supercilium forms upper edge of *often completely grey surround to ear-coverts*.
		• Upperparts and upperside of tail almost uniformly coloured (tail slightly darker grey-brown).
		• Underparts pale; cream-coloured breast-sides, flanks and centre of throat contrast with white belly an[...] faint white submoustachial-stripe.
		• Dark tertials with *pale brown fringes*, contrasting little; in ad ♀ in autumn whitish fringes.
		• Almost complete white eye-ring of even width ⇔ in Spectacled eye-ring broken on front- and rear-si[...] with upper half often broader than lower.
		• Faint brown to dark sandy-coloured wing-panel.
		• When definite 1w, greyish head is indicative of ♂ (ad ♀ also with greyish head).
		• Faint orange orbital-ring (in 1w ♀ brownish).
		• In 1w dark iris.

geog var		*S.c. cantillans* (southern Europe east to Italy)
1s ♂/ad ♂		• Underparts red-orange, paler orange on flanks. Only centre of belly white.
note		• *S.c. inornata* (north-western Africa) like *cantillans* but underparts of ♂ more tending towards pure orang[...]

geog var		*S.c. albistriata* (Balkans and western Turkey)
all plum		• Upperparts slightly paler than in *cantillans*, more slaty-grey in ad ♂; upperparts dark sandy-coloured[...] in 1w.
		• Prim-projection generally longer than in *cantillans*, c.90%.
1s ♂/ad ♂		• Dark brick-red to dark pink-red concentrated on throat and breast (lacking orange); paler flanks usua[...] sharply demarcated from *white of belly extending to breast* (white of belly almost extending to level with wing-bend) ⇔ *cantillans* ad ♂.
		• Broader submoustachial-stripe than in *cantillans* ad ♂.
1s ♀/ad ♀		• Upperparts generally colder grey than in *cantillans* and underparts whiter without rufous wash.
1w		• Often distinctly paler and greyer than *cantillans*.
		• Pale eye-ring weak.
voice		• Call: 'tjrek' or 'tjret', often uttered like 'tjrek-tjrek' ⇔ in *cantillans* lower pitched, single and monosyllabic 'tjuk' of 'tukk'.

Moltoni's Warbler *Sylvia moltonii* L 12.5cm 4

all plum		• Almost identical to Subalpine Warbler.
ad ♂		• Underparts nearly completely coloured and with obvious pink wash, not distinctly orange as in Subalpine *cantillans* or brick-red as in Subalpine *albistriata*.
		• White submoustachial-stripe short and narrow.

moult ⇒
- 1w moult completely in winter range; 1s fresh in spring. Moult strategy in ad very variable, some ind moult completely in winter, others moult completely in summer or arrest moult at end of summer. Fresh plumage in spring indicative.

oice ⇒
- Call normally only diagnostic feature: *Wren-like rattle.*

énétries's Warbler *Sylvia mystacea*   L 12.5cm 4.9"

ll plum ⇒
- Tertial-centres slightly darker grey (♂) or grey-brown (♀) with broad, diffuse grey fringes.
- Prim-projection c.40-50% with usually 6 prim-tips beyond tertials, spacings of which slightly increase towards wing-tips ⇔ Sardinian Warbler.
- Blackish tail with white outer-edge and large white tips to outer tail-feathers; strongly contrasting pattern on underside of tail, as in Sardinian ⇔ Subalpine Warbler.
- Underparts with white background, flanks and breast-sides only very slightly darker ⇔ e.g. Sardinian.
- Base of lower mandible pinkish (sometimes pale grey) ⇔ in Sardinian grey.
- Longest alula feather dark with rather broad white outer-edge, especially conspicuous in ♀-type plumage ⇔ in Sardinian narrower and inconspicuous.
- Bill slightly stronger than in Sardinian with especially broader base.
- Legs pink-brown, usually slightly paler than in Sardinian.
- Slightly smaller size than Sardinian (but overlaps with eastern subspecies of Sardinian *momus*).
- Tail less rounded than in Sardinian (both species can show almost straight-ended tail).

s ♂/ad ♂
- Black cap fading away from up to ear-coverts and rear-crown, gradually merging into grey hind-neck and mantle (mantle often with sandy-coloured wash) ⇔ Sardinian ad ♂. Extremes in both species overlap in head-pattern.
- Variable amount of pink on underparts (often almost none in western subspecies *rubescens*). In strongly coloured ind (only *mystacea*) pink throat and white submoustachial-stripe, resembling Subalpine ♂.
- Iris red-orange ⇔ in all other plumages darker except in some 1s ♂.
- Orange to whitish eye-ring; pale red orbital-ring ⇔ in Sardinian both red.

s ♂
- Like ad ♂ but upperparts and crown with brownish spots.

w/1s ♀/ ad ♀
- Pale grey-brown head (in some ad ♀ dark spots on crown) and almost *uniform pale grey-brown upperparts* contrasting with blackish tail ⇔ in Sardinian ♀ stronger colour contrast between head and upperparts but less contrast between upperparts and tail.
- 1w ♂ often with greyer cov and blackish on crown and ear-coverts showing through (Sardinian 1w ♂ with already completely black head).
- Whitish eye-ring ⇔ Sardinian.
- Iris dark, brownish (also in ad ♀). 1w ♂ often with paler iris in autumn ⇔ all ♀-types.
- Old worn prim, prim-cov and outer greater cov contrast with fresher median cov, inner greater cov and tertials (different generations in ♀ often difficult to see).

hav
- Waves tail in both horizontal and vertical direction ⇔ in Sardinian rarely seen, in Subalpine (almost) never.

og var   *S.m. rubescens* (south-eastern Turkey and Middle East)

♂
- Underparts almost white, no or very slight pink wash on underparts; when present restricted to breast.
- Black on head almost restricted to front-side, fading away from rear-side of eye and middle of crown.
- Upperparts paler than in *mystacea*.

♀
- In general slightly paler than *mystacea*.

rdinian Warbler *Sylvia melanocephala*   L 13.5cm 5.3"

plum
- Conspicuous white throat contrasts with dark head and breast(-sides).
- Dark grey tertial-centres with rather well-defined grey (♂-type) or brown fringes (most ♀-type).
- Prim-projection c.30-40%; usually 5 evenly-spaced prim-tips beyond tertials.
- Blackish tail with white outer-edge and sharply demarcated white tips on (t2-t3)t4-t6; t6 with entirely white outer web, creating strongly contrasting pattern on underside of tail (as in Ménétries's Warbler).
- Base of lower mandible usually grey (about 50% of length). Rest of bill blackish.
- Legs yellow-brown to red-brown.

♂/ad ♂
- Black cap (extending to hind-neck) contrasts strongly with white throat.
- Completely grey upperparts.
- Red orbital-ring conspicuous against black head.
- Flanks and breast-sides grey (sometimes with brown wash).

♀ ⇒
- Warm rufous-brown underparts (especially flanks and breast-sides) contrasting with white throat (but see geog var).
- Brown upperparts.
- Greyish head with often darker, sometimes blackish, ear-coverts (dark ear-coverts more often in *momus*, see geog var).
- Orange orbital-ring.
- Some (older?) ind resemble ♂ due to black cap (but grey hind-neck) and red orbital-ring. Upperparts brownish ⇔ ♂.
- Dark iris.
- Sometimes pale eye-ring.
- In autumn plumage largely as ad due to usually well-advanced post-juv moult.

♂
- Like ad ♂ but upperparts and underparts with brown wash or brownish spots.

♀
- Like ad ♀ but head (especially crown) browner.
- Old juv prim and prim-cov worn, in ♂ distinctly browner than grey ad-type feathers (e.g. greater cov), in ♀ inconspicuous due to mainly brown plumage.

og var   *S.m. melanocephala* (Canary Islands and Mediterranean area, excluding extreme east)

plum
- Underparts largely dark grey (♂) to grey-brown (♀), only centre of underparts paler.
- In general slightly darker than *momus*.

geog var	*S.m. momus* (Middle East)
all plum	• Underparts paler than *melanocephala*. Grey (♂) or cream-coloured (♀) on underparts restricted to flanks and breast-sides; little or no contrast between white throat and pale breast ⇔ *melanocephala*. • Smaller than *melanocephala* with finer bill.
ad ♂	• Black head has sharper border and is more strongly contrasting with grey upperparts than in *melanocepha* • Upperparts grey (paler than in *melanocephala*), when fresh with faint brownish wash. • Tertial-fringes paler and more sharply demarcated than in *melanocephala*; pale grey to whitish.
ad ♀	• Paler head and paler, greyer upperparts than *melanocephala* (but ear-coverts often dark).
note	• Dark-headed morph of ♀ occurs within this subspecies, these like ♀ but with blackish head like ♂ usually with brown or grey spots within the black.

Cyprus Warbler *Sylvia melanothorax*   L 13cm 5.

all plum	⇒	• Very dark to black tertials and greater cov with *narrow well-defined* whitish fringes, as in Rüppell's Warbler but more narrow. ♀ with less conspicuous pale fringes to greater cov than ♂.
	⇒	• Prim-projection c.60% with 5-6 prim-tips beyond tertials ⇔ Rüppell's.
	⇒	• Undertail-cov with conspicuous dark bases and pale tips resembling Barred Warbler 1w. • Narrow white eye-ring. • Yellow to pink-orange basal half of lower mandible. • Legs yellow-orange to red-brown. • Structure and size like Sardinian Warbler. • Rump and uppertail-cov dark, hardly any contrast with tail ⇔ Rüppell's.
ad		• Iris orange-red, darker in winter.
ad ♂		• Whole underparts black-spotted, with spots formed by dark bases and pale tips to feathers. • Black cap as in Sardinian ad ♂ and broad white submoustachial-stripe ⇔ in Rüppell's black on hea of ad ♂ does not conceal whole ear-coverts. • Dark grey upperparts, slightly darker than in Rüppell's ad ♂.
ad ♀		• Spots on underparts usually less numerous and (much) smaller than in ♂, concentrated on throat an breast (much variation, some older ♀ approach ad ♂ in this respect). • Blackish around eye and on fore-crown.
♀/1w		• Crown in ad ♀ dark spotted (also sometimes in Rüppell's older ♀ and 1w/1s ♂); in 1w ♀ no dark spots on crown. • Underparts grey-brown, normally with warm rufous wash towards rear-flanks. • Grey-brown upperparts, less warm than in Sardinian. • Often pale spot on and/or above lores ⇔ Sardinian. • 1w ♂ with dark spots on underparts and patchy black cap (as strongly marked ad ♀). • 1w ♀ usually without black spots on underparts. Head concolorous with upperparts ⇔ Sardinian.
1w/1s		• Usually outer prim moulted, inner still juv; moult-limit in prim (also in Eastern Orphean Warbler 1s). • Iris dark brown, in 1s red-brown.
behav		• Like Sardinian (see behav Ménétries's Warbler).

Rüppell's Warbler *Sylvia rueppellii*   L 13.5cm 5

all plum	⇒	• Dark tertials and greater cov with *well-defined whitish fringes* (as in Cyprus Warbler) and median cov with pale tips, creating distinct wing-bars in fresh plumage.
	⇒	• *Pale grey uppertail-cov and rump* conspicuous, contrasting with dark tail.
	⇒	• Rather long prim-projection c.80% with 6-7 prim-tips beyond tertials ⇔ all smaller *Sylvia* warblers except Subalpine Warbler. • Strong, slightly downcurved bill, mainly caused by curved culmen. • Size as Common Whitethroat, distinctly larger than Cyprus, Subalpine, Ménétries's Warbler and Sardinian Warbler. • Pale underparts with faint grey to cream-coloured flanks and grey breast-sides ⇔ in Sardinian and Cyprus darker underparts. • Pale grey basal half of lower mandible (extreme base often pinkish). • Black alula often strongly contrasting, especially in non-ad ♂. • Usually faint dark bases to undertail-cov creating diffuse dark spots (sometimes no spots at all).
ad		• Orange-red iris, red orbital-ring. • Pale grey (♂) to grey-brown (♀) upperparts ⇔ in Cyprus darker. • In fresh autumn plumage conspicuous white tips to prim ⇔ 1w.
ad ♂/ 1s ♂	⇒	• Black cap fades away on ear-coverts; completely black throat separated by broad white submoustachial-stripe.
ad ♀	⇒	• White submoustachial-stripe bordered by (very variable) dark spotted throat and dark ear-coverts. Many ind with uniform white throat up to 3cy.
1s ♀/1w		• Dark brownish iris, in 1s orange-brown. • Usually completely whitish throat; head variable dark grey and gradually merging into (grey-)brown upperparts. • Upperparts grey-brown. • Sometimes very faint submoustachial-stripe when throat greyish. • 1w ♂ with greyish head, later in autumn black spots on throat ⇔ in 1w ♀ more grey-brown; thro unpatterned white. • In 1w tertials and greater cov with pale brown fringes and tips (tips to prim not conspicuously pale ⇔ ad autumn); in 1s usually distinctly worn.

Asian Desert Warbler and African Desert Warbler

all plum	⇒	• (Orange- or pink-)yellow legs and bill with dark culmen and tip; iris yellow. • Upperparts orange-brown. • Rump and uppertail-cov deep rufous-orange.

- Small size, hardly any larger than Willow Warbler.
- Undergoes complete autumn moult, no moult-limit (in autumn often less worn than 1w). Prim with almost black tips ⇔ 1w.
- Prim and tail-feathers juv, with often distinctly worn tips, sometimes resulting in very short prim-projection. Prim with dark grey tips ⇔ ad.

sian Desert Warbler *Sylvia nana* L 12cm 4.7"

plum ⇒
- See introduction to Asian Desert Warbler and African Desert Warbler.
- Narrow dark tertial-centres.
- Tail tri-coloured: broad white outer-edge (t6 white, t4-5 with white tip), rufous outer webs of t1-5 and narrow dark centre of t1.
- Usually rather obvious colour contrast between upperparts and rufous (closed) tail, uppertail-cov and lower part of rump ⇔ in African Desert Warbler fainter or no colour contrast.
- Cream-coloured underparts; breast-sides rather dark ⇔ in African whiter.
- Legs and bill-base yellow.
- Alula contrastingly dark with narrow pale fringe ⇔ in African broad pale fringe along outer-edge and less dark centre often hidden under cov.

rican Desert Warbler *Sylvia deserti* L 12cm 4.7"

plum ⇒
- See introduction to Asian Desert Warbler and African Desert Warbler.
- Uniform tertials and t1 without obvious dark centres.
- Rather uniform warm sandy-coloured upperparts and crown (less colour contrast between upperparts, rump and tail than in Asian Desert Warbler).
- Legs and bill-base with pink wash.

abian Warbler *Sylvia leucomelaena* L 15.5cm 6.1"

plum ⇒
- Short prim-projection c.25%.
- Conspicuous long *rounded tail*.
- Similar in size to Western/Eastern Orphean Warbler with large rounded head; under field conditions looks bulkier, possibly caused by quiet behaviour.
- Dark eye (ad with small pale spots in iris, only visible at very close range).

⇒
- Broken white eye-ring, in ♀ eye-ring usually fainter ⇔ Western/Eastern Orphean.
- Rather sharply demarcated whitish fringes on tertials ⇔ Western/Eastern Orphean.
- Black tail with white outer-edge on t6 and tip of t5 and t6 (usually only visible on underside); tail strongly contrasting with paler upperparts ⇔ in Western/Eastern Orphean less black tail with complete white outer-side.
- Whitish underparts with brown-grey wash on flanks (as in Eastern Orphean).
- Black (ad ♂) or black-brown (♀ and 1s ♂) cap extending further towards mantle than in Western/Eastern Orphean.

⇒
- Completely deep brown upperparts and *rufous-brown fringes* to tertials and greater cov.
- Rather distinct but short supercilium between eye and bill (often only white spot above lores), normally also present in 1w ♀.

hav
- Holds tail in line with body or slightly downwards, sometimes flicks tail downwards (giving bulbul-like impression) ⇔ other *Sylvia*.
- Movements often distinctly quieter than other *Sylvia*.

og var   *S.l. negevensis* (Israel)

- Pale grey upperparts ⇔ in *leucomelaena* (Arabia, not in WP) grey-brown upperparts.

stern Orphean Warbler and Eastern Orphean Warbler

plum
- Tertials lack distinct pale fringes and almost concolorous with rest of wing and upperparts.
- Strong bill.
- Thick slaty-grey legs.
- Long prim-projection c.70% with 6-7 visible prim-tips.
- Eye-ring indistinct or absent (latter in ad ♂).
- Much white in tail-sides (see geog var; juv with slightly less white in tail).

⇒
- Pale iris (pale grey to yellow-white in ♂, dull grey-white in ♀).
- Black ear-coverts faintly bordered with dark grey (♀) or black cap (♂).
- In fresh autumn plumage conspicuous white tips to prim ⇔ 1w.

♀/1w
-1s
- Dark ear-coverts contrast with browner crown; lores paler.
- Dark iris (iris becomes paler in 1s, in ♂ sooner than in ♀).
- In 1w moult-limit in greater cov; in most Western in 1s too ⇔ in Eastern 1s normally all greater cov 2nd generation.

te
- Resembles large Lesser Whitethroat but with no distinct pale eye-ring, usually dark centres to undertail-cov (in Eastern always), longer tail, larger size, stronger bill and longer prim-projection.

stern Orphean Warbler *Sylvia hortensis* L 15cm 5.9"

plum ⇒
- See introduction to Western Orphean Warbler and Eastern Orphean Warbler.
- Underparts (especially flanks) *warm grey-brown* (white throat strongly contrasting) ⇔ in Eastern Orphean Warbler underparts paler with greyish flanks. Undertail-cov almost white, sometimes with faint dark centres but in most ind uniform ⇔ Eastern.
- Generally darker than Eastern with more grey-brown upperparts (♀ browner than ♂) ⇔ in Eastern upperparts greyer.
- t6 with elongated white wedge on inner web, extending to base ⇔ in Eastern more variable, ranging

voice	from similar to Western to short, more diagonal white wedge, sometimes only sloping white tip (latter not in Western). • Brown upperparts faintly bordered with greyish head and blackish ear-coverts ⇔ Eastern. • Song: quiet, thrush-like and rather simple with many repetitions and regular phrases. • Call: most common a rather thick 'tack', like Blackcap, but gives 'tjek' or 'tjuk-tjuk'.

Eastern Orphean Warbler *Sylvia crassirostris* L 15.5cm 6.

all plum	⇒	• See introduction to Western Orphean Warbler and Eastern Orphean Warbler. • Underparts whiter than in Western Orphean Warbler. • Dark centres to undertail-cov, creating faintly scaled pattern ⇔ Lesser Whitethroat and most Western • Bill longer than in Western (no overlap) with often more strongly curved culmen. • For pattern of t6, see Western. • Upperparts greyer and paler than in Western.
1s ♂/ad ♂		• Black cap larger, more distinctly bordered and more strongly contrasting with upperparts than in Western ad ♂.
1w/1s		• Crown paler than in Western 1w/1s.
1s	⇒	• Outer prim moulted, inner still juv; moult-limit in prim (also in Cyprus Warbler 1s) ⇔ Western 1s.
voice		• Song: faster, fuller and more varied than in Western with typical rolling, and both more Nightingale-lik whistles and more scratching tones. • Call: like Western (see Western) but perhaps less variable.

Barred Warbler *Sylvia nisoria* L 16.5cm 6

all plum	⇒	• Relatively strong, thrush-like bill with *conspicuous pinkish* basal part of lower mandible. • Long prim-projection c.80%.
ad		• Obvious white tips to tail-feathers (large on t6, becoming smaller towards central tail-feathers, t1 without white tip) creating conspicuous white tail-corners, visible especially in flight (in 1w at most ve slightly present). • 2 whitish wing-bars formed by pale tips to median cov and greater cov and white tips to tertials. • Pale yellowish iris.
ad ♂		• Whole underparts barred. • Upperparts with blue-grey wash.
ad ♀/1s ♂		• Flanks scaled, central part of underparts unpatterned. • Upperparts grey-brown. • 1s ♂ and ad ♀ similar but 1s ♂ with worn juv prim and slightly duller iris.
1w/1s	⇒	• Rather distinctly patterned wings with pale tips and fringes to sec, cov and tertials. • Dark 'V'-shaped spots on undertail-cov (dark undertail-cov with pale fringes). • Faint supercilium, dark ear-coverts. • Usually rather pale brown-grey upperparts. • Dirty-white underparts, in fresh autumn plumage diffusely spotted. • Iris dark to medium grey.

Lesser Whitethroat *Sylvia curruca* L 13cm 5

geog var	*S.c. curruca* (western Europe to eastern Asia, north of all other (sub)species)
all plum	• Dark ear-coverts contrast with slightly paler grey crown. • Pale underparts with grey-brown flanks contrast with white throat. • Cold grey-brown upperparts. • In fresh plumage, white eye-ring of which lower half usually broader. • Legs dark grey. • Often faint supercilium. • Tertials lack distinct dark centres. • Grey uppertail-cov and rump ⇔ Common Whitethroat. • Prim-projection c.70%.
ad	• Usually pale greyish iris.
1w	• Dark iris. • Pale outer-side of tail narrow and not pure white.
1s	• Prim and prim-cov brown and worn ⇔ in ad fresher and greyer.
geog var	*S.c. halimodendri* (central Asia south of *curruca* and *blythi*)
all plum	• Slightly paler, more rufous-brown/yellow-brown mantle, scaps and greater cov than in *curruca*; pale brown hind-neck (rather) forms well-defined border with grey crown. • Crown somewhat paler and greyer (in spring pure grey) than in *curruca* and therefore slightly more contrast between pale crown and dark ear-coverts. • Paler, more rufous tertials than *curruca*. • More white in t6 than *curruca* (no dark patterning along shaft of t6) and t5 with rather large white ti • Whiter underparts than *curruca* without distinct contrast between underparts and throat.
geog var	*S.c. minula* (central and eastern Asia)
all plum	• Pale sandy-brown or ochre upperparts gradually merging into greyish head; forehead and lores dark • Distinctly smaller than *curruca* with finer, shorter bill. • Underparts cream-coloured, slightly more deeply coloured on flanks. Slight contrast between relativ pale upperparts and relatively dark underparts. • Prim-projection short c.50% with 6 prim-tips beyond tertials. • Iris pale, often yellowish. • Relative pale upperside of tail.

- Lores dark but ear-coverts often hardly any darker than neck-side.
- Long tail with almost completely white t6 and white tips to t4 and t5 ⇔ in *curruca* pale pattern on t6 rather diffuse and dark around tip of shaft; t5 with at most very slight pale patterning.
- Pale bill-base.

ehav
- Restless, almost *Phylloscopus*-like, regularly flicks tail.

ote
- *S.c. margelanica* (not recorded in WP) similar to *minula* plumage-wise but distinctly larger with more blue-grey uppertail-cov contrasting with sandy-coloured upperparts and darker tail.

eog var   *S.c. blythi* (Siberia)

l plum
- On present knowledge similar to *halimodendri*; tail-pattern possibly more like *curruca* with slight dark patterning along shaft of t6 and only small white tip to t5.

oice eastern
- Call: along with a 'tek' call similar to *curruca*, often gives stuttering rattle (slightly reminiscent of
axa
  call of Sardianian Warbler but less sharp), while other inds give a nasal 'tjèèèèh'. It is possible that these different calls refer to different taxa.
- Song: very different from *curruca* and much more similar to southern *Sylvia* species. Completely warbling song (as often shortly given at start of song of *curruca*). Recognisable *curruca*-like rattle regular mixed in song, but sometimes completely lacking.

ote geog var
- *Lesser Whitethroat complex is currently being thoroughly investigated (e.g. by DNA analysis) and will probably result in the reclassification of the whole complex.*
- Identification of above-mentioned (sub)species is complicated because perhaps almost all have clinal zone with one or more other (sub)species.

me's Whitethroat *Sylvia althaea*   L 14cm 5.5"

l plum
- Dark grey head (darker than in Lesser Whitethroat *curruca* and more uniform) gradually merging into dark grey-brown upperparts ⇔ in Lesser *curruca* upperparts paler.
- Larger than Lesser *curruca* with stronger bill.
- Dark ear-coverts hardly contrasting with crown ⇔ in Lesser *curruca* crown paler than ear-coverts.
- Pale fringes to sec and tertials creating wing-panel in fresh plumage.
- Breast-sides brown-grey, flanks greyer than in Lesser *curruca*.
- t6 with very much pure white.

ote
- Lesser subspecies *caucasica* plumage-wise rather similar but smaller with finer bill and less white in t6.

mmon Whitethroat *Sylvia communis*   L 14cm 5.5"

plum
- Broad rufous fringes to tertials, sec and greater cov creating rufous wing-panel (also in Spectacled Warbler).
- Relatively thick bill.
- Prim-projection c.70% with 6-7 prim-tips beyond tertials.
- Dark tertial-centres; centres with rounded tips.
- Rather a lot of white in outer-side of tail (t6 largely whitish but not bright white and diffusely bordered with dark parts) but not strongly contrasting due to rather pale rest of tail.
- Narrow white eye-ring.
- Mantle rather rufous grey-brown in *communis* (but see geographic variation).
- Legs yellow-brown to orange.
- Rather pale brown-orange iris.

♂/ad ♂
- Blue-grey head (blue-grey lacking in some 1s).
- Pinkish breast.

♀/1w
- Crown concolorous with upperparts. Lores pale. Some ad ♀ with slightly greyish wash on head.
- Underparts browner than in ad ♂.

J
- Similar to ad ♀; dark iris.
- Prim, prim-cov and alula (almost) completely juv, usually worn.

og var   *S.c. icterops* (Middle East)

plum
- Upperparts brown-grey, lacks rufous-brown mantle ⇔ *communis*.
- Wing-panel paler and less rufous than in *communis*.
- Legs slightly more orange than in *communis*.

♂
- Distinct blue-grey head extending into mantle (head often rather dark) ⇔ in *communis* blue-grey does not extend to mantle.

ult   ⇒
- Usually moults completely in winter (in some western populations not complete); in spring fresh, in autumn worn ⇔ *communis*.

te geog var
- *S.c. volgensis* (eastern Europe and western Siberia) intermediate (possibly sometimes identical to *icterops*) and forms clinal bridge between *communis* and *icterops*.

rden Warbler *Sylvia borin*   L 14cm 5.5"

plum   ⇒
- Long prim-projection c.90%.
- Pale broken eye-ring; dark eye conspicuous.
- Lacks obvious patterning but greyish neck-side and faint supercilium.
- Relatively thick bill.
- Diffuse paler neck-side.
- Usually large pale and uniform area around bill-base.
- Legs thick and grey.
- Pale tips to tertials.
- Undertail-cov and vent often conspicuously white.
- Tail-feathers pointed ⇔ in ad rounded.

ult
- Complete spring moult; ad in autumn often distinctly worn ⇔ 1w fresh.

Blackcap *Sylvia atricapilla*   L 14.5cm 5.

all plum	• Uniform grey-brown (♀) to grey (♂) upperparts. • Silver-grey to grey-brown underparts; white undertail-cov, sometimes with weak dark feather-centres • Pale half-ring below eye. • Wings uniform. • Prim-projection c.70% ⇔ in Garden Warbler 100%.
1s ♂/ad ♂ ⇒	• Black cap.
♀ /juv ⇒	• Red-brown cap; in 1w ♂ in early autumn black crown with brown spots.
1s	• Prim, prim-cov and alula (almost) completely juv, usually worn compared to fresher rest of wing.
geog var	*S.a. heineken* (Madeira and Canary Islands)
ad	• Underparts darker grey than in *atricapilla*; throat not distinctly paler than neck-side ⇔ in *atricapilla* throat whitish.
note	• In melanistic morph (probably only in subspecies *heineken* and *gularis*, Azores) ♂ with entirely black head and breast; in ♀ whole plumage with rufous-brown wash.

Locustella **warblers**

• Longest undertail-cov broad and strongly rounded, almost as long or longer than t6 (not in Gray's Grasshopper Warble ⇔ *Acrocephalus* warblers.
• Very strongly rounded tail.
• Curved outer prim.
• Pale outer edge on (closed) wing.

Pallas's Grasshopper Warbler *Locustella certhiola*   L 13.5cm 5

all plum ⇒	• Blackish tertial-centres with cream-coloured outer edge and white spot on tip of inner web; rest of inner web with or without only very narrow pale fringe. Sometimes white spot almost absent in *rubescens* (see geog var).
⇒	• White tips to dark tail-feathers; t1 without white tip ⇔ in Grasshopper Warbler narrow pale fringes around tips of all tail-feathers when fresh.
	• Tail-feathers broad and faintly barred ⇔ Grasshopper.
	• Usually faintly marked rufous-brown rump and uppertail-cov, contrasting with very dark tail and dark streaked mantle (but see geog var). Longest uppertail-cov with large dark centre.
	• Strongly marked wings with pale fringes and sometimes whitish tips to greater cov and median cov, creating diffuse wing-bars (especially in ad). Whole of wing darker than upperparts.
	• Usually distinct supercilium (sometimes almost as in Sedge Warbler) but sometimes narrow and indistinct (see geog var).
	• Dark streaked greyish crown and distinct eye-stripe; rear-crown/hind-neck sometimes with grey was
	• Upperparts streaked on rufous-brown ground-colour. Grey-brown, usually almost unmarked hind-nec creating pale band between dark patterned crown and mantle.
	• Undertail-cov unpatterned or faintly patterned with diffuse dark centres ⇔ Grasshopper.
	• Prim-projection usually longer than in Grasshopper (c.80-100%).
	• Relatively strong bill, especially at base.
ad	• Rather faint uniform brown breast-band.
juv ⇒	• Finely streaked breast, creating weak breast-band; rest of underparts unpatterned. • Underparts with yellow wash ⇔ in ad whiter.
moult	• No or restricted partial post-juv moult. 1w moult completed in winter like ad, thus 1s like ad. • Some ad moult partially in summer with sometimes some prim moulted prior to migration.
geog var	*L.c. certhiola* (western and central Siberia)
all plum	• Paler background than in *rubescens*; upperparts with moderately broad streaking, almost absent on forehead and rump. • Supercilium long and distinct. • Hind-neck and neck-sides greyish.
geog var	*L.c. rubescens* (north-eastern Siberia)
all plum	• Dark rufous-brown without grey or olive colours; heavily and broadly streaked upperparts including uppertail-cov. • Supercilium relatively indistinct. • Deep-rufous rump faintly streaked. • Underparts, especially undertail-cov, warm-brown. • White tips to tertials often indistinct • Flight- and tail-feathers very dark.
geog var	*L.c. centralasiae* (southern central Asia)
	• Only indistinct and narrow streaking on upperparts and crown, nearly absent on forehead and rump; ground-colour relatively pale. • Supercilium moderately distinct. • Flight- and tail-feathers less dark than in other subspecies.
note geog var	• Some ind very difficult to identify to subspecies.

nceolated Warbler *Locustella lanceolata* — L 12cm 4.7"

l plum ⇒
- Undertail-cov sharply streaked with narrow dark lines, often broadening slightly towards tip but *not broadening towards base* ⇔ in Grasshopper Warbler large dark triangular centres to undertail-cov, broadest at base.
- Breast usually sharply streaked over large part, streaking often stronger on breast-sides and sharp streaks on flanks ⇔ in Grasshopper streaking usually restricted to upper breast (but variable in both species).
- Blackish tertial-centres with narrow, well-defined and evenly broad pale fringes; also sharply demarcated on inner webs ⇔ Grasshopper. In ad tertial fringe at tip of inner web often white and broadening slightly, in this respect resembling Pallas's Grasshopper Warbler.
- Undertail-cov cream-coloured to pale brown, often with paler tip; longest undertail-cov often lacks dark streak ⇔ in Grasshopper whitish undertail-cov.
- Mantle heavily streaked with broad continuous bars ⇔ in Grasshopper rows of dark spots on mantle (worn Grasshopper ad in late summer can also show continuous bars).
- Rather short prim-projection ≤ 50% with evenly-spaced prim tips ⇔ in Grasshopper prim-projection c.70% with prim tip spacings slightly increasing.
- Usually slightly stronger head-pattern than Grasshopper with narrow malar-stripe (malar-stripe usually absent in Grasshopper).
- Slightly shorter and less full tail than Grasshopper; tail sometimes looks rather narrow.
- Rump/uppertail-cov usually strongly patterned ⇔ Grasshopper.
- Longest tertial considerably longer than secondaries ⇔ in most Grasshopper longest tertial shorter, sometimes hardly longer than secondaries.
- Shorter, slightly thicker bill than Grasshopper; more triangular head-profile.
- (Yellow-)brown ground-colour on upperparts ⇔ in Grasshopper more green-brown.
- Short thick streaks on underparts.

d
v
- Evenly fresh plumage ⇔ in ad moult very variable, usually 2 generations of prim in autumn; strong wear points to ad.
- Fine, often slightly diffuse streaks on underparts, but variable and some ind have strong and well-defined streaks.

oult
hav
- Very restricted partial post-juv moult. 1w moults completely in winter like ad, thus 1s as ad.
- Only trembles with lower mandible during song ⇔ Grasshopper trembles especially with throat and tail.

te
- Sometimes paler brown-yellowish fringes on feathers of wings and upperparts, these ind very contrasting. Some Grasshopper also with paler fringes but less contrasting due to less dark feather centres.

asshopper Warbler *Locustella naevia* — L 13cm 5.1"

plum
- Undertail-cov strongly marked with dark triangular spots.
- Faint supercilium ⇔ Sedge Warbler.
- (Green-)brown, dark spotted upperparts.
- Underparts white to yellow-brownish with variable amount of streaking (sometimes unpatterned on underparts except undertail-cov).
- Tertials with cream-coloured fringes and dark centres; pale fringe widens towards base ⇔ Lanceolated Warbler.
- Legs pale pinkish.
- In spring sometimes wholly dark bill.

w
- Wing- and tail-feathers fresh ⇔ in ad worn in autumn.
- Underparts often with yellowish wash.

oult
- Very restricted partial post-juv moult. 1w moults completely in winter like ad, thus 1s as ad.
- Some ad moult partially or completely in late summer, with sometimes some prim moulted prior to migration.

te
- Variable in patterning on both underparts and upperparts: some ind with little patterning on underparts, strongly patterned ind resemble Lanceolated (which see for differences).
- See Lanceolated for other field marks.

og var   *L.n. straminea* (Siberia and western Asia)

plum
- Smaller and paler (greyer) than *naevia* with more strongly contrasting streaking on upperparts and (when present) underparts.
- Underparts often with little or no patterning, especially in 1w.
- Tail strongly graduated (see note).

te
- Only some ind identifiable by measurements: combination of p2 ≤ p4, wing-length ≤ 60mm, (slight) emarginations on outer web of p4 and distance between tip of t1 and t6 21mm.

er Warbler *Locustella fluviatilis* — L 15cm 5.9"

plum ⇒
- Distinct large pale tips to dark undertail-cov.
- Throat- and breast patterning vary from very faintly and diffusely spotted to strongly streaked.
- Green-brown to earth-brown upperparts with colder shading (upperparts usually darker than in Savi's Warbler).
- (Very) faint supercilium.
- Legs usually pale (brown-)pink.
- No emarginations on outer web of prim (as in Savi's).
- Very full tail, exaggerated by long undertail-cov.
- Prim-projection c.100% (as in Savi's). p2 longer or equal to p3 (as in Savi's) ⇔ all other passerines except some Great Reed Warblers.
- Lower mandible often conspicuously pink ⇔ in Savi's more brown-yellow.

juv/1w	• Wing- and tail-feathers fresh ⇔ in ad worn in autumn.
moult	• Probably no or very restricted partial post-juv moult. 1w moults completely in winter like ad, thus 1s as ad.
	• Ad partially moults some outer prim in summer, in late winter starts complete moult.
note	• See also Savi's.

Savi's Warbler *Locustella luscinioides* L 14.5cm 5

all plum	• Dark, somewhat *rufous-brown* upperparts (see geog var) ⇔ River Warbler.
	• Typical *Locustella*-structure (see above) lacking conspicuous patterning.
	• Rather faint, narrow supercilium.
	• Prim-projection c.80-100%. p2 longer or equal to p3 (as in River) ⇔ other passerines except some Great Reed Warblers.
	• Brown undertail-cov with diffuse paler tips; pale tips smaller and especially more ill-defined than in River (see geog var).
	• Brown flanks and undertail-cov.
	• No emarginations on outer web of prim (also in River).
	• Legs normally rather dark pink-brown.
	• Breast sometimes diffusely patterned ⇔ in River more well-marked.
	• Often whitish shaft on sec, prim, tail-feathers and tertials ⇔ in River normally hardly any paler (and in other unstreaked brown warblers).
juv/1w	• Wing- and tail-feathers fresh ⇔ in ad worn in autumn.
	• Centres of tertials, cov and sec darker than in ad.
1s	• 2 generations of prim (central fresh), rarely completely worn juv wings.
moult	• Probably very restricted or no partial post-juv moult. 1w moults completely in winter like ad, thus 1s as ad.
	• Some ad moult partially or completely from late summer on, continuing in winter area or on stop-over area in North Africa.
geog var	*L.l. fusca* (western to central Asia)
all plum	• Colder and paler brown upperparts than in *luscinioides*, more like River but paler.
	• Breast faintly streaked (resembles River but streaking more diffuse).
	• Rather distinct pale tips to undertail-cov (resembles River but less well-defined).

Gray's Grasshopper Warbler *Locustella fasciolata* L 15cm 5

all plum	• Large *Locustella* with rather strong bill. Slight resemblance to large River Warbler but undertail-cov uniform orange-yellow.
	• Rather short supercilium often more marked than in River and Savi's Warbler and due to rather dark lores.
	• Very fine stripes on ear-coverts.
	• Rather strong contrast between grey-brown breast(-band) and flanks and pale belly.
	• Uniform chestnut-brown upperparts when fresh in autumn; ad s more grey-brown.
	• Legs pale, pink-orange.
ad	• Grey underparts with warmer coloured flanks, vent and undertail-cov.
	• Blue-grey wash on head-side and supercilium.
juv/1w	• Yellow-brown underparts and supercilium; throat and breast with fine dark patterning.
	• Wings fresh ⇔ in ad worn.
moult	• Probably no or very restricted partial post-juv moult. 1w moults completely in winter like ad, thus 1s as ad.
	• Some ad moult partially in summer, with sometimes some prim moulted prior to migration.
note	• Extremely skulking.

Hippolais warblers and allies

Upcher's Warbler *Hippolais languida* L 15cm 5

all plum	• Larger than Eastern Olivaceous Warbler with relatively large head and usually strong bill.
	• Uneven spacing between tips of tertials: tip of middle tertials closer to tip of longest than to shortest
	• If not too worn, distinct whitish wing-panel which is often weaker than in Olive-tree but more distinct than in Eastern Olivaceous.
	• Dark tail thick and full; distinct whitish sides contrast rather strongly with dark upperside (similar to Olive-tree Warbler) ⇔ in Eastern Olivaceous less white in tail-side and less strong contrast.
	• Supercilium often extending shortly behind eye; behind eye usually as distinct as between eye and b ⇔ Olive-tree.
	• Legs rather dark brown-grey.
	• Rather dark wings (when fresh usually with obvious pale tips to prim) and tail contrast with paler upperparts, especially in more worn ind.
	• Long prim-projection c.80% ⇔ Eastern Olivaceous.
	• Completely pale, yellow to pinkish lower mandible.
	• p1 reaches at most slightly beyond tip of prim-cov ⇔ in Eastern Olivaceous p1 extends well beyond of prim-cov and in Olive-tree does not extend beyond prim-cov.
	• Upperparts generally greyer than in Eastern Olivaceous but some overlap (approaching Olive-tree).
1w	• Wings and tail fresh ⇔ in ad worn in autumn.
fl all plum	• White tail-sides usually clearly visible.
	• Flycatcher-like flight.
behav	• In breeding range regularly perches for prolonged periods on rocks and forages regularly on ground other *Hippolais* and Eastern Olivaceous.

- Waves tail horizontally and vertically; on migration tail sometimes flicked vertically like in Eastern Olivaceous but sometimes also upwards. Often 'wing-flicks'.
- Glides before landing (as in Olive-tree ⇔ Eastern Olivaceous).

Olive-tree Warbler *Hippolais olivetorum*   L 17cm 6.7"

all plum ⇒
⇒
- Long, strong bill with completely *orange-yellow lower mandible*.
- Very long prim-projection ± 100% with 7-8 prim-tips beyond tertials and rather even distances between visible prim-tips ⇔ in Upcher's Warbler usually 7 prim beyond tertials. p1 very short and not visible under field conditions.
- Conspicuous whitish wing-panel and fringes to tertials but these can, due to wear, completely disappear (ad autumn).
- Short, narrow supercilium restricted to above lores and short, weak dark eye-line. Supercilium often bordered by thin dark line on upperside.
- Blackish centres to tertials and flight-feathers contrast with *greyish to slaty-grey upperparts*.
- Uniform grey ear-coverts.
- Diffuse grey rear-flanks.
- Often weak dark patterning on undertail-cov.
- Full, long blackish tail with conspicuous white tail-sides.
- Legs strong and long, medium- to dark brown-grey.

juv/1w
moult
behav
- Wings and tail fresh; possibly no post-juv moult at all in breeding range ⇔ ad worn in autumn.
- Both ad and juv moult completely in winter and possibly do not moult at all in breeding range.
- Regularly waves (sometimes with tail spread) and dips tail, irrespective of season ⇔ Upcher's waves and dips tail mainly in breeding season.

Icterine Warbler *Hippolais icterina*   L 13cm 5.1"

all plum ⇒
- Long prim-projection c.80-100% with usually 7 prim-tips beyond tertials (sometimes 6 or 8).
- Conspicuous pale wing-panel ⇔ in Melodious Warbler often less conspicuous (wing-panel in ad of both species often indistinct from summer onwards).
- Upperparts rather pale grey-green.
- Yellow underparts; some 1w in autumn lack yellow on underparts.
- Prim-projection almost as long as tail-projection beyond wing-tip ⇔ Melodious.
- Faintly patterned or unpatterned lores (as in Melodious).
- p1 same length or slightly longer than prim-cov ⇔ Melodious.
- Legs grey to greyish ⇔ in Melodious brownish (however in some ind greyish).
- Supercilium usually reaches only slightly behind eye (as in Melodious).
- Angular head-profile ⇔ Melodious.

juv/1w ♀
moult
note
- Wings and tail fresh and no post-juv moult at all in breeding range ⇔ ad worn in autumn.
- Both ad and juv moult completely in winter.
- Some ind lack yellow on underparts and show greyer upperparts (as in some Melodious) and could therefore mistaken for e.g. (Western) Olivaceous Warbler.

Differences from (Western) Olivaceous:
- Indistinct, not white, outer-side of tail.
- Short p1 (in Western and Eastern Olivaceous Warbler p1 always reaches beyond prim-cov).
- Long prim-projection with strong uneven spacing between tips of projected prim.

Melodious Warbler *Hippolais polyglotta*   L 12.5cm 4.9"

all plum ⇒
⇒
- Tail-projection beyond wing-tips *c.2x prim-projection* ⇔ in Icterine Warbler equal to or shorter than prim-projection.
- Prim-projection c.60% with 5-6 (sometimes 7) prim-tips beyond tertials.
- Yellow underparts (see note in Icterine), sometimes slightly warmer brown-yellow on breast.
- Faint pale outer-side of outer tail-feathers, less conspicuous than in Icterine.
- p1 reaches relatively far beyond prim-cov; p2 obviously shorter than p3 (falling level with p6-p7) ⇔ in Icterine p1 does not or at most very slightly extends beyond prim-cov; p2 hardly shorter than p3 (falling level with p4).
- Slightly rounder head-profile than Icterine.
- Legs brown but in 1w often greyish (when legs brown then good distinction from Icterine).
- Pale wing-panel usually faint; when fresh, often rather distinct.

1w
moult
note
- Wings and tail fresh ⇔ in ad worn in autumn.
- Upperparts often more green-brown, warmer and less grey-green than in Icterine.
- From arrival in Europe in spring already moderately worn due to early winter moult ⇔ Icterine moults much later in winter and is therefore fresher in spring.
- See note under Icterine.

Eastern Olivaceous Warbler *Iduna pallida*   L 13cm 5.1"

all plum
- Obvious pale wing-panel due to pale fringes to outer web of sec and tertials (and in *elaeica* also often also *pale tips to sec*) ⇔ in Booted Warbler, Sykes's Warbler and Western Olivaceous Warbler wing-panel when present very faint, in *Acrocephalus* warblers always absent.
- Supercilium rather narrow and only distinct between eye and bill, usually fading away directly behind eye and extending up to one eye-diameter behind eye. Often slightly more distinct and longer than in Western, but less distinct than in Sykes's.
- Rather long and relative thick bill (when seen from above or below has broad bill-base); lower mandible entirely pale yellow-orange; culmen dark. Extreme tip often relatively strongly downcurved ⇔ in Sykes's often slightly more evenly tapering to tip, but variable.
- No yellow and green in plumage. Upperparts paler and greyer than in *Acrocephalus* warblers.

215

- Pale tip and fringe on (t4) t5 and t6 more distinct than in Booted and Sykes's (usually more distinct and whiter on inner web, especially towards tip) ⇔ in Blyth's Reed Warbler almost absent.
- Rather long prim-projection c.70% (true for *elaeica*, in other subspecies slightly shorter prim-projection) ⇔ Booted and Sykes's.
- Underparts white with faint brown wash on flanks.
- No distinct dark lateral crown-stripe (as in Sykes's) ⇔ Booted.
- 3 emarginations (p3-p5) on outer web of prim (rarely faint 4th on p6) ⇔ in Booted and Sykes's normally 4.
- Rather angular head-profile with often flat fore-crown and sometimes raised rear-crown feathers (also often in Olive-tree Warbler and Upcher's Warbler).
- Undertail-cov often rather long, sometimes reaching beyond wing-tip (as in Blyth's Reed).
- Relatively long tail almost straight-ended but central and outer tail-feathers (t1 and t6) slightly shorter (in Booted and Sykes's t1 and t6 often obviously shorter).

1w	• Wings and tail fresh ⇔ in ad worn in autumn.
	• Diffuse pale tips to greater and median cov (when well developed resembling Barred Warbler 1w).
behav ⇒	• Regularly flicks tail downwards continuously and sometimes holds tail downwards, often simultaneously with 'tjeck' call ⇔ Booted and Sykes's flick tail faster, shallower and in all directions; Western rarely moves tail at all.
voice	• Song: rather monotone and some parts reminiscent of Reed Warbler song.
	• Call: rather thick 'tjeck' often given simultaneously with downwards tail-flick (see behav).

geog var		*I.p. pallida* (north-eastern Africa)
all plum		• Smallest olivaceous warbler with relatively long tail
		• Upperparts slightly browner and warmer than other subspecies, especially less grey than *elaeica*.
		• Pale wing-panel usually faint, sometimes absent.
		• Prim-projection shorter than other subspecies; ± 50%.

geog var		*I.p. elaeica* (south-eastern Europe, Middle East)
all plum		• Slightly smaller than Western with slightly greyer upperparts (often with green-brown wash). Larger than Booted with often greyer upperparts.
		• Underparts nearly completely white, flanks faintly cream-coloured.
		• Usually pale wing-panel and small pale tips to sec (*narrow pale rear edge of arm*) ⇔ e.g. Sykes's.
		• Rather dark prim and tail-feathers (⇔ e.g. Western).

geog var		*I.p. reiseri* (north-western Africa directly south of and partially overlapping with range of Western)
all plum		• Much smaller and more *Phylloscopus*-like than Western (which overlaps in range) with shorter bill.
		• Prim-projection short: ± 50%.
		• Pale yellowish bill with only culmen dark.
		• Upperparts sandy brown, slightly paler than Western (with distinct pale wing-panel ⇔ Western).
		• Supercilium sometimes extending behind eye.
		• Usually much white on tips of inner webs of t5 and t6.
		• Underparts, especially flanks, faint cream-coloured (in Western usually browner).
		• More sandy-coloured than other subspecies, especially on hind-neck, crown and forehead.

Western Olivaceous Warbler *Iduna opaca* L 14cm 5.

all plum ⇒		• Long bill with *very broad bill-base* (when seen from above or below *sides convex*) ⇔ in Eastern Olivaceous Warbler sides straight. Lower mandible entirely pale as in Eastern.
		• Upperparts and wings uniform, no pale wing-panel ⇔ Eastern.
		• Largest olivaceous warbler, larger than Eastern. Can resemble Upcher's Warbler but paler tail.
		• Tail slightly longer and fuller than in Eastern.
		• Legs thicker than in Eastern.
		• Upperparts pale grey-brown, usually slightly browner than Eastern (especially on back and rump) but differences small and dependent on bleaching and state of wear.
		• Usually less white in t5 and t6 than in Eastern (only evenly narrow fringe around tip).
		• Faint head-pattern (pale lores and ear-coverts concolorous with crown and neck-side); supercilium extending to above eye ⇔ in Eastern usually faint dark loral-spot and slightly darker ear-coverts.
1w		• Wings and tail fresh ⇔ in ad worn in autumn.
behav		• No conspicuous tail movements.

Booted Warbler *Iduna caligata* L 12cm 4.

all plum ⇒		• Obvious, usually broad supercilium ending (rather) faintly behind eye, also *broad above and directly behind eye* ⇔ Sykes's Warbler. Head-pattern resembles Paddyfield Warbler but fainter.
		• Short prim-projection c.40-60% with 5-6 prim-tips beyond tertials.
		• Rather pale (grey-)brown upperparts, in fresh plumage often slightly darker brown.
		• Usually relatively short bill (long billed ind occur) with dark culmen; pale lower mandible with dark tip ⇔ in Eastern Olivaceous Warbler and Sykes's longer bill with entirely pale lower mandible (although in Sykes's often small dark 'shadow' present on lower mandible).
		• Rather dark tertial-centres (in worn ad sometimes even blackish) with (usually) *dark shaft* ⇔ in Sykes's tertial-centres paler and dark shaft faint or absent (in *Phylloscopus* shaft of tertials paler or concolorous with dark centre).
		• Dark lateral crown-stripe rather well-defined.
		• Pale tip and outer edge of t5 and t6 but less conspicuous and more diffusely demarcated than in Eastern Olivaceous and most Sykes's, sometimes hardly any paler outer-side of tail (see Sykes's).
		• Conspicuous large and dark eye, exaggerated by only faint eye-stripe ⇔ Paddyfield.

- Supercilium often pinched in on upperside directly before eye ⇔ Sykes's, Eastern Olivaceous and Paddyfield.
- Central tail-feathers (t1) shorter than other tail-feathers (as in Sykes's and less obvious in Eastern Olivaceous) ⇔ in *Acrocephalus* same length or longer.
- Normally 4 emarginations on outer web of prim (emargination on p6 often faint, sometimes absent) ⇔ in Eastern Olivaceous 3.
- Long p1 (as in Sykes's) reaches far beyond prim-cov (> visible part of prim-cov) ⇔ in Eastern Olivaceous p1 shorter, reaches less far behind prim-cov, often ≤ visible part of prim-grey.
- Legs grey-pink to grey-brown, often with slightly darker toes ⇔ in Eastern Olivaceous more uniform and more brown-grey.
- Pale fringes to sec, tertials and cov contrast rather strongly with dark feather centres (in 1w in autumn) ⇔ most *Phylloscopus*.

w
- Wings and tail fresh ⇔ in ad worn in autumn but some ad start prim-moult in late summer.
- Legs sometimes greyish.

ehav
oice
- Moves tail quickly in all directions, as in Sykes's ⇔ Eastern Olivaceous.
- Song: rather soft, very fast and continuous stream of repeated harsh notes (same theme constantly repeated). Typically starting quietly then slowly increasing in volume ⇔ Sykes's.
- Call: dry, somewhat scratching 'dsrek', obviously longer than call of Sykes's.

otes
- For more differences with Paddyfield see Paddyfield account.
- See also Sykes's.

kes's Warbler *Iduna rama*   L 12.5cm 4.9"

l plum
- Head paler and more faintly marked than in Booted due to shorter supercilium *concentrated between bill and eye and normally merging with eye-ring and not or hardly extending behind eye*. At most small and faint dark loral-spot, no or hardly any eye-stripe and dark lateral crown-stripe faint or absent (effect of shadow).
- Long, thin bill, usually distinctly longer than in Booted Warbler. When seen from above or below sides straighter (not concave as in Booted) but differences less clear than between Western Olivaceous Warbler and Eastern Olivaceous Warbler.
- Long tail.
- Rather uniform pale wings, *tertial-centres only slightly or not at all darker than rest of wing* (no pale wing-panel and pale tips to sec as in Eastern Olivaceous *elaeica*), but dark tertial shafts often present ⇔ in Booted distinctly dark tertial- and alula-centre.
- Short prim-projection c.30-40%; often slightly shorter than in Booted and much shorter than in Eastern Olivaceous.
- Pale tip and fringe of t5 and t6 more distinct and more sharply demarcated than in Booted, *also extending onto inner web* ⇔ Booted.
- Upperparts paler than in Booted and Blyth's Reed, without rufous-brown wash. Generally more similar to pale Blyth's Reed than to pale Booted.
- Entirely pale orange lower mandible as in Eastern Olivaceous. Sometimes very small dark spot on tip of lower mandible. Upper mandible generally paler than in Booted due to broader pale cutting edge.
- Central tail-feathers (t1) shorter than others (as in Booted and olivaceus warblers) ⇔ in other *Iduna* and *Acrocephalus* longer.
- Extreme bill-tip straighter than in Eastern Olivaceous.
- Slightly larger size than Booted but smaller than Eastern Olivaceous.
- Long p1 reaches far beyond prim-cov (as in Booted), often further than visible part of prim-cov ⇔ in Eastern Olivaceous not as far as visible part of prim-cov.
- 4th emargination on outer web, also usually distinct on p6 (⇔ in Booted faint); emarginations on outer web fall before sec-tips (in Eastern Olivaceous about level with sec-tips).
- Leg colour nearly as in Booted but generally darker, often more grey-brown. In 1w sometimes greyish (as in Booted 1w).
- Often has whitish underparts with at most only faint grey brown wash on flanks ⇔ in Booted buffish wash on flanks and vent.

J
- Wings and tail fresh ⇔ in ad worn in autumn but some ad start prim-moult in late summer.
- Pale fringes to wing feathers narrow or almost absent ⇔ Booted 1w.

hav
ce
- Like Booted, but more inclined to stay in higher vegetation (at least in breeding range).
- Song: rather similar to Booted but more loud and sharp (without hesitant start) with more cracking and whistling notes and no constant repeatition of same theme.
- Call: short 'tek', very similar to 'tek' calls of Lesser Whitethroat, Bluethroat and some *Acrocephalus* warbler species.

ck-billed Warbler *Iduna aedon*   L 17cm 6.7"

plum ⇒
⇒
⇒
- No supercilium but diffuse, *large pale spot on lores* (sometimes sickle-shaped).
- Long tail *strongly rounded*.
- Strong bill with distinctly curved distal part of culmen. Completely pale lower mandible; upper mandible usually dark except cutting-edge (sometimes only culmen dark).
- Short prim-projection c.60% with 5-6 prim-tips beyond tertials.
- Rather pale underparts but flanks and undertail-cov usually deep ochre-yellow.
- Forehead often darker, creating capped effect.
- Rounded head-shape.
- Weakly rufous rump and broad weakly rufous fringes on flight-feathers and tail-feathers.
- Wings and tail fresh ⇔ in ad worn in autumn.

ult
- 1w and ad undergo complete moult in winter; in spring still rather fresh.

Reed warblers

Paddyfield Warbler *Acrocephalus agricola*

L 13cm 5.

all plum ⇒	• Short prim-projection c.40-60% with 5-6 prim-tips beyond tertials.
⇒	• Broad white supercilium reaches far behind eye.
	• Dark upper mandible; lower mandible *pale pinkish with large dark tip.*
	• Dark crown sides exaggerate supercilium.
	• Relatively pale iris.
	• Dark eye- and loral-stripe; eye-stripe usually widens behind eye ⇔ in e.g. Booted usually faint eye- o loral-stripe.
	• Long tail, usually rather strongly rounded.
	• Whitish underparts, especially throat and central part of upper breast (only slightly darker wash on flanks). In spring breast-side and flanks often warm cream-brown contrasting with white central part of underparts.
	• Usually faint pale neck-side.
	• Generally smaller than Reed Warbler (usually slightly larger than Booted but overlap).
	• Tertials usually rather dark (especially outer webs) with pale fringes; sometimes paler, then with black shaft-streak as in Booted.
	• 2-3 emarginations on outer webs of prim-projection (p3-p4 (p5)).
	• p1 reaches only slightly beyond prim-cov ⇔ in e.g. Booted far beyond.
	• Legs dark brown, sometimes paler, often with pinkish wash.
	• In some ind faint pale outer-edge of t6 (but less so than e.g. in Booted).
	• When fresh, often rufous-brown to rufous rump and uppertail-cov ⇔ Booted.
1w	• Wings and tail fresh ⇔ in ad worn in autumn.

Blyth's Reed Warbler *Acrocephalus dumetorum*

L 13.5cm 5

all plum ⇒	• Wings uniform brown, *also slightly paler outer-edge of flight-feathers obviously brown* ⇔ in Reed Warbler, Marsh Warbler and Eastern/Western Olivaceous Warbler paler outer-edge obviously paler to whitish.
⇒	• Almost uniform tertials (with at most faint dark centres), concolorous with rest of wing and upperpart ⇔ in other small unstreaked *Acrocephalus* (except some Paddyfield Warblers and most Sykes's Warbler) darker tertial-centres.
	• Uniform upperparts; cold brown in ad, slightly warmer in 1w.
	• Usually conspicuous supercilium, concentrated between eye and bill (broad above lores), extending o slightly behind eye (sometimes also in Marsh Warbler and Reed Warbler).
	• Underparts whitish with grey-brown wash on flanks; undertail-cov white of faint cream-coloured ⇔ Reed underparts browner, including undertail-cov.
	• Long slender bill with fine tip; lower mandible often with faint dark tip ⇔ in Reed, Marsh and Eastern/Western Olivaceous Warbler completely pale lower mandible.
	• Legs usually darker brown than in other small unstreaked *Acrocephalus*, in 1w usually greyish but variable.
	• Prim-projection relatively short, 60-70% with 6-7 evenly-spaced prim-tips beyond tertials.
	• p2 distinctly shorter than p3, falling level with p5-7 ⇔ in Reed and Marsh p2 almost same length as p3, at max falling level with p5.
	• Emarginations on outer webs of p3 and p4 distinct and falling level with longest and middle tertial-ti ⇔ in Reed, Marsh, Sykes's Warbler and Eastern/Western Olivaceous emargination on outer web(s) more towards wing-tip.
	• Usually low and flat forehead.
ad	• No colour difference between prim and tail-feathers ⇔ in Marsh prim slightly paler than tail-feathers
	• No or hardly any pale tips to tail-feathers ⇔ in Marsh normally distinct.
	• In spring inner web of alula dark, often forming darkest area on closed wing (outer web normally pal concolorous with rest of wing) ⇔ in Marsh in spring dark alula (outer web especially very dark) with narrow well-defined white outer edge.
1w	• Slightly warmer brown on upperparts than ad, *especially on outer edge of flight-feathers.*
	• Legs often conspicuously grey, toes paler.
	• Wings and tail fresh ⇔ in ad worn in autumn.
behav	• Frequently holds tail upwards.
voice	• Song: quiet with many repetitions and much mimicry (sometimes reminiscent of Song Thrush). Whistling and nasal tones uttered directly after each other giving the impression of two birds singing together.
	• Call: Sharp and powerful, Lesser Whitethroat-like 'tek', often uttered in short series. Marsh can sometimes utter 'tek'-like call but normally less short and sharp.

Marsh Warbler *Acrocephalus palustris*

L 14cm

all plum	• *Contrasting wings* with blackish centre of alula and pale fringes to tertials.
	• Underparts pale; normally just weakly darker flanks and breast-sides ⇔ Reed Warbler. Underparts often with variable yellow wash ⇔ Reed.
	• Grey-brown to yellow-brown upperparts, 1w slightly deeper brown; rump not rufous ⇔ Reed.
	• Legs greyish to yellow-brown (in 1w sometimes very pale, dull yellow) with usually pale claws ⇔ ir Reed claws usually dark.
	• Long prim-projection usually 100% with 7-8 prim-tips beyond tertials (spacings between prim-tips rather even).
	• Prim-tips with pale fringes when not too worn.
	• Rump usually concolorous with rest of upperparts (in 1w somewhat rufous-brown) ⇔ in Reed usua distinctly rufous-brown.

- Only emargination on outer web of p3.
- Slightly blunter and shorter bill than Reed but much overlap.
- Almost round nostril ⇔ in Reed more oval-shaped but much overlap.
- Eye-ring and supercilium about equally distinct ⇔ in Reed usually more obvious eye-ring.

d
- Longest tertials extends beyond sec-tips (sometimes also in 1w) ⇔ in Reed and Blyth's Reed Warbler longest tertials and tips of sec at same level.
- In spring pale underparts with citrine-yellow wash; less brown flanks than in most Reed.
- In spring in Europe fresh plumage due to complete pre-breeding moult in Africa ⇔ Reed and Blyth's Reed on arrival in spring in Europe already slightly worn due to complete post-breeding moult in late autumn/winter (but see Caspian Reed Warbler *fuscus*).

w
- Wings and tail fresh ⇔ in ad worn in autumn.

oice
- Song: phrases interspersed by short pauses, much variation and almost completely comprising mimicry, except often used and *typical* 'wrrreet wrrreet wrrreet'.
- Call: often similar to Reed Warbler but sometimes slightly less coarse 'tjeh tjeh tjeh tjeh'. Rarely also more 'tjek'-like calls (see Blyth's Reed).

ote
- Almost all features overlap with Reed.
- See also Blyth's Reed.

eed Warbler *Acrocephalus scirpaceus*　　　　　　　　　　　　　L 13.5cm 5.3"

ll plum
- Brown upperparts; rump warmer brown than mantle and tail.
- White throat contrasts with brown flanks and breast ⇔ Marsh Warbler.
- Usually dark claws ⇔ Marsh.
- Prim-projection c.70-100% with 7-8 prim-tips beyond tertials (spacings between prim-tips almost equal).
- Legs grey-brown to red-brown, generally darker and greyer than in Marsh (especially in imm).
- Only emargination on outer web of p3 (sometimes also faintly on p4).
- Tip of upper mandible hangs slightly over lower mandible ⇔ Marsh.
- Long, slender bill with culmen and ridge of lower mandible parallel ⇔ in Marsh slightly deeper bill-base.
- Usually oval nostril (in Marsh only faintly oval).
- Eye-ring usually more obvious than supercilium.

w
- Slightly warmer brown on underparts than ad.
- Wings and tail fresh ⇔ in ad worn in autumn.

oult
- Both ad and juv moult completely in winter.

oice
- Song: dull and monotone stream of jittery notes, sometimes interspersed by short whistles.
- Call: nasal and low-pitched, rattling 'trrehh trrehh trrehh' ⇔ call of Marsh often very similar (see Marsh).

ote
- Almost all field marks overlap with Marsh.

Caspian Reed Warbler *A.s. fuscus* (Middle East and north and east of Caspian Sea)

l plum
- Usually pale tips and fringes to t3-t6, normally more obvious than in Marsh and *scirpaceus*.
- Pale grey-brown upperparts, especially hind-neck (or neck-sides) and crown greyish; rump and uppertail-cov paler, slightly warmer sandy-coloured (see note) ⇔ in *scirpaceus* warmer brown upperparts; rump and uppertail-cov deep warm brown.
- Usually very pale underparts, only flanks faint brown-grey, therefore resembling Marsh (but no yellow on underparts as in Marsh) or sometimes (Eastern) Olivaceous Warbler.
- Faint pale fringes to cov and flight-feathers (when not too worn) ⇔ almost lacking in *scirpaceus*.
- One emargination on outer web of prim-projection (p3), sometimes faint 2nd (p4). 2nd more often present than in *scirpaceus*, never in Marsh. Emargination on outer web of p3 level with sec-tips ⇔ in Marsh more towards wing-tip.

w
- Slightly warmer brown than ad, especially on rump.

oult
- Some populations moult later than *scirpaceus* (especially populations with longest migration route); plumage fresher in spring with darker prim and pale tips (like Marsh).

ote
- Ground-colour of plumage and measurements very variable. Ind from populations with long migration route larger and with longer wings than *scirpaceus*, other populations (e.g. from Israel) small and short-winged. Some ind as warm coloured as *scirpaceus* and indistinguishable on plumage only. Small part of population distinctly grey on upperparts without warmer colour on rump (mainly from eastern part of range).

Differences from Eastern Olivaceous Warbler:

- White in tail-feathers restricted to extreme tip.
- No pale wing-panel.
- Upperparts and upperwing darker.
- Short p1, at most only marginally extending beyond prim-cov.
- Well marked eye-ring below eye.
- One obvious emargination on outer web at p3 ⇔ in Eastern Olivaceous 2, sometimes 3.
- Slender bill-base; no orange-yellow at bill-base.
- Legs darker.
- Lacks pale tips to sec.
- Longer prim-projection with 7-8 prim-tips beyond tertials and p2 only slightly shorter than p3 (wing-tip).

dge Warbler *Acrocephalus schoenobaenus*　　　　　　　　　　　L 12.5cm 4.9"

plum
- Very conspicuous supercilium; faint pale median crown-stripe.
- Dark lores and moustachial-stripe creating severe facial impression.
- Mantle faintly streaked.

	• Whitish tertial-fringes ⇔ Moustached Warbler.
	• Rump and uppertail-cov unstreaked and somewhat rufous-brown, often colour contrast with colder brown back and mantle.
	• Contrasting wings, feathers with dark centres and pale fringes.
	• Legs brownish.
juv	• Normally faintly streaked or speckled breast (⇔ ad) but in some ind not or hardly developed.
	• Pale central crown-stripe, faint and not well-defined ⇔ Aquatic Warbler.
	• Wings and tail fresh ⇔ in ad often heavily worn in autumn.
moult	• Both ad and juv moult completely in winter.

Aquatic Warbler *Acrocephalus paludicola* L 12.5cm 4.

all plum	⇒	• Well-defined *pale median crown-stripe* (often broadening before bill and becoming slightly cream-coloured).
	⇒	• 2 pale bands on mantle, extending onto inner web of tertials.
	⇒	• Almost *uniform pale lores*; moustachial-stripe faint or absent ⇔ Sedge Warbler.
		• Very contrasting wings; feathers with dark centres and very broad pale fringes ⇔ Sedge.
		• Pointed tail-feathers, most conspicuous in slightly elongated t1; in flight pointed tail.
		• More yellow overall than Sedge.
		• Legs pinkish ⇔ in Sedge darker and more brownish.
ad		• Fine dark shaft-streaks on breast and along flanks ⇔ juv and Sedge.
juv		• Entire plumage fresh and usually distinctly yellowish (probably completely juv in Europe) ⇔ in ad largely worn.
		• Most ind with (almost) plain underparts but small area with obvious breast-spotting and in some ind with some streaks along flank.

Moustached Warbler *Acrocephalus melanopogon* L 13cm 5.

all plum	⇒	• Short prim-projection *only c.30%* ⇔ in Sedge Warbler c.100%.
	⇒	• Rufous-brown upperparts, flanks (especially rear-flanks) and breast; underparts darker than in Sedge
		• Very conspicuous broad white supercilium, widening behind eye and ending rectangularly.
		• Very dark crown and ear-coverts contrast with white supercilium and throat. Middle of crown dark brown, side of crown black; no pale median crown-stripe as in Sedge (in worn Sedge ad in autumn sometimes almost completely dark centre of crown).
		• Tertial-fringes (almost) concolorous with upperparts ⇔ in Sedge contrasting whitish tertial-fringes.
		• Wing formula very different from Sedge: p1 reaches far behind prim-cov, p2 considerably shorter than p3 and at least 3 emarginations on outer web of prim ⇔ in Sedge p1 shorter than prim-cov, p2 almos as long as p3 (wing-tip) and only 1 emargination on outer web of prim.
		• Eye- and moustachial-stripe usually more distinct than in Sedge.
		• Legs dark ⇔ in Sedge usually pale.
		• Mantle rather strongly streaked, stronger than in (most) Sedge.
moult		• Both juv and ad moult completely at end of summer.
behav		• Often forages in reed-stems just above water.
note		• Ageing in autumn usually impossible (both juv and ad moult completely at end of summer); retained worn feathers point to ad.

geog var	**Eastern Moustached Warbler** *A.m. mimicus* (from Middle East eastwards)
all plum	• Less rufous upperparts and underparts and often slightly longer prim-projection than *melanopogon*.
note	• Migratory ⇔ *melanopogon*.

Great Reed Warbler *Acrocephalus arundinaceus* L 18cm 7.

all plum	• Head dominated by broad, dark loral-stripe and usually rather broad supercilium.
	• Long prim-projection c.100% with 7-8 prim-tips beyond tertials (distances between prim-tips rather even).
	• Strong bill, ending somewhat bluntly; at least pale basal half of lower mandible.
	• Rather rufous-brown upperparts; rump and uppertail-cov palest and warmest coloured part of upperparts.
	• Pale underparts with cream-brown wash mainly on flanks and undertail-cov.
	• Legs thick and usually rather pale brown-grey, often with pink wash, sometimes darker.
1w	• Wings and tail fresh ⇔ in ad worn in autumn.
moult	• Both ad and 1w moult completely in winter.

geog var	*A.a. zarudnyi* (Asia)
all plum	• Paler on underparts and slightly colder brown on upperparts than *arundinaceus*; bill-structure as in *arundinaceus*. Can resemble eastern subspecies of Clamorous Reed Warbler *brunnescens* but underparts paler.

Oriental Reed Warbler *Acrocephalus orientalis* L 17.5cm 6.

all plum	• Strongly resembles Great Reed Warbler but with *well-defined thin streaks* on throat and upper-breas
	• Whitish tips to tail-feathers.
	• Short prim-projection c.70% with little spacing between 7 prim-tips beyond tertials ⇔ Great and Bas Reed Warbler.
	• Underparts nearly white with brown wash on flanks.
	• Upperparts grey-brown as on Great *zarudnyi* and Basra.
	• Legs greyish.
	• Whitish supercilium extending rather far behind eye.

- Strong bill running more parallel and ending more bluntly than in Great.
- Obvious loral-stripe but less dominant than in Great.

oult
- Both ad and juv moult completely in early autumn, in spring usually with distinct wear ⇔ Great and Basra moult in winter range and are more fresh in spring.

lamorous Reed Warbler *Acrocephalus stentoreus*   L 17cm 6.7"

Features mentioned below apply to *stentoreus* (Egypt) and *levantina* (Israel).

l plum ⇒
⇒
- Dark underparts; *flanks and undertail-cov rufous-brown* ⇔ Great Reed Warbler.
- Short prim-projection c.60% with only 5-6 prim-tips beyond tertials.
- Short narrow supercilium not extending behind eye.
- Deep rufous-brown upperparts.
- Long bill with more slender base than in Great.
- Legs dark greyish.
- Somewhat flatter forehead than in Great.
- Long tail.

ote
- Regularly occurs in variable dark morph. In darkest ind completely dark bill, black-brown upperparts, underparts almost as dark as upperparts and head almost completely dark without supercilium.

eog var   *A.s. brunnescens* (east of Caspian Sea and around Persian Gulf)

l plum
- Prim-projection c.70% with 6-7 prim beyond tertials.
- Upperparts colder olive-brown than in *stentoreus*.
- Underparts paler with less dark undertail-cov than in *stentoreus*.
- Supercilium pure white and mainly before eye.
- Bill-structure between Great and *stentoreus*.
- Shape of tail and leg colour as in *stentoreus*.

ote
- Probably does not occur in dark morph ⇔ *stentoreus* and *levantina*.
- Northern populations migratory ⇔ *stentoreus* and *levantina*.

pe Verde Warbler *Acrocephalus brevipennis*   L 14.5cm 5.7"

plum
- Slightly larger than Reed Warbler and Marsh Warbler with longer bill and legs.
- Short prim-projection ≤ 50%.
- Upperparts and underparts more brown-grey than Reed and Marsh.
- Legs grey.

ehav
ote
- Forages regularly on ground.
- Endemic to Cape Verde Islands.
- Closely related to Greater Swamp Warbler *A. rufescens* (Africa).

sra Reed Warbler *Acrocephalus griseldis*   L 15cm 5.9"

plum ⇒
⇒
- Conspicuous long and slender bill with culmen relatively strongly curved near bill-tip, often giving impression of slightly downcurved bill.
- Dark sec, prim and especially tail-feathers contrast rather strongly with white underparts; only pale grey-brown flanks (undertail-cov whitish).
- Long prim-projection c.100%.
- Grey-brown upperparts.
- Only one emargination on outer web of p3 ⇔ in other large reed warblers 2, but 2nd often indistinct.
- Conspicuous, very pale supercilium; above eye pure white and extending rather far behind eye. Behind eye often (much) narrower and fainter than between eye and bill.
- Pale half eye-ring under eye often conspicuous.
- Legs rather dark greyish.
- Wings and tail fresh ⇔ in ad worn in autumn.

ult
- 1w and ad undergo complete moult in winter; in spring still rather fresh.

Cisticolas and allies

ting Cisticola *Cisticola juncidis*   L 10.5cm 4.1"

plum ⇒
⇒
- Very short prim-projection < 20%.
- Strongly rounded tail with white terminal band (visible especially on under-side during song-flight).
- No distinct eye- and loral-stripe; eye conspicuous.
- Long dark tertials with narrow, well-defined pale fringes.
- Underparts unpatterned; flanks with brown-pink wash.
- Culmen relatively strongly curved.
- Legs pale pinkish.
- Well-defined pale-dark streaked crown and upperparts (on upperparts forming narrow pale lines); rear-head almost uniform.

juv
- Ad and (most) juv moult completely in autumn and plumage thereafter identical.
- Late hatched ind retain some outer prim into 2cy.

hav ⇒
- Usually persistent bounding song-flight with loud penetrating 'tsip...tsip...tsip'.

ceful Prinia *Prinia gracilis*   L 10.5cm 4.1"

plum ⇒
- Faintly patterned head ⇔ Scrub Warbler.
- Very long, strongly rounded tail.
- Tips of underside of tail-feathers with black-white pattern.
- Grey-brown underparts.

ad/juv	• Entirely whitish underparts ⇔ Scrub Warbler. • See Zitting Cisticola.

Cricket Warbler *Spiloptila clamans* L 11.5cm 4.

all plum	⇒	• Somewhat resembles Graceful Prinia (similar structure due to e.g. long tail and short wing) but *upperparts uniform cream-brown*.
	⇒	• Strongly patterned wing due to pale tips to *black median cov and greater cov creating wing-bars* ⇔ Graceful Prinia. • Black lateral crown-stripe. • Pale grey rear-head. • Well-defined black tertial-centres with broad pale fringes ⇔ Graceful Prinia. • Underparts pale cream.

Scrub Warbler *Scotocerca inquieta* L 10.5cm 4.

all plum	⇒	• Distinct eye-stripe and supercilium ⇔ Graceful Prinia. • Very long rounded tail. • Dark tail-feathers (only t1 paler) with pale tips. • Greyish upperparts. • Whitish underparts with somewhat rufous flanks.
geog var		*S.i. saharae* (north-western Africa except west coast of Morocco)
all plum		• Upperparts browner, less greyish than in *inquieta*. • Pale iris ⇔ in *inquieta* dark. • Supercilium cream-coloured ⇔ in *inquieta* white.
geog var		*S.i. theresae* (south-western Morocco)
		• Like *saharae* but darker with bolder streaks on crown, hind-neck and underparts.
ad/juv		• See Zitting Cisticola but in some ind prim retained into 2cy, those then more worn than in ad.

Waxwings

Bohemian Waxwing *Bombycilla garrulus* L 20cm 7

ad ♂	• White tips to visible prim, creating white hooks on tips (in some ad ♀ very narrow). • Broad yellow terminal tail-band. • Sharply defined black throat patch.
♀	• Black throat patch usually rather weakly defined. • Narrow yellow terminal tail-band.
juv	• Diffusely streaked underparts.
1w	• Lacks pale tips to prim (only pale fringes along outer web).
fl all plum	• Silhouette often resembles Common Starling.
note	• Japanese Waxwing *B. japonica* sometimes recorded as (most probably) escape. Differs from Bohemia Waxwing by red-tipped tail-feathers, lack of white tips to sec and prim-cov and smaller size. Ad with white prim tips, reddish wing-bar and blue-grey edge to prim and tail-feathers. Under certain feeding conditions (in captivity) colour of tail-feather tips sometimes subdued.

Cedar Waxwing *Bombycilla cedrorum* L 18cm 7

all plum	⇒	• White undertail-cov ⇔ in Bohemian Waxwing red-brown.
	⇒	• Almost uniform upperwing, only inner web of tertials with white fringes ⇔ in Bohemian conspicuous white tips to prim, prim-cov and sec. • White supercilium ⇔ in Bohemian none. • Except juv, yellow wash on underparts, belly especially yellowish. • Smaller than Bohemian.

Grey Hypocolius *Hypocolius ampelinus* L 17.5cm 6

all plum ad ♂	• Greyish plumage with *long tail* and broad dark terminal band. • Black mask extending over ear-coverts; crown pale. • Large white tips to outer prim. • Grey upperparts and upperside of tail.
ad ♀	• Plumage mainly grey-brown. • Dark prim-tips with narrow white fringes along tips ⇔ ad ♂. • Only faint mask ⇔ ad ♂.
1s	• Like ad but moult-limit in greater cov (outer juv darker and with pale fringes). Part of tail-feathers ar all prim still juv but pattern little different from ad-type.
fl ad ♂	• Black hand with *large white tips to all prim*.
fl ad ♀	• Completely grey brown wings with faint dark trailing edge along hand.

Wallcreeper, nuthatches and treecreepers

Wallcreeper *Tichodroma muraria* L 16.5cm

all plum	• Bright pink-red cov (except greater cov), base of flight-feathers and prim-cov. • Pale grey upperparts contrast with dark wings. • Long, slender bill.

- Black tail with pale grey terminal band.
- Black throat and breast.
- Usually diffuse greyish patch on throat.
- White throat and breast merging into grey rest of underparts.
- Juv wing and tail retained but at most only very slightly different from those of ad.
- Like miniature Eurasian Hoopoe with very strong rounded wings.
- Variable amount of white spots on outer prim, usually 4 (like 'mirrors' in large gulls).

üper's Nuthatch *Sitta krueperi*   L 12cm 4.7"

- Large orange breast patch.
- Orange undertail-cov with white tips (as in Eurasian Nuthatch).
- Blue-grey underparts; white throat.
- Black cap extending from bill to halfway along crown.
- Narrow black eye-stripe.
- Slightly duller markings than ♂ and usually with fainter eye-stripe, sometimes broken on lores.

rsican Nuthatch *Sitta whiteheadi*   L 11.5cm 4.5"

- Relatively narrow and often diffuse eye-stripe for a nuthatch, slightly fading away above ear-coverts; broad white supercilium.
- Dirty grey-brown underparts.
- Black cap merging faintly into blue-grey upperparts.
- Dark blue-grey cap, usually only slightly darker than upperparts.
- Slightly less well marked than ♂.
- Only nuthatch on Corsica.

gerian Nuthatch *Sitta ledanti*   L 12cm 4.7"

- Underparts with variable 'dirty' orange-brown wash; undertail-cov with weak dark centres ⇔ Corsican Nuthatch.
- Rather long, strong bill.
- Black cap extending from bill to halfway along crown (as in Krüper's Nuthatch).
- Eye-stripe as in Corsican ad.
- A 'washed out' version of ♂ with grey cap and diffuse eye-stripe.

d-breasted Nuthatch *Sitta canadensis*   L 11.5cm 4.5"

- Very broad white supercilium extending to hind-neck and not extending over bill.
- Broad eye-stripe widens on neck-side.
- Undertail-cov uniform ⇔ Eurasian Nuthatch.
- Orange underparts.
- Black crown.
- Cream-coloured to orange wash on underparts (less deeply coloured than ♂)
- Dark crown but not black.

rasian Nuthatch *Sitta europaea*   L 13.5cm 5.3"

- Orange undertail-cov with sharply demarcated white spots.
- Grey-blue upperparts.
- Broad, long black eye-stripe.
- Orange underparts but depth of colour very variable (see geog var).
- Prim and prim-cov still juv, in 2cy worn but often only slight difference with ad, sometimes moult-limit in greater cov.

S.e. caesia (central Europe)

- Underparts varying from almost completely orange to faint rufous.

Siberian Nuthatch *S.e. asiatica* (Siberia)

- Smaller size with smaller bill than other subspecies.
- Obvious white supercilium.
- Completely white underparts, only undertail-cov at most orange with white spots.
- Upperparts paler and greyer than in *europaea* and *caesia*.
- Often narrow white wing-bar over greater cov.
- More prone to irruptions than other subspecies, in some winters invasions into Scandinavia and Baltic region.

S.e. europaea (Scandinavia)

- Upperparts pale blue-grey.
- Underparts mainly white, orange restricted to rear-flanks, vent and undertail-cov.
- White throat and breast, orange from belly to undertail-cov.

stern Rock Nuthatch *Sitta tephronota*   L 17cm 6.7"

- Very long black eye-stripe widens on hind-neck and ends abruptly ⇔ Western Rock Nuthatch.
- Much larger than Western with stronger bill.
- Legs grey (as in Western).
- Pale blue-grey upperparts.

note	• Plumage as in Western but generally slightly warmer rufous on vent and undertail-cov (see note).
	• Differences with Western most pronounced where ranges approach/overlap. In eastern part of range (where Western does not occur) eye-stripe narrower and vent and undertail-cov less deeply coloured than in Western. Western in western part of range (where Eastern does not occur) with rather deeply coloured vent and undertail-cov and eye-stripe widening on hind-neck.

Western Rock Nuthatch *Sitta neumayer*   L 15cm 5

all plum	• Underparts whitish with orange wash on belly, vent and undertail-cov, but without sharp white spots undertail-cov characteristic of Eurasian Nuthatch.
	• No white in tail ⇔ Eurasian.
	• Long black eye-stripe narrowing on hind-neck ⇔ Eurasian.
	• Pale blue-grey upperparts.
	• Relatively long bill.
	• Legs grey ⇔ in Eurasian flesh-coloured.
note	• See note Eastern Rock Nuthatch.

Eurasian Treecreeper *Certhia familiaris*   L 13.5cm 5

all plum	• Underparts whiter than Short-toed Treecreeper (which see for other differences).
	• Upperparts paler medium-brown than Short-toed, often with warmer-toned rump.
1w	• See Short-toed 1w.
voice	• Song: descending, rather short verse, starting high and thin, with some fuller notes in middle and ending in a trill. Structure of verse like song of Willow Warbler, sound more like song of European Blu Tit ⇔ in Short-toed rising in pitch.
	• Call: very high pitched, thin 'sriii' or 'siii' (latter lacking 'r'-tone) *quickly repeated* ⇔ 'normal' call of Short-toed. Note that Short-toed has a less frequent call which is rather similar to call of Eurasian but slightly less high-pitched (more similar to call of Redwing) and normally not repeated quickly.

geog var	*C.f. familiaris* (northern Europe)
ad	• When fresh, pale upperparts due to numerous white spots.
	• Rump rufous-brown to rufous.

geog var	*C.f. macrodactyla* (central Europe)
ad	• Darker and browner on upperparts (but rump often cinnamon-coloured) than *familiaris* and weaker supercilium (nearly as Short-toed).
	• Underparts not completely white; flanks and vent with brown wash.
	• Tips to prim pale grey instead of white ⇔ Short-toed and *familiaris*.

geog var	*C.f. britannica* (Britain)
ad	• Mostly resembles *macrodactyla* but upperparts slightly darker and slightly more rufous-brown.
	• Underparts paler than *macrodactyla* but flanks, vent and undertail-cov with rufous wash ⇔ *familiaris*.

geog var	*C.f. corsa* (Corsica)
ad	• By far longest bill of all subspecies and similar to Short-toed.
	• Upperparts sharply streaked white.
	• Outer webs of prim brighter rufous than in other subspecies.

Short-toed Treecreeper *Certhia brachydactyla*   L 13cm 5

all plum	• Bill longer than in Eurasian Treecreeper.
	• Wing-bar on prim formed by pointed blocks, like row of teeth ⇔ in Eurasian often blunter blocks.
	• Pale spot on p4 (as part of bar over prim) small or absent ⇔ in Eurasian obviously present and ofter placed slightly higher making wing-bar curve upwards.
	• Hind-claw slightly shorter than rear-toe ⇔ in Eurasian both about same length.
	• Isolated small pale tips on projected prim ⇔ in Eurasian pale fringe around tip, extending along inner web.
	• Longest alula-feather normally with pale outer-edge ⇔ in Eurasian absent (or sometimes very narro
	• Flanks, vent and undertail-cov with brown-grey wash (but in some ind in fresh plumage almost whit ⇔ in Eurasian completely white underparts (in both Eurasian *macrodactyla* and *britannica* often slig (rufous)brown wash on undertail-cov/vent).
	• Distance between tip of p7 and p8 relatively small (< 2 x distance between p6 and p7) ⇔ in Eurasi distance between p7 and p8 large, > 2 x distance between p6 and p7.
	• Inner webs of tertials rather dark with often diffuse darker tip ⇔ in Eurasian almost uniform pale gr
	• White throat contrasts with slightly darker rest of underparts ⇔ Eurasian.
	• Supercilium between eye and bill fainter ⇔ in Eurasian usually as distinct before eye as behind.
	• Pale crown-streaks fade away towards fore-crown ⇔ in Eurasian evenly distinct over whole crown.
1w	• Outer prim-cov with elongated wedge-shaped pale tips, concentrated on outer-web ⇔ in ad pale tips smaller (sometimes even absent), more triangular or round and evenly distributed on both sides of shaft.
voice	• Song: see Eurasian.
	• Call: normally full 'tjüü, tjüü, tjüü', or with final note higher or lower 'tjüü, tjüü, tjee' or 'tjee, tjee, tjee tüü'. Less frequently high Redwing-like call, see Eurasian.

Wrens

ren *Troglodytes troglodytes*   L 9.5cm 3.7"

l plum
- Barred tail-feathers and flight-feathers.
- Very small with fine long bill.
- Long narrow supercilium.

w-1s
- Sometimes moult-limit in greater cov; juv-type warm-brown without pale tips, ad-type slightly greyer and often with pale or white tips.

eog var | Multiple subspecies in e.g. Iceland (*islandicus*) and islands north of Britain and west of Norway.

l plum
- Larger with longer bill than subspecies of mainland Europe.
- Upperparts usually darker than subspecies of mainland Europe (except e.g. *hirtensis* of St Kilda, Scotland).
- Underparts in some subspecies dark and strongly barred (e.g. *zetlandicus* from Shetland, Scotland).

ote
- Often found in rocky habitats, especially coasts.

Mockingbirds and allies

orthern Mockingbird *Mimus polyglottos*   L 25cm 10"

plum
- Conspicuous wing pattern; 2 white wing-bars, white prim-cov and white spot on prim-base (flight).
- Long tail with broad white outer side.
- Pale iris.
- Dark, slightly downcurved bill.
- Legs long.
- Upperparts grey; underparts pale brown-grey.

own Thrasher *Toxostoma rufum*   L 29cm 11.5"

plum
- Size as Blackbird.
- Very long rounded tail.
- Pale underparts with thrush-like dark spots, usually forming long streaks.
- Upperparts and tail completely rufous-brown.
- Pale iris.
- Two pale wing-bars.

ey Catbird *Dumetella carolinensis*   L 21.5cm 8.5"

plum
- Almost completely dark slaty-grey.
- Black cap and tail.
- Rufous undertail-cov.
- Smaller than Common Starling.

v
- Moult-limit in tertials and/or cov; juv prim brownish.
- Iris dark brown ⇔ in ad red-brown.

Starlings

stram's Starling *Onychognathus tristramii*   L 25.5cm 10"

plum
- Dark with pale orange prim with black tips (especially conspicuous in flight but also visible when perched).
- Longer tail than in Common Starling (somewhat Blackbird-like silhouette).
- Slightly decurved bill.

♂
- Deep-black with purple gloss.

♀
- Like ♂ but less glossy; greyish head and breast.

♂
- Like ad ♂ but prim-cov also orange.

let-backed Starling *Cinnyricinclus leucogaster*   L 16.5cm 6.5"

♂
- Entire upperside including head and upperside of tail uniform dark violet. Underparts milky white. In back-light looks black-and-white.

♀/imm
- Upperside brown with yellowish fringes to all feathers of wing.
- Head yellow-brown with numerous dark streaks.
- Underparts white with numerous well-defined dark spots in irregular lines.

urian Starling *Agropsar sturninus*   L 19cm 7.5"

olum
- Structure like Common Starling but bill shorter and thicker and smaller size.
- Underparts uniform pale grey.
- Pied wings with 2 wing-bars and pale base to sec, prim and prim-cov.
- Pale scaps creating conspicuous pale band.
- Dark mantle and crown (in ad ♂ black; in imm/ad ♀ brown).
- Pale uniform head-side; eye conspicuous.
- Underparts pale grey.
- Purple gloss on upperparts and green gloss on wings ⇔ 1w.
- Dark grey (♂) to grey-brown (♀) upperparts contrast with paler head (contrast in ♂ larger than in ♀).

♂
- Purple and green gloss on mantle and wings ⇔ juv/ad ♀.
- Sharply streaked neck ⇔ juv/ad ♀.

♀
- No obvious gloss-colour on upperparts and wing.
- Pale crown ⇔ ad.

Starlings

fl all plum	• Broad wing-bar.
	• Pale rump and uppertail-cov.
	• Pale underwing.
fl ♂	• Pale rump-patch well-defined.
fl ♀	• Pale rump very weakly bordered and larger than in ♂.

Spotless Starling *Sturnus unicolor*   L 21cm 8

all plum	• ♂ with uniform dark eye, ♀ with paler iris and often whitish circle around iris.
ad	• Feathers on throat and usually also neck-side strongly elongated, creating rough 'beard' ⇔ in Common Starling shaft less strongly elongated (no overlap in length of shaft in ad ♂ of both species).
	• Purplish gloss over plumage but under certain conditions looks greenish.
	• Legs pure pink ⇔ most Common.
	• In summer bill of ♂ like Common, in ♀ summer with pinkish base.
ad ♀	• Less deep black and less glossy than ad ♂.
ad s	• Uniform black (♂) or brown-black (♀).
juv	• Dark grey-brown with only narrow paler fringes to cov, prim, sec, tail-feathers and tertials.
	• Underparts almost as dark as upperparts with only slightly paler throat and central part of underparts ⇔ in Common juv distinctly pale throat and paler central part of underparts.
1w	• ♂ and ♀ with fine white spots on head and underparts, undertail-cov with narrow 'V'-shaped mark, ♀ with narrow pale fringes to all feathers of wings (in ♂ hardly any).
	• Pale fringes to cov and scaps narrow, pale tips to vent and undertail-cov narrow 'V'-shaped ⇔ in Common pale marks on vent and undertail-cov broad and triangular.
1s	• Often identical to ad (but see 1w) but some ind still with one or more juv sec (browner and more wor than neighbouring ad-type) ⇔ Common.
moult 1w	• Juv moults as in juv Common completely into 1w but timing more variable (e.g. depending on hatching time); complete moulted 1w (like ad w) from August, while complete juv ind are recorded to as late as September.
fl all plum ⇒	• Very dark underwing-cov contrast with rest of underwing ⇔ in Common underwing-cov dark brown with broad pale fringes, lacking obvious contrast with rest of underwing.

Common Starling *Sturnus vulgaris*   L 21cm 8

all plum	• ♂ with uniform dark eye, ♀ with paler iris and often *whitish circle* around iris.
ad	• Throat-feathers with elongated shafts (in ad ♂ longer than in ad ♀; in 2cy ♂ as in ad ♀).
ad ♂ s	• Blue-grey bill-base.
♀	• Yellow bill (in summer bill-base whitish).
juv	• Grey-brown with paler throat and diffusely streaked underparts (*zetlandicus* from Shetland Islands considerably darker with uniform black-brown underparts and only narrow pale fringes to feathers of wings.
1w	• Early start of complete moult towards 1w. In midsummer conspicuous mix of juv and ad-type feather thereafter mostly like ad (but see also ad).
1w-1s	• 2nd generation tail-feathers with rather rounded tips, rather ill-defined pale fringes and ill-defined da subterminal fringe ⇔ in ad tail-feathers more pointed with sharper and blacker subterminal fringe.

Rose-coloured Starling *Pastor roseus*   L 21cm

all plum ⇒	• Shorter and thicker bill than Common Starling with rather deep base and *curved culmen*.
ad ♂ s	• Bright pink upperparts, scaps and central part of underparts.
	• Long crest, often hanging down to hind-neck; throat-feathers distinctly elongated.
	• Black parts glossy, head with purple gloss.
	• Black base of lower mandible sharply demarcated from rest of bill.
ad ♀ s	• Like ad ♂ s (and usually difficult to distinguish form ad ♂ s) but black parts usually slightly duller pink parts usually slightly less deeply coloured.
	• Crest shorter than in ad ♂, not hanging down to hind neck and throat-feathers not or less elongate
	• Usually pale fringes to uppertail cov and undertail-cov.
	• Variable dark base of lower mandible, sometimes black and sharply defined as in ad ♂.
ad w	• Pink parts much duller than in ad s and head with small pale speckles.
juv	• *Orange-yellow* bill with usually dark culmen and tip.
	• Dark wings and tail contrast with pale underparts.
	• Diffuse, pale sandy rump.
1w	• Like ad w but upperparts and underparts dull brown-grey or grey-brown.
	• Often still some juv sec with pale fringes.
1s	• In ♂ shorter crest than ad ♂.
	• Pink parts duller, sometimes whitish.
moult	• Retains largely juv plumage to winter (but moult-timing very variable) ⇔ Common juv.
	• Ad moult completely in winter range ⇔ Common.
note	• Leucistic Common juv can theoretically be almost identical to Rose-coloured juv but bill-structure characteristic.

Common Myna *Acridotheres tristis*   L 23c

all plum	• Black head with thick yellow bill and bare yellow spot behind eye.
	• Upperparts and underparts warm dark grey-brown; undertail-cov pale.
	• White prim-cov and base of sec creating large white spot on closed wing.
	• Legs thick, yellow.
	• Pale outer-edge to tail.
fl all plum	• White prim-cov and base of sec creating large white panel on upperwing.
	• White underwing-cov and base of sec contrast strongly with dark rest of underwing.

Sunbirds

gmy Sunbird *Anthreptes platurus* L 10cm 3.9" (excl central tail-feathers of ad ♂ s)

plum	
♂ s	• Short downcurved bill.
	• Strongly elongated central tail-feathers, almost as long as body-length.
	• Blackish upperparts, head and breast with green gloss.
	• Yellow belly, vent and undertail-cov.
♂ w	• Like ♀ with black-spotted throat and green gloss on cov.
	• Grey brown upperparts.
	• Yellow underparts.
	• Narrow supercilium and eye-stripe.

e Valley Sunbird *Anthreptes metallicus* L 10cm 3.9" (excl central tail-feathers of ad ♂ s)

plum	
♂ s ⇒	• Similar to Pygmy Sunbird in equivalent plumage, except ad ♂ s.
♀/1w	• Lower part of dark breast with purple gloss ⇔ Pygmy ad ♂ s
	• Slightly more distinct supercilium and eye-stripe than Pygmy ad ♀/1w.
	• Only central part of underparts yellow; throat, flanks and undertail-cov whiter ⇔ Pygmy ad ♀/1w.
	• Upperparts slightly greyer than in Pygmy ad ♀/1w.
te	• Except ad ♂ s possibly indistinguishable from Pygmy, although species do not normally overlap in range.

estine Sunbird *Nectarinia osea* L 10.5cm 4.1"

plum	
♂ s	• Long downcurved bill.
♂ w	• Black plumage with purple to green gloss.
	• Like ♀ with dark spots on underparts and darker wings with purple gloss.
	• Almost completely brown-grey with slightly darker wings and tail.

rple Sunbird *Cinnyris asiaticus* L 10cm 3.9"

plum	
♂ s	• Rather short downcurved bill, slightly less curved and slightly shorter than in Palestine Sunbird.
♂ w	• Completely dark with (green-)blue and purple gloss, more green than Palestine.
	• Resembles ad ♀ but with dark vertical stripe over underparts and black wings with green gloss on cov.
♀	• Upperparts grey-brown; underparts whitish with yellow wash ⇔ in Palestine no yellow wash.
	• White tips to outer tail-feathers.
♂	• Like ad ♀ but tail black and wings mix of juv and black ad ♂-type feathers.

ning Sunbird *Cinnyris habessinicus* L 12cm 4.7"

plum	
♂ s	• Medium-long strongly downcurved bill.
	• Green gloss on head, mantle and upper breast and *purple forehead*.
♀	• Broad red breast-band, on upper- and lower sides bordered by blue line. Yellow patch on breast-side.
	• Upperparts brown, underparts pale grey. Long supercilium.
	• Dark tail with narrow pale sides.

Dippers

ite-throated Dipper *Cinclus cinclus* L 18.5cm 7.3"

plum	
	• Thickset dark songbird with very conspicuous white breast and throat.
	• Nearly as ad but small white tips to outer greater cov and prim-cov; sometimes moult-limit in greater cov. Later in winter prim-cov worn/bleached.
	• Iris grey-brown to medium dark brown ⇔ in ad warmer brown, often chestnut.
	• Tail-feathers, prim and sometimes other parts of wing still juv and obviously brown and worn.
av	• Dives and swims, sometimes with wings open.

g var Black-bellied Dipper *C.c. cinclus* (northern Europe)

• Dark parts of underparts uniformly coloured, very dark brown.

g var *C.c. aquaticus* (central Europe)

• Deep warm red-brown lower breast and belly (creating very broad red-brown band ⇔ *gularis*). Some ♀ with almost dark belly and only very slightly browner lower breast, such ind very difficult to separate from other subspecies.
• Paler upperparts, hind-neck and crown than *cinclus*.

g var *C.c. gularis* (England, Wales and parts of Scotland)

• Red-brown lower breast; more narrower red-brown band than in *aquaticus* (subspecies *hibernicus* (Ireland and western Scotland) darker on underparts and with even narrower red-brown band on lower breast. But see darker-bellied *aquaticus* (above).

Thrushes

te's Thrush *Zoothera aurea* L 29cm 11.5"

lum ⇒	
⇒	• Whole underparts densely marked with dark *sickle-shaped spots* ⇔ in Mistle Thrush juv has rounded spots.
	• Boldly patterned wings with e.g. pale band over prim-cov and flight-feathers.

Thrushes

	• Long bill.
juv-1w	• Ageing often difficult but 1w usually with moult-limit in greater cov; juv greater cov (outer) shorter and with larger and more symmetrical shaped pale tips than ad-type.
	• White tips to t3 and t4 smaller and more diffusely bordered than in ad.
fl all plum ⇒	• Underwing with strongly contrasting white and dark bands. Marginal and lesser cov white, median cov and greater cov black, base of flight-feathers white, tips to flight-feathers dark.
⇒	• Strongly patterned upperwing with pale band over base of prim and dark band over central part of flight-feathers.
	• Large white corners to tail-tip (in 1w smaller than in ad).
behav	• Shy. Usually walks by sneaking over ground.

Siberian Thrush *Geokichla sibirica*   L 21cm 8

all plum	• Legs very pale yellow-brown.
	• Black-white patterned undertail-cov.
	• Strong bill.
ad ♂	• Very dark plumage (with grey-blue wash) and very broad, conspicuous white supercilium and pale b over middle of belly and vent.
1w ♂	• Like ad ♂ but supercilium patchy, pale patterning on ear-coverts and pale submoustachial-stripe. Wings often more brown-grey.
ad ♀/1w ⇒	• Long supercilium connected with pale rear border of ear-coverts (sometimes broken).
	• Pale centre of ear-coverts, pale submoustachial-stripe and throat.
	• 2 rather faint wing-bars over greater cov and median cov.
	• Obvious submoustachial- and malar stripe.
	• Middle of belly pale.
(1w) ♀	• Densely spotted breast and flanks.
	• Upperparts dark brown.
1w-1s	• Moult-limit in greater cov.
	• Juv wings brownish.
fl all plum	• Underwing pattern similar to White's Thrush.
	• White tips to t4, t5 and t6.

Varied Thrush *Ixoreus naevius*   L 24cm

all plum	• Pied-patterned with deep cream-colored supercilium, throat, belly, wing-bars and prim-base.
	• Uniform grey upperparts.
ad ♂	• Black breast-band and ear-coverts.
ad ♀	• Like ad ♂ but black parts (breast-band and ear-coverts) greyish and cream-coloured parts less vivi
fl all plum	• Underwing pattern as in Siberian Thrush and White's Thrush but contrasting less strongly.

Wood Thrush *Hylocichla mustelina*   L 20cm

all plum	• Uniform orange-brown upperparts (hind-neck and crown rufous).
	• White underparts almost completely marked with well-defined, rounded black spots; flanks also with white background ⇔ *Catharus* thrushes.
	• Fine pale streaked ear-coverts.
	• Relatively short tail.
	• Strong bill ⇔ *Catharus* thushes.

Hermit Thrush *Catharus guttatus*   L 17.5cm

all plum ⇒	• Rather narrow but well-defined pale eye-ring.
⇒	• Rufous tail, uppertail-cov and outer webs of prim, (slightly) contrasting with upperparts.
	• Rather bold and well-defined breast spotting concentrated on centre of breast; often joining togethe into stripes.
	• Supercilium often rather conspicuous but less broad than in Swainson's Thrush due to rather dark lores.
	• Paler basal part of lower mandible but less distinct than in Swainson's, Bicknell's Thrush and Grey-cheeked Thrush.
	• Faintly notched tail.
	• Greyish head-side, sometimes completely brown (then concolorous with crown).
1w	• Pale tips to greater cov creating wing-bar.
fl all plum ⇒	• Dark band over pale underwing-cov (as in other *Catharus* thrushes).
behav	• Frequently flicks wings and tail.

Swainson's Thrush *Catharus ustulatus*   L 17.5cm

all plum ⇒	• Conspicuous broad yellowish eye-ring.
⇒	• Broad but short yellowish supercilium merging into usually uniform pale lores ⇔ in Song Thrush supercilium extending behind eye and obvious loral-stripe.
	• Upperparts uniform medium-brown (not cold brown as in Grey-cheeked Thrush).
	• Rather distinct spotting on breast on yellowish ground-colour, fainter spotting continues on to dirty white belly ⇔ Song.
	• Ear-coverts usually paler than crown (see Hermit Thrush).
	• Grey-brown flanks.
1w	• See Hermit.
fl all plum	• See Hermit.

ey-cheeked Thrush *Catharus minimus*   L 18.5cm 7.3"

| plum |
• Narrow indistinct eye-ring, often incomplete.
• Generally cold grey-brown.
• Head-side and breast-sides greyish; ear-coverts slightly spotted.
• Well-defined dense spotting on upper breast, fading towards belly (often more strongly spotted than Swainson's Thrush).
• Underparts white/brown-grey without yellow.

v
• See Hermit Thrush.

all plum
• See Hermit.

cknell's Thrush *Catharus bicknelli*   L 17cm 6.7"

| plum |
• Like Grey-cheeked Thrush but upperparts and tail slightly warmer brown.
• Prim-projection shorter than in Grey-cheeked, c.80%.
• Basal half of lower mandible yellow; pale basal part of lower mandible larger than in Grey-cheeked (≥ half of bill length) ⇔ in Grey-cheeked more flesh-coloured and more restricted to base.
• Head-side more uniform and browner than in Grey-cheeked.
• Rufous upper-tail, resembles Hermit Thrush.
• Outer webs of prim with rufous wash.

v
• See Hermit.

all plum
• See Hermit.

te
• Not yet recorded in WP, although some previous records of Grey-cheeked may in fact have referred to this species.

ery *Catharus fuscescens*   L 17.5cm 6.9"

| plum ⇒ ⇒ |
• Completely rufous-brown upperparts (sometimes more yellow-brown).
• Uniform diffuse pale lores.
• Narrow eye-ring mainly behind eye, sometimes entirely absent ⇔ Swainson's Thrush.
• Faint malar stripe at most ⇔ stronger in other *Catharus* thrushes.
• Faint brown breast spotting, concentrated on upper-breast ⇔ in other *Catharus* thrushes spotting blackish.
• Head-side often with greyish wash.
• Pale grey flanks ⇔ in other *Catharus* thrushes darker brown-grey.

v
• See Hermit Thrush.

all plum
• See Hermit.

kell's Thrush *Turdus unicolor*   L 21cm 8.5"

⇒
• Eye-ring yellow.
• Legs yellow.

♂
• Blue-grey upperparts and head.
• Bright yellow bill.
• Uniform grey throat, breast, upper part of belly and flanks; rest of underparts white.

♀
• Like faintly coloured ad ♂ with faint supercilium; malar stripe extending into poorly developed breast patterning.
• Bill dull yellow.

all plum
• Underwing-cov orange; underside of flight-feathers very dark grey.

g Ouzel *Turdus torquatus*   L 25.5cm 10"

| plum ⇒ |
• Pale fringes to cov, tertials and sec (creating pale wash over closed wing).
• Long prim-projection c.100% ⇔ in Blackbird c.70%.
• Yellow bill, often with dark culmen.
• No conspicuous pale orbital-ring ⇔ Blackbird.

♂
• Mainly black with large white sickle-shaped breast patch.
• Bill yellow.

♀
• Resembles ad ♂ but slightly duller brown-black with faint pale scales on mantle and underparts (some ad ♀ very similar to ♂).
• Bill duller yellow than in ♂.
• Breast-patch often not pure white ⇔ ad ♂.
• Breast-patch rather distinct (in 1w ♂) to completely absent (in 1w ♀). In 1w ♀ breast often darker than rest of underparts.
• Pale throat and submoustachial-stripe.
• Distinct pale scales on underparts.
• Moult-limit in greater cov.

g var   Southern Ring Ouzel *T.t. alpestris* (central Europe)

• Underparts strongly scaled white with pale bases to feathers ⇔ *torquatus*.
• Pale fringes to wing-feathers broader than in *torquatus*.

g var   Caucasian Ring Ouzel *T.t. amicorum* (Caucasus)

• Underparts as in *torquatus*; wings (especially sec and greater cov) with completely pale grey outer webs or broad pale grey fringes on outer webs.

ckbird *Turdus merula*   L 26cm 10"

♂
• Completely black with orange-yellow orbital-ring and bill.

♀
• Dark brown but paler throat and pale brown breast with dark streaking. Underparts rather variable,

	some ind with paler underparts and dark spots or almost orange breast.
1w-1s	• Pale orbital-ring.
	• Moult-limit in greater cov.
	• Juv prim brownish.
	• In 1w bill dark.
1w ♂	• Completely dull black often with juv outer greater cov with pale tips.
	• Dark bill and no conspicuous pale eye-ring.
geog var	*T.m. mauritanicus* (north-western Africa)
all plum	• Smaller size than *merula*.
ad ♀	• Darker and especially greyer than *merula* with yellow bill.

Eyebrowed Thrush *Turdus obscurus* L 22cm 8

all plum ⇒	• Uniform orange breast and flanks (sometimes faint in 1w); rest of underparts uniform white.
	• Obvious supercilium contrasts with dark eye-stripe.
	• Legs very pale flesh-coloured with whitish nails.
ad ♂	• Grey unpatterned throat and ear-coverts.
ad ♀/1w	• White throat sometimes with black streaking; dark brown-grey ear-coverts with fine pale streaks.
	• Little or no colour difference between head and upperparts (1w ♂ often already with greyer head).
1w-1s	• Moult-limit in greater cov or all greater cov still juv with pale tips ⇔ ad.
fl all plum ⇒	• Pale underwing, underwing-cov *pale brown-grey*.

Dusky Thrush *Turdus eunomus* L 24.5cm 9

all plum ⇒	• Blackish spotted underparts (⇔ Naumann's Thrush); central part of underparts uniform white.
⇒	• Very conspicuous whitish supercilium, usually broadening behind eye ⇔ in Naumann's more cream-colored to rufous.
	• Dark tail with only narrow (rufous) brown outer edge on base of outer tail-feathers.
ad ⇒	• Large red-brown wing-panel (in ad ♂ creating uninterrupted panel over median cov, greater cov, sec and tertials).
	• Blackish crown and ear-coverts.
	• Patterned upperparts with blackish centres to mantle feathers and scaps ⇔ Naumann's.
ad ♂	• Red-brown outer webs of greater cov, on closed wing creating uniform red-brown band ⇔ in ad ♀ only red-brown outer fringes of greater cov, not creating uniform red-brown panel.
ad ♀	• Usually resembles ad ♂; some older ♀ difficult to separate from ad ♂.
1w	• Head-pattern and black patterning on underparts resembles ad but red-brown on wings (much) less conspicuous with at least brown fringes to sec, usually also on tertials, greater cov and prim. In som 1w ♂ brown wing-panel already well developed.
	• Moult-limit in greater cov; outer greater cov and tertials still juv with pale tips.
	• In least patterned ind broad pale neck-sides most conspicuous part.
	• In 1w ♂ throat often almost unpatterned white ⇔ in 1w ♀ often wholly streaked.
fl all plum	• Rufous underwing.

Naumann's Thrush *Turdus naumanni* L 23.5cm

all plum	• Long, usually cream-coloured to rufous supercilium (usually conspicuous, but sometimes very diffuse
	• Rufous to whitish wing-panel (outer edge of greater cov and sec).
	• Mainly rufous tail becoming slightly darker towards tip (closed tail mainly dark due to rufous inner w of tail-feathers). In 1w ♀ least amount of rufous in tail.
♂/ad ♀ ⇒	• Flanks strongly *rufous- to orange spotted* (coloured feather centres with broad pale fringes), central part of underparts uniform white.
♂	• Variable amount of rufous spotting on mantle and scaps (in 1w ♂ sometimes absent ⇔ ♀ usually has uniform upperparts).
	• Rufous uppertail-cov.
ad ♀	• Nearly uniform upperparts with sometimes some rufous and/or blackish spots.
	• Dark spotted submoustachial-stripe area.
1w-1s	• Moult-limit in greater cov; outer greater cov still juv with pale tips.
	• Black spotted malar area and breast.
1w ♂	• Orange supercilium and strong orange spotted underparts lacking dark patterning (not possible to s majority of less well-coloured ind).
1w ♀	• Often not possible to sex but ind with at most very slight rufous edges to greater cov and only weak orange spotted underparts with grey and blackish spots intermixed most probably ♀.
	• Rufous wash on underparts and at least some feathers with rufous centres. *Vent and undertail-cov patterned* ⇔ in Red-throated Thrush 1w ♀ completely white unpatterned vent and undertail-cov.
	• Upperparts grey-brown without rufous spots on mantle and scaps ⇔ 1w ♂.
fl all plum	• See Dusky.

Dusky Thrush/Naumann's Thrush intermediates

Intermediates could show following mixed features:

all plum ⇒	• Dark brown to dark rufous spotted underparts (brownish feather centres with usually black subterminal fringes).
	• Faint head-pattern, usually more like Naumann's than Dusky.
	• Faint dark but not blackish centres to mantle feathers and scaps.
	• Intermediate amount of rufous-brown in tail.

Black-throated Thrush *Turdus atrogularis* — L 24.5cm 9.5"

all plum	• Cold brown-grey to pure grey upperparts.
	• Completely dark tail.
ad	• Black face, no supercilium ⇔ in 1w diffuse supercilium and black isolated loral-stripe.
ad ♂	• Uninterrupted black face, throat and breast; rest of underparts almost uniform grey-white.
ad ♀	• Like ad ♂ but throat pale spotted.
	• Dark-spotted breast-band on dark background ⇔ in 1w ♀ hardly creating any breast-band.
w	• Normally moult-limit in greater cov.
w ♂	• Black breast with pale scales; rest of underparts with fine dark shaft-streaks.
	• Throat completely streaked ⇔ 1w ♀.
w ♀	• Underparts whitish with rows of dark spots and stripes, lacking distinct darker breast.
	• Pale submoustachial-stripe usually more obvious than supercilium.
all plum ⇒	• Rufous underwing-cov, especially greater cov.

Red-throated Thrush *Turdus ruficollis* — L 24.5cm 9.5"

all plum ⇒	• Mainly red-brown tail. In 1w dark outer webs to tail-feathers.
	• Cold brown-grey upperparts as in Black-throated Thrush.
ad ♂ ⇒	• Uniform red-orange supercilium, face, throat and breast.
ad ♀	• Like ♂ but throat usually paler and some dark spots on throat and breast.
w	• Red-brown inner webs to tail-feathers, broader at base of outer tail-feathers (can recall tail pattern of Bluethroat).
	• Normally moult-limit in greater cov.
w ♂	• Head- and breast-pattern nearly as in ad ♀ (ageing by pale tips to greater cov and tertials in 1w).
	• Red-orange breast with pale scales.
w ♀ ⇒	• *Faint orange wash around breast and neck-side.* Throat and breast rather strongly marked with black spots, creating rather bold submoustachial-stripe and breast-side pattern (see also Naumann's Thrush 1w ♀).
all plum ⇒	• Rufous underwing-cov, especially greater cov as in Black-throated.

Hybrid Black-throated Thrush x Red-throated Thrush

all plum	• Intermediate amount of red-brown in tail.
ad ♂	• Very dark red throat and breast, usually not uniform but with black spots.

Fieldfare *Turdus pilaris* — L 25cm 10"

all plum ⇒	• Grey upperside of head, rump and uppertail-cov contrast with black tail and brown mantle.
	• Except juv strongly 'V'-shaped marked underparts; breast with deep cream-coloured ground-colour.
w-1s	• Often moult-limit in greater cov.
	• Grey head with rather faint supercilium.
all plum ⇒	• White underwing-cov contrast with rather dark underside of flight-feathers.

Song Thrush *Turdus philomelos* — L 21cm 8.5"

ad/1w	• Uniform, somewhat rufous-brown upperparts ⇔ Mistle Thrush brown-grey. (But in nominate form from Sweden eastwards both upperparts and tail greyer).
	• Spots on underparts triangular.
	• Rather faint supercilium.
	• Spots fade away and join together on flanks (but see geog var) ⇔ Mistle.
	• In both ad and 1w pale tips to greater cov and median cov; ageing under field conditions more difficult than in most other thrushes, but pale tips on juv-type feathers triangular, in ad-type half round.
w	• Tail-feathers pointed ⇔ in ad rounded.
all plum ⇒	• Yellow-brown underwing-cov.

geog var	*T.p. clarkei* (Britain, Ireland and western Europe)
all plum	• Upperparts warm-brown; rump tinged green-brown.

geog var	*T.p. hebridensis* (Outer Hebrides)
all plum	• Upperparts dark earth-brown.
	• Underparts with pale background and strongly spotted over entire underside.
	• Rump and uppertail-cov greyish (like *philomelos* from central and eastern Europe eastwards).
all plum	• Underwing-cov slightly deeper orange than in other subspecies.

Redwing *Turdus iliacus* — L 21cm 8.5"

all plum ⇒	• Conspicuous long supercilium and submoustachial-stripe.
⇒	• Brown-orange flanks.
	• Uniform dark brown upperparts and tail (darker than Song Thrush).
	• Streaked underparts ⇔ most other thrushes more distinctly spotted.
	• Diffuse dark breast-sides formed by brown ground-colour of breast (middle of breast normally with white background), sometimes giving impression of broken breast-band (see *coburni*).
w	• At least some juv greater cov and/or tertials retained (with triangular pale tips) until late winter (2 generations).
	• Tail-feathers pointed ⇔ in ad rounded.
all plum ⇒	• Underwing-cov brown-orange, concolorous with flanks.

Thrushes/'Brown' flycatchers

geog var	*T.i. coburni* (Iceland and Faroe Islands)
all plum	• Usually whole breast with dark brown ground-colour; breast darker than in *iliacus* with hardly any paler streaking. • Bolder and blacker streaking on underparts (especially throat and breast). • Ear-coverts darker (almost black) than in *iliacus* with hardly any pale patterning. • Legs usually darker and browner than in *iliacus*. • Upperparts slightly darker than in *iliacus*. • Slightly larger than *iliacus*.
note	• Differences from *iliacus* probably too small and variable for safe identification of ind outside normal range (unless biometrics taken outside overlap zone with *iliacus*).

Mistle Thrush *Turdus viscivorus*   L 27.5cm 1"

all plum ⇒	• Greyish head-side and dark spot on rear-side of ear-coverts. • Brown-grey upperparts; rump paler than rest of upperparts. • Contrasting upperwing with dark centres and pale fringes to tertials and cov. • Often dark spot on breast-sides; merging of breast-spots (like broken breast-band, as in Redwing). • Half round spots on flanks and belly, not joining together on flanks ⇔ Song. • Very long prim-projection > 100%.
1w(-1s)	• Ageing sometimes difficult due to overlap in pattern between juv-type and ad-type coverts but when moult-limit in greater cov is present it is characteristic; outer greater cov still juv, *shorter* with often broader pale fringes around tips. Ad has variable pale fringes to greater cov and some ind have small triangular tips to median cov. • Outer tail-feathers narrower and more pointed compared to ad.
fl all plum	• White underwing-cov. • White tips to outer tail-feathers.
geog var	*T.v. deichleri* (north-western Africa, Corsica and Sardinia)
ad	• Pale fringes to sec often creating distinct wing-panel. • Upperparts greyer than in *viscivorus*. • Bill longer and slightly more slender than in *viscivorus*.

American Robin *Turdus migratorius*   L 24cm 9."

all plum	• Red-orange underparts; often slightly paler in ad ♀; scaled in 1w. • Broken white eye-ring and short broken supercilium. • Yellow bill with dark culmen and tip. • Black spots on undertail-cov. • Ear-coverts and crown black spotted (in some ad ♂ almost uniform black). • White tips to outer tail-feathers.
ad ♂	• Almost uniform grey upperparts and upperwing.
ad ♀	• Like ad ♂ but more faintly patterned and coloured, often with brown wash on grey upperparts; many ind difficult to separate from ad ♀.
1w	• Mainly as ad, but moult-limit in greater cov; retained juv greater cov and median cov with pale tip.

'Brown' flycatchers

Asian Brown Flycatcher *Muscicapa dauurica*   L 13cm 5."

all plum ⇒ ⇒	• Broad pale eye-ring, *broadest behind eye* (see also Dark-sided Flycatcher). • Long prim-projection c.100%. • Uniform grey-brown upperparts, hind-neck and crown. • Pale basal part of lower mandible (see also Dark-sided). • Broad whitish loral area. • Underparts uniform dirty whitish (also throat ⇔ Dark-sided), slightly brownish breast-sides.
ad	• White tertial-fringes. • Diffuse submoustachial- and malar stripe ⇔ in 1w absent or very diffuse.
juv-1w	• Thickened pale tips to tertials and greater cov. • Often somewhat cream-coloured tertial-fringes and wing-bar over greater cov.
1s	• Distinctly worn wings.
moult	• Ad moults completely after breeding season, in autumn fresh, in spring variably worn with new tertial ⇔ Dark-sided ad moults in winter, in autumn worn, in spring both ad and 1s fresh.
note	• See also Dark-sided.

Dark-sided Flycatcher *Muscicapa sibirica*   L 13cm 5."

all plum	• Very long prim-projection c.120% ⇔ in Asian Brown Flycatcher c.100%. • Pale eye-ring, broadest behind eye (usually slightly smaller than in Asian Brown). • Short bill with broad base; pale part of base of lower mandible restricted to centre, sides dark ⇔ in Asian Brown whole pale base of lower mandible, including sides. • Cream-coloured lores (sometimes whitish) often with dark spot directly before eye ⇔ Asian Brown. • Head mainly dark without distinct patterning, only regular faint submoustachial-stripe and malar strip. Sometimes weak crown-streaking. • p1 shorter than prim-cov ⇔ Asian Brown. • 2 emarginations on outer webs of prim (p3-p4) ⇔ in Asian Brown 3 (p3-p5).
ad ⇒	• Dark spots on undertail-cov (sometimes seemingly lacking or hidden by overlying feathers). • Breast and flanks diffusely streaked, creating almost uninterrupted dark breast and flanks. Extent of patterning on underparts variable, least marked ind resembling Asian Brown.

v-1w
- Breast and flanks less diffusely streaked than in ad, individual streaks more visible.
- Cream-coloured wing-bar over greater cov.

oult
- See Asian Brown.

te
- Not recorded in WP.

ey-streaked Flycatcher *Muscicapa griseisticta* L 14cm 5.5"

plum
- Wholly white underparts rather heavily streaked, also on flanks. Flank streaking much more well-defined and on whiter ground-colour than in Dark-sided Flycatcher and Spotted Flycatcher.
- Crown and forehead not or very faintly streaked.
- Thick, rather short bill.
- More distinct head-pattern than Dark-sided with more distinct submoustachial- and malar stripe.
- Undertail-cov unpatterned white ⇔ most Dark-sided.
- Prim-projection very long, longer than in Spotted (>100%).

v-1w
- See Spotted.

te
- Not recorded in WP.

otted Flycatcher *Muscicapa striata* L 14cm 5.5"

plum ⇒
- Distinctly streaked crown ⇔ all congeners.
- Brown-grey upperparts.
- Diffusely streaked breast; rest of underparts whitish, almost unmarked.
- Narrow white tertial- and greater cov-fringes.
- Prim-projection at least 100%.
- No white in tail.

-1w
- Pale tips to greater cov creating pale wing-bar.
- Distinct white tertial-fringes, thicker at tip of outer web.

og var
M.s. tyrrhenica (Corsica and Sardinia) and *M.s. balearica* (Balearic Islands)

plum
- Prim-projection slightly shorter than in striata.
- Upperparts warmer (*tyrrhenica*), paler brown (*balearica*) than in *striata*.
- Underparts almost unstreaked but with broad, faint spots.

e
- Ind outside normal range not identifiable with certainty.

Scrub-robins and robins

ous Scrub-robin *Cercotrichas galactotes* L 16cm 6.3"

plum
- Deep rufous rump and tail contrast with mantle and scaps (in western *galactotes* very little contrast).
- Obvious supercilium and eye- and moustachial-stripe.
- Dark centres and pale fringes on all wing feathers.
- Pale tips to tail-feathers (except t1); pale tips becoming larger from t2 to t6.
- Black subterminal patterning on tail-feathers (except t1).

g var
C.g syriacus (south-eastern Europe)

- Brown-grey mantle and scaps (making rufous tail and uppertail-cov contrast more strongly with upperparts than in *galactotes*).
- Tail shorter with smaller white tips and broader subterminal black markings on tail-feathers than in *galactotes*.
- t1 often darker than other tail-feathers ⇔ *galactotes*.
- Stronger head-pattern than in *galactotes* with whiter supercilium, larger pale spot below eye and darker lateral crown-stripe, eye-stripe and moustachial-stripe.

g var
C.g. familiaris (central Asia)

- Like *syriacus* but slightly paler, underparts almost white.

ck Scrub-robin *Cercotrichas podobe* L 21.5cm 8.5"

lum
- Typical structure of bush robin, tail and legs considerably longer than in Rufous Scrub-robin and tail often held upwards.
- Entirely black (in some lighting conditions blue-black) except pale tips to undertail-cov and white tips to tail-feathers.
- Very long rounded tail.

1
- Moults probably completely in 1cy, then in spring like ad.

av
- Confiding and very manoeuvrable.

opean Robin *Erithacus rubecula* L 13.5cm 5.3"

- In autumn and winter greater cov of one generation, sometimes with yellow tips forming wing-bar as in 1w.
- Lacks reddish throat and breast.
- Fine pale spotted head, mantle, throat and breast.
- Pale tips to greater cov creating rather broad wing-bar ⇔ in Thrush Nightingale and Common Nightingale juv narrow.

1s
- 2 generations of greater cov; outer juv greater cov more uniform with yellow tip, inner ad-type feathers sometimes with (smaller) yellow tip. Wing-bar usually more obvious than in ad.
- Tail-feathers pointed ⇔ in ad rounded.
- In 1s wings and tail worn.

geog var	*E.r. melophilus* (Britain and Scandinavia)
ad	• Upperparts rufous-brown, especially uppertail-cov and tail base. • Rear-flanks, vent and undertail-cov browner than in *rubecula*, less contrasting with upperparts. • Face and breast deeper and darker orange-red than in *rubecula*.
note geog var	• Above-mentioned differences with *rubecula* from European mainland often very slight and insufficien for single out of range ind to be identified with certainty.

Tenerife Robin *Erithacus superbus*   L 13cm 5

ad	• Deep orange-red face and breast, contrasting strongly with white belly. • Broad eye-ring especially at rear-side. • Grey border between orange-red of breast and brown of upperparts broader than in European Robin and usually extending over fore-crown. • Upperparts more grey-brown than in European, especially in spring.
note	• Occurs on Gran Canaria and Tenerife; European is found on western Canary Islands.

Rufous-tailed Robin *Luscinia sibilans*   L 13cm 5

all plum	• Deep rufous outer webs on prim; tail-feathers completely rufous. • Greyish underparts with rounded pale spots (underparts appear dark scaled). • Large eye with conspicuous whitish eye-ring. • Long pink legs. • Upperparts olive-brown with rufous wash.
1w	• Pale tips to greater cov and often moult-limit.

Nightingales and Asian chats

Thrush Nightingale *Luscinia luscinia*   L 16cm

all plum ⇒	• Dark grey-brown upperparts contrast with red-brown tail ⇔ in Common Nightingale upperparts pale and slight colour contrast between brown mantle and red-brown rump, uppertail-cov and tail. • Eye-ring relatively faint, especially on front side ⇔ in Common distinct. • Diffuse fine streaking or flecking on breast and often flanks ⇔ in Common none. • p1 ≤ prim-cov ⇔ in Common p1 ≥ prim-cov. • p2 long, approx level with or longer than p4 ⇔ in Common p2 approx level with or shorter than p5. • Only emargination on outer web on p3 ⇔ in Common on p3 and p4. • Often diffuse dark tips to undertail-cov ⇔ in Common none. • Two-toned alula ⇔ in Common more uniform. • Diffuse pale throat usually more distinct than in Common. • Often yellow gape-line. • Lores (almost) concolorous with crown ⇔ in Common usually paler. • Usually faint malar streaking ⇔ in Common usually none. • 7-8 prim-tips beyond tertials ⇔ in Common 7.
1w	• 2 generations of greater cov; outer juv greater cov with pale tips. • Tail-feathers pointed ⇔ in ad rounded. • In 1s wings and tail worn.
voice	• Song: very loud and far-carrying. Like Common but more variable with many cracking and clicking notes. • Call: high-pitched, long, flat 'héééép' ⇔ in Common rising in pitch. Also low Great Reed Warbler-lik 'trrrruh' (like Common).

Common Nightingale *Luscinia megarhynchos*   L 16cm

all plum	• Warm rufous-brown upperparts and tail (little colour difference between tail and upperparts, see Thrush Nightingale). • Faint grey-blue supercilium, lores and neck-side and grey wash over head and underparts ⇔ Thrus • Eye-ring thick and conspicuous ⇔ Thrush.
1w	• 2 generations of greater cov; outer juv greater cov with pale tips. • Tail-feathers pointed ⇔ in ad rounded. • In 1s wings and tail worn.
voice	• See Thrush.
note	• See Thrush for differences with Common.
geog var	*L.m. africana* (eastern Turkey and Caucasus)
all plum	• Somewhat intermediate between *megarhynchos* and *golzii* with dark, duller brown-grey upperparts Underparts rather pale with grey-brown breast. • Size as *megarhynchos*, thus smaller than *golzii*.
geog var	*L.(m.) golzii* (central Asia)
all plum	• Paler and more grey-brown than *megarhynchos*. • Broad, diffuse supercilium. • Distinct pale fringes on almost all cov, tertials and flight-feathers. • Dark ear-coverts and lores contrast with whitish throat. • Rufous tail as on *megarhynchos* but slightly less deep coloured. • Pale spots on undertail-cov. • Slightly larger size and longer tail than *megarhynchos*.

berian Rubythroat *Luscinia calliope*   L 15.5cm 6.1"

plum	• Very dark to black lores sharply demarcated from submoustachial-stripe and supercilium.
	• Uniform grey-brown upperparts.
	• Legs conspicuously long, pale to rather dark with pinkish wash.
	• Relatively deep bill-base.
	• Prim-projection c.80% ⇔ in Bluethroat c.60%.

d ♂/ ⇒ • Broad black lores and bright white supercilium and submoustachial-stripe creating characteristic
w ♂   head-pattern.
        • Bright pink-red throat-patch bordered by narrow black line. In some ♂ (almost exclusive 1w ♂) head-
          pattern incl throat-patch less well developed.

d ♀   • Brown-grey breast and neck-side, in most ad ♂ pure grey.
        • In some (older?) ♀ reddish throat-patch well developed but in most such ind throat-patch with withish
          lower border ⇔ ♂.

d ♀/1w • Narrow malar-stripe ⇔ in Bluethroat broader, broadening towards neck-side.
        • Rather short supercilium extending to just behind eye ⇔ in Bluethroat longer.
        • Rather diffuse pale throat, in 1w without red. Some ad ♀ also lacking any red.
        • Dark grey-brown breast merges into slightly warmer brown flanks.

w   • Small pale tips to tertials and greater cov. Often moult-limit in greater cov, then inner (ad-type) lacking
          pale tips.
        • Tail-feathers pointed ⇔ ad.

uethroat *Luscinia svecica*   L 13.5cm 5.3"

plum ⇒	• Reddish base of outer tail-feathers.
d	• Conspicuous whitish supercilium.
	• Grey-brown upperparts (in eastern subspecies *volgae* and *pallidogularis* more greyish).

d ♂   • Blue throat/breast bordered on underside by black breast-band and then by orange-red breast-band.
■ ♀   • Very variable, some ind strongly resembling ♂ but blue and red areas less uniform. In extreme
         ♂-like ad ♀ much blue on malar area but hint of pale submoustachial-stripe and/or dark malar-
         stripe retained.

/1w ⇒ • Strong head-pattern with obvious supercilium, dark lores, (pale) submoustachial-stripe, (dark) malar-
         stripe and pale throat.
       • Dark spotted breast-band (especially in 1w-1s ♀).
       • Some (mostly older) ad ♀ s resemble ad ♂ (due to red and blue on throat and breast) but with
         obvious submoustachial-stripe ⇔ ad ♂ s. Other ind (1s ♀) strongly resemble 1w.

w   • Cream-coloured wedge-shaped tips to greater cov and tertials; 1w ♂ with blue and red on breast
         and/or throat, like faintly patterned ad ♂ or older ad ♀.
w ♀   • No or hardly any blue or red on breast and/or throat.
s   • Moult-limit in greater cov often difficult to see under field conditions ⇔ most other thrushes. Strongly
         worn prim and prim-cov also often in ad.

og var   *L.s. svecica* (northern Europe to western Alaska and mountains of central Europe)
■ ♂ s   • Usually large brick-red spot in centre of blue throat/breast. Spot usually round or triangular and
            concolorous with or darker than brick-red breast-band.

og var   *L.s. pallidogularis* (south-western Siberia)
plum   • Upperparts more grey than brown.
          • Smaller than *cyanecula* and *svecica*.
♂   • Very variable breast-pattern, some ind with much blue, others with much red and/or white-encircled
            blue and red parts.
te   • *Volgae* (range between *cyanecula* and *pallidogularis*) very variable; field marks intermediate between
            cyanecula and *pallidogularis* with central breast patch usually red with white speckles.

og var   *L.s. cyanecula* (central and eastern Europe)
♂ s   • White spot in centre of blue throat (size of spot variable). Some ind with variable amount of orange
            tipped feathers in white spot.
♂ w   • In winter plumage white spot often hidden under rufous feather tips (in spring tips worn away). Some
            ind in autumn with wholly reddish spot, in spring again moulted to white.
♀ s   • Ind with ♂-like plumage often with rufous central breast spot as in true red-spotted subspecies.

og var   *L.s. magna* (eastern Turkey to Iran)
♂   • Completely blue breast and throat without central spot.
          • No or very restricted black band below blue breast.
          • Larger than *cyanecula* and *svecica*.
e   • Within populations of *cyanecula* ind with completely blue breast without white central spot occur, but
            rest of plumage and size similar to *cyanecula* (so-called 'wolfi'-variant).

og var   *L.s. azuricollis* (mountains of central Spain)
plum   • Larger size.
♂   • Completely blue-breasted without central spot like *magna*.
          • No or very restricted black band below blue breast like *magna*,
          • More cream-coloured supercilium and blue in loral-stripe than in *cyanecula*.

Siberian Blue Robin *Luscinia cyane*
L 15cm 5.

all plum ⇒	• Legs long, *conspicuously pale pinkish*.
	• Large conspicuous eye (in ad ♂ not conspicuous due to blackish mask).
	• Relatively strong bill.
	• Short tail; blue in ♂ and partly blue in ad ♀.
	• Prim-projection c.80%.
ad ♂	• Upperparts and upperside of head cobalt blue (blue difficult to see in shadow). 1s ♂ like ad s but (juv wings brownish.
	• Mainly white underparts, contrasting strongly with upperparts. Especially strong contrast between wh throat and blackish ear-coverts.
1w ♂	• Like ad ♀ with deep blue rump and uppertail-cov, but also with at least some blue in lesser cov, medium cov, scaps and/or tertials.
♀/1w	• Deep blue (some ad ♀/almost all 1w ♂) to at most bluish (1w ♀) wash on tail, especially on basal part (blue usually difficult to see and often entirely absent in 1w ♀).
	• Juv tertials and greater cov with faint cream-coloured tips and often distinct moult-limit in greater co
	• Diffusely spotted breast and flanks; lacks distinct bordered white throat and orange flanks of Red-flanked Bluetail.
	• Faint supercilium; distinct pale eye-ring.
1s	• Distinct moult-limit between new greater cov and tertials and old prim and prim-cov (less distinct in 1s ♀

Red-flanked Bluetail *Tarsiger cyanurus*
L 13.5cm 5

all plum ⇒	• Orange flanks (in many ind fore-flanks bright orange, duller lower on flank).
	• Cobalt blue tail and uppertail-cov (blue difficult to see in shadow).
	• Rather narrow whitish throat-patch usually bordered by dark throat-side of ear-coverts and breast.
	• Broad pale eye-ring conspicuous against rest of almost uniform head-side.
ad ♂ s	• Entirely blue upperparts and upperwing (brightest on rump).
	• White supercilium (still rather broad in early spring but disappearing almost completely over course of summer).
	• Fringes of sec and prim brown to blue and often show a mix of brown and blue (not age-related).
ad ♂ autumn	• Grey-brown upperparts (scaps blue).
	• Broader supercilium than in ad ♂ s.
	• Lesser cov creating bright blue spot on brownish upperwing.
ad ♀/1w	• Uniform grey-brown upperparts.
	• Dull blue tail-feathers and uppertail-cov (in 1w ♂ generally deeper blue).
1w	• Moult-limit in greater cov and/or tertials diagnostic for age but often still completely juv greater cov and/or tertials; juv greater cov and tertials with weak pale tips, but sometimes difficult to see ⇔ ad.
	• Pointed tail-feathers ⇔ in ad slightly rounded, but structure sometimes quite close to juv.
1w ♂	• Similar to 1w ♀ but in some ind already some blue on cov, scaps and/or tertials.
1s ♂	• Like ad ♀ but some ind with bright blue lesser cov and slight blue on tertials and scaps.

White-throated Robin *Irania gutturalis*
L 17cm 6

all plum ⇒	• Long uniform blackish tail.
	• Long slender bill.
	• Dark alula contrasts with paler grey rest of wing and upperparts.
	• Legs relatively long.
ad ♂	• Black face, ear-coverts and rear-side of throat.
	• Whitish vertical stripe over middle of throat extending to upper breast (width of stripe very variable).
	• Deep orange breast and belly (vent and undertail-cov white), in some ind dull rufous breast and belly
	• Long white supercilium.
	• Blue-grey upperparts.
ad ♀/1w ⇒	• Orange flanks and undertail-cov, but in some 1w (♀?) not or hardly developed.
	• Upperparts uniform cold brown-grey.
	• No (or very faint) supercilium but obvious pale eye-ring.
	• Diffuse pale throat and faint submoustachial-stripe.
	• 1w with moult-limit in greater cov, outer cov with pale tips. Prim-cov with pale tips.
1s	• Distinct moult-limit between new greater cov and tertials and old prim and prim-cov (less distinct in 1s

Redstarts

Eversmann's Redstart *Phoenicurus erythronotus*
L 15cm !

♂ ⇒	• Wing-pattern: *uninterrupted white band* over lesser cov, inner median cov and inner greater cov.
⇒	• Upperparts and throat red (upperparts with greyish wash in fresh plumage, autumn) ⇔ all other redstarts.
♀	• Like Common ♀ but broad pale fringes on tertials and flight-feathers and faint wing-bars along gre cov and median cov.
1s	• Moult-limit between eventually new greater cov and tertials and old prim and prim-cov (difficult to s in 1s ♀).
behav	• Pumps tail, not vibrating ⇔ Common.

Black Redstart *Phoenicurus ochruros*
L 14cm

all plum	• 4 emarginations on outer web of prim (p3-p6) ⇔ in Common Redstart 3 (p3-p5).
	• Distance between p5 (longest prim) and p6 less than half of distance between p6 and p7 ⇔ in Common distances between p5-p6 and p6-p7 nearly same (in Common wing-tip often formed by p4
ad ♂	• See geog var.

♀
- Both upper- and underparts dark brown-grey (European subspecies) ⇔ in Common underparts pale with orange-brown wash.

1w
- Not spotted like Common juv but similar to ad ♀.

1w-1s
- Similar to ad ♀; some 1w-1s ♂ strongly resemble ad ♂ ('*paradoxus*'-morph) but browner juv wings with pale brown feather fringes, at most some greater cov and tertials replaced by ad-type feathers, pale patch on lower belly, throat with grey intermix, upperparts with variable brown-orange juv feathers and weak dark tip on t6.
- See also Common 1w.

note
- ♂ acquires full ad plumage as late as after 2 or 3 years. Some ♂ acquire ad-like plumage in 1cy except distinct pale wing-panel, see '*paradoxus*'-morph in 1w-1s.

geog var

Caucasian Black Redstart *P.o. ochruros* (eastern Turkey, Caucasus, northern Iran)

ad ♂
- Variable amount of rusty red on vent and lower belly but extending no further than middle of belly ⇔ *semirufus* and *phoenicuroides*.
- No distinct white wing-panel ⇔ *gibraltariensis*.
- In many respects between European *gibraltariensis* and Asian subspecies *semirufus* and *phoenicuroides*, therefore sometimes seen as intermediate population.

geog var

P.o. gibraltariensis (western and central Europe)

ad ♂
- Black throat and breast gradually merge into dark grey belly and pale grey vent; undertail-cov rufous.
- Grey crown and hind-neck gradually merge into slightly darker grey upperparts.
- White fringes to tertials and sec creating large but rather diffuse wing-panel (in summer can almost completely disappear by wear).

geog var

P.o. aterrimus (Iberian Peninsula, North Africa)

ad ♂ ⇒
- Deep black upperparts, scaps and greater cov.
- Sharply defined grey crown (black hind-neck ⇔ *gibraltariensis*)
- Underparts deep black to belly (whitish vent and rufous undertail-cov as in *gibraltariensis*).
- White fringes to tertials and sec creating large but rather diffuse wing-panel (in summer can almost completely disappear by wear).

geog var

P.o. semirufus (south-eastern Europe, western Asia)

plum
ad ♂
- No distinct white wing-panel ⇔ *gibraltariensis*.
- Resembles Common with red underparts but upperparts more blackish instead of slaty grey.
- Black throat-patch extending well over breast ⇔ Common.
- Supercilium fainter than in Common.

note ♀
- ♀ Ehrenberg's Redstart *P.p. samamisicus* (occurring in range of *semirufus* and *phoenicuroides*) paler than Common *phoenicurus*. Under field conditions *semirufus* and *phoenicuroides* ♀ distinctly darker than *samamisicus* ♀.

note geog var
- Identification of *phoenicuroides* and *semirufus* in Europe complicated by hybrid ♂-type Black x Common which can especially resemble *phoenicuroides*.
- In northern Spain *aterrimus* and *gibraltariensis* occur next to each other in different habitats (*gibraltariensis* in villages and cities, *aterrimus* on stony hill-sides).

geog var

Eastern Black Redstart *P.o. phoenicuroides* (Asia)

ad ♂
- Like *semirufus* but upperparts less deep black. Reddish underparts extending further (to wing-bend), resembling Common.
- No distinct white wing-panel ⇔ *gibraltariensis*.
- Paler than in *gibraltariensis*, therefore more similar to Common ♀ *phoenicurus* (see all plum and note ♀) with slightly paler throat.
- Rufous to reddish wash on (rear-)flanks, not extending to throat.

note
- Hybrid Black x Common can strongly resemble *phoenicuroides* but normally has white wing-panel and whitish vent and belly. Wing structure intermediate with distance between p5-p6 always larger than half of distance between p6-p7 (see all plum).

Common Redstart *Phoenicurus phoenicurus*   L 14cm 5.5"

ad ♂
- Slaty grey upperparts, orange underparts, black throat and white supercilium (in autumn more faintly patterned but with black lores ⇔ 1w).

♀/1w
- Thickened eye-ring on rear-side.
- Underparts pale with orange-brown wash and whitish throat ⇔ Black Redstart.

juv
- Spotted like Robin juv but t5 and t6 red; t1 black.

ad ♂
- Lores and throat mottled pale ⇔ in ad lores solid black.
- Newly moulted lesser cov and median cov with greyish fringes ⇔ ♀ autumn. Rufous wing-bar along greater cov is not an ageing feature.
- Tail-feathers rather pointed, t1-pair narrower than other tail-feathers ⇔ in ad tail-feathers rounded and t1-pair as broad as other tail-feathers.
- Inner prim with distinct pale tips ⇔ in ad very narrow pale fringes.
- 1w ♀ often difficult to distinguish from ad ♀ as both have rufous wing-bar along greater cov.
- Largely old wings, brownish and worn.

geog var

Ehrenberg's Redstart *P.p. samamisicus* (western to central Asia south of *phoenicuriodes*)

ad ♂
- Whitish fringes on tertials (except inner), sec and prim to p3 creating distinct wing-panel. Wing-panel

pure white ⇔ in *phoenicurus* with wing-panel normally some buff near feather-tips.

1w ♂
- White fringes to outer 2 tertials and inner sec *broadening at base* and often slightly narrowing at tip ⇔ *phoenicurus*.
- Upperparts generally greyer and darker than in *phoenicurus*.
- Black throat often larger than in *phoenicurus*, with black on to upper breast and neck-side.
- Whitish fringes to tertials and sec narrower and less numerous than in ad (not extending onto prim), often only innermost sec and outer tertials edged white, rest of tertials with buff fringes. White fringe broadening at base ⇔ in *phoenicurus* broadening towards tip. Correct ageing essential due to similar between 1w ♂ and *phoenicurus* ad ♂.
- More adult-like than *phoenicurus* probably due to earlier and more extensive moult towards 1w than *phoenicurus*. Often all median and large part of greater cov moulted in autumn (with grey fringes and therefore strongly contrasting) ⇔ *phoenicurus*.
- Upperparts greyer than in *phoenicurus* 1w. Correct ageing essential; *phoenicurus* ad with greyer upperparts than *phoenicurus* 1w.

1s
- Only ind which show obvious broadening of white at base of outer tertials and inner sec distinguishable, others identical to *phoenicurus* in field conditions. Correct ageing essential!

opm
- Some *phoenicurus* ad ♂ with broad pale fringes to all tertials and most or all sec, but in contrast to *samamisicus* fringes evenly broad often tending to buff towards tips and no or hardly any white on outer-edge of prim (and in *samamisicus* inner tertial almost lacks white). These ind often with distinct white feather-tips on lower part of black throat, creating white borderline.

Moussier's Redstart *Phoenicurus moussieri*   L 12.5cm 4

all plum
- Short prim-projection c.40% ⇔ Common Redstart.
- Small size.

ad ♂
- Black upperside of head with very conspicuous broad white supercilium extending to neck-side.
- Entirely orange-red underparts.
- Well-defined bright white wing-panel (also in 1w ♂).
- Black mantle and back.

♀
- Underparts bright orange-red with slightly paler throat-patch.
- Very faint, pale wing-panel.

behav
- Often perches on top of vegetation like Whinchat or Common Stonechat.

Güldenstädt's Redstart *Phoenicurus erythrogastrus*   L 15.5cm 6

all plum ⇒
- Large size.

ad ♂
- Black head with well-defined white cap to hind-neck.
- Large white wing-patch extending over whole base of flight-feathers (also in 1w ♂).
- Dark red underparts; throat and upper breast black.

ad ♀
- Like large less contrasting Common Redstart ♀.
- Central tail-feathers (t1) dull grey-brown, hardly contrasting with rest of tail ⇔ in Common ♀ t1 contrastingly dark.

Blackstart *Cercomela melanura*   L 15cm 5

ad ⇒
- Completely black tail and uppertail-cov.
- Completely grey upperparts and upperside of head.
- Black alula contrasts slightly with dark grey rest of wing.

fl all plum
- Uniform pale underwing.

behav
- Often confiding.

Stonechats

Whinchat *Saxicola rubetra*   L 13cm 5

all plum
- Broad, very obvious supercilium.
- Inner prim with white base on outer web, creating *white spot at base of inner-hand*.
- Long prim-projection c.100%.
- Mantle feathers and scaps with dark centres creating rows of large dark drop-shaped spots (not in a ♂ s).

ad ♂
- Blackish ear-coverts and crown.
- In spring deep orange throat and breast.
- Extensive white patterning on prim-cov creating distinct pale spot ⇔ in ad ♀ some pale pattering at base, in 1w ♀ prim-cov wholly dark.
- Inner greater cov largely white, other greater cov very dark ⇔ ♀.

ad ♀
♂ autumn
- Less contrastingly patterned on head and wings than ad ♂ (inner greater cov usually with little or no whi
- Dark speckled breast.

1w ♂
- Inner 3 greater cov largely white ⇔ 1w ♀ (when perched usually difficult to see because inner grea cov normally obscured by scaps).
- Outer prim-cov with white base ⇔ in 1w ♀ no white.

1w-1s
- Moult-limit in greater cov (in ♀ often very difficult to see).

fl all plum
- White tail corners formed by white base of outer tail-feathers.
- Rump and uppertail-cov heavily streaked ⇔ in European Stonechat finely or almost unstreaked.

Canary Islands Stonechat *Saxicola dacotiae*   L 12cm

all plum
- Orange breast; white throat.
- Narrow white stripe formed by white inner greater cov (as in European Stonechat but narrower).
- Completely dark tail ⇔ Whinchat.

⇒	• Dark head with *narrow white supercilium*.
	• White band through neck-side.
♀	• Rather pale grey-brown upperparts with faint streaking on mantle and rump.
⌐	• Uniform wings without white stripe.
⊦te	• Endemic to Fuerteventura.

┐ropean Stonechat *Saxicola torquatus*   L 12.5cm 4.9"

plum	• Short prim-projection c.50-70%.
	• Completely dark tail ⇔ in Whinchat white corner at tail base.
	• Inner greater cov white (somewhat variable but generally most white in ad ♂, least in 1w ♀).
♂ s	• Broad white band through neck-side.
	• Blackish head and throat.
	• Orange underparts, most extensive on breast, gradual merging into whitish undertail-cov.
w	• 1w slightly resembles ad ♀ due to brown tips to feathers of head and upperparts but throat, lores and ear-coverts blackish (in ad ♂ w solid deep black) and conspicuous white band through neck-side. Band through neck-side often partially orange in fresh plumage.
	• At least some pure white on uppertail-cov and/or neck-side ⇔ all ♀.
♀	• (Very) faint supercilium.
	• Dark head and throat but not blackish as in ad ♂, paler in autumn due to pale feather-tips.
	• Underparts as in ad ♂ but slightly duller orange.
	• Faint pale patch on neck-side ⇔ in (1w) ♂ at least some pure white but in fresh plumage largely concealed by brown feather-tips.
⌐-1s	• Largely as ad of equivalent sex but moult-limit in greater cov. In 1s still old prim and prim-cov.
	• Tail-feathers pointed, but in some ind more rounded and almost as ad.
⌐ ♀	• Like ad ♀ with rather pale head.
⌐ ♂	• Largely as ad ♂ autumn but black of head more concealed by brown feather-tips.
⌐ll plum	• Rather dark underwing-cov (darker in ♂ than in ♀) ⇔ Whinchat.
⌐g var	*S.t. rubicola* (Mainland of Europe to Caucasus)
	• Normally whitish rump, sometimes unpatterned. Uppertail-cov normally at least slightly patterned but in extreme ind unmarked, then similar to Siberian Stonechat.
	• Rather large white patch on neck-side but smaller than in Siberian.
	• Orange breast (and usually flanks); central part of belly white, resembling Siberian ⇔ *hibernans*.
	• In fresh plumage pale brown fringes on feathers of upperparts and head.
⌐g var	*S.t. hibernans* (Britain and western parts of Netherlands, Belgium and France)
plum	• Darker than *rubicola*.
	• Underparts almost entirely dark orange-red ⇔ *rubicola*.
	• Relatively small white neck-side patch.
	• Feather-fringes on upperparts and head dark chestnut, paler in summer.
	• Underparts almost entirely orange.
⌐e geog var	• Only extremes of *rubicola* and *hibernans* identifiable and only in fresh plumage. Both subspecies have clinal zone in western part of European mainland. Ind with features of *rubicola* breed within range of *hibernans* and vice versa.

┐erian Stonechat *Saxicola maurus*   L 12.5cm 4.9"

plum ⇒	• Unmarked whitish to orange (in autumn normally buff) rump and uppertail-cov (in some 1w ♀ faint brown streaking on rump) ⇔ in European Stonechat ♂ often uppertail-cov and/or part of rump whitish but at least uppertail-cov streaked.
	• Variable but generally more white on inner greater cov than in European, often creating conspicuous white patch.
	• Prim-projection c.90% with projected prim elongated ⇔ in European slightly shorter and projected prim more triangular.
	• Flanks uniform ⇔ in European (especially ♀) sometimes diffuse dark patterning.
s	• Very strong contrast between very dark upperparts and very pale underparts ⇔ European.
	• Broad white band on neck-side, extending to hind-neck; neck-side regularly orange until late in spring ⇔ European.
	• Orange only on breast (sometimes extending slightly further), rest of underparts often but not always conspicuously white, strongly contrasting with very dark upperparts.
♂ s	• (Almost) uniform black upperparts ⇔ in European ad ♂ dark brown.
♂	• Like ad ♂ s but less black upperparts with fine pale patterning and often hint of supercilium.
⇒	• Upperparts and underparts both paler than in European; upperparts with pale sandy-coloured fringes to feathers, creating broad pale streaks. Pale fringes on fresh feathers broader than in European with summer plumage features less obvious than in European; sexing more difficult than in European.
	• Broad pale buff fringes on tertials and sec creating large pale wing-panel.
⌐-1s	• Moult-limit in greater cov (often not present in 1w). In 1s old prim and prim-cov retained. 1s ♂ with paler, sandier streaked upperparts than ad (⇔ in European more buff or brownish streaked), but when worn upperparts become very dark to black.
⌐w	• Ad ♂ w with dark throat and black lores and ear-coverts. 1w ♂ rather similar to ♀ w, but throat, ear-coverts and lores often less white, becoming darker in winter due to wear.
♀ /1w ⇒	• Whitish throat. Ad ♀ retains pale throat to summer ⇔ European.
	• Usually obvious broad supercilium (sometimes resembling Whinchat).
	• Underparts white with faint orange cast on breast-side and flanks ⇔ in European underparts darker.
⌐	• Very dark underwing-cov and black axillaries with at most narrow fringes ⇔ in European ♂ dark

239

underwing-cov with distinct pale fringes and grey axillaries.
- Underside of flight-feathers with whitish fringes on inner webs; underwing relatively pale (exaggerat contrast with black axillaries and underwing-cov) ⇔ in European greyer fringes and underwing dark slightly contrasting with axillaries and underwing-cov.

geog var — **Caspian Stonechat** *S.m. variegatus* (steppes of Lower Volga to eastern Caucasus)

all plum ⇒
- Much white in tail, tail-pattern resembles that of Pied or Black-eared Wheatear (white inner web of t. t6 can extend completely to feather tip) ⇔ in *maurus* sometimes very small pale base on outer tail-feathers (in *armenicus* about quarter of tail-base pale but not extending to inner web).
- Uppertail-cov and rump often pure white, without creamy wash on rump as in *maurus* (pale rump ar larger than in *maurus*).
- Slightly larger than *maurus*.

ad ♂ s
- Breast deep orange-red.
- Very large white neck-side patch.
- Large white spot on inner cov.

1w ♂
- Almost complete black throat (⇔ *maurus*), when fresh with white scales.

♀/1w
- Upperparts pale brown (slightly paler than in *maurus*).

Pied Stonechat *Saxicola caprata* L 13cm ⁵

all plum
ad ♂
- Slightly larger than European Stonechat with stronger bill.
- Mainly black plumage with white vent, undertail-cov, uppertail-cov, rump and central part of belly.
- White inner cov creating conspicuous vertical white stripe (as in European).

ad ♀ ⇒
- Mainly grey-brown with rufous wash on underparts and deeper rufous rump.
- Pale throat and faint supercilium.
- Pale vent, undertail-cov and central part of belly.

1w ♂
- Like ad ♂ but duller black.

1w
- Rather broad pale fringes to cov.

Northern Anteater-chat *Myrmecocichla aethiops* L 17.5cm

all plum
- Large size with Common Starling-like structure.
- Completely dark brown-black.

fl all plum
- Pale inner webs to all prim creating very conspicuous pale panel (usually also visible when perched)

Wheatears

Isabelline Wheatear *Oenanthe isabellina* L 15.5cm

all plum ⇒
- Black centre of alula contrasts with *paler centre of greater cov and median cov* ⇔ in Northern Wheatear blackish centre of both alula and cov.
- Border between white of rump and brown back falls in line with tertial-tips ⇔ in Northern border further towards back.
- Broad whitish supercilium, especially distinct between eye and bill, fainter behind eye and tending slightly towards cream-coloured ⇔ in Northern the other way around. Supercilium sometimes disappears behind eye or almost absent (especially in ♀?)
- Black terminal tail-band broader than visible white part of outer tail-feathers (in all wheatears when perched amount of black in tail often difficult to judge; even species with relatively little black sometimes appear to show completely black tail).
- Usually diffuse pale area below eye and pale submoustachial area or wholly whitish throat.
- Underparts paler than in Northern, especially conspicuous in autumn because Northern 1w/♀ often has deep cream-coloured breast-band. Little contrast between upperparts and underparts.
- Ear-coverts not distinctly darker than crown, often paler ⇔ most Northern ad ♀/1w autumn.
- Slightly larger than Northern with relatively larger head.
- Prim-projection c.100%, slightly shorter than in Northern. Prim-projection > tail-projection beyond wing-tips ⇔ Desert Wheatear.
- Long bill with relatively deep base.
- Lores usually contrastingly dark (especially in spring), broad and well-defined (in ♀ sometimes har present) ⇔ most Northern.
- Wing-tips usually reach only slightly beyond undertail-cov ⇔ Northern.

1w/1s
- Moult-limit in greater cov, inner moulted feathers fresher and longer than outer ones.
- In 1w pale fringes to prim-cov frayed ⇔ in ad narrower and not frayed.
- 1s with worn wings, especially prim.

ad ♂
- Well-defined black loral-stripe (sometimes also in 1w ♂).

1w/ad
- Prim, sec and tertials dark brownish (2cy Northern in spring and summer also often has more brown win

fl all plum ⇒
- Tail-pattern: broad terminal tail-band, broader than black 'leg of the T' ⇔ in Northern smaller than of the T'.

⇒
- White to cream-coloured axillaries and underwing-cov and pale bases to flight-feathers; whole of underwing very pale, conspicuous on take-off ⇔ Northern.
- Grey-brownish upperwing due to relatively pale centre of prim (not blackish) ⇔ almost all other wheatears.

behav
- Frequently moves tail up and down.

Northern Wheatear *Oenanthe oenanthe* L 15cm

all plum
- Tail-pattern: black terminal tail-band evenly broad, 'leg of the T' slightly longer than width of termin tail-band.
- Prim-projection c.120%; prim-projection > tail-projection beyond wing-tips.

♂ ⇒
♀ w/1w
- Pure grey mantle and scaps.
- Supercilium two-toned: cream-coloured before eye, white above and behind.
- Rufous ear-coverts.
- Grey-brown mantle (upperparts more greyish in spring in ad ♀).
- Pale fringes to prim-cov frayed ⇔ in ad narrower and not frayed.
- For general ageing criteria, see Pied Wheatear 1w.
- Wings with brownish wash and pale fringes to cov (normally no moult-limit in greater cov).
- Mantle often with brownish wash (disappearing later in spring).

all plum
- Blackish upperwing.
- Rather dark underwing-cov but in ad ♂ not black as in most 'black-throated' wheatears ad ♂.

e
- See Isabelline Wheatear for more field marks.

og var
Greenland Wheatear *O.o. leucorhoa* (Iceland and Greenland)

plum
- Generally slightly larger than *oenanthe*, with longer prim-projection and legs. Measurements often conclusive.
- Terminal tail-band generally slightly broader than in *oenanthe*.

♂
♀/1w
- Almost completely orange-brown throat, breast and belly (sometimes also in *oenanthe*).
- Often somewhat rufous underparts.

e
- Identification on plumage only not conclusive.

ebohm's Wheatear *Oenanthe seebohmi* L 14.5cm 5.7"

plum
- Terminal tail-band narrower than in Northern Wheatear.

♂
- Large black throat-patch, black sometimes connecting with wing-bend (as in Desert Wheatear ♂).
- Underparts whiter than in Northern, (almost) no orange on breast.

♀
- (Dark) grey mottled throat; distinct black loral-stripe.
- Upperparts pale sandy-coloured.
- For general ageing criteria, see Pied Wheatear 1w.

♂
- Black underwing-cov (in ♀ pale streaks on dark underwing-cov) ⇔ Northern.

d Wheatear *Oenanthe pleschanka* L 15cm 5.9"

plum
♂ s
- Long prim-projection ≥ 100%.
- Large black throat-patch broadly connected to scaps by black neck-side (often also visible in ad ♂ autumn and some 1w ♂) ⇔ Eastern Black-eared Wheatear.
- White crown extending onto hind-neck to mantle ⇔ Cyprus Wheatear ad.

♂ w
- Whole wings and feathers of upperparts with narrow white fringes (worn away during winter). Wings and feathers of upperparts deeper black than in 1w ♂ with narrower pale fringes.

♂ autumn
- Pale fringes to all feathers of wings and lower part of black throat concealed by pale feather tips therefore sometimes resembling 1w ♂, but prim deep black; *sec at base without pale fringes* (creating solid black panel below greater cov) and lores and upperside of throat uniform black without pale feather tips.

♀ s
- Uniform dark cold brown upperparts, breast and throat ⇔ in Eastern Black-eared upperparts warmer brown.

♀ autumn/
w
- Feathers of upperparts (including scaps) with brown-black centres and pale fringes, forming diffuse pale scales (in 1w sometimes indistinct dark centres due to broad pale fringes). When dark centres present, then diagnostic against Eastern/Western Black-eared.
- Often rather dark throat (in 1w ♀ greyish throat and upper breast) merging into orange breast, lacking pale border between throat and breast (1w ♀ normally lacks orange on breast) ⇔ in Eastern/Western Black-eared pale border present.
- Cov, tertials and flight-feathers with pale fringes.
- Usually strong contrast between dark upperparts and pale underparts.
- Ageing often difficult in autumn ♀ but see 1w.
- Prim-cov with slightly frayed broad white fringes ⇔ in ad autumn often narrower and sharply bordered, not frayed.
- Prim brown to brown-black often with pointed and worn tips ⇔ in ad deep black and fresh looking. Confirmation of exact colour needs good field conditions and viewing from different angles.
- Pale fringes to sec complete and cream-coloured in 1w of both sexes and most ad ♀ ⇔ in ad ♂ fringes often whitish, disappearing towards base, creating solid black panel below greater cov.
- Tail-feathers relatively narrow and with small point at shaft-tip ⇔ in ad broad and rounded.
- Sometimes moult-limit visible in greater cov; outer retained juv greater cov slightly shorter and duller than inner, often difficult to see. Often all cov still juv with broad cream-coloured fringes ⇔ ad.
- Wings with brown wash and pale fringes to cov. Inner greater cov often moulted in 1w, longer and blacker than retained outer ones.
- 1s ♂ sometimes with brown mantle and back and often grey-brown crown.

plum
- Tail-pattern: variable but terminal band always widens on outer tail-feather(s) and narrows between t2-t5 (sometimes terminal tail-band almost broken at t3 and t4).
- White-throated morph *'vittata'* occurs mainly in Asia (but some hybrid Eastern Black-eared x Pied from eastern Europe probably very similar). ♂ with completely white throat and variable broad black breast-band (some ind lack breast-band and resemble Eastern Black-eared ♂. ♀ with pale throat (also in spring) but not pure white (base of throat feathers grey); therefore strongly resembles Eastern Black-eared ♀ -type but upperparts cold brown.

rus Wheatear *Oenanthe cypriaca* L 14cm 5.5"

lum ⇒
- Except ad s, dark grey-brown crown, (almost) concolorous with throat ⇔ in Pied Wheatear dark crown greyer and paler, normally obviously paler than throat.

⇒
- (Except ad ♂ s which has (almost) completely white crown), white supercilium extending along rear-

	side of ear-coverts to hind-neck, creating border between dark neck-side and crown. Supercilium of rather narrow and well-defined ⇔ in Pied normally broader and diffusely bordered.
	• White rump slightly smaller than in Pied, extending at most to tip of shortest tertials ⇔ in Pied extending to base of shortest tertials or even higher.
	• Prim-projection c.100%, slightly shorter than in most Pied.
	• p1 obviously longer than prim-cov ⇔ in Pied hardly longer.
	• Smaller and more compact than Pied with relatively large head.
ad s	• Pale area on rear-head/hind-neck not extending onto mantle and *not broadening towards neck-side* ⇔ Pied ♂.
	• ♀ only slightly duller coloured than ♂ with darker crown, from summer almost identical to ♂.
ad ♀/1w	• Upperparts and crown black-brown (crown often whitish in summer).
	• Deep orange-brown lower breast and belly ⇔ in Pied in autumn orange wash only on lower breast and belly.
	• Large dark throat-patch.
1w	• For general ageing criteria, see Pied 1w.
1s	• Prim browner and more worn than in ad.
fl all plum ⇒	• Tail-pattern: black terminal band broader than in Pied and probably always complete (not broken at and t4 like in some Pied).

Eastern Black-eared Wheatear and Western Black-eared Wheatear

all plum ⇒	• Orange to brown-grey breast-band. When dark-throated then separated from dark throat by pale line when pale-throated then pale throat contrasting with dark breast and ear-coverts. Not in most ad s.
ad	• Lower part of scaps (almost) as dark as wings ⇔ Desert Wheatear and Northern Wheatear.
	• Ad w like ad s but wings and scaps with narrow pale fringes and, when dark-throated, throat with p scales. In general differences between ad w and ad s far less than in Pied Wheatear.
ad ♂	• Uniform pale orange-brown to greyish or even almost white upperparts and underparts.
	• White-throated ind differ usually by throat colour from Pied (note that white-throated Pied occurs, se Pied note).
ad ♂ autumn	• Mainly black wings with only narrow pale fringes to tertials, sec and greater cov not extending to ba in many ind median cov and lesser cov almost lack pale fringes ⇔ Pied ad autumn normally with considerably more and broader pale fringes to feathers of wings and body (and therefore often mor strongly resembling 1w).
	• Deep black prim ⇔ 1w ♂.
ad ♀ s	• Usually faint dark (not black) throat-patch, but like ♂ also occurrs in pale-throated morph. Later in summer throat-patch becomes darker.
1w	• Pale fringes to *all* feathers of wings ⇔ most ad autumn.
	• For general ageing criteria, see Pied 1w.
1s ♂	• Pale parts can bleach to white in summer in both species.
ad w/1w	• When dark-throated then dark throat separated by pale line from orange-coloured breast (probably especially in Western) ⇔ Pied ad ♀ autumn/1w.
	• Almost uniform upperparts (⇔ in Pied 1w scaled upperparts), varying between grey-brown (Easter and orange-brown (Western).
	• Scaps with faint dark centres, less so in ♀ (mainly concealed by broad pale feather-fringes).
	• Evenly broad, diffuse orange breast-band.
1w/1s	• In 1w sometimes moult-limit in greater cov, inner moulted feathers deeper black and longer than o In 1s obvious differences between new jet-black feathers and old brown ones (in Eastern more bro feathers with pale fringes than in Western) ⇔ in ad all feathers black.
fl all plum	• Tail-pattern: very variable but tail-band widens on outer-side of tail and narrows strongly between t (in ad t2-t4 sometimes entirely white, imm with generally more black in tail). Tail-pattern like Pied (including variation).

Eastern Black-eared Wheatear *Oenanthe melanoleuca*   L 14.5cm

all plum	• See introduction to Eastern Black-eared Wheatear and Western Black-eared Wheatear.
	• Generally colder (brown) than Western Black-eared Wheatear and in that respect more similar to Pi Wheatear.
	• Prim-projection c.100% (generally longer than in Western).
ad ♂	• Relatively large amount of black above eye ⇔ in Western normally very little or no black above eye
	• Black on forehead; black of mask extends in band over bill (in most 1s ♂ less black on forehead a thus more similar to Western) ⇔ in Western very little or no black above bill.
	• Mantle and crown very variable: greyish, completely white or cream yellow, crown usually diffusely patchy or washed greyish with more coloured mantle ⇔ in Western crown, hind-neck and mantle warmer coloured and especially more uniform and 'cleaner'. Western 1s ♂ sometimes also almost white on both upperparts as underparts.
	• In black-throated morph large throat-patch extending to breast and covering whole ear-coverts (throat-patch larger and more angular on rear-side of ear-coverts than in Western with largest thr patch). In some ind (especially older ad?) throat-patch extendis onto neck-side and almost conne with wings.
	• Coloured underparts (when present directly connected to black throat ⇔ in Western often pale line between coloured underparts and black throat.
	• Large number of scaps black (relatively narrow pale mantle area) ⇔ in Western fewer scaps black (broader pale mantle area).
	• Occurs in white- and black-throated morph (as in Western) but no obvious intermediate types as in Western. Black-throated morph more common ⇔ Western.
ad ♂ autumn /1s ♂	• Typical ind with brown-grey upperparts ⇔ in typical Western deep orange-brown.

♂
- Often still looks rather immature with distinct paler fringes to feathers of wings and dirty grey wash on mantle and crown (and often distinct supercilium) ⇔ in Western 1s ♂ more uniform upperparts and blacker wings, similar to ad ♂ with only slightly browner old feathers.
- Wings black-brown ⇔ in Western deeper black.

w/ad ♀
- Rather dark grey-brown crown, mantle, back and breast, usually colder coloured and often less uniform and clean than Western ad ♀. In Pied 1w upperparts normally darker and more scaled due to darker feather-bases.
- Often dark brown breast-sides ⇔ in Western breast-sides not distinctly darker.

w ♂
- Most ind resemble Pied 1w ♂ (some strongly so!), but dark throat-patch or mask normally separated from dark wings by pale neck-side (however sometimes very difficult to see due to presence of pale feather-tips which conceal bases of all feathers) ⇔ in Pied 1w ♂ throat-patch extends onto neck-side but often difficult to see.
- Upperparts often paler, browner and more uniform than in Pied 1w ♂ (for differences with Western, see 1w/ad ♀).

te
- See also Western.

Eastern Black-eared Wheatear *Oenanthe hispanica* L 14.5cm 5.7"

plum
- See introduction to Eastern Black-eared Wheatear and Western Black-eared Wheatear.
- Prim-projection 80-100% (usually slightly shorter than in Eastern).

♂
- Mask/throat-patch very variable; *normally no black above eye and bill*. In black-throated ind with largest throat-patch black sometimes extends to forehead with very narrow rim over bill (see Eastern).
- Mantle, crown and breast (deep) orange-yellow to orange-brown; especially in spring warmer coloured than Eastern, in summer more bleached and colder coloured, then much like Eastern. 1s ♂ sometimes almost completely black and white (like some Eastern).
- Occurs in both white- and black-throated morph and many intermediates ⇔ in Eastern more or less stable white- and black-throated morph. White-throated morph more common ⇔ Eastern.

♀
- Uniform yellow-brown to dark brown mantle, back and breast; usually warmer coloured than in Eastern ad ♀. Upperparts distinctly *more uniform and 'cleaner'* than in Eastern (as in 1s ♂).

♂
- See Eastern 1s ♂.

te
- See Eastern for more field marks.

Desert Wheatear *Oenanthe deserti* L 15cm 5.9"

plum ⇒
- *Whitish fringes* on cov, tertials and sec, especially inner lesser cov creating very pale wing-bend (worn away in summer, then wings black except for inner lesser cov).
⇒
- Visible part of tail completely black (in all wheatears when perched amount of black in tail often difficult to judge; even species with relatively little black sometimes seems to show completely black tail).
- Prim-projection c.100%. Prim-projection ≤ tail-projection beyond wing-tips ⇔ Northern Wheatear and Isabelline Wheatear.
- Fine bill.
- In autumn rump often cream-coloured.
- Scaps concolorous with mantle ⇔ in Eastern/Western Black-eared Wheatear ad and most imm scaps darker than mantle.
- Black throat connected with black wing-bend.
- For general ageing criteria, see Pied Wheatear 1w.

♂
- Like ad ♂ but fringes to cov (especially prim-cov) broader pale cream-coloured (later white) and dark throat with pale wash (small pale feather-tips) ⇔ in fresh ad in autumn fringes whiter and narrower and fringes to greater cov and prim-cov almost absent.

♀/ad ♀ w
- Lores not distinctly darker than crown ⇔ Northern and Isabelline.
- Upperparts with grey wash.
- Ear-coverts darker than crown ⇔ Isabelline.

1s
- Often moult-limit in greater cov, but can be difficult to judge; sometimes all greater cov moulted, but in many 1w all greater cov still retained.
- Cov and flight-feathers with relatively broad pale fringes, characteristic of this age when prim-cov have obvious pale and frayed fringes.
- Prim brown-black ⇔ in ad deep black (see Pied 1w).

I plum
- Tail-pattern: nearly completely black tail (except base of outer tail-feathers).

g var
- *O.d. homochroa* (North Africa), *O.d. deserti* (Middle East) and *O.d. atrogularis* (Asia)

plum
- *Homochroa palest*, most sandy-coloured and smallest subspecies; eastern subspecies larger and darker; atrogularis browner. Vagrants in north-western Europe probably largely belong to eastern subspecies.

Finsch's Wheatear *Oenanthe finschii* L 15.5cm 6.1"

plum ⇒
- Relatively short wings, prim-projection only c.80% (wing-tip reaches at most to black tail base).
- Relatively large head and thick neck.

♂ ⇒
- Whitish to cream-coloured cap, mantle and back; pale back conspicuous, especially in flight, appearing as pale band between dark wings, as in Eastern/Western Black-eared Wheatear.
- Broad connection of black throat to black wings as in Pied Wheatear ad ♂.

♀
- Rufous-brown ear-coverts.
- Older ♀ with ♂-like dark throat and ear-coverts.
- Brown-grey mantle and scaps.
- Some ♀ in winter dark grey on upperparts.

♀/1w
- Broad cream-coloured to greyish fringes on cov, tertials and flight-feathers.
- Broad *greyish* fringes to cov ⇔ all other wheatears.

1w	• For general ageing criteria, see Pied 1w.
1w/1s	• Usually moult-limit in greater cov, sometimes all greater cov moulted. In 1s prim and some cov still j but difference with ad-type feathers hardly visible.
fl all plum ⇒	• Tail-pattern: small white tips to tail-feathers (except t1) creating pale terminal tail fringe. Black tail-band relatively narrow and of even width.
	• Pale inner webs of prim creating diffuse pale wash over hand but less distinct than in Eastern/Weste Mourning Wheatear.

Red-rumped Wheatear *Oenanthe moesta* L 15.5cm €

all plum ⇒	• Greater cov and median cov with *broad pale fringes* (only wheatear *ad* with broad pale fringes to cov in spring).
	• Relatively large head with rather strong bill.
	• Relatively short prim-projection c.80% (wing-tip reaches at most to black of tail base).
	• Slightly larger than Northern Wheatear.
ad ♂	• Obvious contrast between pale grey crown and hind-neck and dark grey upperparts.
	• Broad white supercilium.
	• Black throat broadly connected to black wing-bend.
	• Underparts dirty white.
ad ♀ ⇒	• Nearly *uniform orange head* contrasts with grey mantle.
	• Rufous wing-panel formed by rufous fringes to mainly sec and tertials.
	• Grey-brown upperparts; whitish underparts (underparts normally distinctly paler than in Persian Wheatear).
1w	• For general ageing criteria, see Pied Wheatear 1w.
1w/1s	• Usually moult-limit in greater cov, sometimes all greater cov moulted. In 1s prim and part of cov still but difference with ad-type feathers difficult to see.
behav	• Pumps tail and often flicks tail downwards.
	• Often flies with spread tail ⇔ Red-tailed/Kurdistan Wheatear.
fl all plum ⇒	• Tail-pattern: almost completely black tail with orange base of outer tail-feathers, in ♀ slightly more orange at base, less black in tail.
	• Dark grey upperwing; pale inner webs of prim creating pale wash over upperside of hand ⇔ Kurdistan/Red-tailed.
	• Rump pale cream-coloured.

geog var	*O.m. moesta* (North Africa) compared to *O.m. brooksbanki* (Middle East)
ad	• Generally darker upperparts (blackish when worn) than *brooksbanki*.
	• Orange undertail-cov, uppertail-cov and base of outer tail-feathers ⇔ in *brooksbanki* duller coloured
♀	• Upperparts more rufous (in *brooksbanki* more grey).

Kurdistan Wheatear and Red-tailed Wheatear

all plum ⇒	• No contrast between grey-brown mantle and crown ⇔ Red-rumped Wheatear.
	• Orange-red vent, undertail-cov, uppertail-cov and rump (sometimes hardly any orange-red in ♀).
	• Size as Northern Wheatear (⇔ Red-rumped is larger) with relatively large head.
1w	• For general ageing criteria, see Pied Wheateear 1w.
fl all plum ⇒	• Pale underwing (in Red-tailed completely pale, in Kurdistan slightly darker underwing-cov) ⇔ in Re rumped ad ♂ blackish underwing-cov as in most 'black-throated' wheatears ad ♂.
	• Uniform dark upperwing ⇔ Red-rumped.
	• Rufous rump and uppertail-cov.
note	• Some ind appear intermediate between Red-tailed and Kurdistan; some Kurdistan ♀ with rufous tail-base.

Kurdistan Wheatear *Oenanthe xanthoprymna* L 14.5cm

ad	• See introduction to Kurdistan Wheatear and Red-tailed Wheatear
	• Hed-orange uppertail cov, rump, undertail-cov and vent (in ad ♂ regularly extends to belly and flan
ad ♂	• Grey crown, mantle and scaps.
	• White supercilium.
	• Large black throat-patch to wing-bend.
1w ♂	• Like ad ♂ but upperparts browner and throat less deep black with brown feather tips.
ad ♀	• Usually diffuse dark throat-patch (in 1s ♀ pale throat); some (older) ♀ resemble ad ♂ ⇔ Red-tail Wheatear all plum.
	• Pale throat in some 1s resembling both sexes of Red-tailed, but lacks distinct blue-grey neck-side a breast (see also flight all plum).
	• Dark grey-brown upperparts and only slightly paler underparts (upperparts darker than in Red-taile
fl all plum ⇒	• Tail-pattern: *white corners of tail-base* with evenly broad terminal band. Some (1w/1s ♂) ♀ with rufous tail and very similar to Red-tailed, maybe intermediate.

Red-tailed Wheatear *Oenanthe chrysopygia* L 14.5cm

ad ⇒	• See introduction to Kurdistan Wheatear and Red-tailed Wheatear
	• Blue-grey neck-side and breast ⇔ Kurdistan Wheatear ♀.
	• Grey-brown upperparts, only slightly paler underparts.
	• Rufous ear-coverts and rufous wash on belly; undertail-cov deeper reddish.
	• Sexes almost alike ⇔ Kurdistan.
fl all plum ⇒	• Tail-pattern: red tail with evenly broad terminal band ⇔ Kurdistan.
	• Uniform dark brown upperwing.

riable Wheatear *Oenanthe picata*

og var — *O.p. picata* (eastern part of Middle East, e.g. Iran)

♂
- Resembles larger Hume's Wheatear but black throat extending further to breast; back largely black ⇔ in Hume's white back and black mantle.
- Undertail-cov buffish.
- Dull black ⇔ Hume's glossy black.

♀
- Pattern as in ad ♂ but black parts with brown wash.

all plum
- For general ageing criteria, see Pied Wheatear 1w.
- Terminal tail-band of even width.

og var — *O.p. opistholeuca* (central Asia)

- Resembles both black morph of Eastern Mourning Wheatear (but no pale inner web on flight-feathers) and White-crowned Black Wheatear imm (but with complete tail-band).
- Dark parts dark grey, slightly contrasting with black wings ⇔ White-crowned Black imm and black morph of Eastern Mourning.
- Ear-coverts weak red-brown.
- Border between white and black on underparts at vent situated directly behind legs (see White-crowned Black imm and black morph of Eastern Mourning).

♀
- Like ad ♂ but black parts with brown wash.

all plum
- Terminal tail-band of even width.

og var — *O.p. capistrata* (central Asia)

♂
- Resembles Pied ad ♂ but underparts always completely white; crown in spring uniform grey.

♀
- Resembles Pied ad ♀ and very difficult to distinguish from if tail-pattern cannot be seen.

all plum
- Terminal tail-band of even width ⇔ Pied.

stern Mourning Wheatear *Oenanthe lugens*

plum
- Legs sometimes dark grey instead of black as in most other wheatears.
⇒ • White underparts except orange-yellow undertail-cov (see Western Mourning Wheatear and geog var).
- Like Pied Wheatear ad ♂ (black mantle, back and throat-patch broadly connected to black wings).
- White cap extending less far to mantle than in Pied ad ♂ and usually widens at most very slightly on hind-neck.
- Sometimes still white tips to prim-cov and tertials in spring (as in autumn plumage of other wheatears).
- Ad ♀ almost identical to ♂ ⇔ Western.

♀
- For general ageing criteria, see Pied 1w.

/1s
- Distinct moult-limit in greater cov, inner moulted feathers deeper black and longer than outer.

all plum
- White inner webs of flight-feathers creating conspicuous pale wash over upperwing (also strong contrast on underwing).
- Tail-pattern: rather narrow terminal tail-band of even width ⇔ Pied.
- Very small white tips to tail-feathers except central pair, creating narrow white terminal tail-fringe (as on Finsch's Wheatear but still narrower).

e
- In Jordan almost completely dark morph occurs ('Basalt Wheatear') with black underparts except white undertail-cov; border between white and black behind legs situated at vent ⇔ White-crowned Black Wheatear 1w.

og var — *O.l. persica* (southern Iran)

plum
- Larger and more elongated than *lugens* with especially longer wings and bill.
- Often lacks pale tips to prim-cov.
- Undertail-cov deeper orange-brown than in *lugens*.
- Crown often with brown or grey wash.
- Tail-band slightly broader than in *lugens*.

d
- White on inner webs less extensive than in *lugens* (similar to Western).

stern Mourning Wheatear *Oenanthe halophila*

♂
- Like Eastern Mourning Wheatear but faint orange-yellow undertail-cov, sometimes absent ⇔ in Eastern more distinct orange-yellow undertail-cov.

♀
- Pale grey-brown on upperparts and head with variable darker throat and ear-coverts from completely pale-throated to almost black-throated (dark-throated ind more common in eastern part of range, otherwise throat becomes darker by wear).
- Broad faintly bordered supercilium.
- Can resemble Finsch's Wheatear ad ♀ (normally no overlap in range) but longer prim-projection and more contrasting due to blackish wings and paler grey-brown upperparts.
- For general ageing criteria, see Pied Wheatear 1w.

1s
- Distinct moult-limit in greater cov. In ♂ distinct colour difference, in ♀ difference in amount of wear more useful (inner moulted feathers fresher and longer than outer).

l plum
- Pale wash over prim much fainter and diffuser than in Eastern.
- Tail pattern as in Eastern.

oded Wheatear *Oenanthe monacha*

plum
- Large with long body, long bill and short legs.
♂ ⇒ • Black throat and breast, rest of underparts white.
- White cap.

1w ♂	• Superficially like ad ♂ but yellow-brown tail (pattern as in ♀).
1w	• For general ageing criteria, see Pied Wheatear 1w.
ad ♀/1w ⇒	• Orange rump, uppertail-cov and tail (slightly more black on tip of outer tail-feathers than ad ♂).
⇒	• Upperparts and underparts rather uniform pale brown.
	• All feathers on wings with dark centres and pale fringes.
1w/1s ♂	• Obvious/distinct moult-limit in greater cov; inner moulted feathers deeper black and longer than oute... Moult-limit in 1w/1s ♀ probably detectable by amount of wear.
fl all plum ⇒	• Only small black tips to outer tail-feathers, creating no tail-band (tail-pattern similar to White-crown... Black Wheatear).
	• Butterfly-like foraging flight.

Hume's Wheatear *Oenanthe alboniger*   L 18cm 7

all plum ⇒	• Glossy black head, throat, mantle and wings.
	• Large size with large head and relatively strong bill ⇔ Variable Wheatear *picata*.
	• Sexes alike, imm with brown wash over black parts.
	• Border between black throat and white underparts directly above wing-bend ⇔ in Variable *picata* border higher up.
1w	• For general ageing criteria, see Pied 1w.
1w/1s	• Prim and probably some cov still juv; difference with ad-type feathers probably detectable by amoun... of wear.
fl all plum	• White uppertail-cov, rump and back.
	• Broad black and straight terminal tail-band.

White-crowned Black Wheatear *Oenanthe leucopyga*   L 17.5cm 6

all plum	• Relatively strongly curved culmen.
ad	• Completely black except white crown, rump, uppertail-cov, undertail-cov and vent.
	• Border between white and black level with legs or slightly before ⇔ Eastern Mourning Wheatear dark morph.
imm	• Lacks (partial) white crown to spring of 2nd cy.
1w	• For general ageing criteria, see Pied Wheatear 1w.
1w/1s	• Juv prim and some cov retained, usually distinct difference between brown juv and black ad-type feathers. Juv feathers often with pale fringes or tips to 2cy.
fl all plum ⇒	• Very little black in tail; in ad usually entirely white outer tail-feathers; sometimes (usually imm) narro... chequered terminal tail-band (pattern and variation nearly similar to Hooded Wheatear) ⇔ Black Wheatear and Eastern Mourning dark morph.
geog var	*O.l. ernesti* (Middle East)
all plum	• Slightly larger than *leucopyga* with longer bill.
ad	• Generally more gloss on black parts of plumage than in *leucopyga*.

Black Wheatear *Oenanthe leucura*   L 17cm

all plum ⇒	• Large with relatively strong bill.
	• Completely black, except white rump, uppertail-cov, undertail-cov, vent and basal part of outer tail-feathers. White not reaching legs ⇔ White-crowned Black Wheatear.
ad ♂	• Dull black.
ad ♀	• Black-brown.
1w ♂	• Contrast between black body and brown juv wings (some greater cov black).
1w/1s	• Moult-limit in greater cov; inner moulted feathers deeper black and longer than outer.
fl all plum ⇒	• *Broad* black tail-band of even width ⇔ White-crowned Black.

Rock thrushes

Rufous-tailed Rock Thrush *Monticola saxatilis*   L 18.5cm

all plum	• Thickset, short-tailed thrush (tail projects only slightly beyond wing-tips).
	• Red tail, except t1 (resembles redstarts).
	• Very long prim-projection (± 130%).
ad ♂ ⇒	• White-spotted back, upper part of rump and part of scaps.
ad ♂ s	• Grey-blue head, throat, mantle and uppertail-cov.
ad ♂ w	• Underparts strongly patterned with black feather-centres and white fringes (forming scaled underpa...
	• Summer plumage obtained by wear (as e.g. in redstarts).
ad ♀	• Strongly patterned head and upperparts (like large Robin juv).
	• Barred underparts with rufous wash.
1w	• Like ad w but broader pale fringes to wing-feathers.
1s	• Like ad of equivalent sex but prim old and brown and often moult-limit in greater cov.

Blue Rock Thrush *Monticola solitarius*   L 22cm

all plum	• Size like Common Starling; long bill and tail.
ad ♂	• Dull dark blue except black wings and tail (blue often difficult to see in shadow).
ad ♀ ⇒	• Underparts barred on rather pale background.
	• Uniform dark grey-brown to blue-grey upperparts.
1w-1s	• Like ad but moult-limit in greater cov.
note	• ♀ somewhat resembles Siberian Thrush ♀ but in latter e.g. much paler belly, vent and undertail-c... pale legs and stronger head-pattern.

Ficedula **flycatchers**

d-breasted Flycatcher *Ficedula parva* L 11.5cm 4.5"

plum ⇒
- White basal half of at least t4-t6 creating distinct white corner to tail-base.
- Distinct, complete pale eye-ring.
- Uniform (grey-)brown upperparts.
- Unmarked pale underparts.
- Usually paler base of lower mandible (see Taiga Flycatcher).
- Dark (usually not black, see Taiga) uppertail-cov contrast with upperparts.

♂
- Greyish head and breast-sides.
- Orange-red throat-patch usually extending on to breast (in 2s ♂ smaller and more orange throat-patch).
- Part of wing (normally some inner sec, tertials, greater cov and some median cov) retained juv feathers with pale tips sometimes still present (but often worn off).

♂
♀/1w
- Like ad ♀ but in some ind very faint orange throat-patch (see Taiga).
- White underparts with cream-coloured breast and fore-flanks.

w ⇒
- Narrow pale outer-edges and small pale tips to tertials ⇔ in ad w broad diffuse outer-edges to tertials.
- Rather faint cream-coloured to brown-orange wing-bar over greater cov.

iga Flycatcher *Ficedula albicilla* L 12cm 4.7"

plum
- Completely dark bill (only extreme base of lower mandible sometimes paler) ⇔ on Red-breasted Flycatcher pale lower mandible with dark tip. In some Red-breasted almost completely dark lower mandible.
- Pale grey breast and upper belly ⇔ Red-breasted.
- (Glossy) black longest uppertail-cov, as black or even deeper black than tail; *strongly contrasting* with grey brown upperparts ⇔ on Red-breasted dark brown longest uppertail-cov (sometimes almost black).
- Dark grey-brown upperparts (slightly darker and colder coloured than in Red-breasted).
- Dark (brown) crown often creating capped appearance (especially in ad ♂/1s ♂) ⇔ Red-breasted all plum.
- General field marks such as tail-patterning and eye-ring as in Red-breasted.
- Blackish flight-feathers ⇔ in Red-breasted usually brownish.

♂ s ⇒
- Small red-orange throat-patch extends only over throat and upper part of breast, *surrounded by broad grey breast-band* ⇔ Red-breasted ad ♂.
- Grey-brown crown concolorous with upperparts ⇔ on Red-breasted completely blue-grey head.
- Diffuse pale lores.

♂
- Nearly as ad ♂; orange-red throat-patch already developed in 1w; in spring of 2cy ♂ looks like ad ♂ with juv (worn) cov and flight-feathers ⇔ on Red-breasted ♂ orange-red throat-patch develops as late as in 3cy ♂ (in some Red-breasted 1s ♂ faint orange-yellow throat-patch).

♂ w
/1w ⇒
- Ad ♀-like winter plumage ⇔ in Red-breasted ad ♂ no distinct winter plumage.
- *Grey* to brownish-grey breast and upper belly contrast with rather distinct whitish throat-patch ⇔ in Red-breasted ♀/1w almost uniform warm cream-coloured breast and flanks and larger ill-defined paler throat.
- Pale whitish tips to greater cov and prim-cov worn away more quickly than (yellow-brown tip) in Red-breasted.

J
- Whitish outer-edge on tertials connected with thickening at tertial-tip ⇔ in Red-breasted 1w more narrow and buff fringes, which are less distinct. Pattern more similar to 1w black-and-white flycatchers than to 1w Red-breasted.

ice
- Call: rattling like Red-breasted but dryer and much faster (twice as fast as Red-breasted) with more than 10 notes per call (not countable by human ear) ⇔ in Red-breasted about 5 notes per call and just countable.

gimaki Flycatcher *Ficedula mugimaki* L 13cm 5.1"

♂
- Characteristic blue-black head and upperparts, white outer-side of tail-base, white tertial-fringes and fringes on inner greater cov and white supercilium only behind eye.
- Orange-red throat, breast and upper belly; rest of underparts whitish.

♀
- Like faintly marked and strongly bleached ad ♂ with brown-grey upperparts, orange throat and breast and white tips only on greater cov.

J
- Similar to ad ♀.
- Like ad but prim, prim-cov and outer cov obviously brown.

te
- Only record in WP regarded as escape.

ck-and-white flycatchers

first step to identifying especially ♀-type black-and-white flycatchers is correct ageing, as some important field rks only apply for one plumage type. Identification of all plumages of black-and-white flycatchers is complicated by tence of hybrids (at least Pied Flycatcher x Collared Flycatcher) and/or large individual variation. Some ind, especially utumn, are not identifiable with certainty.

J
- White outer-edges on tertials thickened at tip.
- Greater cov with white tips, on outer web thickened (creating notched wing-bar) ⇔ ad.
- Dark brown prim (often already blackish in Collared Flycatcher 1w, especially ♂).
- In Collared and Pied Flycatcher sometimes (partial) 2nd wing-bar due to pale tips to retained juv median cov. Presence of juv median cov depends on extent of post-juv moult (in Semicollared Flycatcher 2nd wing-bar normal on sec).
- Similar to ad of equivalent sex but prim, prim-cov and outer cov obviously brown (in ♀ much more difficult to see than in ♂).
- Species-specific prim-spot (much) smaller than in ad or absent.
- Species-specific patch on forehead (much) smaller than in ad.

Semicollared Flycatcher *Ficedula semitorquata* L 12.5cm

all plum ⇒	• White tips to median cov creating whitish-chequered, obvious wing-bar (in some plumages of Pied Flycatcher and Collared Flycatcher also but in these more faint, less white and less distinctly uninterrupted). In Atlas Flycatcher 1s/ad s sometimes present.
ad	• Often large white prim-spot (but generally smaller than in Collared), extending to p4.
ad ♂/1s ♂⇒	• *Much white in tail* ⇔ Collared and Pied. t6 and t5 with large white centres to inner web, t6 often wit white fringe along inner web and completely white outer web. Sometimes less white in tail but outer web of t6 always completely or largely white ⇔ Pied (and hybrid Collard x Pied).
ad ♂ s	• Wing-bar over median cov often merging with large amount of white on greater cov, therefore less conspicuous. • Usually narrow white stripe on neck-side but variable, sometimes identical to Pied. • 'Melted' double white patch on forehead (size generally between Pied and Collared). • Diffuse grey rump-patch ⇔ on Collared larger and whiter.
1s	• See introduction to black-and-white flycatchers.
ad ♀ ⇒	• *Narrow* tertial-fringes, slightly broader at base ⇔ Pied and Collared. • *Narrow evenly broad* pale (normally not white) fringes along tail-sides extending around tip of t6 (sometimes also on t5). Inner web of t6 rather pale grey-brown. Normally no white on basal part of inner web ⇔ Pied and Collared ad ♀. • Wing-bar over median cov important in this plumage (in autumn ageing essential first step, see introduction to black-and-white flycatchers). • Wings and tail (especially t6) often not black but variable dark grey (t6 often with dark subterminal fringe surrounding tip) ⇔ Collared to lesser extent Pied. • Rather large prim-spot, generally smaller than in Collared ad ♀ s (but Collared 1s ♀ usually same, ageing essential!). Prim-spot usually extending to p4 (as in most Collared). • Brown-grey upperparts, similar to Collared ♀ s (paler and especially colder grey than in Pied ♀). • Uppertail-cov slightly paler than black upper-tail, not black as in Collared, Atlas and Pied *iberiae*.
ad ♂ w	• Like ad ♀ but upperparts darker and deep black flight-feathers. • Wing-bar over median cov usually conspicuous (⇔ Collared) but sometimes absent.
1w (ageing see above)	• 2nd wing-bar over median cov often conspicuous but in this plumage of less value as often also present in Pied and Collared 1w. • Rest of plumage like ad ♀, including tail-pattern.
voice	• Call: more whistling than call of Collared and descending in pitch 'tjuuup', somewhat reminiscent of of Siberian Chiffchaff. Also slightly rising, short 'tjeep'. • Song: slow like Collared but less variable in pitch and with more clear trembles.

Collared Flycatcher *Ficedula albicollis* L 12.5cm

all plum	• Prim-spot normally extending to outer-edge of wing (in most ind to p4, in ad often to p3, in 1w ♀ o not further than p5) ⇔ in Pied Flycatcher not extending to outer-edge of wing, not further than p5, i most to p6. • Slightly longer prim-projection than Pied (± 100%).
ad	• Large, often somewhat rectangular prim-spot, reaching distinctly below prim-cov.
ad ♂ s/1s ♂	• *Completely white collar* (varying in width). • *Little or no* white in tail (at most white outer web of t6 and t5). • Large white spot on forehead (in 1s ♂ sometimes smaller). • Diffuse greyish to white spot on rump/lower part of back.
ad ♂ w	• Like ad ♀ but deep black sec, prim and central tail-feathers. • Narrow white tail-sides like in Pied. Tail-feathers moulted in winter to summer-type (almost) without whi • Sometimes faint pale collar.
1s	• See introduction to black-and-white flycatchers. • In ♂ sometimes collar broken at rear-side by dark band (also in hybrid Collared x Pied, never in pur ad ♂ s).
ad ♀/1s ♀	• Grey-brown upperparts with diffuse grey hind-neck and rump and blackish uppertail-cov (in 1s brow grey upperparts, paler and greyer than ♀ Pied). • White in outer web of t6 and t5 often extending to tip and in most ind also some white in outer web t4 ⇔ most Pied. • Tertials with broad white bases and narrowly edged white at tips (narrower than in most Pied).
1w (ageing see above)	• Like ad ♀ (w), including tail-pattern but prim-spot usually smaller and often broadly white-surround on tips of tertials as in Pied 1w. • In 1w ♂ often already deep black prim and central tail-feathers, outer tail-feathers more grey-brow ⇔ Pied 1w. • In 1w ♂ white fringes on tertials conspicuously broad ⇔ in 1w ♀ rather narrow. • Sometimes faint 2nd wing-bar over median cov (in ad typical for Semicollared Flycatcher) usually interrupted and not pure white (like in Pied 1w).
voice	• Song: characteristic, rather slow and mixed in pitch, strongly variable trilling notes, some parts of so reminiscent of song of European Robin ⇔ Pied. • Call: single-toned, rather drawn-out, rather dry and flat 'eeehp' ⇔ Pied and Semicollared.

Pied Flycatcher *Ficedula hypoleuca* L 12.5cm

all plum	• Small prim-spot creating narrow stripe along prim-cov, rarely reaching beyond tip of longest prim-cc More concentrated on inner prim and at most extending to p5, not to outer-edge of wing ⇔ Collared Flycatcher ad. • Rather little white in outer-side of tail, broadening towards base (in Collared broadening at base is o less distinct). Often extending up to inner web of t6 but normally not reaching tip (sometimes almost white in tail in ad ♂ s). Generally no large differences in tail-pattern between 1w, 1s/ad ♀ and 1s/a ♂ ⇔ Collared and Semicollared Flycatcher.

d ♂ s ⇒
- Small double white patch on forehead, sometimes 'melted'.
- Brown morph (mainly occurring in western Europe) resembles ad ♀ s but darker brown-grey on upperparts, black rump and sometimes also uppertail-cov, much white in tertials and greater cov and pale patch on forehead.

s
♀ s
- See introduction to black-and-white flycatchers (for brown-type ♂ applies same as for ♀).
- Brown upperparts ⇔ Collared and Semicollared ♀ s.
- Much white on tertials, strongly broadening towards base but also rather broad surround to tip ⇔ Collared and Semicollared.

d w
- Sometimes faint 2nd wing-bar over median cov.
- Dark brown prim ⇔ in most Collared and Semicollared ad w black.

w (ageing see above)
- Breast and throat with brown wash exaggerating white submoustachial-stripe ⇔ in Collared and Semicollared 1w less distinct.
- Rest of plumage like ad ♀, including tail-pattern, but any ind with only diffuse border and dirty-white at outer-edge of t5 and t6 is ♀ and ind with much and bright white at outer-edge of t5 and t6 is ♂. Pattern in between former occurs in both ♂ and ♀.
- Sometimes faint 2nd wing-bar over median cov (in other plumages typical for Semicollared) usually interrupted and not pure white (like in Pied 1w). See introduction to black-and-white flycatchers.

ice
- Call a short, repeated 'peet' or 'weet'.
- Song a short series of low- and high-pitched whistles ⇔ Collared.

og var
Iberian Pied Flycatcher *F.h. iberiae* (Iberian Peninsula)

♂ s
- Intermediate between Atlas Flycatcher and *hypoleuca* but more similar to Atlas with larger grey rump-patch, larger patch on forehead, more white in tertials, completely white greater cov and larger prim-spot than *hypoleuca*.

las Flycatcher *Ficedula speculigera*   L 12.5cm 4.9"

♂ s ⇒
- All greater cov completely white *from base onwards* ⇔ in hybrid and pure Collared Flycatcher dark base of at least outer greater cov.

⇒
- Completely black tail or very limited amount of white in sides (as in most Collared ad ♂ s).
- Narrow white band through neck-side, extending slightly further than in Pied Flycatcher. In some ind similar to Semicollared Flycatcher and hybrid Collared x Pied.
- (Very) large white forehead- and prim-spot (as in Collared). Patch on forehead, when well-developed, largest of all black-and-white flycatchers.
- Black parts deep black as in Collared ad ♂ s.

♀
- Pale grey rump-patch (as in Semicollared).
- Regularly one or more white tips to median cov (but not forming complete wing-bar as in Semicollared).
- Insufficient information, on current knowledge not distinguishable from Pied with certainty.
- See introduction to black-and-white flycatchers.

♂
- No white on neck-side. Any black-and-white flycatcher 1s ♂ with white on neck(-side) but no complete collar is either odd Collared or hybrid Collared x Pied.
- Tail completely juv (brown with white outer sides) or mix of ad and juv feathers ⇔ in Collared 1s ♂ (almost) completely black tail.

ce
- Call like Pied. Song reminiscent of Pied but possibly slower and lower pitched.

Accentors

nnock *Prunella modularis*   L 14cm 5.5"

plum
- Bold (diffusely) streaked flanks.
- Heavily streaked mantle.
- White tips to greater cov creating narrow wing-bar.

⇒
- *Grey-blue throat*, breast, neck-side and supercilium.
- Heavily streaked underparts, breast and throat ⇔ ad.
- Pale base of lower mandible.
- Lacks grey-blue tones.

/1s
- Juv prim, tail-feathers and usually greater cov and tertials retained but differences with ad-type feathers usually difficult to see (in most other *Prunella* usually easier to see). Juv tail-feathers pointed ⇔ in ad rounded.

erian Accentor *Prunella montanella*   L 14cm 5.5"

plum
- Uniform cream-coloured supercilium, throat, breast and sometimes also part of belly (usually no colour difference with supercilium) ⇔ in Black-throated Accentor whiter supercilium.
- Distinct, usually somewhat chequered wing-bar over greater cov ⇔ in Black-throated often less distinct.
- Rufous-brown mantle-stripes and (when present) flank streaks; in some ind heavier, more black streaked, resembling Black-throated.
- Grey middle of crown, as in Black-throated.
- White tips to tertials usually more obvious than in Black-throated.

1s
e
- See Alpine Accentor.
- See Black-throated.

de's Accentor *Prunella ocularis*   L 13.5cm 5.3"

lum ⇒
- Faint malar striping ⇔ absent in Siberian Accentor and Black-throated Accentor.
- Rather broad, pure white supercilium.
- Upperparts cold grey-brown with black streaking ⇔ Siberian and Black-throated.
- Underparts rather strongly but diffusely streaked ⇔ Siberian and Black-throated.

- Centre of crown brownish ⇔ Siberian and Black-throated.
- Wing-bars often hardly developed.
- White to yellowish throat.

Black-throated Accentor *Prunella atrogularis*   L 14cm 5

all plum		• Rather cold brown upperparts with black stripes on mantle and scaps ⇔ Siberian Accentor.
		• Whitish supercilium with usually yellowish wash (often pure white in summer) ⇔ in Siberian normally deeper cream-coloured.
		• Underparts with well-defined border between cream-yellow flanks and white central part of underpa ⇔ in Siberian central part of underparts more gradually becoming paler.
		• Centre of flanks streaked blackish ⇔ Siberian.
		• Rather faint wing-bar.
		• Broad, grey middle of crown (often broader than in Siberian).
ad	⇒	• Black throat patch (in 1w often faintly present).
1w	⇒	• Some ind lack black patterning on throat (1w ♀ ?), in these ind throat more whitish with *throat paler than breast* ⇔ Siberian.
1w/1s		• See Alpine Accentor but usually some inner greater cov new.
note		• See Siberian.

Alpine Accentor *Prunella collaris*   L 16.5cm 6

all plum	⇒	• Long prim-projection 100% ⇔ in Dunnock c.50%.
	⇒	• Dark greater cov creating broad dark band on upperwing (also visible in flight).
		• Bold rufous streaked flanks.
		• Strong dark patterned undertail-cov ⇔ Dunnock all plum.
		• White tips to median cov and greater cov creating chequered wing-bars (broader than in Dunnock).
		• White throat patch with small dark spots.
		• Yellow basal half of lower mandible (also in Dunnock imm but less conspicuous) and extreme base o upper mandible.
juv		• Underparts evenly streaked; lacks rufous flanks.
1w/1s		• Like ad but prim, tail-feathers, often tertials and all or most greater cov still juv. Juv greater cov with broad white tips which often connect to create continuous wing-bar (pattern of greater cov different form already moulted ad-type median cov) ⇔ in ad greater cov with small rounded white tips which create row of spots, no continuous wing-bar.
		• Prim and tail-feathers rather pointed and worn at tips and tertials with worn edges ⇔ in ad pale fringes along rounded tips of prim and tail-feathers and broad pale fringes to tertials.

Avadavats, silverbills and waxbills

Red Avadavat *Amandava amandava*   L 10 cm

ad	• Red bill, rump and uppertail-cov.
ad ♂ s	• Completely dark red with rounded white spots on underparts, cov and tertials. Belly to undertail-cov and tail darker.
ad ♀ / ad ♂ w	• Grey-brown with underparts slightly paler except for red rump and uppertail-cov. ♂ also has pinkish belly.
	• Dark mask, in ♀ less well marked.
1w	• Like ad ♀ but only rump reddish.
	• Buff wing-bars ⇔ in ad pale spotted.
note	• Introduced in Portugal.

African Silverbill *Lonchura cantans*   L 11cm

all plum	• Like Indian Silverbill (see note) but underparts and flanks completely white.
	• Head-side darker than in Indian, not much paler than crown.
fl all plum ⇒	• Hump and uppertail-cov entirely dark ⇔ Indian.
note	• Introduced Indian Silverbill *L. malabarica* has in all plum thick dark grey bill, uniform brown upperpa outer-side of wing contrasting dark, crown dark streaked and white underparts with brown wash on flanks (flanks faintly barred). In flight white rump and uppertail-cov conspicuous ⇔ African.

Common Waxbill *Estrilda astrild*   L 10 cr

all plum	• Completely brown upperside incl rump and tail (diffusely barred) ⇔ in other waxbills rump and/or t contrasting with upperparts in various ways.
	• Red mask.
	• Dark undertail-cov.
ad	• Red bill.
	• Central part of underparts reddish ⇔ imm.
imm	• Dark bill.
	• Underparts uniform brownish.
note	• Introduced in Portugal.

Old World sparrows

House Sparrow *Passer domesticus*   L 15cm

ad ♂ s	• Grey crown and ear-coverts.
	• Large black throat/breast-patch.
	• Black bill.

d ♂ w
- More faint head-pattern than ad s.
- Small black throat-patch.
- Pale bill.

♀
- Broad diffuse supercilium, only behind eye.
- Faint off-white wing-bar over median cov.
- Resembles weakly patterned ad ♀.

oult
- Both ad and juv moult completely in autumn, 1w similar to ad.

lian Sparrow *Passer italiae*   L 15cm 5.9"

♂ s
- Brown crown as in Spanish Sparrow.
- White ear-coverts as in Spanish.
- Upperparts and black throat/breast-patch as in House Sparrow.

♀ /1w
- Indistinguishable from House and/or Spanish.

te
- Formerly regarded as hybrid population between Spanish and House.

anish Sparrow *Passer hispaniolensis*   L 15cm 5.9"

plum
- Stronger bill than in House Sparrow.
- Long gape-line reaches to almost front-side of eye.
- Somewhat wavy cutting-edge on upper mandible (bunting-like).

♂
- Black breast gradually extending into variable but often heavily patterned belly and flanks (rows of black spots creating broad longitudinal stripes). In fresh autumn plumage visible black on underparts restricted.
- White ear-coverts.
- Chestnut crown.
- Obvious white supercilium, broken above eye.
- Mantle with broad black longitudinal stripes.

♀
- Fine dark shaft streaks on underparts and rump/uppertail-cov, sometimes also on crown (sometimes also in House ad ♀ from June to November but less extensive and more diffuse).
- Pale stripes on mantle more distinct than in House.
- Supercilium longer (both before and behind eye), broader and paler cream-coloured than in House ♀.
- Wing-bars along median cov and greater cov whiter than in House ♀.
- Fringes to tertials, greater cov and flight-feathers sandy-coloured ⇔ in House ♀ usually warmer brown.

ad Sea Sparrow *Passer moabiticus*   L 12.5cm 4.9"

plum ⇒
- Short prim-projection c.40% with only 3, sometimes 4 prim-tips beyond tertials ⇔ in House Sparrow and Spanish Sparrow prim-projection c.70% and 4-5 prim-tips beyond tertials.

♂
- Characteristic head-pattern: grey head with well-defined supercilium and submoustachial-stripe connected with pale stripe on neck-side; black throat-patch.
- Chestnut-brown greater cov and median cov.
- Greyish underparts.

⇒
- Like washed out House, but small, *orange-yellow bill*.
- Grey-brown head-side.
- Pale throat.
- Diffuse but obvious broad eye-ring.
- Obvious, well-defined supercilium behind eye.

o Sparrow *Passer iagoensis*   L 13cm 5.1"

plum
♂
- Smaller than House Sparrow with shorter prim-projection.
- Deep rufous upperparts and supercilium.
- Dark grey crown; grey hind-neck.
- Black eye-stripe and small black throat-patch.

♀ ⇒
- Resembles House ad ♀ but uniform rufous scaps (in House ad ♀ scaps with dark centres) and often more conspicuous and deeper cream-coloured supercilium.
- Bill black ⇔ in House paler.
- Rufous-brown mantle and rump.

n
- Pale lower mandible(-base).

sert Sparrow *Passer simplex*   L 14cm 5.5"

plum
- Pale, unmarked underparts. Variable from almost white to cream-colored.
- Short, thick bill.
- Dark tips to prim, prim-cov and alula and dark centres to tertials.
- Legs very pale.

♂
- Brown-grey to pure grey upperparts and crown.
- Pale sec and outer sides of prim creating conspicuous pale wing-panel.
- Dark base of greater cov creating wing-bar.

♂ s
- Black bill, lores and breast-patch.

♀
- Uniform sandy to brown upperparts and crown.
- Black 'beady eye' conspicuous on pale head.
- Resembles weakly patterned ad.

ult
- Both ad and juv moult completely in autumn, 1w similar to ad.

es
- North-western African *saharae* generally paler than *simplex* (north-eastern Africa), but individual variation large and field marks in both taxa probably wholly overlapping.
- Isolated central Asian subspecies(?) *zarudnyi* not in WP but occurs relatively close to east border of WP (mainly Turkmenistan). In this taxon underparts almost white (like palest *simplex/saharae*). ♂ with

colder grey upperparts, including rump (⇔ in *simplex/saharae* pale cream-coloured) and more extensive black mask and throat-patch. ♀ strongly resembles ♂ including black wing-bar and sligh more diffuse mask and throat-patch, thus very different from *simplex/saharae* ♀.

Tree Sparrow *Passer montanus*   L 13.5cm 5

ad	• Chestnut-brown crown.
	• White collar.
	• White ear-coverts with large dark spot in centre.
	• Underparts (sometimes only flanks) and rump grey-brown ⇔ in House Sparrow grey.
	• Only black throat-patch (underparts lack black).
	• White tips to both median cov and greater cov creating two white wing-bars ⇔ in House pale tips to greater cov less distinct.
	• Sexes alike.
juv	• Resembles faintly patterned ad; sometimes rather similar to hybrid House x Tree due to faint head-pattern and faint grey centre of crown.
moult	• Both ad and juv moult completely in autumn, 1w similar to ad.

Golden Sparrow *Passer luteus*   L 13cm 5

ad ♂	• Uniform deep yellow head and underparts.
	• Red-brown mantle and greater cov.
	• Bill black.
ad ♀/juv	• Bunting-like wing-pattern with two wing-bars and broad pale tertial-fringes (in combination with bunting-like head somewhat resembles Yellow-breasted Bunting juv/ad ♀ but differs e.g. by long pr projection c.100%).
	• Yellow-brown head and upperparts; crown darker brown.
	• Underparts uniform pale; breast more cream-coloured.
	• Pale bill.

Pale Rock Sparrow *Carpospiza brachydactyla*   L 15cm 5

all plum	⇒	• Rather uniform dull grey-brown upperparts and head with faint supercilium, submoustachial- and malar-stripes.
	⇒	• *Very long* prim-projection c.100-120% and short tail-projection beyond wing-tips.
		• White tips to tail-feathers as in Rock Sparrow but slightly smaller.
		• Median cov with well-defined dark centres and white fringes, creating distinct wing-bar; weaker 2nd wing-bar over greater cov.
		• Pale outer webs to sec creating pale wing-panel ⇔ Yellow-throated Sparrow.
		• Curved (convex) culmen.
		• Scaps with diffuse dark centres.
		• Breast and flanks almost concolorous with upperparts; belly whitish.

Yellow-throated Sparrow *Gymnoris xanthocollis*   L 14cm 5

all plum	⇒	• Very broad white wing-bar over median cov (Common Chaffinch-like), more distinct than in Pale Rock Sparrow.
		• No white in tail ⇔ Pale Rock.
		• No pale wing-panel ⇔ Pale Rock.
		• Underparts and upperparts similar to Pale Rock Sparrow but greyer, scaps almost uniform and underparts slightly whiter.
		• Nearly uniform head with faint (dark) eye-stripe; at most faint supercilium.
		• Rather slender bill with straight culmen ⇔ in Pale Rock thick bill with convex culmen.
		• Prim-projection c.80%.
ad ♂	⇒	• In breeding season black bill and yellow spot under white throat.
	⇒	• Rufous lesser cov, especially visible in flight.

Rock Sparrow *Petronia petronia*   L 16cm ■

all plum	⇒	• Strongly patterned head with long broad rectangular-ending supercilium, dark lateral crown-stripe and pale median crown-stripe.
	⇒	• Heavy cone-shaped bill with pink to yellow lower mandible.
	⇒	• Long prim-projection c.100%.
		• Dark uppertail-cov and undertail-cov with large pale tips.
		• Heavily streaked mantle, resembling Spanish Sparrow ad ♀ in fresh plumage.
		• Heavily streaked underparts; broad dark brown stripes extending along flanks to undertail-cov.
		• Pale tips to outer webs of tail-feathers except t1.
		• Pale outer web on basal part of outer prim creating diffuse pale prim-spot.
ad		• Small yellow spot on throat (often hidden by overlying feathers).
geog var		*P.p. barbara* (north-western Africa)
ad		• Greyer and less heavily marked than *petronia*.
		• Slightly larger size and larger bill than *petronia*.

White-winged Snowfinch *Montifringilla nivalis*   L 18cm

all plum	• Completely white arm (also visible when perched); black hand.
	• Long, almost white tail (t1 and tips of rest of tail-feathers dark).
	• Uniform brown upperparts.

♂
- Grey head with dark lores.
- Large black throat-patch (in fresh plumage hidden behind pale feather-tips).
- In summer black bill ⟺ in ad ♀ s grey-brown with diffuse dark tip.
- Prim-cov white, often with small black spot on tips ⟺ ♀ (see below).

♀
- Small black throat-patch or completely absent.
- Head brown-grey; lores hardly darker.
- Prim-cov variable from completely dark (probably 1w-1s) to largely white with dark tips (probably in older ind).

w/imm
- Yellow bill (often more orange in ♂).

ault imm
- Complete in 1st cy, after moult resembles ad but see ad ♀.

og var   *M.n. alpicola* (Caucasus)
- Brown wash over greyish head; crown darker.

Wagtails

low wagtails' (all taxa from Yellow Wagtail through to Black-headed Wagtail)

♂ w
- Like ad ♂ s but head less brightly coloured and patterned with green-brown spots or wash on head and/or upperparts.
- Underparts duller yellow than in ad ♂ s.
- In most ind hints of head-pattern of ad ♂ showing through.
- Usually much duller coloured than ♂ with only yellow wash on underparts; some (older) ♀ more brightly coloured and resembling ad ♂.
- Moult-limit in cov; sometimes absent or difficult to judge, when present characteristic ⟺ ad.
- Underparts whitish with brown breast and variable amount of yellow on underparts, often only undertail-cov and vent with yellow wash.
- Pale base to lower mandible.
- In some ♂ yellow belly and undertail-cov, very similar to ad ♀ ⟺ in ♀ mainly (dirty) white with some yellow on underparts.
- Some ind (mostly ♀) lacking yellow altogether on underparts and superficially resembling Citrine Wagtail 1w (see account of that species for differences). These grey-and-white ind occur almost exclusively in eastern 'yellow wagtail' taxa.
- Often difficult to distinguish from ad under field conditions but distinct worn prim and very worn, short outer greater cov indicative. Note that moult-limit in greater cov in itself is no ageing feature as ad s also shows moult-limit caused by partial spring moult but moult-limit less well-defined than in most 1s.

low Wagtail *Motacilla flavissima*   L 15.5cm 6.1"

♂ s
- Broad yellow supercilium and ear-coverts. Crown and eye-stripe normally darker greenish but some ind completely yellow-headed (like Yellow-headed Wagtail).
- Upperparts relatively pale brown-green to grey-green.

♂ w
- Like dark variant of ad s with paler throat (some 1s ♂ nearly identical).

♀ s
- Many ind like Blue-headed Wagtail and Sykes's Wagtail ad ♀ s but supercilium often more yellow (characteristic when obviously yellow).
- Yellow of underparts often extending to throat ⟺ Blue-headed and Sykes's.
- Pale centre of ear-coverts often larger and more yellow than in most Blue-headed and Sykes's.

e
- 'Channel Wagtail' (hybrid Blue-headed x Yellow Wagtail) occurs along Continental coast of English Channel between Belgium and northern France. ♂ often rather similar to Sykes's due to pale blue-grey head and broad white stripe over ear-coverts. Sykes's normally with yellow throat, stronger head-pattern with darker loral-stripe and more rasping call than Blue-headed and Yellow.
- Dark variant of Yellow ♂ can resemble Green-headed Wagtail *M. taivana* of east Asia due to uniform dark green ear-coverts and crown and yellow supercilium. In *taivana* grey-black ear-coverts and fore-crown (becoming dark green towards rear), darker brown-green upperparts and rasping call resembling Citrine.

ow-headed Wagtail *Motacilla lutea*   L 15.5cm 6.1"

olum
- Probably indistinguishable from all ♀-type and extreme yellow-headed Yellow Wagtail ♂.
  All field marks mentioned below probably fall within variation of Yellow.

♂ s
- Almost uniform yellow head resembles Citrine Wagtail but rear-crown, hind-neck and eye-stripe/ear-coverts sometimes darker (concolorous with mantle) ⟺ in Yellow rarely almost uniform yellow head.
- Wing-bar over median cov very broad, often extending over more than half of visible part of median cov ⟺ in most Yellow usually c.30% of visible part of median cov.
- Usually deeper yellow underparts than Yellow, whole underparts evenly yellow.
- Upperparts olive-green without trace of grey wash ⟺ most Yellow.
- Rump often paler (yellow-green) than in most Yellow.

♀ s
- Like Yellow ad ♀ s.

e-headed Wagtail *Motacilla flava*   L 15.5cm 6.1"

olum
- Obvious supercilium.

♂ s
- Blue-grey crown, hind-neck and ear-coverts.
- Ear-coverts usually only slightly darker than crown.
- Yellow throat but relatively large number of spring ind (probably 1s) with more or less white throat. White throat has indistinct border with yellow breast (in 1s sometimes bordered by dark spots) ⟺ Ashy-headed Wagtail and Spanish Wagtail.

♀ s
- Brown to greyish hind-neck and ear-coverts, whitish throat.

Wagtails

geog var	**Sykes's Wagtail** *M.f. beema* (Russia to western Siberia)
ad ♂ s	• Well-defined loral-stripe reaching bill. Broad white supercilium extending to upper mandible (supercilium broader above lores than in Blue-headed).
	• White stripe in centre of blue-grey ear-coverts, which together with conspicuous supercilium, broad eye-stripe and submoustachial-stripe creates rather stripy head-pattern.
	• Yellow throat, often with white chin and broad white submoustachial-stripe.
	• Head normally paler grey-blue than in Blue-headed but variable in both forms.
	• Often slightly more greenish upperparts than Blue-headed.
ad ♀ s	• Like Blue-headed ad ♀ s but head-pattern usually stronger, more like ad ♂ s (white in ear-coverts, supercilium and eye-stripe). Similar to Yellow ad ♀ s which lacks yellow on supercilium and ear-cove
1w	• Most ind with pure pale grey upperparts and white underparts lacking yellow ⇔ in Blue-headed and Grey-headed Wagtail 1w sometimes white underparts (normally brownish-yellow) but mantle and sca grey-brown, contrasting with grey back and rump.
	• When juv cov with large white tips retained than resembles Citrine 1w.

White-headed Wagtail *Motacilla leucocephala*　　　　　　　　　L 15.5cm €

ad ♂ s	• Head almost entirely white, ear-coverts and crown often very pale greyish.
ad ♀ s	• Like pale headed Sykes's Wagtail ad ♀ s but crown, lores and forehead normally paler grey. Ear-coverts finely pale speckled. See note ad ♂ s.
note ad ♂ s	• Status in WP unclear: at least some white-headed yellow wagtails in western Europe appear to be partially leucistic ind. Some ind show faint eye-/loral-stripe and/or whitish parts on mantle and breas

Eastern Yellow Wagtail *Motacilla tschutschensis* and *'simillima'*　　　　L 15.5cm €

all plum	• Basically similar to all corresponding plumages of Blue-headed Wagtail but with ear-coverts normally more uniformly dark, ranging from pale grey in 1w to almost black in some ad ♂.
1w	• 'Grey-and-white' ind much more common than in western taxa with many greyish ind; greenish wash on scaps.
note	• Some of the 'grey-and-white' 'yellow wagtails' occurring in western Europe in autumn possibly belo to this taxon.
voice ⇒	• Rasping flight-call, slightly similar to Citrine Wagtail ⇔ north-western 'yellow wagtail' taxa.

Grey-headed Wagtail *Motacilla thunbergi*　　　　　　　　　　　L 15.5cm

all plum	• Culmen slightly straighter than in other 'yellow wagtails', bill looks slightly upcurved (probably sometimes also in other subspecies).
ad ♂ s	• Dark blue-grey crown and hind-neck; very dark, often black lores and front-side of ear-coverts. Sometimes very little contrast between rear-side of ear-coverts and crown, then resembling Black-headed Wagtail but rear-crown and hind-neck at least slightly blue-grey and less sharply demarcate from mantle than in Black-headed.
	• Often dark breast(-side) patterning.
	• No or very narrow and short supercilium.
	• Upperparts often darker than in other 'yellow wagtails'.
	• Yellow throat; variable white submoustachial-stripe creating border with black ear-coverts (sometim also in Black-headed).
ad ♂ w	• Like ad ♂ s but head with green-brown spots or wash.
	• Underparts fainter yellow than in summer plumage.
ad ♀ s	• Dark greyish head with at most faint supercilium.
	• Ear-coverts uniformly dark ⇔ Blue-headed ad ♀ s.
	• Broad black loral-stripe.
1s ♂	• White throat but less sharply demarcated from breast than in Ashy-headed Wagtail, Spanish Wagtail and Egyptian Wagtail.

Spanish Wagtail *Motacilla iberiae*　　　　　　　　　　　　　　L 15cm

all plum	• Slightly smaller than other 'yellow wagtails' except Egyptian Wagtail.
ad ♂ s	• Entirely white throat sharply demarcated from yellow underparts (see Blue-headed).
	• Front-side of crown and/or lores dark grey to black and normally uniformly dark ear-coverts or at m very small pale patch in centre (in summer plumage ear-coverts often slightly darker than crown).
	• Distinct supercilium but variable, normally narrower than in Blue-headed, sometimes disappearing above lores and/or eye (see Ashy-headed Wagtail).
	• Dark blue-grey crown and hind-neck (in winter plumage with dark green-brown spots).
	• Sometimes white eye-ring below eye but often absent.
	• Flanks often with diffuse dark spots (as in Egyptian and Ashy-headed).
ad ♀ s	• Similar to Egyptian and Ashy-headed and most not separable. Differs from most Blue-headed by we defined white throat, narrower supercilium and darker ear-coverts without pale centre.
voice	• Rasping flight-call ⇔ north-western 'yellow wagtail' taxa.
note voice	• Especially of the spring, part of song is mixed in with flight-call, which is rasping in all taxa. These phra are typically only descending; flight-call has quick rise and fall in pitch.

Ashy-headed Wagtail *Motacilla cinereocapilla*　　　　　　　　　L 15.5cm

ad ♂ s	• Similar to Spanish Wagtail but without distinct supercilium; supercilium absent or restricted to white spot above or directly behind eye.
	• Front-side of crown and lores blackish, creating weak mask ⇔ in Grey-headed Wagtail front-side c crown and lores only a little darker than rest of head.
	• Rear-side of ear-coverts concolorous with crown ⇔ in Grey-headed slightly darker than crown.
	• White eye-ring below eye lacking, above eye sometimes present in combination with supercilium.

- Breast-sides with or without at most very slightly dark patterning ⇔ Grey-headed.
- Flanks often with diffuse dark spots (as in Spanish and Egyptian Wagtail).

♀ s
- Like Spanish ad ♀ s but supercilium normally faint or absent.

ice
- Rasping flight-call ⇔ north-western 'yellow wagtail' taxa.

te voice
- See Spanish.

og var Egyptian Wagtail *M. c. pygmaea* (Egypt)

plum
- Smaller size than other 'yellow wagtails' (except Spanish Wagtail).
- Like Ashy-headed Wagtail and usually not separable.

♂ s
- Supercilium usually absent.
- Crown and hind-neck often with green wash.
- Upperparts and underparts usually less strongly coloured than in Ashy-headed.
- Throat often not pure white.

♀ s
- As Ashy-headed ad ♀ s.

ck-headed Wagtail *Motacilla feldegg*   L 15.5cm 6.1"

♂ s ⇒
- Entirely uniform black (glossy) cap extending to mantle with *well-defined border between pale mantle and black hind-neck* ⇔ Grey-headed Wagtail. In early spring border between black head and paler upperparts less well-defined due to greenish or brownish feather tips (remains of winter plumage).
- Usually no distinct dark spots on breast(-side) (but often patch on breast-sides) ⇔ most Grey-headed.
- Normally yellow throat directly connected to black parts of head (without white submoustachial-stripe) although variable, with narrow white submoustachial-stripe sometimes present (possibly more likely in 1s or indication of intergrade, see note).
- Sometimes narrow white supercilium or white spot before and/or behind eye (see note), probably more likely in 1s or indication of intergrade. Such ind mainly occur at edge of range with other taxa from 'yellow wagtail' complex.
- Mantle normally slightly paler and greener than in Grey-headed.

♀ s
- Dark head with or without only indistinct supercilium.
- Almost complete, conspicuous pale eye-ring.
- Uniform dark ear-coverts ⇔ Blue-headed Wagtail.
- Upperparts often greyer than in Blue-headed and Grey-headed.
- Underparts often whiter than in Blue-headed and Grey-headed.

te
- *M.f. 'superciliaris'* (mainly east of Balkans) with conspicuous (but variable) white or yellow supercilium and eye-ring; *M.f. 'dombrowski'* (mainly Romania) with distinct supercilium and eye-ring, dark grey cap and white submoustachial-stripe (like Grey-headed with supercilium and eye-ring); *M.f. 'melanogrisea'* (Volga Delta and east of Caspian Sea) with white submoustachial-stripe to almost completely white throat and completely black cap but cap more diffusely bordered and does not extend as far towards mantle as in Black-headed. Above-mentioned 'forms' are intergrades between Black-headed and other subspecies, mainly Yellow-headed Wagtail, Blue-headed and Sykes's Wagtail.

ce
- Rasping flight-call ⇔ north-western 'yellow wagtail' taxa.

te voice
- See Spanish Wagtail.

rine Wagtail *Motacilla citreola*   L 16cm 6.3"

plum
- Long, slightly curved hind claw (as long as hind-toe) ⇔ in 'white wagtails' hind claw shorter and more curved; in 'yellow wagtails' variable and can be rather long, especially in eastern taxa, therefore some ind overlap with Citrine.
- Very broad white wing-bars over median cov and greater cov and broad white outer edge on tertials.
- Upperparts entirely greyish (except in brief juv plumage).
- Relatively long tarsus.

♂ s
- See geog var.

♂
- Most ind resemble ad ♂ s but often less colourful; often distinct wear of prim-cov, prim and outer greater cov (see 1s). Some ind strongly resemble (older) ad ♀ due to faint yellow underparts, dark crown, rather dark ear-coverts and dark spots on breast. Yellow forehead, very broad yellow supercilium and eventually some black patterning on upper mantle separate such ind from ad ♀.

w/ad ♀ s
- Dark ear-coverts and crown; ear-coverts completely framed in yellow (yellow throat, supercilium and rear-side of ear-coverts).
- Brightness of yellow decreases from throat to vent (undertail-cov and often vent whitish).
- ♀ variable in amount of yellow on underparts and some 1s with dark breast-band (rarely in ad).

⇒
- Ear-coverts completely whitish framed by supercilium, rear-side of ear-coverts and submoustachial-stripe. Narrow black eye-stripe and moustacial stripe often distinct.

⇒
- Undertail-cov white ⇔ in 'yellow wagtails' almost always slightly yellow (but see Sykes's Wagtail 1w).
- Pale (yellow-)brown forehead; supercilium before eye merges with weakly patterned lores ⇔ in most 'yellow wagtails' 1w has dark loral-stripe and more sharply bordered supercilium before eye.
- Dark lateral crown-stripe.
- Black bill (rarely slightly paler at base) ⇔ 'yellow wagtails' 1w.
- Pale centre of grey ear-coverts.
- Ear-coverts in general often darker than in 'yellow wagtails' 1w.
- Black tertials with sharp white fringes ⇔ in 'yellow wagtails' often diffuse grey outer web and white fringe not sharply defined.
- Grey upperparts ⇔ in 'yellow wagtails' 1w with brown wash (but see Sykes's 1w).
- Belly and undertail-cov white; flanks often grey.
- Broad white wing-bars and tertial-fringes but sometimes hardly different from most 'yellow wagtail' 1w.
- Grey rump becomes darker towards tail; uppertail-cov blackish.

note 1w	• White 1w with (almost) completely pale surrounds to ear-coverts can cause confusion, but has (besid[e] short, curved hind-claw) *dark border of lateral crown-sides between eye and bill*, often dirty-yellow face, more uniform ear-coverts and narrower white wing-bars and fringes to tertials and sec. Rear-si[de] of ear-coverts usually cuts through pale surrounding.
1s	• Brownish and usually distinctly worn prim, prim-cov and outer greater cov, creating distinct moult-lin[e] in greater cov (moult-limit in greater cov also present in ad in spring but less obvious). • 1s ♀ like 1w but yellow head-pattern and yellow throat; rest of underparts usually dull pale yellow.
geog var	*M.c. citreola* (northern Russia)
ad ♂	• Medium grey to dark grey upperparts; most ind with broad black collar, extending distinctly over win[g] bend and strongly broadening on upper part of mantle. • Upperparts sometimes with brownish wash ⇔ *werae*. • Flanks rather dark brown-grey. • Underparts usually deeper yellow than in *werae*. • Some ind with variable dark patterning on middle of crown (more often in 1s).
geog var	*M.c. werae* (central Asia to eastern Europe)
all plum ad ♂	• Slightly smaller than *citreola* with slightly shorter tarsus (but much overlap). • Pale grey upperparts with usually a faintly bordered, narrow, evenly broad blackish collar. In some ind collar almost lacking completely. • Upperparts paler, more pure grey than in *citreola*. • Underparts often rather pale yellow, also in 3cy+ ⇔ in most *citreola* deeper yellow from 3cy. • Flanks pale grey. • Generally slightly smaller wing-bars than in *citreola* (dark centres to median cov and greater cov larger).
ad ♀/1w	• Not identifiable with certainty under field conditions, but ad ♀ possibly never has dark patterning on upperparts and crown (also applies to many (young ♀ and) ad ♀ *citreola*).
note	• Due to large overlap, many *werae* ad ♂ s are indistinguishable from *citreola*.
geog var	*M.c. calcarata* (southern central Asia)
ad ♂	• Completely black upperparts. • Greater cov with more white than in *citreola* and especially *werae* (dark centres to median cov and greater cov small). • Deeper yellow underparts than *citreola* and yellow often extending to undertail-cov.
ad ♀	• Like *citreola* but some ind with black spots on upperparts and yellow to undertail-cov.
note	• Not recorded in WP. Some ind in range of *citreola* have very dark upperparts.

Grey Wagtail *Motacilla cinerea* L 18.5cm ⌀

all plum ⇒	• Broad white tertial-fringes contrast strongly with rest of faintly patterned wing; *only narrow wing-ba[r]* ⇔ in 'yellow wagtails' pale wing-bars at least as broad and conspicuous as tertial-fringes.
⇒	• Bright *yellow uppertail-cov* ⇔ in 'yellow wagtails' grey-brown to yellow-green.
⇒	• Legs *(pale) brown* to dark grey, relatively short ⇔ in all other wagtails very dark to black. • Blue-grey upperside. • Variable amount of yellow on underparts (undertail-cov and vent always bright yellow); *flanks white*. • Very long tail (also conspicuous in flight) with much white in outer-side (see geog var). • Long supercilium (short in juv and some ♀).
ad ♂ s	• Black throat; broad white submoustachial-stripe. • Breast and central part of belly deeper yellow than in ad ♀ s.
ad ♀ s	• Patchy black throat; in some ind almost white. • Underparts faint yellow, except undertail-cov and vent.
ad ♂ w	• Like ad ♂ s but throat white, often contrasting with yellow underparts.
ad ♀ w	• Like ad ♀ s but throat, ear-coverts and supercilium often faint cream-coloured ⇔ ad ♂ w. • Underparts, except undertail-cov and vent, largely whitish.
juv	• Warm yellow breast, yellow fading away towards undertail-cov. • Pinkish base of lower mandible (sometimes retained up to 1w).
1w	• Like ad ♀ w but moult-limit in greater cov (different generations under field conditions often only discernable by difference in length).
1s	• Prim worn (sometimes distinctly bleached) and often obvious moult-limit in greater cov (also ad sho[w] moult-limit in greater cov but less obvious).
fl all plum ⇒	• Underwing with contrasting broad pale wing-bar at base of sec.
behav	• Often pumps tail and rear body.
geog var	*M.c. schmitzi* (Madeira) and *M.c. patriciae* (Azores)
all plum	• Tail shorter than in *cinerea* with less white on tail-sides (especially in *patriciae* little white in t4 and dark base to t5 and t6). • Bill longer than *cinerea*, especially in *patriciae*.
ad ♂ s	• Upperparts darker grey than in *cinerea*. • Supercilium shorter and narrower than in *cinerea*, often hardly extending above lore. • Submoustachial-stripe narrower than in *cinerea*. • Underparts deeper yellow than in *cinerea*.
ad ♀	• Differences with *cinerea* same as in ad ♂ but less distinct.

ite Wagtail *Motacilla alba* — L 17.5cm 6.9"

- **plum**
  - Grey upperparts.
- **♂ s**
  - Black crown and hind-neck rather sharply demarcated from grey upperparts; forehead white.
- **♀ s**
  - Black crown and hind-neck faintly demarcated from grey upperparts; grey extending to rear-head.
- **w**
  - Only black breast-band; throat white.
  - In ♂ uniform black cap, faintly demarcated from hind-neck (as in ad ♀ s). In ad ♀ wholly grey or patchy black cap.
  - ♀ with uniform grey crown ⇔ in 1w ♂ often some black on crown and white forehead, as in ad ♀ w.
  - Face with yellowish wash (sometimes also faint in ad ♀ w) and often diffuse dark ear-coverts ⇔ in Pied Wagtail 1w whiter head-side.
  - Moult-limit in greater cov.
  - Often conspicuous moult-limit on greater cov (also moult-limit in ad on greater cov but less conspicuous) and old brown prim.
  - Patchy black crown (sometimes completely grey without black spots in 1s ♀); white flecked forehead.
- **e geog var**
  - *M.a. baicalensis* (central Siberia, possible vagrant to WP)
  - Resembles White *alba* but ad s with white upper part of throat and sec with very broad white fringes and tips to greater cov and median cov (on closed wing only dark centres and bases visible). However, White in east of range (e.g. Middle East) has more white in greater cov and median cov.
- **e**
  - East Siberian Wagtail *Motacilla ocularis* (eastern Siberia, possible vagrant to WP) differs from *alba* by *dark eye-stripe* and relatively large amount of white on greater cov and median cov in ad (dark centres in 1w-1s).

d Wagtail *Motacilla yarrellii* — L 17.5cm 6.9"

- **plum**
  - Upperparts dark grey to black (in 1w upperparts often not darker than in darkest White Wagtail).
  - Dark grey flanks and breast-sides.
  - Black uppertail-cov and rump ⇔ in White dark grey, only longest uppertail-cov blackish.
  - 2 broad white wing-bars; large amount of white especially in greater cov.
- **♂**
  - Black upperparts (also in winter plumage).
- **♀**
  - Very dark grey upperparts often with black spots.
- **w**
  - Only black breast-band; throat white (as in White ad w).
  - Dark (often completely black) crown and hind-neck ⇔ White 1w. In autumn combination of moult-limit in greater cov (definite 1w), blackish crown and relatively white face and forehead indicative.
  - Like ad ♀ but often conspicuous moult-limit in greater cov (ad shows moult-limit in greater cov but less conspicuous) and old brown prim.

sked Wagtail *Motacilla personata* — L 17.5cm 6.9"

- **lum**
  - Median cov and greater cov mainly white (in ad ♂ almost entirely white, in 1w greater cov dark centred, creating large white wing panel.
  - Upperparts grey.
- **♂ s ⇒**
  - Black head and breast joined together; white forehead connected with white mask.
- **♀ s**
  - Like ad ♂ but centres of greater cov faint grey and crown often less uniform black.
- **w/1w ♀**
  - White throat and submoustachial-stripe, narrow black malar- and moustachial-stripe.
- **♂ w**
  - Like ad ♂ s but crown sometimes less black and hind-neck grey.
- **♀ w**
  - Like ad ♂ w but crown grey spotted.
  - Like ad w but greater cov with diffuse dark centres and moult-limit in greater cov and tertials.
  - Crown grey, in 1w ♂ crown darker at border with white mask. In 1w ♀ crown completely grey.

ur Wagtail *Motacilla leucopsis* — L 17.5cm 6.9"

- **lum**
  - Median cov and greater cov white (in juv cov with dark centres) creating large white wing panel.
  - Black rump ⇔ in White Wagtail *baicalensis* grey.
  - Pure white flanks (and rest of underparts).
- **♂ ⇒**
  - Jet black upperparts.
  - Wholly white rear-head and white front of crown extending high up.
  - White throat (also in summer plumage), black breast-patch isolated.
- **♀**
  - Like ad ♂ but upperparts very dark grey instead of jet black.
  - Black breast-patch smaller than ♂ (not extending to throat).
  - Upperparts grey (in ♂ upperparts with black patches and darker crown).
  - Outer (juv) greater cov with dark centres.
  - In some ind dark breast pattern lacking altogether.
  - Like ad of equivalent sex but often still some juv outer greater cov present (with darker centres).
  - Some ♀ with medium grey upperparts resembling White *baicalensis* but lesser cov black and black breast-patch small unlike White *baicalensis*.

occan Wagtail *Motacilla subpersonata* — L 17.5cm 16"

- **♂ s**
  - Black eye-stripe conspicuous.
  - Mainly black head and breast, except white forehead and supercilium; white moustachial-stripe and white, sickle-shaped spot below eye.
  - White spot on neck-side.
- **♀ s**
  - Like ad ♂ but dark parts of head less deep black, often with grey spots.
- **♂/1w**
  - White throat.
  - Black loral-stripe and dark rear-side of ear-coverts ⇔ White Wagtail.

African Pied Wagtail *Motacilla aguimp*

L 18.5cm

all plum ⇒	• Unique combination of broad white supercilium, white throat, dark ear-coverts and breast-band.
	• Much white in closed wing; median cov often completely white (juv-type median cov with dark shaft-streaks).
	• White spot on neck-side.
ad	• Black upperparts, crown, ear-coverts and breast-band. Ad ♂ s deep glossy black; in ad ♀ w dull black to grey except black crown. See note ad.
imm	• Juv greater cov with large dark centres ⇔ ad.
	• Upperparts often patchy grey-brown.
	• Moult-limit in greater cov with outer greater cov distinctly shorter than inner (also ad shows moult-li in greater cov but less conspicuous).
note ad	• Both 'summer plumage' and 'winter plumage' occur whole year round.

Forest Wagtail *Dendronanthus indicus*

L 17cm

all plum	• Unmistakable with black wings and 2 very broad pale wing-bars.
	• Double breast-band with vertical central part.
	• Brown-grey upperparts.
	• Long narrow supercilium.
1w	• Similar to ad. Completes post-juv moult very early, timing almost same as ad ⇔ other wagtails.

Pipits

First-summer pipits

•Slightly more worn prim, sec and tail-feathers than in ad, but often this is only visible in the hand; sometimes some strongly worn outer greater cov.

•Often 3 generations of greater cov (juv, winter moulted ad-type and spring moulted ad-type feather) ⇔ in ad max 2.

Richard's Pipit *Anthus richardi*

L 18.5cm

all plum ⇒	• Conspicuously disproportionate with very long tail resembling wagtail, long legs with very long, sligh curved hind-claw, long bill and often relatively long neck.
⇒	• t6 (almost) completely white; t5 with long white wedge ⇔ Blyth's Pipit. Sometimes little white in t5 then narrow white wedge almost parallel to shaft ⇔ Blyth's.
	• Relatively heavy thrush-like bill; culmen rather strongly curved near tip ⇔ in Blyth's bill more pointe due to straighter culmen.
	• Pale lores, as in Blyth's ⇔ Tawny Pipit.
	• Long supercilium extending far behind eye and ending or more of less rectangularly.
	• Breast densely streaked with rather short, thick stripes; rest of underparts unpatterned.
	• Often some colour contrast between cream-coloured breast and white rest of underparts.
ad ⇒	• Ad-type median cov with dark, often diffuse *pointed* centre and broad cream-coloured fringe ⇔ Blyth's. Shape of centre variable, sometimes more square and therefore similar to Blyth's.
1s	• See 'First-summer pipits'.
juv-1w	• Centres of juv-type median cov as in ad but with narrower, better-defined and more whitish fringe. often with some ad-type median cov. Often still remnants of juv plumage on upperparts in autumn western Europe ⇔ in Blyth's normally none.
	• Besides different pattern also obvious difference in length between short juv-type and long ad-type feather. Post-juv moult of cov often in waves which can create moult-limit between ad-type feather combination with retained juv-type feathers then thus 3 generations.
behav	• Often hovers before landing in grass or other vegetation, as in Blyth's (does not normally hover befo landing on bare ground).
note	• See also Blyth's.

Blyth's Pipit *Anthus godlewskii*

L 16.5cm

all plum	• Smaller size than Richard's (about size of Tawny Pipit); bill shorter with straighter culmen; *more triangular and pointed*.
	• Ad-type median cov with *well-defined* black, almost *rectangular* centre ⇔ in Richard's more triang and especially *more diffuse* centre.
	• t6 with large white wedge on tip, t5 variable from only white near tip to white wedge extending tov base as in Richard's Pipit but wedge running more diagonal ⇔ Richard's.
	• Broad whitish to faint cream-coloured tips to ad-type median cov ⇔ in Richard's smaller and deep cream-coloured tip. Patterning of median cov and greater cov (wing-bars) in general more contrast than in Richard's. Juv-type median cov with large, triangular centre and narrow pale fringe, very si to juv-type of Richard's.
	• In general more contrasting than Richard's with whiter (and therefore more conspicuous) wing-bar tertial-edges and often more marked whitish mantle-stripes.
	• Tail, tarsus and hind-claw shorter than in Richard's (hind-claw variable but often shorter than hind
	• Supercilium fades away behind eye, not extending far back (*often whiter directly behind eye*) ⇔ Richard's.
	• Crown often evenly streaked ⇔ in Richard's crown sides often slightly more heavily streaked than of crown.
	• Usually distinctly and evenly streaked mantle due to dark feather-centres and contrasting pale fri ⇔ in Richard's usually messier and less contrasting streaked mantle.
	• Underparts with rather even orange-brown wash ⇔ in Richard's often more colour contrast betwe cream-coloured breast and white rest of underparts.
	• Malar-stripe often forms spotted triangle ⇔ in Richard's often more uniform dark triangle.
	• Streaked breast as in Richard's but often finer and more regular.

/-1w
- Juv greater cov, especially inner ones, with blunt-tipped dark centres (reflecting ad-type pattern) ⇔ in Richard's with more pointed centres.
- See 'First-summer pipits'.

hav
- See Richard's.

ice ⇒
- Call: rather reminiscent of Richard's but slightly higher pitched, more nasal and longer (more drawn-out), with less emphatic 'r'-sound, sounding like 'psiuuw'. Often tending towards disyllabic. Common call sometimes mixed with characteristic *short nasal 'tjiep-tjiep'* ⇔ in Richard's only more House Sparrow like 'shreew' call.

te
- See Richard's.

ˈwny Pipit *Anthus campestris* L 17cm 6.7"

plum ⇒
- Usually broad dark loral-stripe, narrow but *conspicuous moustachial- and malar-stripe* and long broad supercilium.
- Tertial-fringe warm-buff (often deepest coloured part of upperparts).
- Long and pale legs.
- Relatively short hind-claw.
- Much white in outer side of tail; t6 almost completely white, t5 with white outer web and long narrow white wedge along inner web.

⇒
- Almost uniform pale yellow-brown underparts (only some faint streaks on breast-sides); belly whiter.
- Median cov creating conspicuous row due to contrasting broad, triangular black centres and broad pale fringes.
- Faintly patterned pale brown-grey upperparts (rump and uppertail-cov often yellow-brown).

ˈ-1w
- Upperparts heavily scaled but quickly moulted to ad-type upperparts; often some dark juv scaps (pale in ad) and most cov and tertials retained late into autumn (moult-limit). Juv-type cov with large black centres and white fringes ⇔ in ad smaller black centres with cream-coloured fringes.
- Breast streaked, usually continuing along flanks but, as applies for upperparts, quickly moulted; underparts later in autumn more as in ad.
- See 'First-summer pipits'.

ˈe juv
- Variable post-juv moult, some 1cy in autumn difficult to separate from ad; others still nearly as juv. In most 1w still some juv mantle feathers and/or scaps with dark centres, distinctly streaked breast(-side) and moult-limit in median cov.

ult ad
- Ad moult often only partially in breeding range (especially in northern populations) and continues moult in winter range. In autumn sometimes moult-limit in cov as in 1w but retained feathers more heavily worn than retained juv feathers in 1w.

ˈthelot's Pipit *Anthus berthelotii* L 14cm 5.5"

ˈɔlum
- Upperparts faintly streaked.
- Well-defined streaking on breast, ill-defined streaking extending onto flanks; underparts with white background.
- Conspicuous long white supercilium.
- Pale neck-side isolates dark ear-coverts (resembles Citrine Wagtail juv).
- Legs more towards rear of body than in other pipits.
- Brown-grey upperparts, in spring/summer evenly worn (no spring moult).
- Dark somewhat rufous-brown upperparts with obvious dark mantle-stripes.
- Moult-limit when present characteristic.
- Endemic to Canary Islands and Madeira.

ˈg-billed Pipit *Anthus similis* L 17cm 6.7"

ˈɔlum ⇒
- Pale parts of outer tail-feather (t6) relatively small and yellow-brown to grey ⇔ in Tawny Pipit white.
- Upperparts with blue-grey wash.
- Underparts nearly uniformly coloured, often *warm dull brown* ⇔ in Tawny more yellow-brown with more contrasting pale belly.
- Long bill with relatively strongly curved culmen; tip seemingly hanging down.
- Larger than Tawny with longer tail; structure more similar to Richard's Pipit than to Tawny.
- Supercilium long but narrow, curved down and fading away towards rear ⇔ in Tawny broader, straighter and ending abruptly.
- Narrow long dark loral-stripe of even width ⇔ in Tawny broad at eye, narrowing near bill.
- Submoustachial- and malar-stripe faint or absent ⇔ Tawny.
- Rather short-legged.
- Ear-coverts darker and more uniform than in Tawny.
- Dark tail contrasts with rest of plumage.

⇒
- Median cov with *diffuse dark centres* and visible black shaft-streaks ⇔ all larger pipits.
- Rather dull, almost unpatterned head with conspicuous dark eye ⇔ in Tawny stronger head-pattern.
- Faint breast- and mantle streaking. Breast streaking normally more obvious than in Tawny.

1w
- Resembles Tawny juv-1w but in general less contrastingly patterned (which see for differences with ad) but with more contrasting dark tail (as in all plum).
- Breast streaking distinct but less well-defined than in Tawny juv-1w.
- See Tawny juv-1w for more features.
- See 'First-summer pipits'.

plum
- Tail looks full.

ˈe-backed Pipit *Anthus hodgsoni* L 15cm 5.9"

ˈɪum ⇒
- Almost uniform or faintly streaked upperparts.

⇒
- Conspicuous *two-toned* supercilium; *cream-coloured before eye*, white behind eye. Supercilium extending further back than in Tree Pipit (about 2x diameter of eye).

Pipits

⇒	• Green-brown tertial-fringes (⇔ in Tree paler), concolorous or only slightly paler than upperparts.
	• Supercilium (behind eye) as white or even whiter than wing-bar over greater cov ⇔ in Tree the other way around.
	• Pale and dark spot on rear-side of ear-coverts; eye-stripe cuts through supercilium behind eye. Strong patterned Tree can approach such pattern but in Olive-backed dark spot on rear-side of ear-coverts (almost) as dark as breast streaking ⇔ Tree.
	• Lateral crown-stripe broader than rest of crown streaking ⇔ in Tree evenly streaked crown.
	• Heavily streaked breast and flanks with large well-defined longitudinal stripes; stripes along flanks becoming slightly narrower but often not as thin as in Tree.
	• In fresh plumage (autumn) conspicuous dark yellow background of throat, breast and flanks; centre of breast white ⇔ in Tree completely cream-coloured breast.
	• Legs pale pinkish.
	• Short, rather strongly curved hind-claw (as in Tree).
	• Often very short prim-projection ⇔ in Tree none.
1w	• See Tree Pipit.
1s	• See 'First-summer pipits'.
behav	• Often pumps tail like Tree but more persistent.

Tree Pipit Anthus trivialis   L 15cm 5

all plum ⇒	• Usually rather heavy breast streaking *becoming thinner on flanks*.
	• Stronger head-pattern than Meadow Pipit with short eye-/loral-stripe (breaking through eye-ring at front), more obvious submoustachial- and malar-stripe and usually more obvious supercilium behind eye. Rear-side of ear-coverts usually with variable pale and dark spot (extremes approach Olive-backed Pipit) ⇔ Meadow.
	• Median cov conspicuous due to large whitish tips and dark centres.
	• Stronger bill than in Meadow (and Olive-backed) due to deeper base; lower mandible with pinkish base ⇔ Meadow.
	• Underparts two-toned: cream-coloured breast and flanks, white belly (in summer less distinct due to bleaching).
	• Hind-claw relatively short and rather strongly curved ⇔ Meadow.
	• Legs with pinkish wash ⇔ Meadow.
1w	• Some ind show moult-limit in cov and/or tertials in autumn. Most ind still with complete set of juv cov and tertials and under field conditions not possible to age.
1s	• See 'First-summer pipits'.
behav	• Often pumps tail like Olive-backed ⇔ Meadow.

Pechora Pipit Anthus gustavi   L 14.5cm

all plum ⇒	• Conspicuous pale 'snipe-stripes' on upperparts.
⇒	• Only pipit with *obvious prim-projection*, c.30%.
	• 2 broad white wing-bars.
	• Dark streaked rump (as in Red-throated Pipit). Rump feathers with evenly broad black shaft-streaks in Red-throated broad black triangular centres.
	• Dark streaked, rufous crown creating somewhat capped effect.
	• Eye-ring at front broken by dark, short loral-stripe; loral-stripe not reaching bill.
	• Moustachial- and malar-stripe faint, thin or absent.
	• Relatively deep bill(-base) with pinkish base of lower mandible.
	• Large neck-side patch connected with bold, sharp breast streaking; bold streaking continues along flanks.
	• Scaps with large dark centres.
	• Finely streaked hind-neck (in similar pipits very diffuse or unstreaked).
	• Rather short tail.
	• Yellowish to rufous wash on breast contrasts with white belly, almost creating breast-band as in Olive-backed Pipit and Tree Pipit (in summer disappearing through wear).
1w	• Normally identical to ad. No post-juv moult of cov and/or tertials.
1s	• See 'First-summer pipits'.
behav	• Often hovers before landing, as in Richard's Pipit and Blyth's Pipit ⇔ most other small pipits.
	• Usually does not call when flushed ⇔ other pipits.
	• Often skulking ⇔ other pipits.

Meadow Pipit Anthus pratensis   L 14.5cm

all plum	• Pale lores, faint eye-stripe behind eye and complete eye-ring creates open-faced impression.
	• Rather heavily streaked mantle and crown.
	• Short, slender bill (with grey-brown base of lower mandible).
	• Hind-claw long and slightly curved ⇔ in Tree Pipit strongly curved.
	• Rather heavily streaked on breast and along flanks (except juv).
	• Breast streaks often clot together on middle of breast.
	• Rump and uppertail-cov at most faintly marked ⇔ Red-throated Pipit and Pechora Pipit.
juv	• No or faint flank streaking.
1w	• Juv-type median cov often with obvious 'tooth' on dark centre and whiter tip than in ad.
	• Post-juv moult variable; in southern populations often more developed with moult-limit in cov and tertials, in northern populations often no moult-limit late into autumn.
1s	• See 'First-summer pipits'.
note	• Some ind from western populations (*whistleri*) with variable warm coloured underparts; the most strongly coloured ind can resemble Red-throated Pipit or Buff-bellied Pipit.

Pipits

d-throated Pipit *Anthus cervinus*   L 14.5cm 5.7"

plum ⇒
⇒
- Strongly streaked rump and uppertail-cov (as in Pechora Pipit).
- Scaps with blackish centres ⇔ in Meadow Pipit only faint darker centres, often restricted to shaft-streaks.
- Pale stripes along mantle feathers conspicuous (sometimes also in Meadow), exaggerated by dark feather centres.
- Dark tertials with well-defined whitish fringes along outer webs, extending partially along inner webs ⇔ in Meadow cream-coloured fringes along outer webs only.
- Slender bill with yellowish base of lower mandible ⇔ in Meadow more grey-brown.
- 2 obvious wing-bars, usually slightly broader than in Meadow.
- Longest undertail-cov with dark pointed centre.
- Brown-red to pinkish head-side, supercilium, throat and breast but very variable; varies from very little colour restricted to throat (normally ♀) to completely deep coloured face, throat and breast without dark streaking (normally ♂). See also note in Meadow.

v
- Large neck-side patch connected with heavy breast streaking, extending along flanks in (usually) 2 rows.
- Usually uniform ear-coverts and rather obvious moustachial-stripe ⇔ in Meadow often pale centre of ear-coverts and at most faint moustachial-stripe.
- Underparts with uniform ground-colour ⇔ in most Meadow obvious yellow-brown wash on flanks.
- Juv greater cov, median cov and tertials normally almost completely retained in 1w (⇔ many other pipits), rarely moult-limit. Retained cov and tertials more worn than in ad.
- Some ind without coloured supercilium, throat and/or breast, as in 1w.
- See 'First-summer pipits'.

ter Pipit *Anthus spinoletta*   L 16cm 6.3"

plum ⇒
- Rump *rufous-brown* ⇔ Rock Pipit, Buff-bellied Pipit.
- Pure white outer-side of tail ⇔ in Rock dirty grey, sometimes whiter.
- Supercilium broad and white ⇔ in Rock almost always less distinct.
- Legs dark, blackish (sometimes paler).
- Dark lores.
- Upperparts only faintly patterned (*spinoletta*, see geog var), wing-bars therefore conspicuous.
- Long bill.

s ⇒
- Fresh plumage with blue-grey head contrasting with *brown wash* on upperparts (especially rump), colour contrast between mantle and hind-neck ⇔ in Rock (*littoralis*) summer plumage pure blue-grey upperparts and usually less developed with contrast between old feathers (tertials and most cov) and new summer-type feathers. Other ind of Rock like winter plumage and distinctly worn (all *petrosus* and some *littoralis*).
- Pinkish breast fading into whitish rest of underparts.
- Usually little streaking on breast and along flanks but variable (sometimes hardly streaked on underparts).
- Malar-stripe faint or absent ⇔ Rock s.
- Basal part of lower mandible yellow (as in Rock and Buff-bellied) ⇔ in ad s bill entirely black.
- Rather narrow streaking on white underparts; streaking on flanks smaller and more well-marked than in Rock.
- Upperparts brown-grey, paler and greyer than in Rock w.
- Under field conditions difficult to age with certainty because patterns of juv and ad-type cov overlap. Distinct moult-limit characteristic but in fresh autumn plumage apparent moult-limit regular in both ad and 1w due to smaller pale tips to inner greater cov.
- See 'First-summer pipits'.

g var   *A.s. spinoletta* (Europe east to Balkans)
plum
- Eye-ring broken at front- and rear-side.
- Dark lores.
- Brown-pink breast; belly white.
- Upperparts rather faintly streaked.
- Some ind with rather obvious streaking on flanks and breast-sides and malar-stripe; rather similar to Rock *littoralis* with strongly developed summer plumage.
- Rather strongly and darkly streaked underparts ⇔ *coutelli* and *blakistoni*.

g var   *A.s. coutelli* (western Asia)
plum
- Loral-stripe often slightly less developed than in *spinoletta* (between *spinoletta* and *blakistoni*).
- Upperparts paler and more strongly streaked than in *spinoletta* (also obviously streaked in winter plumage).
- Underparts completely pink-yellow (also belly ⇔ *spinoletta*) with very slight or no streaking.
- Underparts with brownish streaking on yellow-brown ground-colour ⇔ *spinoletta* w.

g var   *A.s. blakistoni* (central and eastern Asia)
lum
- Upperparts palest of all subspecies; rather distinctly streaked.
- Pale lores and (almost) complete eye-ring, as in Buff-bellied *japonicus*. Differs from Buff-bellied *japonicus* by longer bill, more obviously streaked upperparts, in winter plumage only faint brown streaked underparts and dark legs.
- Underparts with or without very little streaking and paler than in other subspecies with only faint pink-orange wash ⇔ Buff-bellied.
- Not recorded in WP.

Rock Pipit *Anthus petrosus*

L 16cm 6

all plum	⇒	• Crown, hind-neck and mantle without colour contrast; brown, often with green wash ⇔ Water Pipit.
		• Supercilium faint (sometimes more obvious in *littoralis* ad with well-developed summer plumage) ⇔ Water.
		• Grey-brown rump ⇔ in Water all plum obviously brown.
		• Long bill (as in Water).
		• Legs (rather) dark, red-brown.
		• Obvious malar-stripe, including in summer plumage (see geog var *petrosus*) ⇔ most Water s.
		• Dark lores.
		• Outer side of tail pale brown-grey, rarely whiter ⇔ most other pipits.
w	⇒	• Broad but *ill-defined* streaking on breast and along flanks on yellow-brown ground-colour ⇔ in Water whiter ground-colour and more well-defined streaking on underparts.
		• Faintly and diffusely streaked dark green-brown upperparts.
		• Basal part of bill yellowish but usually less bright yellow than in Water.
		• In spring often still old worn tertials (often no spring moult of tertials, especially in *petrosus*) ⇔ in Water spring moult more complete with e.g. fresh tertials.
1w		• Under field conditions difficult to age with certainty because patterns of juv and ad-type cov overlap distinct mouth-limit characteristic.
1s		• See 'First-summer pipits'.

geog var	*A.p. petrosus* (Britain, western France)
ad s	• No real summer plumage; dirty white underparts with heavy streaking. Hardly any spring moult, plumage differs only slightly from winter plumage and obviously worn ⇔ most *littoralis* and Water.

geog var	*A.p. littoralis* (Scandinavia)
all plum	• Supercilium sometimes rather distinct but rarely as obvious as in Water.
	• In general slightly more contrastingly patterned than *petrosus*.
ad s	• In ind with distinct summer plumage (most cases) streaking on underparts more restricted than in *petrosus* but flanks rather heavily and diffusely streaked ⇔ Water ad s.
	• Often brown-pink breast but usually less extensive than in Water s, some ind developing at most only slight summer plumage like *petrosus*.
	• Upperparts blue-grey without brown wash ⇔ Water.
note geog var	• In winter plumage and undeveloped summer plumage subspecies not separable on plumage.

Buff-bellied Pipit *Anthus rubescens*

L 15.5cm

all plum	• Centre of tertials and tail-feathers very dark to black and distinctly contrasting with upperparts ⇔ in Water Pipit and most Rock Pipit paler and at most very slightly contrasting.
	• Complete pale eye-ring ⇔ in Water and Rock broken by dark loral-stripe.
	• Pale lores ⇔ Water and Rock.
	• Distinct moustachial-stripe ⇔ in Water and Rock faint.
	• Rather slender, Meadow Pipit-like bill, sometimes longer than in Meadow ⇔ Water.
	• t6 largely white, only dark wedge at basal part of inner web; t5 with relatively much white on tip; sometimes small white tip to t4 (see geog var) ⇔ in Water less white on inner web of t6 and no or little white tip on t5.
	• Distinct (in *rubescens* often slightly cream-coloured) supercilium, usually ending rectangularly.
	• Rump concolorous with rest of upperparts or sometimes greyer ⇔ in Water browner.
	• Upperparts almost unmarked (crown only faintly streaked) but in *japonicus* sometimes more strongly marked.
	• Crown and upperparts uniformly coloured (hind-neck sometimes greyer) ⇔ in Water crown and hind-neck often greyer than mantle.
	• Sometimes diffuse pale centre of ear-coverts ⇔ in Water and Rock no paler centre.
ad s	• Cream-coloured to brown-orange underparts ⇔ in Water more pinkish. See also note in Meadow.
	• Grey-brown to blue grey upperparts with only faint streaking or even spotting.
	• Breast rather well-marked with short well-defined streaks, often extending along flanks. Some *rubescens* with restricted and very fine streaking on underparts ⇔ *japonicus* (see geog var).
	• Malar-stripe normally distinct ⇔ in Water faint or absent.
1w	• See Water 1w.
1s	• See 'First-summer pipits'.

geog var	**American Buff-bellied Pipit** *A.r. rubescens* (North America to western Greenland)
all plum	• Wing-bars cream-coloured to whitish and rather diffusely bordered, especially over greater cov ⇔ *japonicus*.
	• Legs usually dark brown to blackish (sometimes grey or even pale) ⇔ in *japonicus* usually pale.
	• Upperparts greyish, often with slight olive wash.
	• Most ind with more white on tip of t5 than in *japonicus* (see all plum).
(1)w	• Rather broad but short streaking on breast, diffuser on breast-sides and flanks; whole underparts with brown-yellow wash (whiter later in winter) ⇔ *japonicus*.
	• Upperparts medium brown-grey, when fresh with olive wash ⇔ *japonicus*.

geog var	**Siberian Buff-bellied Pipit** *A.r. japonicus* (central and eastern Asia)
all plum	• Wing-bars conspicuously white ⇔ *rubescens*.
	• Legs rather pale pinkish to (red-)brown ⇔ most *rubescens*.
	• Upperparts moderately streaked ⇔ in *rubescens* weakly.
	• Complete eye-ring and supercilium whiter and more distinct than in *rubescens*.

- Malar-stripe is rather conspicuous; being more broad, more uniform and deeper black than in *rubescens*.
- Heavy and well-defined blackish streaked and/or spotted underparts on white background, often creating slight breast-band ⇔ Water and *rubescens*.
- Upperparts dark brown-grey ⇔ in *rubescens* slightly paler and greyer.

Finches

•mmon Chaffinch *Fringilla coelebs*   L 15cm 5.9"

plum ⇒
- White lesser cov creating conspicuous white 'shoulder' (in flight very conspicuous).
- Broad pale wing-bar (over greater cov) and pale spot at prim-base.
- Bluish hind-neck and crown.
- Orange-red underparts.
- Brown mantle.

w
- Dark stripes on hind-neck and along crown-sides.
- Dark grey-brown mantle, hind-neck and crown.
- Whitish underparts with grey-brown wash on breast and flanks.
- Pale nape patch (as in Brambling and Yellowhammer) but often absent in summer.

ʋ-1s
- Like ad of equivalent sex but sometimes moult-limit in greater cov (juv outer greater cov greyer than ad-type with smaller white tips; different generations in ♀ often hardly visible). Prim, tail-feathers and tertials juv, less deep black and later in winter more worn than in ad (juv tail-feathers narrow and pointed).
- Juv t1-pair uniform grey ⇔ in ad t1 with black subterminal spot.

♂
- Sometimes still dark stripes on rear-head/nape.

•og var
Atlas Chaffinch *F.c. africana* (north-western Africa)

plum ⇒
- Much more white in tail than *coelebs*. Especially in ♂ t4-t6 almost completely white; t3 often with white wedge near tip ⇔ in *coelebs* t6 largely white, t5 with white distal half and dark base and sometimes small white mark at tip of t4.

♂
- Grey-blue head with black lores and forehead.
- Broken white eye-ring.
- Moss-green mantle, scaps and back.
- Salmon-coloured throat and breast gradually merging into white undertail-cov (ind from western part of distribution (e.g. Morocco) deeper coloured).

♀
- Underparts greyer (without brown wash) than in *coelebs* ♀.
- Variable green wash on mantle and scaps.
- Pale blue-grey collar.

ce
- Song: rather similar to *coelebs* but slightly lower pitched, see also *spodiogenys*.
- Call: sparrow-like 'chep' ⇔ *coelebs*.

•og var
Tunisian Chaffinch *F.c. spodiogenys* (north-western Africa east of *africana*)

plum
♂
- Tail-pattern as in *africana* (see above).
- Very similar to *africana* but underparts not or only slightly coloured, dirty-grey to whitish.
- Head paler grey than in *africana*.
- Green on upperparts restricted to mantle ⇔ *africana*.
- White around eye vaguely bordered, upper and lower half of eye-ring merging more into each other and more concentrated behind eye than in *africana*.
- Fringes on tertials and sec and tips of greater cov whiter and slightly broader than in *africana* (in *africana* often yellow in wing-bar over greater cov).

ce
- Song: quite unlike song of *africana*; shorter and more monotone.
- Call similar to *africana*.

•g var
Chaffinch subspecies of Atlantic Islands (*tintillon*, *palmae*, *ombrosia* and *maderensis*)
All are probably best regarded as separate group. General features are:

plum
♂
- Bill stronger and longer than in *coelebs*, *africana* and *spodiogenys*.
- Pinkish underparts and face (eye within pink ⇔ *africana* and *spodiogenys*.).

•g var
F.c. tintillon (Gran Canaria, Tenerife and La Gomera)

♂
- Completely dark grey-blue mantle, hind-neck and crown; rump green.

•g var
F.c. palmae (La Palma)

♂
- Like *tintillon* but whole upperparts (including rump) dark blue.
- Less pink on underparts than *tintillon*, belly white.

♀
- Neck-side often conspicuously pale (also in *tintillon* but often less obvious).

•g var
F.c. ombrosia (El Hierro)

♂
- Upperparts green-brown (green when worn).
- Underparts like *tintillon* but flanks greyer.

♀
- Neck-side hardly any paler ⇔ *palmae* and *tintillon*.

•g var
F.c. maderensis (Madeira)

♂
- Like *tintillon* but mantle greenish.

geog var	*F.c. moreletti* (Azores)
ad	• Dark eye-stripe ⇔ other island taxa.
ad ♂	• Like *ombrosia* (upperparts green-brown) but flanks greyer.

Blue Chaffinch *Fringilla teydea*   L 17cm 6

all plum	• Strong bill. • Conspicuous white broken eye-ring. • 2 broad blue-grey, diffuse wing-bars (see geog var). • Only diffusely bordered and off-white in tail.
ad ♂	• Completely grey-blue upperparts and head; underparts paler and slightly greyer.
ad ♀	• Uniform grey-brown head. • Uniform grey underparts; white undertail-cov.
1w ♂	• Like ad ♀ but centres of feathers of upperparts greyer.
1w-1s	• 2 generations of greater cov (juv greater cov with narrower whiter tip); prim, tail-feathers and tertials juv (juv tail-feathers pointed).
geog var	*F.t. polatzeki* (Gran Canaria)
ad ♂	• Like *teydea* (Tenerife) but wing-bars whiter and more well-defined. • Black forehead. • White belly, vent and undertail-cov.

Brambling *Fringilla montifringilla*   L 15cm

all plum ⇒	• *Orange wing-bend* (lesser cov, median cov and scaps) and greater cov with whitish or orange tips creating characteristic wing-pattern (stripe over greater cov evenly broad ⇔ in Common Chaffinch broadening towards inner-wing). • Orange breast. • Black rounded spots on rear-flanks.
ad ♂ s	• Completely black head, mantle and bill.
ad ♂ w	• Rather dark patchy head.
1w-1s	• Like ad w of equivalent sex but moult-limit in greater cov (juv outer greater cov dark grey with white tips, inner ad-type black with orange tips). Prim, tail-feathers and tertials juv, less deep black and m worn than in ad (juv tail-feathers pointed). In 1w ♂ often dark centres to lesser cov (in ♀ always) ⇔ ad ♂. • Tail-feathers pointed ⇔ in ad rounded.
1w ♂	• Often some lesser cov with dark centres ⇔ in ad ♂ uniform orange.
1w ♀	• All lesser cov with dark centres, lesser cov as a whole dark with little orange ⇔ in ad ♀ some less cov with dark spot in centre, lesser cov as a whole orange with some dark patterning.
ad ♀/1w	• Grey neck-side. • Pale centre of crown and hind-neck bordered by dark stripes down neck-side.
fl all plum ⇒ ⇒	• *Almost completely dark tail* (only white in basal part of t6 and grey tip of t5 and t6). • Elongated white back/rump-patch.

Red-fronted Serin *Serinus pusillus*   L 12cm

all plum	• Dark general impression due to e.g. very heavily streaked upperparts and underparts (vent and undertail-cov pale). In worn plumage (from about June) uniform black head and breast. • Legs and bill black. • 2 brown-yellow wing-bars (becoming whitish from winter). • Green-yellow fringes to prim, greater cov and base of tail-feathers.
ad	• Large red patch on forehead (larger in ♂ than in ♀). • Almost black head (more black in ♂ than ♀).
ad ♀	• In some ad ♀ grey streaked (rear-)crown; others with entirely black crown as in ad ♂.
juv-1w ⇒	• Dark with *orange-brown crown and ear-coverts*; black lores.
fl all plum	• Diffuse yellowish rump-patch.

European Serin *Serinus serinus*   L 11.5cm

all plum	• Heavily streaked underparts, especially flanks. • Supercilium (yellow in ad) connected with pale ear-coverts surround. • Legs pale. • Short stumpy bill ⇔ in Eurasian Siskin long and pointed. • Dark lores ⇔ Syrian Serin all plum. • 2 well-defined dirty-white to yellowish wing-bars ⇔ in Eurasian Siskin broader yellowish wing-bars and yellow prim-base.
ad	• Diffuse pale nape-patch. • Rump bright and unstreaked yellow.
ad ♂	• More and brighter yellow on head and breast than ad ♀. • Centre of breast unstreaked ⇔ ad ♀. • Forehead unstreaked yellow ⇔ in ad ♀ crown and forehead dark streaked.
ad ♀	• Some ind with very little yellow.
juv	• Lacks bright yellow; yellow-brownish where yellow is in ad. Upperparts including rump streaked ⇔ ad rump unstreaked. • Wing-bars yellow-brown.
1w-1s	• Like ad of equivalent sex but usually moult-limit in greater cov and sometimes some tail-feathers new (old ones very pointed). In southern populations post-juv moult (almost) complete, then as ad (see ad ♂).

all plum ⇒
- Tail completely dark (⇔ Eurasian Siskin); small, unstreaked bright yellow rump (almost identical to Eurasian Siskin).

ote
- Some escaped descendants of Atlantic Canary can resemble European Serin but are e.g. larger with shorter prim-projection (in European Serin prim-projection 100%). Yellow-fronted Canary *S. mozambicus* (regular escape) differs by e.g. completely yellow and uniform underparts, black eye- and malar-stripe, broad yellow supercilium, short prim-projection and white tips to tail-feathers.

rian Serin *Serinus syriacus*   L 12.5cm 4.9"

plum ⇒
- Long tail.
- Bright yellow throat, forehead and area around bill (ad ♀ dull yellow). In ♂ bright yellow eye-ring; rest of head greyish.
- No streaking on underparts (in ♀ some streaking on flanks); grey flanks ⇔ other canaries.
- Yellow-green greater cov and median cov ⇔ other canaries.
- Green-yellow fringes to prim; outer sec creating faint wing-panel.
- When worn (from winter) narrow grey wing-bar over greater cov and grey fringes to tertials.
- Legs and bill dark.

√
y-1s
- Head and underparts uniform pale brown-grey; cov yellow-brown.
- Like ad of equivalent sex but tail-feathers, prim and usually some greater cov juv (difference with ad often difficult to see); sometimes t1 new.

all plum
- Greenish median cov and greater cov contrast with darker rest of wing.
- Small diffuse yellowish rump-patch.
- Green-yellow fringes to tail-feathers creating pale tail-sides.

antic Canary *Serinus canaria*   L 13cm 5.1"

plum
- Pale bill ⇔ in European Serin rather dark.
- Relatively fine streaking on flanks ⇔ European Serin.
- Sharply streaked upperparts.

♂
- Completely green-yellow underparts.

♀
- Greyish breast and neck-side.
- Faint yellow-grey underparts.
- Like ad ♀ but no yellow or greenish colours (except on rump).
- Diffuse pale stripe above and under eye.

all plum
- Yellow streaked rump, relatively inconspicuous (only faintly paler than rest of upperparts) ⇔ other *Serinus* species.
- Completely dark tail.

ril Finch *Carduelis citrinella*   L 12cm 4.7"

plum ⇒
- 2 broad yellowish but somewhat diffuse wing-bars (browner in juv); faintly bordered on upperside.
- Rather long tail.

♂
- No streaking on underparts; upperparts at most faintly streaked.
- Grey rear-head, neck-side and flanks.
- Green-yellow forehead, throat and underparts ⇔ ad ♀.
- Grey-green mantle.

♀
- Duller and more grey than ad ♂. Forehead and chin dull yellow and throat greyish.
- Wing-bars narrower than in ♂.
- Mantle faintly streaked.
- Grey-brown plumage without yellow or green, resembling European Goldfinch juv but darker and wing-bars pale brown instead of yellow.
- Faint streaking on underparts; strongly streaked upperparts.

-1s
- Like ad but usually moult-limit in greater cov; sec, prim, tail-feathers and usually some tertials juv. In ind with advanced post-juv moult (usually ♂) all tertials new, contrasting with old sec.

all plum
- Rump faint yellow-green, but in ad ♂ often bright green-yellow.
- Dark tail with pale green edges of outer tail-feathers.

rsican Finch *Carduelis corsicanus*   L 12cm 4.7"

⇒
- Like Citril Finch but brown faintly streaked mantle and scaps.
- Slightly more yellow on underparts than Citril.

♂
♀
- Yellow on forehead and face brighter but less extensive than in Citril.
- Brown-grey crown and hind-neck ⇔ ad ♂.
- Underparts only faint yellow.

ll plum
e
- Rump yellow-grey ⇔ Citril.
- Sexual dimorphism greater than in Citril.

opean Greenfinch *Carduelis chloris*   L 15.5cm 6.1"

plum
- Grey tertials with black centres or inner webs.
- Strong pale cone-shaped bill.
- Long prim-projection c.100%.
- Bright yellow outer-webs of prim creating distinct yellow outer-edge on closed wing, in flight creating yellow panel over prim. Sec lack yellow.
- Broad yellow base of tail-sides.

♂
- More yellow in prim and especially tail-feathers than in ad ♀/1w, and t4-t6 with completely yellow basal part ⇔ in ad ♀ yellow almost restricted to outer webs.
- Upperparts and underparts uniform deep grey-green.

♀
- Mantle and scaps green-brown, diffusely streaked.

	• Green-grey underparts sometimes with diffuse dark streaks. Some ind with much yellow-green and more similar to ad ♂ (but see tail-pattern in ad ♂). • Narrower yellow outer webs to prim than in ad ♂, not creating uniform patch. • Crown mainly grey ⇔ in ad ♂ mainly yellow-green.
juv-1w	• Underparts paler than in ad with rather well-defined longitudinal stripes. • Upperparts greyish with rather well-defined streaking.
1w-1s	• Similar to ad of equivalent sex but duller coloured; usually moult-limit in greater cov (in ♀ often difficult to see) but post-juv moult sometimes almost complete, then under field conditions like ad. • Tail-feathers often obviously worn ⇔ ad.
note	• Grey-capped Greenfinch *C. sinica* resembles European Greenfinch and can occur as escape. Differences are: basal part of outer webs of sec also yellow (which together with yellow on prim crea long yellow wing-bar in flight), grey-blue crown and hind-neck, pale pinkish bill which contrasts strongly with blackish face, browner upperparts, brown wash on underparts, less yellow on outer we of prim and yellow concentrated on basal part of prim.

European Goldfinch *Carduelis carduelis* L 13cm 5

all plum	• Bright yellow basal part of all flight-feathers and tips of greater cov. • Long pointed pale bill. • Much white in central part of tail-feathers. • Large pale tips to tertials.
ad	• Red face and forehead, white central part of head-side, black crown and hind-neck. • Uniform grey-brown mantle, scaps, breast-sides and flanks; rest of underparts whitish.
ad ♂	• Red reaches to behind eye ⇔ ad ♀.
juv	• Lacks characteristic head-pattern of ad; pale streaked, greyish head. • Grey-brown streaked mantle, scaps, breast-sides and flanks.
1w-1s	• Similar to ad but usually moult-limit in greater cov (often difficult to see); post-juv moult sometimes almost complete, then under field conditions like ad.
fl all plum	• Black upperwing with broad bright yellow wing-bar over basal part of flight-feathers and tips of greater • White rump.
geog var	*C.c. britannica* (Britain and possibly western Netherlands)
all plum	• Generally slightly smaller than *carduelis*.
ad	• Slightly darker brown on upperparts and breast-sides than *carduelis*. • Pale parts on head-side less white than in *carduelis*.
note	• Differences with *carduelis* from mainland of Europe probably too small and variable in both taxa for safe identification of single ind outside normal range.

Eurasian Siskin *Carduelis spinus* L 12cm

all plum ⇒	• Characteristic wing-pattern: 2 broad yellow or yellowish wing-bars over median cov and greater cov pale wing-panel over sec and yellow spot on prim-base. • Long pointed bill. • Long prim-projection more than 100%.
ad ♂	• Black crown and throat-patch ⇔ in ♀ -type grey. • Tail-feathers with completely yellow basal part ⇔ in ad ♀ yellow almost restricted to outer webs. • Rump uniform yellowish ⇔ in ♀ -type diffusely streaked. • Rather faintly streaked flanks.
ad ♀/1w	• Mantle broadly streaked ⇔ in ad ♂ weak and narrow. • Less yellow than ad ♂.
1w-1s	• Like ad of equivalent sex but moult-limit in greater cov; prim, tail-feathers and tertials juv (juv tail-feathers pointed).

Linnet *Carduelis cannabina* L 12.5cm

all plum	• Greyish head with *pale areas above and below eye* (faint supercilium, eye-ring below eye and vertic stripe over cheek) and broad, faint dark moustachial-stripe (also in Twite) forming characteristic head-pattern. • Broad white inner-edge of especially outer tail-feathers (much white at tail-base) ⇔ in Twite narrow white inner-edges. • Whitish outer webs of prim (also in Twite but less distinct; in Twite more obvious pale spot on sec). • Legs brown to dark grey (in juv often paler). • Faintly streaked or uniform upperparts ⇔ in Twite more heavily streaked. • Greyish bill ⇔ in Twite yellow in autumn, becoming darker in spring.
ad ♂ s	• Red fore-crown and breast, especially breast-sides (often extending on to flanks). • Uniform rufous-brown mantle, scaps and cov (in ad ♂ w mantle-feathers and scaps with dark centres).
ad ♀	• Mantle, scaps and cov grey-brown (not rufous-brown as in ad ♂).
ad w	• ♂ rather similar to ♀ due to e.g. streaked upperparts but with weak reddish on breast and warme brown scaps and cov.
1w-1s	• Similar to ad of equivalent sex but usually moult-limit in greater cov, in southern populations somet post-juv moult almost complete, then under field conditions like ad.

Twite *Carduelis flavirostris* L 13cm

all plum	• Heavily streaked mantle, breast and flanks ⇔ in Linnet faint and diffuse (in Linnet juv slightly more strongly streaked breast and flanks). • Ground-colour of head, breast and mantle warm yellow-brown.

- Whitish wing-bar over greater cov ⇔ in Linnet faint and brownish.
- Pale fringes to central part of sec creating narrow pale wing-panel (also in Linnet but usually less distinct).

♂/1w ♂
- Small pinkish rump-patch.
- Rump streaked, when fresh sometimes with faint pink wash but pink usually absent ⇔ ♂.
- Dark, with heavily streaked upperparts and underparts.
- Pale, usually yellowish bill (darker in spring and summer).

v-1s
- Like ad but moult-limit in greater cov; prim, tail-feathers and usually tertials juv (juv tail-feathers pointed but difference with ad sometimes very slight). Ageing difficult, little difference in pattern between juv and ad-type feathers. Different generations in greater cov and tertials only recognizable by difference in wear.

ice
- Call: dry and nasal 'jiieet', slightly rising in pitch. Higher-pitched and more monotone than call of Linnet.

og var *C.f. brevirostris* (Turkey to Iran)

- Ground-colour paler than in *flavirostris* with dark streaks contrasting more strongly.
- Underparts paler than *flavirostris* with well-defined dark patterning on breast-sides.
- Pale fringes to flight-feathers more distinct than in *flavirostris* (more similar to pattern of Linnet).
- Rump pale pink to almost white.

og var *C.f. pipilans* (Britain)

- In general darker and more warmly coloured than *flavirostris*.
- Underparts heavily streaked with streaking extending further on to flanks (middle of belly hardly any paler) ⇔ in *flavirostris* usually distinct whitish belly.
- Wing-bar over greater cov orange-brown ⇔ in *flavirostris* more yellow-brown.
- Neck-side and hind-neck (almost) concolorous with upperparts ⇔ in *flavirostris* neck-side and hind-neck paler than upperparts.

ser Redpoll and Common Redpoll

plum
- Heavily streaked mantle, scaps and underparts, especially flanks ⇔ Linnet.
- 2 pale wing-bars, of which lower (over greater cov) most distinct.
- Red fore-crown patch; small black throat-patch.
- Undertail-cov streaked.
- Culmen often slightly concave (pinched in) ⇔ in Arctic Redpoll straight.
- Legs black.
- In summer often heavily worn and much darker on upperparts and head than in autumn.

♂
- Pink-red throat and breast (becoming more extensive in spring and summer due to wear).

♀
- Pink-red throat and breast absent (sometimes some red spots).

-1s
- Like ad but sometimes moult-limit in greater cov; prim, tail-feathers and tertials juv (juv tail-feathers pointed but difference from ad sometimes very difficult to see). In ♂ pink-red on throat and breast but rarely as extensive as in ad ♂.
- Head with sandy-coloured wash.

sser Redpoll *Carduelis cabaret*   L 12cm 4.7"

plum
- See introduction to Lesser Redpoll and Common Redpoll
- Heavily streaked *deep yellow-brown flanks and breast* contrast with white central part of belly and vent.
- Dark warm yellow-brown upperparts, scaps, head and breast; upperparts heavily streaked, normally without paler central area ⇔ in Common Redpoll more cold grey-brown with obvious paler central area.
- Prim-projection ≤ 100% ⇔ in Common longer. Short tail.
- Flanks heavily streaked; undertail-cov weakly streaked.
- Rump normally distinctly streaked, with pink wash in ad ♂.
- Generally only slightly smaller than Common with overlap.
- Cream-coloured wing-bars ⇔ in Common white.
- Cream-coloured wash on undertail-cov ⇔ Common.
- Often complete eye-ring ⇔ in Common eye-ring often eye-ring only distinct below eye.

♂
- From spring onwards dark red throat and breast ⇔ in Common paler red.

mmon Redpoll *Carduelis flammea*   L 13.5cm 5.3"

plum
- See introduction to Lesser Redpoll and Common Redpoll
- Grey-brown upperparts with slightly paler streaks; head often greyer than upperparts.
- Often whitish underparts with variable amount of streaking (underparts sometimes almost unpatterned).
- Long prim-projection > 100%; elongated rear-end.
- Wing-bars white (in fresh juv pale brown).
- Rump pale on white background, often wholly streaked but in some ind unstreaked central area.
- Dark patch on ear-coverts.
- Undertail-cov with arrow-shaped dark centres but in some ind completely unstreaked as in Arctic Redpoll.
- Some ind exceptionally pale and very similar to Arctic (see that account for differences).

♂
- From spring onwards orange-red throat and breast, sometimes extending to flanks (in some ind throat and breast dull darker red and more like Lesser Redpoll).

og var *C.f. rostrata* (southern Greenland, northern Labrador and Baffin island)

plum
- Large size (larger than *islandica*), generally larger than *flammea*.
- Relatively strong bill with deep base and slightly convex culmen (sometimes stronger than in *islandica*).

ad ♂	• Upperparts brown (lacking grey when fresh) and heavily streaked (darker than *islandica* and resemb large Lesser but often still darker).
	• Flank streaking often bold but diffuse ⇔ *islandica*.
	• Undertail-cov with large triangular centres.
	• Head, throat and breast warm yellow-brown (like Lesser and *islandica*).
	• Broad wing-bar over greater cov.
	• Head faintly patterned.
	• Rarely pink-red on breast; no pink on rump ⇔ most Lesser.

geog var	*C.f. islandica* (Iceland)
all plum	• Large size, generally larger than *flammea*.
	• Relatively strong bill with deep base and slightly convex culmen (but often less strong than in *rostra*
	• Upperparts often greyer and paler than in *rostrata*.
	• Underparts whitish with heavy streaking (often in 3 lines) on flanks (especially distinct in paler type).
	• Head, throat and breast warm yellow-brown (like Lesser and *rostrata*).
	• Broad wing-bar over greater cov (like *rostrata*).
	• Head faintly patterned (like *rostrata*).
ad ♂	• Pale type (see note) sometimes with pink-red on breast; no pink on rump ⇔ most Lesser.
note	• Very variable and possibly hybrid population with Arctic *hornemanni*. Occurs in 2 types; dark type ve similar to *rostrata*; pale type can be very similar to Arctic due to large white unstreaked rump, sometimes more pinkish breast in ♂ and 'loose plumage' but often with distinct patterning on flank and undertail-cov.

Arctic Redpoll *Carduelis hornemanni*   L 12.5cm

geog var	Coues's Redpoll *C.h. exilipes* (northern Europe)
all plum	• Unstreaked white rump (in ♂ sometimes with pink wash) extending high up to between tertials. In Common Redpoll whitish rump with sometimes small part unstreaked, but dark streaking increasing between tertials.
	• Pure white flanks with little or no streaking; streaking normally narrow and not extending far back.
	• Undertail-cov with evenly narrow dark shaft streak on longest undertail-cov (sometimes completely unstreaked) ⇔ in Common rarely unstreaked.
	• Pale rear scaps.
	• Uppertail-cov with greyish centres and pale fringes.
	• Ear-coverts almost concolorous with rest of rear-head ⇔ in Common ear-coverts normally darker.
	• Small, short bill ⇔ in Common normally longer bill.
	• Tail often slightly longer than in Common.
	• Distinct supercilium, often obviously running over forehead ⇔ Common.
	• Upperparts with yellow-brown to white ground-colour (often 2 whitish central mantle-stripes with yellow-brown sides of mantle) but see *hornemanni* ⇔ in Common more grey-brown ground-colour.
	• Dark bases of sec often creating rather strongly contrasting dark patch (sometimes also in Common
	• Broad white wing-bar over greater cov.
	• Often has 'Rook-like' 'full' tight feathering.
	• Often pale hind-neck.
	• Often broad head and thick neck.
	• Often 'full' rear-end due to 'fuller' undertail-cov than in Common.
	• Often smaller red patch on forehead than in Common.
♂	• Pinkish wash on breast and often on rump (latter especially in ad ♂ but also in some 1w ♂) ⇔ in Common more extensive and more tending towards orange-red.
	• Often very pale, mostly white and grey, with brown restricted to scaps.
	• 1w ♂ similar to ad ♂ but often slightly less bright.
♀	• Upperparts with less white background than in ♂.
	• Mantle more heavily streaked than in ♂, unstreaked white part of rump often smaller than in ♂.
1w-1s	• Like ad, ageing often difficult but tail-feathers more pointed than in ad and often more worn (greate cov often completely juv, of no use for ageing).
	• Pale fringes to juv tertials sometimes worn ⇔ in ad fresh in autumn.
	• Head with sandy-coloured wash contrasting with whitish background of underparts.

geog var	Hornemann's Redpoll *C.h. hornemanni* (Greenland and arctic Canada)
all plum	• Distinctly larger than *exilipes*; stronger bill with especially deeper base, larger head with steep forehead, longer wings (prim-projection > 100%) and obviously long tail.
	• When fresh (autumn/winter) rear-side of head warm 'chamois-leather-coloured', contrasting with w background of rest of plumage. Contrast between colour of head and body stronger than in *exilipes*.
	• Mantle and scaps with multiple whitish stripes, hardly any colour difference between these 2 feathe tracts ⇔ *exilipes*.
	• Ground-colour of whole plumage almost pure white with broad white fringes to tertials and tail-feathers.
	• Very large white rump-area, often extending along sides of back, rarely with pinkish wash ⇔ *exilip* Rump-area sometimes faintly streaked ⇔ *exilipes*.
	• Underparts white with very narrow streaking along flanks (sometimes streaking completely absent in ♂).
	• Undertail-cov sometimes with some very fine shaft-streaks.
	• Thigh feathering fuller than in *exilipes*.
	• Only rather small red patch on fore-crown.
	• Uppertail-cov often largely white with blackish shaft-streaks.
ad ♂	• Often only some pink on breast ⇔ in 1w no pink.

o-barred Crossbill *Loxia leucoptera*   L 15cm 5.9"

plum
- 2 broad white Common Chaffinch-like wing-bars; wing-bar over greater cov broadening towards inner-wing.
- Large white tips to tertials, (almost) separated by black shaft-streak.
- Generally more slender and less strongly curved mandibles than in other crossbills, making bill look longer (but variable as in all crossbills). In imm of all species of crossbill mandibles often less strongly curved than in ad.
- p8 falls beyond tertials (wing-tip formed by p3 or p3/p4) ⇔ in Common Crossbill p8 falls approximately level with longest tertial-tip.
- Often fine dark shaft-streaks on underparts.
- Scaps and mantle-feathers with very dark bases; upperparts becoming darker due to wear.

♂
- Bright red head, upperparts and underparts. Flanks, vent and undertail-cov grey.

♀
- Green-yellow rump and often head, rest of upperparts and underparts. Upperparts and underparts mix with grey especially on flanks, vent and undertail-cov.
- Mantle finely streaked/spotted.
- Strongly streaked upperparts and underparts (as in all crossbills juv ⇔ ad ♀), wing-bars already developed but usually narrower than in ad.
- Underparts with mainly grey background ⇔ in ad ♀ mainly green.
- As well as individual variation, very variable due to extended breeding season. Thus 1cy ind can be at a range of different stages of development and consequently show different moult timings; some 1w ♂ completely orange, others nearly still complete juv at same time or with mix of green-yellow and red-orange underparts and upperparts.
- Moult-limit in greater cov indicative, early hatched ind go through complete moult in autumn like ad.
- Prim, tail-feathers and tertials juv, less deep black and later in winter more worn than in ad (juv tail-feathers narrow and pointed). Rest of plumage very variable, some ♂ already entirely red.

ce
- Call: weaker, dryer and more rasping than call of Common: 'chret-chret-chret'. Also characteristic low-pitched, nasal, trumpettering 'weep' and sometimes low pitch 'chrou-ee'.

a
- Common juv-1w have pale wing-bars (but often not white), sometimes even quite broad in combination with pale tertial-fringes, however never as broad as in Two-barred. Common however normally lacks dark centres to scaps, lacks shaft-streaks on underparts and shows slightly different colour and structure. Pale fringes to tertials and greater cov normally consist of evenly broad fringes which do not broaden around tip as in Two-barred and wing-bar does not broaden towards inner-wing but often disappears on inner greater cov. However, fringes and wing-bars broaden on some ind; these are possibly hybrid Common x Two-barred.

g var
White-winged Crossbill *L.l. leucoptera* (North America)

olum
- Distinctly smaller than *bifasciata* (Eurasia) with bill obviously more slender (both in frontal and dorsal view) and longer.
- Both upperparts and underparts darker than *bifasciata* due to larger dark centres (upperparts) and more obvious shaft-streaks (underparts) than in *bifasciata*.
- Prim, sec and tail-feathers deeper black than in *bifasciata*.
- Lores and rear-side of ear-coverts dark.
- Crown often dark spotted.

e geog var
- Not recorded in WP but potential vagrant to north-western Europe.

nmon Crossbill *Loxia curvirostra*   L 16cm 6.3"

olum
- Rather strong bill with evenly curved culmen.
- Lower mandible rather slender ⇔ Parrot Crossbill.
- Obvious corner between culmen and forehead ⇔ Parrot sometimes seems to lacks forehead.

♂
- Deep red plumage with blackish wings and tail.

♀
- Yellow-green rump, rest of plumage greenish with often grey wash on neck-side and along flanks. Underparts very diffusely streaked ⇔ juv.
- Rump bright green-yellow ⇔ juv.
- Streaked head, upperparts and underparts with grey-brown ground-colour.

1w
- Remiges, tertials and (some) greater cov browner and more worn than in ad.
- Whitish fringes on cov, creating wing-bar (sometimes also in ad but then greenish in ♀ or reddish in ♂).
- See also Two-barred Crossbill 1w.
- See Two-barred 1s. In 1s ♂ fringes to flight-feathers greenish ⇔ ad ♂ reddish.

e
- At least 6 types distinguishable on basis of voice and bill-structure; possible cluster of species.

e geog var
- Numerous subspecies which clinally show more grey on feather bases from north to south, in ♂ same cline from red to pink, in ♀ from yellow-green to almost wholly grey in *poliogyna* (North Africa).

ttish Crossbill *Loxia scotica*   L 16.5cm 6.5"

olum
- Measurements intermediate between Common Crossbill and Parrot Crossbill; plumages as in Parrot.
- Only 'identifiable' on basis of range and possibly voice.

e
- Flight-call: deep 'kjuup-kjuup', strongly reminiscent of call of Parrot and certain types of Common but slightly sharper and with rather obvious 'j'-sounds Identification by human ear normally not possible.

rot Crossbill *Loxia pytyopsittacus*   L 17cm 6.7"

lum
- Large bill (lower mandible especially thicker than in Common Crossbill).
- Both mandibles strongly curved to almost square corner (⇔ in Common less strongly curved); bill looks square, which is exaggerated by thickening of lower mandible; tip of lower mandible does not usually extend above upper mandible (also in some Common and most Scottish Crossbill).

	• Larger size in direct comparison with Common.
	• Larger head and thicker neck than in Common.
	• Often paler cutting edges on both mandibles than in Common.
	• Seems to lack forehead because bill runs in almost straight line into crown.
	• Slightly flatter crown makes head appear more angular than in Common.
	• Eye relatively small and situated slightly closer to front of head than in Common.
ad ♂	• See Common ad ♂.
ad ♀	• See Common ad ♀.
juv	• See Common juv.
juv-1w	• Remiges, tertials and (some) greater cov browner and more worn than in ad at same time of year.
	• Whitish fringes to cov, creating wing-bar (sometimes also in ad but then greenish in ♀ or reddish in ♂).
	• See also Two-barred Crossbill 1w.
1s	• See Two-barred 1s. In 1s ♂ fringes to flight-feathers green ⇔ ad ♂.
voice	• Flight-call: pure, deep and full 'kuup-kuup', more full and lower-pitched than most types of Common but very similar to certain types of Common. Identification by human ear normally not possible.

Asian Crimson-winged Finch *Rhodopechys sanguineus*   L 14cm

all plum	• Characteristic patterned head with blackish cap, broad supercilium and brown ear-coverts with pale surround.
	• Dark brown upperparts, breast and flanks; flanks contrast strongly with white central part of belly and breast.
	• Pink outer-edge to flight-feathers creating large pink wing-panel.
	• Long prim-projection > 100%.
	• Grey-brown to yellow bill (yellow in spring).
1w	• Mainly as ad but pink edges to wing-feathers more vague.
1s	• Prim, tail-feathers, tertials and (some) greater cov juv, less deep black and later in winter more worn than in ad (juv tail-feathers pointed).
fl all plum	• Pinkish rump and tail-base.
	• Pink to whitish outer-edge to sec, prim and prim-cov creating pale fan over whole wing, similar to upperwing of Desert Finch but greater cov dark ⇔ Desert.

African Crimson-winged Finch *Rhodopechys alienus*   L 14cm

all plum	• See Asian Crimson-winged Finch.
♂	• Less black on crown than Asian and hind-neck and neck-side grey without reddish-brown.
	• Generally with less deep black patterning and less pink (more brown) than Asian (pink restricted to fringes of sec, prim and prim-cov).
	• Upperparts and underparts more uniform without obvious blackish feather-centres ⇔ Asian.

Desert Finch *Rhodospiza obsoleta*   L 13.5cm

ad	• Pink outer-edge to greater cov, prim-cov and sec; white outer-edge on prim.
	• Uniform cream-brown upperparts, head, breast and flanks; rest of underparts white.
	• Longest tertials covering much of closed wing.
ad s	• Black bill.
ad w	• Pale bill.
ad ♂ ⇒	• Black lores and tertial-centres ⇔ ad ♀.
1w ♂	• Pale lores but black tertial-centres as in ad ♂.
1w	• See Asian Crimson-winged Finch 1w.
1s	• See Asian Crimson-winged 1s.
fl all plum	• Large white fringes to outer side of basal part of tail-feathers creating large white corners at tail-ba (large amount of white in tail).

Mongolian Finch *Bucanetes mongolicus*   L 12.5cm

all plum ⇒	• *Pale bases of greater cov and pale outer-edge to sec* creating contrastingly patterned wing (less obvious in ad ♀) ⇔ Trumpeter Finch.
⇒	• Rather pale, *brown bill* ⇔ Trumpeter ad ♂.
⇒	• Legs brown-yellow ⇔ Trumpeter ad ♂.
	• Upperparts faintly streaked ⇔ in Trumpeter unstreaked.
	• Slightly smaller bill than Trumpeter.
	• Brown head and upperparts, no colour difference between rear-crown and mantle (ad ♀ slightly pa than ad ♂).
	• Both upperparts and underparts uniformly coloured ⇔ Trumpeter.
ad ♂	• Pink on greater cov and tail-base and weakly pink on crown ⇔ in ad ♀ slightly or not at all pink.
ad ♀	• Like faintly patterned and coloured ad ♂.
juv	• 2 obvious wing-bars ⇔ Trumpeter juv.
	• Pale fringes to sec creating pale wing-patch ⇔ Trumpeter juv.
1w	• See Asian Crimson-winged Finch 1w.
1s	• See Asian Crimson-winged 1s.
fl all plum	• Whitish panel on arm.
	• Small grey-brown rump-patch bordered pink ⇔ in Trumpeter ad ♂ completely pink rump and uppertail-cov.
	• White corners at tail-base ⇔ in Trumpeter pale pink.

mpeter Finch *Bucanetes githagineus*
L 12.5cm 4.9"

plum
- Very thick cone-shaped bill with deep base.
- Legs reddish to flesh-coloured.

♂ s
- Pink-red bill.
- Pink underparts (especially flanks) and fringes to greater cov and outer tail-feathers.
- Pink rump and uppertail-cov (flight).
- Bluish head, brown upperparts.

w/ad ♀ s/
- Grey-brown bill.
w
- Sandy brown upperparts and underparts, sometimes pink wash on underparts.
- Pale bill.
- Nearly uniform grey-brown upperparts.

n
- For general ageing criteria see Asian Crimson-winged Finch 1w/1s.
- Moult-limit in wings; post-juv moult sometimes/almost complete, then like ad.

♂
- At least some blue-grey on head and pink on rump, uppertail-cov, underparts and cov but often much fainter than in ad ♂ s.
- Orange bill.

mmon Rosefinch *Carpodacus erythrinus*
L 14.5cm 5.7"

plum ⇒
- Thick bill with convex culmen.
⇒
- Pale outer-edge to tertials and 2 pale wing-bars over greater cov and median cov.

♂
- Red head, breast and rump.
- Wing-bars and sometimes tertial-fringes with red wash.

♀/1s ♂
- Uniform grey-brown head with conspicuous dark eye.
- Faintly streaked grey-brown upperparts.
- Throat and breast extensively streaked, fading away towards vent; undertail-cov unstreaked.
- Some 1s ♂ with variable amount of pink to reddish feathers on head, breast and rump. These ind differ from ad ♂ by narrow whitish wing-bars (worn greater cov and median cov) and worn tail-feathers.
- Like ad ♀ but plumage fresher, wing-bars broader than ad ♀ in autumn and tertial-fringes sometimes more cream-coloured. Fresh plumage ⇔ ad and 2cy in autumn.

ult
- Moults in winter range. Ad and 2cy in autumn worn ⇔ 1w.

es
- Indigo Bunting ad ♀ w and 1w represent possible pitfall (see there).
- House Finch *C. mexicanus* can occur as an escape and is a possible vagrant to WP; resembles Common Rosefinch in all plum but with heavier and more diffuse streaking on the flanks and a more curved culmen.

ai Rosefinch *Carpodacus synoicus*
L 14cm 5.5"

plum
- Short thick bill, slightly less heavy and stumpy than in Common Rosefinch.
♂
- Head, underparts and rump mainly pink-red.
- Patchy white supercilium, forehead and ear-coverts.
- Underparts become gradually paler towards undertail-cov.
- Pink-red rump.

♀/imm
- Nearly completely grey-brown plumage with little difference between slightly darker upperparts and paler underparts.
- Upperparts faintly streaked; underparts uniform.
- Faint wing-bars and tertial-patterning ⇔ Common ad ♀/imm.
- Dark eye conspicuous in uniform pale head.
- Like ad ♀ but tail-feathers, prim and greater cov retained juv feathers, browner and more worn than in ad. In some 1s ♂ slight pinkish wash on head and underparts.

as's Rosefinch *Carpodacus roseus*
L 15.5cm 6.1"

plum
- Well-defined whitish tertial-fringes.
- 2 broad wing-bars over greater cov and median cov, brightest and broadest over median cov ⇔ in Common Rosefinch wing-bars narrower and of even width.

♂
- Heavily dark streaked reddish upperparts.
- Red head and underparts, becoming fainter on vent.
- White speckled crown, forehead and throat.

♀/imm
- Orange wash on head and rump.
- Heavily streaked underparts and upperparts.
- Like ad ♀ but tail-feathers, prim and greater cov retained juv feathers, browner and more worn than in ad. In some 1s ♂ more pinkish-red on crown, underparts and rump.

e
- All records in WP regarded as escapes.

icasian Great Rosefinch *Carpodacus rubicilla*
L 20cm 8"

lum
- Very large with long tail.
- Large pale bill.

♂
- Pink-red head and underparts; *underparts with evenly white spotting.*
- Uniform grey-brown mantle and back; rump pink-red.

♀/imm
- Completely grey-brown.
- Faintly streaked upperparts; heavily and diffusely streaked underparts.
- Like ad ♀ but tail-feathers, prim and greater cov retained juv feathers, browner and more worn than in ad.

Pine Grosbeak *Pinicola enucleator*
L 20.5cm &

all plum ⇒	• Size of Common Starling.
	• Black wings with 2 wing-bars; greater cov with white outer-edges and tips ⇔ Common Rosefinch.
	• Complete and broad white outer-edges to tertials ⇔ in Common Rosefinch narrower pale fringes around distal part of tertials (also extending on inner web).
	• Thick bill with strongly curved culmen; tip of upper mandible falls over tip of lower mandible.
	• Flanks and underparts from belly onwards becoming grey; in *alascensis* (North America) more grey on underparts.
ad	• Central tail-feathers (t1) broad and more rounded than in 1w.
ad ♂	• Red head, upperparts and underparts.
ad ♂/1w ♂	• Well-defined black centres to mantle feathers and scaps ⇔ in ad ♀/1w ♀ weak dark centres at m
ad ♀	• Yellow-green head, upperparts and underparts.
1w ♂	• Yellow-orange head and variable amount of orange-yellow or yellow-green on upperparts and underparts; scaps and flanks usually grey. Some 1w ♂ similar to ad ♀ but centres to mantle feath and scaps often darker.
juv-1w	• Greater cov with narrow white fringes (difference with ad usually small); in 1w often moult-limit in greater cov.
1s	• Like ad ♀ but tail-feathers, prim and greater cov (and sometimes median cov) retained juv feathers browner and more worn than in ad. Some ♂ with some orange or pinkish-red patterning, especially head and breast.

Long-tailed Rosefinch *Uragus sibiricus*
L 17cm

all plum	• Long black tail with broad white sides (t6 completely white, t5 with white outer web).
	• Stubby, pale bill.
	• 2 broad white wing bars, upper wing bar (along tips of median cov) broadest.
	• Crown and ear-coverts greyish.
ad ♂	• Pink-red rump, centre of underparts and loral area, most bright in summer. Mantle quite heavily streaked dark and whitish with only faint pinkish wash.
1s ♂	• Mainly like ad ♀ but more grey and in most ind pinkish-red wash on underparts.
ad ♀	• Under- and upperparts mainly yellow-brown; pink-red restricted to rump.
1w	• Like ad ♀ but rump lacking pink colour and wing bars often slightly buffish.

Eurasian Bullfinch *Pyrrhula pyrrhula*
L 16.5cm

ad	• Black wings with broad white wing-bar; black tail, cap and bill.
	• Large white rump-patch.
	• Uniform grey upperparts.
ad ♂	• Uniform pale red underparts.
ad ♀	• Uniform grey-brown underparts.
juv	• Like ad ♀ but uniform grey-brown head (lacks black cap) and brownish upperparts.
	• Wing-bar buff.
	• Pale grey-brown bill.
1w	• Like ad but sometimes still some juv outer greater cov with diffuse grey-brown tips.
1s	• Like ad but tail-feathers, prim and some greater cov retained juv feathers, browner and more worn than in ad. Moult-limit in greater cov often conspicious.

geog var	**Northern Bullfinch** *P.p. pyrrhula* (Scandinavia)
all plum	• *Larger* and paler than other European subspecies (i.e. *europoea*, central Europe).
	• Underside of wing-bar often with saw-toothed shape caused by white extending to feather edges ⇔ other European subspecies (i.e. *europoea*).
ad ♀	• Upperparts greyish (nape often more extensive) and underparts warm brown with slight purple was little contrast between upperparts and underparts ⇔ European subspecies (i.e. *europoea*) more pur brown on both upperparts and underparts.
note	• Part of population with Two-barred Crossbill or Trumpeter Finch-like trumpetering call.

geog var	*P.p. iberiae* (Iberian Peninsula)
all plum	• Smaller than other European subspecies.
ad	• Upperparts and underparts darker than in other European subspecies.

Azores Bullfinch *Pyrrhula murina*
L 17.5cm

ad	• Sexes almost alike and similar to Eurasian Bullfinch ♀ but upperparts more grey-brown.
	• Bill thicker than in Eurasian.
	• Rump and wing-bar grey (⇔ in Eurasian white) and pale area on rump smaller.
note	• Occurs only on São Miguel, Azores (where Eurasian does not occur).

Hawfinch *Coccothraustes coccothraustes*
L 17.5cm

ad	• Large head with extremely heavy cone-shaped bill.
	• Pale cov creating broad band.
	• Grey neck-side and hind-neck contrast with dark brown upperparts and yellow-brown head.
	• Bill varies from grey-black in spring via brown in autumn to brown-yellow in winter.
ad ♂	• Inner sec rather dark with purple-blue outer-webs.
	• More vividly coloured than ♀ with strongly developed spade-shape broadening on inner flight-feath
ad ♀	• Sec with pale edges, creating wing-panel.

- Underparts strongly spotted.
- Like ad but tail-feathers and prim retained juv feathers, browner and more worn than in ad. In 1s ♀ spade-shape does not broaden; in 1s ♂ broadening of spade-shape sometimes less well developed than in ad.

l plum
- *Broad long pale wing-bar* formed by pale band over cov and white band over prim.
- Short tail with broad white terminal band.

Evening Grosbeak *Hesperiphona vespertina*   L 19cm 7.5"

lum
♂
- Very large *green-grey bill* (resembling Hawfinch).
- Dark head with very conspicuous broad yellow supercilium.
- Tertials, inner sec and greater cov completely white (creating large uninterrupted wing-panel); rest of wings and tail black.
- Green-yellow scaps, back, rump, vent and undertail-cov.
- Underparts yellow.

♀
- Tertials, inner sec and greater cov white with grey centres.
- White spot on prim-base.
- Greyish head, upperparts and upperparts.
- Greyish head, underparts and upperparts. Hind-neck and neck-sides green.
- White spots in tail-tip and on uppertail-cov.
- Similar to ad ♀.
- Like ad but tail-feathers, prim and often tertials retained juv feathers, greyer and more worn than in ad.

Buntings and New World sparrows

Snow Bunting *Plectrophenax nivalis*   L 17cm 6.7"

♂
- Black bill.
- Completely white greater cov (usually inner two greater cov patterned like tertials).
- Prim-cov completely white or only with black tips.

♂ s
♀
- Completely white head and black upperparts.
- Dark bases to all greater cov.
- Prim-cov (largely) dark-looking in the field (at most white bases to inner-webs).
- Rather pale lesser cov and median cov ⇔ 1w ♀.

♀ s
- Dark streaked ear-coverts and crown.
- Yellow bill with small dark tip.
- Cream-brown ear-coverts framed white (frame often broader and more complete in ♂).
- Very pointed tail-feathers ⇔ in ad rounded.

♂
- Like ad ♂ but base of outer greater cov dark.
- Head darker than in ad ♂ w.
- Prim-cov as in ad ♀.

♀
- Dark greater cov with only slightly paler tips; median cov and lesser cov only slightly paler.
- Little white in sec.
- Prim-cov wholly dark.
- Prim and tail-feathers (largely) worn.

plum
- Very broad white sides to tail.
- White arm contrasts with black hand.
- No partial spring-moult but summer plumage acquired by wear.

var   *P.n. insulae* (Iceland)

um
- Darker upperparts and breast-band than *nivalis*, dark tips to outer tail-feathers and dark outer webs to sec.

♂ s
♂
- Mainly black rump and uppertail-cov ⇔ on *nivalis* especially whiter rump.
- Dark bases to greater cov as in *nivalis* ad ♀.
- Ad ♀ w differs from *nivalis* ad ♀ w by completely dark prim-cov ⇔ in *nivalis* ad ♀ has pale bases to prim-cov.

Lapland Bunting *Calcarius lapponicus*   L 15cm 6.1"

um ⇒
- Rufous outer webs to greater cov creating *broad rufous wing-panel* (inconspicuous in worn summer plumage).

⇒
- Very long prim-projection ≥ 100% with very large spacings between visible prim-tips.
- Pale uniform lores, creating open face (not in ad ♂ s).
- Broad whitish wing-bars (much narrower when worn).
- Pale yellowish bill with dark tip (dull yellow to grey-brown in imm and winter plumage).
- Flanks streaked; belly uniform white.
- Very broad pale supercilium extending to hind-neck.
- Pale cream-coloured stripes on mantle.
- Deep rufous-brown fringes to tertials and greater cov (inconspicuous in worn summer plumage).
- Legs blackish ⇔ most other buntings.
- Rump distinctly streaked/spotted ⇔ most other buntings.
- Lark-like long hind-claw.
- t6 nearly completely white; t5 with only very narrow white wedge on tip.
- Red-brown hind-neck and neck-side.

♂ s
♂ s
- Black head and breast; broad supercilium bends behind ear-coverts towards breast-sides.
- Like ad w/1w with pale ear-coverts, submoustachial-stripe and throat but later in summer crown darker and rufous hind-neck more extensive.
- Pale ear-coverts completely surrounded by black.

273

Buntings and New World sparrows

w ♂	• Rufous-brown hind-neck (also in 1w ♂') ⇔ in ♀ brown-grey.
ad w	• Dark scaled breast; streaked flanks.
1w	• Fine breast streaking ⇔ ad.
	• Greater cov and median cov with diffuse white tips ⇔ in ad w large, well-defined, bright white tips
1s	• Like ad s of equivalent sex but prim and tail-feathers browner and worn; 1s ♂ not uniform black on breast.
voice	• Flight-call: rolling 'prrt', drier and often shorter than flight-call of Snow Bunting. Often mixed with 'tj (as in Snow).
geog var	*C.l. subcalcaratus* (western Greenland and Canada)
all plum	• Generally slightly larger and darker than *lapponicus* but with wide overlapping range.
	• Bill generally longer and deeper at base.
	• Feather fringes possibly paler than in *lapponicus*.
note geog var	• In North America often very tame, subspecies in WP usually not.
	• Probably a regular winter visitor to north-western Europe but currently only identifiable by measurements.

Dickcissel *Spiza americana*   L 16cm

all plum	• Yellow patch on breast (faint or sometimes lacking in 1w ♀).
	• Long, pale cone-shaped bill with dark culmen.
	• Rufous lesser cov and median cov (most conspicuous in ad/1w ♂').
	• Conspicuous yellow to cream-coloured supercilium.
	• Very flat forehead, often in straight line with culmen (seems to lack forehead).
	• Heavily streaked mantle.
	• Uniform ear-coverts, dark crown (streaked in non-ad ♂').
	• Ear-coverts bordered by supercilium and submoustachial-stripe but not dark-framed ⇔ many bun
ad ♂' s	• Grey neck and head with yellow supercilium and submoustachial-stripe; large black 'V'-shaped spo throat/upper breast.
1w ♀	• Mainly grey-brown with pale throat and narrow malar-stripe (sometimes yellow on breast and supercilium at least).

Rose-breasted Grosbeak *Pheucticus ludovicianus*   L 20c

all plum ⇒	• Large white tips to median cov, greater cov and tertials.
	• Very large bill resembling Hawfinch.
	• White spot at prim-base (in 1w ♀ sometimes hardly present).
	• Striking supercilium and pale median crown-stripe (except ad ♂' s).
	• Legs blue-grey.
♀/1w	• Uniform dark ear-coverts bordered by submoustachial-stripe and very conspicuous long white supercilium.
	• Breast and flanks dark streaked.
1w ♂'	• Deep cream ground-colour of underparts (especially breast and flanks), often with some pink-red s on breast ⇔ in 1w ♀ more whitish background.
fl all plum	• Yellow (♀) to orange-pink (♂') underwing-cov.

Indigo Bunting *Passerina cyanea*   L 14cm

all plum	• Rather strongly curved culmen.
	• Legs normally very dark, when paler they appear purple-brown.
♂'	• In summer plumage completely bright blue; in winter plumage mottled mix of grey-brown and blue undertail-cov white.
1w/ad ♀	• Uniform cinnamon-brown head and upperparts with dark eye.
	• Broad diffuse wing-bars. 1w often with moult-limit in greater cov; inner ad-type longer and with b yellow-brown fringes on tips, juv outer short with narrow whitish fringes.
	• Breast very diffusely streaked.
	• Sometimes faint bluish outer-edges to sec, prim and especially tail-feathers, when present characteristic.
	• 1w ♂' like ad ♂' w but with less blue spots on upperparts and underparts, 1w ♀ without blue sp
notes	• Lazuli Bunting *P. amoena* (North America, not accepted in WP as wild vagrant) resembles Indigo in ♀ and imm plumages but with unstreaked orange breast and 2 distinct wing-bars.
	• Common Rosefinch ad ♀/1w can possibly form pitfall due to similar plain head with distinct dark and somewhat similar (but thicker) bill-shape. Wing-bars in Common Rosefinch ad ♀/1w white in of yellow-brown, fringes to flight-feathers pale lemon instead of weak brownish, upperparts cold brown-grey and legs pale.

Eastern Towhee *Pipilo erythrophthalmus*   L 21cm

all plum	• Broad orange patch extends along flanks; central part of belly white.
	• Cream-coloured vent and undertail-cov.
	• Long dark tail with broad white fringes.
	• White base to outer prim.
	• Broad pale tertial-fringes.
	• Dark cone-shaped bill.
ad ♂'	• Black upperparts, head and breast.
ad ♀	• Brown upperparts, head and breast.
1w	• Resembles ad but flight-feathers browner.

k Sparrow *Chondestes grammacus* L 16.5cm 6.5"

olum ⇒ • Large amount of white in tail-sides and on tip of tail.
• Diffuse pale spot at prim-base.
• 2 faint cream-coloured wing-bars.
⇒ • Strong head-pattern with broad supercilium, red-brown lateral crown-stripe and ear-coverts, large pale spot under eye, narrow white median crown-stripe and conspicuous submoustachial- and malar-stripe.
• Upperparts grey-brown with typical bunting pattern; tertial-fringes as in American sparrows (see '*Emberiza* buntings').
• Underparts uniform, except dark spot on centre of breast.
• Grey-brown wash on flanks; rest of underparts white.
• Head-pattern less distinct than in ad.
• Breast faintly and diffusely spotted and streaked.
-1s • Prim and tail-feathers worn from 2cy spring on.

annah Sparrow *Passerculus sandwichensis* L 14cm 5.5"

olum ⇒ • Dark, heavily and sharply streaked underparts and upperparts; pale streaks on upperparts.
⇒ • No or very short prim-projection.
• Yellow supercilium; yellow mainly concentrated between eye and bill. In some ind hardly any yellow in supercilium.
• No white in tail (except some ind from western populations).
• Pale median crown-stripe.
• Rather slender pointed bill.
• Brown ear-coverts sharply demarcated from long black waving eye- and moustachial-stripe; rear-side of ear-coverts not bordered.
1s • Prim and tail-feathers worn from 2cy spring on.

g var **Ipswich Sparrow** *P.s. princeps*

•lum • Like large pale *sandwichensis*.
• Underparts brown spotted and/or streaked (patterning paler pinkish-brown on flanks) ⇔ in *sandwichensis* very dark spotted and/or streaked underparts.
• Streaking on underparts narrower than in *sandwichensis*.
• Upperparts grey-brown with pale (almost white) stripes on mantle.
• Often regarded as separate species.

Sparrow *Passerella iliaca* L 17.5cm 6.9"

•lum ⇒ • Red-brown tail and *unstreaked red-brown uppertail-cov* (rump grey).
⇒ • Underparts with red-brown spots (belly and vent unpatterned white).
• Upperside of supercilium rather faintly bordered with crown ⇔ Song Sparrow.
• No white in tail.
• Crown red-brown streaked on usually grey ground-colour.
• Upperparts and wings mainly red-brown.
• 2 narrow pale wing-bars over median cov and greater cov.
• Grey supercilium and hind-neck, as in Song.
• Very broad rufous tertial-fringes becoming narrower towards tips.
• Pale bill with dark culmen ⇔ Song.
• Prim-projection c.70%.
1s • Prim and tail-feathers worn from 2cy spring onwards.
• Many, rather different (sub)species. Above applies for at least northern subspecies, the only subspecies recorded in WP.

g Sparrow *Melospiza melodia* L 16cm 6.3"

•lum ⇒ • Grey centre of ear-coverts ⇔ Fox Sparrow.
⇒ • Moustachial- and malar-stripe blackish; broad malar-stripe usually most obvious feature on head.
• Short prim-projection c.30%.
• Grey supercilium and hind-neck as in Fox.
• Breast streaking often joins together in centre to form large black spot (as in many other American sparrows which have not been recorded in WP) ⇔ Fox.
• Underparts strongly streaked, blackish on breast, sometimes red-brown towards rear-flanks.
• Upperparts contrastingly streaked ⇔ Fox.
• Uppertail-cov streaked ⇔ Fox.
• Long notched tail (rounded when closed) ⇔ Savannah Sparrow.
• No white in tail.
• Broad, brown tertial-fringes becoming narrower towards tips (see also Fox).
1s • Some ind with recognisable juv prim (more worn and pointed than ad-type) and sometimes moult-limit with outer prim new.

te-crowned Sparrow *Zonotrichia leucophrys* L 17.5cm 6.9"

•um • Pale pink to yellowish bill ⇔ in White-throated Sparrow dark greyish.
• Underparts rather evenly brown-grey and unmarked, flanks brown (belly not distinctly paler ⇔ White-throated).
• No white in tail.
• Throat slightly or not at all paler than breast; when paler throat present then very ill-defined ⇔ White-throated.
• Uppertail-cov and rump brown and unstreaked as in White-throated.

ad	• Lores grey (western populations) or black (e.g. north-eastern population and some ind from western populations). • Uniform grey neck-side, head-side, throat, breast and upper belly. • Black eye-stripe and lateral crown-stripe; white supercilium (to above eye) and median crown-strip ⇔ 1w.
1w	• Brown crown-sides and eye-stripe; supercilium pale brown-grey ⇔ in ad crown-sides and eye-stri black; supercilium white. • Lores grey; supercilium almost fading away above lore ⇔ in White-throated 1w supercilium extend to bill. • Uniform unstreaked underparts; greyish on breast, cream-coloured on belly to undertail-cov ⇔ Whi throated 1w. • Malar-stripe faint ⇔ White-throated 1w.
1w-1s	• Prim and tail-feathers worn from 2cy spring onwards. Body-plumage of 1w plumage retained until April.

White-throated Sparrow *Zonotrichia albicollis* L 17cm

all plum	• Well-defined pale throat (in tawny-type less well-defined, see note) ⇔ White-crowned Sparrow. • White wing-bars over greater cov and median cov. • Dark grey bill ⇔ in White-crowned usually paler yellowish to pink. • Heavily streaked, rather rufous-brown mantle ⇔ in White-crowned more faintly streaked and more brown-grey. • No white in tail.
ad ⇒	• Broad two-toned supercilium, yellow between eye and bill; in tawny-type often uniformly coloured (cream-coloured) or two-toned and browner between bill and eye, see note.
1w	• Diffusely but rather strongly streaked breast (breast/flanks streaked to 1s) ⇔ in ad streaking on underparts very faint. White-crowned unpatterned on underparts in all plum. • Head-pattern less well-defined than ad with less pure white supercilium and median crown-stripe, browner rather than black lateral crown-stripes. • Faint malar-stripe ⇔ in ad none. • Evenly broad supercilium extends to bill ⇔ White-crowned 1w. • Dark brown eye-stripe and lateral crown-stripe ⇔ pale brown in White-crowned 1w.
note	• Polymorphic; tawny-type much more weakly patterned and white parts mainly replaced by buff.
1w-1s	• Prim and tail-feathers slightly worn from 2cy spring onwards. Body-plumage of 1w plumage (partia retained until April.

Dark-eyed Junco *Junco hyemalis* L 15.5cm

all plum ⇒	• Uniform greyish breast and grey to grey-brown flanks, *sharply demarcated from white belly*, vent a undertail-cov. • Pale pinkish bill. • Much white in outer sides of tail. • Legs pale grey-brown.
♂	• Completely dark grey upperside, head, breast and flanks.
♀	• Grey-brown upperparts, crown, flanks and fringes to tertials and sec.
1w	• Resembles ad but browner (1w ♂ resembles ad ♀), usually with moult-limit in greater cov.
1s	• Juv prim retained, brown and worn.
note	• Many noticeably different (sub)species. Above applies at least for northern *hyemalis*, the only subspecies recorded in WP.

Emberiza buntings

Most Eurasian buntings show characteristic tertial-pattern consisting of dark centre with pale fringe which strongly widens on outer web, creating pale wedge in dark centre (except Grey-necked Bunting, Corn Bunting, Rock Bunting, Black-headed Bunting and Red-headed Bunting). These and North American sparrows show evenly broad tertial-fring

Black-faced Bunting *Emberiza spodocephala* L 14cm

all plum ⇒	• Two-toned bill; dark upper mandible, *pale pinkish lower mandible*. • Uniform (blue-)grey neck-side. • Heavily streaked mantle but without distinct paler stripes ⇔ e.g. Common Reed Bunting. • Grey lesser cov. • Unstreaked greyish rump slightly paler than rest of upperparts. • Short prim-projection c.40%. • Tail-pattern: in western *spodocephala* and *oligoxantha* t6 with white starting from base of outer we running diagonally towards inner web creating dark-tipped outer web and dark base to inner web; with large white wedge in distal part of inner web; outer web completely dark. Both with diagonal border with dark base. • Wing-bars indistinct (rufous-)brown (as in Reed, although sometimes slightly paler).
ad ♂	• Black face, blue-grey rest of head and breast. • Yellowish wash on underparts.
1w/♀ ⇒	• Colour and patterning resembles Dunnock. • Usually rather faint supercilium, distinct pale submoustachial-stripe and dark malar-stripe; *submoustachial-stripe more distinct than supercilium; submoustachial-stripe palest and most conspicuous part of head*. • (Nearly) uniform ear-coverts with or without only faint pale spot on rear-side of ear-coverts ⇔ in m other similar ♀ -type buntings conspicuous pale spot in dark ear-coverts. • 1w ♂ often with yellowish wash on underparts and grey on central crown and ear-coverts (latter fe also in ad ♀). Neck-sides in 1w ♂ often rather broadly grey ⇔ in 1w ♀ narrow and indistinct.

- 1w ♀ with fine dark streaks in pale central crown-stripe ⇔ in 1w ♂ uniformly pale.
- Like ad of equivalent sex but juv wing and tail-feathers usually more worn than in ad, often rather distinct.

ce
- Call high-pitched 'tsip' or almost disyllabic 'tsleet'. Difficult to distinguish from other 'ticking' buntings.

e geog var
- Most western subspecies (such as *oligoxantha*) lacking olive on upperparts and with least yellow on underparts (in 1w no yellow at all); upperparts most heavily streaked; *oligoxantha* intergrades with *spodocephala* towards east; *spodocephala* slightly more finely streaked on upperparts and ♂ with weak yellowish underparts.

e Bunting *Emberiza leucocephalos* L 16.5cm 6.5"

plum ⇒
- No yellow in plumage, *underparts with pure white background* ⇔ in Yellowhammer at least some yellow wash on belly.
- Rufous rump and uppertail-cov (like Yellowhammer and Black-headed Bunting); uppertail-cov with variable dark shaft-streaks or dark centres.
- Whitish outer-edges to prim ⇔ in Yellowhammer yellowish.
- Rufous scaps contrast with heavily streaked grey-brown upperparts.
- Grey lesser cov.
- Tail pattern resembles Yellowhammer but more white on inner web of t5 and t6, *white often extending on to feather-base* ⇔ in Yellowhammer white more restricted to distal part.
- Slightly larger and longer tailed than Yellowhammer.
- Bill-base (including cutting edges) often grey or sometimes flesh-coloured (especially in ad) ⇔ in Yellowhammer grey, in no plumage flesh-coloured.

♂ s
- White crown and ear-coverts, both white areas black-bordered (in ad ♀ w head-pattern less obvious).
- Red-brown throat and supercilium.

♂ w
- Like faintly patterned ad ♂ s.
- (Nearly uniform) dark chestnut throat and obvious white spot/stripe at border between throat and breast.

♂
- Like ad ♂ w but underparts more heavily streaked, pale spot at border between throat and breast more narrow.
- Throat often paler and crown darker (paler crown-patch smaller) than in ad ♂ w.
- Upperparts heavily streaked with obvious paler mantle-stripes than in ad ♂ w.

♀
- Like very faintly patterned ad ♂ with faint red-brown wash on supercilium and breast (in winter red-brown hardly visible) and faint paler centre of crown.

w/1w ⇒
- Dark ear-coverts with distinct pale spot on rear-side, in 1w ♂ extending to bill as in ad ♂.
- Well-defined crown-streaking; lateral crown-stripe extending to neck-side ⇔ in Yellowhammer crown evenly and more diffusely streaked.
- Whitish throat (in 1w ♂ darker with white spots) ⇔ ad ♂.
- Underparts with slightly finer and sharper streaking than in Yellowhammer (1w ♂ heavily streaked).
- In ad ♀ and 1w ♂ centre of crown paler (in ad ♂ w white crown-patch). 1w ♀ lacks paler crown centre.
- Bill usually rather obviously two-toned ⇔ in most Yellowhammer more uniformly coloured.
- Pale spot on nape ⇔ in Yellowhammer (when present in some ad) fainter.
- Scaps (and often fringes to greater cov) deeper rufous than in Yellowhammer.

♀
- Like ad w ♀ but lacks red-brown on head and breast. Centre of crown not paler.
- Generally grey-brown without any yellow.
- Submoustachial-stripe rather distinct ⇔ in Yellowhammer fainter or absent.
- Usually broad well-defined malar streaking ⇔ in Yellowhammer ♀ w narrower and fainter.
- Pale wing-bars more distinct (whiter) than in Yellowhammer.
- Grey neck-side usually faintly streaked ⇔ in Yellowhammer ♀ w uniform grey.
- Stronger head-pattern than Yellowhammer with distinct whitish to grey broad supercilium (head-pattern sometimes resembles Lapland Bunting).
- Like ad of equivalent sex but juv prim and tail-feathers usually more worn than in ad, often difficult to see.
- Underwing-cov with white background ⇔ in Yellowhammer yellow.

e
- Both song and call very similar to Yellowhammer.

d Yellowhammer x Pine Bunting

whammer and Pine Bunting hybridise over a broad zone. Most ind are normally obviously recognisable by mixed field
s, with 'white-headed' and 'yellow-headed' types most common. White-headed type often with white throat,
rcilium, ear-coverts, crown and throat. Yellow-headed type with yellow supercilium, crown and ear-coverts and often
rown throat. Cross-backs often strongly similar to one or other species.

whammer-type hybrid

w fringes to prim.
owish underwing-cov.
ow on head (submoustachial-stripe area).
y or blackish lores.
her) distinct malar- or submoustachial-stripe.
te or yellowish supercilium.
-brown streaking on underparts.

Bunting-type hybrid

te background to underwing-cov.
ish ear-coverts and/or crown.
ng red-brown throat.

Yellowhammer *Emberiza citrinella* L 16cm

all plum	• Red-brown rump and uppertail-cov, usually faintly streaked. • Heavily but rather diffusely streaked underparts (ad ♂ s only streaked on flanks) ⇔ in Cirl Bunting sharply streaked. • Some ind appear to lack yellow in plumage (only 1w ♀ ?) except (sometimes hardly visible) yellowi outer-edges to prim and most sec. Under good viewing conditions always some *yellow visible on be*
ad	• Tail-pattern: large white wedge on inner web of t5 and t6, both with diagonal border and dark base.
ad ♂ s	• Yellow head with narrow eye-, moustachial- and lateral crown-stripe (at most faint malar-stripe ⇔ ♀ s). • Yellow underparts with diffuse brown breast-band.
ad ♂ w/ad ♀	• Yellow head with obvious eye-, moustachial -, malar- and lateral crown-stripes. In ad ♂ w yellow supercilium and submoustachial-stripe most conspicuous features on head. • Diffuse pale spot on nape ⇔ in Cirl none (in Pine Bunting often more obvious).
1w	• Rather faintly patterned head (lacking obvious supercilium) with diffuse streaking on crown and fair supercilium, submoustachial-stripe and malar-stripe. • Often moult-limit in greater cov.
1s	• Like ad ♀ but juv prim and tail-feathers usually more worn than in ad, often difficult to see. Some ♂ more like ad ♂.
voice	• Call 'treet' or 'treeuw', also more rasping 'triehh' or truuhh' sound. Sometimes short, sharp 'tseet'.

Cirl Bunting *Emberiza cirlus* L 15.5cm

all plum	⇒	• Greyish rump (uppertail-cov often somewhat rufous) ⇔ Yellowhammer all plum. • Short prim-projection c.30–40%. • Uniform hind-neck and neck-side ⇔ in Yellowhammer diffuse pale nape patch.
ad		• Tail-pattern: white wedge on inner web of t6 (c.70% white) and t5 (c.60% white) with diagonal bor and dark base.
ad ♂		• Black throat, yellow streak over ear-coverts and broad black eye-stripe. Dark crown and hind-neck Bright yellow supercilium isolated in dark head. • Grey-green breast and brown breast-sides; rest of underparts yellow (flanks faintly streaked). • Relatively faintly streaked upperparts (scaps uniformly rufous).
♀/1w	⇒	• Underparts and neck-side with *fine well-defined streaks* ⇔ in Yellowhammer heavily streaked underparts and unpatterned neck-side. • Rufous scaps contrast with greyish upperparts and grey brown lesser cov. • Rather distinct head-pattern (with broad dark eye-, moustachial- and malar-stripes). • Greyish upperparts heavily and sharply streaked. • Greyish neck-side and breast-sides.
1w		• Often moult-limit in greater cov, sometimes 2 generations of tail-feathers.
1s		• Like ad of equivalent sex but juv prim and tail-feathers usually more worn than in ad, often difficult to see.
voice		• Flight-call sharp, thin 'zitt'.
note		• Hybrid Pine Bunting x Yellowhammer ♂ can be superficially similar to Cirl but usually with rufous and uppertail-cov, uniform yellow lores and rufous throat.

Rock Bunting *Emberiza cia* L 15.5cm

all plum	• Lacks tertial-pattern of most *Emberiza* buntings (see '*Emberiza* buntings'). • Grey lesser cov. • 2 white wing-bars, over median cov and greater cov (when worn in spring/summer wing-bars can completely disappear). • Two-toned bill; dark grey upper mandible, pale grey lower mandible. • Tail-pattern: much white in tail-sides, pattern similar to Yellowhammer.
ad	• Completely black surrounding of ear-coverts and black lateral crown-stripe. • Grey head, neck and upper-breast; upper-breast unstreaked ⇔ in House Bunting streaked or diffus spotted grey breast. • (Nearly) uniform rufous underparts and rump.
ad ♂	• Head, especially supercilium and ear-coverts, paler grey than breast (in ad ♀/1w head more even grey and slightly darker). • Head-streaking black ⇔ in ♀ lateral crown-stripe with brown. • Grey breast sharply demarcated from rufous underparts ⇔ in ♀ more weakly bordered and colo duller.
1w	• Like faint ad with cream-grey head, white throat and white submoustachial-stripe. • Often moult-limit in greater cov.
1s	• Like ad of equivalent sex but juv prim and tail-feathers usually more worn than in ad, often difficult to see.
note	• Godlewski's Bunting *E. godlewskii* (not recorded in WP) strongly resembles Rock Bunting but has re instead of black head-stripes and deeper brown-orange underparts, rump and scaps.

Meadow Bunting *Emberiza cioides* L 16cm

ad ♂	⇒	• Resembles Pine Bunting ad ♂ but dark *chestnut-brown crown*, grey neck-side and *uniform white throat*.
ad ♀		• Resembles Pine ad ♀ but cream-coloured *unstreaked underparts* and pure white supercilium. • Tail-pattern: t6 white (also outer web) except dark wedge on basal part of inner web; t5 with white outer web and white wedge on tip of inner web. Both feathers have very sloping borders and dark bases.
note		• All records in WP regarded as escapes.

iolated Bunting *Emberiza striolata* L 13.5cm 5.3"

plum ⇒ • Two-toned bill; dark upper mandible, orange lower mandible.
   ⇒ • *Orange* tail-sides ⇔ e.g. Rock Bunting.
- No conspicuous wing-bars.
- Upperparts rather strongly streaked.
- Dark centres to median cov ⇔ in House Bunting none.
- Greyish, strongly streaked head (with conspicuous whitish supercilium and submoustachial-stripe), neck and breast.
- Brown-grey, rather faintly streaked upperparts.
- Faint rufous underparts.
- Head less greyish than in ad ♂.
- Supercilium and submoustachial-stripe cream-coloured, not whitish.
- Greyer upperparts with less well-defined streaking than in ad ♂.
- Similar to ad of equivalent sex but sometimes still moult-limit in greater cov and/or tertials. Post-juv moult often almost complete, then under field conditions like ad.

use Bunting *Emberiza sahari* L 13.5cm 5.3"

plum ⇒ • Upperparts nearly uniform rufous ⇔ Striolated Bunting.
- Head greyer and less strongly streaked than in Striolated (no white supercilium and moustachial-stripe hardly present).
- Underparts deeper rufous than in Striolated.
- Resembles to some extent an 'intermediate' between Striolated and Rock Bunting.
- Well-defined grey breast and rufous underparts.
- Slightly duller and less well-patterned than ♂.
- Resembles ad of equivalent sex but normally moult-limit in most wing feather groups including prim.

ereous Bunting *Emberiza cineracea* L 16.5cm 6.5"

plum ⇒ • Grey bill.
   ⇒ • Brown-grey (nearly) unstreaked rump and uppertail-cov.
- Upperparts faintly streaked.
- Rather distinct whitish wing-bars.
- Usually conspicuous pale eye-ring.
- Underparts hardly patterned.
- Tail-pattern: relatively small white tips to t6 and t5 with normally straight border and dark rest of feather.
-1w • Faintly streaked grey-brown breast and flanks, contrasting with whitish belly.
- Like ad of equivalent sex, but juv prim and tail-feathers usually more worn than in ad (features which are often difficult to see).

g var *E.c. cineracea* (Greece and western Turkey)

♂ s • Diffuse yellow throat, submoustachial-stripe and supercilium.
- Uniform grey underparts with white central part of belly and vent.
- Undertail-cov uniform white ⇔ *semenowi*.
♀ s • Very faintly streaked greyish underparts and upperparts.
- Diffuse pale throat and submoustachial-stripe.

g var *E.c. semenowi* (eastern Turkey, western Iran)

♂ s ⇒ • Completely yellowish underparts.
- Crown brighter yellow than in *cineracea*.
♀ • Yellowish head, throat and submoustachial-stripe, nearly as *cineracea* ♂ but streaked crown ⇔ *cineracea* ♂.
e geog var • Intermediate ind with e.g. weak yellow central part of underparts and wholly white undertail-cov regularly occur (i.e. on migration in Israel).

olan Bunting *Emberiza hortulana* L 15.5cm 6.1"

plum ⇒ • Long pointed orange-red bill.
- Conspicuous *pale yellowish* eye-ring (often whitish, especially in imm).
- Grey-brown upperparts; rump and uppertail-cov slightly more rufous ⇔ in Cretzschmar's Bunting more red-brown, especially rump.
- Brown tertial-fringes ⇔ Cretzschmar's.
- Prim-projection c.30-60% with 2-3 prim-tips beyond tertials. When prim under tertials visible, then rather wide distances between prim-tips.
- Tail-pattern: t6 with large broad white wedge or completely white distal part of inner web; t5 similar to t6 but with slightly less white. Both with diagonal border and dark base.
♂ s ⇒ • Uniform green-grey to blue-grey head and breast; *yellow submoustachial-stripe* and throat; unstreaked rufous underparts.
♀ s • Somewhat like ad ♂ s but head and breast less coloured and dark shaft-streaks on crown, breast and sometimes rest of underparts.
♀/ad ♂ w • Dark malar-stripe connected with finely streaked breast. Grey-green head and breast less distinct and underparts less deep rufous than in summer plumage of equivalent sex. In ad ♀ w colours paler and duller and head and breast more strongly streaked than in ad ♂ w; ad ♂ w with more yellow throat and more rufous underparts than ad ♀ w.
- Strong, almost pipit-like spotted underparts (especially on breast and flanks) connected with malar-stripe ⇔ in Cretzschmar's juv underparts slightly more faintly spotted.

279

Buntings and New World sparrows

1w	• Upperparts strongly streaked ⇔ Cretzschmar's juv often slightly more faintly streaked on upperpart • Similar to ad w of equivalent sex but underparts often more streaked (flanks ⇔ ad) and often moult-limit in cov and tertials. 1w ♂ similar to ad ♀ w.
ad ♀/1s ♀	• Conspicuous black spotted malar-stripe contrasts strongly with well-defined (pale) submoustachial-stri • Head and breast with greenish wash. • Sometimes very faint supercilium ⇔ in Cretzschmar's none. • Ear-coverts usually slightly darker than crown ⇔ Cretzschmar's.
moult	• In ad completed in late summer. Summer plumage acquired by partial spring moult ⇔ most other buntings. • In 1w only body, cov and tertials.
fl all plum ⇒	• Underwing-cov pale yellowish ⇔ Cretzschmar's.
voice	• Flight-calls: interchanging deep liquid 'tjuup' and higher-pitched, dry 'sleet'.

Cretzschmar's Bunting *Emberiza caesia* L 15cm

all plum ⇒	• Rump and uppertail-cov rufous, rump unstreaked or with faint streaking ⇔ in Ortolan Bunting rump grey-brown and rather obviously streaked. • Shorter and less pointed bill than Ortolan with often darker culmen. • Short prim-projection c.20% with usually only one or two prim beyond long overhanging tertials. Wh prim visible under tertials, then short distances between prim-tips ⇔ Ortolan. • Whitish eye-ring without yellow wash ⇔ most Ortolan. • Rufous-brown tertial-fringes ⇔ Ortolan. • No supercilium (⇔ rarely present in Ortolan and always diffuse). • Scaps with narrow black centres ⇔ in Ortolan broader black centres to scaps. • Uneven tertial-spacing. Central tertial often relatively long with distance between shortest and centra tertial longer than between central and longest (as in Grey-necked Bunting) ⇔ in Ortolan distances evenly spaced. This feature is variable in Cretzschmar's, and is only useful in cases where all tertial are obviously of the same generation.
ad	• Tail-pattern: white tips to t5 and t6 but white in t5 smaller (overall less white in tail-feathers than Ortolan) with *less sloping* border towards dark base than in Ortolan; t4 often with small white tip ⇔ most Ortolan.
ad ♂ s ⇒	• Grey-blue head and breast; *orange lores, submoustachial-stripe and throat.* • Underparts almost uniform deep rufous ⇔ in ad ♀ s paler and with pale scales (pale feather tips).
ad ♀ s	• Like ad ♂ s but head and breast less deep blue; lores, submoustachial-stripe and throat duller coloured and fine dark shaft-streaks on crown and breast (more ♂-like than Ortolan ad ♀).
ad ♀/ad ♂w	• Dark malar-stripe connected to finely streaked breast. Grey-blue head and breast less distinct and underparts less deep rufous than in summer plumage of equivalent sex. In ad ♀ w colours paler an head and breast more strongly streaked than in ad ♂ w; ad ♂ w with browner throat and more ru underparts than ad ♀ w.
juv	• Spotted centre of breast, fading away on flanks; rest of underparts unpatterned ⇔ Ortolan juv. • Faint pale loral-spot ⇔ most Ortolan • Rufous-brown underparts to undertail-cov.
1w	• Many ind similar to ad w of equivalent sex but underparts often more streaked and often moult-limi cov and tertials. 1w ♂ similar to ad ♀ w.
1s ♀	• Malar-stripe faint ⇔ Ortolan 1s ♀. • Upperparts less strongly streaked than in Ortolan 1s ♀.
juv-1w	• Like 1s ♀ but head lacks grey.
fl all plum ⇒	• Underwing-cov pale rufous ⇔ Ortolan.
moult	• See Ortolan.
voice	• Flight-calls: rather similar to Ortolan, but often gives sharper 'tsreep'.

Grey-necked Bunting *Emberiza buchanani* L 15cm

all plum ⇒ ⇒	• Rufous-brown scaps contrast with brown-grey upperparts. • *Faintly and narrowly streaked* brown-grey mantle ⇔ Ortolan Bunting and Cretzschmar's Bunting. • Lacks tertial-pattern of most *Emberiza* buntings (see '*Emberiza* buntings') but often weak broadenin pale fringes to outer-webs. • Underparts pink-orange faintly pale scaled; *(upper-)breast more fiercely coloured*; vent and undertail-cov whitish. No grey breast-band ⇔ Ortolan and Cretzschmar's. • Long tail. • Culmen not darker than rest of bill ⇔ Ortolan and Cretzschmar's. • Brown-grey, almost uniform rump, only narrow dark shaft-streaks. • Grey lesser cov. • Whitish eye-ring. • Generally smaller than Ortolan. • Uneven tertial-spacing ⇔ Ortolan (see Cretzschmar's all plum).
1w/ad ⇒	• Pale grey-blue head and hind-neck/neck-side; *grey-blue not extending to centre of breast*. Wine- red underparts. • Slight sexual dimorphism; ♂ slightly more richly coloured. • White-yellow submoustachial-stripe and throat. • Tail-pattern: t6 with much white and diagonal bordered with dark base; t5 similarly patterned but w slightly less white; t4 lacks white.
1w	• Many ind already like ad, but 1w ♂ with faint wine-red underparts, 1w ♀ mainly cream-coloured underparts and almost without red. • Underparts, neck-side and crown very finely streaked. • Moult-limit in cov.
1s	• Like ad of equivalent sex but often some juv greater cov, tertials and all prim and tail-feathers usua more worn than in ad, often difficult to see.

•ice
- Flight-calls: rather similar to Ortolan and Cretzschmar's, but includes short 'tseep' and deeper 'tsuup' in repertoire.

estnut-eared Bunting *Emberiza fucata* L 16cm 6.3"

plum ⇒
- Characteristic breast-pattern: fine dark spots creating *broad patchy band*, with variable rufous breast-band underneath.

⇒
- On closed wing almost no prim-projection; long tertials cover prim almost completely (when wing slightly hanging down, prim-projection seemingly visible).
- Submoustachial-stripe joins black-spotted breast-pattern.
- Pale eye-ring.
- Rufous-brown ear-coverts, scaps and rump (rump unstreaked, uppertail-cov grey-brown and streaked).
- Pointed tail-feathers (in 1w more pointed than in ad, as in Chestnut Bunting).

♂ s
- Greyish head and breast. Rufous-brown ear-coverts, scaps and breast-pattern most conspicuous in this plumage (♀ more faintly patterned).

⇒
- Supercilium between eye and bill bronze-coloured.
- Only t6 with white ⇔ in ad also small white wedge on t5.

low-browed Bunting *Emberiza chrysophrys* L 15cm 5.9"

plum ⇒
- Strong head-pattern with long yellow supercilium (in non-ad s yellow only usually between eye and bill), very dark lateral crown-stripe, narrow pale median crown-stripe and broad pale submoustachial-stripe.
- Deep red-brown central part of mantle; rest of mantle brown-grey with heavy, black streaks.
- Ear-coverts with complete dark surrounding and pale spot on rear-side (like Rustic Bunting w).
- Large pale grey-brown bill with dark culmen, sometimes upper mandible completely dark.
- Two pale wing-bars over median cov and greater cov.
- Red-brown rump and uppertail-cov (uppertail-cov with dark shaft-streaks).

s
- ♂ with black ear-coverts and crown (in ♀ dark brown).
- Well-defined blackish streaking on underparts.
- Tail-pattern: very broad white wedge over inner web of t6, tip around shaft dark; t5 with long but narrower white wedge.

w
- Well-defined, rather thin, dark red-brown streaking on underparts.
- Sometimes very little yellow in supercilium in 1w.
- Malar-stripe usually rather distinct, resembling Common Reed Bunting.

ult
- Partial spring moult, in autumn sexes almost same.

stic Bunting *Emberiza rustica* L 14cm 5.5"

plum ⇒
- Broad rufous breast- and flank-streaking (in ad s creating closed breast-band) contrasting with uniform white lower breast and belly.

⇒
- *Finely pale scaled* chestnut rump.
- 2 whitish wing-bars over median cov and greater cov.
- Rather long prim-projection c.70% with strong uneven spacings between visible prim-tips.
- Straight or slight concave culmen ⇔ in Common Reed Bunting slightly convex.
- Rufous neck-side (in 1w ♀ very narrow) ⇔ Reed all plum.
- Angular head-profile with crest-like point on rear-crown.
- White rear-crown except in ad ♂ s.

♂ s
- Black ear-coverts and crown.

♀ s / 1s ♂
- Dark parts of head not completely black.

w / 1w
- Very broad long supercilium, white (ad) to pale cream-colored (1w), broadest and brightest behind eye.
- Submoustachial-stripe as distinct as supercilium (behind eye) ⇔ Reed and most Little Bunting.
- Narrow pale median crown-stripe.
- Usually bright and well-defined pale spot on rear-side of ear-coverts.
- Tail-pattern: t6 largely white; t5 with white wedge on inner web.

♂
- Sides of crown and surrounding of ear-coverts solid blackish ⇔ in w ♀ browner.
- Rather broad chestnut-brown band across hind-neck ⇔ in w ♀ narrow or absent.
- Like ad of equivalent sex (although 1s ♂ sometimes resembles ad ♀) but some juv prim, tail usually more worn than in ad and sometimes moult-limit in greater cov.
- 1s ♂ with broad, completely chestnut neck ⇔ in ad ♀ more narrow and mix of brown and grey.

ult
- Partial spring moult, in autumn sexes almost alike.

av
- Regularly flicks wings ⇔ Reed.

e Bunting *Emberiza pusilla* L 12.5cm 4.9"

lum ⇒
- Lores, ear-coverts and median crown-stripe red-brown. Supercilium broad, paler behind eye.
- Usually finely streaked breast and flanks.
- Colour-contrast between grey-brown mantle and deeper chestnut scaps ⇔ Rustic Bunting and Common Reed Bunting.
- Malar-stripe narrow; moustachial-stripe often (almost) absent, when present not extending to bill.
- Tail-pattern: t6 with rather narrow diagonal white wedge over largest part of inner web, dark around shaft-tip; t5 with very little white on inner web along shaft-tip.
- Submoustachial-stripe paler than supercilium before and above eye.
- Small bill with straight culmen.
- Usually obvious pale eye-ring.
- Greyish neck-side.
- Brown-grey lesser cov (often not visible due to overhanging scaps); in spring grey.
- Strongly developed tertial-pattern typical of *Emberiza* buntings (see '*Emberiza* buntings').
- 2 pale wing-bars but often not very distinct ⇔ in Reed wing-bars indistinct red-brown (similar to rest of feather-fringes of wing).

1s moult	• Like ad of equivalent sex some juv prim and tail usually more worn than in ad, often difficult to see. • Partial spring moult; in autumn sexes alike, in spring ♂ deeper and more extensive chestnut-brown rear-crown and throat.

Chestnut Bunting *Emberiza rutila* L 13cm

all plum ⇒ ⇒	• Deep rufous unstreaked lower back and rump (in juv streaked). • No white in tail; sometimes greyish t6. • Pointed tail-feathers (also in ad). • Prim-projection c.40%. • Yellow to yellowish underparts.
ad ♂ s	• Completely rufous head, breast, cov and upperparts.
ad ♀/imm	• Almost uniform dark ear-coverts (without distinct paler centre). • Submoustachial-stripe often most conspicuous part of head.
ad ♀	• Faint head-pattern with faint supercilium and faint pale ear-coverts surrounding (somewhat resembling Yellow-breasted Bunting but head-pattern much fainter and without distinct pale centre ear-coverts). • Rather faintly streaked green-brown mantle. • Breast and flanks faintly and diffusely streaked. • In some ind faint rufous crown-sides and ear-coverts and rufous wash on breast.
juv	• Strong well-defined streaking on underparts and upperparts; *breast and throat finely streaked*. • Head-pattern somewhat resembling Yellow-breasted juv but less conspicuous, supercilium with dark streaking. • Pattern of median cov as in Yellow-breasted juv.
1s	• Like ad of equivalent sex (1s ♂ less colourful than ad ♂) but some juv prim and tail usually more worn than in ad, often difficult to see.

Yellow-breasted Bunting *Emberiza aureola* L 15cm

all plum	• Short prim-projection c.20-30% (due to long tertials hanging far over tips of sec). • Streaked rump and uppertail-cov ⇔ in Yellowhammer unstreaked red-brown rump. • Relatively short tail (sometimes conspicuous in flight). • Tail-pattern: little white in t6, white starting from base of outer web and running diagonally towards inner web, creating dark-tipped outer web and dark-based inner web; t5 variable, from completely c to small white wedge on tip. • 2 pale wing-bars ⇔ Chestnut Bunting and Yellowhammer.
ad ♂ s	• Red-brown crown and mantle. • Solid black face, ear-coverts and throat. • Yellow underparts with narrow dark brown breast-band. • Completely white mantle and lesser cov creating white 'shoulder'.
ad ♂ w	• Like ad ♂ s but much duller; bright colours hidden under pale fringes of all fresh feathers (summer plumage acquired with wear).
ad ♀/juv ⇒ ⇒	• Bright *yellowish stripe on neck-side* (part of pale ear-coverts surround). • Strong head-pattern: dark ear-coverts (with pale centre) *completely* surrounded by pale with conspicuous broad supercilium as upper border. In ad ♀ very broad whitish supercilium. • Mantle heavily streaked dark; 1 or 2 pairs of contrasting pale stripes. • Breast(-side) and flanks finely streaked; amount of streaking very variable. In ad ♀ w underparts (almost) unstreaked. • Narrow pale median crown-stripe.
juv	• Like ad ♀ s but often with distinct malar-stripe and variable amount of streaking on underparts; streaking finer than in ad ♀ s and usually creating complete breast-band. • Yellow on underparts varies from bright pale yellow to yellow-brown. • Median cov with less white and narrower, more pointed dark centres than in ad ♀. Dark shaft (almo extending to feather-tip ⇔ ad ♀. See note. • Tail-feathers pointed.
1s ♂	• Variable; resembles ad ♀ s but red-brown breast-sides, dark ear-coverts and dark spots on throat. • Wing-bar over median cov narrower than in ad ♂ s, like ad ♀.
1s ♀ moult	• Variable; like ad ♀ but median cov with juv-like pattern and sometimes old juv tertials. • Partial spring moult, in autumn sexes almost alike.
note	• Migrates in mainly juv plumage to winter range (⇔ most other *Emberiza* buntings), median cov pat useful for ageing in western Europe.

Common Reed Bunting *Emberiza schoeniclus* L 14.5cm

all plum ⇒	• Mainly *red-brown feather-fringes on mantle and wings*; tips of median cov and greater cov concolo with fringes; no conspicuous wing-bars. • Convex culmen. • Tail-pattern: t6 almost completely white except for dark wedge on base of inner web; t5 with slight less white. Both with distinct diagonal border and dark base.
ad ♂ s	• Black head and breast with conspicuous submoustachial-stripe. • Broad white collar.
ad ♂ w	• In fresh autumn plumage strongly resembles ad ♀, later in winter head gradually becomes blacke and collar whiter. • Breast patterning concentrated on centre ⇔ in ♀ breast evenly streaked.
♂	• Grey(ish) rump (sometimes present in ad ♀ in worn summer plumage).
ad ♀ s	• Dark head with faint supercilium and whitish throat; malar-stripe very broad.
♀/ad w/1w ⇒	• Conspicuous malar-stripe, broadening towards breast. Moustachial-stripe extends up to bill. • Crown evenly streaked ⇔ Rustic Bunting.

- Faint dark lateral crown-stripe ⇔ Pallas's Reed Bunting.
- Like ad of equivalent sex but some juv prim and tail retained; amount of wear not reliable ageing character from April onwards.

og var   *E.s. reiseri* (south-eastern Europe)

plum
- Conspicuously thick bill with curved culmen.
- Larger and darker than north-west European subspecies.

og var   *E.s. passerina* (north-western Siberia)

plum
- Slender bill with usually straight culmen.
- Upperparts slightly paler than European subspecies with narrower dark shaft-streaks.
- Rump usually greyish.

og var   *E.s. pallidor* (south-western Siberia)

plum
- Usually distinctly larger than European subspecies.
- Much paler than *passerina* with yellow-brown ground-colour of upperparts and narrow dark shaft-streaks.
- Underparts almost white with narrow pale brown streaking on breast and flanks.
- Rump usually greyish.

te geog var
- Numerous subspecies within WP, often difficult to distinguish. Two main groups recognisable, often referred to as thin-billed and thick-billed (thin-billed *schoeniclus*-group in north, thick-billed *pyrrhuloides*-group in south). Above-mentioned *reiseri* and *pallidor* belong to *pyrrhuloides*-group; *passerina* belongs to *schoeniclus*-group.

llas's Reed Bunting *Emberiza pallasi*　　　　　　　　　　　　　　L 13cm 5.1"

plum ⇒
- Pale *cream-coloured* fringes and especially tips to cov creating wing-bars, in ♂ also pale fringe to remiges. In ♀-type often distinct colour contrast between red-brown fringe to remiges and pale tips to greater cov.
- Overall smaller and paler than Common Reed Bunting.
- Two-toned bill; very dark to black upper mandible and (partially) pale lower mandible; in almost all ad ♂ and (some?) ad ♀ in summer bill completely black.
- (Except juv) only flanks finely streaked, sometimes underparts almost unstreaked (in ad ♂ s uniform white).
- Pale rump.
- Grey or grey-brown lesser cov ⇔ in Common Reed all plum red-brown.
- Pale mantle- and scap-lines very conspicuous, often creating two evenly broad pale stripes ⇔ in Common Reed at most one distinct broad pale stripe and a weak second.
- No dark lateral crown-stripe ⇔ Common Reed (not applicable to ad ♂ s).
- Relatively small bill with straight culmen.
- Relatively long tail.
- Legs rather pale, pink-brown ⇔ in Common Reed normally darker, more red-brown).
- Tail-pattern: t6 similar to Common Reed; t5 with less white than in Common Reed and with less sloping (usually almost straight) border with dark base.

♂ s
- Mantle heavily streaked blackish with *almost white stripes*; upperparts almost black and white ⇔ Common Reed.
- Head-pattern resembles Common Reed ad ♂ s but submoustachial-stripe widens near neck-side and black does not extend as far towards breast as in Common Reed.
- Collar not completely white, *often cream-coloured* ⇔ Common Reed.
- Whitish rump.

autumn ⇒
- Broad *warm buff neck-side*, often retained into spring.
- Broad pale cream-coloured and blackish stripes on mantle.
- Underparts only faintly streaked red-brown ⇔ Common Reed ♀.
- Underparts heavily but diffuse streaked ⇔ ad.

/1w ⇒
- Dark spot on lower edge of ear-coverts; no complete dark ear-coverts surround as in Common Reed ♀/1w.
- Supercilium fading behind eye ⇔ Common Reed.
- Usually pinkish base to lower mandible.
- Like ad of equivalent sex but some juv prim and tail retained; amount of wear probably not a reliable character for ageing later in spring (as in Common Reed).

ce ⇒
- Call: House Sparrow-like 'chreep' or disyllabic 'tsi-lee' (later more reminiscent to call of Greenish Warbler). Also more Tawny Pipit-like 'tsloe'. Calls very different from Common Reed.

d-headed Bunting *Emberiza bruniceps*　　　　　　　　　　　　　　L 16cm 6.3"

plum
- No distinct white in tail (as in Black-headed Bunting); sometimes white wedge on t6 (in Black-headed only rarely).
- Strong grey bill but generally slightly smaller and thinner than in Black-headed.
- Slightly smaller and more slender than Black-headed.
- Tertials with evenly broad pale fringes (unlike tertial-pattern of most *Emberiza* buntings; see introduction '*Emberiza* buntings'), as in Black-headed.
- Slightly shorter prim-projection than Black-headed (50-60%) with 4-5 prim tips beyond tertials. Slightly shorter wings give impression of slightly longer tail than in Black-headed (see Black-headed for differences between prim tip spacing).
⇒
- Yellow rump.

ad ♂ s	• Brown head and breast; rest of underparts yellow.
	• Grey-green mantle and scaps.
ad ♀	• Older ♀ easier to identify as colour-pattern resembles ♂.
	• Upperparts grey-brown, nowhere rufous ⇔ most Black-headed ad ♀.
	• Rump in summer usually rather distinctly yellow, in autumn grey-green.
	• Mantle in spring with black streaking ⇔ in Black-headed more diffuse and dark brownish.
♀/1w	• Nearly uniform head without submoustachial- and/or malar-stripe; ear-coverts not or slightly darker than crown ⇔ in most Black-headed often weak submoustachial-stripe and ear-coverts often darke
	• Little and faint crown streaking, forehead almost unstreaked ⇔ most Black-headed ♀/1w.
	• Cold grey-brown upperparts (sometimes also in Black-headed ♀/1w); rump greyish, often yellow-g sometimes green-yellowish.
	• Upperparts generally more heavily patterned (creating better developed streaks) than in Black-heade ♀/1w.
	• Cream-coloured fringes to cov and flight-feathers ⇔ in Black-headed ♀/1w often more whitish (bu due to wear very variable in both species).
	• Underparts very variable; (brown-)yellow (often with dark shaft-streaking on breast and flanks) to uniform whitish ⇔ in Black-headed ♀/1w rarely shaft-streaking. Often undertail-cov, vent and belly the most deeply coloured.
1w	• Wings and tail fresh (prim with pale fringes around tips) ⇔ in ad worn in autumn.
	• Lores and direct surrounding concolorous with rest of head ⇔ Black-headed 1w.
1s	• 1w probably moults completely in winter; 1s plumage similar to ad.
moult	• See Black-headed.
note 1w	• Some ind not distinguishable with certainty from Black-headed 1w.

Black-headed Bunting *Emberiza melanocephala*   L 16.5cm €

all plum	• Rufous-brown to largely yellow rump in heavily worn ad ♂ s (in many imm and ♀ less distinct) ⇔ Red-headed Bunting yellow(ish).
	• Long strong bill, generally slightly longer than in Red-headed.
	• No distinct white in tail.
	• Underparts unstreaked; in some non-ad ind faint breast-streaking and/or flank streaking, as in Red-head
	• Tertials with evenly broad pale fringes (unlike tertial-pattern of most *Emberiza* buntings; see '*Ember* buntings'), as in Red-headed.
	• No or very faint supercilium, as in Red-headed.
	• Rather long prim-projection c.70% with 4-5 (6) prim-tips beyond tertials ⇔ Red-headed.
	• Often 3 larger spacings between prim-tips; inner 3 prim more bunched ⇔ in Red-headed often 2 larger spacings; inner 4 prim more bunched. Often difficult to see and only useful in obvious cases.
ad ♂ s	• Black hood, yellow throat and neck-side (in spring head sometimes still with grey-brown or yellowis patterning, remains of feather tips that have not yet worn off).
	• Uniform red-brown upperparts and breast-sides (some mantle feathers and scaps sometimes brown grey with dark shaft-streaks like ♀, possibly 1s). Worn ind often with yellowish rump.
	• Completely yellow underparts.
♀/1w	• Obviously streaked crown ⇔ Red-headed ♀/1w.
	• Upperparts finely streaked (more distinct in 1w) *with rufous wash, especially on rump* (in older ♀ rufous wash more obvious). When rufous wash present then diagnostic difference from Red-headed ♀-type. Streaks often closely spaced ⇔ in Red-headed often more connected to long streaks.
	• Yellowish undertail-cov as in Red-headed (sometimes absent).
	• Ear-coverts usually darker than rest of head ⇔ Red-headed ♀.
	• Older ♀ easier to identify as colour-pattern resembles ♂.
	• Whitish fringes to cov and flight-feathers ⇔ in Red-headed often more cream-coloured but very variable in both species.
1w	• Wings and tail fresh (prim with pale fringes around tips) ⇔ in ad worn in autumn.
	• When some rufous-brown present on upperparts then a distinguishing feature from Red-headed.
	• Pale face, especially around lores.
1s	• 1w moults completely in winter; In 1s like ad (but see ad ♂ s).
moult	• Ad at least moults completely in early winter. In summer only some body-moult in ♂, in ♀ normall none (together with Red-headed, only bunting with this moult strategy).
note	• See Red-headed.

Corn Bunting *Emberiza calandra*   L 17.5cm

all plum ⇒	• No white in tail.
	• Evenly patterned without conspicuous field marks.
	• Large size with large pale bill.
	• Streaking on underparts often joins together to form large spot at centre of breast.
	• (Very) faint supercilium, faint pale spot on ear-coverts; distinct submoustachial-stripe and variable p central crown-streak.
	• Breast and head with numerous dark, small, well-defined streaks; long stripes on flanks.
	• Upperparts, mantle and back streaked; rump and uppertail-cov unstreaked or faintly patterned.
	• Evenly broad tertial-surrounding ⇔ most Eurasian buntings.
	• Prim-projection c.40%.
juv	• Mantle heavily streaked and/or scaled.
	• Fringes to cov and tertials whitish, sharply bordered and of even width.
	• Breast rather heavily streaked and/or spotted.
1w/1s	• Juv moults completely in autumn; after moult like ad.

bolink *Dolichonyx oryzivorus*   L 17.5cm 6.9"

plum ⇒
- Blackish tertials with *well-defined narrow pale fringes* ⇔ Yellow-breasted Bunting and most other European buntings.
- Rather long prim-projection c.80% with prim-tips rather evenly spaced ⇔ Yellow-breasted Bunting.
- Legs rather pale (red-)brown (sometimes darker in ad ♂ s).
- No white in tail and very pointed tail-feathers ⇔ Yellow-breasted Bunting.
- Rather flat crown usually continues in almost straight line from culmen.
- Relatively small head; relatively long neck sometimes conspicuous.

♂ s
- Completely black underparts and fore-part of head; rear-head cream-coloured; uppertail-cov, rump and scaps white.

♀/(1)w ⇒
- No (or very faint) malar- and moustachial-stripe ⇔ Yellow-breasted Bunting ♀/1w (Yellow-breasted Bunting ad ♀ often lacks distinct malar-stripe).
- Broad dark lateral crown-stripe, pale median crown-stripe and dark eye-stripe; lores uniform.
- Breast-sides faintly and diffusely spotted; flanks heavily and sharply streaked.
- Ear-coverts only faintly dark-bordered on rear-side ⇔ Yellow-breasted Bunting ♀/1w.
- Broad pale stripes on heavily streaked mantle; rump and uppertail-cov less heavily streaked.
- Pale bill with usually dark culmen and tip ⇔ in Yellow-breasted Bunting often dark upper mandible.
- Brown-yellow wash on underparts.

ll plum
- Long pointed wings.

ult
- Moults completely in both summer and winter; ageing and sexing in autumn usually impossible.

e
- Some ♀-type weavers of the African genus *Euplectes* resemble Bobolink ♀/(1)w but differ e.g. by lacking prim-projection.

Icterids

wn-headed Cowbird *Molothrus ater*   L 19cm 7.5"

plum
- Size as Common Starling.
- Rather large cone-shaped bill.

♂
- Black with blue-green gloss; dark brown head.

♀
- Grey-brown overall with slightly paler throat and faint submoustachial- and malar stripe.
- Under- and upperparts diffusely streaked.
- Like ad ♀ but juv feathers with pale tips; after October like ad.

mmon Grackle *Quiscalus quiscula*   L 31cm 12"

plum ⇒
- Long rounded tail often with slightly up-curved sides.
- Yellow iris (in juv dark iris).
- Short prim-projection c.50%.
- Dark with blue to purple gloss on head and breast.
- Wings and tail with greenish gloss.

e
- Two colour morphs: bronze morph (interior North America) bronze-coloured except purple-blue head and breast; purple morph (east coast of North America) mantle, scaps and underparts faintly glossy spotted with various colours.
- Glossy-starlings from the African genus *Lamprotornis* are sometimes mistaken for North American grackles. Glossy-starlings usually show shorter, straight-ended tail (without up-curved sides) and conspicuous large eye.
- WP records are regarded as escapes.

ow-headed Blackbird *Xanthocephalus xanthocephalus*   L 24cm 9.5"

plum
- Size about as Blackbird but ♀ distinctly smaller than ♂.

♂
- Black with golden-yellow head (dark lores) and breast. In fresh plumage (from autumn) yellow less deep and often with dark spots.
- White prim-cov.

♀
- Dark but not completely black lores ⇔ in 1w/ad ♂ black lores.
- Black-brown with yellowish breast, supercilium and submoustachial-stripe; prim-cov completely dark.
- Regularly white patterning on belly, throat and neck-side.

♂
- Browner than ad ♂ with yellowish head and breast with dark scales.
- White tips to prim-cov.

♀
- Completely brown with little yellow restricted around head.
- Brown worn prim, sec and large part of cov.

imore Oriole *Icterus galbula*   L 22.5cm 9"

lum ⇒
- Long, very pointed bill.
⇒
- Yellowish tail with diffuse darker centre (in ad ♂ black tail-base and central tail-feathers with well-defined large yellow-orange corners). Underside of tail entirely yellow to orange.
- White tertial-fringes, white fringes to sec and white wing-bars creating boldly patterned wing.
- Deep yellow-orange rump.
- Legs thick, blue-grey.

♂
- Completely black head and upperparts.
- Deep orange underparts.

♀
- Orange underparts.
- Blackish upperparts.
- Variable dark-spotted head with faint supercilium and pale throat.
- Green-grey to greenish mantle and back with faint dark streaks.
- 2 white wing-bars of which upper (over median cov) broadest.

	• Very faint head-pattern with very faint supercilium, submoustachial- and malar stripe; ear-coverts slightly darker.
	• Moult-limit in greater cov.
1w ♂	• Deeper yellow-orange underparts than 1w ♀; some yellow in median cov (in 1w ♀ completely whit and darker streaks on mantle and scaps than in 1w ♀.
1w ♀	• Orange breast, rest of underparts sometimes greyish.

New World warblers

Black-and-white Warbler *Mniotilta varia*　　　　　　　　　　　L 13.5cm £

all plum ⇒	• Completely or mainly streaked black-and-white.
	• White outer-edges of tertials creating white stripe connected with wing-bars.
	• Broad white supercilium and median crown-stripe.
	• Long, slightly downcurved bill.
ad ♂	• Throat and ear-coverts black (ad ♂ s) or black spotted, sometimes unpatterned white (ad ♂ w).
♀/1w ♂	• White throat.
	• Pale ear-coverts, black eye-stripe.
♀	• Pale brown wash over vent and undertail-cov (especially in 1w ♀).
1s	• Tail-feathers and prim retained juv feathers, duller and more worn than cov; tail-feathers pointed ⇔ ad. Often slightly less solidly coloured and patterned than ad s.
behav	• Moves in nuthatch-like manner through trees.

Golden-winged Warbler *Vermivora chrysoptera*　　　　　　　　　L 12.5cm ♦

all plum ⇒	• Yellow cov creating *conspicuous wing-panel*.
	• Upperparts cold-grey.
	• Yellow forecrown (indistinct in 1w ♀).
	• Underparts grey but undertail-cov white.
	• Tail pattern: much white on inner webs of t4-t6.
♂	• Bold head-pattern with black ear-coverts and throat (also in 1w ♂); white supercilium and submoustachial-stripe.
♀	• Dark grey ear-coverts and grey throat.

Blue-winged Warbler *Vermivora pinus*　　　　　　　　　　　　　L 12.5cm

all plum	• Blue-grey wings with 2 white wing-bars (very broad in ad ♂, narrow in 1w ♀).
	• Upperparts and hind-neck to rear-crown yellow-green.
	• Tail pattern: much white on inner webs of t4-t6.
♂ ⇒	• Yellow crown and underparts (undertail-cov white) ⇔ in Golden-winged Warbler grey underparts.
	• Black lores and short eye-stripe.
♀	• Yellow supercilium; crown yellow-green like upperparts.

Tennessee Warbler *Vermivora peregrina*　　　　　　　　　　　　L 12.5cm

all plum ⇒	• Straight, very pointed bill with grey lower mandible (⇔ *Phylloscopus* warblers).
	• Rather faint eye-stripe and supercilium (more distinct in ad ♂ s).
	• Long prim-projection c.100% (⇔ most *Phylloscopus* warblers).
	• Only small pale spots on inner webs of outer tail-feathers (♂) or no white in tail (♀) ⇔ *Dendroica* warblers.
	• Diffuse cream-yellow wing-bar over greater cov and sometimes also (even) fainter wing-bar over median cov. In ad s usually worn away.
ad ⇒	• Pale grey to whitish underparts, vent and undertail-cov bright-white.
ad ♂ s	• Grey head and neck-side.
	• Greenish upperparts.
ad ♂ w	• Similar to ad ♀.
ad ♀	• Brown-green upperparts.
	• Greyish wash on crown.
	• Yellow wash on throat.
1w	• Brown-green upperparts.
	• Brown-yellow underparts contrasting with whitish to pale yellowish undertail-cov.
	• 2 very narrow, usually indistinct wing-bars (very faint or absent in ad).
	• Obvious pale tips to prim.

Northern Parula *Parula americana*　　　　　　　　　　　　　　L 11.5cm

all plum	• Green-brown mantle, contrasting with grey-blue scaps and wing (more green-brown on upperparts in 1w).
	• Yellow throat, *often with dark breast-band* (black and red-brown, more faint in ♀-type) and yellow upper part of belly; rest of underparts white. 1w ♀ lacks breast-band so throat and breast are wholly yellow.
	• Broken eye-ring.
	• Small size with short tail.
	• 2 broad white wing-bars, on greater cov not extending to inner ones.
	• Yellowish lower mandible.
ad ♂	• Black lores, no supercilium. Breast-band consists of black and chestnut bar. Ad ♂ with some ches along flanks.
♂ w	• Like s but grey lores and green wash over whole of upperparts. Breast-band fainter than in s.
♀ s	• Very similar to ♂ w.

- Green fringes along sec and tertials ⇔ in ad ♂ grey-blue, in ad ♀ green-grey.
- Like ad of equivalent sex but in 1w ♀ dark breast-band completely lacking; in 1w ♂ upperparts greener than in ad ♂.
- See Black-and-white Warbler 1s.

erican Yellow Warbler *Dendroica petechia* L 12.5cm 4.9"

plum ⇒
- No supercilium and eye-stripe; almost uniform pale head with often diffuse, broad pale eye-ring.
- Completely yellow underparts (sometimes yellow-brown in 1w ♀).
- Bright-yellow inner webs on all tail-feathers (in 1w less broad) ⇔ in other *Dendroica* warblers white in tail.
- Pale yellowish fringes to all sec, prim, tertials and cov; tertial-fringes whitish in ad ♀/1w.
- Relatively thick bill.
- Legs pale brown-yellow (in ad s often reddish).

♂
- Underparts reddish streaked (sometimes also faintly present in 1w ♂ and ad ♀).
- Yellow-brown to yellow-green upperparts (yellow-brown ⇔ ad).

ll plum
- Yellow underwing-cov.
- See Black-and-white Warbler 1s, but also often moult-limit in greater cov and tail-feathers with less yellow in juv feathers.

estnut-sided Warbler *Dendroica pensylvanica* L 12.5cm 4.9"

plum ⇒
- Red-brown patches extend along breast-sides and flanks (fainter in ad w; not extending to rear-flanks in ad ♀; absent in 1w ♀ and most 1w ♂).
- Yellow to green-yellow crown.
- Upperparts with dark streaks (in ad s very broad).

♂ s
- Black eye- and moustachial-stripe; ear-coverts white; yellow crown.

♀ s
- Like ad ♂ s but red-brown patches not extending on to rear-flanks and lores paler; greenish crown.

⇒
- Grey head-side without patterning.
- Underparts whitish with variable red-brown flanks (in 1w ♀ lacking, in 1w ♂ and ad ♀ often faint).

⇒
- *Bright-green* mantle, hind-neck and crown (crown often slightly more yellow).
- Pale eye-ring.
- 2 broad white-yellow wing-bars over greater cov and median cov.
- Dark wings and tail contrast with rest of plumage.
- Tail pattern: white inner webs on t4-t6; in 1w on t5 and t6 (extending to base of t6 on ad).
- Upperparts finely (♂) or at most very slightly (♀) dark spotted ⇔ ad (but ad ♀ often similar to 1w ♂).
- See Black-and-white Warbler 1s.

ck-throated Blue Warbler *Dendroica caerulescens* L 13.5cm 5.3"

plum ⇒
- Large well-defined *white prim-spot* (often absent in 1w ♀).
- Legs brown to black (toes often paler).
- Tail pattern: very similar Cape May Warbler but dark tips not complete, white extending to feather-tips along inner-side.

♂/1s ♂
- Uniform dark blue upperparts and crown.
- Black throat and flank; rest of underparts white.

♀/1s ♀
- Very different from ad ♂/1s ♂; upperparts uniform greenish, underparts uniform yellow-brown.
- Narrow, long, well-defined supercilium and eye-ring conspicuous due to dark lores and ear-coverts.
- Pale cream-coloured throat contrasts strongly with dark ear-coverts.
- Bluish outer-edge to tail-feathers.
- Like ad of equivalent sex but 1w ♀ with browner upperparts and lacks prim-spot. 1w ♂ with green wash on blue upperparts.
- See Black-and-white Warbler 1s.

ck-throated Green Warbler *Dendroica virens* L 12.5cm 4.9"

plum ⇒
- *Uniform green-yellow upperparts*, distinctly contrasting with wing.

⇒
- Yellow spot on vent; belly and undertail-cov white.
- Diffuse dark ear-coverts bordered by broad yellow supercilium and very broad yellow submoustachial-stripe completely surrounding ear-coverts.
- 2 well-defined white wing-bars.
- Tail pattern: almost completely white inner webs of t4-t6, with outer web also white on basal half; t4 with less white, especially in 1w ♀.

♂
- Black throat and breast; heavily streaked flanks (ad ♂ w as ad ♀ s).

♀ s
- Like ad ♂ s but black parts not uniform and head-pattern less well-defined.

♀/ ♂ ⇒
- Black malar-stripe extending into large black patch on breast-sides, continuing in 2 broad rows of black spots along flanks.
- 1w ♀ with pale throat and diffusely streaked underparts. In 1w ♂ black spotted breast and throat (nearly as ad ♀ s or ad ♂ w).
- See Black-and-white Warbler 1s.

ckburnian Warbler *Dendroica fusca* L 12.5cm 4.9"

lum ⇒
- *Pale mantle-stripes* on dark upperparts.

⇒
- Pale median crown-stripe (only on forehead).
- Yellow to orange supercilium conspicuous, broadening behind eye.
- Uniform dark ear-coverts.
- Half eye-ring under eye conspicuous.

	• Tail pattern: white inner webs to t4-t6, extending to outer web at base; 1w ♀ with white on distal p of outer webs of t5 and t6 only.
	• Streaking from breast-sides along flanks.
ad ♂	• Vivid-orange supercilium, neck-side, throat and breast; black crown and ear-coverts (ad ♂ w slightl less strongly coloured).
	• Large white wing-panel over median cov and greater cov.
	• Black upperparts.
ad ♀	• Orange-yellow throat and breast; rest of underparts whiter.
	• 2 broad white well-defined wing-bars.
1w	• Like ad ♀ but throat pale yellow and head-pattern less well-defined. 1w ♀ faintly patterned and almost lacks yellow.
1s	• See Black-and-white Warbler 1s.

Cape May Warbler *Dendroica tigrina*   L 12.5cm ◂

all plum ⇒	• Very pointed bill with slightly *curved culmen*.
	• Underparts densely and relatively finely streaked, denser and finer than in Magnolia Warbler (1w ♀ sometimes very diffusely streaked).
	• (Green-)yellow rump, *faintly bordered* ⇔ Magnolia and Yellow-rumped Warbler.
	• Bright greenish fringes to flight-feathers and whitish outer-edges to greater cov.
	• 2 whitish wing-bars, broader over median cov than over greater cov.
	• Tail pattern: much white on inner webs of t3-t6, except tip and base; amount of white decreasing fro out- to inner-side.
ad ♂ s	• Bright yellow neck-side; red-brown ear-coverts, black crown.
ad ♂ ⇒	• Completely white median cov and largely white greater cov creating conspicuous wing-panel.
	• Yellow underparts with well-defined black streaking.
	• Ad ♂ w like ad ♂ s but head-pattern much fainter.
ad ♀/1w ⇒	• Pale (yellowish) spot on neck-side.
	• Greyish underparts with diffuse streaking and yellow wash.
	• Green-grey upperparts and crown; upperparts with faint streaking.
	• Broad yellow but somewhat diffuse supercilium.
1w	• Like ad ♀ but more faintly patterned and coloured (underparts often at most very slightly yellow; upperparts usually uniform).
1s	• See Black-and-white Warbler 1s. In ♂ crown spotted and less chestnut on head-side.

Magnolia Warbler *Dendroica magnolia*   L 12.5cm

all plum ⇒	• Tail pattern: *white central tail-band* comprising large white spots on centres of all tail-feathers exce t1 (on upperside only visible on spread tail).
⇒	• Variably streaked and spotted yellow underparts except bright-white belly, vent and undertail-cov.
	• Bright yellow, well-defined rump-patch (as in Yellow-rumped Warbler).
	• 2 well-defined white wing-bars over greater cov and median cov.
	• Blue-grey cap and hind-neck.
	• Pale eye-ring.
ad s	• Yellow underparts with broad black stripes, thickening on breast to form breast-band (vent and undertail-cov bright white).
	• Broad white supercilium behind eye.
	• Black spotted (ad ♀) or completely black upperparts (ad ♂) except yellow rump-patch.
	• Dark ear-coverts and lores (uniform black in ad ♂).
	• Mainly white greater cov and median cov creating conspicuous wing-panel.
ad w	• Grey head.
	• Greenish upperparts; scaps with dark centres.
	• Complete pale eye-ring.
1w	• Like ad w but diffuse grey breast-band and unpatterned scaps.
	• 1w ♀ almost uniform on underparts.
1s	• See Black-and-white Warbler 1s.

Yellow-rumped Warbler *Dendroica coronata*   L 14cm

all plum ⇒	• Brownish head (except ad s) with conspicuous white eye-ring broken at front- and rear-side; narrow white supercilium (sometimes almost absent).
⇒	• Mantle with rather heavy dark streaks.
	• Tail pattern: relatively small rounded white spot on inner webs of t4-t6, becoming smaller from oute side to inner-side, not extending to base (1w ♀ lacks white on t4).
	• Yellow to orange-brown spot on fore-flanks (in 1w ♀ often absent).
	• Pale throat (white in ad s) extending to under dark ear-coverts.
	• Bright yellow rump, sharply bordered.
	• Rather heavily streaked underparts (especially breast-sides and flanks).
	• 2 white wing-bars.
	• Pale spot above lores (isolated part of supercilium), pale brown in 1w.
	• Blue-grey outer-edges to sec, prim, cov, uppertail-cov and tail-feathers (often not very conspicuous
ad	• Yellow crown-patch.
ad ♂ s	• Upperparts and fore-crown blue-grey (in ad ♀ s with brown wash) and black ear-coverts.
ad w	• Crown, ear-coverts and mantle brown.
1s	• See Black-and-white Warbler 1s.
note	• 'Audubon's Warbler' *D.c. auduboni* (western North America, not recorded in WP) has dark ear-cover hardly bordered by pale neck-side, lacks supercilium, in ad at least some yellow on throat and less white in tail than 'Myrtle Warbler' *D.c. coronata* (on underside of tail resembles elongated white spo

base and tip of tail broadly black-bordered ⇔ *coronata*); *auduboni* 1w has more obvious wing-bars and only diffusely streaked underparts.

n Warbler *Dendroica palmarum*   L 14cm 5.5"

lum ⇒
⇒
⇒
- Undertail-cov bright yellow.
- Tail pattern: straight-ended, white tips to inner webs of t5 and t6 (very conspicuous when flushed).
- Obvious supercilium, eye- and loral-stripe and weaker submoustachial- and malar-stripe somewhat resembling pipit.
- (Grey-)brown upperparts with faint dark streaks.
- Relatively long, slender bill.
- Yellowish underparts (in *palmarum* belly whitish) with faint streaking on breast and flanks.
- Broad but diffuse pale brown wing-bars, mainly over greater cov.
- Red-brown crown.
- See Black-and-white Warbler 1s.

g var   *D.p. hypochrysea* (south-eastern Canada and north-eastern United States)

lum
- Completely yellowish underparts.
- Underparts with red-brown streaking.

kpoll Warbler *Dendroica striata*   L 14cm 5.5"

lum
- Legs grey to *pale yellowish*, toes yellowish; when legs darker then pale yellowish souls.
- 2 white wing-bars, somewhat broken by dark shaft-streaks on upperside ⇔ Bay-breasted Warbler
- Whitish tertial-fringes.
- Undertail-cov white ⇔ in Bay-breasted cream-coloured.
- Conspicuous eye-stripe (not in ad s ♂).
- Tail pattern: relatively small subterminal white spot on inner webs of (t4), t5 and t6.

♂ s
- Black cap, white ear-coverts and long black malar-stripe.
- White underparts with fine black streaking.
- Greyish upperparts with bold dark streaks.

♀ s
- Like ad ♂ s but sharply streaked crown and patchy malar stripe connected with finely streaked flanks.
- Green-yellow upperparts with dark streaking; underparts yellowish, especially breast and flanks.
- Variable amount of streaking on underparts, ♂ with more distinct malar-stripe.
- Like ad w with usually faint, diffuse breast patterning, sometimes connected with faint malar-stripe.
- Breast and flanks usually more yellow than in ad w.
- See Black-and-white Warbler 1s.

breasted Warbler *Dendroica castanea*   L 14cm 5.5"

um
- Long prim-projection c.100% ⇔ in Blackpoll Warbler often slightly shorter.
- Legs dark ⇔ Blackpoll.
- 3 emarginations on outer webs of prim (p3-p5) ⇔ in Blackpoll 2 (p3-p4).
- 2 broad well-defined white wing-bars, often slightly broader than in Blackpoll.
- Tail pattern as in Blackpoll.

♂ s ⇒
- Dark orange-red breast-sides and flanks.
- Dark orange-red crown, throat, breast-sides and flanks.
- Large black mask.
- Large yellowish neck-side patch.

♀ s
- Like ad ♂ s but much more faintly patterned and coloured; dark mask spotted, eye-ring conspicuous ⇔ ad ♂ s.

/1w ⇒
- Brown-yellow breast (rear-flanks and undertail-cov more cream-coloured to red-brown), underparts usually lack streaking ⇔ in Blackpoll diffuse but obvious streaking on breast (sides) and white undertail-cov.
- Yellow-green to yellow-brown upperparts with faint streaking in 1w ⇔ in Blackpoll upperparts more grey-green with faint to rather heavy streaking.
- Neck-side conspicuously pale yellow-green to cream-coloured.
- Conspicuous eye-ring broken by eye-stripe at front- and rear-side.
- See Black-and-white Warbler 1s.

lean Warbler *Dendroica cerulea*   L 12cm 4.7"

um
- Smallest *Dendroica* warbler with shortest tail.
- Tail pattern: small white spots on distal part of t4-t6.
- 2 very broad white wing-bars.
- Broad supercilium (usually faint in ad ♂ s) and conspicuous eye-stripe.

/1s ♂
- Deep grey-blue upperparts and head, mantle diffusely streaked.
- White throat and neck-side sharply defined.
- White underparts with dark blue breast-band and streaking along flanks.

/1s ♀
- Bright blue-green unpatterned upperparts; crown with blue wash.
- Dirty white underparts with yellow wash, undertail-cov pure white.
- Like ad ♀ but underparts more yellowish and almost unpatterned. In 1w ♂ rather well-defined flank streaking.
- See Black-and-white Warbler 1s. In ♂ upperparts duller, breast-band thinner and no or very small white spot on t2.

American Redstart *Setophaga ruticilla*   L 13.5cm,

all plum	• Red (ad ♂) or yellow (ad ♀ and 1w) basal part of tail-feathers (except t1) creating very conspicuo tail-corner.
ad ♂	• Black wings with broad red wing-bar over base of flight-feathers.
ad ♀/1w ⇒	• Bright yellow wing-patch *at base of flight-feathers* (in many 1w ♀ no yellow in wing); rest of wing uniform dark brown.
	• Pale, unstreaked underparts with yellow or orange patch on breast-sides.
	• Blue-grey wash on head; throat paler.
	• Uniform brown upperparts.
	• Relatively long rounded tail.
1s	• ♂ similar to ad ♀ but dark lores and some with black spots on head and underparts and orange flanks. Wings largely worn.
behav	• Very manoeuvrable; has remarkable whirling foraging flight through tree and scrub (resembles fora behaviour sometimes seen in bonelli's warblers).

Ovenbird *Seiurus aurocapilla*   L 15cm

all plum ⇒	• Conspicuous large dark eye with pale eye-ring and orange median crown-stripe demarcated from lateral crown-stripe.
	• Underparts white with thrush-like stripes and spots.
	• Upperparts and majority of head uniform olive-brown.
	• Throat uniform white; submoustachial- and malar-stripe conspicuous.
	• Legs pale pinkish.
	• Pale bill.
1w	• Tertials with weak rufous tips ⇔ ad.
behav	• Outside breeding season stays mainly on ground; walks with almost mammal-like gait.

Northern Waterthrush *Seiurus noveboracensis*   L 15cm

all plum ⇒	• Yellowish to white background on underparts with heavy streaking on to rear-flanks.
	• Supercilium usually yellowish and narrowing towards rear ⇔ Louisiana Waterthrush.
	• Throat finely spotted, sometimes very little ⇔ in Louisiana usually completely unpatterned.
	• Breast-sides and neck-side sharply spotted ⇔ in Louisiana faint and diffuse streaking.
	• Legs brownish to pink.
	• Very long conspicuous supercilium, extending to rear-side of ear-coverts (at rear-side slightly narrc and sometimes becoming pale brown ⇔ Louisiana).
	• Uniform dark green-brown upperparts.
1w	• Tertials with weak cream-coloured tips ⇔ ad.
fl all plum	• Very dark underwing.

Louisiana Waterthrush *Seiurus motacilla*   L 15.5cm

all plum ⇒	• Supercilium white, extending very far and broadening behind ear-coverts; supercilium above lores not bright white.
	• Underparts with almost completely white background and contrasting *brownish (sometimes somev rufous) flanks and undertail-cov* ⇔ Northern Waterthrush lacks contrasting flank colour.
	• Strong, long bill, usually distinctly stronger than in most Northern.
	• Legs bright pink (especially in spring).
	• Throat usually unspotted.
	• Breast-sides and neck-side usually diffusely patterned.
	• Pale half eye-ring under eye usually whiter and more distinct than in Northern.
1w	• Tertials with weak cream-coloured edges ⇔ ad.
fl all plum	• Very dark underwing.

Common Yellowthroat *Geothlypis trichas*   L 12.5cm

all plum	• Uniform green-brown upperparts and top of head.
	• Short prim-projection c.50%.
	• Yellow throat and upper breast.
	• Legs pale flesh-coloured.
	• Rather long pointed bill.
	• No white on rounded tail.
ad ♂	• Black mask with pale grey upper-edge extending to neck-side.
ad ♀ ⇒	• Dark ear-coverts ⇔ Hooded Warbler.
	• Yellowish undertail-cov and throat; rest of underparts grey-brown. Yellow on throat sharply demarc from dark ear-coverts.
	• Flank and breast-sides brown, sometimes forming breast-band.
	• Very faint supercilium ⇔ in Hooded and Wilson's Warbler broad and distinct.
1w	• Like ad ♀ but in 1w ♀ yellow on throat faint or absent.
	• 1w ♂ with faint dark mask.
1s	• Most ind with (some) old juv prim, tail-feathers and tertials, other ind completely moulted and similar t

Hooded Warbler *Wilsonia citrina*   L 13.5cm

all plum ⇒	• Pale inner webs to t3-t6 (in 1w t4-t6) ⇔ in Wilson's Warbler no white in tail.
⇒	• Dark lores (usually faint).
	• Uniform yellow-green upperparts.
	• Yellow underparts.

• Legs orange.
• Black head with large yellow mask (1w ♂ like ad ♂).
• Black band over crown and rear-side of ear-coverts resembling head-pattern of ad ♂. Sometimes there is no black on head in ♀, but this may be only in 1s ♀.
• Yellow face and forehead; *dark lores.*
• Pale ear-coverts ⇔ Wilson's 1w.
• See Common Yellowthroat 1s.

son's Warbler *Wilsonia pusilla*   L 12cm 4.7"

plum ⇒
• Lores uniform yellow ⇔ Hooded Warbler.
• Uniform yellow-green upperparts.
• Yellow underparts.
• Pale grey-brown base to lower mandible ⇔ Hooded.
• Legs orange.
• Faint dark ear-coverts ⇔ Hooded.
• No white in tail.
• Black cap contrasts with yellow forehead and yellow supercilium.
⇒ • Dark crown, not black as in ad ♂.
• Like ad ♀.
• See Black-and-white Warbler 1s.

ada Warbler *Wilsonia canadensis*   L 13.5cm 5.3"

plum ⇒
• Upperparts, wings and rear-side of head uniform dark blue-grey.
• Underparts yellow; undertail-cov white.
• Breast streaked with some long stripes; in 1w ♀ very faint, in ad ♂ well-defined and broad.
• Conspicuous pale complete eye-ring.
• Short yellow supercilium between eye and bill (in 1w ♀ faintly bordered, in ad ♂ sharp).
• Legs pale orange.
• No white in tail.
♂ • Throat black-bordered at sides towards head-side; black forehead (fainter in ad ♂ w).
• Breast streaked black (forming breast-band).
♀ • Breast faintly streaked; black on head restricted to speckling on crown and ear-coverts.
• Like ad but uniform blue-grey head with faint yellow supercilium; breast only diffusely streaked (almost unmarked in some 1w ♀).
• See Black-and-white Warbler 1s.

Tanagers

mer Tanager *Piranga rubra*   L 19.5cm 7.7"

um ⇒
• Wings contrast at most very slightly with upperparts ⇔ Scarlet Tanager.
• Strong, long, pale bill ⇔ in Scarlet shorter and darker (in Scarlet 1w often paler).
• Eye-ring broken by diffuse dark lores ⇔ Scarlet.
• Long crown-feathers, often creating short crest.
♂ ⇒ • Completely red with slightly darker wings.
♂ ⇒ • Variable amount of red on head, upperparts and underparts (usually head and breast patchy red, rest of body yellow-green) ⇔ in Scarlet 1s ♂ completely red body as in ad ♂.
w ♂ • Mainly green-yellow with grey wash on upperparts and crown.
• Variable amount of reddish spots, sometimes none.
plum ⇒ • Uniform yellowish to pink underwing-cov ⇔ Scarlet.

let Tanager *Piranga olivacea*   L 17.5cm 6.9"

um
• Rather short dark bill.
• Complete eye-ring; lores uniformly pale (eye-ring not conspicuous in ad ♂ s).
• Underparts green-yellow, except ad ♂ s.
♂ s • Completely deep red except black wings and tail.
♂ w • Like ad ♀ but wings completely deep black.
w ⇒ • Dark wings contrast with uniform green-yellow upperparts ⇔ Summer Tanager.
• Very distinct moult-limit in cov and/or scaps with brown-grey juv-type and deep black ad-type feathers.
plum ⇒ • Whitish underwing-cov ⇔ Summer.

Bibliography

For this book numerous photographs and the following journals and books have been consulted.

Journals
British Birds
Alula
Dutch Birding
Birding World
Limicola

Books
Alström, P. And Mild, K. 2003. *Pipits & Wagtails of Europe, Asia and North America*. Christopher Helm, London.
Baker, K. 1993. *Identification Guide to European Non-Passerines*. BTO, Thetford.
van den Berg, A.B. and Bosman, C.A.W. 1999, 2001. *Rare Birds of the Netherlands*. Pica Press, Sussex.
van den Berg, A.B., van Loon, A.J., and Oreel, G.J (*Dutch Birding*). 1990. *Vogels nieuw in Nederland*. Zomer and Keuning, Ede.
Blomdahl, A., Breife, B. and Holmström, N. 2003. *Flight Identification of European Seabirds*. Christopher Helm, London.
Byers, C., Olsson, U. and Curson, J. 1995. *Buntings and Sparrows: A Guide to the Buntings and North American Sparrows*. Pica Press, Sussex.
Clark, W.S. 1999. *A Field Guide to the Raptors or Europe, the Middle East, and North America*. Oxford University Press, Oxford.
Clark, W.S. and Yosef, R. 1998. *Raptor In-hand Identification Guide*. International Birding Centre, Eilat.
Cleere, N. and Nurney, D. 1998. *Nightjars: A Guide to Nightjars and Related Nightbirds*. Pica Press, Sussex.
Clement, P., Harris, A. and Davis, J. 1993. *Finches and Sparrows: An Identification Guide*. Christopher Helm, London.
Clement, P. and Hathway, R. 2000. *Thrushes*. Christopher Helm, London.
Cramp, S. and Simmons, K.E.L. (eds). 1977. *The Birds of the Western Palearctic*. Volume 1. Oxford University Press, Oxford.
Cramp, S. and Simmons, K.E.L. (eds). 1980. *The Birds of the Western Palearctic*. Volume 2. Oxford University Press, Oxford.
Cramp, S. and Simmons, K.E.L. (eds). 1983. *The Birds of the Western Palearctic*. Volume 3. Oxford University Press, Oxford.
Cramp, S (ed). 1985. *The Birds of the Western Palearctic*. Volume 4. Oxford University Press, Oxford.
Cramp, S (ed). 1988. *The Birds of the Western Palearctic*. Volume 5. Oxford University Press, Oxford.
Cramp, S (ed). 1992. *The Birds of the Western Palearctic*. Volume 6. Oxford University Press, Oxford.
Cramp, S. and Perrins, C.M. (eds). 1993. *The Birds of the Western Palearctic*. Volume 7. Oxford University Press, Oxford.
Cramp, S. and Perrins, C.M. (eds). 1994. *The Birds of the Western Palearctic*. Volume 8. Oxford University Press, Oxford.
Cramp, S. and Perrins, C.M. (eds). 1994. *The Birds of the Western Palearctic*. Volume 9. Oxford University Press, Oxford.
Dunn, J. and Garrett, K. 1997. *Warblers. A Field Guide to Warblers of North America*. Houghton Mifflin Harcourt, Boston.
Enticott, J. and Tipling, D. 1997. *Photographic Handbook of the Seabirds of the World*. New Holland Publishers, London.
Ferguson-Lees, J. and Christie, D.A. 2001. *Raptors of the World*. Christopher Helm, London.
Forsman, D. 1993. *Roofvogels van Noordwest-Europa*. GMB Uitgeverij, Haarlem.
Forsman, D. 1999. *The Raptors of Europe and the Middle East: A Handbook of Field Identification*. T and A.D. Poyser, London.
Grant, P.J. 1986. *Gulls: A Guide to Identification*. Second edition. T and A.D. Poyser, London.
Grimmett, R., Inskipp, C. and Inskipp, T. 1999. *Pocket Guide to the Birds of the Indian Subcontinent*. Christopher H London.
Harris, A., Tucker, L. and Vinicombe, K. 1989. *The Macmillan Field Guide to Bird Identification*. Macmilla London.
Harris, A., Shirihai, H. and Christie, D.A. 1996. *The Macmillan Birder's Guide to European and Middle Eas Birds*. Macmillan, London.
Hayman, P., Marchant, J. and Prater, T. 1986. *Shorebird An Identification Guide to the Waders of the World*. Christopher Helm, London.
Hollom, P.A.D., Porter, R.F., Christensen, S. and Willis, I. 1988. *Birds of the Middle East and North Africa*. T and A.D. Poyser, London.
Jonsson, L. 1992. *Birds of Europe with North Africa and Middle East*. Christopher Helm, London.
Kanouchi, T., Abe, N. and Ueda, H. 1998. *Wild Birds of Japan*. Yama-Kei Publishers, Tokyo.
Lefranc, N. and Worfolk, T. 1997. *Shrikes: A Guide to th Shrikes of the World*. Pica Press, Sussex.
Lewington, I., Alström, P. and Colston, P. 1991. *A Field Guide to the Rare Birds of Britain and Europe*. HarperCollins, London.
MacKinnon, J. and Phillipps, K. 2000. *A Field Guide to Birds of China*. Oxford University Press, Oxford.
Mitchell, D. and Young, S. 1997. *Photographic Handboc the Rare Birds or Britain and Europe*. New Holland Publishers, London.
National Geographic Society. 1999. *Field Guide to the E of North America*. Third edition. National Geographic Society, Washington D.C.
Olsen, K.M. 1992. *Jagers. De jagers van het Noordelijk Halfrond*. GMB Uitgeverij, Haarlem.
Olsen, K.M. and Larsson, H. 1994. *Terns of Europe and North America*. Christopher Helm, London.
Olsen, K.M. and Larsson, H. 1997. *Skuas and Jaegers: Guide to the Skuas and Jaegers of the World*. Pica Press, London.
Paulson, D. 2005. *Shorebirds of North America: The Photographic Guide*. Princeton University Press, Prince
Porter, R.F., Christensen, S. and Schiermacker-Hansen, 1996. *Field Guide to the Birds of the Middle East*. T a A.D. Poyser, London.
Porter, R.F., Christensen, S., Nielsen, B.P. and Willis, I. 1 *Vliegbeelden van Europese roofvogels*. Sovon, Baarn.
Prater, A.J., Marchant, J.H. and Vuorinen, J. 1977. *Guide Identification and Ageing of Holarctic Waders*. BTO, Tri
Rasmussen, P.C. and Anderton, J.C. 2005. *Birds of Sou Asia. The Ripley Guide*. Volumes 1 and 2. Lynx Edicio Barcelona.
Robson, C. 2009. *A Field Guide to the Birds of South-E Asia*. New Holland Publishers, London.
Rosair, D. and Cottridge, D. 1995. *Photographic Guide the Waders of the World*. Hamlyn, London.
Shirihai, H. 1996. *The Birds or Israel*. T and A.D. Poyse London.
Shirihai, H., Gargallo, G., Helbig, A.J., Harris, A. and Cottridge, D. 2001. *Sylvia Warblers. Identification, Taxonomy and Phylogeny of the Genus Sylvia*. Christopher Helm, London.
Shirihai, H. and Jarrett, B. 2002. *A Complete Guide to Antarctic Wildlife*. Alula Press, Degerby.
Sibley, D. 2000. *The North American Bird Guide*. Chanticleer Press, New York.
Snow, D.W. and Perrins, C.M. (eds). 1998. *The Birds o Western Palearctic. Concise Edition*. Volumes 1 and 2 Oxford University Press, Oxford.
Stevenson, T. and Fanshawe, J. 2002. *Field Guide to t Birds of East Africa*. T and A.D. Poyser, London.
Svensson, L. 1992. *Identification Guide to European Passerines*. Fourth edition. BTO, Tring.
Svensson, L., Grant, P.J., Mullarney, K. and Zetterströn 1999. *Collins Bird Guide*. HarperCollins, London.
Vinicombe, K. and Cottridge, D.M. 1996. *Rare Birds in E and Ireland: A Photographic Record*. HarperCollins, Lo

Other Birding Books by New Holland

Index

Roman = English name, *Italic = Latin name.*

A

Accentor, Alpine 250
Accentor, Black-throated 250
Accentor, Radde's 249
Accentor, Siberian 249
Accipiter badius 68
Accipiter brevipes 68
Accipiter gentilis 67
Accipiter gentilis atricapillus 68
Accipiter gentilis buteoides 68
Accipiter nisus 68
Acridotheres tristis 226
Acrocephalus agricola 218
Acrocephalus arundinaceus 220
Acrocephalus arundinaceus zarudnyi 220
Acrocephalus brevipennis 221
Acrocephalus dumetorum 218
Acrocephalus griseldis 221
Acrocephalus melanopogon 220
Acrocephalus melanopogon mimicus 220
Acrocephalus orientalis 220
Acrocephalus paludicola 220
Acrocephalus palustris 218
Acrocephalus rufescens 221
Acrocephalus schoenobaenus 219
Acrocephalus scirpaceus 219
Acrocephalus scirpaceus fuscus 219
Acrocephalus stentoreus 221
Acrocephalus stentoreus brunnescens 221
Actitis hypoleucos 114
Actitis macularius 114
Aegithalos caudatus 197
Aegithalos caudatus europaeus 197
Aegithalos caudatus irbii 197
Aegithalos caudatus rosaceus 197
Aegithalos caudatus siculus 197
Aegithalos caudatus tephronotus 197
Aegolius funereus 164
Aegypius monachus 63
Aenigmatolimnas marginalis 84
Aethia cristatella 154
Aethia psittacula 154
Agropsar sturninus 225
Aix galericulata 20
Aix sponsa 20
Alaemon alaudipes 189
Alauda arvensis 192
Alauda gulgula 192
Alauda razae 193
Albatross, Atlantic Yellow-nosed 36
Albatross, Black-browed 36
Albatross, Campbell Islands 36
Albatross, Grey-headed 36
Albatross, Indian Yellow-nosed 36
Albatross, Shy 37
Albatross, Wandering 37
Alca torda 153
Alcedo atthis 168
Alectoris barbara 32
Alectoris chukar 32
Alectoris graeca 32
Alectoris graeca whitakeri 32
Alectoris rufa 32
Alle alle 154
Alopochen aegyptiaca 16
Amandava amandava 250
Ammomanes cinctura 188
Ammomanes deserti 188
Ammomanes deserti algeriensis 188
Ammomanes deserti annae 189
Ammomanes deserti isabellinus 189
Ammomanes deserti payni 188
Ammoperdix griseogularis 32

Ammoperdix heyi 33
Anas acuta 29
Anas americana 26
Anas capensis 27
Anas carolinensis 28
Anas clypeata 30
Anas crecca 28
Anas cyanoptera 30
Anas discors 30
Anas erythrorhyncha 29
Anas falcata 27
Anas formosa 27
Anas penelope 26
Anas platyrhynchos 28
Anas querquedula 29
Anas rhynchotis 30
Anas rubripes 29
Anas sibilatrix 26
Anas strepera 27
Anhinga 48
Anhinga anhinga 48
Anhinga melanogaster 48
Anhinga rufa 48
Anous minutus 143
Anous stolidus 143
Anser albifrons 12
Anser albifrons flavirostris 12
Anser albifrons frontalis 12
Anser albifrons gambeli 12
Anser anser 13
Anser anser rubrirostris 13
Anser brachyrhynchus 12
Anser caerulescens 10
Anser caerulescens atlanticus 11
Anser erythropus 13
Anser fabalis 11
Anser fabalis johanseni 11
Anser fabalis middendorffii 12
Anser rossii 11
Anser serrirostris 12
Anteater-chat, Northern 240
Anthreptes metallicus 227
Anthreptes platurus 227
Anthus berthelotii 259
Anthus campestris 259
Anthus cervinus 261
Anthus godlewskii 258
Anthus gustavi 260
Anthus hodgsoni 259
Anthus petrosus 262
Anthus petrosus littoralis 262
Anthus pratensis 260
Anthus pratensis whistleri 260
Anthus richardi 258
Anthus rubescens 262
Anthus rubescens japonicus 262
Anthus similis 259
Anthus spinoletta 261
Anthus spinoletta blakistoni 261
Anthus spinoletta coutelli 261
Anthus trivialis 260
Apus affinis 168
Apus alexandri 166
Apus apus 166
Apus apus pekinensis 166
Apus caffer 167
Apus melba 166
Apus pacificus 167
Apus pallidus 167
Apus pallidus brehmorum 167
Apus pallidus illyricus 167
Apus unicolor 166
Aquila adalberti 76
Aquila chrysaetos 73
Aquila chrysaetos homeyeri 73
Aquila clanga 72
Aquila clanga 'fulvescens' 72
Aquila fasciata 74

Aquila heliaca 75
Aquila nipalensis 74
Aquila pennata 73
Aquila pomarina 72
Aquila rapax 75
Aquila verreauxii 74
Ardea bournei 54
Ardea cinerea 54
Ardea cinerea monicae 54
Ardea goliath 55
Ardea herodias 54
Ardea melanocephala 54
Ardea purpurea 54
Ardeola bacchus 51
Ardeola grayii 51
Ardeola ralloides 51
Ardeotis arabs 87
Arenaria interpres 118
Arenaria interpres morinella 118
Asio capensis 164
Asio flammeus 164
Asio otus 164
Athene noctua 163
Athene noctua glaux 163
Athene noctua indigena 163
Athene noctua lilith 163
Athene noctua saharae 163
Auk, Little 154
Auklet, Crested 154
Auklet, Parakeet 154
Avadavat, Red 250
Avocet, Pied 88
Aythya affinis 19
Aythya americana 17
Aythya collaris 18
Aythya ferina 17
Aythya fuligula 19
Aythya marila 19
Aythya nyroca 18
Aythya valisineria 17

B

Babbler, Afghan 197
Babbler, Arabian 197
Babbler, Fulvous 198
Babbler, Iraq 197
Bartramia longicauda 113
Bateleur 63
Bee-eater, Blue-cheeked 169
Bee-eater, European 169
Bee-eater, Little Green 168
Bittern, American 50
Bittern, Dwarf 50
Bittern, Eurasian 49
Bittern, Least 50
Bittern, Little 50
Bittern, Schrenck's 50
Blackbird 229
Blackbird, Yellow-headed 285
Blackcap 212
Blackstart 238
Bluetail, Red-flanked 236
Bluethroat 235
Bobolink 285
Bombycilla cedrorum 222
Bombycilla garrulus 222
Bombycilla japonica 222
Booby, Brown 45
Booby, Masked 45
Booby, Red-footed 45
Botaurus lentiginosus 50
Botaurus stellaris 49
Brachyramphus perdix 154
Brambling 264
Brant, Black 15
Branta bernicla 15
Branta canadensis 13
Branta canadensis fulva 14

ta canadensis interior 13
ta canadensis maxima 14
ta canadensis moffitti 14
ta canadensis occidentalis 14
ta canadensis parvipes 14
ta hrota 15
a hutchinsii 14
a hutchinsii hutchinsii 14
a hutchinsii leucopareia 15
a hutchinsii minima 14
a hutchinsii taverneri 14
a leucopsis 15
a nigricans 15
a ruficollis 15
ascalaphus 162
ascalaphus desertorum 162
bubo 162
scandiaca 161
virginianus 162
zeylonensis 162
lcus coromandus 52
lcus ibis 52
netes githagineus 271
netes mongolicus 270
phala albeola 24
ohala clangula 24
ohala islandica 24
ehead 24
l, Common 196
l, Red-vented 196
l, White-eared 196
l, White-spectacled 196
nch, Azores 272
nch, Eurasian 272
nch, Northern 272
eria bulwerii 39
eria fallax 39
ng, Black-faced 276
ng, Black-headed 284
ng, Chestnut 282
ng, Chestnut-eared 281
ng, Cinereous 279
ng, Cirl 278
ng, Common Reed 282
ng, Corn 284
ng, Cretzschmar's 280
ng, Godlewski's 278
ng, Grey-necked 280
ng, House 279
ng, Indigo 274
ng, Lapland 273
ng, Little 281
ng, Meadow 278
ng, Ortolan 279
ng, Pallas's Reed 283
ng, Pine 277
ng, Red-headed 283
ng, Rock 278
ng, Rustic 281
ng, Snow 273
ng, Striolated 279
ng, Yellow-breasted 282
ng, Yellow-browed 281
nus oedicnemus 89
nus senegalensis 89
lark, Kordofan 187
rd, Arabian 87
rd, Denham's 87
rd, Great 87
rd, Houbara 87
rd, Little 87
rd, Macqueen's 87
d, Nubian 87
bannermani 70
buteo 69
buteo insularum 70
buteo menetriesi 70
buteo rothschildi 70

Buteo buteo vulpinus 70
Buteo lagopus 71
Buteo lagopus sanctijohannis 72
Buteo rufinus 70
Buteo rufinus cirtensis 71
Buteo swainsoni 69
Butorides striata 51
Butorides virescens 51
Buttonquail, Small 88
Buzzard, Cape Verde 70
Buzzard, Common 69
Buzzard, Long-legged 70
Buzzard, Rough-legged 71
Buzzard, Steppe 70

C
Calandrella acutirostris 190
Calandrella brachydactyla 190
Calandrella brachydactyla longipennis 190
Calandrella cheleensis 191
Calandrella cheleensis niethammeri 191
Calandrella cheleensis persica 191
Calandrella rufescens 191
Calcarius lapponicus 273
Calcarius lapponicus subcalcaratus 274
Calidris acuminata 103
Calidris alba 98
Calidris alpina arctica 105
Calidris alpina hudsonia 105
Calidris alpina sakhalina 105
Calidris alpina schinzii 105
Calidris bairdii 102
Calidris canutus 98
Calidris canutus islandica 98
Calidris ferruginea 103
Calidris fuscicollis 102
Calidris himantopus 104
Calidris maritima 104
Calidris mauri 99
Calidris melanotos 103
Calidris minuta 100
Calidris minutilla 101
Calidris pusilla 99
Calidris ruficollis 100
Calidris subminuta 101
Calidris temminckii 101
Calidris tenuirostris 98
Calonectris borealis 40
Calonectris diomedea 40
Calonectris edwardsii 40
Calonectris leucomelas 40
Canary, Atlantic 265
Canvasback 17
Capercaillie 32
Caprimulgus aegyptius 165
Caprimulgus aegyptius saharae 165
Caprimulgus europeus 165
Caprimulgus nubicus 164
Caprimulgus ruficollis 165
Caprimulgus ruficollis desertorum 165
Carduelis cabaret 267
Carduelis cannabina 266
Carduelis carduelis 266
Carduelis carduelis britannica 266
Carduelis chloris 265
Carduelis citrinella 265
Carduelis corsicanus 265
Carduelis flammea 267
Carduelis flammea islandica 268
Carduelis flammea rostrata 267
Carduelis flavirostris 266
Carduelis flavirostris brevirostris 267
Carduelis flavirostris pipilans 267
Carduelis hornemanni 268
Carduelis hornemanni exilipes 268
Carduelis sinica 266
Carduelis spinus 266
Carpodacus erythrinus 271

Carpodacus mexicanus 271
Carpodacus roseus 271
Carpodacus rubicilla 271
Carpodacus synoicus 271
Carpospiza brachydactyla 252
Casmerodius albus 53
Casmerodius albus egretta 53
Casmerodius albus modesta 53
Catbird, Grey 225
Catharus bicknelli 229
Catharus fuscescens 229
Catharus guttatus 228
Catharus minimus 229
Catharus ustulatus 228
Cecropis daurica 195
Cecropis daurica daurica 196
Cecropis daurica rufula 195
Centropus senegalensis 160
Cepphus grylle 154
Cepphus grylle mandtii 154
Cercomela melanura 238
Cercotrichas galactotes 233
Cercotrichas galactotes familiaris 233
Cercotrichas galactotes syriacus 233
Cercotrichas podobe 233
Certhia brachydactyla 224
Certhia familiaris 224
Certhia familiaris britannica 224
Certhia familiaris corsa 224
Certhia familiaris macrodactyla 224
Ceryle alcyon 168
Ceryle rudis 168
Cettia cetti 196
Cettia cetti albiventris 196
Cettia cetti orientalis 197
Chaetura pelagica 166
Chaffinch, Atlas 263
Chaffinch, Blue 264
Chaffinch, Common 263
Chaffinch, Tunisian 263
Chanting-goshawk, Dark 67
Charadrius alexandrinus 92
Charadrius asiaticus 94
Charadrius dubius 90
Charadrius hiaticula 91
Charadrius hiaticula tundrae 91
Charadrius leschenaultii 93
Charadrius leschenaultii columbinus 94
Charadrius leschenaultii crassirostris 94
Charadrius leschenaultii leschenaultii 94
Charadrius mongolus 92
Charadrius mongolus atrifrons 93
Charadrius mongolus pamirensis 93
Charadrius mongolus schaeferi 93
Charadrius mongolus stegmanni 93
Charadrius morinellus 94
Charadrius pecuarius 92
Charadrius semipalmatus 91
Charadrius tricollaris 92
Charadrius veredus 94
Charadrius vociferus 91
Chersophilus duponti 189
Chersophilus duponti margaritae 189
Chiffchaff, Canary Islands 203
Chiffchaff, Caucasian 203
Chiffchaff, Common 202
Chiffchaff, Iberian 203
Chiffchaff, Siberian 202
Chlamydotis macqueenii 87
Chlamydotis undulata 87
Chlamydotis undulata fuerteventurae 87
Chlidonias hybrida 146
Chlidonias leucopterus 147
Chlidonias niger 146
Chlidonias surinamensis 147
Chondestes grammacus 275
Chordeiles minor 165
Chough, Alpine 181

Index

Chough, Red-billed 181
Choicocephalus brunnicephalus 125
Chroicocephalus cirrocephalus 125
Chroicocephalus genei 124
Chroicocephalus philadelphia 124
Chroicocephalus ridibundus 124
Chrysococcyx caprius 159
Chrysococcyx klaas 159
Chrysolophus amherstiae 34
Chrysolophus pictus 34
Ciconia abdimii 55
Ciconia ciconia 55
Ciconia nigra 55
Cinclus cinclus 227
Cinclus cinclus aquaticus 227
Cinclus cinclus gularis 227
Cinnyricinclus leucogaster 225
Cinnyris asiaticus 227
Cinnyris habessinicus 227
Circaetus gallicus 63
Circus aeruginosus 64
Circus cyaneus 64
Circus cyaneus hudsonius 65
Circus macrourus 65
Circus pygargus 66
Circus spilonotus 64
Cisticola juncidis 221
Cisticola, Zitting 221
Clamator glandarius 159
Clamator jacobinus 159
Clangula hyemalis 23
Coccothraustes coccothraustes 272
Coccyzus americanus 160
Coccyzus erythrophthalmus 160
Colaptes auratus 170
Colius macrourus 158
Columba bollii 157
Columba eversmanni 156
Columba junoniae 157
Columba livia 156
Columba oenas 156
Columba palumbus 156
Columba trocaz 157
Coot, American 85
Coot, Common 85
Coot, Red-knobbed 86
Coracias abyssinicus 169
Coracias benghalensis 169
Coracias garrulus 169
Cormorant, Double-crested 47
Cormorant, Great 46
Cormorant, Long-tailed 48
Cormorant, Pygmy 47
Cormorant, Socotra 47
Corncrake 84
Corvus corax 183
Corvus corax tingitanus 183
Corvus cornix 182
Corvus cornix pallescens 182
Corvus cornix sharpii 182
Corvus corone 182
Corvus dauuricus 182
Corvus frugilegus 182
Corvus monedula 181
Corvus monedula soemmerringii 182
Corvus monedula spermologus 181
Corvus rhipidurus 183
Corvus ruficollis 183
Corvus splendens 182
Coturnix coturnix 33
Coturnix japonica 33
Coucal, Senegal 160
Courser, Cream-coloured 89
Courser, Temminck's 89
Cowbird, Brown-headed 285
Crab-plover 88
Crake, African 84
Crake, Baillon's 84

Crake, Little 83
Crake, Spotted 83
Crake, Striped 84
Crane, Common 86
Crane, Demoiselle 86
Crane, Sandhill 86
Crane, Siberian 86
Crecopsis egregia 84
Crex crex 84
Crossbill, Common 269
Crossbill, Parrot 269
Crossbill, Scottish 269
Crossbill, Two-barred 269
Crossbill, White-winged 269
Crow, Carrion 182
Crow, Hooded 182
Crow, House 182
Crow, Pied *Corvus albus* 182
Cuckoo, Black-billed 160
Cuckoo, Common 159
Cuckoo, Didric 159
Cuckoo, Great Spotted 159
Cuckoo, Jacobin 159
Cuckoo, Klaas's 159
Cuckoo, Oriental 159
Cuckoo, Yellow-billed 160
Cuculus canorus 159
Cuculus optatus 159
Curlew, Eskimo 112
Curlew, Eurasian 113
Curlew, Little 112
Curlew, Slender-billed 113
Cursorius cursor 89
Cursorius temminckii 89
Cyanistes caeruleus 185
Cyanistes cyanus 185
Cyanistes flavipectus 185
Cyanistes hedwigii 185
Cyanistes ombriosus 185
Cyanistes palmensis 185
Cyanistes teneriffae 184
Cyanistes ultramarinus 185
Cyanopica cooki 181
Cyanopica cyanus 181
Cygnus bewickii 10
Cygnus columbianus 10
Cygnus cygnus 10
Cygnus olor 10
Cypsiurus parvus 168

D
Daption capense 38
Darter, African 48
Darter, Oriental 48
Delichon urbicum 195
Dendrocopos leucotos 172
Dendrocopos leucotos lilfordi 172
Dendrocopos major 171
Dendrocopos major numidus 171
Dendrocopos medius 172
Dendrocopos minor 172
Dendrocopos syriacus 171
Dendrocygna bicolor 10
Dendrocygna javanica 10
Dendrocygna viduata 10
Dendroica caerulescens 287
Dendroica castanea 289
Dendroica cerulea 289
Dendroica coronata 288
Dendroica coronata auduboni 288
Dendroica fusca 287
Dendroica magnolia 288
Dendroica palmarum 289
Dendroica palmarum hypochrysea 289
Dendroica pensylvanica 287
Dendroica petechia 287
Dendroica striata 289
Dendroica tigrina 288

Dendroica virens 287
Dendronanthus indicus 258
Dickcissel 274
Diomedea exulans 37
Dipper, Black-bellied 227
Dipper, White-throated 227
Diver, Black-throated 35
Diver, Great Northern 35
Diver, Pacific 35
Diver, Red-throated 34
Diver, White-billed 36
Dolichonyx oryzivorus 285
Dotterel, Eurasian 94
Dove, African Collared 157
Dove, Collared 157
Dove, Laughing 158
Dove, Mourning 158
Dove, Namaqua 158
Dove, Oriental Turtle 157
Dove, Rock 156
Dove, Stock 156
Dove, Turtle 157
Dove, Yellow-eyed Stock 156
Dowitcher, Asiatic 110
Dowitcher, Long-billed 109
Dowitcher, Short-billed 109
Dromas ardeola 88
Dryocopus martius 171
Duck, American Black 29
Duck, Falcated 27
Duck, Ferruginous 18
Duck, Fulvous Whistling 10
Duck, Harlequin 22
Duck, Lesser Whistling 10
Duck, Long-tailed 23
Duck, Mandarin 20
Duck, Marbled 30
Duck, Red-billed 29
Duck, Ring-necked 18
Duck, Ruddy 20
Duck, Tufted 19
Duck, White-faced Whistling 10
Duck, White-headed 20
Duck, Wood 20
Dumetella carolinensis 225
Dunlin *Calidris alpina* 104
Dunnock 249

E
Eagle, African Fish 61
Eagle, Bald 61
Eagle, Bonelli's 74
Eagle, Booted 73
Eagle, Eastern Imperial 75
Eagle, Golden 73
Eagle, Greater Spotted 72
Eagle, Lesser Spotted 72
Eagle, Pallas's Fish 61
Eagle, Short-toed 63
Eagle, Spanish Imperial 76
Eagle, Steppe 74
Eagle, Tawny 75
Eagle, Verreaux's 74
Eagle, White-tailed 61
Egret, American Great 53
Egret, Cattle 52
Egret, Eastern Cattle 52
Egret, Great White 53
Egret, Indian Reef 53
Egret, Intermediate 53
Egret, Little 53
Egret, Snowy 52
Egret, Western Reef 52
Egretta ardesiaca 52
Egretta caerulea 52
Egretta garzetta 53
Egretta gularis 52
Egretta gularis schistacea 53

etta intermedia 53
etta thula 52
etta tricolor 52
r, Common 20
r, Dresser's 21
r, King 21
r, Northern 20
r, Pacific 21
r, Spectacled 21
r, Steller's 22
oides forficatus 59
us caeruleus 59
eriza aureola 282
eriza bruniceps 283
eriza buchanani 280
eriza caesia 280
eriza calandra 284
eriza chrysophrys 281
eriza cia 278
eriza cineracea 279
eriza cineracea semenowi 279
eriza cioides 278
eriza cirlus 278
eriza citrinella 278
eriza fucata 281
eriza godlewskii 278
eriza hortulana 279
eriza leucocephalos 277
eriza melanocephala 284
eriza pallasi 283
eriza pusilla 281
eriza rustica 281
eriza rutila 282
eriza sahari 279
eriza schoeniclus 282
eriza schoeniclus pallidor 283
eriza schoeniclus passerina 283
eriza schoeniclus reiseri 283
eriza spodocephala 276
eriza spodocephala oligoxantha 276
eriza striolata 279
idonax alnorum 173
idonax minimus 173
donax traillii 173
idonax virescens 173
alauda dunni 188
alauda dunni eremodites 188
ophila alpestris 193
ophila alpestris altas 193
ophila alpestris flava 193
ophila alpestris penicillata 193
ophila bilopha 193
opterix nigriceps 187
opterix nigriceps albifrons 188
opterix nigriceps melanauchen 188
opterix nigriceps nigriceps 188
opterix signatus 187
acus rubecula 233
acus rubecula melophilus 234
acus superbus 234
da astrild 250
namys scolopaceus 160
stomus glaucurus 169

alexandri 77
amurensis 78
biarmicus 80
biarmicus erlangeri 80
biarmicus feldeggii 80
biarmicus tanypterus 81
cherrug 81
cherrug 'saceroides' 81
columbarius 78
columbarius aesalon 78
columbarius columbarius 78
columbarius pallidus 79
columbarius subaesalon 79

Falco concolor 80
Falco eleonorae 79
Falco madens 82
Falco naumanni 76
Falco neglectus 77
Falco pelegrinoides 82
Falco peregrinus 81
Falco peregrinus brookei 82
Falco peregrinus calidus 82
Falco peregrinus tundrinus 82
Falco rusticolus 81
Falco sparverius 77
Falco subbuteo 79
Falco tinnunculus 77
Falco vespertinus 77
Falcon, Amur 78
Falcon, Barbary 82
Falcon, Cape Verde 82
Falcon, Eleonora's 79
Falcon, Gyr 81
Falcon, Lanner 80
Falcon, Mediterranean Peregrine 82
Falcon, Peregrine 81
Falcon, Red-footed 77
Falcon, Saker 81
Falcon, Sooty 80
Falcon, Tundra Peregrine 82
Ficedula albicilla 247
Ficedula albicollis 248
Ficedula hypoleuca 248
Ficedula hypoleuca iberiae 249
Ficedula mugimaki 247
Ficedula parva 247
Ficedula semitorquata 248
Ficedula speculigera 249
Fieldfare 231
Finch, African Crimson-winged 270
Finch, Asian Crimson-winged 270
Finch, Citril 265
Finch, Corsican 265
Finch, Desert 270
Finch, House 271
Finch, Mongolian 270
Finch, Trumpeter 271
Firecrest 184
Firecrest, Madeira 184
Fiscal, Grey-backed 179
Flamingo, American 56
Flamingo, Chilean 57
Flamingo, Greater 56
Flamingo, Lesser 56
Flicker, Northern 170
Flycatcher, Acadian 173
Flycatcher, Alder 173
Flycatcher, Asian Brown 232
Flycatcher, Atlas 249
Flycatcher, Collared 248
Flycatcher, Dark-sided 232
Flycatcher, Fork-tailed 173
Flycatcher, Grey-streaked 233
Flycatcher, Iberian Pied 249
Flycatcher, Least 173
Flycatcher, Mugimaki 247
Flycatcher, Pied 248
Flycatcher, Red-breasted 247
Flycatcher, Semicollared 248
Flycatcher, Spotted 233
Flycatcher, Taiga 247
Flycatcher, Willow 173
Francolin, Black 33
Francolin, Double-spurred 33
Francolinus francolinus 33
Fratercula arctica 154
Fratercula cirrhata 155
Fregata aquila 49
Fregata ariel 49
Fregata magnificens 49
Fregata minor 49

Frigatebird, Ascension 49
Frigatebird, Great 49
Frigatebird, Lesser 49
Frigatebird, Magnificent 49
Fringilla coelebs 263
Fringilla coelebs africana 263
Fringilla coelebs maderensis 263
Fringilla coelebs moreletti 264
Fringilla coelebs ombriosa 263
Fringilla coelebs palmae 263
Fringilla coelebs spodiogenys 263
Fringilla coelebs tintillon 263
Fringilla montifringilla 264
Fringilla teydea 264
Fulica americana 85
Fulica atra 85
Fulica cristata 86
Fulmar 37
Fulmarus glacialis 37

G
Gadwall 27
Galerida cristata 191
Galerida macrorhyncha 191
Galerida macrorhyncha randonii 191
Galerida theklae 192
Galerida theklae carolinae 192
Galerida theklae ruficolor 192
Gallinago delicata 107
Gallinago gallinago 106
Gallinago media 107
Gallinago megala 108
Gallinago stenura 108
Gallinula angulata 84
Gallinula chloropus 84
Gallinule, Allen's 85
Gallinule, American Purple 85
Gannet, Cape 46
Gannet, Northern 46
Garganey 29
Garrulus glandarius 180
Garrulus glandarius atricapillus 180
Garrulus glandarius cervicalis 180
Gavia adamsii 36
Gavia arctica 35
Gavia immer 35
Gavia pacifica 35
Gavia stellata 34
Gelochelidon nilotica 145
Geokichla sibirica 228
Geothlypis trichas 290
Geronticus eremita 56
Glareola maldivarum 90
Glareola nordmanni 90
Glareola pratincola 89
Glaucidium passerinum 162
Godwit, Bar-tailed 111
Godwit, Black-tailed 111
Godwit, Hudsonian 111
Godwit, Icelandic Black-tailed 111
Goldcrest 183
Goldeneye, Barrow's 24
Goldeneye, Common 24
Goldfinch, European 266
Goosander 25
Goose, Aleutian Cackling 15
Goose, Atlantic Canada 13
Goose, Barnacle 15
Goose, Cackling 14
Goose, Canada 13
Goose, Dark Cackling 14
Goose, Dark-bellied Brent 15
Goose, Dusky Canada 14
Goose, Egyptian 16
Goose, Eurasian White-fronted 12
Goose, Greater Snow 11
Goose, Greenland White-fronted 12
Goose, 'Grey-bellied' Brent 15

Index

Goose, Greylag 13
Goose, Hutchins's Cackling 14
Goose, Intermediate Canada 14
Goose, Lesser Snow 11
Goose, Lesser White-fronted 13
Goose, Pale-bellied Brent 15
Goose, Pink-footed 12
Goose, Red-breasted 15
Goose, Ross's 11
Goose, Snow 10
Goose, Spur-winged 16
Goose, Taiga Bean 11
Goose, Taverner's Cackling 14
Goose, Todd's Canada 13
Goose, Tundra Bean 12
Goose, White-fronted 12
Goshawk, Gabar 67
Goshawk, Northern 67
Grackle, Common 285
Grebe, Black-necked 58
Grebe, Great Crested 57
Grebe, Little 57
Grebe, Pied-billed 57
Grebe, Red-necked 57
Grebe, Slavonian 58
Greenfinch, European 265
Greenfinch, Grey-capped 266
Greenshank 116
Grosbeak, Evening 273
Grosbeak, Pine 272
Grosbeak, Rose-breasted 274
Grouse, Black 31
Grouse, Caucasian Black 31
Grouse, Hazel 31
Grouse, Red 31
Grouse, Willow 31
Grus canadensis 86
Grus grus 86
Grus leucogeranus 86
Grus virgo 86
Guillemot, Black 154
Guillemot, Brünnich's 153
Guillemot, Common 153
Guineafowl, Helmeted 34
Gull, American Herring 138
Gull, Armenian 137
Gull, Audouin's 127
Gull, Baltic 133
Gull, Baraba 138
Gull, Black-headed 124
Gull, Bonaparte's 124
Gull, Brown-headed 125
Gull, Cape 143
Gull, Caspian 137
Gull, Common 129
Gull, Franklin's 126
Gull, Glaucous 142
Gull, Glaucous-winged 139
Gull, Great Black-backed 143
Gull, Great Black-headed 128
Gull, Grey-headed 125
Gull, Herring 134
Gull, Heuglin's 133
Gull, Iceland 141
Gull, Ivory 123
Gull, Kamtchatka 130
Gull, Kelp 143
Gull, Kumlien's 141
Gull, Laughing 126
Gull, Lesser Black-backed 132
Gull, Little 125
Gull, Mediterranean 127
Gull, 'Nelson's' 140, 142
Gull, Pallas's 128
Gull, Relict 127
Gull, Ring-billed 130
Gull, Ross's 125
Gull, Sabine's 123

Gull, Short-billed 129
Gull, Slaty-backed 142
Gull, Slender-billed 124
Gull, Sooty 128
Gull, Thayer's 140
Gull, White-eyed 129
Gull, Yellow-legged 135
Gymnoris xanthocollis 252
Gypaetus barbatus 62
Gyps africanus 63
Gyps fulvus 62
Gyps rueppellii 62

H
Haematopus ostralegus 88
Halcyon leucocephala 168
Halcyon smyrnensis 168
Haliaeetus albicilla 61
Haliaeetus leucocephalus 61
Haliaeetus leucoryphus 61
Haliaeetus vocifer 61
Harrier, Eastern Marsh 64
Harrier, Hen 64
Harrier, Montagu's 66
Harrier, Northern 65
Harrier, Pallid 65
Harrier, Western Marsh 64
Hawfinch 272
Hawk, Rough-legged 72
Hawk, Swainson's 69
Heron, Black 52
Heron, Black-headed 54
Heron, Bourne's 54
Heron, Chinese Pond 51
Heron, Goliath 55
Heron, Great Blue 54
Heron, Green 51
Heron, Grey 54
Heron, Indian Pond 51
Heron, Little Blue 52
Heron, Night 50
Heron, Purple 54
Heron, Squacco 51
Heron, Striated 51
Heron, Tricolored 52
Hesperiphona vespertina 273
Himantopus himantopus 88
Himantopus mexicanus 88
Hippolais icterina 215
Hippolais languida 214
Hippolais olivetorum 215
Hippolais polyglotta 215
Hirundapus caudacutus 166
Hirundo aethiopica 195
Hirundo rustica 195
Hirundo rustica erythrogaster 195
Hirundo rustica savignii 195
Hirundo rustica transitiva 195
Hirundo smithii 195
Histrionicus histrionicus 22
Hobby 79
Honey-buzzard, European 58
Honey-buzzard, Oriental 58
Hoopoe, Eurasian 169
Hydrobates melitensis 44
Hydrobates pelagicus 44
Hydrocoloeus minutus 125
Hydrocoloeus rosea 125
Hydroprogne caspia 146
Hylocichla mustelina 228
Hypocolius ampelinus 222
Hypocolius, Grey 222

I
Ibis, African Sacred 56
Ibis, Glossy 55
Ibis, Northern Bald 56
Ibis, White-faced 56

Icterus galbula 285
Iduna aedon 217
Iduna caligata 216
Iduna opaca 216
Iduna pallida 215
Iduna pallida elaeica 216
Iduna pallida reiseri 216
Iduna rama 217
Irania gutturalis 236
Ixobrychus eurhythmus 50
Ixobrychus exilis 50
Ixobrychus minutus 50
Ixobrychus sturmii 50
Ixoreus naevius 228

J
Jackdaw, Daurian 182
Jackdaw, Western 181
Jay, Eurasian 180
Jay, Siberian 180
Junco hyemalis 276
Junco, Dark-eyed 276
Jynx torquilla 170

K
Kestrel, Alexander's 77
Kestrel, American 77
Kestrel, Common 77
Kestrel, Lesser 76
Kestrel, Neglected 77
Killdeer 91
Kingfisher, Belted 168
Kingfisher, Common 168
Kingfisher, Grey-headed 168
Kingfisher, Pied 168
Kingfisher, White-throated 168
Kinglet, Azores 183
Kinglet, Canary Islands 184
Kinglet, Ruby-crowned 183
Kite, Black 59
Kite, Black-eared 60
Kite, Black-winged 59
Kite, Cape Verde 60
Kite, Red 60
Kite, Swallow-tailed 59
Kite, Yellow-billed 60
Kittiwake 123
Knot, Great 98
Knot, Red 98
Koel, Asian 160

L
Lagopus lagopus 31
Lagopus muta 31
Lagopus muta millaisi 31
Lagopus scoticus 31
Lammergeier 62
Lanius collurio 177
Lanius collurio 'kobylini' 177
Lanius cristatus 174
Lanius excubitor 177
Lanius excubitor homeyeri 178
Lanius excubitor sibericus 178
Lanius excubitoroides 179
Lanius isabellinus 176
Lanius isabellinus arenarius 176
Lanius meridionalis 178
Lanius meridionalis algeriensis 179
Lanius meridionalis aucheri 179
Lanius meridionalis elegans 178
Lanius meridionalis koenigi 178
Lanius minor 177
Lanius nubicus 180
Lanius pallidirostris 179
Lanius phoenicuroides 175
Lanius phoenicuroides 'karelini' 176
Lanius schach 177
Lanius senator 179

us senator badius 180
us senator niloticus 180
us senator rutilans 180
ving, Black-headed 97
ving, Northern 97
ving, Red-wattled 97
ving, Sociable 97
ving, Spur-winged 96
ving, White-tailed 97
American Horned 193
Asian Short-toed 191
Atlas Horned 193
Bar-tailed 188
Bimaculated 189
Black 190
Calandra 189
Caucasian Horned 193
Crested 191
Desert 188
Dunn's 188
Dupont's 189
Greater Short-toed 190
Hoopoe 189
Horned 193
Hume's Short-toed 190
Lesser Short-toed 191
Magreb 191
Mongolian 190
Raso 193
Shore 193
Temminck's 193
Thekla 192
Thick-billed 189
White-winged 190
s argentatus 134
s argentatus 'omissus' 135
s armenicus 137
atricilla 126
audouinii 127
cachinnans 137
cachinnans barabensis 138
canus 129
canus brachyrhynchos 129
canus heinei 130
canus kamtschatschensis 130
delawarensis 130
dominicanus 143
dominicanus vetula 143
fuscus 132
fuscus graellsii 132
fuscus intermedius 132
glaucescens 139
glaucoides 141
glaucoides kumlieni 141
hemprichii 128
heuglini 133
heuglini 'taimyrensis' 134
hyperboreus 142
ichthyaetus 128
leucophthalmus 129
marinus 143
melanocephalus 127
michahellis 135
michahellis atlantis 136
pipixcan 126
relictus 127
schistisagus 142
smithsonianus 138
thayeri 140
otilos crumeniferus 55
la falcinellus 105
la falcinellus sibirica 105
dromus griseus 109
dromus griseus caurinus 109
dromus griseus hendersoni 109
dromus scolopaceus 109
dromus semipalmatus 110
a haemastica 111

Limosa lapponica 111
Limosa limosa 111
Limosa limosa islandica 111
Linnet 266
Locustella certhiola 212
Locustella certhiola centralasiae 212
Locustella certhiola rubescens 212
Locustella fasciolata 214
Locustella fluviatilis 213
Locustella lanceolata 213
Locustella luscinioides 214
Locustella luscinioides fusca 214
Locustella naevia 213
Locustella naevia straminea 213
Lonchura cantans 250
Lonchura malabarica 250
Lophodytes cucullatus 25
Lophophanes cristatus 185
Loxia curvirostra 269
Loxia leucoptera 269
Loxia pytyopsittacus 269
Loxia scotica 269
Lullula arborea 192
Luscinia calliope 235
Luscinia cyane 236
Luscinia luscinia 234
Luscinia megarhynchos 234
Luscinia megarhynchos africana 234
Luscinia megarhynchos golzii 234
Luscinia sibilans 234
Luscinia svecica 235
Luscinia svecica azuricollis 235
Luscinia svecica cyanecula 235
Luscinia svecica magna 235
Luscinia svecica pallidogularis 235
Lymnocryptes minimus 106

M
Macronectes giganteus 37
Macronectes halli 37
Magpie, Azure-winged 181
Magpie, Eurasian 181
Magpie, Iberian 181
Magpie, Magreb 181
Mallard 28
Marmaronetta angustirostris 30
Martin, Banded 193
Martin, Brown-throated 193
Martin, Crag 194
Martin, House 195
Martin, Pale Crag 194
Martin, Pale Sand 194
Martin, Purple 194
Martin, Sand 194
Melanitta americana 22
Melanitta deglandi 23
Melanitta deglandi stejnegeri 23
Melanitta fusca 23
Melanitta nigra 22
Melanitta perspicillata 23
Melanocorypha bimaculata 189
Melanocorypha calandra 189
Melanocorypha leucoptera 190
Melanocorypha mongolica 190
Melanocorypha yeltoniensis 190
Melierax metabates 67
Melospiza melodia 275
Merganser, Common 26
Merganser, Hooded 25
Merganser, Red-breasted 25
Mergellus albellus 25
Mergus merganser 25
Mergus merganser americanus 26
Mergus serrator 25
Merlin 78
Merlin, Pallid 79
Merlin, Taiga 78
Merops apiaster 169

Merops orientalis 168
Merops orientalis cleopatra 168
Merops orientalis cyanophrys 169
Merops persicus 169
Merops persicus chrysocercus 169
Micronisus gabar 67
Milvus aegyptius 60
Milvus aegyptius parasiticus 60
Milvus fasciicauda 60
Milvus lineatus 60
Milvus migrans 59
Milvus milvus 60
Mimus polyglottos 225
Mirafra cordofanica 187
Mniotilta varia 286
Mockingbird, Northern 225
Molothrus ater 285
Monticola saxatilis 246
Monticola solitarius 246
Montifringilla nivalis 252
Montifringilla nivalis alpicola 253
Moorhen, Common 84
Moorhen, Lesser 84
Morus bassanus 46
Morus capensis 46
Motacilla aguimp 258
Motacilla alba 257
Motacilla alba baicalensis 257
Motacilla cinerea 256
Motacilla cinerea patriciae 256
Motacilla cinerea schmitzi 256
Motacilla cinereocapilla 254
Motacilla cinereocapilla pygmaea 255
Motacilla citreola 255
Motacilla citreola calcarata 256
Motacilla citreola citreola 256
Motacilla citreola werae 256
Motacilla feldegg 255
Motacilla feldegg 'dombrowski' 255
Motacilla feldegg 'melanogrisea' 255
Motacilla feldegg 'superciliaris' 255
Motacilla flava 253
Motacilla flava beema 254
Motacilla flavissima 253
Motacilla iberiae 254
Motacilla leucocephala 254
*Motacilla leucopsis*257
Motacilla lutea 253
Motacilla ocularis 257
Motacilla personata 257
Motacilla 'simillima' 254
Motacilla subpersonata 257
Motacilla taivana 253
Motacilla thunbergi 254
Motacilla tschutschensis 254
Motacilla yarrellii 257
Mousebird, Blue-naped 158
Murrelet, Ancient 154
Murrelet, Long-billed 154
Muscicapa dauurica 232
Muscicapa griseisticta 233
Muscicapa sibirica 232
Muscicapa striata 233
Muscicapa striata balearica 233
Muscicapa striata tyrrhenica 233
Mycteria ibis 55
Myiopsitta monachus 158
Myna, Common 226
Myrmecocichla aethiops 240

N
Necrosyrtes monachus 62
Nectarinia osea 227
Needletail, White-throated 166
Neophron percnopterus 62
Neotis denhami 87
Neotis nuba 87
Netta erythrophthalma 17

Netta rufina 17
Nettapus coromandelianus 16
Nighthawk, Common 165
Nightingale, Common 234
Nightingale, Thrush 234
Nightjar, Egyptian 165
Nightjar, European 165
Nightjar, Nubian 165
Nightjar, Red-necked 165
Noddy, Black 143
Noddy, Brown 143
Nucifraga caryocatactes 181
Nucifraga caryocatactes macrorhynchos 181
Numenius arquata 113
Numenius arquata orientalis 113
Numenius borealis 112
Numenius hudsonicus 113
Numenius minutus 112
Numenius phaeopus 112
Numenius phaeopus alboaxillaris 112
Numenius phaeopus variegatus 112
Numenius tenuirostris 113
Numida meleagris 34
Nutcracker, Slender-billed 181
Nutcracker, Spotted 181
Nuthatch, Algerian 223
Nuthatch, Corsican 223
Nuthatch, Eastern Rock 223
Nuthatch, Eurasian 223
Nuthatch, Krüper's 223
Nuthatch, Red-breasted 223
Nuthatch, Siberian 223
Nuthatch, Western Rock 224
Nycticorax nycticorax 50
Nycticorax nycticorax hoactli 51

O
Oceanites oceanicus 43
Oceanodroma castro 44
Oceanodroma leucorhoa 44
Oceanodroma markhami 44
Oceanodroma matsudairae 44
Oceanodroma monorhis 44
Oena capensis 158
Oenanthe alboniger 246
Oenanthe chrysopygia 244
Oenanthe cypriaca 241
Oenanthe deserti 243
Oenanthe deserti atrogularis 243
Oenanthe deserti homochroa 243
Oenanthe finschii 243
Oenanthe halophila 245
Oenanthe hispanica 243
Oenanthe isabellina 240
Oenanthe leucopyga 246
Oenanthe leucopyga ernesti 246
Oenanthe leucura 246
Oenanthe lugens 245
Oenanthe lugens persica 245
Oenanthe melanoleuca 242
Oenanthe moesta 244
Oenanthe moesta brooksbanki 244
Oenanthe monacha 245
Oenanthe oenanthe 240
Oenanthe oenanthe leucorhoa 241
Oenanthe picata 245
Oenanthe picata capistrata 245
Oenanthe picata opistholeuca 245
Oenanthe pleschanka 241
Oenanthe pleschanka 'vittata' 241
Oenanthe seebohmi 241
Oenanthe xanthoprymna 244
Onychognathus tristramii 225
Onychoprion aleutica 144
Onychoprion anaethetus 144
Onychoprion anaethetus melanoptera 144
Onychoprion fuscata 144
Oriole, Baltimore 285

Oriole, Eurasian Golden 174
Oriolus oriolus 174
Osprey 76
Otis tarda 87
Otus brucei 161
Otus scops 161
Ouzel, Caucasian Ring 229
Ouzel, Ring 229
Ouzel, Southern Ring 229
Ovenbird 290
Owl, Barn 160
Owl, Brown Fish 162
Owl, Cape Verde Barn 161
Owl, Dark-breasted Barn 161
Owl, Eurasian Eagle 162
Owl, Eurasian Pygmy 162
Owl, Eurasian Scops 161
Owl, Great Grey 164
Owl, Great Horned 162
Owl, Hume's 163
Owl, Lilith's 163
Owl, Little 163
Owl, Long-eared 164
Owl, Marsh 164
Owl, Northern Hawk 162
Owl, Pale-breasted Barn 161
Owl, Pharaoh Eagle 162
Owl, Short-eared 164
Owl, Snowy 160
Owl, Striated Scops 161
Owl, Tawny 163
Owl, Tengmalm's 164
Owl, Ural 163
Oxyura jamaicensis 20
Oxyura leucocephala 20
Oystercatcher 88

P
Pagophila eburnea 123
Painted-snipe, Greater 88
Pandion haliaetus 76
Panurus biarmicus 187
Parakeet, Monk 158
Parakeet, Ring-necked 158
Partridge, Barbary 32
Partridge, Chukar 32
Partridge, Grey 33
Partridge, Red-legged 32
Partridge, Rock 32
Partridge, Sand 33
Partridge, See-see 32
Parula americana 286
Parula, Northern 286
Parus major 185
Passer domesticus 250
Passer hispaniolensis 251
Passer iagoensis 251
Passer italiae 251
Passer luteus 252
Passer moabiticus 251
Passer montanus 252
Passer simplex 251
Passerculus sandwichensis 275
Passerculus sandwichensis princeps 275
Passerella iliaca 275
Passerina cyanea 274
Pastor roseus 226
Pelagodroma grallaria 43
Pelagodroma marina 43
Pelagodroma tropica 43
Pelecanus crispus 48
Pelecanus erythrorhynchos 48
Pelecanus onocrotalus 48
Pelecanus rufescens 49
Pelican, American White 48
Pelican, Dalmatian 48
Pelican, Pink-backed 49
Pelican, White 48

Perdix perdix 33
Periparus ater 186
Periparus ater britannicus 186
Periparus ater cypriotes 186
Periparus ater hibernicus 186
Periparus ater ledouci 186
Perisoreus infaustus 180
Pernis apivorus 58
Pernis ptilorhyncus 58
Petrel, Atlantic 38
Petrel, Bermuda 39
Petrel, Black-capped 39
Petrel, Bulwer's 39
Petrel, Cape 38
Petrel, Desertas 38
Petrel, Fea's 38
Petrel, Herald 39
Petrel, Jouanin's 39
Petrel, Northern Giant 37
Petrel, Soft-plumaged 38
Petrel, Southern Giant 37
Petrel, Zino's 38
Petrochelidon pyrrhonota 196
Petronia petronia 252
Petronia petronia barbara 252
Phaethon aethereus 45
Phaethon aethereus indicus 45
Phaethon lepturus 45
Phalacrocorax africanus 48
Phalacrocorax aristotelis 47
Phalacrocorax aristotelis desmaresti
Phalacrocorax aristotelis riggenbach
Phalacrocorax auritus 47
Phalacrocorax carbo 46
Phalacrocorax carbo lucidus 46
Phalacrocorax carbo maroccanus 46
Phalacrocorax carbo sinensis 46
Phalacrocorax nigrogularis 47
Phalacrocorax pygmeus 47
Phalarope, Grey 119
Phalarope, Red 119
Phalarope, Red-necked 119
Phalarope, Wilson's 119
Phalaropus fulicarius 119
Phalaropus lobatus 119
Phalaropus tricolor 119
Phasianus colchicus 33
Pheasant, Common 33
Pheasant, Golden 34
Pheasant, Lady Amherst's 34
Pheasant, Reeves's 34
Pheucticus ludovicianus 274
Philomachus pugnax 106
Phoebe, Eastern 173
Phoenicopterus chilensis 57
Phoenicopterus minor 56
Phoenicopterus roseus 56
Phoenicopterus ruber 56
Phoenicurus erythrogastrus 238
Phoenicurus erythronotus 236
Phoenicurus moussieri 238
Phoenicurus ochruros 236
Phoenicurus ochruros aterrimus 237
Phoenicurus ochruros gibraltariensi
Phoenicurus ochruros semirufus 23
Phoenicurus ochruros phoenicuroide
Phoenicurus phoenicurus 237
Phoenicurus phoenicurus samamisicu
Phylloscopus bonelli 201
Phylloscopus borealis 199
Phylloscopus canariensis 203
Phylloscopus collybita 202
Phylloscopus collybita abietinus 202
Phylloscopus collybita tristis 202
Phylloscopus coronatus 198
Phylloscopus fuscatus 200
Phylloscopus humei 200
Phylloscopus ibericus 203

oscopus inornatus 200
oscopus lorenzii 203
oscopus neglectus 202
oscopus nitidus 198
oscopus orientalis 201
oscopus plumbeitarsus 198
oscopus proregulus 199
oscopus schwarzi 200
oscopus sibilatrix 201
oscopus trochiloides 199
oscopus trochilus 203
oscopus trochilus acredula 204
oscopus trochilus yakutensis 204
mauritanica 181
oica 181
des tridactylus 172
des tridactylus alpinus 172
canus 170
sharpei 170
vaillantii 170
viridis 170
n, Bolle's 157
n, Laurel 157
n, Trocaz 157
ola enucleator 272
l, Northern 29
erythrophthalmus 274
American Buff-bellied 262
Berthelot's 259
Blyth's 258
Buff-bellied 262
Long-billed 259
Meadow 260
Olive-backed 259
Pechora 260
Red-throated 261
Richard's 258
Rock 262
Siberian Buff-bellied 262
Tawny 259
Tree 260
Water 261
ga olivacea 291
ga rubra 291
ea leucorodia 56
ophenax nivalis 273
ophenax nivalis insulae 273
opterus gambensis 16
dis chichi 56
dis falcinellus 55
, American Golden 95
, Anatolian Sand 94
, Caspian 94
, Egyptian 89
, European Golden 96
, Greater Sand 93
, Grey 96
, Kentish 92
, Kittlitz's 92
, Lesser Sand 92
, Little Ringed 90
, Mongolian 93
, Oriental 94
Pacific Golden 95
, Ringed 91
, Semipalmated 91
, Three-banded 92
lis apricaria 96
lis dominica 95
lis fulva 95
lis squatarola 96
nus aegyptius 89
rd, Common 17
rd, Red-crested 17
rd, Southern 17
ps auritus 58
ps cristatus 57
ps grisegena 57

Podiceps grisegena holboellii 57
Podiceps nigricollis 58
Podilymbus podiceps 57
Poecile cinctus 187
Poecile lugubris 186
Poecile lugubris anatoliae 186
Poecile montana 186
Poecile montana borealis 186
Poecile montana kleinschmidti 186
Poecile palustris 186
Polysticta stelleri 22
Porphyrio alleni 85
Porphyrio madagascariensis 85
Porphyrio martinica 85
Porphyrio poliocephalus 85
Porphyrio poliocephalus caspius 85
Porphyrio poliocephalus seistanicus 85
Porphyrio porphyrio 85
Porzana carolina 83
Porzana parva 83
Porzana porzana 83
Porzana pusilla 84
Pratincole, Black-winged 90
Pratincole, Collared 89
Pratincole, Oriental 90
Prinia gracilis 221
Prinia, Graceful 221
Progne subis 194
Prunella atrogularis 250
Prunella collaris 250
Prunella modularis 249
Prunella montanella 249
Prunella ocularis 249
Psittacula krameri 158
Ptarmigan 31
Pternistis bicalcaratus 33
Pterocles alchata 156
Pterocles alchata caudacutus 156
Pterocles coronatus 155
Pterocles exustus 155
Pterocles lichtensteinii 155
Pterocles orientalis 155
Pterocles senegallus 155
Pterodroma arminjoniana 39
Pterodroma cahow 39
Pterodroma deserta 38
Pterodroma feae 38
Pterodroma hasitata 39
Pterodroma incerta 38
Pterodroma madeira 38
Pterodroma mollis 38
Ptynoprogne obsoleta 194
Ptynoprogne obsoleta presaharica 195
Ptynoprogne rupestris 194
Puffin, Atlantic 154
Puffin, Tufted 155
Puffinus bailloni 43
Puffinus baroli 42
Puffinus boydi 42
Puffinus carneipes 41
Puffinus gravis 41
Puffinus griseus 41
Puffinus lherminieri 42
Puffinus mauretanicus 41
Puffinus pacificus 40
Puffinus persicus 43
Puffinus puffinus 41
Puffinus yelkouan 42
Pycnonotus barbatus 196
Pycnonotus cafer 196
Pycnonotus leucotis196
Pycnonotus xanthopygos 196
Pygmy-goose, Cotton 16
Pyrrhocorax graculus 181
Pyrrhocorax pyrrhocorax 181
Pyrrhula murina 272
Pyrrhula pyrrhula 272
Pyrrhula pyrrhula iberiae 272

Q
Quail, Common 33
Quail, Japanese 33
Quiscalus quiscula 285

R
Rail, Water 83
Rallus aquaticus 83
Ramphocoris clotbey 189
Raven, Brown-necked 183
Raven, Common 183
Raven, Fan-tailed 183
Razorbill 153
Recurvirostra avosetta 88
Redhead 17
Redpoll, Arctic 268
Redpoll, Common 267
Redpoll, Coues's 268
Redpoll, Hornemann's 268
Redpoll, Lesser 267
Redshank, Common 118
Redshank, Spotted 116
Redstart, American 290
Redstart, Black 236
Redstart, Caucasian Black 237
Redstart, Common 237
Redstart, Eastern Black 237
Redstart, Ehrenberg's 237
Redstart, Eversmann's 236
Redstart, Güldenstädt's 238
Redstart, Moussier's 238
Redwing 231
Regulus azoricus 183
Regulus azoricus inermis 183
Regulus azoricus sanctaemariae 183
Regulus calendula 183
Regulus ignicapilla 184
Regulus madeirensis 184
Regulus regulus 183
Regulus teneriffae 184
Remiz pendulinus 184
Remiz pendulinus caspius 184
Remiz pendulinus coronatus 184
Remiz pendulinus macronyx 184
Rhodopechys alienus 270
Rhodopechys sanguineus 270
Rhodophoneus cruentus 174
Rhodospiza obsoleta 270
Riparia cincta 193
Riparia diluta 194
Riparia paludicola 193
Riparia riparia 194
Rissa tridactyla 123
Robin, American 232
Robin, European 233
Robin, Rufous-tailed 234
Robin, Siberian Blue 236
Robin, Tenerife 234
Robin, White-throated 236
Roller, Abyssinian 169
Roller, Broad-billed 169
Roller, European 169
Roller, Indian 169
Rook 182
Rosefinch, Caucasian Great 271
Rosefinch, Common 271
Rosefinch, Long-tailed 272
Rosefinch, Pallas's 271
Rosefinch, Sinai 271
Rostratula benghalensis 88
Rubythroat, Siberian 235
Ruff 106
Rynchops flavirostris 152
Rynchops niger 153

S
Sanderling 98
Sandgrouse, Black-bellied 155

Sandgrouse, Chestnut-bellied 155
Sandgrouse, Crowned 155
Sandgrouse, Lichtenstein's 155
Sandgrouse, Pallas's 156
Sandgrouse, Pin-tailed 156
Sandgrouse, Spotted 155
Sandpiper, Baird's 102
Sandpiper, Broad-billed 105
Sandpiper, Buff-breasted 106
Sandpiper, Common 114
Sandpiper, Curlew 103
Sandpiper, Green 115
Sandpiper, Least 101
Sandpiper, Marsh 117
Sandpiper, Pectoral 103
Sandpiper, Purple 104
Sandpiper, Semipalmated 99
Sandpiper, Sharp-tailed 103
Sandpiper, Solitary 115
Sandpiper, Spotted 114
Sandpiper, Stilt 104
Sandpiper, Terek 114
Sandpiper, Upland 113
Sandpiper, Western 99
Sandpiper, White-rumped 102
Sandpiper, Wood 118
Sapsucker, Yellow-bellied 171
Saxicola caprata 240
Saxicola dacotiae 238
Saxicola maurus 239
Saxicola maurus variegatus 240
Saxicola rubetra 238
Saxicola torquatus 239
Saxicola torquatus hibernans 239
Saxicola torquatus rubicola 239
Sayornis phoebe 173
Scaup, Greater 19
Scaup, Lesser 19
Scolopax minor 111
Scolopax rusticola 110
Scoter, Black 22
Scoter, Common 22
Scoter, Stejneger's 23
Scoter, Surf 23
Scoter, Velvet 23
Scoter, White-winged 23
Scotocerca inquieta 222
Scotocerca inquieta saharae 222
Scotocerca inquieta theresae 222
Scrub-robin, Black 233
Scrub-robin, Rufous 233
Seiurus aurocapilla 290
Seiurus motacilla 290
Seiurus noveboracensis 290
Serin, European 264
Serin, Red-fronted 264
Serin, Syrian 265
Serinus canaria 265
Serinus pusillus 264
Serinus serinus 264
Serinus syriacus 265
Setophaga ruticilla 290
Shag 47
Shearwater, Audubon's 42
Shearwater, Balearic 41
Shearwater, Barolo 42
Shearwater, Boyd's 42
Shearwater, Cape Verde 40
Shearwater, Cory's 40
Shearwater, Flesh-footed 41
Shearwater, Great 41
Shearwater, Manx 41
Shearwater, Persian 43
Shearwater, Scopoli's 40
Shearwater, Sooty 41
Shearwater, Streaked 40
Shearwater, Tropical 43
Shearwater, Wedge-tailed 40

Shearwater, Yelkouan 42
Shelduck, Cape 16
Shelduck, Common 16
Shelduck, Paradise 16
Shelduck, Ruddy 16
Shikra 68
Shoveler, Australian 30
Shoveler, Northern 30
Shrike, Balearic Woodchat 180
Shrike, Brown 174
Shrike, 'Chinese' 176
Shrike, Daurian 176
Shrike, Desert Grey 178
Shrike, Great Grey 177
Shrike, 'Isabelline' 175
Shrike, Lesser Grey 177
Shrike, Levant Grey 179
Shrike, Long-tailed 177
Shrike, Masked 180
Shrike, Red-backed 177
Shrike, Red-tailed 175
Shrike, Rosy-patched 174
Shrike, Southern Grey 178
Shrike, Steppe Grey 179
Shrike, Woodchat 179
Silverbill, African 250
Silverbill, Indian 250
Siskin, Eurasian 266
Sitta canadensis 223
Sitta europaea 223
Sitta europaea asiatica 223
Sitta europaea caesia 223
Sitta krueperi 223
Sitta ledanti 223
Sitta neumayer 224
Sitta tephronota 223
Sitta whiteheadi 223
Skimmer, African 152
Skimmer, Black 153
Skua, Arctic 120
Skua, Brown 123
Skua, Great 122
Skua, Long-tailed 121
Skua, Pomarine 120
Skua, South Polar 122
Skylark 192
Skylark, Oriental 192
Smew 25
Snipe, Common 106
Snipe, Great 107
Snipe, Jack 106
Snipe, Pintail 108
Snipe, Swinhoe's 108
Snipe, Wilson's 107
Snowcock, Caspian 32
Snowcock, Caucasian 32
Snowfinch, White-winged 252
Somateria fischeri 21
Somateria mollissima 20
Somateria mollissima borealis 20
Somateria mollissima dresseri 21
Somateria mollissima faeroeensis 21
Somateria mollissima v-nigra 21
Somateria spectabilis 21
Sora 83
Sparrow, Dead Sea 251
Sparrow, Desert 251
Sparrow, Fox 275
Sparrow, Golden 252
Sparrow, House 250
Sparrow, Iago 251
Sparrow, Ipswich 275
Sparrow, Italian 251
Sparrow, Lark 275
Sparrow, Pale Rock 252
Sparrow, Rock 252
Sparrow, Savannah 275
Sparrow, Song 275

Sparrow, Spanish 251
Sparrow, Tree 252
Sparrow, White-crowned 275
Sparrow, White-throated 276
Sparrow, Yellow-throated 252
Sparrowhawk, Eurasian 68
Sparrowhawk, Levant 68
Sparrow-lark, Black-crowned 187
Sparrow-lark, Chestnut-headed 187
Sphyrapicus varius 171
Spiloptila clamans 222
Spiza americana 274
Spoonbill, Eurasian 56
Starling, Common 226
Starling, Daurian 225
Starling, Rose-coloured 226
Starling, Spotless 226
Starling, Tristram's 225
Starling, Violet-backed 225
Stercorarius antarcticus 123
Stercorarius antarcticus lonnbergi 12
Stercorarius longicaudus 121
Stercorarius longicaudus pallescens 122
Stercorarius maccormicki 122
Stercorarius parasiticus 120
Stercorarius pomarinus 120
Stercorarius skua 122
Sterna dougallii 152
Sterna forsteri 150
Sterna hirundo 150
Sterna hirundo longipennis 151
Sterna paradisaea 151
Sterna repressa 152
Sternula albifrons 145
Sternula antillarum 145
Sternula saundersi 145
Stilt, Black-necked 88
Stilt, Black-winged 88
Stint, Little 100
Stint, Long-toed 101
Stint, Red-necked 100
Stint, Temminck's 101
Stonechat, Canary Islands 238
Stonechat, Caspian 240
Stonechat, European 239
Stonechat, Pied 240
Stonechat, Siberian 239
Stone-curlew 89
Stork, Abdim's 55
Stork, Black 55
Stork, Marabou 55
Stork, White 55
Stork, Yellow-billed 55
Storm-petrel, Black-bellied 43
Storm-petrel, European 44
Storm-petrel, Leach's 44
Storm-petrel, Madeiran 44
Storm-petrel, Markham's 44
Storm-petrel, Matsudaira's 44
Storm-petrel, Mediterranean 44
Storm-petrel, Swinhoe's 44
Storm-petrel, White-bellied 43
Storm-petrel, White-faced 43
Storm-petrel, Wilson's 43
Streptopelia decaocto 157
Streptopelia orientalis 157
Streptopelia orientalis meena 158
Streptopelia risoria 157
Streptopelia senegalensis 158
Streptopelia turtur 157
Strix aluco 163
Strix aluco mauritanica 163
Strix butleri 163
Strix nebulosa 164
Strix uralensis 163
Strix uralensis macroura 164
Sturnus unicolor 226

...us vulgaris 226
dactylatra 45
leucogaster 45
leucogaster plotus 46
sula 45
ird, Nile Valley 227
ird, Palestine 227
ird, Purple 227
ird, Pygmy 227
ird, Shining 227
ia ulula 162
ia ulula caparoch 162
low, American Barn 195
low, Barn 195
low, Cliff 196
low, Ethiopian 195
ow, Red-rumped 195
low, Tree 194
low, Wire-tailed 195
np-hen, African 85
np-hen, Grey-headed 85
np-hen, Western 85
, Bewick's 10
, Mute 10
, Whistling 10
, Whooper 10
African Palm 168
Alpine 166
Cape Verde 166
Chimney 166
Common 166
Little 168
Pacific 167
Pallid 167
Plain 166
White-rumped 167
althaea 211
atricapilla 212
atricapilla heineken 212
balearica 204
borin 211
cantillans 206
cantillans albistriata 206
cantillans cantillans 206
communis 211
communis icterops 211
communis volgensis 211
conspicillata 205
crassirostris 210
curruca 210
curruca blythi 211
curruca halimodendri 210
curruca minula 210
deserti 209
deserticola 205
hortensis 209
leucomelaena 209
leucomelaena negevensis 209
melanocephala 207
melanocephala momus 208
melanothorax 208
moltonii 206
mystacea 207
mystacea rubescens 207
nana 209
nisoria 210
rueppellii 208
sarda 204
undata 205
undata dartfordiensis 205
boramphus antiquus 154
icus reevesii 34
ptes paradoxus 156

aptus ruficollis 57
ineta bicolor 194
a cana 16

Tadorna ferruginea 16
Tadorna tadorna 16
Tadorna variegata 16
Tanager, Scarlet 291
Tanager, Summer 291
Tarsiger cyanurus 236
Tattler, Grey-tailed 115
Tattler, Wandering 115
Tchagra senegalus 174
Tchagra, Black-crowned 174
Teal, Baikal 27
Teal, Blue-winged 30
Teal, Cape 27
Teal, Cinnamon 30
Teal, Common 28
Teal, Green-winged 28
Terathopius ecaudatus 63
Tern, Aleutian 144
Tern, American Black 147
Tern, Arctic 151
Tern, Black 146
Tern, Bridled 144
Tern, Cabot's 148
Tern, Caspian 146
Tern, Cayenne 148
Tern, Common 150
Tern, Elegant 149
Tern, Forster's 150
Tern, Great Crested 149
Tern, Gull-billed 145
Tern, Least 145
Tern, Lesser Crested 150
Tern, Little 145
Tern, Roseate 152
Tern, Royal 149
Tern, Sandwich 148
Tern, Saunders's 145
Tern, Sooty 144
Tern, Whiskered 146
Tern, White-cheeked 152
Tern, White-winged Black 147
Tetrao mlokosiewiczi 31
Tetrao tetrix 31
Tetrao urogallus 32
Tetraogallus caspius 32
Tetraogallus caucasicus 32
Tetrastes bonasia 31
Tetrax tetrax 87
Thalassarche carteri 36
Thalassarche cauta 37
Thalassarche chlororhynchos 36
Thalassarche chrysostoma 36
Thalassarche impavida 36
Thalassarche melanophris 36
Thalasseus acuflavida eurygnatha 148
Thalasseus acuflavida 148
Thalasseus bengalensis 150
Thalasseus bergii 149
Thalasseus bergii thalassina 150
Thalasseus bergii velox 150
Thalasseus elegans 149
Thalasseus maxima 149
Thalasseus maxima albididorsalis 149
Thalasseus sandvicensis 148
Thick-knee, Senegal 89
Thrasher, Brown 225
Threskiornis aethiopicus 56
Thrush, Bicknell's 229
Thrush, Black-throated 231
Thrush, Blue Rock 246
Thrush, Dusky 230
Thrush, Eyebrowed 230
Thrush, Grey-cheeked 229
Thrush, Hermit 228
Thrush, Mistle 231
Thrush, Naumann's 230
Thrush, Red-throated 231
Thrush, Rufous-tailed Rock 246

Thrush, Siberian 228
Thrush, Song 231
Thrush, Swainson's 228
Thrush, Tickell's 229
Thrush, Varied 228
Thrush, White's 227
Thrush, Wood 228
Tichodroma muraria 222
Tit, Azure 185
Tit, Bearded 187
Tit, Coal 186
Tit, Crested 185
Tit, European Blue 185
Tit, Gran Canaria Blue 185
Tit, Great 185
Tit, Hierro Blue 185
Tit, Long-tailed 197
Tit, Marsh 186
Tit, Palma Blue 185
Tit, Penduline 184
Tit, 'Pleske's' 185
Tit, Siberian 187
Tit, Sombre 186
Tit, Tenerife Blue 184
Tit, Ultramarine Blue 185
Tit, Willow 186
Tit, Yellow-breasted 185
Torgos tracheliotus 63
Towhee, Eastern 274
Toxostoma rufum 225
Treecreeper, Eurasian 224
Treecreeper, Short-toed 224
Tringa brevipes 115
Tringa erythropus 116
Tringa flavipes 117
Tringa glareola 118
Tringa incanus 115
Tringa melanoleuca 116
Tringa nebularia 116
Tringa ochropus 115
Tringa semipalmata 117
Tringa semipalmata inornata 117
Tringa solitaria 115
Tringa solitaria cinnamomea 115
Tringa stagnatilis 117
Tringa totanus 118
Tringa totanus robusta 118
Troglodytes troglodytes 225
Troglodytes troglodytes hirtensis 225
Troglodytes troglodytes zetlandicus 225
Tropicbird, Red-billed 45
Tropicbird, White-tailed 45
Tryngites subruficollis 106
Turdoides altirostris 197
Turdoides fulva 198
Turdoides huttoni 197
Turdoides huttoni salvadori 197
Turdoides squamiceps 197
Turdus atrogularis 231
Turdus eunomus 230
Turdus iliacus 231
Turdus iliacus coburni 232
Turdus merula 229
Turdus merula mauritanicus 230
Turdus migratorius 232
Turdus naumanni 230
Turdus obscurus 230
Turdus philomelos 231
Turdus philomelos clarkei 231
Turdus philomelos hebridensis 231
Turdus pilarus 231
Turdus ruficollis 231
Turdus torquatus 229
Turdus torquatus alpestris 229
Turdus torquatus amicorum 229
Turdus unicolor 229
Turdus viscivorus 232
Turdus viscivorus deichleri 232

Index

Turnix sylvaticus 88
Turnstone, Ruddy 118
Twite 266
Tyrannus savana 173
Tyto alba 160
Tyto alba erlangeri 161
Tyto alba gracilirostris 161
Tyto alba guttata 161
Tyto alba schmitzi 161
Tyto detorta 161

U
Upupa epops 169
Uragus sibiricus 272
Uria aalge 153
Uria aalge albionis 153
Uria lomvia 153

V
Vanellus gregarius 97
Vanellus indicus 97
Vanellus leucurus 97
Vanellus spinosus 96
Vanellus tectus 97
Vanellus vanellus 97
Veery 229
Vermivora chrysoptera 286
Vermivora peregrina 286
Vermivora pinus 286
Vireo flavifrons 173
Vireo griseus 173
Vireo olivaceus 174
Vireo philadelphicus 174
Vireo, Philadelphia 174
Vireo, Red-eyed 174
Vireo, White-eyed 173
Vireo, Yellow-throated 173
Vulture, African White-backed 63
Vulture, Egyptian 62
Vulture, Eurasian Black 63
Vulture, Griffon 62
Vulture, Hooded 62
Vulture, Lappet-faced 63
Vulture, Rüppell's 62

W
Wagtail, African Pied 258
Wagtail, Amur 257
Wagtail, Ashy-headed 254
Wagtail, Black-headed 255
Wagtail, Blue-headed 253
Wagtail, 'Channel' 253
Wagtail, Citrine 255
Wagtail, East Siberian 257
Wagtail, Eastern Yellow 254
Wagtail, Egyptian 255
Wagtail, Forest 258
Wagtail, Green-headed 253
Wagtail, Grey 256
Wagtail, Grey-headed 254
Wagtail, Masked 257
Wagtail, Moroccan 257
Wagtail, Pied 257
Wagtail, Spanish 254
Wagtail, Sykes's 254
Wagtail, White 257
Wagtail, White-headed 254
Wagtail, Yellow 253
Wagtail, Yellow-headed 253
Wallcreeper 222
Warbler, African Desert 209
Warbler, American Yellow 287
Warbler, Aquatic 220
Warbler, Arabian 209
Warbler, Arctic 199
Warbler, Asian Desert 209
Warbler, Audubon's 288
Warbler, Balearic 204

Warbler, Barred 210
Warbler, Basra Reed 221
Warbler, Bay-breasted 289
Warbler, Black-and-white 286
Warbler, Blackburnian 287
Warbler, Blackpoll 289
Warbler, Black-throated Blue 287
Warbler, Black-throated Green 287
Warbler, Blue-winged 286
Warbler, Blyth's Reed 218
Warbler, Booted 216
Warbler, Canada 291
Warbler, Cape May 288
Warbler, Cape Verde 221
Warbler, Caspian Reed 219
Warbler, Cerulean 289
Warbler, Cetti's 196
Warbler, Chestnut-sided 287
Warbler, Clamorous Reed 221
Warbler, Cricket 222
Warbler, Cyprus 208
Warbler, Dartford 205
Warbler, Dusky 200
Warbler, Eastern Bonelli's 201
Warbler, Eastern Crowned 198
Warbler, Eastern Moustached 220
Warbler, Eastern Olivaceous 215
Warbler, Eastern Orphean 210
Warbler, Garden 211
Warbler, Golden-winged 286
Warbler, Grasshopper 213
Warbler, Gray's Grasshopper 214
Warbler, Great Reed 220
Warbler, Greater Swamp 221
Warbler, Green 198
Warbler, Greenish 199
Warbler, Hooded 290
Warbler, Hume's Leaf 200
Warbler, Icterine 215
Warbler, Lanceolated 213
Warbler, Magnolia 288
Warbler, Marmora's 204
Warbler, Marsh 218
Warbler, Melodious 215
Warbler, Ménétries's 207
Warbler, Moltoni's 206
Warbler, Moustached 220
Warbler, Myrtle 288
Warbler, Olive-tree 215
Warbler, Oriental Reed 220
Warbler, Paddyfield 218
Warbler, Pallas's Grasshopper 212
Warbler, Pallas's Leaf 199
Warbler, Palm 289
Warbler, Plain Leaf 202
Warbler, Radde's 200
Warbler, Reed 219
Warbler, River 213
Warbler, Rüppell's 208
Warbler, Sardinian 207
Warbler, Savi's 214
Warbler, Scrub 222
Warbler, Sedge 219
Warbler, Spectacled 205
Warbler, Subalpine 206
Warbler, Sykes's 217
Warbler, Tennessee 286
Warbler, Thick-billed 217
Warbler, Tristram's 205
Warbler, Two-barred Greenish 198
Warbler, Upcher's 214
Warbler, Western Bonelli's 201
Warbler, Western Olivaceous 216
Warbler, Western Orphean 209
Warbler, Willow 203
Warbler, Wilson's 291
Warbler, Wood 201
Warbler, Yellow-browed 200

Warbler, Yellow-rumped 288
Waterthrush, Louisiana 290
Waterthrush, Northern 290
Waxbill, Common 250
Waxwing, Bohemian 222
Waxwing, Cedar 222
Waxwing, Japanese 222
Wheatear, 'Basalt' 245
Wheatear, Black 246
Wheatear, Cyprus 241
Wheatear, Desert 243
Wheatear, Eastern Black-eared 242
Wheatear, Eastern Mourning 245
Wheatear, Finsch's 243
Wheatear, Greenland 241
Wheatear, Hooded 245
Wheatear, Hume's 246
Wheatear, Isabelline 240
Wheatear, Kurdistan 244
Wheatear, Northern 240
Wheatear, Pied 241
Wheatear, Red-rumped 244
Wheatear, Red-tailed 244
Wheatear, Seebohm's 241
Wheatear, Variable 245
Wheatear, Western Black-eared 243
Wheatear, Western Mourning 245
Wheatear, White-crowned Black 246
Whimbrel, Eurasian 112
Whimbrel, Hudsonian 113
Whinchat 238
Whitethroat, Common 211
Whitethroat, Hume's 211
Whitethroat, Lesser 210
Wigeon, American 26
Wigeon, Chiloe 26
Wigeon, Eurasian 26
Willet 117
Willet, Eastern 117
Willet, Western 117
Wilsonia canadensis 291
Wilsonia citrina 290
Wilsonia pusilla 291
Woodcock, American 111
Woodcock, Eurasian 110
Woodlark 192
Woodpecker, Black 171
Woodpecker, Great Spotted 171
Woodpecker, Green 170
Woodpecker, Grey-headed 170
Woodpecker, Iberian Green 170
Woodpecker, Lesser Spotted 172
Woodpecker, Levaillant's Green 170
Woodpecker, Lilford's 172
Woodpecker, Middle Spotted 172
Woodpecker, Syrian 171
Woodpecker, Three-toed 172
Woodpecker, White-backed 172
Woodpigeon 156
Wren 225
Wryneck 170

X
Xanthocephalus xanthocephalus 288
Xema sabini 123
Xenus cinereus 114

Y
Yellowhammer 278
Yellowlegs, Greater 116
Yellowlegs, Lesser 117
Yellowthroat, Common 290

Z
Zenaida macroura 158
Zonotrichia albicollis 276
Zonotrichia leucophrys 275
Zoothera aurea 227